SAT
SUCCESS

SAT*

SUCCESS

Peterson's Study Guide to English and Math Skills for College Entrance Examinations

Fourth Edition

Joan Carris
with Michael R. Crystal and William R. McQuade

Peterson's Guides
Princeton, New Jersey

SAT questions selected from *Introducing the New SAT,* College Entrance Examination Board, 1993 and SAT Question and Answer Booklets, College Entrance Examination Board, 1989. Reprinted by permission of Educational Testing Service, the copyright owner of the test questions.

Permission to reprint the above material does not constitute review or endorsement by Educational Testing Service or the College Board of this publication as a whole or of any other questions or testing information it may contain.

Excerpts from *The Conscience of Words, Brother to a Dragonfly, The Troubled People Book, Ice, Quetzalcoatl, The Uncollected Wodehouse,* and *Jane Austen* copyright © by Crossroad/Continuum Publishing Company, New York, New York.

Excerpts from *Germany: 2000 Years* and "The Son" (within *The Little Comedy and Other Stories*) copyright © by Frederick Ungar Publishing Company, New York, New York.

Excerpt from *What's What* copyright © by the Hammond Publishing Company, Maplewood, New Jersey.

Excerpts from *Animal Behavior: Ecology and Evolution* and *It Began with a Stone* copyright © by John Wiley & Sons, Publishers, New York, New York.

Excerpts from *Junior Year in Britain* and *Jobs for English Majors and Other Smart People* copyright © by Peterson's Guides, Princeton, New Jersey.

Swedberg, R., *Economics and Sociology: Redefining Their Boundaries.* Copyright © 1990 by Princeton University Press. 409 words used with permission.

Library of Congress Cataloging-in-Publication Data

Carris, Joan Davenport.
    SAT success : Peterson's study guide to English and math skills for college entrance examinations / Joan Davenport Carris with William R. McQuade and Michael R. Crystal. — 4th ed.
        p.   cm.
    ISBN 1-56079-393-7
    1. Universities and colleges—United States—Entrance examinations—Study guides. 2. Scholastic aptitude test—Study guides. I. McQuade, William R. II. Crystal, Michael R., 1964– .
    III. Title.

LB2353.57.C364 1994
378.1'662—dc20   94-2714
                                                                                                                        CIP

Composition and design by Peterson's Guides

Printed in the United States of America

10 9 8 7 6 5

Contents

Acknowledgments

For this edition of *SAT* Success* we wish to thank many contributors, because their time, care, and expertise are represented on these pages.

When confronted with scholarly differences of opinion on matters debatable, we used the following authorities: *Webster's Ninth New Collegiate Dictionary;* Willard Espy's *O Thou Improper, Thou Uncommon Noun,* 1978; *Building Word Power,* by J. R. Orgel and A. M. Works, 1955; *Bulfinch's Mythology,* edited by Edmund Fuller, 1959; *Dictionary of English Word-Roots,* by Robert W. L. Smith, 1966; *Dictionary of Word Origins,* by Joseph T. Shipley, 1964; and *The Oxford Dictionary of English Etymology,* edited by C. T. Onions, 1983.

Because of generous permission from the following publishers, we have outstanding reading passages for practice and as part of our Practice SATs. First, to Crossroad/Continuum Publishing Company, thanks for excerpts from *The Conscience of Words,* by Elias Canetti, 1979; *Brother to a Dragonfly,* by Will D. Campbell, 1977; *Quetzalcoatl,* by José Lopez Portillo, 1976; *The Troubled People Book,* by Paul G. Quinnett, 1985; *The Uncollected Wodehouse,* by P. G. Wodehouse, 1976; and *Jane Austen,* by J. Dwyer, 1989.

Thanks to the Frederick Ungar Publishing Company for excerpts from *Germany: 2000 Years,* by Kurt F. Reinhardt, 1961.

Thanks also to the Hammond Publishing Company for an excerpt from its pictorial compendium *What's What,* by David Fisher and Reginald Bragonier Jr., 1982.

The excellent science passages are here, for the most part, through the courtesy of John Wiley & Sons, including *Animal Behavior: Ecology and Evolution,* by C. J. Barnard, 1983; *It Began with a Stone,* by Henry Faul and Carol Faul, 1983; and *The Sky at Night 10* by Patrick Moore, 1992, as well as a social science passage from *The Big Fix* by J. R. Adams.

Princeton University Press is acknowledged gratefully for passages from *Economics and Sociology,* edited by R. Swedberg, 1990.

Peterson's Guides supplied materials from *Junior Year in Britain,* by Barbara Hanson Pierce, 1979, and from *Jobs for English Majors and Other Smart People,* by John L. Munschauer, 1981.

Additional sources for reading passages and appropriate quotations were supplied by people long gone but certainly not forgotten. We say thanks to the following classic authors: Jane Austen, for a brief excerpt from *Mansfield Park;* Benjamin Franklin, the *Autobiography;* Washington Irving, author of *The Sketch Book,* from which we excerpted the opening to "The Country Church"; Oscar Wilde, for excerpts from "Lord Arthur Savile's Crime" and from "The Decay of Lying"; and H. D. Thoreau for an excerpt from *A Week on the Concord and Merrimack Rivers.* We also thank Chief Justice Earl Warren and Justice William Douglas of the Supreme Court of the United States for excerpts from their opinions on *Terry v. Ohio,* 1968.

Last, and we hope in a most prominent spot, a loud and hearty thank-you to our editors and to the proofreaders and careful, patient folks in the art and production departments—those who turn manuscripts into books.

Thank heavens for each one of you—we'd hate to be in this all alone!

Unit 1: Plain Talk About You and the SAT and PSAT

Let's not waste time bemoaning the low verbal scores (in the 420s) or the math scores (mid-470s) on these tests, okay? Instead, let's talk truth about you and your education.

If you are lucky enough to go to a good school with teachers who care about you and your schoolwork, count your blessings. You and your community are working together to see that you will go somewhere in life. You'll probably score respectably on the PSAT and SAT. Even so, you should study the Red Alert pages and do the practice tests in this book, along with exercises to strengthen your weak points . . . just in case . . . just to give you extra confidence.

If, however, you live in a poor neighborhood where books are rare, or in a neighborhood with weak, undemanding schools, both the PSAT and the SAT will be a real challenge.

(But not insurmountable. Read on.)

If you watch a lot of TV or spend 20+ hours a week playing sports and never read for pleasure, you'll find the verbal section very tough.

If you've always taken the easier courses in school, these tests will come as a jolt. Your scores may even tell admissions personnel that you are not ready for college work.

> If your neighborhood or the adults in your life have not asked for ALL YOU'VE GOT, THEN YOU HAVE TO SET THINGS RIGHT. You must teach yourself what they have failed to teach you or you have failed to learn—whatever.
> **FACT: The only lifestyle that leads to success is one which asks a lot from us.**

Remember that if you're determined to do something, you can do it. Do you think Neil Armstrong's mom believed him when he said he wanted to walk on the moon? Give me a break! She thought he was a dear boy, just a trifle loony. But guess who eventually walked on the moon?

DETERMINATION TO DO SOMETHING IS THE ONLY WAY YOU WILL GET WHERE YOU WANT TO GO—to college, to the career of your dreams, or to the moon. Now let's get cracking.

STEP 1.   Keep going forward in this book. The knowledge you learn in these pages can boost you into college or into a fine trade or professional school. Learn all you can if you want a say in your future life.

You do want a say in your future, don't you?

STEP 2.   Take the Diagnostic SAT so you can plan an intelligent review schedule.

FACTS ABOUT THE PSAT AND SAT

STANDARDIZED TESTS IN GENERAL

The tests used most frequently by colleges and universities in the United States for the evaluation of applicants for admission or for their placement in courses are the American College Testing Program's ACT Assessment Program, known as the ACT, and the College Board's newly renamed Scholastic Assessment Tests, known as the SAT. The PSAT, or Preliminary Scholastic Assessment Test, is a preview of the SAT and is commonly taken early in the junior year of high school.

THE PSAT

The full acronym for the PSAT includes the letters NMSQT. The NMSQT section of the title means that it is the qualifying test for the nationwide competition run by the National Merit Scholarship Corporation.

The College Board and the National Merit Scholarship Corporation distribute the *Student Bulletin,* which explains the purpose and uses of test results, the eligibility requirements for students, the steps in the competition, and the scholarships offered. Being a National Merit Finalist or Semifinalist, or receiving a Letter of Commendation, is worth a great deal when you apply to college. Doing well on the PSAT is worth any extra effort you can muster.

The PSAT is a standardized test of developed verbal and mathematical abilities. It has two verbal sections totaling 58 questions and two math sections with 50 total questions. Testing time is two hours, not counting a short break in the middle.

THE PSAT

One 30-minute Verbal Section:
>   16 Sentence Completions
>   13 Critical Reading Questions (2 passages)

One 30-minute Math Section:
>   25 Multiple-Choice Questions on arithmetic, algebra, geometry

Time Out

Another 30-minute Verbal Section:
>   12 Analogies
>   11 Critical Reading Questions (paired passages)
>   6 Critical Reading Questions (1 passage)

Another 30-minute Math Section:
>   15 Quantitative Comparison Questions on arithmetic, algebra, geometry
>   10 Questions; Student-Produced Answers, Recorded on Grid

The PSAT does not ask for facts, as such, although you will use all of your verbal and math knowledge to answer the questions. Like the SAT I (see below), the PSAT tests your ability to reason and think logically.

If you are preparing to take the PSAT, this book will be of tremendous help. *Its quizzes and practice tests ask questions just like those on the PSAT.* Students with learning differences or other special needs will find that special arrangements can be made to accommodate them and should check with their counselor.

THE SAT I: REASONING TEST

Test-takers who survive a PSAT know what to expect on the SAT in their senior year—more of the same.

An SAT is just a longer PSAT, with 78 verbal questions: 19 analogies, 19 sentence completions, and 40 critical reading questions. There are 60 math questions: 35 multiple-choice questions on basic arithmetic, algebra, and geometry; 15 quantitative comparison questions covering the same body of knowledge; and 10 questions for which you compute the answer and enter it on a numbered grid. In chart form, an SAT looks like this:

THE SAT

Verbal 1: 30 Questions—30 minutes
>   9 Sentence Completions
>   6 Analogies
>   15 Critical Reading Questions (2 passages)

Verbal 2: 35 Questions—30 minutes
>   10 Sentence Completions
>   13 Analogies
>   12 Critical Reading Questions (1 long passage)

Verbal 3: 13 Questions—15 minutes
>   Analysis of 2 Reading Passages on a Related Topic

Math 1: 25 Questions—30 minutes
>   All multiple-choice on arithmetic, algebra, and geometry

Math 2: 25 Questions—30 minutes
>   15 Quantitative Comparisons
>   10 Student-Produced Answers—Recorded on Grid

Math 3: 10 Questions—15 minutes
>   All multiple-choice as in Math 1

On the test itself, the verbal and math sections are interspersed. Everyone taking an SAT should get hold of the publication *Taking the SAT* from the College Board. If you haven't received yours, talk to your guidance department right away. You'll find invaluable information about the test as well as test-taking advice in that pamphlet.

WHAT ABOUT RECENT CHANGES?

The PSAT and SAT were slightly redesigned in 1993 and '94, but the changes are not drastic. In fact, many test-takers will be more comfortable with the "new" tests because the antonyms (which everyone hated) are gone, and the reading passages appear to be not so difficult. Even difficult reading is okay—if you have enough time. But students have always cried for more time on SATs and PSATs.

Now, if there's a serious time crunch, it's apt to be on the math half of the exam, where multiple concepts are tested in lots of the problems, making them knottier to solve.

A quick way to spot the differences between the old and new tests is by looking at these brief lists:

PSATs and SATs

Verbal Changes

- No antonym questions
- Longer reading passages
- Questions testing critical reading skills (this book's strength—see pages 69–95)
- Questions on vocabulary in context
- No Test of Standard Written English (TSWE) segment in the SAT I

Math Changes

- Calculator use allowed
- Questions asking you to compute answers and record them on a numbered grid
- Application of math principles to more complex reasoning problems

VERBAL REASONING QUESTIONS ON THE PSAT AND SAT I

Analogy questions on PSATs and SATs ask you to analyze the relationship in a given pair of words and find another pair showing the same relationship, choosing among five answers. You can practice and get very good at analogies, but you will get them all right *only* if you have a fat vocabulary. At least 25% are pure vocabulary questions.

Sentence completion questions are based on the social and natural sciences and the humanities. Selecting correct answers depends on your full understanding of what the sentence is saying—its meaning and its logic. As with all PSAT and SAT questions, more than a quarter of them will demand an educated vocabulary.

Reading comprehension questions expect you to read with a careful, logical, discerning eye. On PSATs and SATs, you'll be reading four passages, one of which is a double passage that presents a topic from two viewpoints. Reading passages are longer and more interesting than those in the past, so that your chance of staying involved as you read is greater and that should help your score. Just over half of the verbal questions come from these passages, and several questions test the meanings of words in context. And again, these questions require a college-level vocabulary.

A BIG, STRONG VOCABULARY IS THE KEY TO DOING WELL ON THE VERBAL QUESTIONS.

Test of Standard Written English: This 30-minute segment of the past SAT has been removed from the SAT I and has become part of the *SAT II: Writing Test.* This new achievement test contains grammar and usage sections exactly like those on the past TSWE plus an essay topic requiring a written response. You'll have 20 minutes to write the essay, which will be read and scored by two separate readers—just as the English Composition Achievement essay is currently scored. Because of this change, college admissions personnel will now see a "classroom sample" of every applicant's writing if they require a score from the SAT II: Writing Test.

MATH REASONING QUESTIONS ON THE PSAT AND SAT I

According to the College Board, the math portions of the new exams reflect changes in the current high school climate—most notably, the widespread use of calculators and calculator-based instruction. The tests' emphasis on your ability to apply mathematical concepts and interpret data has been increased. Both tests call upon your ability to solve math/algebra reasoning questions and math/geometry reasoning questions.

Better than half of the math questions are the same old thing—*multiple-choice questions* with 5 answer choices. *Quantitative comparison questions* are 25 percent of the exam. (They were 33 percent of the old tests.) These questions, which have only 4 answer choices, depend upon logic and common sense as well as basic mathematical principles for solution.

The remaining portion of the exam consists of questions requiring you to compute the answers and record them on a special grid on the answer sheet. These are definitely not multiple choice or even multiple guess! Although you may use a calculator (no hand-held computers), no question requires a calculator for its solution. In early test trials, students scored slightly higher using calculators—perhaps because they were accustomed to using them in the classroom and felt more comfortable or because they could always check their work for accuracy. However, you've got to decide what's most comfortable for you—don't make the mistake of feeling that you must use a calculator because it's allowed.

SING HALLELUJAH!

Read this and feel glad. You really are working with the right book. Why? Because we don't just present endless problems to work, we explain HOW TO DO THEM! We always have. Other books mainly offer lists and say, "Learn all this stuff." We say, "Read this material, practice with it, then test yourself with real questions." You need this knowledge forever, you know, not just for a test.

For instance . . . is geometry merely a dim memory? No sweat. All the critical stuff is in this book.

Is your vocabulary teeny-tiny? Uh-oh. The PSAT and SAT are giant vocabulary tests. Luckily, **you are holding the most reliable, computer-analyzed word list on the market.** These are the words and roots you must know—the ones that appear on SATs and PSATs year after year.

Last, this book has a sense of humor. Learning goes better when you're enjoying yourself. We don't get our humor from poking fun at the test-makers, either. How can that possibly help you? Turn to the section titled Words From Special Places (p. 114–125) and read some bits. See?

HOW CAN I LEARN ALL THIS MATERIAL?

Don't underestimate your brain. It can store everything in this book and lots more. Most people die with zillions of brain cells unused. What a waste.

For example, look at any vocabulary lesson. You'll probably know at least half of the words, maybe more. That leaves about 15-20 words to learn for each lesson. Follow the book's suggestions about how to do it by making flash cards, working with a friend or establishing a prep group, asking teachers for help, and so on. Your brain is the finest thing you own, so dust it off and put it to work.

Set a schedule for review and be faithful. Things on a schedule always get done, just ask Bill and Hillary.

Tell yourself you WILL do this thing and do it right.

What you need to know is in this book.

What are you waiting for?

SCORING HIGH ON THE PSAT AND SAT

WILL YOUR SCORES VARY FROM TEST TO TEST?

Test takers should know that variation in scores for an individual is normal. A student might test 600 as the first verbal score on an SAT. A few months later, this same student could score as low as 550 or as high as 650. Needless to say, this variation is one reason for suggesting that students take these exams *more than once*. It is also the reason for students, parents, teachers, and college admission officials to take *any* test result with a large box of salt.

HOW MUCH CAN YOU RAISE YOUR SCORE?

The authors' teaching experience has shown that a well-motivated, average student can raise a verbal or a math score, or both . . . and raise these scores significantly. For students who take Joan Carris's course, a jump in verbal score of 60-150 points is customary, and Bill McQuade has seen similar leaps in students' math scores through his own teaching. After the test is over, put it out of your mind. You gave it your all, and now it's over. Surely you are eager to go on to other things, such as graduation from high school. Fortunately, college admission officers know all of this. They know that a student is not a test score. They put the test score into its proper perspective, and all readers of this book should do likewise.

Unit 2: The Diagnostic SAT

Finding out where you stand now is a good basis for planning any review course. Knowing how you score today on a typical SAT will tell you which specific areas need the most review. Here's how to do it:

1. Set yourself up in a quiet place at home, with a timer.
2. Find the answer sheet at the back of this book.
3. Set the timer for 30 minutes per test segment (15 minutes for the final verbal and math segments) and do your absolute best, pretending that this is the real thing.
4. When you have completed all segments, score them and find where you stand on the scaled score.
5. Answer the analysis questions carefully. This section is the most important of all. It tells you where you are brilliant and how you can become so in areas that proved downright nasty.
6. And now, you can begin an intelligent series of review lessons based on what you KNOW YOU MUST KNOW.

THE TEST

Before starting the test, locate the answer sheet at the back of this book and tear it out.

SECTION 1	Time — 30 minutes	30 Questions

The following sentences need a word or words to complete their meaning. Choose the word or words that best fit the meaning of each sentence.

1. Captain Jack's ----, prompt, and intelligent reactions were often necessary to save his ship and her crew from disaster.

    (A) wise   (B) decisive   (C) swift   (D) capricious
    (E) astronomical

2. Drawn to home waters by a blend of acute senses of smell and taste, the spawning salmon combats ---- to reach the ---- of native streams.

    (A) all other life. .peace
    (B) nature. .solitude
    (C) any obstacle. .sanctuary
    (D) defensively. .origin
    (E) daily. .regions

3. The soft, rhythmic ---- of an owl's wings at night belies its ---- skill as a ruthless predator.

    (A) flap. .dangerous
    (B) beat. .dubious
    (C) occasion. .obvious
    (D) whir. .formidable
    (E) singing. .scheming

4. Apparently ---- now, scientists still hope that the enigmatic sources responsible for the "common cold" will one day be ----.

    (A) difficult. .captured
    (B) numberless. .recorded
    (C) accessible. .exposed
    (D) ill-defined. .enumerated
    (E) flagrant. .contained

5. Leukemia is a long and weary process of disease, ---- for a fortunate few, marching ---- toward death for others.

    (A) vanquished. .inexorably
    (B) mitigated. .vainly
    (C) conquered. .peacefully
    (D) doomed. .swiftly
    (E) foretold. .inevitably

5

6. Many team members were abrupt, even ---- at times, about responding to suggestions from their young, inexperienced swim team coach.

(A) pleasant
(B) curt
(C) uninterested
(D) insolent
(E) ignorant

7. The urban sophisticate and the more ---- rural dweller appear at odds only to the mind unaccustomed to ---- into mankind's common motivations.

(A) bumptious. .looking
(B) ingenuous. .delving
(C) casual. .searching
(D) bucolic. .probing
(E) naive. .analysis

8. Once an enemy's true nature is ----, an opponent has some chance to ---- the situation and perhaps gain the upper hand.

(A) superimposed. .recreate
(B) exposed. .arbitrate
(C) disguised. .ameliorate
(D) veiled. .understand
(E) manifest. .reverse

9. In general, ---- behavior on the part of administration aggravates an already tense worker problem instead of ---- it.

(A) humorless. .worsening
(B) responsible. .soothing
(C) autocratic. .alleviating
(D) irresponsible. .condoning
(E) meretricious. .maximizing

The following questions are based on analogous relationships. Choose the lettered pair that best expresses a relationship similar to the pair in capital letters.

10. FLIGHT : WINGS ::

(A) dancing : costume
(B) walking : legs
(C) gardening : tools
(D) swimming : gills
(E) sailing : instruction

11. PUP : SEAL ::

(A) student : teacher
(B) herd : sheep
(C) whelp : dog
(D) child : teenager
(E) veal : calf

12. LEAF : TREE ::

(A) pebble : rock
(B) plant : vegetation
(C) scene : book
(D) drink : water
(E) eagle : bird

13. IDEA : ABSTRACT ::

(A) theory : vague
(B) speech : entertaining
(C) project : innovative
(D) practice : medical
(E) earth : concrete

14. SPRING : FUTURE ::

(A) youth : promise
(B) art : career
(C) law : safety
(D) summer : flowers
(E) disease : death

15. EUPHONY : PLEASURE ::

(A) contortion : anger
(B) artistry : consideration
(C) satiety : discomfort
(D) ruckus : unease
(E) energy : enervation

Questions on the following reading passages should be answered based on what is stated or implied in the passage.

The Toltecs began to know great abundance and enjoy the generous gifts of the land, as had been foretold by Quetzalcoatl.

Line "He has great powers. He has made us rich. We
(5) have not known hunger since he arrived. Where he places his eyes and hands, everything is abundance and beauty."

Tula grew. People came from afar to admire its growth. Many asked permission to settle down and
(10) enjoy its abundance, which was distributed according to the needs of the people. They were all content because they all had more than they had ever had. Many worked. They were busy all day.

Quetzalcoatl had spent six years among the
(15) Toltecs. The granaries were full when he decided:

"There is prosperity and abundance in all the land. Let us extend it beyond the mountains. We shall go to the land of the Chichimecs. It is time to take my mission to them. I shall make them better,
(20) I shall gather them in towns, I shall teach them to till the land and to build their homes."

"Let us leave them in their land as they are now," Topiltzin argued. "They are barbarous, their life is violent and disorderly. They roam freely,

(25) like the wind in the mountains and the plains, with nothing to keep them. Leave them where they are. There is much that we must do in our own land."

"I do not belong to this land alone. They are all my friends, and I am to give to all of them. I shall

(30) take the gods of Tula to them," Quetzalcoatl said.

"Think carefully. You do not know them. They do not understand words. They are like savage animals, like jaguars," Topiltzin insisted.

"I shall go," said Quetzalcoatl. "My life must

(35) be accomplished. This time you will not accompany me because you do not have the will to go. I shall leave soon with some of my followers."

"Do not go with so few people! I shall accompany you with skillful warriors who are

(40) used to killing Chichimecs and avoiding their traps," Topiltzin insisted.

"I am not going there with violence. I shall go to them as I came here, to take them the gifts of life and the doctrine of sin and redemption."

(45) "You have not spoken of sin and redemption for a long time," Tatle remarked. He had been listening intently to the dialogue, and was then close to seventeen years of age. "You have not come near the Tree you planted in the square in a

(50) long time. The Tree has no shoots, it has not grown, it looks sad and lonely."

"During this time, Tatle, I have often thought of it. There was confusion in my spirit. Now the Tree orders me to spread good in other lands, to make

(55) others happy. It will soon have shoots."

16. The passage is most probably recounting

(A) history
(B) a paradox
(C) a contemporary life
(D) a myth or legend
(E) an allegorical tale

17. It can be inferred from the passage that

I. the city of Tula owed its growth to Quetzalcoatl

II. Quetzalcoatl believed he had been entrusted with a sacred mission

III. the followers of Quetzalcoatl will dissuade him from going to the land of the Chichimecs

IV. the society of the Toltecs was monotheistic

V. Quetzalcoatl's Tree was a symbol for him and the Toltecs

(A) I, III, and V
(B) I, II, and V
(C) II only
(D) I, II, and IV
(E) II, IV, and V

18. According to the passage, the prosperity of Tula

(A) was due to the Toltecs' godlike behavior
(B) occurred prior to Quetzalcoatl's appearance
(C) was a relatively recent development
(D) caused alarm among Quetzalcoatl's followers
(E) was yet to be established

19. When Tatle refers to Quetzalcoatl's Tree, saying that the Tree is "sad and lonely" in line 51, he means that

(A) the Tree is dying
(B) the Toltecs have ignored the Tree
(C) the Tree is bereft of friends
(D) there should have been celebrations around the Tree
(E) Quetzalcoatl has forgotten the Tree's significance

20. The "shoots" mentioned in line 55 refer to

(A) the spread of Quetzalcoatl's beliefs to other areas
(B) the Tree's growing roots and branches yet to develop
(C) the Toltecs' outlying settlements
(D) the "savage animals, like jaguars," line 33
(E) the distribution of Tula's riches, lines 10–11

21. Which of the following is NOT an objection Topiltzin raises to Quetzalcoatl's plan?

(A) the Chichimecs may pose a danger to Quetzalcoatl's party
(B) the Chichimecs move around a great deal
(C) the Chichimecs do not speak Quetzalcoatl's language
(D) Quetzalcoatl still has work to accomplish in Tula
(E) Quetzalcoatl cannot help the Chichimecs as he has the Toltecs

The most important function of vitamin A (retinol) in the body is in forming and keeping healthy the epithelial tissue, which is the shield the body forms to
Line protect it from infections and other external hazards.
(5) Skin is epithelial tissue; so are the mucous linings of the mouth, the stomach, and the intestines (small and large), and the mucous linings in the respiratory, genital, and urinary tracts.

Rich sources of vitamin A include liver, kidney,
(10) fish liver oil, eggs, whole milk, and yellow and green vegetables (carrots, sweet potatoes, squash, spinach, broccoli) and some fruits. Eating liver and kidney once a week, eggs three times a week, and vegetables and fruits daily should give us all the
(15) vitamin A we need.

The major source of vitamin A in our diets is yellow and green vegetables. In these foods, vitamin A is in the form of carotene. Our bodies have the capacity to convert carotene to vitamin A (20) in the intestines and in the liver. However, we always have very small amounts of carotene circulating in the blood. This does not seem to have much value since the body uses only vitamin A.

(25) Carotenes are usually yellow, orange, or reddish in color. In some vegetables, this color is masked by the green of chlorophyll. Not every green vegetable contains carotenes. Remember the ones that do contain carotenes include spinach, (30) broccoli, and kale.

There are many carotenes and they vary in their nutritional quality. Some are converted to vitamin A more efficiently than others. Beta-carotene is the most efficiently converted form and therefore it (35) has the highest nutritional value of all the carotenes. However, this form is seldom found alone. Most yellow and green vegetables contain a mixture of carotenes. The intensity of the color, yellow or green, is usually a reliable measure of (40) the content of carotenes or vitamin A.

A deficiency of vitamin A causes the skin and the mucous linings to become dry, flat, and scaly. This invites infections and allows germs to penetrate into the body. Our resistance to (45) infectious diseases of all kinds is very much dependent on having enough vitamin A and a healthy epithelial tissue. So our parents were very wise in insisting on a spoonful of cod liver oil with breakfast during the winter months, when green (50) and yellow vegetables weren't plentiful.

We shouldn't forget, either, that the epithelial tissue around the eye cavity dries up in vitamin A deficiency. In its advanced stage, this leads to a disease, xerophthalmia (pronounced zer-of- (55) thalmia), in which the tear secretion stops, eyelids swell and become sticky (as bacteria infects them and fills them with pus), and eventually bacterial infection of the eye causes ulcerations on the cornea and blindness.

(60) This condition is common in many countries where vitamin A is lacking in the diet. One estimate put the number of children going blind each year because of vitamin A deficiency at 80,000, with about half of them dying of this (65) deficiency.

In North America, the evidence for vitamin A deficiency, while not alarming, should be of concern. We should be concerned that recent surveys found many Canadian and American (70) children have low concentrations of the vitamin in the blood. Analysis of livers of adult accident victims in the U.S. and Canada showed many to have below-average or low concentrations of vitamin A. This is an indication of a long-term (75) deficiency state.

Recent studies also showed that the absence of vitamin A increases the susceptibility of the epithelial tissue not only to infections but also to carcinogens. This opens a new vista that suggests (80) vitamin A protects the body from carcinogenic substances.

22. According to the passage, people need vitamin A to

(A) form and maintain epithelial tissue
(B) circulate blood properly
(C) assist in digestion and food absorption
(D) maintain proper muscle tone
(E) assist them in adhering to a diet

23. The carotene circulating in the blood is of little value because

(A) it is indigestible
(B) the body uses only vitamin A
(C) it is of inferior quality to vitamin A
(D) it is a carotene mixture
(E) beta-carotene cannot be absorbed

24. Of the carotenes,

(A) few convert to vitamin A efficiently
(B) most are in yellow vegetables
(C) beta-carotene has the highest nutritional value
(D) that found in liver is most nutritional
(E) the ones masked by deep green color are of least value nutritionally

25. It can be inferred from the passage that a person deficient in vitamin A would be prone to

(A) heart attacks
(B) kidney problems
(C) gallstones
(D) colds and other respiratory infections
(E) muscular aches and pains

26. According to the passage, the eye disease xerophthalmia is caused by

(A) vitamin A deficiency
(B) lack of beta-carotene in the diet
(C) excess tear secretions
(D) improper hygiene
(E) swollen eyelids

27. The passage mentions all of the following as parts of the body that would be adversely affected by vitamin A deficiency EXCEPT the

(A) eyes
(B) bones
(C) skin
(D) stomach lining
(E) urinary tract

28. In line 19, the word "capacity" most nearly means

    (A) role
    (B) volume
    (C) ability
    (D) suitability
    (E) maximum amount

29. The author views the evidence that many North Americans have a vitamin A deficiency with

    (A) doubt about the reliability of the tests that yielded this evidence
    (B) anger over North Americans' unwillingness to eat foods high in vitamin A
    (C) regret over the relative inaccessibility of green and yellow vegetables at certain times of the year

    (D) alarm over the high probability that many of these North Americans will go blind
    (E) dismay at the possibility that these North Americans may be subject to various diseases

30. The passage suggests that one reason for eating green and yellow vegetables regularly is to

    (A) prevent heart and lung diseases
    (B) maintain the tissues of the ears, eyes, and nose
    (C) enable the body to form carotenes in the bloodstream
    (D) help the body resist the effects of carcinogenic substances
    (E) facilitate the body's conversion of vitamin A into beta-carotene

> **STOP** Do not go on to the next section of the test until you have set your timer.

| **SECTION 2** | **Time — 30 minutes** | **25 Questions** |

> In this section solve each problem, and then choose the most appropriate answer from the choices given.

1. All of the following pairs (x,y) satisfy the inequality $y \leq x^2$ EXCEPT

   (A) $(1,-2)$ (B) $(2,4)$ (C) $(-2,4)$
   (D) $(-3,4)$ (E) $(-1,2)$

Test No.	% Correct
1	90%
2	75%
3	95%
4	90%
5	85%

2. The above table shows the percent correct Olga received on each of five 60-question tests. What was the total number of questions Olga answered correctly during the five tests?

   (A) 87 (B) 255 (C) 261 (D) 270 (E) 300

3. A boy bicycles 1 mile south and then 2 miles east. Bicycling in which of the following directions will bring him back to his starting point?

   (A) 2 miles west and 1 mile north
   (B) 2 miles east and 1 mile north
   (C) 1 mile west and 2 miles north
   (D) 2 miles west and 1 mile south
   (E) 3 miles north

4. A right triangle that is also an isosceles triangle has a 90° angle and an $x°$ angle. $x =$

   (A) 35 (B) 45 (C) 55 (D) 75 (E) 90

5. The area A of a rectangle is given by the formula $A = \ell w$ where ℓ is the length and w is the width. What is the width of a rectangle when $\ell = 150$ and $A = 1,050$?

   (A) 7 (B) 15.75 (C) 70 (D) 157.5 (E) 700

6. The image above is the face of a clock as it would be seen in a mirror. What is the time shown?

   (A) 1:20 (B) 4:05 (C) 11:40 (D) 12:05
   (E) 12:20

7. In a given month, Friday is the 21st day of the month. What day of the week was the 1st of the month?

    (A) Monday   (B) Thursday   (C) Friday
    (D) Saturday   (E) Sunday

8. Two numbers a and b can be arranged in two different orders, (a,b) and (b,a). In how many different orders can three numbers be arranged?

    (A) 2   (B) 3   (C) 4   (D) 5   (E) 6

9. If $x + 3y = 4(3y)$, then $x =$

    (A) $3y$
    (B) $4y$
    (C) $9y$
    (D) $12y$
    (E) It cannot be determined from the information given.

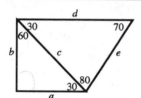

10. What is the area of the right triangle formed by halving a square with perimeter 36 along its diagonal?

    (A) 9   (B) 18   (C) $18 + 9\sqrt{2}$ (D) 40.5
    (E) 81

Note: Figure not drawn to scale.

11. Which of the five line segments shown above is the longest?

    (A) a (B) b (C) c (D) d (E) e

12. If $a = x$ and $b = y$ and $xy = 0$, then which of the following is true?

    (A) $a = 0$
    (B) $b = 0$
    (C) $a = 0$ and $b = a$
    (D) $a = 0$ or $b = 0$
    (E) None of the above

13. If $156.00 is divided among three people in the ratio of $\frac{1}{2} : \frac{1}{3} : \frac{1}{4}$, what is the *difference* between the greatest share received and the least share received?

    (A) $34.67   (B) $36   (C) $39   (D) $48
    (E) $72

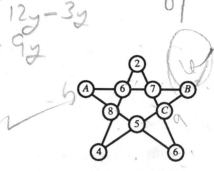

14. If the sums of four circles along any line segment of the star are all equal, then $B =$

    (A) 3
    (B) 4
    (C) 6
    (D) 7
    (E) It cannot be determined from the information given.

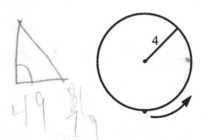

15. A bug starts walking around a circle with radius 4. If after having taken four steps he has walked around 25% of the circle, how long are each of his steps?

    (A) $\dfrac{2}{\pi}$ (B) $\dfrac{4}{\pi}$ (C) π (D) $\dfrac{\pi}{4}$ (E) $\dfrac{\pi}{2}$

16. Of the total number of days in a week, what fraction of them occur only 52 times in a leap year?

    (A) $\dfrac{1}{7}$ (B) $\dfrac{2}{7}$ (C) $\dfrac{3}{7}$ (D) $\dfrac{4}{7}$ (E) $\dfrac{5}{7}$

17. In a cube, in how many places are three edges mutually perpendicular?

    (A) 0   (B) 2   (C) 4   (D) 8   (E) 12

$$N = (2,4,6)$$
$$D = (3,6,9)$$

18. What is the square root of the difference between the greatest and least fractions that can be formed by choosing one number from set N to be the numerator of the fraction and one number from set D to be the denominator of the fraction?

    (A) $\dfrac{4}{3}$ (B) $\dfrac{3}{4}$ (C) 0   (D) $\dfrac{9}{16}$ (E) $\dfrac{16}{9}$

Questions 19 and 20 refer to the following definition:

$$\begin{vmatrix} a & b \\ c & d \end{vmatrix} = \frac{1}{ad - bc}$$

19. Which of the following is undefined?

(A) $\begin{vmatrix} 1 & 2 \\ 3 & 4 \end{vmatrix}$ (B) $\begin{vmatrix} 2 & 3 \\ 5 & 7 \end{vmatrix}$ (C) $\begin{vmatrix} 4 & 3 \\ 8 & 6 \end{vmatrix}$

(D) $\begin{vmatrix} 2 & -2 \\ 4 & 4 \end{vmatrix}$ (E) $\begin{vmatrix} -3 & -2 \\ 6 & -4 \end{vmatrix}$

20. $\begin{vmatrix} 4 & 4 \\ 3 & 5 \end{vmatrix}$ equals which of the following?

(A) $\begin{vmatrix} 4 & 5 \\ 4 & 3 \end{vmatrix}$ (B) $\begin{vmatrix} 2 & 0 \\ 6 & 4 \end{vmatrix}$ (C) $\begin{vmatrix} -3 & -4 \\ -5 & 4 \end{vmatrix}$

(D) $\begin{vmatrix} 5 & 6 \\ 5 & 2 \end{vmatrix}$ (E) $\begin{vmatrix} 7 & 2 \\ 10 & 0 \end{vmatrix}$

21. At a casino there are three tables. The payoff at the first table is 10:1, at the second 30:1, and at the third 40:1. If a woman bets $10.00 at each table and wins at two of the tables, what is the difference between her maximum and minimum possible gross winnings?

(A) $200   (B) $300   (C) $400   (D) $500
(E) $600

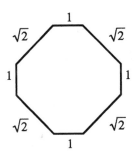

Note: Figure not drawn to scale.

22. The sides of an octagon alternate in length. As pictured above, each side with length 1 is next to a side of length $\sqrt{2}$. What is the area of the octagon?

(A) 5   (B) 6   (C) 7   (D) 8   (E) 9

23. What is the area of the square with vertices at the points (0,2), (0,–2), (2,0), and (–2,0)?

(A) 4   (B) 6   (C) 8   (D) 12   (E) 16

24. A typewriter that cost $250 two years ago now costs $100. What was the percent decrease in price?

(A) 30%   (B) 60%   (C) 75%   (D) 150%
(E) 250%

25. Six equilateral triangles with side 1 are joined to form a hexagon. A circle is circumscribed about the hexagon. What is the area of the shaded region in the figure above?

(A) $\pi - \dfrac{\sqrt{3}}{2}$

(B) $\pi - \dfrac{3\sqrt{3}}{2}$

(C) $\dfrac{\pi\sqrt{3}}{3}$

(D) $2\pi - \dfrac{\sqrt{3}}{2}$

(E) $2\pi - 3\sqrt{3}$

STOP   Do not go on to the next section of the test until you have set your timer.

SECTION 3   Time — 30 minutes   35 Questions

The following sentences need a word or words to complete their meaning. Choose the word or words that best fit the meaning of each sentence.

1. Most readers enthusiastically recommend Swift's social satire, mainly because they enjoy its ----.

   (A) cultural awareness   (B) biting humor
   (C) humane approach   (D) polite critique
   (E) breadth of vocabulary

2. We explained our late arrival due to a(n) ---- circumstance—a very flat tire; even so, we were marked tardy, as the rules on tardiness are ----.

   (A) annoying. .arbitrary
   (B) freakish. .a nuisance
   (C) extenuating. .inflexible
   (D) unfortunate. .regrettable
   (E) embarrassing. .inexcusable

3. A small nation that ignores the ---- of a foreign government may awake one day to the ---- of its own.

   (A) wisdom. .continuance
   (B) ambition. .pressure
   (C) force. .enhancement
   (D) prestige. .flourishing
   (E) colonialism. .downfall

4. The size and simplicity of an Indian tipi lead us to conclude that it was designed more for ---- than for ----.

   (A) easiness. .feasibility
   (B) livability. .ease
   (C) practicality. .ostentation
   (D) pretense. .usefulness
   (E) tradition. .efficiency

5. Modern transportation, though more ---- than older modes of transport, seldom offers the ---- atmosphere that was an inherent part of a conveyance like the stagecoach.

   (A) crowded. .genial
   (B) up-to-date. .unfortunate
   (C) numerous. .enforced
   (D) efficient. .convivial
   (E) progressive. .stylish

6. Although certain herbicides appear ---- to farmers who are deeply concerned with profit and loss, they have also ---- bird populations dependent on formerly weedy ditches and hedgerows.

   (A) beneficial. .decimated
   (B) useful. .augmented
   (C) dangerous. .disturbed
   (D) mandatory. .enhanced
   (E) costly. .banished

7. To avid playgoers, the return of classic theater dramas is ----, but it is surely ---- as well, emphasizing as it does the dismaying lack of quality in many modern productions.

   (A) welcome. .ironic
   (B) endless. .fitting
   (C) deplorable. .pragmatic
   (D) inane. .regrettable
   (E) inconsequential. .ludicrous

8. Perhaps the earliest chorus on earth, the primeval spring chorale of the frogs heralded both ---- and the ---- of emerging life forms.

   (A) artistry. .awareness
   (B) mating time. .dawn
   (C) morning. .confusion
   (D) unpredictability. .era
   (E) modernity. .complexity

9. Changed from its original meaning, the word *sophistry* now has a negative ----, suggesting a(n) ---- argument resulting from skillful, deceitful tactics.

   (A) feeling. .reprehensible
   (B) significance. .debatable
   (C) connotation. .specious
   (D) interpretation. .formidable
   (E) cast. .open-ended

10. The rabbit named Fiver in *Watership Down*, a beloved animal fantasy, appeared ---- and timorous to his fellows, yet he eventually proved his value as an oracle through repeated, ---- predictions.

   (A) nervous. .unwarranted
   (B) weak. .fallacious
   (C) untoward. .direful
   (D) unstable. .unerring
   (E) autocratic. .insightful

11. GYMNASIUM : EXERCISE ::

(A) courtyard : entertainment
(B) house : dwelling
(C) university : study
(D) mall : recreation
(E) laboratory : microscope

12. OVERTURE : PERFORMANCE ::

(A) planet : heavens
(B) day : month
(C) birth : growth
(D) plan : architecture
(E) prologue : book

13. SALESPERSON : COMMISSION ::

(A) theatergoer : ticket
(B) bank teller : interest
(C) professor : tenure
(D) pharmacist : prescription
(E) waiter : tip

14. JOKE : SPEECH ::

(A) fact : theme
(B) seasoning : stew
(C) design : apparel
(D) droplet : torrent
(E) humor : comedy

15. HEW : TREE ::

(A) compose : speech
(B) taunt : bully
(C) observe : silence
(D) defame : reputation
(E) believe : code

16. COURT : JUSTICE ::

(A) school : instructors
(B) textbook : enlightenment
(C) graveyard : tombs
(D) office : records
(E) library : tranquillity

17. SHADOW : SUBSTANCE ::

(A) supposition : proof
(B) dawn : dusk
(C) moisture : atmosphere
(D) theory : hypothesis
(E) ghost : apparition

18. NOTICEABLE : LURID ::

(A) imperfect : flawed
(B) humorous : boring
(C) huge : enormous
(D) difficult : grueling
(E) perceptive : shrewd

19. CONTRITE : REMORSE ::

(A) angry : haste
(B) hearty : hunger
(C) exasperated : hysteria
(D) envious : jealousy
(E) jocose : cupidity

20. EXPRESSION : DISARMING ::

(A) construction : unique
(B) physique : lithe
(C) facade : antique
(D) wit : impenetrable
(E) outlook : ingenuous

21. DISCONCERTED : APLOMB ::

(A) antic : reserve
(B) static : balance
(C) audacious : appetite
(D) austere : restraint
(E) animated : spirit

22. BELIEF : RECANT ::

(A) ill will : harbor
(B) truth : acknowledge
(C) knowledge : disavow
(D) tenet : embrace
(E) credo : espouse

23. PROPAGANDA : INDOCTRINATE ::

(A) litigation : decide
(B) mythology : instruct
(C) science : advance
(D) solicitation : reward
(E) rhetoric : stupefy

Bank runs are the bogeymen of American bank regulators. The regulators' ultimate nightmare is a line of angry depositors clamoring for their money
Line at the doors of closed savings institutions. Often it
(5) seems that all other concerns, including preventing bank fraud, take second place behind shoring up confidence in the savings system.

This concern for the public's confidence in savings institutions leads to some strange policies. (10) One example is the secrecy shrouding the results of regular bank examinations. After a great deal of technical analysis of the records of individual savings institutions, bank examiners boil down their findings to one number: the institution's (15) rating. On a scale of one to five, one is the best, five the worst. This number is easy to understand. Yet it is one of the most closely guarded secrets in the federal government. Bank regulators are afraid that the number is *too* easy to understand. The (20) public would pull its funds from a savings institution with a "five" rating, causing a run. The institution would probably fail. And that, the regulators say, would be bad.

It may not be obvious to the public why a (25) poorly managed outfit should be protected as it continues to collect their money. Since a "five" rating usually results from fraud or mismanagement, bank regulators may be inadvertently covering up criminal behavior. The (30) explanation has been that a run on a sick bank might lead to a panic at healthy banks, thus endangering the economy and collapsing the financial system.

History would indeed make one fear a bank (35) panic. In the past 150 years, mobs at the closed brass doors of a bank have been more directly tied to the onset of economic depression than have the most violent of stock market crashes. The run itself, though, isn't the problem. It's what (40) government does afterward that causes the damage.

Runs, however, do catch people's attention. A simple bank run may be thoroughly "rational." Depositors suddenly receive new information and (45) question the safety of their bank. Knowing the bank can't pay everyone, they rush to get there while it still has money. It's rational, but turbulent. For instance, a contemporary account of the Cincinnati Bank Riot of 1842 describes how a (50) crowd forcibly entered a closed bank and commenced the demolition of everything they could lay their hands on.

"Irrational" runs are even more dangerous. The Cincinnati crowd trashed only the banks that they (55) felt had cheated them with worthless currency. What bank regulators fear is that a rational run will spread to healthy banks, causing an irrational panic. If solvent banks have trouble paying their depositors, the crisis of confidence could shake the (60) entire financial system. The outstanding example is the onset of the Great Depression, which was marked by not one but three waves of bank panics before President Roosevelt declared the Bank Holiday of March 1933.

(65) However, bank failures by themselves do not trigger a panic. The trauma of the Great Depression has obscured the memory of a wave of bank closings during the 1920s, when some 4,400 savings institutions failed. Yet despite the high (70) number of bank closings, there was no general panic. What was the difference between the routine bank failures of the 1920s and the waves of bank closings in the early depression?

The most persuasive answer is that the (75) depression bank panics were part and parcel of the mechanism that created the Great Depression in the first place. No less an authority than Milton Friedman argues that the downturn of 1929 would have ended in 1930 as a severe but standard (80) recession if it had not been for disastrous bungling by the people in charge of the nation's money supply. Friedman maintains that the economy waxes and wanes in direct response to expansion and contraction in the money supply. According to (85) Friedman's analysis, the bank runs of the 1930s caused the money supply to contract by taking deposits out of circulation. The Federal Reserve System should have compensated by pumping more money into the system. Instead it did just the (90) opposite, contracting the available money and so strangling the economy. Bank runs became more intense, removing even more deposits from the financial system and diminishing the money stock even further.

(95) In this light, the bank panics of 1932 and 1933 were not so unreasonable after all. If the banking system as a whole is riding a downward spiral, it makes sense to try to step off. Blaming bank panics on the depositors is backward. Sound banks (100) became swept up in a panic along with the bad because a disastrous economic policy was victimizing both.

The Federal Reserve System, accepting Friedman's analysis, now plans to counter any (105) future runs on savings institutions by making more funds available. Thus, bank regulators' fears about causing a panic, and the secrecy these fears have brought about, are no longer justified. Indeed, depositors are not likely to stage a run at a healthy (110) bank unless they doubt its condition. A panic is far more likely to result from poor information or rumor than from reliable information.

24. The main purpose of the passage is to

(A) explain the difference between rational and irrational bank runs

(B) provide a new interpretation of the causes of the bank runs of the 1920s

(C) refute bank regulators' assumption that bank fraud and mismanagement are the primary cause of widespread bank runs

(D) suggest that the secrecy brought about by bank regulators' fear of widespread bank panics is unnecessary

(E) argue that Federal Reserve System policies should be changed

25. By calling bank runs "the bogeymen of American bank regulators" (line 1), the author suggests that bank regulators

(A) fear the violence that sometimes accompanies bank runs
(B) allow superstition to determine their behavior
(C) are unnecessarily frightened of a largely imaginary danger
(D) believe that bank runs constitute a serious, though somewhat overblown, threat
(E) fail to distinguish between rational and irrational bank runs

26. To the author, the policy of keeping the results of bank examinations secret is primarily

(A) a necessary evil
(B) a disservice to the public
(C) an inadequate response to an enormous problem
(D) an understandable but misguided practice
(E) a deliberately deceptive procedure

27. "It may not be obvious . . ." in line 24 conveys a sense of

(A) irony about the reasons for keeping the results of bank examinations secret
(B) regret over bank regulators' inability to trust the public's perceptions
(C) amazement over the incompetence of some bank managers
(D) resentment against public misunderstanding of bank regulators' motives
(E) doubt about the correlation between bank runs and general economic depressions

28. The passage suggests that bank regulators fear bank runs primarily because the regulators

(A) know that bank runs usually pose a serious threat to public safety
(B) believe that series of bank runs cause general economic depressions
(C) assume that rational runs are more dangerous than are irrational runs
(D) wish to forestall disclosure of possible fraud or incompetence on the part of bank managers
(E) do not trust the Federal Reserve System to react appropriately to such runs

29. The author of the passage suggests that which of the following would occur if the results of bank examinations were released to the public?

(A) Public confidence in the Federal Reserve System would increase.
(B) Bank runs would be confined primarily to banks that suffer from fraud or mismanagement.
(C) Bank failures would evoke less violent responses on the part of depositors.

(D) Economic recessions would usually lead to major depressions.
(E) The Federal Reserve System would have to pump money into the economy more often.

30. According to the passage, the primary difference between "rational" bank runs and "irrational" bank runs is that "rational" runs

(A) are more likely to provoke violence than are irrational runs
(B) are more likely to endanger the whole economy than are irrational runs
(C) are more likely to cause banks to run out of money than are irrational runs
(D) result from misinterpretation of old information about banks while irrational runs result from the reception of new information
(E) have unhealthy, often mismanaged banks as their targets while irrational runs target healthy, solvent banks

31. The author cites the Cincinnati Bank Riot of 1842 in lines 48-52 primarily in order to

(A) explain why bank runs attract a great deal of attention
(B) argue that violence almost inevitably accompanies public distrust in savings institutions
(C) demonstrate the difference between the bank failures of the 1920s and earlier bank runs
(D) provide an example of a bank run that could have been prevented by more effective government action
(E) illustrate the mechanism whereby rational bank runs often lead to irrational panics

32. The author discusses the bank closings of the 1920s (lines 66-71) primarily in order to establish that

(A) large numbers of bank closings often precede the onset of a general economic depression
(B) proper government intervention in the face of bank closings can prevent a general bank panic
(C) the public prefers not to remember the difficulties caused by large numbers of bank closings
(D) large numbers of "rational" bank runs need not lead to large numbers of irrational bank runs
(E) the runs triggered by those closings were more "rational" than the bank runs of the 1930s

33. The word "wave" in line 67 most nearly means

(A) cycle
(B) up-and-down movement
(C) persistent condition
(D) surge
(E) signal

34. The phrase "disastrous bungling" in line 80 refers to which of the following actions?

    (A) Banks failed to pay their depositors.
    (B) Bank regulators inadvertently encouraged irrational bank runs.
    (C) Depositors caused the money supply to contract by removing their money from banks.
    (D) The federal government failed to take action to keep a minor economic recession from becoming a major depression.
    (E) The Federal Reserve System took money out of circulation.

35. The word "contract" in line 86 most nearly means

    (A) arrange
    (B) agree
    (C) decrease
    (D) acquire
    (E) bind

STOP   Do not go on to the next section of the test until you have set your timer.

SECTION 4	Time — 30 minutes	25 Questions

Questions 1–15 each consist of two quantities. You are to compare the two quantities and write for your answer:

- A   if the quantity in Column A is greater;
- B   if the quantity in Column B is greater;
- C   if the two quantities are equal;
- D   if the relationship between the two quantities cannot be determined from the information given.

Information that may be used to determine the relationship between the two quantities is centered above the two columns.

	Column A	Column B
1.	2^8	8^2

Five years ago it cost 20¢ more to buy blue ribbon than to buy red ribbon.

2.	The cost of red ribbon now	The cost of blue ribbon now

50% of y equals 180

3.	y	90

$t < s$

4.	The average of t and s	s

5.	The number of prime numbers that are between 1 and 100	The number of odd numbers that are between 1 and 100
6.	The product of a negative number and a positive number	The product of two negative numbers

$x^2 < 25$
$y^3 < 125$

7.	x	y

Column A	Column B

The area of the shaded region in square R > the area of the shaded region in square S.

Note: Figure not drawn to scale.

8.	Area square R	Area square S

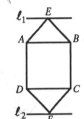

$\ell_1 \| \ell_2 \| AB \| CD$
$ABCD$ is a square.

Note: Figure not drawn to scale.

9.	Area of $\triangle AEB$	Area of $\triangle DFC$

$b \neq 0$

10.	$a - b$	$a + b$

Note: Figure not drawn to scale.

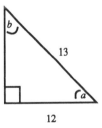

11.	a	b

$s^2 < 9$
$t^2 < 4$

12.	s	t

Let $\boxed{n}$ be defined by the equation
$$\boxed{n} = (n+1)^2$$

13.	$\dfrac{\boxed{8}}{\boxed{4}}$	$\boxed{2}$

Column A   Column B

$$0 < a < x$$
$$0 < b < y$$

14. $\dfrac{x+a}{y-b}$ $\dfrac{x-a}{y+b}$

15. The volume of a   The volume of a
    cube   rectangular solid

On the answer sheet are a set of ten blank grids. For each of the following problems, write the solution in the first row of the corresponding grid. For each box from the first row with a number, slash, or decimal point in it, fill in the corresponding square under the box. If there is more than one correct solution, grid in only one solution.

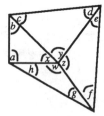

16. In the figure above, what is the value of:
    $(a + b - x) + (c + d - y) + (e + f - z) + (g + h - w)$?

$$4x + 3y = 15$$
$$-2x - 3y = -9$$

17. Given the two equations above, what is the value of $\dfrac{y}{x}$?

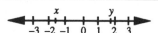

Note: Figure not drawn to scale.

18. What is the only possible *integer* value that can be the length of $\overline{xy}$?

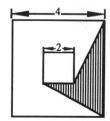

Note: Figure not drawn to scale.

Two concentric squares with parallel sides are drawn as above.

19. What is the area of the shaded region?

$$\frac{1}{2} < y < \frac{3}{4}$$

20. What is a possible value for $\sqrt{y}$?

21. Two cars start off at the same point on a straight highway facing opposite directions. Each car drives for 3 miles, takes a left turn, and then drives for 4 miles. How many miles apart are the two cars?

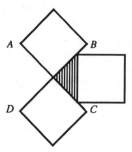

22. In the figure above, BD and AC are both line segments. All three squares shown have an area of 16. What is the area of the shaded isosceles triangle?

23. A man walks 6 miles at 4 miles per hour. At what speed would he need to travel during the next $2\frac{1}{2}$ hours to have an average speed of 6 miles per hour during the complete trip?

24. In 1983 a certain lamp cost $16.00. Each year from 1983 to 1987 the price went up by 50%. What was the price (in dollars) of the lamp in 1987?

25. What is the maximum number of 6 × 10 rectangles that can be placed in a 28 × 105 rectangle if there is no overlapping of the smaller rectangles and the edges of the small rectangles are parallel to the edges of the enclosing rectangle?

STOP Do not go on to the next section of the test until you have set your timer.

SECTION **5**   Time — 15 minutes   **13 Questions**

Questions on the following reading passages should be answered based on what is <u>stated</u> or <u>implied</u> in the passage.

Passage 1

In this passage, published in 1849, the writer reflects on the view from a canoe on a New England river.

The trees made an admirable fence to the landscape, skirting the horizon on every side. The single trees and the groves left standing on the
Line interval appeared naturally disposed, though the
(5) farmer had consulted only his convenience, for he too falls into the scheme of Nature. Art can never match the luxury and superfluity of Nature. In the former all is seen; it cannot afford concealed wealth, and is miserly in comparison; but Nature,
(10) even when she is scant and thin outwardly, satisfies us still by the assurance of a certain generosity at the roots. In swamps, where there is only here and there an evergreen tree amid the quaking moss and cranberry beds, the bareness
(15) does not suggest poverty. The single spruce, which I had hardly noticed in gardens, attracts me in such places, and now first I understand why people try to make them grow about their houses. But though there may be very perfect specimens in front-yard
(20) plots, their beauty is for the most part ineffectual there, for there is no such assurance, as in a swamp, of kindred wealth beneath and around them, to make them show to advantage. As we have said, Nature is a greater and more perfect art,
(25) the art of God; though, referred to herself, she is genius; and there is a similarity between her operations and human art even in the details and trifles. When the overhanging pine drops into the water, the sun and water, and the wind rubbing it
(30) against the shore, wear its boughs into fantastic shapes, white and smooth, as if turned in a lathe. Human art has wisely imitated those forms into which all matter is most inclined to run, such as foliage and fruit. Our art leaves its shavings and its
(35) dust about; Nature's art exhibits itself even in the shavings and the dust which we make, as the curled shavings drop from a wood plane, and borings cluster round an auger. She has perfected herself by an eternity of practice.

Passage 2

This passage, published in 1891, consists of an imaginary dialogue that takes place in an English country house.

(40) *Cyril [coming in through the open window from the terrace].* My dear Vivian, don't coop

yourself up all day in the library. It is a perfectly lovely afternoon. The air is exquisite. There is a mist upon the woods, like the purple bloom upon a plum. Let us go and lie on the grass and enjoy
(45) Nature.
Vivian. Enjoy Nature! I am glad to say that I have entirely lost that faculty. People tell us that Art makes us love Nature more than we loved her before; that it reveals her secrets to us; and that
(50) after a careful study of Corot and Constable we see things in her that had escaped our observation. My own experience is that the more we study Art, the less we care for Nature. What Art really reveals to us is Nature's lack of design, her curious crudities,
(55) her extraordinary monotony, her absolutely unfinished condition. Nature has good intentions, of course, but, as Aristotle once said, she cannot carry them out. When I look at a landscape I cannot help seeing all its defects. It is fortunate for
(60) us, however, that Nature is so imperfect, as otherwise we should have no art at all. Art is our spirited protest, our gallant attempt to teach Nature her proper place. As for the infinite variety of Nature, that is a pure myth. It is not to be found in
(65) Nature herself. It resides in the imagination, or fancy, or cultivated blindness of the person who looks at her.
Cyril. Well, you need not look at the landscape. You can lie on the grass and talk.
(70) *Vivian.* But Nature is so uncomfortable. Grass is hard and lumpy and damp, and full of dreadful crawling insects. Why, even the poorest workman could make you a more comfortable seat than the whole of Nature can. I don't complain. If Nature
(75) had been comfortable, we would never have invented architecture, and I prefer houses to the open air.

1. In line 4, "disposed" most nearly means

   (A) discarded
   (B) arranged
   (C) inclined
   (D) decided
   (E) transferred

2. The author of Passage 1 uses the phrase "a certain generosity at the roots" (lines 11-12) to suggest that

   (A) human art is merely an imitation of natural beauty
   (B) an observer must look very closely at a natural phenomenon to appreciate its beauty
   (C) nature's chief beauty lies in the way growing things are sustained by the abundance around them

(D) natural beauty is always abundant even if the abundance is not immediately apparent

(E) the richness of the soil from which trees and other plants grow is itself beautiful

3. For the author of Passage 1, the reason a spruce tree growing naturally in a swamp is more beautiful than is a spruce tree cultivated in a front yard is that the spruce tree in the swamp

(A) has not been spoiled by human intervention

(B) has been worn into interesting shapes by the sun and wind

(C) is surrounded by other naturally occurring phenomena

(D) is more likely to be healthy and therefore beautiful

(E) stands out against the relative poverty of its immediate environment

4. The "overhanging pine" in line 28 is presented as an example of

(A) a natural phenomenon that is more beautiful than anything a human artist could produce

(B) a natural form that is similar to art produced by human beings

(C) the beauty that results when natural processes of erosion affect growing things

(D) the great variety of forms that natural beauty can take

(E) the contrast between plants growing in the wild and those cultivated by humans

5. The contrast between the "shavings" and "dust" of human art and those of nature's art in lines 34-38 serves primarily to show that

(A) human art imitates natural forms

(B) human art is more wasteful than is nature's art

(C) nature's art is more carefully designed than is human art

(D) nature's art sometimes appears less abundant to the casual observer than does human art

(E) nature's art can make beautiful forms out of the leavings of human art

6. Cyril's speech in lines 40-46 serves primarily to

(A) characterize Cyril as a great lover of natural beauty

(B) characterize Vivian as a thoughtful person who reads a great deal

(C) establish the fact that Cyril has been outdoors while Vivian has been indoors

(D) outline a conventional notion of natural beauty to which Vivian can respond

(E) introduce the contrast between human art and natural beauty

7. Which of the following does Vivian in Passage 2 see as a positive outcome of nature's limitations?

(A) Nature's unfinished quality inspires people to create art.

(B) Nature's monotony makes people appreciate artistic variety.

(C) Nature's meager scope ensures that nature rarely intrudes on human life.

(D) Studying nature is relatively easy because natural phenomena exhibit so little variety.

(E) Observers must use their imaginations to see beauty in nature.

8. In Passage 2, Vivian mentions all of the following as defects of nature EXCEPT that nature is

(A) full of imperfections

(B) emotionally unsatisfying

(C) unable to deliver on its well-meant intentions

(D) less well designed than is art

(E) less interesting than is art

9. The word "poorest" in line 73 most nearly means

(A) most humble

(B) most pitiable

(C) most destitute

(D) least valuable

(E) least competent

10. Vivian would most likely say that the author of Passage 1 sees so much beauty in nature because he

(A) gives nature credit for her good intentions

(B) has too little appreciation for human art

(C) brings the beauty to nature from his own mind

(D) transfers his appreciation of beautiful human artifacts to similar natural phenomena

(E) ignores the lack of comfort in natural surroundings

11. One technique that the author of Passage 1 and Vivian in Passage 2 both employ is

(A) personification of nature as female

(B) comparison of specific artistic and natural forms

(C) use of nature metaphors to describe artistic endeavors

(D) use of specific artists as examples

(E) citation of earlier writers as authorities

12. In contrast to the tone of Passage 1, the tone of Vivian's speeches in Passage 2 is more

(A) inflammatory

(B) epigrammatic

(C) antiquated

(D) polished

(E) dramatic

13. Vivian would most likely react to the assertion by the author of Passage 1 that nature "has perfected herself by an eternity of practice" (lines 38-39) with

(A) dubious acquiescence
(B) studied indifference
(C) condescending pity
(D) lofty dismissal
(E) intense outrage

STOP Do not go on to the next section of the test until you have set your timer.

SECTION 6   Time — 15 minutes   **10 Questions**

In this section solve each problem, and then choose the most appropriate answer from the choices given.

1. $\left(\frac{1}{2}\right)\left(\frac{2}{3}\right)\left(\frac{3}{4}\right)\left(\frac{4}{5}\right)\left(\frac{5}{6}\right) = \frac{1}{x}$ $x =$

(A) $\frac{1}{6}$ (B) $\frac{11}{15}$ (C) $\frac{15}{11}$ (D) $\frac{23}{12}$ (E) 6

2. The statement $\frac{A}{B} = C$ implies that all of the following equations are correct EXCEPT

(A) $B = A \cdot C$
(B) $C = A \div B$
(C) $A = B \cdot C$
(D) $A = C \cdot B$
(E) All of the above statements are correct.

3. If $\frac{3}{4}$ the area of a square is 12, what is its area?

(A) 9 (B) 15 (C) 16 (D) 20 (E) 26

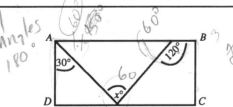

Note: Figure not drawn to scale.

4. In the figure above, $ABCD$ is a rectangle. $x =$
(A) 150 (B) 125 (C) 100 (D) 75 (E) 60

5. If the sum of $a - 2$, a, $a + 2$, and $a + 4$ is 0, then $a =$
(A) –2 (B) –1 (C) 0 (D) 2 (E) 4

6. If $x = \frac{1}{2}y$, and $w = 2x$, then y written in terms of w is

(A) $\frac{1}{4}w$ (B) $\frac{1}{2}w$ (C) w (D) $2w$ (E) $4w$

7. Which of the following statements is/are necessarily true?

I. If $\frac{n}{2}$ is an even number, then $\frac{n}{4}$ is an even number.

II. If $\frac{n}{4}$ is an even number, then $\frac{n}{2}$ is an even number.

III. If $\frac{n}{4}$ is an odd number, then $\frac{n}{2}$ is an even number.

(A) I only
(B) II only
(C) I and II only
(D) I and III only
(E) II and III only

8. $a = \frac{1}{x}$
$b = 9a$
$c = \frac{1}{b}$
$d = 9c$
$e = \frac{1}{d}$
$x =$
(A) a (B) b (C) c (D) d (E) e

9. If $b \neq a$, then $\frac{b}{a-b} - \frac{a}{b-a} =$

(A) –1
(B) 0
(C) 1
(D) $\frac{b-a}{a-b}$
(E) $\frac{a+b}{a-b}$

10. If $x^2 + y^2 = 15$ and $xy = 5$, then $x + y =$

   (A) 5 only
   (B) −5 only
   (C) 5 or −5
   (D) 5 or 10
   (E) 10 or −10

STOP   You have completed the test. You may go
back and review the questions in this section only.

THE ANSWERS

Verbal Sections

	Section 1		Section 3		Section 5
1. B	24. C	1. B	24. D	1. B	
2. C	25. D	2. C	25. C	2. D	
3. D	26. A	3. E	26. B	3. C	
4. D	27. B	4. C	27. A	4. B	
5. A	28. C	5. D	28. B	5. E	
6. B	29. E	6. A	29. B	6. D	
7. B	30. D	7. A	30. E	7. A	
8. E		8. B	31. A	8. B	
9. C		9. C	32. D	9. E	
10. B		10. D	33. D	10. C	
11. C		11. C	34. E	11. A	
12. C		12. E	35. C	12. E	
13. E		13. E		13. D	
14. A		14. B			
15. D		15. D			
16. D		16. B			
17. B		17. A			
18. C		18. D			
19. E		19. D			
20. A		20. B			
21. E		21. A			
22. A		22. C			
23. B		23. A			

Correct Answer Total _____
Wrong Answer Total _____

Math Sections

	Section 2		Section 4		Section 6
1. E	18. A	*1. A	†18. 3	1. E	
2. C	19. C	*2. D	†19. 3	2. A	
3. A	20. B	*3. A	†20. .8	3. C	
4. B	21. B	*4. B	(actually,	4. E	
5. A	22. C	*5. B	any value	5. B	
6. C	23. C	*6. B	between	6. C	
7. D	24. B	*7. D	.708 and	7. E	
8. E	25. B	*8. A	.865)	8. D	
9. C		*9. D	†21. 10	9. E	
10. D		*10. D	†22. 4	10. C	
11. D		*11. B	†23. 7.2 or 36/5		
12. D		*12. D	†24. 81		
13. B		*13. B	†25. 40		
14. C		*14. A			
15. E		*15. D			
16. E		†16. 0			
17. D		†17. 1/3 or .333			

*Questions with 4 answer choices
†Grid-in problems

Correct Answer Total _____
Wrong Answer Totals:

Sections 2 and 6 _____

Section 4, questions 1–15 _____

SCORING THE TEST

Verbal Sections 1, 3, and 5

1. Write the total number of questions answered correctly in space ① .
2. Multiply this correct answer total by 7.7 and write that product in space ② .
3. Add 200 and put the sum in space ③ .
4. Now, count the number of questions answered incorrectly—the number of wrong answers—and write this total in space ④ .
5. Multiply the value in space ④ by 2.5 and put this product in space ⑤ .
6. Subtract the value in space ⑤ from the total in space ③ (your right answer total) and put the result in space ⑥ . This number in space ⑥ is your *approximate* score.

Verbal Score Sheet

Total # Correct: ①_____   × 7.7 = ②_____

                                                          +   200

                              Positive Score ③_____

Total # Incorrect: ④_____   × 2.5 = ⑤ −_____

                              Approximate SAT score: ⑥_____

Math Sections 2, 4, and 6

Write the total number of questions you answered correctly in space ① . Multiply this by 10 and put the product in space ② . Add 200 and put the sum in space ③ . Write the *total* number of questions you answered incorrectly from sections 2 and 6 in space ④ . Multiply this by 2.5 and put the product in space ⑤ . Write the total number of quantitative comparison questions you answered incorrectly from section 4, questions 1-15, in space ⑥ . Multiply this by 3.33 and place the product in space ⑦. Place the sum of the values in spaces ⑤ and ⑦ in space ⑧. Subtract the value in space ⑧ from the value in space ③ and place the difference in space ⑨. This is your *approximate* score.

This is only an approximate score because your actual score not only depends on how well you do, but also on how well everyone else does who is taking the test with you. For example, if you make 20 mistakes but a lot of people only made 10 mistakes, your score will be lower than if you make 20 mistakes and everyone else makes 30 mistakes.

Math Score Sheet

Total # Correct: ①_____   × 10 = ②_____

                                                          +   200

                              Positive Score ③_____

incorrect multiple choice
from sections 2 and 6   ④_____   × 2.5 = ⑤ −_____

incorrect quantitative
comparison from section 2,
questions 1-15   ⑥_____   × 3.33 = ⑦_____

                              Negative score: ⑧_____
                              Approximate SAT score: ⑨_____

About Your Score

If you scored somewhat lower than you expected, fret not. This diagnostic SAT is often harder for students than real SATs, and most people score a bit lower. A *real* test will be a treat, then, won't it? Also, now you can analyze what caused you to lose points and do something about the problem before the actual test day.

Take a look at the evaluation sheet that follows. It will help to guide your study during further test preparation. And don't look at the columns that show what you did *wrong* as your sole evaluation. What did you do *right?* If you do certain things well, you know you can learn to do *other* things well, too.

Composite # = 10 - evenly

EVALUATION OF THE DIAGNOSTIC SAT

VERBAL QUESTIONS

Sentence Completions

_____ right   _____ wrong   (19 total questions)

Difficulty encountered:
_____ 1st half of question set (easy to medium)
_____ 2nd half of question set (more difficult)

Unknown words include _____

_____

Re-read the sentences and check out the vocabulary.
If you see that vocabulary is your real problem, spend the majority of your review time learning words.

Analogies

_____ right   _____ wrong   (19 total questions)

Difficulty encountered:
_____ 1st half of question set (easy to medium)
_____ 2nd half of question set (more difficult)

Unknown words include _____

_____

Relationships misunderstood or puzzling are _____

_____

_____

Were you always able to express the given relationship in a sentence or phrase? _____ If not, please look at the answers now and create a sentence or phrase that correctly states the given relationships. (Now, of course, these problems will seem much easier.)

Reading Comprehension Questions

_____ right   _____ wrong   (40 total questions)

Unknown words include _____

_____

Question type(s) that gave trouble? _____

_____

Conclusions

My best kinds of questions are _____

My worst question types are _____

Areas for serious review are _____

_____

Timing Problems?

If you ran out of time on any segments, remember that practice will make you faster. It will also give you a feel for a 30-minute test period—part of the "test smarts" you want to perfect.

Vocabulary Alert . . . One More Time

If you couldn't answer several questions because you didn't know words in the question or in the answers, then your problem is really VOCABULARY. Half (or more) of your review time should be spent learning the words in the Vocabulary Unit, pp. 127–226.

MATH QUESTIONS

Total number of problems worked correctly _____

Total missed _____

Total omitted problems _____

Any missed in problems numbered 1 to 12 in section 2? (These are normally simpler problems.) _____

If any missed, list why: (carelessness, moving too fast, unknown formula, etc.) _____

_____

_____

Other problems missed were in the areas of _____

_____

_____

Quantitative comparison problems worked correctly _____

Quantitative comparison problems missed _____

Do you need to study Math Lessons 15 and 16 to improve performance in this area? _____

Problems worked correctly tested which concepts? (These can be considered areas of strength.) _____

_____

_____

Conclusions

Best kinds of problems include _____

_____

(Merely skim over these topics in the Lessons as a refresher.)

I need to review and work practice problems in the areas of _____

_____

_____

Lessons I plan to STUDY include _____

_____

Timing Problems?

Folks who run out of time on PSAT and SAT math segments can get faster with practice, but only up to a point. Work too fast and you may begin to make errors. The only way to time yourself intelligently on these exams is by practicing at home, with a timer, until you find what works best for you. Racing madly through problems is a lousy idea.

RED ALERT
ABSOLUTELY VITAL HELP

You really need to know everything on these red-bordered pages. This information will:

- Give you confidence
- Point you to right answers
- Help you with logic and reasoning skills
- Buy you extra time for each test segment

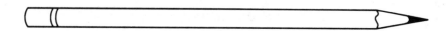

WHAT IS YOUR REAL TEST GOAL??

The dream score for most people is not a perfect 800 but somewhere between 500 and 700, which is more attainable. Most students know what realistic goals are for them. To set yours intelligently, check out this chart.

Goal	Maximum Mistakes Allowed		Maximum Omitted Questions
700 or above	3 (V) 4 (M)	+	1 (V) 3 – 4 (M)
600 or above	8 (V) 8 (M)	+	5 – 6 (V) 6 – 8 (M)
500 or above	12 (V) 12 (M)	+	12 – 14 (V) 14 – 16 (M)

In words, this chart says:

- You can work slowly and accurately, miss some questions and omit many, and still score over 600.
- You can bobble over a third of the math questions and almost that many verbal questions and still score over 500.

Given reasonable preparation, you can set a sensible goal and reach it.

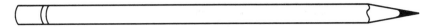

WHAT IS EACH QUESTION WORTH?

Each question on the verbal half of an SAT is worth approximately 7.7 points and 10 points on a PSAT, no matter how easy or hard or how long it took you to find it. Each math question is worth 10 points—a bit more than that on a PSAT. Remember that on an SAT, only 78 verbal questions and 60 math questions count for score. The experimental set of questions never counts toward your score.

 Do all of the simpler questions first, collecting as many right answers as possible. Don't invest precious minutes of agony in questions you are apt to miss.

 Always save the stumpers for last.

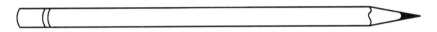

???   WHAT ABOUT GUESSING   ???

Should You Guess? Always make an educated guess whenever you can eliminate one or two wrong answers. The more wrong answers you can eliminate, the better your chances.

What Is an Educated Guess? An educated guess is based on some knowledge and/or a gut feeling arising from your awareness of the subject. Educated guessers eliminate wrong answers carefully, one by one.

Is There a Guessing Penalty? Yes, but it's minor when compared with omitting many questions. You lose one fourth of a correct answer for every wrong answer throughout most of the test. For the 20 quantitative comparison questions, which have only 4 answer choices, you lose one third of a right answer. There is no penalty for wrong answers on math grid-ins.

How Many Points Can Guessing Earn You? Because probability is on your side, here's how educated guessing works for you:

 On a set of 10 multiple-choice math questions, you answer the first 6 correctly, without guessing. You make educated guesses on the next 2 and get them right, but you guess wrong on the last 2 and miss both. Remember that one fourth of the points you can earn are taken off for each wrong answer.

 Given about 10 points for each right answer, here's your score for this 10-question set:
$$60 + 20 = 80 - 5 = 75$$

If you had not guessed, your score would have been only 60 points!
Wouldn't you really rather have 75 points?

How Do You Make an Educated Guess? Good guesses result from using every bit of information in the test itself and in YOU.

 For Verbal Questions, ask:
  What kind of question is this? What is the REAL question here?
  How long will it take to get the answer? If lots of time is needed, circle and come back later.
  What help can I get from the answer choices? E.g., part of speech needed for the correct answer.
  Which is the wacko answer? There's nearly always one hilarious choice. Find it and you're down to 4 choices. That's progress.
  Do I need negative or positive words here?
  Is there a word root or known prefix (or both) in any of these mystery words?
  Do any of these words look or sound like words in a foreign language I know?
  Have I spotted all the real clues (key words, for instance) to the right answer in this problem?
 For Math Questions, ask:
  What type of problem is this—one of arithmetic mainly or algebra, geometry, or logic?
  How much, if any, abstract reasoning is needed?
  How much would it help if I drew a picture? (Usually, an excellent idea.)
  What is the shortcut around lengthy computation here? (Be alert. You are not expected to do lengthy computation.)
  Which units should I work in? The answers will tell you. Usually it's better to work in the smaller unit. E.g., inches not feet.

What is the range of possible answers? Again, the answers will tell you. As with reading comprehension questions (see p. 74), one answer choice is typically too big or broad, one is too small or narrow, one is wacky, one is very tempting but wrong, and one is CORRECT.

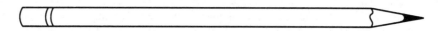

WHEN SHOULD YOU OMIT A QUESTION?

Do not answer a question if you feel that it comes from outer space. When you've never seen the rotten words before, and they have no recognizable roots or prefixes, or the math is obviously Einstein level—well, you know the feeling. Whenever it swamps you, omit the question.

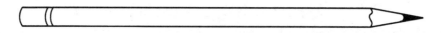

NEVER POUNCE

Only an idiot grabs the first good-looking answer. Smart folks eliminate wrong answers one by one, carefully. Most questions will offer you one RIGHT answer plus one or more VERY TEMPTING answers. Cross out incorrect choices one by one until you isolate the answer that is EXACTLY RIGHT.

WHERE ARE THE KILLER QUESTIONS?

To be honest, any question you can't answer correctly becomes a killer question. You'll generally find the first half of every verbal question segment—or the first 10–15 questions on a 30-minute math segment—to be fairly simple.

From halfway to three quarters of the way through a question set you can find some real stinkers, but most of the time these problems will bring on only a mild sweat.

Most (notice we didn't say *all*) of the killer questions will be the last few in any batch.

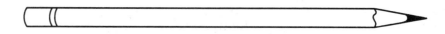

KNOW THYSELF

After some PSAT or SAT practice—certainly after all these years of school—you can probably say which kinds of questions you do best. *Always do those first.* That's how you establish a good mental attitude for the work period and also how you collect points for right answers.

Do your second-best kind of question next, and so on. Saving the worst for last makes all kinds of sense. You probably wouldn't score as many right answers on questions you hate, so who cares if you run out of time doing them?

WATCH YOUR WATCH

Always wear a watch to a test. Lay it on the desk in front of you and plan each 30-minute test segment, allocating the minutes as you need them. Some proctors forget to warn you time is flitting by, but you need to know. For many students, time is the worst enemy on a PSAT or SAT.

When practicing at home, always time yourself. Learn how long it takes to do various question sets. Decide which questions to skip if you need to gain extra time. You can use each minute to your advantage, but only if you have practiced how to do it.

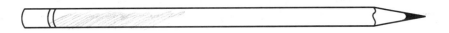

USE YOUR TEST BOOKLET

The test booklet itself is your only scrap paper, so go ahead and write on it. Especially, draw math diagrams or pictures. Remember, too, that each page corner is a right angle. Use the edges of the booklet's pages to measure line segments or compare them in math problems. And, of course, cross out wrong answers as you eliminate them, for every single problem.

DON'T FALL OFF THE TROLLEY

Check each question number to see that its answer is being recorded in the correct place on the answer sheet. If you discover you've written answers in the wrong slots, you'll be furious.

OR: Complete a question set, then transfer the answers in a batch from the test booklet to the answer sheet. You'll rarely put an answer in the wrong slot this way.

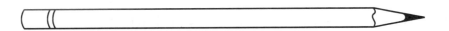

WHAT'S DONE IS DONE

Let your answers rest in peace. Go back and change an answer only if you have plenty of time to reconsider and be certain that the afterthought answer is the correct one.

RED ALERT   RED ALERT   RED ALERT   RED ALERT   RED ALERT

TERRIFIC, SPECIFIC HELP FOR
THE VERBAL QUESTIONS

The verbal questions on any standardized test can be a slippery lot. The English language is extraordinarily expressive to begin with, and it is constantly growing because of worldwide use. No wonder students cry, "There are so many words!"

All those words are the key factor in the PSAT and SAT. The words in this book are especially vital to know. Also, memorize the hints in this unit so that you do your best on all the verbal questions.

VERBAL QUESTIONS ON THE PSAT AND SAT	
PSAT	**SAT**
2 verbal sections 58 questions in two 30-minute segments	3 verbal sections* 78 questions in two 30-minute segments & one 15-minute segment
16 sentence completions 12 analogies 30 reading comp questions	19 sentence completions 19 analogies 40 reading comp questions

*You may get another verbal segment of experimental questions, which do not count toward score.

A BIG PERCENTAGE

Of the 78 verbal questions that count toward your SAT score, 40 are questions based on reading comprehension. On a PSAT, 30 of the 58 questions test your reading skills. **Learning to "read critically," as the College Board puts it, is indeed critical.**

This emphasis on reading skill is on purpose; in college, roughly 90 percent of your work is apt to depend on your reading ability.

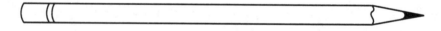

The Key to it All

A big fat vocabulary is the key to success on the verbal half of this test. Besides reading to beef up your storehouse of words, use flashcards. They really work, they're not babyish, and you'll be learning the words as you make the cards! They can tuck into your pants pockets and sit on your bedside chair or table—going everywhere you go until you've learned them. And you really CAN learn hundreds in a few weeks, working alone or with a buddy.

VOCABULARY TIP: Simplify, Simplify

Learn to see all the small bits in each word. A big, scary word is often a friend draped in prefixes and suffixes. Strip away these extra garments before you assume it's an unknown word.

Examples:

PREDETERMINATION = pre + determin + ation
[before + determine = deciding ahead of time]

IMPOVERISH = im + pover + ish
[im + poverty + ish = to make awfully poor]

IRRELEVANCY = ir + relevanc + y
[not + relevant + y = lack of importance or significance]

While not all words break down like this, over half of English words do. That's why knowing roots and prefixes is so important.

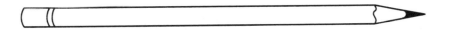

HELP WITH ANALOGIES

Of the 78 verbal questions on an SAT, 19 are analogies; they are 12 of the total 58 verbal questions on a PSAT. That's a sizable percentage both places—a solid 25% on the SAT, and about 150 of the possible 600 points. With practice, you can become good at these questions, you really can.

Keep in mind that **the colon : means "is related to" and the double colon :: means "just as."** For example:

cap : head :: boot : foot

A cap is related to the head just as a boot is to the foot.
or
A cap protects the head just as a boot protects the foot.
or
A cap covers the head just as a boot covers the foot.
or
A cap is worn on the head just as a boot is worn on the foot.

This analogy shows us everyday items in their customary roles. It is one of many basic analogy types.

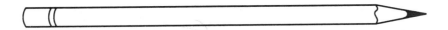

Know the Basic Kinds of Analogies

A quick peek at pp. 54–56 will show you the basic analogous relationships. Once you're familiar with these repeating varieties, the majority of analogy questions will become much simpler.

Identify the analogy type whenever possible. *By identifying the type of analogy, you are deciding what the real question is, a critical step in problem solving.* Read those two given words and ask: Is this a part-to-whole relationship? A question of degree? An item related to its typical location? In what specific way are these two words joined together in this question?

Examples:

EYELET : SHOE ::   Part of a Whole Thing
    An eyelet is one part of a shoe.

DELUGE : FLOOD ::   Cause and Effect (or Typical Result)
    A deluge of rain can result in a flood.

ACTIVITY : FEVERISH ::   Great Degree of Something
    A great degree of activity is termed feverish.

TEARS : SALT ::   Object with a Natural Component
    Salt is a natural component of tears.

OCEAN : PLANKTON ::   Object Related to Natural Location
    Plankton naturally occurs in the ocean.

EXPRESSION : WINSOME ::   "Near-cliché" Expression
    An appealing expression is commonly called winsome.

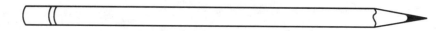

Always Make a Partial Sentence

In order to locate a matching pair (the correct answer) for each given pair (the question), you must turn those two given words into a partial sentence, as in the foregoing examples, and then think of a completing pair that expresses the same relationship.

Examples:

BEE : HIVE :: becomes
    A bee lives in a hive just as *another live thing* : *lives in this*

BIBLIOGRAPHY : BOOKS :: becomes
    a bibliography is a list of sourcebooks just as
    some other compilation : *lists these definite things*

COMPACT : AUTOMOBILE :: becomes
    a compact is a small automobile just as
    another small thing : *represents this general group*

MANAGER : OFFICE :: becomes
    a manager runs the office just as *some other "head"* : *is in charge of a specific place*

People Alert

Suppose the original pair in a question looks like this:

ARTIST : EASEL ::

The first word represents a person and the second, a tool used in that person's work. A perfect answer choice will show a person in the first slot and a logical tool in the second. Certainly, the first word should be a live being, not something inanimate.

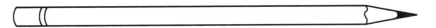

Negative or Positive?

If the given analogous pair has a definitely negative word or words, then the completing pair will **usually** be similar, although no rule works all the time here.

Examples:

APPEARANCE : DOWNCAST :: TONE : DOLEFUL
(negative descriptive adjective on each side)

Use the same thought processes to do "by nature" analogies.

CELEBRATION : JOYOUS :: SACRAMENT : SOLEMN
(a celebration is joyous by nature, just as a sacrament is solemn)

THIEF : SURREPTITIOUS :: LIAR : DUPLICITOUS
(negative person type with logically negative adjective on each side)

EXPRESSION : PLEASING :: REVIEW : RAVE
(a desirable expression is pleasing, just as a desirable review is a rave)

Watch for "good outcomes" or "bad outcomes"—those cause and effect analogies. Both pairs must be alike in outcome.

CARELESSNESS: ACCIDENT :: INDULGENCE : OBESITY

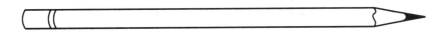

Can't Understand the Given Pair?

What if you cannot understand the relationship in the given pair? You study it and still no clue. Aaaargh!

Now, **examine the answers.** Try to determine their relationships. Many times you can, and these relationships will send you back to the original pair. In this way, you can often figure out the given pair and match it correctly.

Test Each Answer Choice

Never consider an answer choice that is a "bad pair"—words that lack a clear and logical relationship to each other. Here are some bad pairs offered as answer choices on recent SATs.

INSPIRE : PAINTER (vague at best)
BEGIN : RECOMMENCE (doublespeak)
STIMULATE : MOTIVATE (true synonyms here—would rarely occur, if ever, in given pair)
DISTRUSTFUL : ACQUAINTANCE (oh yeah?)
HALFHEARTED : PERSUADE (hunh?)
DISTURBANCE : QUELLED (well, maybe, in a real pinch)

Remember, whenever you can eliminate one or more answer choices, make an educated guess.

Timing?

There are 12 analogies in a batch on PSATs and 13 in the larger batch on an SAT. You should try to complete either of these sets in 5 or 6 minutes at most. Remember that you'll need at least half of every time period for the critical reading questions.

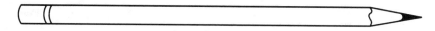

HELP WITH SENTENCE COMPLETIONS

Sentence completion questions require you to fill in empty slots with words or phrases that best complete the meaning of the sentences as shown. There are 19 sentences on an SAT and 16 on a PSAT, and they often gobble way too much time. Like analogies, sentence completion questions are about 25% of your total score. Get them right and you've pocketed another 150 points. In fact, if you get all the analogies and sentence completion questions correct, you'll have a score of 500. Practice is the real secret—lots of practice—plus the following guidelines.

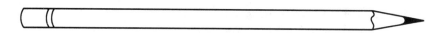

What Kind of Sentence Is This?

The first step toward a correct answer is asking, "What kind of sentence is this?" each time. You must understand what the sentence really says—and therefore what is missing—before you can go on an answer hunt. The **four main kinds of sentences are:**

(1) **cause and effect**   (Because of one thing, something else happened or resulted.)
(2) **definition**   (Words in the sentence define the word or phrase to be filled in—a real gift.)
(3) **contrast**   (What you need will be the opposite of an existing word or idea.)
(4) **comparison**   (What you need will logically complete or blend with the sentence meaning.)

Examples:

(1) Due to the heavy rains, the abundance of topsoil has gradually ---- into low-lying river beds.
     (*Cause and Effect*—Word filled in must explain how the rains caused the topsoil to end up in the river.)

(2) He's by nature a ---- person, quick to fly off the handle when things go wrong.
     (*Definition*—Word filled in must describe a person "quick to fly off the handle when things go wrong.")

(3) Since he's normally prompt, I was astonished when his car arrived so ----. *late*
     (*Contrast*—Word filled in must be the opposite of "normally prompt," or you wouldn't be "astonished.")

(4) Known for her sunny nature and ---- disposition, Maria easily won the Congeniality Award.
     (*Comparison*—Word filled in must go well with "sunny nature" and "congeniality" to make logical sense.)

Key Word Alert

Every sentence has clues pointing to the correct answer. These clues are in the form of **key words that unlock the sense of the sentence.**

In sentence (1) on the preceding page, the key words "due to" told you it was a cause and effect sentence. The entire last half of sentence (2) was your key to look for a word that would fit the given description or definition. Sentence (3) gives you "Since" and "normally prompt" and "astonished" as keys to meaning. And sentence (4) capitalized "Congeniality Award," which would be pretty hard to overlook.

Note these highlighted key words:

Example: **Although** he **customarily** longed to soar above the clouds, **today's** ~~glummy~~ forecast had him **tapping his fingers** ---- on the flight plan. (It's a crummy forecast and he doesn't want to fly, or he wouldn't be tapping his fingers, would he?)

Example: **Thanks to** decades of ---- **efforts** on the part of environmentalists, the **trapping** of **innocent dolphin** in nets designed for tuna ---- in large part. (These must be "good" efforts resulting in far fewer trapped dolphin, or we wouldn't be saying, "Thanks to." Note that the verb must be supplied for the main clause.)

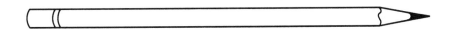

Common Key Words to Know

Concentrate on these words. They send strong signals to a reader who's alert. Though many are "little words," they often shape the *entire meaning of a sentence.*

WORDS SIGNALING A MEANING SHIFT AND/OR CONTRAST

but	moreover	in spite of
yet	curiously	nonetheless
since	however	on the contrary
unless	although	even so
due to	ironically	on the other hand
oddly	uncharacteristically	nevertheless
because	strangely	while

WORDS SIGNALING COMPARISON OR COORDINATION

and	similarly	or
too	alike, like	commonly
along with	plus, also	

ADVERBS

And many verbs, e.g., "reflected" and "mirrored." In general, **pay attention to all adverbs.** Words like "pitifully," "tiredly," "testily" give you giant clues about attitude or tone of voice.

VERBS

Watch all verbs, too. "Grumbled" is not the same as "talked." "Stomped" is not the same as "walked."

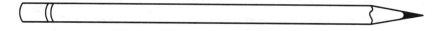

Get Your Own Answer in Mind

Knowing what you're looking for makes finding it much simpler. After reading each sentence, think of appropriate words to fill in the blanks *before* looking at all those answers. This technique works well for all but the most difficult questions.

Right now, turn to the sentence completion practice questions on pp. 65–68. Cover the answers for several sentences and get your own ideas in mind before you embark on your hunt, eliminating choices one by one. The more you practice this technique, the better you will get and the more natural it will feel.

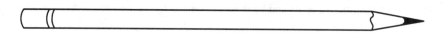

Both Words Must Fit Perfectly

In two-word completions, both words filled in must be exactly right. If one of the two offered is wrong or only half right, the entire answer is wrong and should be crossed out.

Example:

, to avoid

While it is easy to castigate television for its ---- effects on today's students, we need to step back and view the topic with more ----, remembering the many excellent offerings from public television.
(A) known. .objectivity (B) appalling. .excitement
(C) salutary. .approval (D) negative. .pessimism
(E) deleterious. .charity

You think: What is the sentence really saying here? Even if you don't know the word "castigate," the only sensible meaning for it is a negative one; otherwise it would not be so easy to pick on TV. Reading the entire sentence should tell you that *the first half picks on TV and the second half says, whoa. What about all that great stuff on public TV?*

SO, you need a negative word for the first blank and a positive word for the second blank.

Checking answers:

(A) known. .objectivity

The word "known" is weak here. It doesn't say anything. You should eliminate this answer, although "objectivity" is super.

(B) appalling. .excitement

"Appalling" works well, as it is very negative. But if you "step back" from something, you don't show "excitement"; you're trying to gain objectivity to reconsider. "Excitement" is a poor choice. Cross out this answer.

(C) salutary. .approval

"Salutary" (think of *salud* in Spanish) means promoting good health, a dopey choice here. Cross out immediately.

(D) negative. .pessimism

"Negative" is a fine choice, but "pessimism" is dead wrong. We need a positive word here, remember? Cross out this choice.

(E) deleterious. .charity

Wow. What if you don't know "deleterious"? Still, you eliminated all the other choices. This has to be IT. Also, "de-" is usually a negative prefix and "charity" works extremely well. **Even if you don't know "deleterious," choose this answer anyway. This is the process of elimination at its best.**

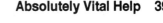

Check for Standard American Idiom

Don't choose any answer that makes the completed sentence sound weird or ungrammatical. If the chosen word or phrase doesn't result in standard American English, it's wrong.

Example:

> **I wish you wouldn't ---- me when I'm trying to make a carefully considered decision.**
> (A) wheedle   (B) carp   (C) distract
> (D) entice   (E) interfere

You think: What is the real meaning of this sentence?

Answer: This person doesn't want to be bothered while making a decision. In that case, *only the idiomatically correct* "distract" me, answer (C), works here.

Checking Answers: See why the others won't work?

(A) wheedle	wheedle me when I'm trying. . . .	Nope.
(B) carp	carp me (?)	Would have to be "carp at me."
(D) entice	entice me	Makes no logical sense here.
(E) interfere	interfere me	Unidiomatic. Missing a word.

Always read your final selection to yourself, asking, Is this standard American English?

Again . . . Simplify, Simplify

Remove any extra words or phrases from sentences. Keep the sense of the sentence, but clean it up to work with it.

Example:

> **Jeff strained to apply himself to the demanding task at hand, willing the task itself to keep ---- at bay, even though he sensed the approach of the storm, as ominous and menacing as those he ---- in childhood.**

You think: Grown-up Jeff is still afraid of storms.

You simplify 39 words: Jeff worked hard to avoid fear while a terrible storm approached—something he'd always dreaded. (15 words)

Example:

> **That Poe, who was haunted by an ever-present dread of madness and tuberculosis, became America's first master of the horror story seems somehow ----.**

You think: Yes. He wrote horror. It's only logical.

You simplify 23 words: Poe as our first master of horror seems logical or inevitable. (11 words)

(You can omit everything between the commas because you know it! You'll remember it as you eliminate, so you don't have to repeat the whole sentence with each new answer test.)

No Rule Works All the Time

One oft-suggested idea is that the tougher sentences have tougher vocabulary words as correct answer choices. Yes, sometimes they do, but not always. In the past ten years, some amazingly complex sentences have been completed properly with very simple words. No rule works all the time.

Timing?

In general, you should spend no more than 5-6 minutes on a set of 9 or 10 sentence completion questions, and you can reduce this time with practice.

When finding the answer depends on difficult, unfamiliar vocabulary, and it does occasionally, you may choose to omit the question.

HELP!   **READING COMPREHENSION QUESTIONS**   **HELP!**

If you want to comprehend what you read more fully, there are techniques you need to know. Mainly, you need to practice reading in a knowledgeable way. How to do it? Read on.

Read and Do Pages 69–95

While a bit of preparation with analogies and sentence completion questions does the job for many people, that approach won't work with reading comprehension questions. Strong reading skills take time to perfect, and they're more important than any other skills you possess. Success in any field—even math, technical studies, or science—hinges on these critical reading analysis skills.

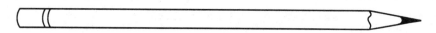

Basic Vital Facts

All reading sections on PSATs and SATs are typical of college-level material, requiring you to have a large, broad vocabulary.

One 30-minute segment on a current SAT has two reading passages, with a total of 15 questions. Another 30-minute segment has a passage nearly 100 lines long, on which 12 questions are asked. The final 15-minute portion features a pair of passages on which 13 questions are asked. Future tests may juggle number of questions per segment; the total number of critical reading questions will still be 40.

Passages come from the following subject areas: social and physical sciences (e.g., history, psychology, chemistry, biology) and fiction. You'll see one fiction passage for sure, and one featuring women or racial minorities.

Remember that these questions are over half of your test. Do well on them and the school of your dreams will be dying for you to enroll.

Key Words Again

Key words really are key. For instance, the tiny words "but" and "yet" signal a shift in meaning. "However" is the same as "but." Each word counts, no matter how small or seemingly minor. Look at these two sentences:

Laura was *usually punctual but* today seemed to be different.
(*You think:* **But . . .** today she's going to be late!)

Laura was *usually punctual, and* today seemed no different.
(*You think:* **And** today she'll be on time, as usual.) A teeny, tiny change? No way. This was a major change.

As you read a passage, pay attention to these "loaded words." Be sure to review the Red Alert on p. 37.

Eliminating Answers . . . One More Time

It is always smart to eliminate answers one by one on any multiple-choice test, but it is screamingly important on reading comprehension questions. Two of the answers are usually acceptable in many people's minds. **But** only one will be the correct answer. You'll lose one fourth of a right answer whenever you act rashly. Be careful. You must be able to defend your answer choice with material stated or implied in the passage. Move with deliberation, not haste.

Read Questions First—Before the Passage

Read the basic idea of each question, not the whole thing plus all answer choices. It takes only seconds, but then, as you read, you'll know what you're reading for. After all, your goal on a timed test is to locate right answers as quickly as possible. This technique often saves time.

Some people loathe this idea and cannot force themselves to do it. Never follow advice that you know would hurt your performance. If you develop a way to answer questions that serves you well, keep on using it.

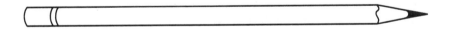

What Kinds of Questions Are Asked?

Think for a minute and you'll know what kinds of questions can be asked. Somebody will want to know if you discovered:

1. The **main theme or central idea** of the passage
2. **Basic facts** contained in the material
3. The **attitude or tone of the author**
4. The **implications** of the material, including the drawing of **logical conclusions**
5. The **organization or technique** of the passage
6. The use of **vocabulary in context**

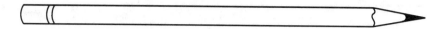

What Kinds of Answers Are Offered?

Although no rule is infallible, the answers offered for these questions usually fall into these categories:

1. **Too big,** too broad, too comprehensive in some way
   The right answer cannot cover this much ground.
2. **Too narrow,** too restricted in outlook, too limited in scope
   This answer is incomplete, treating only a part of the question asked.
3. **Off the mark,** wacko, out in left field
   Locating a totally hilarious answer is fun. Chuckle out loud, thereby amazing other test takers.
4. **Awfully close,** a very tempting answer
   This is the next-best answer. Be wary.
5. **A quote or near-quote** of the passage
   Again, be wary. Correct answers rarely parrot the passage exactly.
6. **Impressive,** weighty, professorial-sounding, and **maybe lengthy** as well
   These answers are rarely correct.
7. **Specific, succinct,** and **meaty—to the point**
   Pay attention. Good answers are like this.

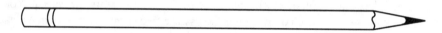

Order of Difficulty

Reading comprehension questions are in no particular order as to difficulty. The first question may be the toughest; the last can be the simplest. If you see that a question is going to take a long time, save it for last and keep your eye on the clock.

While reading passages used to occur on SATs in order of their difficulty (relatively speaking), current test samples are using passages that simply reflect educated writing, which should be clear to anyone aiming for college. These passages are on roughly 11th to 13th grade level.

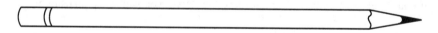

Learn Your Skills

As you practice with SAT-type reading passages, watch your progress. Is reading comprehension your strongest area? If so, be sure to save enough time. The general advice is to save these slower reading comprehension questions for last, but it may be bad advice for *you*. One major purpose of PSAT/SAT preparation is learning your own strengths on these tests.

A Favorite Question

The most common question about a PSAT or SAT passage is one on the central theme or main point. Various ways of asking this question read:

1. The author's main point is . . . ?
2. An appropriate title for this passage would be . . . ?
3. The primary function of this passage is to . . . ?
4. This passage suggests that . . . ?
5. The content of this passage answers primarily which question? (5 choices, all phrased as questions)
6. This passage is primarily concerned with . . . ?

First, read the entire piece quickly, with the goal of finding the main point. As you read, ask yourself, What is this piece really saying? Look for a central theme in the first or lead paragraph, the most logical place. If it's not there, watch for a meaty, summation-type sentence near the end of the passage.

Also, each paragraph has a point to make, especially in nonfiction. A change in focus or additional information is the reason for paragraphing. Keep these added points in mind.

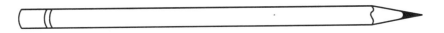

Be Involved as You Read

Only four reading passages, one of them a double passage with contrasting points of view, now appear on SATs and PSATs. Passages are longer, and each has more questions than previous tests.

YOU CANNOT ANSWER THESE QUESTIONS CORRECTLY UNLESS YOU STAY INVOLVED AS YOU READ AND KNOW EXACTLY WHAT THE PASSAGE IS SAYING. You can't just cruise through the passage hunting specific answers. That method simply will not work well. Instead, **block out the world as you read.** If you do that, these passages aren't bad according to juniors who took PSATs in the fall of '93.

Read the questions first, before you read the passage, to guide your reading a bit better. You will read each question again—carefully—when you know what the passage says—as you mark an answer for every question.

Mark the passages with symbols that help you—perhaps ******* beside meaty sentences; **circles** around words that give you tone, attitude, or mood; and **underlining** for facts. Devise your own system if you like, but do try it. Marking the passage keeps you involved as you read, and for difficult or dull passages this technique keeps you awake, too.

This is the "critical reading" skill so necessary for scoring well on the "new" SAT I and PSAT, according to the College Board. This is the kind of involved reading that *SAT Success* **has always taught, unlike other books that suggest you merely skim the passages in search of answers.**

Remember . . . you read it here first!!

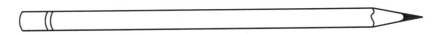

Timing?

Most students need at least half of each 30-minute verbal segment for reading comprehension questions. Many people need 20 minutes for these questions. You must know before the big day how much time you require. Find out by practicing with the verbal segments in this book, and always set a timer.

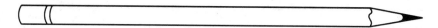

What About Those Paired Passages?

The test section that has two passages that express both similarities and differences is very similar to the other reading comprehension sections. Most of the questions are about only one of the passages, and all questions are of the same types: main point, facts, author attitude, implications, vocabulary, and technique.

Answer Questions on Passage 1 First

The first few questions that follow the two passages will be about Passage 1 only. Skim them over, read Passage 1, and then answer those questions. In a short time, you will have already answered a third or more of the questions.

Make the Comparisons as You Go Along

Being involved as you read is even more important when reading paired passages. As you read the second passage, be alert for the similarities and differences between it and the first one. Circle parts of the second passage that show these similarities and differences. Then you'll be ready to answer either questions about Passage 2 alone or questions that compare the two passages.

NECESSARY KNOW-HOW FOR THE MATH QUESTIONS

The math questions on PSATs and SATs are some of the easiest problems you'll see . . . and some of the hardest. (And in between are the in-between ones.) But unlike the rather general preparation for the verbal sections, which is accompanied by prayer and the burning of much midnight oil, preparing for the math sections is a more structured process. That's the nature of mathematics, and perhaps one reason the average math score is always about 50 points higher than the average verbal score. For these questions, we know exactly what to study. And it's right here in this book.

MATH QUESTIONS ON THE PSAT AND SAT	
PSAT	**SAT**
2 math sections 50 questions in two 30-minute segments	3 math sections* 60 questions in two 30-minute segments & one 15-minute segment
15 quantitative comparison problems 10 grid-in-answer and 25 multiple choice in arithmetic, algebra & geometry	15 quantitative comparison problems 10 grid-in-answer and 40 multiple choice in arithmetic, algebra & geometry

*You may get one other 30-minute math segment of experimental questions, which do not count toward score.

BASIC KNOWLEDGE

Check out—no, **memorize**—the Glossary of Formulas and Relationships on pp. 392–393. Each item is a critical bit of information, sure to be useful on PSATs and SATs—and all through college. Learn anything in this glossary that you do not know extremely well. Also, **memorize the test directions** for general problems and for grid-in problems and quantitative comparison problems. (See pages 230, 252, and 370.) There is never enough time on Test Day to pore over these directions.

UNIT ALERT

If a problem is presented in different units, such as inches and feet, remember to convert and work the problem all in inches or all in feet. *It is usually much easier to work with the smaller unit.*

PICK AND PLUG

If a multiple-choice problem says, "Solve for *x*," it is a gift. Go directly to the answer choices and plug in the most logical choice. Usually, answer choices are arranged in increasing order, small to large.

As your first test, pick a middle-sized answer and plug it in. Is it too little? If so, then you need answers with bigger numbers. If this middle-sized answer is too big, then test only the answer choices with smaller numbers. Using this method, you should never have to test more than 3 answer choices.

Example: If $\dfrac{72 \times 4}{x} = 48$, then $x = ?$

   (A) 4   (B) 6   (C) 8   (D) 9   (E) 12

Solution: If you don't see an easy way to work the problem, then this is a good time to pick and plug. Start in the middle to save time: $\dfrac{72 \times 4}{8} = 36$, *not 48*. An answer of 36 is too small; therefore, divide by a smaller number to get a bigger result. Try *answer (B) 6*.

   Trying *answer (B) 6*, gives this equation:

$\dfrac{72 \times 4}{6} = 48$ Yahoo! Exactly correct.

SIMPLIFY, SIMPLIFY . . . NOT JUST FOR VERBAL QUESTIONS

This is one guideline that applies to every question on a PSAT or SAT—or any other test.

   Some problems contain TOO MUCH INFORMATION. Weed out that which is unnecessary as you set up equations, and don't worry if you do not use all the information given.

   Whenever two equal quantities appear, such as $a = b$, put an a in place of every b to simplify the equation.

Example: <u>Column A</u>   <u>Column B</u>

$$a = b = c$$

            $a + b$ $b + c$

Solution: Okay, since a is equal to b and also to c, you can substitute a for every b and c. You can rewrite Column A as $a + a$, and Column B becomes $a + a$.

   Thus, $2a = 2a$, no matter what the value of a. You'll select *answer (C)* for this quantitative comparison problem. (Remember, *answer (C)* always means that both quantities are equal.)

SNEAKY MULTIPLICATION AND DIVISION

Multiplication doesn't *always* make things bigger. For example, $3Y$ is not always greater than $2Y$. If you plug in -1 for Y, then $3Y = -3$, and $2Y = -2$, making $2Y$ the bigger quantity in this case.

   Likewise, dividing doesn't always make something smaller. For example, $4 \div X$ is not always less than $10 \div X$. If you plug in -1 for X, then $4 \div -1 = -4$, and $10 \div -1 = -10$, making $4 \div X$ *greater than* $10 \div X$.

QUANTITATIVE COMPARISONS—ALERT!

Memorize the foregoing about sneaky multiplication and division because it is ABSOLUTELY VITAL KNOWLEDGE when working quantitative comparison problems. **Always plug in –1, 0, 1, and a fraction (e.g., $\frac{1}{2}$) before jumping to a sadly incorrect conclusion about which is bigger or smaller,** or whether the two quantities are equal.

- Quantitative comparison problems make up one third of your math questions. They are worth practice time.
- Memorize the directions to these problems right now.
- Only 4 answer choices count on these problems. NEVER mark answer (E). There is no answer (E).
- For only these problems, the penalty is one third of a right answer off (not one fourth, as with the multiple-choice questions) for every problem missed.
- These problems are normally quick, and few are killers. Study pp. 362, 363, and 370 and then relax.

SPECIFIC TIPS FOR QUANTITATIVE COMPARISON PROBLEMS

1. In these problems, don't assume that a variable represents a positive number.

Example:

Column A		Column B
	$X \neq 0$	
$3X$		$4X$

Solution: If $X = 1$, then Column B is greater than Column A, right? But, if $X = -1$, then Column A is greater than Column B. Therefore, the correct answer to the problem would be *answer (D)*, "*It cannot be determined from the information given.*"

2. If the quantities being compared do NOT involve variables, never choose answer (D), "*It cannot be determined. . . .*"

Example:

Column A		Column B
The sum of the interior		The sum of the exterior
angles of a right triangle	180	angles of a trapezoid

Solution: Note right away that the sum of the interior angles of a triangle is **a constant, 180°, not a variable!** Likewise, the sum of the exterior angles of a trapezoid, or any polygon, is always 360°—again, **a constant, not a variable!** Here, then, the correct choice is answer (B). (Confused? Check Lesson 12, "Geometry of Polygons and Polyhedrons.")

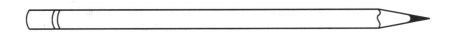

INSPECT THOSE ANSWERS

Remember that an answer can be represented in more than one way. If you're fairly sure you did a problem correctly, check to see if the answer you got is the same as one of the answer choices given for the problem, *but in a different form.*

For example, you may have solved a problem and gotten $\frac{2m}{a} - L$ as an answer and you're sure it is correct. On the test, however, the correct answer is given as $\frac{2m - aL}{a}$. Who's correct? You both are: $\frac{2m}{a} - L$ and $\frac{2m - aL}{a}$ are the same value written in different forms.

CONFUSED BY VARIABLES?

If the variables in a problem confuse you, try using numbers.

Example: If $x = 2\sqrt{c} - 1$ and $y = 2c$, what is y in terms of x?

(A) $\dfrac{(x-1)^2}{4}$

(B) $2(x+1)^2$

(C) $\dfrac{(x+2)^2}{2}$

(D) $\dfrac{(x+1)^2}{2}$

(E) $\dfrac{(x+1)^2}{4}$

Solution: Since x and y are defined in terms of c, choose any value for c; let's try 1. Now solve for x and y when $c = 1$. Then, $x = 1$ and $y = 2$. Plug $x = 1$ into the answer choices until you get a value of 2 because we are looking for which answer choice is equal to y. In *answer (D)*,

$$\frac{(x+1)^2}{2} = \frac{(1+1)^2}{2} = \frac{4}{2} = 2 = y \text{ when } c = 1$$

You found the correct answer.

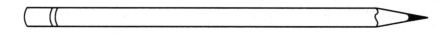

CHECK OUT INEQUALITIES

Inequalities are tricky. You must know the twelve rules on pp. 275–276 to work problems correctly. The lesson on inequalities is only four pages long, but it is terribly important. You need to understand inequalities to do well on these tests.

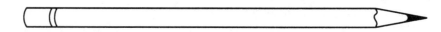

A MAGIC SWITCH

If you're having trouble, turn algebraic answers into numerical problems for quicker solution.

Example: If W is an even integer, which of the following is an odd integer?
    (A) $W - 4$ (B) $(W - 2)$ (C) $(W + 1) + 3$ (D) $(W - 1) - 4$ (E) $2(W + 3)$

Solution: Pick any even integer and plug that number in for W. Suppose you try the even number 2:

(A)	$2 - 4 = -2$	NO
(B)	$(2 - 2) = 0$	NO
(C)	$(2 + 1) + 3 = 6$	NO
(D)	$(2 - 1) - 4 = -3$	YES
(E)	$2(2 + 3) = 10$	NO

Only *answer (D)* -3 can be correct, as it is the only odd integer.

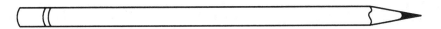

A SHADY PROBLEM

When finding the area of a shaded region, break the figure down into its separate parts or solve by subtracting areas.

Example: $ABEG$ is a rectangle. F is the midpoint of GE; H is the midpoint of BE; E is the midpoint of FD; $AB = 12$; $AG = 8$. Find the area of the shaded region.

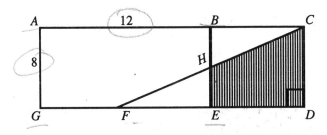

Note: Figure not drawn to scale.

(A) 24   (B) 36   (C) 42   (D) 48   (E) 96

Solution: The shaded region is a trapezoid, but you do not need to know the formula for its area if you recognize the large triangle FDC. By subtracting the area of $\triangle FEH$ from the area of $\triangle FDC$, you get the area of $HEDC$.

$FE = 6$, so $ED = 6$, $HE = 4$, and $CD = 8$.

The area of $\triangle FEH = \dfrac{1}{2}(4)(6) = 12$.

The area of $\triangle FDC = \dfrac{1}{2}(8)(12) = 48$.

Thus, the shaded portion has an area of $48 - 12$, or 36.
Only *answer (B) 36* is correct.

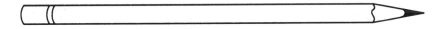

BEING DETERMINED

Being determined to do something well is a powerful force. Even though problems become more difficult near the end of each testing segment, difficult problems can be overcome. Remember that the PSAT and SAT require knowledge of basic skills in arithmetic, algebra, and geometry. If you master the fundamentals in these areas—and practice—and stay determined to do it—you can solve even the toughest problems.

SHORT OF TIME?

If you're in panic mode and preparing for an SAT or PSAT, spend your math reviewing time on the following topics:

- Your main area of weakness
- Fractions and decimals (Lesson 7)
- Percentage (Lesson 8)
- Geometry (Lessons 11, 12, and 13)
- Quantitative comparisons (Lessons 15 and 16; remember that this set of questions tests ALL skills)
- The diagnostic and practice tests

HOW TO USE THIS BOOK—THE STUDY PLANS

You can prepare for your PSAT or SAT several ways. Our suggestions include the **9-Week Plan,** which is used by many people; the **18-Week,** or **Semester, Plan** favored by schools; and the **Panic Plan,** for folks who have only a couple of weeks to get ready. Obviously, the more relaxed and careful your preparation can be, the better. Your goal is real learning that you can use throughout life.

Making a plan for study is crucial. Check out these plans. Choose one now and get going. You know you can raise your scores if you try hard enough.

THE 9-WEEK PLAN—2 LESSONS PER WEEK

Week 1:   **Lesson 1**
   To guide your study:
      First: **Do the complete Diagnostic SAT, pp. 5–22, and the self-evaluation that follows.**
      Then: **Read the Red Alert pages, 28–49,** that precede these plans. **This is truly vital information.**
      Verbal: Read: Introduction to Success, pp. 1–4
                      How to Answer Analogy Questions, pp. 53–61
                Do: Prefixes, pp. 96–100
                      Plagued Pairs and Quiz, pp. 127–133
      Math :   Read: The Red Alert pages—in case you forgot, pp. 45–49
                Do: Lesson 1: The Basics of Arithmetic and all practice problems, pp. 253–261

   Lesson 2
      Verbal: Practice Analogy Questions, pp. 56–59
                Review Prefixes and do Quiz, pp. 96–100
                Vocabulary List 1 and Quiz, pp. 134–139
      Math: Lesson 2: Polynomials and all practice problems, pp. 261–265

Week 2:   **Lesson 1**
      Verbal: Review prefixes HARD. Go through the Plagued Pairs list and
                      Vocabulary Lists 1 and 2 and CIRCLE ALL PREFIXES.
                Vocabulary List 2 and Quiz, pp. 139–143
      Math: Lesson 3: Solving Linear Equations and all practice problems, pp. 266–274
   Lesson 2
      Verbal: Study Latin/Greek Roots, *acer–mal*, pp. 100–104
                Vocabulary List 3 and Quiz, pp. 143–147
      Math: Lesson 4: Solving Inequalities and all practice problems, pp. 275–279

Week 3:   **Lesson 1**
      Verbal: How to Do Sentence Completion Questions, pp. 62–64
                Review Roots, *acer-mal*, pp. 100–104
                Vocabulary List 4 and Quiz, pp. 148–152
      Math: Lesson 5: Factoring and all practice problems, pp. 279–282
   Lesson 2
      Verbal: Sentence Completions for Practice, pp. 65–68
                Study Latin/Greek Roots, *manu–zo,* pp. 104–109
                Vocabulary List 5 and Quiz, pp. 153–157
      Math: Lesson 6: Radicals and all practice problems, pp. 283–289

Week 4:   **Lesson 1**
      Verbal: Reading Comprehension, pp. 69–73
                Review Latin/Greek Roots, *manu-zo,* pp. 104–109, and take the Quiz, p. 109
                Vocabulary List 6 and Quiz, pp. 157–162
      Math: Lesson 7: Fractions, Decimals, and Averages and all practice problems, pp. 289–304
      Test Practice: **Study the actual SAT questions on Red Alert**, pp. 227–251. See the step-by-step
                      reasoning that leads to right answers.

> **Lesson 2**
>> Verbal: How to Read for Main Point, pp. 73–75
>> Number Roots and Quiz, pp. 111–113
>> Vocabulary List 7 and Quiz, pp. 162–167
>> Math: Lesson 8: Percentage, Ratio, and Proportion and all practice problems, pp. 304–311

Week 5:   **Lesson 1**
>> Verbal: Reading to Decode Author Attitude, Style, and Mood, pp. 75–78
>> Words from Characters in Literature, pp. 114–116
>> Vocabulary List 8 and Quiz, pp. 167–172
>> Math: Lesson 9: Two Equations in Two Unknowns and all practice problems, pp. 313–316

> **Lesson 2**
>> Verbal: Reading to Isolate Key Facts and Examples, pp. 78–81
>> Words from Myth and Legend, pp. 116–119
>> Vocabulary List 9 and Quiz, pp. 172–177
>> Math: Lesson 10: Word Problems and all practice problems, pp. 316–326

Week 6:   **Lesson 1**
>> Verbal: Reading for What Is Suggested or Implied, pp. 81–82
>> Words from Names of People, pp. 119–121
>> Vocabulary List 10 and Quiz, pp. 177–182
>> Math: Lesson 11: Geometry of Angles and all practice problems, pp. 327–332

> **Lesson 2**
>> Verbal: How to Answer Questions on Paired Passages, pp. 84–86
>> Practice Reading Comprehension Passages 1 and 2, pp. 87–89
>> Words from Place Names, pp. 121–122
>> Vocabulary List 11 and Quiz, pp. 182–187
>> Math: Lesson 12: Geometry of Polygons and Polyhedrons and all practice problems, pp. 333–347

Week 7:   **Lesson 1**
>> Verbal: Practice Reading Comprehension Passages 3 and 4, pp. 90–91
>> Summary of Words from Special Places and Quiz, pp. 123–125
>> Vocabulary List 12 and Quiz, pp. 187–192
>> Math: Lesson 13: Geometry of Circles and all practice problems, pp. 349–355

> **Lesson 2**
>> Verbal: Practice Reading Comprehension Passages 5 and 6, pp. 91–93
>> Foreign Words and Phrases, p. 126
>> Vocabulary List 13 and Quiz, pp. 192–198
>> Math: Lesson 14: Coordinate Geometry and all practice problems, pp. 355–361
>> **Test Practice:** **Begin the Practice SAT on p. 394.** Do one verbal section and one math section only and wait to score.

Week 8:   **Lesson 1**
>> Verbal: Practice Reading Comprehension Passages 7 and 8, pp. 94–95
>> Vocabulary List 14 and Quiz, pp. 198–203
>> Math: Lesson 15: Quantitative Comparisons: Arithmetic and Algebra and all practice problems, pp. 362–369
>> **Test Practice:** **Practice SAT,** pp. 401–406; do the second verbal and math sections of the Practice SAT. Correct all four sections completed so far. Consider any errors before completing this practice test in next lesson.

> **Lesson 2**
>> Verbal: Vocabulary Lists 15 and 16 and Quizzes, pp. 203–213
>> Math: Lesson 16: Quantitative Comparisons: Geometry and all practice problems, pp. 370–384
>> **Test Practice:** **Complete the Practice SAT by doing Section 3 Verbal and Section 3 Math.** Total answers and note approximate SAT score. Pinpoint any areas of difficulty.

Week 9:   **Lesson 1**
>> Verbal: Based on areas of difficulty in Practice SAT, review accordingly. How about Roots and Prefixes?
>> Vocabulary List 17 and Quiz, pp. 213–218
>> Math: Lesson 17: Special Topics: Data Interpretation, Pattern Repetition, Funny Functions and all practice problems, pp. 384–388

Lesson 2
> Verbal: Vocabulary List 18 and Quiz, pp. 218–223
> Math: Lesson 18: The Last Three Problems on a Typical SAT, pp. 390–391

As we say several times in this book, practice with *the real thing* is invaluable. The College Board has published a sample SAT for guidance counselors and test preparation instructors to examine. You need to see this test! Ask your counselor about it now. Don't worry about your scores; concentrate on those questions that give you fits. Study those. Learn to think as the test makers think, and you will feel more comfortable as each day goes by. You don't need a perfect score, remember, just a respectable one.

18-WEEK, OR FULL-SEMESTER, PLAN

One glance at the foregoing 9-Week Plan and you can guess what the semester plan is. **One lesson per week** is the job, taking about 4 hours of time for the average student.

This plan is the best, of course, because it is not so rapid or demanding. In a semester you can dramatically increase your vocabulary, your test-taking skills, and your math knowledge. You have time to work every exercise in this book. You don't need a class to keep you company either. Hundreds of kids just like you have done this all by themselves.

Best of luck with your preparation. This long-term study plan is bound to make a big difference in your skills and your score.

THE PANIC PLAN

Most people dislike thinking about a big exam that's coming, especially one with a long-range effect, such as a PSAT or SAT. The whole idea is depressing. Some folks do such a fine job of putting-off-the-thought-and-depression that the exam is upon them almost before they can react.

Well, if you're one of those people, calm down. You can still take quick action that will make your exam a much better experience. There's still time to learn:

- How to avoid common mistakes
- How to get the most right answers possible
- Vital test techniques for this and other tests

How to Do It

Suppose your test is only a couple of weeks away. Here's a plan of action that still gives you time to eat and sleep.

Week 1
> Verbal: Read both sets of Red Alert pages, 28–49 and 227–251. Study these pages slowly and carefully.
>   Read the "How-To" portions in Unit 3 on analogy, sentence completion, and reading comprehension questions.
>   Do practice exercises for the most troublesome kinds of questions. Check all answers.
> Math: Read all those Red Alert pages one more time!
>   Study the Glossary of Important Formulas and Relationships, pp. 392–393 at the end of the
> math   lessons.
>   Work practice problems, reading the answer explanations for all difficult problem types.
>   Work practice problems in Lessons 7 and 8, because these problems are a major portion of PSAT and SAT exams.

Week 2
> Verbal: Practice with the Diagnostic SAT, pp. 5–22, and take the Practice SAT, pp. 394–416. You'll learn a lot by correcting these tests. You'll also learn exactly what to expect for problem types and difficulty level on Test Day. Be sure to set a timer for each test segment.
> Math: Review Lessons 11, 12, and 13 in preparation for the geometry portion of your test (about one third).
>   Learn about quantitative comparison problems, Lessons 15 and 16, as they make up another third of the test.
>   Work all math sections of the Practice SAT, pp. 394–411.
>   Study your booklet *Taking the SAT,* being sure to memorize all test directions.

Unit 3: How to Answer the Verbal Questions

The verbal sections of SATs and PSATs are designed to test how well you understand and work with the English language. Both exams reveal the level of your reading skills and the size of your vocabulary.

Your verbal SAT score is based on 78 questions, from three verbal segments. (See chart in Red Alert pages, p. 32) (An extra verbal section will be experimental questions and won't count toward your score.)

In these three test segments you'll find 19 questions based on analogous relationships, 19 sentence completions, and 40 questions derived from four long reading passages, one a double passage. If you have not "played" with old SATs or seen questions like these before, you may be unnerved by the mere sight of an SAT or PSAT.

But—surprise!—you can get good at answering these questions. YOU CAN LEARN TO THINK LIKE THE TEST-MAKERS. Soon, whenever you read an article in the newspaper, your mind will say to you, "Oh boy. Look alive here. There'll be a question about this part. Better underline." Or: "Aha! An SAT word. They're all over the place!"

The goal of this book is to make you so comfortable with every aspect of SATs and PSATs that nerves go away and confidence takes over.

You need to be in charge of this test, not the other way around, and you can do it by putting yourself on a study plan today. Stay with this course of review and you're bound to raise your score. Tons of kids have done it, why not you??

WHAT SHOULD YOU DO FIRST?

Right now, unless it's night and school is closed, see your adviser or guidance counselor. Ask for a copy of the "new" **SAT I: Reasoning Test** that was published in February 1993 as a preview copy for general information. Also, check the bookstore for a new title from the College Board that offers a sample test and relevant facts. You need to see as many paired passages as possible, just so they seem familiar, and you need to practice your timing with the new, longer reading passages.

Otherwise . . . questions are the same. You can practice tons of analogies in any old SAT available, and in this book. Ditto for all sentence completion questions. Getting a feel for a 30-minute test segment and becoming comfortable with the three basic question types will do wonders for your comfort level . . . and your score . . . on Test Day.

HOW TO ANSWER ANALOGY QUESTIONS

An analogy compares a relationship between two things to a similar relationship between two OTHER THINGS. It relates four things in such a way that the two members of one pair bear the same relationship to each other as the two members of the other pair. *For example:*

acorns : oak :: cones : pine

In other words, acorns grow on an oak as seeds of that tree, just as cones grow on a pine tree as seeds of the pine.

The vital point about analogies is that their terms must be in the same order on both sides of the double colon. If the product of the oak (acorns) appears first on one side, then the product of the pine (cones) must appear first on the other side.

Positioning is critical. If we move any one of those words to a different slot, the analogy falls apart.

COMMON ANALOGOUS RELATIONSHIPS

Analogies fall into patterns or types that tend to repeat over and over. Feeling at home with some of the basic ones will be a help to you on any test featuring analogy questions.

1. Antonyms

zenith : nadir :: pinnacle : valley

Putting this analogy into a sentence, we get: *zenith* is to *nadir* (the absolutely lowest point) as *pinnacle* (a very high peak) is to *valley*. Each side of this analogy shows total opposites; words representing the highest are in the same slots on both sides of the analogy. It works, in other words.

2. Synonyms

wealthy : affluent :: indigent : poverty-stricken

Wealthy is to *affluent,* just as *indigent* is to *poverty-stricken*. This time both sides of the analogy balance because they are synonyms; that is, the words mean the same thing. Each word is in its correct slot.

   Note: While the foregoing examples of antonyms and synonyms are common analogous relationships, you probably won't see them on PSATs or SATs. They are much too simple.

3. Degree

warm : boiling :: cool : frozen

Warm is much less hot than *boiling,* just as *cool* is much less cold than *frozen*. Analogies of degree are favorite toys of people who make up tests. They're fun, rather like a puzzle, and, if you make up a few like this example, you will catch the spirit.

4. Person Related to Tool, Major Trait, or Skill/Interest

writer : pen :: painter : brush

A *writer* uses a *pen* (in his work), just as a *painter* uses a *brush*. Very straightforward, right?

writer : words :: painter : design

A *writer* works with *words,* just as a *painter* works with a *design*. You can see that what was put on the right side of each analogy (*words* and *design*) is that person's "stock in trade." These are popular analogous relationships on tests.

judge : probity :: instructor : knowledge

A *judge* is (or should be) known for *probity* (moral uprightness), just as an *instructor* is (or should be) known for *knowledge*.
   Remember to state the relationship as precisely as you can each time you express the analogy.

5. Person Related to Least Desirable Characteristic

judge : corrupt :: instructor : ignorant

The last thing you'd want a *judge* to be is *corrupt;* the last thing you'd want an *instructor* to be is *ignorant*. Note that two nouns are in the first position on each side of the analogy and two adjectives occupy the second position on each side. To be absolutely correct, an analogy must be set up this way, so that a set of imaginary scales balances to perfection.

6. One of a Kind

peach : fruit :: beet : vegetable

A *peach* is one kind of *fruit;* a *beet* is one kind of *vegetable*.

7. Part of a Whole

core : apple :: heart : tree

The *core* is a part of an *apple*, just as the *heart* is part of a *tree*. Note that both words in the first slots refer to parts in the same location in their respective wholes.

8. Substance Related to End Product

cotton : sheet :: wool : sweater

A *sheet* is typically made of *cotton;* a *sweater* is typically made of *wool.*

9. Cause and Effect (or Typical Result)

irritability : argument :: warmth : friendship

Irritability typically results in (or leads to) an *argument,* just as *warmth* typically results in (or leads to) *friendship.*

10. Noun Related to Logical Action

shears : cut :: hammer : pound

Shears are used to *cut* something; a *hammer* is used to *pound* something.

11. Relationship of Location/Description

letter : signature :: book : index

A *signature* comes last in a *letter,* just as an *index* appears last in a *book.*

buffalo : plains :: seal : ocean

A *buffalo* typically lives on the *plains,* just as a *seal* typically lives in the *ocean.* This does not mean that these animals live *only* in the named places, simply that they are natural inhabitants of those locations.

coin : round :: brick : rectangular

A *coin* is customarily *round* in shape, just as a *brick* is typically *rectangular.* (This does not mean that every brick in the world must be rectangular.)

12. Near-Cliché Expressions

devoted : companion :: vigilant : guardian

The best kind of *companion* is *devoted,* just as the best sort of *guardian* is *vigilant.* (Both are often-used descriptions.)

earnest : plea :: heartfelt : comment

A *plea* with a great deal of emotion in it is often described as *earnest,* just as a deeply felt *comment* is often termed *heartfelt.*

13. Implied Comparisons

clouds : sun :: hypocrisy : truth

Clouds block out (or hide) the *sun,* just as *hypocrisy* blocks out (or hides) the *truth.*

painter : smock :: chef : apron

A *painter* wears a *smock* to protect clothing worn underneath, just as a *chef* wears an *apron* as protection against damage to clothing.

manacles : movement :: blinders : sight

Manacles (handcuffs) restrict or inhibit *movement* of the hands, just as *blinders* (on a racehorse, perhaps) restrict or inhibit *sight*.

Hot Tip: *These implied relationships are now the most common analogy type on the SATs.*

Working on the practice analogies should help you to sort out relationships. Keep in mind that if you narrow your choices down to 2, which is almost always possible, your chance of guessing the correct answer—if you are still stumped—is 1 in 2. That means that, even when you are stumped, you should come up with the correct answer 50 percent of the time.

When Working with Analogies, Remember:

1. Analyze the given analogous pair as precisely as possible.
2. Express the given relationship in a very specific sentence.
3. Choose your own word, or pair of words, to complete the relationship *before* looking at the answers if at all possible.
4. *Eliminate* bad answer choices systematically, one by one. Cross out the wrong answers in your test booklet.
5. Eliminate all answer pairs that do not show a clear and logical relationship to each other. If you cannot see how the two words could *possibly* be related to each other, they are NOT THE CORRECT ANSWER.
6. Keep *negative* vs. *positive* concepts in mind. If one or both sides of an analogy require a negative word, for instance, you can discard any answers that show a positive word in that particular slot.
7. Left with two answer choices, select the *more specific answer*.
8. Keep *human* vs. *animal* vs. *plant* vs. *mineral* concepts in mind. Comparing a human worker, for example, to another human worker is a better analogy than comparing human to animal.
9. Be alert to *live* vs. *inanimate* (nonlive) distinctions. A comparison between a human and an animal is probably more accurate than one between a live thing and an inanimate thing. "A man uses a chisel, just as an otter uses a rock," for example, is a fair analogy that compares how one living thing uses a tool to the way another living thing uses a tool.
10. Use your knowledge of prefixes and roots to help you understand strange-looking words. Negative or positive prefixes will guide you to the right answer choices, if you remember to use them as hints. Similarly, if a word *sounds* strongly negative, it probably is. Words are funny that way; often they sound pleasant or ugly, and that points the way to their meanings. Your ear is a valuable language tool.

PRACTICE ANALOGIES 1

Choose and circle the lettered pair that best expresses a relationship like that of the first pair. Remember to express the relationship in a sentence.

1. VERSE : SONG :: (A) play : drama
   (B) rug : carpet   (C) paper : typewriter
   (D) bicuspid : teeth   (E) barn : door

2. GOOD NEWS : SMILE :: (A) cheer : health
   (B) worry : frown   (C) face : expression
   (D) terror : fright   (E) outlook : optimism

3. FISH : SCHOOL :: (A) chick : hen
   (B) herd : tribe   (C) geese : gaggle
   (D) rooster : coop   (E) mammal : pack

4. FOOD : HUNGER :: (A) acumen : bankruptcy
   (B) hope : fear   (C) desire : greed
   (D) transportation : car   (E) water : thirst

5. STUDIO : ART :: (A) conservatory : music
   (B) school : business   (C) office : contracts
   (D) laboratory : experiments
   (E) museum : crafts

6. SCALPEL : INCISION :: (A) knife : blade
   (B) needle : insertion   (C) awl : repair
   (D) trowel : plaster   (E) plow : furrow

7. MEDIA : NEWS :: (A) home : rule
   (B) government : laws   (C) legislature : bureaus
   (D) library : words   (E) market : vegetables

8. SLEEVE : ARM :: (A) fedora : ankle
   (B) ruching : chest   (C) chapeau : head
   (D) cravat : waist   (E) bustle : leg

9. ACCORD : DISSENSION ::
   (A) chicanery : guile   (B) obloquy : reproach
   (C) refinement : denigration
   (D) gentility : coarseness
   (E) wariness : desiccation

10. TORTUOUS : PATH ::
    (A) wretched : miscreant
    (B) worthless : solution   (C) convoluted : prose
    (D) heinous : crime (E) ignominious : defeat

Note: A few tough words here, right? The vocabulary used in PSAT/SAT questions has become more demanding in recent years. Please learn the words in the foregoing ten questions. Most have appeared on past tests, and many will return to haunt you.

ANSWERS to all quizzes can be found in the back of the book, beginning on p. 417.

PRACTICE ANALOGIES 2

Choose and circle the lettered pair that best expresses a relationship like that of the first pair. Remember to cross out wrong answers as you eliminate them.

1. RAFTERS : WOOD :: (A) cart : harness
   (B) hole : peg   (C) walk : cement
   (D) garden : manure   (E) horse : hide

2. PEDIATRICIAN : CHILDREN ::
   (A) numismatist : therapy
   (B) linguist : language   (C) podiatrist : bones
   (D) lawyer : suits
   (E) playwright : identification

3. PECK : BUSHEL :: (A) quart : half-gallon
   (B) cup : quart   (C) pint : quart
   (D) ounce : cup   (E) pint : gallon

4. GOVERNMENT : ANARCHY :: (A) joy : bliss
   (B) harmony : dissonance   (C) sobriety : mien
   (D) dichotomy : subtraction
   (E) honesty : affluence

5. CAT : FELINE :: (A) tomboy : feminine
   (B) cow : canine   (C) masculine : man
   (D) bull : taurine   (E) woman : virile

6. TURNCOAT : VILIFY :: (A) viper : slay
   (B) pickpocket : describe
   (C) author : confound
   (D) adviser : confirm (E) terrorist : attest

7. DOWNPOUR : FLOOD :: (A) battle : slaughter
   (B) torrent : gullywasher
   (C) altercation : discord
   (D) harmony : accord (E) drizzle : rain

8. WORDS : SPEECH :: (A) peeling : orange
   (B) leaves : tree   (C) pages : book
   (D) potato : skin   (E) seeds : apple

9. EXPRESSION : FACE :: (A) pleasant : smile
   (B) appearance : inside   (C) hair : head
   (D) facade : building   (E) features : look

10. INTIMATE : COMMAND ::
    (A) ameliorate : approve
    (B) extirpate : eradicate   (C) appease : abate
    (D) advocate : aspire (E) suggest : epitomize

Again . . . any words that were stumpers? If so, spend some fruitful minutes in the vocabulary section of this book. Words are grouped alphabetically to speed your quest for answers or meanings. If the word you seek isn't featured in bold type, consult a dictionary.

PRACTICE ANALOGIES 3

Directions as before.

1. TIGER : FEROCIOUS :: (A) deer : timorous
   (B) cow : grumpy   (C) proud : lion
   (D) dog : stealthy   (E) mule : tractable

2. SQUASH : VINE :: (A) berries : quart
   (B) mulberry : tree   (C) buckle : boot
   (D) handle : drawer   (E) peach : fruit

3. HONEY : HIVE :: (A) water : tub
   (B) liquid : bowl   (C) wine : cask
   (D) batter : pan   (E) thermos : soup

4. RADIANCE : GLIMMER :: (A) glow : shine
   (B) sparkle : glitter   (C) dark : light
   (D) heat waves : shimmer   (E) midday : dawn

5. COW : CHEESE :: (A) otter : shell
   (B) pup : whelp   (C) deer : venison
   (D) bee : pollen   (E) cream : goat

6. SCRIVENER : SCROLL ::
   (A) cartwright : tractor   (B) sculptor : chisel
   (C) woodsman : forest
   (D) seamstress : garment
   (E) engraver : stamp

7. DIFFICULT : ARCANE :: (A) assiduous : clear
   (B) engaging : abrupt   (C) tenuous : impalpable
   (D) willful : venerable   (E) acerbic : low-spirited

8. CHILD : MATURE :: (A) bud : burgeon
   (B) spine : flex   (C) shrub : wither
   (D) stalk : support   (E) youth : imitate

9. PLOT : THWART :: (A) goal : wrest
   (B) attempt : frustrate   (C) design : copy
   (D) vignette : abbreviate   (E) scene : dramatize

10. SLOTH : TORPID :: (A) gazelle : willful
    (B) amphibian : gelid
    (C) mammal : carnivorous   (D) ant : assiduous
    (E) bluejay : ascetic

Check your answers at the end of each practice set. Are you becoming a better guesser? *Note when you guess* so that you can watch your progress.

PRACTICE ANALOGIES 4

Directions as before.

1. CYLINDER : ROUND :: (A) octagon : oval
   (B) dome : open   (C) wagon : rectangular
   (D) bulb : square   (E) peg : circular

2. DRENCH : SPRINKLE ::
   (A) suppose : speculate   (B) drive : impel
   (C) refute : confirm   (D) abide : rest
   (E) squander : spend

3. MITTEN : TOUCH :: (A) glove : cover
   (B) head cold : smell   (C) apparel : see
   (D) stomachache : taste   (E) megaphone : hear

4. PERSEVERANCE : SUCCESS ::
   (A) curiosity : knowledge   (B) scrutiny : results
   (C) hope : confirmation   (D) endeavor : trials
   (E) consternation : answer

5. HEED : ADVICE :: (A) rejoice : good fortune
   (B) enjoin : rumor   (C) prevent : acclaim
   (D) vanish : thin air   (E) synchronize : thoughts

6. SLEEP : FITFUL :: (A) dream : wakeful
   (B) idea : ludicrous   (C) design : original
   (D) thought : chaotic   (E) manuscript : trite

7. BEE : SWARM :: (A) wrestler : opponent
   (B) editor : staff   (C) spectator : throng
   (D) athlete : horde   (E) actor : bevy

8. NARCOTIC : DULL :: (A) notice : admit
   (B) inhalant : irritate   (C) bandage : wound
   (D) license : prohibit   (E) unguent : soothe

9. CONSTITUTION : AMENDMENT ::
   (A) index : appendix   (B) will : codicil
   (C) newspaper : headline
   (D) adjunct : corollary   (E) church : nave

10. SHYSTER : DIDDLE :: (A) rover : calculate
    (B) fabricator : foment   (C) critic : quibble
    (D) mountebank : bilk   (E) trickster : debunk

PRACTICE ANALOGIES 5

Directions as before.

1. STREAM : CRAYFISH :: (A) grass : zebra
   (B) heavens : planet   (C) garden : flower
   (D) ground : mole   (E) water : fowl

2. AUTUMN : WITHER :: (A) fall : digress
   (B) winter : retreat   (C) spring : flower
   (D) season : change   (E) summer : heat

3. TOADY : FAWNING :: (A) twerp : ingratiating
   (B) sneak : wily   (C) braggart : circumspect
   (D) sycophant : hardy   (E) jester : carping

4. DATA : COMPUTER :: (A) fodder : cattle
   (B) source : well   (C) idea : title
   (D) bridle : horse   (E) language : calculator

5. AUGUR : FUTURE :: (A) knight : medieval
   (B) poet : century   (C) vanguard : pack
   (D) historian : past   (E) commentator : present

6. STATELY : DEMEANOR ::
   (A) seaworthy : character
   (B) ascetic : deportment   (C) narrow : vessel
   (D) fertile : nature   (E) sober : mien

7. PROGENITOR : HEIR :: (A) ancestor : serf
   (B) author : sire   (C) precursor : lord
   (D) forebear : descendant
   (E) sponsor : candidate

8. RASH : STOIC :: (A) didactic : adherent
   (B) articulate : orator   (C) dubious : scoundrel
   (D) dolorous : spouse   (E) agnostic : cleric

9. JALOPY : DILAPIDATION ::
   (A) clue : authorization   (B) yoke : conjunction
   (C) clasp : separation   (D) desk : aggravation
   (E) statue : dissection

10. WASTREL : DISCIPLINE ::
    (A) transient : permanence
    (B) pariah : longevity   (C) waif : passivity
    (D) vagabond : prudence
    (E) lackey : commitment

BEFORE WE GO ANY FARTHER . . . A VOCABULARY BREAK

Certain words crop up repeatedly in literature, newspapers, speeches . . . *and* on the SAT and PSAT. These words have been used in the foregoing exercises; more are listed in the vocabulary section of this book (pp. 127–226). A few appear in the following exercises. These same words parade by, test after test—and you must know them.

Spend some quiet moments with the following quizzes designed to *teach* you the words without confounding you. For a more exact feel of any strange word, try recalling a sentence in which it was used or the context of its use. Remember that learning *opposites* is a great way to learn new words.

Memorize the ones you don't know well.

Antonym- sound the same, but mean different

Antonyms A

Choose the best antonym for each numbered word from the selections that follow word number 5, and write it on the correct line.

Antonym	Word and Meaning
_____	1. apathy (lack of interest, emotion, or caring)
_____	2. decrepit (broken down, aged, no longer useful)
_____	3. atrophy (to waste away, degenerate, wither)
_____	4. plethora (vast amount, excess amount)
_____	5. capitulate (to yield, give in, give up)

Choices: burgeon, paucity, resist, vigorous, zeal

Antonyms B

Directions as with A.

Antonym	*Word and Meaning*
_____	1. ingenuous (innocent, trusting, naive)
_____	2. staid (serious, sober, sedate, restrained)
_____	3. indifferent (neutral, without prejudice)
_____	4. discerning (astute, perceptive, able to distinguish between one thing and another)
_____	5. revere (to honor or esteem highly, worship)

Choices: exuberant, disdain, sophisticated, obtuse, biased

If these words are becoming all mixed up—like a recipe for goulash—here's an idea. Ask your English teacher to offer 5 minutes of vocabulary review a day. That's 25 minutes a week for all the weeks preceding your exam. You'll be amazed at what you can learn in that amount of regular, concentrated time.

Antonyms C

Directions as with A.

Antonym	*Word and Meaning*
_____	1. rant (to denounce angrily, rave noisily)
_____	2. ignominy (utter shame and disgrace)
_____	3. elucidate (to make perfectly clear, explain)
_____	4. extricate (to disentangle, work one's way out of a predicament)
_____	5. hypocrisy (lack of honesty, sincerity, or truth)

Choices: esteem, embroil, sincerity, talk pleasantly, confound

Antonyms D

Directions as with A.

Antonym	*Word and Meaning*
_____	1. expendable (unnecessary, extra)
_____	2. defunct (useless, dead, finished)
_____	3. copious (superabundant, plentiful)
_____	4. provincial (of narrow, restricted outlook; lacking polish or sophistication)
_____	5. ambiguous (lacking clarity, vague)

Choices: sparse, broad-minded, extant (existing), definite, irreplaceable and vital

PREFIXES TO KEEP IN MIND

Prefixes That Are Usually Negative

a, an	atypical	il, in	inefficient
ab, abs	abdicate	im, ir	irregular
anti	antipathy	mis	mistake
contra	contradict	non	nonsense
counter	counteract	ob	obstacle
de	destruct	of, op	oppose
dif, dis	disagree	un	unwilling
for	forbid		

Prefixes That Are Usually Positive

bene	beneficial	com, co	comply
bon	bonus	eu	euphony
col, con, cor	correlate	pro	promote

Prefixes of Time or Location

ana	anachronism	hyp, hypo	hypodermic
ante	antecedent	inter	interrupt
anti	anticipate	intro, -a	introduce
cata	catacombs	neo	neophyte
circum	circumference	para	paralegal
em, en	embrace	peri	perimeter
enfold	post	postpone	
epi	epidermis	pre	predict
ex, e, ef	exit	re	retract
extra, -o	extracurricular	sub, sup, sus	submarine
fore	forecast	tele	telegraph
	trans	transpose	

Hot Tip: Words are slippery devils, often having more than one meaning. You need to be flexible. Look at the answers first to determine the part of speech. For example, one meaning of *incline* is slope; both are nouns. But wait . . . *incline* also means *to be likely, to tend toward,* as "He is *inclined* to ski whenever he has a chance." Many words can change their part of speech and thereby change their meanings. *Be wary.*

HOW TO ANSWER FILL-IN-THE-BLANK SENTENCE COMPLETION QUESTIONS

Sentence completion questions ask you to select the word or words that best complete the meaning of the sentence. As on other portions of a typical test, 5 answer choices are offered. While sentence completion questions look different from antonym or analogy problems, they are actually much the same. Again, each question tests both the depth and the breadth of your vocabulary and general verbal ability. And again, *practice* with this type of question will enhance your abilities—and that means a higher score.

WHAT ARE YOUR KEYS TO ANSWERS?

Often, the key to a right answer is a very small word, such as *but.* This is true for one-word sentence completion questions as well as sentences asking you to choose two words. A seemingly minor word can point to the meaning of the sentence as a whole. *Until you know the general sense of the sentence, you cannot fill in the blanks correctly.*

When you see *because, since, unless,* or *due to,* your mental antennae should quiver. These words (and others like them) set up a *cause and effect* relationship.

> *Example of a* **Cause and Effect Sentence:**
> Since the drought and winds began, our crops have suffered badly. *(Because of one thing, something else happened.)*

Other words or brief phrases set up a sentence of *contrast: yet, although, but, however, nevertheless, oddly, in spite of, uncharacteristically, strangely, ironically, on the other hand, curiously, nonetheless,* etc.

> *Example of a* **Sentence of Contrast:**
> Ironically, Sara's skill at chess, a game demanding patience and planning, deserted her when she worked math problems. *(The irony is that Sara's chess skills did not come to her aid—a direct contrast to what we expected.)*

Still other words point to a *comparison or coordination* of ideas: *and, or, plus, even,* and many verbs.

> *Examples of* **Comparison or Coordination of Ideas:**
> Her customary optimism and positive encouragement made her a natural leader. *(The words joined by* and *refer to one person and explain* why *she's a natural leader. Given the general sense of this sentence, those two words could never be opposites.)*
> She was hopeful, even buoyant, as we set out on our journey. *(Here, the clue* even *calls for a word meaning hopeful to a greater degree, and* buoyant *fills that requirement. The word that completes this comparison could never have been negative in tone.)*

Some key words serve as a definition of the answer choice you seek. Watch for sentences that hand you the answer on a silver platter.

> *Example of a* **Sentence Giving You a Definition:**
> Reginald was too often guilty of *hypocrisy,* saying one thing when we all knew he believed the opposite.
> Remember to note these "little" words, the *verbs,* and *all adverbs* to clarify the general sense before you start hunting for words to complete the meaning of the sentence.

ONE-WORD SENTENCE COMPLETION QUESTIONS

Example: Choose the word that best completes the meaning of the entire sentence.

> Rae knew that she should ---- the swim practice
> because her inflamed shoulder was stiff and painful.

Step 1.   **Use the information in the given sentence.** Circle or underline words that point to the answer you must have.

Step 2.   **Analyze** the sentence information. Does Rae appear to need or want a swim practice? Is she unable? Is she disabled? Answer: She's in rough shape, poor kid. A tough practice will probably finish her off.

Note the **"little" words** in the sentence: *should* and *because.* For *should,* substitute *ought to* if that helps to clarify meaning and remember *because.* Now your sentence reads:

Rae knew that she OUGHT TO ---- the swim practice
BECAUSE her inflamed shoulder was stiff and painful.

Step 3.   **Get your own answer in mind.** How about "skip the practice" or "avoid the swim practice"? You know she feels that she will not do well because of her inflamed shoulder.

New sentence:

Rae knew that she OUGHT TO SKIP the swim practice
BECAUSE her inflamed shoulder was stiff and painful.

Step 4.   **Look at the answers.** Any answers that show poor Rae going to swim practice will probably not be correct.

Answer choices: (A) cease   (B) endure   (C) forgo   (D) appreciate   (E) suffer

(A) **cease.** Stop going to practice altogether? It is awkward to phrase this sentence "Rae knew that she should *cease* the swim practice." No. Throw out.

(B) **endure.** Too painful for Rae. Do you want the sentence to read that she "should endure the swim practice because her inflamed shoulder was stiff and painful"? No. Throw out.

(C) **forgo.** This answer means she skips or forgets this swim practice, and for a good reason. This one's a keeper.

(D) **appreciate.** How can Rae *appreciate* swimming with a painful shoulder? No. Throw out.

(E) **suffer.** Yes, she'll "suffer" all right. Not a logical choice, so throw out.

Once again, you have systematically shot down all of the bad answers. To do so, you used *four main tools that you will always have in any test:*

1. Every single word in the problem—especially the "little" words.
2. Logic—and your own common sense.
3. The answers as clues.
4. The process of elimination, your ally.

TWO-WORD SENTENCE COMPLETION QUESTIONS

For the two-word fill-in questions you'll follow the same four steps, only this time you may feel extra dependence on the answers as clues. If one of the words in the two-word answer does not fit the meaning you require—and this happens a lot—that whole answer is worthless. For example, if the word offered for the first blank is negative and you need a *positive* word for that slot, just ignore the entire answer. Cross it out immediately.

If the sentence is complex, peppered with commas and extra phrases, *be sure to reword the sentence so that its meaning is absolutely clear to you.* Ignore extra phrases.

Look ahead in your own mind *before* you consult the answer choices.

If your sentence is way off-base when you check the answers, *recast* the sentence *a second time* in your own words until you feel it is right. Then, plug in words that fit the altered meaning.

Example:

Oddly enough, Andy's ---- at lacrosse
never ---- his enthusiasm.

Step 1.   **Use given information, noting key words** that point to the answer you need.

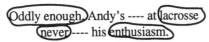

Step 2.   **Analyze** sentence information. Is Andy good at lacrosse or not? If he *is* good at it, then he *ought to be enthusiastic.* So why is it *odd* that he's got enthusiasm? Maybe he isn't very good at it, but he likes it anyway???

What parts of speech do you need? The first blank has to be a noun. The second blank must be the verb for the entire sentence. We probably need a negative noun for the first blank. Any positive word offered as an answer choice for the first blank can be eliminated immediately.

Step 3.   **Get your own answer in mind.** The new sentence for this problem could read:

> Oddly enough, Andy's LACK OF SUCCESS at lacrosse
> never SQUASHED/FLATTENED/RUINED his enthusiasm.

Step 4.   **Check the answer choices, eliminating the unlikely ones, and circling the better ones** as you fit them into your sentence.

(A) achievement. .quenched
(B) woes. .enhanced
(C) triumph. .penetrated
(D) failure. .dampened
(E) downfall. .enlightened

(A) His *achievement* never *quenched* his enthusiasm? Of course it wouldn't! Not logical. Throw out.

(B) His *woes* never *enhanced* his enthusiasm? True, they wouldn't add to it a bit. Not like the trial sentence, but it does make sense. Doesn't fit with *oddly enough,* but still worth retaining for a bit.

(C) His *triumph* never *penetrated* his enthusiasm? Dumb sentence. Throw out.

(D) His *failure* never *dampened* his enthusiasm? Aha! Makes complete sense, and sounds like the trial sentence. Keep!

(E) His *downfall* never *enlightened* his enthusiasm? Another dumb sentence. Throw out.

Of the keepers, answers (B) and (D), answer (D) is clearly superior. When *failure* and *dampened* are plugged into the original sentence, they make complete, logical sense. *All* of the words fit the sentence meaning and convey a unified idea.

Review: Keys to Answers

1. Analyze the sentence to determine its general sense. What is it really saying? Do you need negative (bad) words or positive (good) words as fill-ins?
2. Note all the "little" words and phrases—*so, but, and, yet, since, most, least, although, however, nonetheless, on the other hand, ironically, strangely enough, oddly, moreover, unless, typically, normally, curiously, uncharacteristically, even though, nevertheless,* etc.—that shape the meaning of the sentence.
3. If the sentence is complex, simplify it by substituting your own words. Be faithful to the original sentence meaning.
4. Whomp up your own answer with logical words filled in before you examine the 5 choices.
5. Remember that the typical sentences for these completion-style questions are sentences that (a) **contrast** one thing with another, (b) **compare** or **coordinate** ideas or concepts with one another, and (c) **show cause and effect** relationships. Some sentences **define** the word you need as your answer.

   Be alert for these sentence types because they point the way to the answer. Two adjectives, for instance, joined by the word *and* (and applying to one person) will be close in meaning to one another and are apt to be nearly synonymous; certainly they could not be antonyms.
6. Questions get tougher as you move through any question set. Near the end of a set, the sentences are apt to be convoluted and full of extra phrases, such as *it seems to me* and *according to the experts.* Always remove these extra bits from your mind when converting the mess to your own simpler phraseology.

   Although answer choices may be sophisticated, they can also be startlingly simple. Be careful: *No single rule about answer choices works consistently.*
7. Listen to the sentence in its final form after you've selected your completing word or words. If it sounds awkward, it may be wrong. Remember that your ear is a valuable language tool. You've probably heard the special cadences of English all of your life. Let those rhythms speak to you.

TIMING FOR SENTENCE COMPLETION QUESTIONS

Look ahead to see how many sentence completion questions are on a given portion of your timed test. On an SAT, these questions total 19 of the 78 verbal questions, and they are 16 of the 58 questions on a PSAT.

Students often spend longer on these questions than they should. They forget—or repress—thoughts of long, often uninspiring reading passages that await them later in the test.

Allowing yourself 30 seconds to 1 minute per question ought to be enough. Practice with sentence completion questions should help to make you a speedy, accurate worker. Plan to spend no more than 5–6 minutes on a set of 9 or 10 questions.

SENTENCE COMPLETION FOR PRACTICE 1

For this practice exercise, and all that follow for this type of question, select the word or words that *best* complete the meaning of each sentence.

easy

1. Rob abhors games that seem ---- and calls them "mindless marathons."

   B (A) superficial (B) tedious (C) simple
   (D) enlightening (E) complex

hard

2. The horse named Stockings, always ---- to manage, has the habit of scraping riders off under low-hanging branches.

   (A) weird (B) invigorating (C) difficult
   (D) simple (E) content

3. Because of her age and customary good nature, our family tries to handle Gramma's occasional ---- with tact and humor.

   business

   E (A) illness (B) ideas (C) ailments (D) nastiness
   (E) idiosyncrasies

4. Feeling threatened, our cat Fred viewed the newcomer, a young puppy, with ---- and ---- .

   (A) uncertainty. .unawareness
   C (B) curiosity. .delight
   (C) wariness. .consternation (D) hatred. .terror
   (E) happiness. .alarm

5. If only our cat Fred were more ----, he might learn to view our new puppy with ----, at the very least.

   Delighted

   A (A) sanguine. .detachment (B) fearful. .distaste
   (C) pessimistic. .fondness (D) gloomy. .distrust
   (E) friendly. .enmity

6. Martha says she's tired of essay tests; she believes that their grading is entirely too ----, founded as it is on teacher opinion.

   (A) subjective (B) rigorous (C) objective
   (D) ineffectual (E) persnickety

7. Uncertainty dogged his career; should he gamble on sales or take the safer route and choose customer service? The former alternative offered ----, the latter, ----.

   B (A) boredom. .uncertainty (B) challenge. .security
   (C) little. .much (D) safety. .banality
   (E) excitement. .insecurity

8. "The ---- of building your own house," Marg said excitedly, "is that when it's finished, you know it to be a(n) ---- creation."

   (A) frustration. .modern (B) difficulty. .individual
   (C) satisfaction. .unique (D) contentment. .new
   (E) construction. .complete

9. Johann's ---- in personal relationships is reflected daily in his business decisions; rarely have we known anyone so ----.

   D (A) ineptitude. .skillful (B) acumen. .obtuse
   (C) impatience. .adept (D) finesse. .perspicacious
   (E) acuteness. .wise

10. Although the male lion assiduously pursues a mate during courtship, his later ---- stands in startling contrast to his earlier ----.

    (A) preoccupation. .concern
    (B) contempt. .frustration
    (C) absorption. .fascination
    E (D) isolation. .interest
    (E) indifference. .fervor

SENTENCE COMPLETION FOR PRACTICE 2

Are you remembering to eliminate extra phrases that get in the way? Also keep the need for negative (bad) or positive (good) words in mind. Knowing that you need a really bad word for the first blank, for example, lets you zap out any answer with a positive word first.

1. After listening to one ---- after another, we concluded that our guest speaker hadn't altered his speech in twenty years.

   B (A) remark (B) cliché (C) innuendo
   (D) surprise (E) paradox

2. Originality flourishes on every floor of this museum, as you will discover in each ---- exhibit.

   A (A) arresting (B) delightful (C) distressing
   (D) abundant (E) parsimonious

3. In spite of its ----, the movie we attended rarely revealed ---- or devoted serious attention to its underlying theme.

   (A) penetration. .thoughtful originality
   (B) freshness. .shallow insights
   C (C) novelty. .profound truths
   (D) presentation. .superficial observations
   (E) production. .mental acumen

4. While machines have rescued farmers from a mainly ---- existence, still the ---- on weather plagues their days.

    (A) crop-related. .reliance
    (B) work-oriented. .relationship
    (C) labor-intensive. .dependence
    (D) family-oriented. .changeability
    (E) back-breaking. .independence

5. The natural ---- of fish in our streams ---- our looking further afield for either sustenance or sporting entertainment.

    (A) paucity. .discouraged
    (B) plethora. .encouraged
    (C) absence. .assisted
    (D) amount. .obviated
    (E) abundance. .forestalled

6. A normally intrepid canoeist, Sally, behaving in a most uncharacteristic manner, suggested that we ---- our canoes and ---- the rapids downstream before we continued.

    (A) unload. .avoid   (B) portage. .shoot
    (C) abandon. .swim   (D) beach. .investigate
    (E) bank. .ignore

7. Although our preparations for the debate were ----, the actual debate turned into a surprising and ---- victory for our school.

    (A) acceptable. .stunning   (B) excellent. .thrilling
    (C) flimsy. .amateur   (D) efficient. .welcome
    (E) inadequate. .heartwarming

8. Brent is really quite a(n) ---- soul, but at times he retreats from ---- to consider who he is and where he's going.

    (A) scholarly. .introspection   (B) convivial. .society
    (C) reclusive. .company   (D) withdrawn. .himself
    (E) extroverted. .contemplation

9. Always a popular musical instrument, the clarinet becomes even more ---- when played by a ---- such as Pete Fountain, the famous New Orleans musician.

    (A) euphonious. .novice   (B) daunting. .musician
    (C) appealing. .virtuoso   (D) eclectic. .tyro
    (E) erudite. .master

10. Modern scientists zealously study that ---- known as a living cell, even though they realize that its complexity may cause certain definitive relationships to ---- description for years to come.

    (A) conundrum. .defy   (B) incongruity. .entail
    (C) profundity. .elude   (D) enigma. .bask in
    (E) sphinx. .promulgate

SENTENCE COMPLETION FOR PRACTICE 3

Are you remembering to eliminate answers one by one?

1. Parenting has undergone redefinition in recent years, yet child psychologists believe that the basic parent role is essentially ----.

    (A) unique   (B) altered   (C) valueless
    (D) protection   (E) unchanged

2. Laboratory scientists, often striving for answers to seemingly unanswerable questions, realize that ---- is, and always has been, their finest ally.

    (A) resistance   (B) philanthropy   (C) persistence
    (D) assistance   (E) research

3. As glaciers moved ---- across the face of continents, they left ---- behind them, some in the form of hill-shaped debris known as end moraines.

    (A) grievously. .alteration
    (B) swiftly. .essentially nothing
    (C) slowly. .valleys
    (D) ponderously. .residual landmarks
    (E) alarmingly. .cataclysmic changes

4. Marlene's concern and ---- for orphaned children have at times been misconstrued as ---- and overly protective.

    (A) compassion. .obsessive
    (B) absorption. .considerate
    (C) apathy. .compulsive
    (D) empathy. .corrective
    (E) sympathy. .healthy

5. Although it is acknowledged that certain inoculations guarantee ---- from disease, their ---- use for diseases long eradicated seems questionable.

    (A) illness. .casual   (B) freedom. .indiscriminate
    (C) cessation. .regular   (D) relapses. .customary
    (E) absence. .mandatory

6. One consequence of the ---- popularity of exercise was a veritable ---- of fitness gyms and spas, all in response to our emphasis on physical health.

    (A) sudden. .mushrooming
    (B) questionable. .tidal wave   (C) reliable. .flood
    (D) stunning. .horde   (E) dwindling. .neglect

7. Blamed partially on inbreeding, the ---- of the Saint Bernard's formerly lovable character has been viewed with ---- by all dog breeders who respect the breed itself.

   (A) depression. .suspicion
   (B) enhancement. .much appreciation
   (C) relegation. .alarm
   (D) deterioration. .deep regret
   (E) withdrawal. .approbation

8. Known throughout school as a ---- boxer, Ken is basically ---- in nature and unusually shy, which comes as a surprise to his boxing opponents when they meet outside the ring.

   (A) vaguely timid. .aggressive
   (B) highly talented. .pugnacious
   (C) superbly trained. .dilatory
   (D) somewhat tentative. .obnoxious
   (E) consummately skilled. .retiring

9. Unaware that she had expected her fellow jurors to be ----, Mrs. Cook was relieved and ---- to discover their unified attitude of dedication and serious purpose.

   (A) mendacious. .disturbed
   (B) callous. .overwrought
   (C) nonchalant. .gratified
   (D) unobservant. .delirious
   (E) astute. .dismayed

10. Amazed that anyone could doubt his special insight into the whereabouts of ancient Troy, archaeologist Heinrich Schliemann ---- until the site was discovered just as he had ----.

    (A) acquiesced. .elaborated
    (B) persevered. .foretold
    (C) digressed. .advocated
    (D) persuaded. .articulated
    (E) competed. .predicted

SENTENCE COMPLETION FOR PRACTICE 4

Remember to put the trickier sentences into your own words. Know what sort of word you need for each blank before you eliminate answers.

1. While critics praised the play highly, viewers did not flock to the theater, and the playwright reaped only a(n) ---- reward from its brief run.

   (A) just   (B) modest   (C) embarrassed
   (D) monetary   (E) precise

2. My economics textbook is ---- to read, yet when I read attentively, I understand the theories presented.

   (A) exciting   (B) annoying   (C) objectionable
   (D) demanding   (E) idealistic

3. It would be wrong to dismiss Charles as a fair-weather friend merely because he disagrees with me at times, because, when I honestly need his ----, he is on my side.

   (A) debates   (B) consternation   (C) permission
   (D) comprehension   (E) support

4. Although children need shelter and protection, their need for ---- is just as great if they are to evaluate themselves and their world honestly.

   (A) homes   (B) affection   (C) truth
   (D) adjustment   (E) instruction

5. The considerate personality of Dr. Jekyll underwent a total ---- as he became Mr. Hyde, a(n) ---- character bent on evil.

   (A) alteration. .dubious
   (B) refurbishing. .masterful

   (C) indoctrination. .original
   (D) advancement. .different
   (E) metamorphosis. .ruthless

6. If, as Shelley wrote, "The great instrument of moral good is the imagination," then we must not allow ---- to exclude totally our ----.

   (A) harsh reality. .idealistic goals
   (B) creativity. .fantasies
   (C) unpleasant facts. .daily lives
   (D) religion. .perception of life
   (E) practicality. .constructive ideas

7. Underlying Twain's ----, "Man is the only animal that blushes. Or needs to," is his admitted ---- regarding the flawed human race.

   (A) quote. .fondness   (B) cliché. .disillusionment
   (C) epigram. .cynicism   (D) paradox. .hatred
   (E) statement. .idealism

8. Even though certain forms of cancer now respond well to treatment, others have remained a(n) ---- continuing to puzzle physicians.

   (A) pestilence   (B) allusion   (C) eccentricity
   (D) enigma   (E) provocation

9. Once one of America's most ---- states, possessed of pine forests and winding streams, rolling meadows abundant with wildflowers, and a lengthy coastline of white sand beaches, New Jersey is now largely transformed by that ---- called Industrial Progress.

   (A) idyllic. .idol   (B) controversial. .wizard
   (C) pastoral. .genius   (D) prodigal. .liberal
   (E) provincial. .aesthete

10. Believing himself supported by more than a(n) ----
of evidence, the professor endeavored to prove that
Beowulf was not the ---- his colleagues claimed, but
an actual man whose existence was the basis for the
Old English epic.

    (A) shred. .persona   (B) modicum. .chimera

(C) fabrication. .demon   (D) particle. .heresy
 (E) aggregation. .protagonist

Ahem! Do you know—with absolute certainty—
all of the words in this unit that have been given as
answer choices? If not, it's flashcard time! These words
appear year after year on the SAT and PSAT.

SENTENCE COMPLETION FOR PRACTICE 5

1. Mrs. Davis is clear and direct of speech, yet her
remarks yesterday were uncharacteristically ----.

    (A) sprightly   (B) lucid   (C) superficial
    (D) obscure   (E) servile

2. No one wishes to discourage a sincere desire to ----;
nevertheless, novelty for novelty's sake is a
questionable approach.

    (A) discriminate   (B) innovate   (C) diverge
    (D) revitalize   (E) stagnate

3. I prefer the lively discord of a(n) ---- debate to the
---- restraint of chillingly civilized discourse.

    (A) ready. .cool   (B) alarmist. .admirable
    (C) incessant. .brief   (D) heated. .tempered
    (E) exciting. .trivial

4. It was perhaps inevitable that our highly ---- uncle
would be placed in a nursing home as age ---- his
propensity for unpredictable behavior.

    (A) eccentric. .accentuated
    (B) benevolent. .increased   (C) erratic. .reduced
    (D) pious. .encouraged   (E) wayward. .deterred

5. "If you will confine your testimony to what is ----,"
the judge ordered, "we will learn the answers to our
questions."

    (A) diverse   (B) eloquent   (C) serious
    (D) interesting   (E) relevant

6. Dissension spread among the troops, ---- like a
plague, and equally ---- in its grip.

    (A) unwelcome. .homicidal   (B) infamous. .futile
    (C) virulent. .tenacious   (D) subtle. .stubborn
    (E) contemptible. .conspicuous

7. Bobby accepted his summer exile to camp with ----,
but he ---- the offers of friendship from other
campers and resolutely stayed in his cabin with a
book.

    (A) resignation. .repudiated
    (B) alacrity. .welcomed

(C) complacence. .ignored
(D) gravity. .extolled
(E) reluctance. .derided

8. Not renowned for his mental ----, Mr. Bumble
nonetheless delivered a(n) ---- address in the state
assembly, which, according to all reports, prompted
careful study of hitherto unexamined reports.

    (A) gifts. .banal
    (B) subtleties. .conciliatory
    (C) perception. .dogmatic
    (D) fervor. .impassioned
    (E) acuity. .provocative

9. Known for ---- rather than garrulity, Mrs. Brown
was nonplussed when nominated to be president, a
position that frequently demanded ----.

    (A) amiability. .gravity
    (B) fastidiousness. .precision
    (C) reticence. .eloquence
    (D) impulsiveness. .sobriety
    (E) incoherence. .clarity

10. While some say it is ---- to suggest that an infinitive
may be "split" by an adverb, e.g., *to radically alter,*
we need to ---- each inherited grammatical guideline
in order to make decisions that suit our evolving
language.

    (A) redundant. .evaluate   (B) distasteful. .pursue
    (C) heresy. .scrutinize   (D) expeditious. .examine
    (E) incongruous. .relegate

Phew! You have survived 50 of these dreadful
sentences. Take a break and treat yourself to a giant bowl
of popcorn or a new movie—or *both.*

HOW TO DEVELOP CRITICAL READING SKILLS

FIRST, THE FACTS

On each SAT, 40 of the 78 questions are based on reading comprehension; there are 30 such questions on a PSAT.

Most of these readings are fairly interesting. They seem to have improved recently, maybe as a result of the law requiring ETS to publish used test forms, or maybe because SAT tutors have criticized the reading passages as the worst-written material imaginable.

The reading passages include material from the physical and social sciences. One selection is usually fiction, and another focuses on an ethnic group or on women.

HOW SHOULD YOU READ?

We all do at least two distinct varieties of reading:

1. **Pleasure Reading:** Garfield and his lasagna and/or "The Wildest Girl/Boy in Town."
2. **Information/Study Reading:** the biology book, American history, and how-to manuals, like this one.

As you know, these two kinds of reading are done for very different purposes. The *way* that they are performed must be just as different.

The *kind of reading you want to perfect* is demanding reading because it asks for *all* of you, not just your funny bone. It expects you to be totally involved with the passage. And if you are, the answers are there, waiting for you to spot them and answer the questions with no strain.

KEY WORDS ... ONE MORE TIME

Remember the list of key (or clue) words from p. 37 in the Red Alert section on sentence completion questions? Words such as *but, yet, since, although, except, moreover, unless,* and *nonetheless* will be just as helpful to you in reading comprehension territory. *Key words in sentences signal a shift, a qualification, an anomaly—SOMETHING you should note.* More than half of the questions will come from sentences containing key words. Luckily, the answers must be somewhere in the reading material. The answers will be either stated or implied in the passages, just as the test directions say.

The answers are there. And you will learn how to spot them by doing this unit.

WHAT KINDS OF QUESTIONS ARE ASKED?

If you think for a minute, you'll know what kinds of questions can be asked about a passage only a few paragraphs long. Someone out there will want to know whether or not you grasped:

1. The "main point" or "central theme" of the passage
2. The author's intent, attitude, tone—how the writer *feels* about what he or she is saying
3. The basic facts contained in the material
4. The implications of the material, including the drawing of logical conclusions
5. The organizational techniques the author uses
6. How the author uses certain words—vocabulary in context

WHY ARE READING PASSAGES SUCH A BIG PART OF A VERBAL TEST?

College entrance exams are developed at the request of colleges themselves. ETS, for example, has developed its college entrance tests for the College Board, a group whose members represent a wide variety of colleges and schools. As nearly as possible, these tests are designed to discover how well a student will do with college-level reading material. Your college work will *directly depend* on your ability to read and understand written material. Some authorities have stated that as much as 90 percent of your work in college is reading based. Need I say more?

KNOW THESE FACTS TO RAISE YOUR SCORE

1. Spending too long on a stumper-question can really cost you points. Keep moving throughout any block of questions. Circle the stinkers and come back to them at the end. You must pocket all the right answers you can in each timed segment.
2. You may be the exception—and that's why you need to practice test-taking—but *in general,* students score more right answers by doing the analogies and sentence completion questions FIRST. They're faster for most people.
3. Be sure to save PLENTY OF TIME FOR READING PASSAGES.
4. Questions are *not* arranged in order of difficulty as they tend to be on the rest of an SAT or PSAT. The last question about a passage may be the easiest.
5. Any answer choice is wrong if it contradicts proven facts. Draw on your own storehouse of facts to help you spot wrong answers as well as right ones.

HOW WELL ARE YOU READING NOW?

In order to make the best use of your time, try to determine how well you are reading now. Maybe your reading is developed to a point that you do not need the introductory exercises of this review and can go directly to the section titled "How to Read for the Main Point or Central Theme." If so, you should skip these opening exercises. If not, of course, you should follow this section, step by step.

Try this passage as a self-quiz.

First Try

It has been said many times that we live in an age of anxiety. Psychologists and psychiatrists have told us this is true so many times and in so many ways, it must be so—everyone is a little
Line neurotic, everyone gets uptight, we all have an unresolved conflict
(5) here or there, interpersonal stress is commonplace, no one communicates, we need releases from the pressure we are under.

As a result, our language has changed. Now we talk like psychologists. Where once we had worrywarts we now have obsessive-compulsive neurotics. Where we used to cry at funerals,
(10) we now have grief reactions. Where once we were afraid of things, we now have phobias (some seven hundred by the last count). Does our use of language affect the way we see ourselves? I think so. And what if the language is unclear? When a client says to me he wants to "get it together," I ask get *what* together? If someone says
(15) they are "losing it," what, pray tell, is being lost? Thankfully these particular ailments are fading as clichés should. But now we have burnout—the latest in a long line of quasi-clinical terms that imply a new and unhealthy psychological condition. To illustrate the perils of language, let's examine this new ailment.

Questions

Answer the questions based on material stated or implied in the passage. Try *not* to look back at the passage.

1. The author of this passage is most probably a   (A) teacher   (B) minister   (C) parent   (D) psychologist   (E) librarian
2. The author feels that language   (A) defines us   (B) affects our perception of ourselves   (C) is relatively unimportant   (D) determines entirely how we view ourselves   (E) needs to evolve to reflect increasingly sophisticated knowledge
3. According to the passage, the most recent "quasi-clinical" term is   (A) depression   (B) burnout   (C) manic   (D) stress   (E) interpersonal
4. We can infer that the author's attitude toward mental health clichés is one of   (A) admiration   (B) deep scorn   (C) total detachment   (D) scholarly regard   (E) basic disapproval

These four questions represent material you ought to have retained after one reading.

Answers

1. (D) *psychologist*   Answer (B), minister, may have been tempting, but ministers don't have "clients" (line 13).
2. (B) *affects our perception of ourselves*   Answers (A) and (D) are much too strong and not supported in the passage. Answer (E) may be true but has no support in the passage.
3. (B) *burnout*   (line 17).
4. (E) *basic disapproval*   Answer (B) expresses too strong an emotion; (C) and (D) misinterpret the tone of the passage, which is quite informal.

You might also have remembered some of the psychological jargon, especially a humorous example such as "grief reaction," a pompous expression for crying.

How well did you do? If you got 3 of the 4 answers right, you are reading carefully, *involving yourself* sufficiently in the passage so that you can answer questions immediately after reading. If you got only 1 or 2 answers right, you need to concentrate more fully in order to pull information out of the reading and fix it in your mind.

If your answers were nearly all correct, 3 out of 4 or 4 correct (hallelujah!), you should move on to the section titled "How to Read for the Main Point or Central Theme," on p. 73.

If you had problems with this passage and remembered very little, go to the section titled "Second Try," which follows.

Second Try

Ask yourself what you missed in the first-try reading selection. Was it the author's attitude? Decide exactly why you couldn't answer the questions you missed, and on this second try read more carefully.

Everyone loves Jane Austen's novels—scientists, feminists, college freshmen, traditionalists, even readers who think they don't like fiction. After Shakespeare and perhaps Dickens, Austen is the most universally admired writer in the English language. Her
(5) popularity is extraordinary when one considers that she deals with neither death nor religion nor great moments in history. Her subject is courtship and her stories all end the same way—in happy marriage. Yet no one has ever accused Austen of being shallow or suggested that her novels appeal because of their escapism. Quite
(10) the contrary—her work is usually characterized as wise, witty, and realistic.

In many ways Austen's novels resemble Shakespeare's comedies, which also end in marriage. Both the novels and the comedies demonstrate how much human nature may be revealed
(15) within the confines of a circumscribed environment and a limited plot. Like Shakespeare, Austen makes women her central characters. By using their wits and their moral sensibilities as a substitute for the power they do not have, they bring about a desired end. This element in itself—the success of the weak over the
(20) powerful—may account for some part of Austen's popularity.

The greater part of Austen's appeal, however, is rooted in her ability to combine the seemingly incompatible qualities of romance and irony, engagement and detachment. Rational though she may initially appear from the beauty of her balanced sentences, there is
(25) much in Austen's work that is firmly rooted in the realm of the feelings. Despite her elevation of civility, restraint, good manners, good sense, and duty, Austen's novels are essentially fairy tales—fantasies. They are grounded in realism and made credible by careful observation and sound precepts of moral behavior, but they
(30) are fantasies nevertheless.

Questions

Answer the questions as before, based on material stated or implied in the passage. Try to *remember* what you read. Don't look back if you can help it.

1. The author's attitude toward his or her subject can best be described as
   (A) moderately approving
   (B) enthusiastic and admiring
   (C) that of a typical, biased biographer
   (D) a blend of approval and disapproval
   (E) blindly worshiping

2. We can infer from this passage that most literary critics would admire Austen's work for all of the following EXCEPT
   (A) her insights into human nature
   (B) her revelation of universal truths
   (C) her humor
   (D) her poignant examples of our mortality
   (E) the inventiveness of her heroines

3. The author compares Austen's novels to Shakespeare's comedies primarily in order to
   (A) establish Austen's literary stature
   (B) emphasize the zany wit that both employed
   (C) discuss the role of women in literature
   (D) illustrate how much can be conveyed by very simple vehicles
   (E) reiterate the undying popularity of both authors

4. Given this passage, the author appears to respect Jane Austen the most for
   I. her universality of appeal
   II. her gift in discussing even very painful subjects
   III. her union of irony and romance
   IV. her ability to remain objective as an author while engaging the reader
   V. her unrelentingly rational, realistic approach

   (A) I, III, and IV   (B) II, III, and IV   (C) I, IV, and V   (D) III, IV, and V   (E) I, III, and V

Answers

1. (B) *enthusiastic and admiring*   Only this choice can be adequately defended. This biographer is very much a fan of Jane Austen, which kills answers (A) and (D). We have to question the truth of (C), which suggests that all biographers are biased. And (E) is too strong in tone.
2. (D) *her poignant examples of our mortality*   The passage states in line 6 that Austen never deals with death.
3. (D) *illustrate how much can be conveyed by very simple vehicles*   Reread the second paragraph, paying particular attention to lines 13–16. Remember also that the question asks you to choose the *primary* reason the two authors are being compared. While other answer choices are partially correct here, only answer (D) is comprehensive enough to be totally accurate.
4. (A) *I, III, and IV*   Roman numeral II can be inferred as wrong, since Austen writes of neither death nor religion nor momentous historical events, which are often inherently painful. Roman numeral V is contradicted by the entire last paragraph.

How well did you do? This passage was tougher than the one before. Student judges say that it is "somewhere around medium, not really nasty." And now you have some idea of how you will do on typical SAT and PSAT questions. You can get very good at answering questions like these with practice.

Okay, let's get going.

HOW TO GET BETTER

At this point you should have a good idea of your strengths and weaknesses as a reader. What do you remember well, seemingly without much effort? What is it that escapes you? As you work through the following practice test passages, concentrate on your reading skills so that you become proficient even with difficult material.

Good readers, like good writers, get that way through practice. No one can give you rules, because you're an individual. What works for you may not work for someone else. But you can learn to be a very good reader, just by practicing the skill of *involved* reading. *And there is a class-tested, time-proven way to do it.* Try it. It will make life, and particularly your life during a test, much easier than you might believe.

HOW TO READ FOR THE MAIN POINT OR CENTRAL THEME

Everything written or said has a point to make. Even the simple exclamation "Oh, really?" can make a telling point in just two words. Why speak or write if you *don't* have a point?

Typical questions about the main point on an SAT or PSAT read something like these:

1. The author's main purpose in this passage is . . . ?
2. An appropriate title for this passage would be . . . ?
3. The primary function of this passage is to . . . ?
4. This passage suggests that . . . ?
5. The content of this passage answers primarily which question. . . . (5 answer choices, all phrased as questions)?

In order to find the answer to such questions as quickly as possible, follow these steps:

Step 1. **Skim over all the questions quickly *before* you read the passage.** Unlike other verbal test sections, the reading comprehension section goes better if you know the questions *first.* Then, as you read, you know what to watch for in the written material.

A few students detest this method. Don't follow any suggestion that you hate. Read the passage first, if you feel that is the *only* right way for you.

Step 2. **Look for the main idea** (central theme) in the first paragraph. All opening paragraphs are obligated to tell you *where the piece is going.* However, no rule works all the time, remember? Sometimes you will discover a meaty, summation-type sentence that gives you the central point in the *middle* of the piece. Sometimes, too, it will be *near the very end.*

Step 3. **Read the passage, *rather quickly,*** especially when reading to determine the central idea. As you go, *mark the passage* with asterisks in the margin (as many *** as you like) every time you read a "meaty" sentence that sounds like a central idea, major conclusion, or focal point. These are sentences you'll want to find quickly later.

Step 4. If you are unsure of the main idea after the first paragraph, read quickly to the end of the selection. Concluding sentences are supposed to restate the theme in some fashion, or at least make a summary comment.

Reading for the Main Point: Passage 1

Line

(5)

(10)

There are few places more favorable to the study of character than an English country church. I was once passing a few weeks at the seat of a friend, who resided in the vicinity of one, the appearance of which particularly struck my fancy. It was one of those rich morsels of quaint antiquity which give such a peculiar charm to English landscape. It stood in the midst of a country filled with ancient families, and contained, within its cold and silent aisles, the congregated dust of many noble generations. The interior walls were incrusted with monuments of every age and style. The light streamed through windows dimmed with armorial bearings, richly emblazoned in stained glass. In various parts of the church were tombs of knights, and highborn dames, of gorgeous workmanship, with their effigies in colored marble. On every side

(15) the eye was struck with some instance of aspiring mortality; some
haughty memorial which human pride had erected over its kindred
dust, in this temple of the most humble of all religions.

Answer the question based on what is stated or implied in the passage.

Question

An appropriate title for this passage would be

    (A) Country Churches Throughout England

    (B) Studying Character in a Country Church

    (C) Aspiring Mortality in a Church

    (D) An English Country Church

    (E) The Temple of a Humble Religion

Answer

In this example, we are concerned only with the question about central theme or main idea. Which lines should you have underlined or *** in the passage to help point to the correct answer?

    Look back at the passage to see whether or not you *** line 4, which tells us that the author was "particularly" taken with one specific church. Note that the remainder of the material is devoted to careful description of this same church. Now look again at the possible answers:

    (A) Too *all-inclusive*. Only talked about one church.

    (B) *Too limited* to be the theme. Only one sentence, the first, says that this topic may be pursued eventually.

    (C) Again *too limited*. Mentioned only in line 14.

    (D) *Specific*. Tells exactly what this passage discusses.

    (E) This was the summation sentence, but gives only a *narrow* picture. See lines 14–16.

This example illustrates the variety of answers you'll be offered for main idea questions. In general, you will find:

1. *One answer will cover too much ground.* It will suggest greater coverage of the material than is possible in your sample.
2. *One or more answers will be too restricted,* too narrow in outlook. These answers will highlight only a portion of the material. Your main idea choice must deal with the larger part (greater number of sentences) of the reading passage.
3. *One or more answers are apt to parrot the passage,* repeating exact phraseology, and these are often tempting. But typically, they are too restricted in meaning, and if so they are not what you want.
4. *One answer may be completely "off the wall"* or illogical.
5. *One will be right.* It will be specific, as "An English Country Church" was specific, and it will summarize the *majority* of the sentences in the passage.

Reading for the Main Point: Passage 2

Aberystwyth is a university town and a popular seaside resort on Cardigan Bay. It was quite by accident that the first Welsh college was founded there. A vast Victorian hotel was being built for the
Line summer trade, and it went bankrupt just as some dedicated
(5) Welshmen were trying to figure out how to give Wales its own national university. They bought the building for a fraction of its market value and opened the College's doors. This impressive building, known today as the Old College, sits right on the seafront, dominating the Promenade.
(10)   Aberystwyth is an isolated provincial town, and the University is an integral part of the community's life. People who have studied there are intensely loyal to the University, perhaps because of the striking setting and the social life that the isolation forces upon

(15) them. Prince Charles, Prince of Wales, studied there in 1969. To the north and south, there are some fine stretches of the Cardigan coast, and inland there is rolling moorland. Aberystwyth is the site of the National Library of Wales, which houses over two million printed works and has an unrivaled collection on Celtic Studies.

Answer the question based on what is stated or implied in the passage.

Question

The best title for this selection would be

    (A) Prince Charles at Aberystwyth

    (B) An Old Welsh University Town

    (C) Cardigan Bay Town: Aberystwyth

    (D) Aberystwyth, University in Isolation

    (E) Aberystwyth: University and Celtic Town

Answer

For this passage, examine the answer choices again.

    1. Ask yourself, "What is the main point of paragraph 1?"
    2. What is the main point of paragraph 2?
    3. What one title would encompass *both* paragraphs?

Now eliminate answer choices, one by one.

    (A) Too *restricted*. Prince Charles is mentioned only in line 14.

    (B) Too *broad* a coverage is suggested here.

    (C) More specific, but only fair. Lacks mention of the university. But a keeper for now.

    (D) Gives the wrong idea somehow; only noted in lines 10–14.

    (E) Aha! Cites the university, then the town, just as the passage does.

Of the keepers, answers (C) and (E), answer (E) is better. Your ideal answer almost *has* to refer to the university, since it is the main topic of both paragraphs. (Sentences 1 and 2 [lines 1–3] and lines 10 and 11 point to this title and should have been *** or underlined.)

This approach will work well for nearly all questions dealing with the main topic. It is quick. Also it gives you the focus of the entire passage, and a second reading should provide all of the remaining answers you need.

READING TO DECODE AUTHOR ATTITUDE, STYLE, AND MOOD OF THE PASSAGE

Often, questions based on passages of reading material ask you to determine the authors' attitudes toward their material. How do they *feel* about what they are saying? *Why* are they bothering to write all this down for posterity? And what is the *result* of this attitude—the *mood* of the passage?

Authors *reveal attitude by their word choice*. If they say that the shopping bag ladies of large cities are "pitiable creatures," then you know their feeling is one of *pity* for those ladies. Certain words are very revealing of author attitude, and you must note those words or ideas as you read through a passage for later reference about author attitude.

Passages written mainly to inform do just that, usually without intruding mood or feeling. The tone, therefore, is unimportant, *as long as the authors' feelings* about what they're writing are not part of the message. Educational materials typically are written to inform, and that is their sole purpose. (The words *tone* and *mood* are often interchangeable and since they rarely apply to informative passages shouldn't cause you any problems.)

WHEN TO BEWARE

When reading for authors' attitudes toward their material or the mood (tone) of the passage, *avoid answers that are strongly negative*. Violently critical material—highly disputatious stuff—just isn't going to appear. Authors' attitudes may be *admiring, appreciative, approving, respectful,* or *deferential,* but they never *loathe* the person or group they are writing about—not for the SAT anyway.

If the passage you're reading is fiction—not fact—the author's tone may be *satirical,* as in the following passage, but it will *never* be *dogmatic, pedantic, explanatory,* or *informative, because those tones (moods) are not appropriate for fiction.* On one SAT, the author's attitude toward a fictional subject was one of *detached sympathy,* and the answer choices *cold objectivity, clear distaste,* and *veiled disdain* were decidedly wrong answers.

Some words have *never* been correct answers to describe author attitude, style, or mood of an SAT passage. Avoid like the plague: *ambivalent, condescending, vitriolic, pompous, apathetic, skeptical* (or *suspicious*), and *apologetic.* When you see other words like these, be extremely careful. These words are altogether too pejorative.

In the following brief passages, read for author attitude and mood. After each passage, write in the margin a few words that describe the passage in terms of mood or tone. Answer the questions, and see how closely you pegged the tone of each piece. *Circle* words that guide you to the answers.

Reading for Author Attitude and Mood: Passage 1

"Sylvia!"

"Yes, papa."

"That infernal dog of yours—"

Line   "Oh, papa!"

(5)   "Yes, that infernal dog of yours has been at my carnations again!"

Colonel Reynolds, V.C., glared sternly across the table at Miss Sylvia Reynolds, and Miss Sylvia Reynolds looked in a deprecatory manner back at Colonel Reynolds, V.C.; while the dog in

(10) question—a foppish pug—happening to meet the colonel's eye in transit, crawled unostentatiously under the sideboard, and began to wrestle with a bad conscience.

"Oh, naughty Tommy!" said Miss Reynolds mildly, in the direction of the sideboard.

(15) "Yes, my dear," assented the colonel; "and if you could convey to him the information that if he does it once more—yes, just once more!—I shall shoot him on the spot you would be doing him a kindness." And the colonel bit a large crescent out of his toast, with all the energy and conviction of a man who has thoroughly made up

(20) his mind. "At six o'clock this morning," continued he, in a voice of gentle melancholy, "I happened to look out of my bedroom window, and saw him. He had then destroyed two of my best plants, and was commencing on a third, with every appearance of self-satisfaction. I threw two large brushes and a boot at him."

(25) "Oh, papa! They didn't hit him?"

"No, my dear, they did not. The brushes missed him by several yards, and the boot smashed a fourth carnation. However, I was so fortunate as to attract his attention, and he left off."

"I can't think what makes him do it. I suppose it's bones. He's

(30) got bones buried all over the garden."

"Well, if he does it again, you'll find that there will be a few more bones buried in the garden!" said the colonel grimly; and he subsided into his paper.

Question

The tone of this selection could best be described as   (A) serious   (B) literary   (C) irritable   (D) humorous (E) familial

Answer

The answer to this piece lies in the words chosen by its author, P. G. Wodehouse, one of the most famous English humorists of all time. If you did as suggested and circled words to point to tone or mood, you might have circled lines 9–12, which show the pug wrestling "with a bad conscience." That in itself is a laughable approach, as is the picture of Sylvia's father, whose voice is one of "gentle melancholy," lines 20–21. Last, the Colonel's threat to add a few more bones to the garden isn't treated very seriously by the author, and probably not by Sylvia.

All in all, you can eliminate any serious answers, as this is *not* a serious piece; that gets rid of (A), (B), and (C) in short order. And while it pictures a family at table, the talk is not family centered, which eliminates (E), *familial.* Therefore, by elimination, you choose (D), *humorous,* which does fit the mood of this piece. Its tone is light, and we know that Sylvia is not really frightened by her father, although he'd probably wish her to be at least awed.

Reading for Author Attitude and Mood: Passage 2

The blade on the guillotine is released by a *release cord* or *release button.* The Italian *mannaia* and the Scottish *maiden* were variations of the French guillotine. A *gibbet,* similar to a gallows,
Line has a single, horizontal arm from which the noose was hung. On an
(5) electric chair, electrodes are attached to the prisoner's head and leg to complete the circuit. A *tumbrel* is any vehicle used to bring condemned people to the place of execution.

Question

The literary style of this selection can best be described as   (A) avant-garde   (B) sophisticated   (C) informative (D) emotional   (E) morbid

Answer

Remember that you are going to base your answer choice on exactly what was stated or implied *in the passage itself.* Your feelings are not the subject, no matter how strong they are. Thus, you must ask how authors felt about their material. Did they use adjectives or adverbs to describe the foregoing execution devices? If they did, were the adjectives and adverbs precise and clinical or dredged in feeling and emotion?

It boils down to this: We *don't know* how the author feels about this material. He or she is simply describing it, fact by dry fact, without a shred of emotion anywhere. That leaves all of the answers but one completely out. Only answer (C), *informative,* is left to describe the style of this passage. Like many scientific passages in texts, this one conveys information as its sole purpose.

Reading for Author Attitude and Mood: Passage 3

When I disengaged myself, as above mentioned, from private business, I flattered myself that, by the sufficient though moderate fortune I had acquired, I had secured leisure during the rest of my
Line life for philosophical studies and amusements. I purchased all Dr.
(5) Spence's apparatus, who had come from England to lecture in Philadelphia, and I proceeded in my electrical experiments with great alacrity; but the public, now considering me as a man of leisure, laid hold of me for their purposes, every part of our civil government, and almost at the same time, imposing some duty upon
(10) me. The governor put me into the commission of the peace; the corporation of the city chose me one of the common council and soon after an alderman; and the citizens at large elected me a burgess to represent them in Assembly. This latter station was the more agreeable to me, as I was at length tired with sitting there to
(15) hear debates, in which, as clerk I could take no part, and which were often so uninteresting that I was induced to amuse myself with making magic squares or circles or anything to avoid weariness; and I conceived my becoming a member would enlarge my power of doing good. I would not, however, insinuate that my ambition
(20) was not flattered by all these promotions; it certainly was; for considering my low beginning, they were great things to me; and they were still more pleasing, as being so many spontaneous testimonies of the public's good opinion, and by me entirely unsolicited.

Question

The author's intent in this passage is most likely   (A) to inform   (B) autobiographical   (C) to relate facts   (D) to amuse   (E) to arouse awe

Answer

This passage clearly seems to be about someone's life. In fact, it is a portion of Benjamin Franklin's well-known *Autobiography,* the 1848 version as published by Harper & Brothers. While it does state facts, as suggested by answer (C), and it does give information [answer (A)], answer (B) is more precise and specifically identifies the autobiographical writing form. Answer (B) is correct.

Often, two or even three answers to a mood or author-attitude question seem very tempting. Whenever you can choose the more *specific* answer, you should do so.

Remember that you can accomplish a great deal in a quick reading by *marking words with circles or underlines* that give you the feeling of mood, tone, and author attitude. Then the marked words stand as ready reference when you scan back over the passage seeking answers.

If you feel that circling or underlining is tiresome, time-consuming, or unnecessary, don't do it. Nonetheless, this technique does help many to stay involved with the material. It helps them to concentrate only on the passage, not on a growling stomach or the promise of a wonderful evening to come.

The combined effect of author attitude and purpose *leads* to mood or tone—as a last reminder. This total effect is often called *"the author's point of view."*

READING TO ISOLATE KEY FACTS AND EXAMPLES

A third type of question on college entrance exams dealing with material in reading passages is a question based on facts in the passage. The key point authors wish to make is most often buttressed by facts and examples that help to make the meaning clear and to support their thesis. Overlooking these facts is like not reading the passage at all.

POLLYANNA OR DR. PANGLOSS?

To do well on PSAT and SAT factual passages, keep in mind two characters from literature named Pollyanna and Dr. Pangloss. They were unfailingly positive and even-tempered—no matter what. When you and I would shout and stamp around, *they* might admit to "mild distress." The test makers at ETS must be related to them because they *never print emotionally charged material.* They especially avoid writings of skeptical or censorious authors when they select factual, serious reading passages.

When you see answers expressing strong feelings, be suspicious. Here's a sample of what I mean, using answers from recent SATs. The choices on the left were always wrong, the ones on the right were correct. Remember that this guideline—*avoid answers too strongly worded or too emotional*—applies mainly to serious passages, i.e., history, chemistry, biography, etc.

Too Emotional = Wrong	*Nicely Restrained = Right*
argumentative [too controversial]	impersonal
apologetic [too wimpy]	objective
passionately	analytical
harsh	informative or explanatory
hazy	lucid
defensive	pragmatic or practical
wildly excited	dissatisfaction
opinionated [too negative]	
capricious [as bad as hazy]	
vengeful	

Summary: Factual passages, material about ethnic groups, and "serious" subjects (law, government, medicine, science, education) are indeed serious business to the folks who design your test. They will print material restrained in tone, style, and author attitude—and you must choose answers in this same vein.

READING TECHNIQUE

As you read a sample of written material, *make a check mark in the margin* next to sentences containing examples or facts. A typical question on an SAT is "All *but* one of the following were given as examples in the passage: . . ." And then you must determine which example was *not* mentioned. You cannot do that unless you know what examples *were given* and how to find them *quickly*. If check marks pinpoint the location of each example, your job becomes easier.

These questions should be like gifts, and I think you'll feel that way as soon as you make a habit of marking the passage wherever you see examples or key facts that have been included.

Reading for Facts and Examples: Passage 1

London is the capital of the United Kingdom and one of the great cities of the world. It is also, as the King's College prospectus puts it, "the intellectual, literary, artistic, musical, political, legal,
Line administrative, financial and commercial capital of Great Britain."
(5) It is no wonder that students of all cultures wish to study there. Usually, most sophomores planning a junior year in Britain want to go to London, but students applying to any branch of the University of London should realize that places are few, competition is fierce, University accommodations are scarce, private lodgings are
(10) expensive, the cost of living is high, and urban living can be lonely at times—even in London. There are currently over 38,000 full-time students enrolled in the various branches of the University. In most cases, junior year abroad students are competing for places at the University with full-time undergraduates seeking a London
(15) degree. Consequently, there is a better chance for nondegree admission in those fields that are not already over-subscribed by British undergraduates. Although the admissions pattern may vary from year to year according to departmental enrollments, it is safe to say that, in general, the humanities student will have a far more
(20) difficult time getting into the University of London than will the social or natural scientist.

Question

In the passage, all *but* which one of the following were cited as examples of why students living in London may have problems?   (A) existence is lonely   (B) rooming costs a great deal of money   (C) course offerings are limited (D) competition is keen   (E) the overall cost of living is high

Answer

If you checked lines 8–11, you had your examples marked, ready for quick reference. In those lines, the author outlined all of the difficulties facing a college student who wished to live and study in London. Nowhere did the author say that course offerings were limited, answer (C), and that is the correct answer to this typical question.

In order to anticipate other questions based on facts, with which this reading sample is loaded, you should probably have checked lines 1–4, 8–11, 15–17, and 19–21. That would have prepared you to answer most questions based on facts in this passage. Checking the margin is a quick, relatively painless way to guide you back to answers that you will need.

Question

The author's style in this passage is best described as   (A) apathetic   (B) very enthusiastic   (C) apologetic (D) explanatory   (E) gently negative

Answer

The overall presentation of this material is extremely factual. The author is explaining the applications picture for students interested in the University of London. No more; no less. If you chose (D), *explanatory,* you were right. Answer (B) was too emotional, and all of the others too negative to accurately describe the style of this piece. The author never apologizes for the facts but simply states them.

Reading for Facts and Examples: Passage 2

Interviewers are not going to pull information from a reluctant interviewee. They will simply ask a question that will give you a lead. They feel that one way to assess your abilities is to judge how
Line well you present yourself. Put yourself in a recruiter's shoes and
(5) judge for yourself how well you come across. The recruiter's mission is to screen applicants and refer them to managers who will do the actual hiring. If, in a sales training program interview, you say you are unsure of your interest in sales but wonder about something in administration, the recruiter is going to be annoyed.
(10) He is exhausted from traveling around the country looking for people interested in sales, and you focus on an entirely different job area. What is he supposed to do? Report back to his manager and say, "I have a candidate, a very nice person, but I am not sure he wants to sell"?
(15) If you were in the recruiter's shoes, you would not recommend such a candidate. Nor would you recommend one who says "you know" at the end of each thought, nor one who laces sentences with unnecessary "filler" words. Help the recruiters. They look long and hard for candidates who will be a credit to their judgment. What
(20) they want an interview to be is just what you want it to be—an exchange between two people sincerely trying to establish whether they have a mutual interest, with neither party trying to intimidate or manipulate the other. The recruiters, however, are the questioners; if you are not prepared with answers, you are going to
(25) feel as if you were on trial.

Question

The advice given to an interviewee can best be summarized by:

I. It is important to present yourself well.

II. Be honest about your lack of interest in sales.

III. Express an open interest in administration.

IV. Give direct, clear answers that are well phrased.

V. Prepare penetrating questions beforehand.

(A) I and IV   (B) II and IV   (C) I and III   (D) III and IV   (E) IV and V

Answer

Look back at the passage, and see if you have checked lines 2–4, 5–9, and 15–18, plus 23–25 as a summation sentence. If you have, you can see that Roman numeral I sums up the advice shown by examples in the first paragraph, and Roman numeral IV sums up what the second paragraph is saying. Thus, both can act as themes of the key points to be gleaned from these two paragraphs.

This type of roundup question is not one that students are used to seeing. If you haven't involved yourself sufficiently in the reading passage, it comes as a rather rude shock.

Answer (A), then, *I and IV,* is the correct choice.

Note also that this type of question is a mixture of the Main Point question and the Fact and Example variety.

Vital Reminder: Each paragraph has one major point to make. (That is its contribution to the piece as a whole.) Questions often center on the main point of a paragraph. As you read, *you must note the central idea in each paragraph.*

Question

The author's style and tone in this passage combine to give an overall impression of (A) formality (B) corporate bias (C) encouraging friendliness (D) professional detachment (E) unabashed enthusiasm

Answer

A basically informative, how-to passage will avoid any *bias,* answer (B), as well as strong emotion, answer (E). Answers (A) and (D) are too cold and detached if you consider paragraph 2. That leaves only (C), *encouraging friendliness,* as the correct answer. (Whenever an author speaks to "you"—the reader—directly, as in paragraph 2, the tone warms up considerably.)

READING FOR WHAT IS SUGGESTED OR IMPLIED BUT NOT STATED

A very important word in the directions given for questions based on reading material is the word *implied.* It tells you to read with extreme care, as some questions may be asked about what was *not explicitly* set forth in the passage.

Suppose a reading sample begins: "Unlike the conifers, deciduous trees shed their leaves in the fall and are useful for planting near solar buildings dependent on the winter sun."

Questions

What went *before?* What material is *now* most probably going to be discussed?

Answer

Your acute eye read the words *"Unlike the conifers."* Thus, what went *before* most likely was a discussion of conifers, the cone-bearing, or evergreen, trees that do *not* shed their leaves. And what is *now* coming up is material about the *other* kind of tree, the deciduous tree, that sheds its leaves before winter.

In other words, you must use *every single word* in a reading passage to tell you what *preceded* the little hunk you get to see and what could logically *follow* it. You will use those words to infer or deduce the conclusions or results of what the author is telling you.

JUST *WHAT* WAS IMPLIED?

Practice 1

Reread the passage on p. 73 that we titled "An English Country Church." Then do the following exercise:

Question

The author of this passage implies that his material will discuss   (A) knights and highborn dames   (B) temples of humble religions   (C) his visit in the English countryside   (D) the study of character   (E) other country churches like the one in the first paragraph

Answer

Your clue to this question was in the first sentence, lines 1 and 2. *Often,* the clue to what went *before* or what will *eventually be discussed* is found in the opening sentences of a reading passage. In this case, you can read that the author is interested in the study of character and guess that, even though he now describes one church, he will eventually get around to discussing the *people* that are in the church. Answer (D) is correct. Also, there is no hint anywhere in the passage that any of the other topics mentioned in the answers will be treated.

Practice 2

Reread the passage on p. 76 that was written by P. G. Wodehouse in a humorous style. Then do the following exercise.

Question

We can infer from the passage that the pug dog named Tommy   (A) rarely was in the flower garden   (B) disliked carnations   (C) was in the Colonel's favor most of the time   (D) was a joy to Sylvia, his mistress   (E) had repeatedly destroyed the Colonel's carnations

Answer

Your first clue to the answer was in lines 5 and 6, in the Colonel's comment that the dog had been "at my carnations *again,*" which says that he's done damage in that garden at *other* times. Later, in lines 29 and 30, Sylvia wonders why her dog digs in the garden and says that he has bones buried "all over the garden." Therefore, answer (E), *had repeatedly destroyed the Colonel's carnations,* is the best answer.

We might guess that the pug *disliked carnations,* answer (B), but there is no supporting evidence for that guess, just as there is no evidence to support answer (D), that he was a joy to his mistress. We might find that to be true later, but in this specific sample, only answer (E) is corroborated.

Practice 3

Reread the passage on p. 77 from Benjamin Franklin's *Autobiography.* Then, do this exercise.

Question

We can infer from the passage that the author is now going to expand on which topic?   (A) his business life   (B) his life at home   (C) his family   (D) his retirement from business that led to public service   (E) his avoidance of public service in order to pursue private experiments

Answer

Your answer lies in the first sentence. Right at the beginning, Franklin states that he has retired from business, hopes to pursue private endeavors, but "the public . . . laid hold of me for their purposes." These opening sentences lay the groundwork for his discussion. Thus, answer (D) is the correct answer. All of the other answers either contradict what was said in the passage or do not concern any of the material discussed.

TIMING FOR READING COMPREHENSION QUESTIONS

If you're aiming for a high verbal score, over 700, you must answer each question with great care. (Even so, you can miss 4 and omit 3 or 4, and still score 700.) Because the critical reading questions are OVER HALF of an SAT, you should logically save over half of each 30-minute segment to deal with these questions. (I need 20 minutes.)

The only way to be sure of how much time you need is by practicing with several lengthy or complex reading segments. See how long it takes you to read and answer questions on the longer readings in the upcoming practice passages as well as all passages on the practice and diagnostic SAT.

What if you absolutely loathe these passages? You just cannot skip them, sorry. But you can omit the hairier questions and thereby avoid a total migraine experience. (Review the chart on p. 28 of the first Red Alert section.)

Summary: Know-How for Reading Comprehension Questions

Of all of the sections in your book, this section on reading comprehension is the most significant. Careful, efficient reading is the key to all college entrance tests, even the math portion. If you can learn to *involve yourself* in the written material so that you absorb every single word of it, the correct answers will be much easier to find and enter on your answer sheet.

Remember to use the steps that lead to correct answers:

Step 1.   **Skim the questions *before* reading the passage.** (If this task drives you bats, don't do it. Begin by reading the passage quickly to determine the main idea.)

Step 2.   **Read the passage as quickly as you can, concentrating first on the main points** that the author is making. Be sure to underline or *** meaty, summation-type sentences. If you are ready at the end of the first reading, answer any questions on the main point or central theme of the material.

Step 3.   **Mark the reading passage with check marks** in the margin for fact-filled areas or specific examples on your second reading.

Step 4.   **Mark all words** (a quick slash before the word works well) **that indicate a shift in viewpoint** or something different coming up, e.g., *but, however, although, nevertheless, ironically, atypically, nonetheless,* and *unless.* If a *date* is given, it's there for a reason. Also, **note words that indicate tone or mood.**

Step 5.   **Answer the questions with the elimination method** so that you select your answer because all of the *other* answers cannot be correct.

General Principles

A.   Be sure to save adequate time for the questions on reading passages.

B.   Questions after a reading passage do not appear in order of difficulty.

C.   Always eliminate answers one by one. A quick grab at a likely-looking answer is never smart.

D.   Read as quickly as you can to get the main idea. Then hunt for specific answers to questions. Each paragraph will also have a main point, and you need to find it.

E.   Remember the key word concept (p. 37). Questions will often derive from sentences with key words.

F.   Be wary of lengthy, direct quotes from the reading passage as answer choices. ETS usually rephrases ideas to make them harder to pinpoint.

G.   Use your own factual knowledge. No passage will go against established truth.

H.   Avoid answers to factual passages that express extremely strong emotion; likewise, avoid strongly negative answer choices when determining author attitude, style, and mood (tone).

HOW TO ANSWER QUESTIONS ON PAIRED READING PASSAGES

Another important new feature of the SAT I is paired reading comprehension passages. One verbal section consists entirely of 11-13 questions based on two passages of 350-400 words each. You will need all your critical reading skill to answer questions that ask you to compare two passages. But don't let this section throw you; *the passages and questions are of exactly the same kinds as in the other reading comprehension sections.*

WHAT KINDS OF PASSAGES SHOULD YOU EXPECT?

The subject matter of the paired passages will be the same as in the other sections: science, social science, or humanities. The passages will be related but show some kind of contrast.

What kinds of relationships between the two passages can you expect to see? There are three possibilities:

1. The two passages might disagree about *the same subject.* For instance, the author of Passage 1 might put forward the conventional view that pretend play helps preschool children develop social skills. The author of Passage 2 might argue that more structured activities are a better way to help children learn social skills.

2. The two passages might come to *the same subject with differing perspectives,* perhaps from different disciplines. For instance, Passage 1 might talk about young children's play from a sociological perspective, emphasizing the ways that play helps children learn to get along with each other. Then Passage 2 might talk about play from a psychological perspective, emphasizing how play helps an individual child to mature intellectually and emotionally.

3. The two passages might be about *different subjects but have a similar perspective on their subjects.* For instance, Passage 1 might be about how young children learn social skills through play, while Passage 2 is about how baby zebras interact with each other and with adult zebras. In this case, you would probably find that Passage 2 says that baby zebras learn to interact by playing. And you can be sure that one of the questions will ask you about the similarities between the two passages.

WHAT ABOUT THE QUESTIONS?

Two pieces of good news: First, most of the questions will be about only *one* passage. The first four to six questions following the two passages will be *about Passage 1 only.* The next four to six questions will be *about Passage 2.* The questions will always identify which passage they are about with either line numbers or passage numbers. That will leave *just two to five questions that ask you to compare the two passages.*

The second piece of good news is that the questions will be of exactly the same types you have been studying already: main points, author attitude or mood, facts and examples, what is suggested or implied, vocabulary, or technique and organization. *Both* the questions on individual passages *and* the questions that ask you to compare the two passages will be of these types. (You can be pretty sure that if there is a main point question, it will be among the questions that compare the passages.)

> *Hot tip:* Start out by treating Passage 1 as an individual passage. Read the first few questions and stop when you get to the first question that asks about Passage 2 (that is, if you're comfortable with reading the questions first—if not, just read Passage 1 and then go directly to the first few questions). Then read Passage 1, keeping the questions in mind, and then answer Passage 1 questions. This way you're sure of answering about a third of the questions even if you run out of time.

Questions that Compare the Two Passages

The questions that ask you to compare or contrast the two passages will come at the end of the set of questions. The difficulty of the questions will vary, but in general you'll probably find them harder than questions that ask about only one passage.

But *don't panic.* The questions will still be of the same types:

1. **Main point or central theme** questions will ask you to compare or contrast the main points of the two passages:

> Both passages are primarily concerned with . . .
> The author of Passage 1 and the author of Passage 2 disagree over the central issue of . . .

The main purpose of Passage 1 differs from that of Passage 2 in that Passage 1 is primarily concerned with . . .

2. **Author attitude or mood** questions will compare or contrast the attitudes of the two authors. Your answer options might be words that describe emotions (scorn, approval, doubt) or sentences or phrases describing how one author would respond to the other:

The author of Passage 1 would most likely respond to the assertion by the author of Passage 2 that _____ with . . .

How would the author of Passage 2 respond to the way the author of Passage 1 describes _____ ?

The author of Passage 2 would most likely respond to the argument of the author of Passage 1 by saying that . . .

3. Questions about **facts or examples** will usually compare the way the two authors *use* their facts or examples:

Both passages mention which of the following as an important aspect of _____ ?

The author of Passage 2 believes that the argument presented by the author of Passage 1 is flawed because . . . (This question could be asking either for facts, if the basis of disagreement is specifically stated in Passage 2, or for what is suggested or implied, if the basis of disagreement is not specifically stated.)

4. Questions about **what is suggested or implied** will probably be the most common type. You will need to read carefully to determine how the implications of one passage bear on the implications of the other, or how one passage suggests something about the other passage that is not immediately apparent in the passage:

Both passages suggest that . . .

What additional information would reduce the differences between the _____ described by the two authors?

How would the author of Passage 2 respond to the argument in Passage 1 that _____ ?

The author of Passage 2 would most likely say that the author of Passage 1 asserts that _____ because . . .

With which of the following assumptions made by the author of Passage 2 would the author of Passage 1 be most likely to agree?

5. **Vocabulary** questions will focus on how the two authors use the same or similar words.

In line _____, the author of Passage 1 uses the word _____ differently from the way the author of Passage 2 uses the word in that . . .

Both authors use the word _____ to mean . . .

6. **Technique and organization** questions will usually ask you to compare a specific portion of one passage with either a specific portion or all of the other passage:

The questions at the end of Passage 1 serve to express which of the following reactions to Passage 2?

The example in lines ____ of Passage 2 is most similar to which of the following aspects of Passage 1?

Both passages use which of the following techniques to characterize _____ ?

Reading the Paired Passages

How does reading paired passages differ from reading the other reading comprehension passages? At first, not much. You can start out by reading Passage 1 as an individual passage, answering its questions just as you do in the other reading comprehension sections.

The difference comes when you read Passage 2. As you read, *keep Passage 1 in mind*. Ask yourself questions: What is the similarity between these two passages? Why are they put together in this test? Do they discuss *the same subject* with a substantial disagreement or difference in emphasis? Do they discuss *different subjects* but imply some similarity between the subjects? How would the author of Passage 2 respond to what you have read in Passage 1? Or how would the author of Passage 1 respond to what you are now reading in Passage 2? If you find anything in Passage 2 that seems directly related to Passage 1, circle it and draw an arrow toward Passage 1.

Timing for Reading Paired Passages

You have only 15 minutes. *You must read Passage 1 and answer Passage 1 questions before you tackle Passage 2.* If you can read Passage 1 and answer its questions in five to seven minutes, you'll probably have enough time to answer the other questions, too. If you can't do it in that amount of time, you already will have answered at least a third of the questions.

Skim all the rest of the questions after answering the Passage 1 questions, so that you'll know what to look for both in Passage 2 and in comparing the two passages. After reading Passage 2, answer the questions you find easiest and skip any you find difficult. You may find that the questions focusing only on Passage 2 are easiest to answer. On the other hand, you've just been reading with both passages in mind, so you may have already come up with the answer to one or more of the questions that compare the two passages. In either case, work quickly over the questions to answer the ones you know first. Don't waste time puzzling over a hard question when the next one may be much easier. You can always go back to the harder questions if you have time at the end.

Know-How for Answering Questions on Paired Passages

Use all your know-how for answering other kinds of reading comprehension questions, since the paired passages and questions are of the same types.

Follow these steps to improve your score:

Step 1.   **Skim the questions about Passage 1.** These will be the first questions in the set, and you can tell that the Passage 1 questions have ended when a question refers you to Passage 2 or to a line number in Passage 2. (Again, if you absolutely can't bring yourself to read questions first, don't worry about it. Do what feels comfortable.)

Step 2.   **Read Passage 1 as quickly as you can, looking especially for the author's main points.** You may not need the main point to answer Passage 1 questions, but you'll need it to help you compare the two passages.

Step 3.   **Mark Passage 1** using the system you've already devised for keeping track of central themes, specific facts, key words, and tone or mood.

Step 4.   **Answer Passage 1 questions using the elimination method.**

Step 5.   **Skim all remaining questions.** The first few questions will be about Passage 2 alone and the rest about the two passages. You will get ideas not only about what to look for in Passage 2 but also about the similarities and differences between the two passages.

Step 6.   **Read Passage 2 as quickly as you can,** *keeping Passage 1 in mind.* Ask yourself why these two passages are paired, and mark any parts of Passage 2 that seem especially related to Passage 1.

Step 7.   **Answer remaining questions, skipping difficult ones.** If you have time at the end, you can go back to the hard questions.

PRACTICE READING PASSAGES

The following passages are as close to actual test passages as possible. As on standardized tests, the passages come from a variety of reading materials. No one reads scientific matter or novels exclusively, and skill with all types of reading is necessary for college studies.

As you work with the passages, practice reading and answering questions as rapidly as possible.

PRACTICE PASSAGE 1

For this, and all the following practice reading passages, choose the best answer based on material *stated* or *implied* in the passage.

Sticker races were a frequent game for the dozens of Campbell cousins who gathered at Grandpa Bunt's house on summer Sunday
Line afternoons. They required no equipment and could
(5) be played by every size. Training for the races began on the day we began to go barefooted. I do not recall any criteria, such as how many days from the last frost, but somehow it became known that on a particular day all boy chaps would take
(10) their shoes off. On that day the tender feet of winter began their perilous journey into spring and summer. First in the yard only. Then timidly onto the stomp—that area between the scraped, packed dirt yard surrounding the house, swept clean with
(15) dogwood brooms, and the edge of the fields—and finally into the field, woods, riverbanks and graveled roads. It was not that shoes were looked upon with scorn. We looked forward to the time, generally in late adolescence, when we would
(20) wear them all year. It was a symbol of manhood. (Joe would one day have twenty pairs of shoes in his closet and under his bed at once.) Shoes were, in fact, one's most prized possession. They alone separated a man from what was at once his best
(25) friend and worst enemy—the earth. Best friend because it produced the corn and potatoes to eat, the cotton to try to pay off the mortgage. And worst enemy because it harbored the cottonmouths and rattlers, the sawbriars and stickers, and snow
(30) and ice of winter. The earliest songs we sang had to do with shoes:

Mamma, soon I'll be an angel.
By perhaps, another day.
Give them all my toys, but Mother,
(35) *Put my little shoes away.*

And years later Carl Perkins and Elvis Presley, swinging, gyrating, twisting, rejoicing to the music and lyrics of "Blue Suede Shoes," a song not about a rich dude from the city who impressed the girls
(40) with his daily change of shoes, but a story written in the cotton fields of west Tennessee by a poor boy who saved enough money to pay for the coveted suede, and served notice on the world that it could do anything it would to him but, "Stay off
(45) my blue suede shoes!" The wearing of shoes was a luxury dreamed of. The taking them off in spring an occasion which might as well be celebrated as lamented.

The Sticker Race was no more than a contest to
(50) see who had the toughest feet. The winner was the one who could run the length of Grandpa's Stomp and "brad" the most stickers. The race was run in groups of four, lined up by age or size. "Bradding" meant that the needle points were broken off by
(55) the leather-like soles of the feet with no penetration into the "quick." One was disqualified if he had to stop to pull one out. Those finishing the course were inspected to see if any stickers were present. A tie in the number of stickers went
(60) to the one who crossed the line first. When four boys finished a race the winner stepped aside to compete in the finals and four more began. There was never any tangible prize, just the satisfaction of having the toughest feet in the Campbell
(65) community.

Questions

1. It can be inferred from the passage that the narrator lived

   (A) in a contemporary suburb
   (B) in the country out West
   (C) in the country in the South
   (D) on a communal farm
   (E) near a city

2. The boys in the Campbell community held sticker races because

   (A) it proved who was the toughest
   (B) it was so much fun
   (C) it was more challenging to run barefoot
   (D) it was a symbol of manhood
   (E) it was a game that required no training

3. In this passage, the earth is represented as

   (A) a symbol of manhood
   (B) man's enemy and his best friend
   (C) a source of stickers for races
   (D) a boy's source of proving himself
   (E) a contest between man and nature

4. Which of the following phrases best represents how the narrator felt about this period of his boyhood?

   (A) ambivalent and regretful
   (B) amused yet tolerant
   (C) modest and unassuming
   (D) condescending yet attached
   (E) nostalgic and perceptive

PRACTICE PASSAGES 2—PAIRED PASSAGES

Passage 1

Double stars would seem to be the ideal test of visual acuity: is your vision sharp enough to see the double star as not one but two separate points
Line of light? In theory, the closest-together pair you
(5) could split would show the limit of your eyes' resolving power. In practice, seeing the more faint of two stars is progressively more difficult as the difference in their brightness is greater. (The brightness of stars is expressed as their
(10) "magnitude"; lower numbers indicate brighter stars.) The easiest double star to split should thus be one in which the components have the same magnitude. But if both stars are fairly dim—perhaps fourth-magnitude—are they really easier
(15) to split than are, for instance, a first- and third-magnitude pair?

Distances in the sky are measured by degrees—the moon is about 10 degrees in diameter—but the distances between double stars
(20) are so small that they are measured in seconds, with 3,600 seconds to a degree of arc. Test your eyes to see which of these pairs you can split. The two stars of Alpha Capricorni are 376 seconds apart, with magnitudes of 3.6 and 4.2. The stars of
(25) Alpha Librae, at magnitudes of 2.7 and 5.2, are only 231 seconds apart. Even smaller is the distance between the two stars of Epsilon Lyrae—only 210 seconds—but their magnitudes are very similar: 5.0 and 5.1.
(30) And what about that almost always visible and widest split, the pair in the Big Dipper's handle, Mizar and Alcor? Mizar's magnitude is 2.4, Alcor's 4.0; they are a (comparatively) whopping 708 seconds apart. The pair were
(35) popularly known as Horse and Rider long ago, and another name meant "The Test"—but surely a test of bad rather than of excellent vision. On a good night (clear, moonless, and steady) you should be able to distinguish Alcor; the reason that Mizar
(40) and Alcor were called "The Test" could not have been that only sharp-sighted people could see Alcor in the unpolluted, dark desert skies of medieval Arabia, where this title was coined. We must remember that eyeglasses had not yet been
(45) invented! If you cannot see Alcor just beyond Mizar's glow, even on an excellent night, you should probably consider a visit to the eye doctor.

Passage 2

Centuries ago, it was widely assumed that the heavens are unchangeable. Nothing could be
(50) further from the truth. There are changes going on all the time, both in the long and in the short term. Stars explode into supernovae; Red Giant stars compress themselves into White Dwarves. The fact that such changes do take place leads to
(55) interesting, though perhaps minor, mysteries.

One such mystery concerns Mizar or Zeta Ursae Majoris, the second star in the handle of the Big Dipper. It is easy to see that there is a much fainter star, Alcor, close to Mizar. The distance
(60) between the two is 709 seconds of arc; the magnitudes are 4.0 and 2.4, and Alcor is visible without optical aid on any reasonably clear night. It and Mizar are often nicknamed "Jack and his Rider." Yet the Arabs of a thousand years ago
(65) regarded Alcor as a very difficult naked-eye object. In the thirteenth century Al-Kazwini stated that "people tested their eyesight by this star," and in the fourteenth century Al-Firuzabini called it "The Test."
(70) This is certainly peculiar. The Arabs were notoriously keen-sighted, and their skies were much less light-polluted than ours. Can these stars have changed to become brighter in modern times? It seems improbable. Mizar itself is a well-
(75) known double star, but neither it nor Alcor seems to be the sort of system to vary appreciably over a period of a few centuries.

It has been claimed that the Arabs were referring not to Alcor, but to another star which
(80) lies between it and the Mizar binary. According to W. H. Smyth, this star was first noted by D. Einmart of Nürnberg in 1691, and was reobserved in 1723 by a German astronomer. It is not genuinely associated with the Mizar system
(85) and is actually far distant from Mizar and Alcor; as an eighth-magnitude star, it is well below naked-eye or even binocular visibility. It is no more likely to have dimmed since Arab times than Alcor is to have brightened, but that the Arabs were
(90) wrong is equally unlikely. Thus, the mystery remains unsolved.

Questions

1. It can be inferred from the passage that a person who tries to distinguish the two stars of Epsilon Lyrae (lines 26–29) from each other is most likely to be helped by the fact that

   (A) Epsilon Lyrae appears as a relatively bright star in the sky
   (B) Epsilon Lyrae is relatively widely separated from the moon
   (C) the two stars are relatively widely separated from each other
   (D) the two stars are relatively close in magnitude to each other
   (E) the two stars are not a genuine binary but are distant from each other in space

2. According to Passage 1, a degree is a measurement of the

   (A) resolving power of the eye
   (B) surface temperature of stars
   (C) apparent brightness of stars
   (D) actual distance between stars in space
   (E) apparent distance between stars in the sky

3. Which of the following would a person have to know about the double stars listed in lines 22–29 in order to follow the advice to "Test your eyes to see which of these pairs you can split" (lines 21–22)?

   (A) How large a degree of arc is
   (B) How bright those double stars appear
   (C) Where those double stars appear in the sky
   (D) Which of those pairs of stars is closest together
   (E) How the eyes' resolving power is determined

4. The references to supernovae and to Red Giants in lines 52–53 serve to provide examples of

   (A) ways in which double stars can form
   (B) ways in which stars can change over time
   (C) the mysterious nature of cosmic phenomena
   (D) types of stars of which medieval Arabs were unaware
   (E) kinds of cosmic changes that can be observed with the naked eye

5. In line 70, the word "This" refers to the

   (A) change in Alcor's brightness since medieval times
   (B) great increase in light pollution since medieval times
   (C) suggestion that many medieval Arabs suffered from poor eyesight
   (D) idea that medieval Arabs used Alcor to test their vision
   (E) fact that medieval Arab astronomers gave Alcor a nickname

6. The reference to the observation of an eighth-magnitude star by D. Einmart of Nürnberg in lines 81–82 serves primarily to

   (A) establish that this star was first observed long after the time of the medieval Arabs

   (B) demonstrate the superiority of later astronomical observation techniques over those of the medieval Arabs
   (C) describe how astronomers discovered that this star is not part of the Mizar system
   (D) provide evidence that this star may have dimmed over the course of several centuries
   (E) suggest that Einmart must have used a telescope to see this star

7. The main purpose of Passage 1 differs from that of Passage 2 in that Passage 1 is primarily concerned with

   (A) how double stars come into existence
   (B) using double stars to test one's eyesight
   (C) the possibility that stars can change
   (D) the relative magnitudes of Mizar and Alcor
   (E) various names that have been given to Mizar and Alcor

8. Which of the following is mentioned in both passages as a reason that medieval Arabs should have had less, not more, difficulty in distinguishing Mizar and Alcor than do modern observers?

   (A) The fact that telescopes had not yet been invented
   (B) The relatively large separation between Mizar and Alcor
   (C) The difference in brightness between Mizar and Alcor
   (D) The fact that Mizar itself is now known to be a double star
   (E) The relative lack of pollution in the medieval atmosphere

9. The author of Passage 1 would most likely respond to the assertion in lines 90–91 that "the mystery remains unsolved" by

   (A) explaining how to distinguish double stars from each other
   (B) suggesting that the mystery is not a particularly important one
   (C) pointing out that the medieval Arabs did not have eyeglasses
   (D) refuting the assertion that double stars may change in brightness
   (E) arguing that medieval Arabian astronomers used poor methods to observe the stars

10. The author of Passage 1 would be most likely to disagree with which of the following assumptions made by the author of Passage 2?

    (A) Medieval Arabs probably had very good eyesight.
    (B) Stars can change in brightness over centuries.
    (C) Mizar and Alcor together constitute a double star.
    (D) Medieval Arabs used Mizar and Alcor as a test of eyesight.
    (E) The stars were more clearly visible in medieval Arabia than they are today.

PRACTICE PASSAGE 3

start

While Austria had come out of the first phase
Line of the Napoleonic Wars weakened but not broken,
(5) Prussia had lost more than half her territory,
having been reduced to but four provinces:
Brandenburg, Pomerania, Prussia, and Silesia. Her
economic life was completely paralyzed by the
immense war indemnities and by Napoleon's
(10) "Continental Blockade" of England (decree of
1806), which made it impossible for Prussia to
continue the lucrative export of agricultural
products to the British Isles. The catastrophes of
Jena and Auerstedt made the political leaders of
(15) Prussia realize the mistakes and omissions of the
past decades and made room at last for those
unselfish and patriotic men who had long voiced
their prophetic warnings in vain.
One such man was Baron Karl vom Stein, who
(20) said, "I have but one fatherland which is called
Germany. With my whole heart I am devoted to it,
and not to any of its parts." In 1804 Stein received
an appointment as Prussian Minister of State and
was given charge of the departments of finance
(25) and economics. He immediately seized the
opportunity to carry out some of the much-needed
reforms. An edict of 1805 decreed the suspension
of the inland duties in Prussia which had proven
one of the major stumbling blocks to the
(30) development of a unified national economy. The
substitution of private ownership of industrial
enterprises for State ownership served to break
down the economic system of the mercantile State
and the elimination of the corporate restrictions of
(35) the guilds was to prepare the way for the
introduction of the principle of freedom of trade.
In 1806, Stein's demand for reorganization of
the whole governmental system for the sake of
greater efficiency and responsible leadership went
(40) unheeded, and he was dismissed by royal cabinet
order. Within six months he was recalled and
shortly thereafter published his first great Reform
Edict, having as its main objectives the abolition of
serfdom, the free exchange and disposal of landed
(45) property, and the free choice of occupation. Up to
this time, two thirds of the population of Prussia
had been bound to the soil, unable to leave their
homes of their own free will and obliged to render
personal service to the manorial lord. In the rural
(50) districts the medieval feudal system had survived
essentially untouched.
Stein recognized in the sudden and unparalleled
breakdown of Prussia the result of a political and
social system of bureaucratic and feudalistic
(55) tutelage. A partly paternalistic, partly absolutistic
form of administration had gradually loosened the
mutual bonds of loyalty and unselfish devotion
between the people and their government and had
bred an attitude of irresponsibility and indifference
(60) among all classes of the population. Stein's
program of national regeneration received its
directives from his clear-sighted diagnosis of the
national disease.

Questions

1. According to the passage, which of the following
would *not* be true of the concerns and character of
Karl vom Stein?

   (A) absorption with Germany's economic status in
   the world
   (B) understanding of the nature of the Germanic
   people
   (C) approval of the Prussian governmental
   leadership in the early 1800s
   (D) willingness to act in a decisive, revolutionary
   manner
   (E) perception to judge Prussian history and
   prophesy trouble ahead

2. When Baron vom Stein said of Germany, ". . . I am
devoted to it, and not to any of its parts" (lines 19–
20), he most probably meant that

   (A) he was not concerned with the separate
   Prussian states
   (B) he was interested mainly in Germany's
   international role
   (C) he was involved with leadership, not warring
   factions
   (D) he viewed his country as a single, united entity
   (E) he was interested in Prussia, not Germany

3. The reason given for Prussia's lack of exportation to
Britain was

   (A) Napoleon's blockade of the British islands
   (B) the early phase of the Napoleonic Wars
   (C) lack of agricultural commodities to export
   (D) reduction in commodities produced for export
   (E) Prussian governmental policy on exportation to
   the British Isles

4. According to the author, Germany was hindered in
its establishment of a unified national economy by

   (A) the massive war effort itself
   (B) its policy of imposing inland duties
   (C) the substitution of private ownership in place of
   State ownership
   (D) guilds that had historically operated without
   restrictions
   (E) the catastrophes of Jena and Auerstedt

5. Stein felt that Prussia had broken down as a country primarily because

   (A) the Napoleonic Wars had paralyzed its economy
   (B) Prussia's political leaders paid scant attention to their international role
   (C) the mercantile State had not kept pace with that of other countries
   (D) two thirds of her population was bound to the soil
   (E) her people no longer felt morally or emotionally bound to their homeland

PRACTICE PASSAGE 4

Aside from that, what have I learned from Karl Kraus? What of his have I so thoroughly absorbed that I could no longer separate it from my own *Line* person?

(5) First of all, there is the feeling of absolute responsibility. I had it before me in a form bordering on obsession, and nothing less seemed worthy of life. That model is before me even today, so powerful that all later formulations of the

(10) same demand would have to appear inadequate. There is that wretched word "commitment," which was born to be banal and is now rampant everywhere like weeds. It sounds as if one were an employee of the most important things. True

(15) responsibility is a hundred degrees harder, for it is sovereign and self-determining.

Second of all, Karl Kraus opened my ear, and no one could have done it like him. Since hearing him, it has not been possible for me not to do my

(20) own hearing. He began with the sounds of the city about us, the calls, yells, randomly caught distortions of language, and especially things that were wrong and out of place. It was all funny and terrible at once, and the connection of these two

(25) spheres is something I have taken for granted ever since. Thanks to him, I started realizing that each individual has a linguistic shape distinguishing him from all others. I understood that people talk to but fail to comprehend one another; that their

(30) words are thrusts ricocheting off the words of others; that there is no greater illusion than thinking that language is a means of communication between people. One speaks to another person but in such a way that he does not

(35) understand. One keeps talking and he understands even less. One screams, he screams back; ejaculation, eking out a miserable existence in grammar, takes control of language. The exclamations bounce to and fro like balls, deliver

(40) their blows, and drop to the ground. Seldom does anything penetrate the other person, and if it does, it is usually twisted awry.

Questions

1. The author's attitude toward his subject is one of

   (A) humble adoration
   (B) respectful gratitude
   (C) bemused speculation
   (D) absolute responsibility
   (E) slavish imitation

2. According to the passage, true responsibility

   (A) eludes nearly all of us continually
   (B) is a commitment
   (C) is an employee of most important things
   (D) is preeminent and rooted within us
   (E) is rampant everywhere, like weeds

3. The author credits Karl Kraus with opening his (the author's) ears to

   (A) each person's unique linguistic shape
   (B) the twisting of words awry
   (C) everything linguistically wrong and out of shape
   (D) understanding of individual communication
   (E) exclamations, talking, and screams

4. The great illusion of language, according to both Kraus and the author, is

   (A) that grammar is a miserable existence
   (B) that speech addresses our needs
   (C) believing that language is communication
   (D) one of a funny and terrible alliance
   (E) that each person communicates individually

5. The best translation for "twisted awry" (line 42) as it is used in this context would be

   (A) twisted oddly
   (B) bent awry
   (C) changed positively
   (D) a garbled message
   (E) a clarified meaning

PRACTICE PASSAGE 5

Audrey was out of town when Owen arrived in London, but she returned a week later. The sound of her voice through the telephone did much to
Line cure the restlessness from which he had been
(5) suffering since the conclusion of his holiday. But the thought that she was so near yet so inaccessible produced in him a meditative melancholy which enveloped him like a cloud that would not lift. His manner became distrait. He lost weight.
(10)   If customers were not vaguely pained by his sad, pale face, it was only because the fierce rush of modern commercial life leaves your business man little leisure for observing pallor in bank-clerks. What did pain them was the gentle
(15) dreaminess with which he performed his duties. He was in the Inward Bills Department, one of the features of which was the sudden inrush towards the end of the afternoon, of hatless, energetic young men with leather bags strapped to their left
(20) arms, clamouring for mysterious crackling documents, much fastened with pins. Owen had never quite understood what it was that these young men did want, and now his detached mind refused even more emphatically to grapple with the
(25) problem. He distributed the documents at random with the air of a preoccupied monarch scattering largess to the mob, and the subsequent chaos had to be handled by a wrathful head of the department in person.
(30)   Man's power of endurance is limited. At the end of the second week the overwrought head appealed passionately for relief, and Owen was removed to the Postage Department, where, when he had leisure from answering Audrey's telephone
(35) calls, he entered the addresses of letters in a large book and took them to the post. He was supposed also to stamp them, but a man in love cannot think of everything, and he was apt at times to overlook this formality.

Questions

1. We can assume from the passage that Owen lost weight because

  (A) Audrey had spurned him
  (B) he despised Audrey
  (C) Audrey refused to talk to him
  (D) Audrey was unreachable in person
  (E) he disliked his new job in the Postage Department

2. The "subsequent chaos" in line 27 was a result of

  (A) Owen's romantic preoccupation
  (B) Owen's loss of weight
  (C) Owen's detachment and involvement
  (D) Owen's powers of endurance
  (E) Owen's impending transfer to the Postage Department

3. The style of this passage can best be described as

  (A) devilish invective
  (B) profound irony
  (C) light satire
  (D) amused nostalgia
  (E) reflective musing

4. The word "largess" in line 27 can be interpreted to mean

  (A) worthwhile advice
  (B) valuable gifts
  (C) free favors
  (D) worthless materials
  (E) unavailable papers

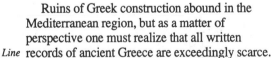

PRACTICE PASSAGE 6

Ruins of Greek construction abound in the Mediterranean region, but as a matter of perspective one must realize that all written
Line records of ancient Greece are exceedingly scarce.
(5) It is difficult to estimate how much Greek literature has survived in any form, but it almost certainly must be less than 1 percent. Very few of the surviving works are in their original form, almost all are corrupted by careless copying over
(10) many centuries, and few contain much information that would permit dating them even

indirectly. Nevertheless, it is clear that ancient Greece was the scene of much geological thinking . . . and that many of the seminal ideas
(15) eventually found their way into printed books.
     The fragmentary kaleidoscope of Greek science records isolated glimpses of important geological understanding. In the sixth century B.C., the Pythagoreans were the first to teach that the Earth
(20) was round because it cast a round shadow on the moon in eclipses. Eratosthenes (ca. 276–ca. 195 B.C.), the second director of the Museum Library in

Alexandria, devised a method of measuring the diameter of the Earth's sphere. He observed that
(25) on the summer solstice, the longest day of the year, the sun stood at an angle of one-fiftieth of a circle from vertical in Alexandria, but was directly overhead in Syene (now Aswan). He had no accurate way of measuring the north-south
(30) distance between the two places (the length of the meridian), but he made a reasonable estimate and calculated a remarkably accurate value for the Earth's diameter. Later commentators have pointed out the obvious sources of error in his
(35) estimate, but that does not diminish the brilliant simplicity and fundamental grandeur of the experiment. There is some uncertainty about the units he used, but his result appears to be only about 20 percent larger than modern
(40) determinations.

Extending his calculations to include some doubtful sun-angle determinations and rough distance estimates, Eratosthenes then attempted to establish a coordinate grid for the whole ancient
(45) world. The result was a distinct improvement in the world map of the day, but the unreliability of the data was recognized and severely criticized by the astronomer Hipparchus of Bithynia (?–after 127 B.C.). In categorically rejecting conclusions
(50) based on inadequate data, Hipparchus was being very scientific, but in failing to concede that an inspired guess is better than no information at all he set geography back a fair distance. It was this same Hipparchus who pioneered the quantitative
(55) approach to astronomy and developed the precession of the equinoxes. Almost all of his original writings are lost and his work is known mostly from references to it in Ptolemy's *Almagest,* written about three centuries after
(60) Hipparchus died.

Herodotus of Halicarnassus (?484–?425 B.C.), the great historian of Greek antiquity, concerned himself mainly with political and military history, but he had traveled as far as the Black Sea,
(65) Mesopotamia, and Egypt and made accurate geological observations. He was aware that earthquakes cause large-scale fracturing and thus may shape the landscape. . . . He noted the sediment carried by the Nile and estimated the
(70) amounts of deposition from the annual floods in the Nile Valley and the growth of the great delta. "Egypt . . . is an acquired country, the gift of the river," he wrote, and throughout those discussions he displayed a remarkable understanding of the
(75) vastness of geologic time.

Questions

1. The word "seminal" in line 14 is used in this passage to suggest which of the following ideas?

    (A) containing the seeds of later development
    (B) fragmented or incomplete
    (C) amorphous or unformed
    (D) revealing primitive thought
    (E) displaying corruption or carelessness

2. An appropriate title for this passage would be

    (A) Eratosthenes and Hipparchus, Greek Geologists
    (B) Greek Achievements: A Loss for Science
    (C) A Fragmentary Greek Kaleidoscope
    (D) Geology in Ancient Greece
    (E) The Grecian Fascination with Geology

3. The author views the achievements of Eratosthenes with

    (A) professional detachment
    (B) slight skepticism
    (C) respect and qualified admiration
    (D) amusement and deep interest
    (E) condescension

4. It can be inferred from the passage that the astronomer Hipparchus was *not*

    (A) scientific in his approach
    (B) particularly flexible or intuitive
    (C) pioneering in his approach
    (D) published in his time
    (E) critical of other scientific studies

5. According to the passage, Greek geological information was

    I. almost all lost
    II. of little value for today's scientists
    III. surprisingly accurate and often grand in scope
    IV. acquired after much thought and calculation
    V. carefully dated and logically explained

    (A) I, III, and V   (B) II and IV   (C) III and V
    (D) I, III, and IV   (E) I, II, and V

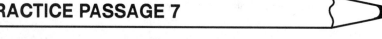

PRACTICE PASSAGE 7

Although a complex nervous system is not
essential for behaviour—protozoans get by quite
nicely with only rudimentary sense cells—the
Line scope and sophistication of behaviour within the
(5) animal kingdom is quite clearly linked with the
evolution of neural complexity. The behavioural
capacities of protozoans and earthworms are
extremely limited compared with those of birds
and mammals. What, then, are the properties of a
(10) nervous system which make complex behaviour
possible?

. . . True nervous systems are only found in
multicellular animals. Here they form a tissue of
discrete, self-contained nerve cells or *neurons*.
(15) Like any other type of animal cell, neurons
comprise an intricate system of cell organelles
surrounded by a cell membrane. . . . Unlike other
animal cells, however, they are specialised for
transmitting electrical messages from one part of
(20) the body to another. This specialisation is reflected
both in their structure and their physiology.

A neuron has three obvious structural
components. The main body of the cell, the *soma*,
is a broad, expanded structure housing the nucleus.
(25) Extending from the soma are two types of
cytoplasm-filled processes called *axons* and
dendrites. Axons carry electrical impulses away
from the soma and pass them on to other neurons
or to muscle fibres. Dendrites receive impulses
(30) from other neurons and transport them to the
soma. All three components are usually
surrounded by *glial cells*. Although glial cells are
not derived from nerve tissue, they come to form a
more or less complex sheath around the axon. In
(35) invertebrates, the glial cell membranes may form a
loose, multilayered sheath in which there is still
room for cytoplasm between the layers. In this
case the arrangement is known as a *tunicated
axon*. In vertebrates the sheath is bound more
(40) tightly so that no gaps are left. The glial cells are
known as Schwann cells and are arranged along
the axon in a characteristic way. Each Schwann
cell covers about 2 mm of axon. Between
neighbouring cells there is a small gap where the
(45) membrane of the axon is exposed to the
extracellular medium. These gaps are known as
the nodes of Ranvier. Axons with this interrupted
Schwann cell sheath are called *myelinated* or
medullated axons. The formation of the myelin
(50) sheath enhances enormously the speed and quality
of impulse conduction.

Questions

1. We can infer from the passage that
   (A) an eagle is more complex in behavior than a
       cow
   (B) cows and eagles are comparably sophisticated
       in behavior
   (C) a sparrow possesses more sophisticated
       behavior patterns than a night crawler
   (D) unicellular organisms possess a specialized
       nervous system
   (E) behavioral capacities of protozoans have yet to
       be fully delineated

2. According to the passage, the components of nerve
   cells that perform jobs opposite to one another are
   (A) the cell organelles and the cell membrane
   (B) the soma and the muscle fibers
   (C) the glial cells and the cytoplasm
   (D) the axons and dendrites
   (E) a tunicated axon and glial cells

3. From information given in the passage, a reader can
   assume that animals possessing myelinated or
   medullated axons
   (A) will receive fewer messages from their nervous
       systems
   (B) will receive interrupted messages from their
       nervous systems due to the gaps known as
       the nodes of Ranvier
   (C) will tend to receive electrical messages at too
       great a speed for assimilation
   (D) will receive electrical messages more quickly
       and with greater accuracy
   (E) will receive specialized electrical messages
       only

4. One major difference between invertebrate and
   vertebrate neurons is
   (A) their structural components
   (B) the tightness of the glial cell sheath
   (C) that of basic neural complexity
   (D) the number of cytoplasm-filled processes
       known as axons and dendrites
   (E) the presence of a glial cell sheath

PRACTICE PASSAGE 8

The *Principia* of Isaac Newton first appeared in 1687 and contained, among many other geophysically fundamental ideas, a calculation of
Line the figure of the Earth based on its rotation as a
(5) body held together only by the force of gravity. It concludes that "the diameter of the Earth at the equator, is to its diameter from pole, as 230 to 229." Newton was impressed by the "diligence and care" of Richer's observations and cites them
(10) as primary experimental proof of the theoretically calculated flattening (*Principia*, book 3, Proposition 20).

In the meantime, Gian Domenico Cassini (1625–1712), another big name brought to Paris
(15) by the new Academy (this time from Bologna), began to organize the great project of extending the meridian of the Paris observatory across all France by ground survey and making astronomical observations of latitude at points along it. It took a
(20) long time, but by 1718 an accurate triangulation network extended from Collioure in the south to Dunkerque in the north. The results of the astronomical observations led Gian Domenico's son and successor as Director of the Paris
(25) Observatory, Jacques Cassini (1677–1756), to announce "definitely" that the length of a degree of arc on the surface of the Earth decreased toward the poles. The Earth, he asserted, was not flattened at the poles as Newton had calculated, but was
(30) pointed (like an American football), and somehow that was construed as a great victory for Cartesian physics over the newfangled Newtonism. It was a matter of observational inaccuracies, but as a subject for popular scientific debate it fitted nicely
(35) with the widely fashionable commentary that surrounded Newton's *Principia*.

The contemporary popular criticism of the *Principia* was rarely illuminating. Some writers praised the work and others condemned it, but
(40) except for a small group of mathematicians and astronomers, few commentators were able to show that they had understood it. The concept of attractive force as a fundamental property of matter was admittedly difficult to grasp. Newton
(45) was a great master of precise language, but his manner of presenting mathematical relationships may have been obscure even to readers with some mathematical training. His Latin must have been a joy to read, compared with the quasi-Latin that
(50) was current at the time, and his grammar was perfect, but the power of his new physics was not obvious.

Questions

1. According to the author, Newton's *Principia* was greeted with

    (A) a fair amount of acclaim
    (B) disgust in scientific quarters
    (C) varying degrees of acceptance
    (D) understanding accompanied by a desire for elucidation
    (E) irritation at Newton's deliberate obfuscation

2. The public reaction to the *Principia* is best understood in the light of which of the following observations?

    (A) The potential of Newtonian physics eluded most people.
    (B) Scientists never trust the work of other scientists.
    (C) Cassini's explanation of an Earth pointed at its poles seemed more logical at the time.
    (D) Everyone appreciated Newton's grasp of grammar and language.
    (E) People were basically unaware of the fundamental properties of matter.

3. As presented in the passage, the concept most unsettling for critics of Newtonian physics was

    (A) the subject of the Earth's rotation
    (B) the idea of an Earth flattened at the poles
    (C) the comparison of Cassini's measurements to Newton's
    (D) Newton's reliance on Richer's observations as support for his calculations
    (E) the theory of gravity's force

4. The author's tone in lines 22–36 is best described as one of

    (A) subtle innuendo
    (B) delicate suggestion
    (C) light irony
    (D) careful exposition
    (E) amused condescension

Unit 4: The Roots of English Words

Were you able to decode most of the strange words in the preceding unit on test techniques? If you have a strong background in languages, particularly Latin, you were probably a good word detective. But if those "aliens" gave you trouble, this unit will remedy your problem. Because 60–70 percent of our language is Latinate at heart, you must know its roots and prefixes to decode many words. Those that will be most helpful are listed on the next few pages.

PREFIXES THAT GIVE INFORMATION

Knowing what a prefix means is vital to dissecting a mystery word. That's why people study roots and prefixes—so that they can puzzle their way through to an understanding *even when faced with a strange word.*

Prefixes are little hunks of letters tacked on at the beginning of a word. But you already know that. You studied prefixes ages ago. And now they're back—not to haunt you, but to help you. *And they will help.* Read them over slowly. Let the examples sink into your brain. Don't worry if a few of the prefix meanings seem contradictory. The different *a* prefixes only seem confusing when read in a list of prefixes. The way a word is used *in context* will lead you to the right prefix meaning.

The prefixes listed here are the vital bits of foreign words that we've appended to our English words. Abbreviations are L for Latin, Gr for Greek, AS for Anglo-Saxon.

Do not memorize prefixes or roots alone. Learn each with one key word that will bring meaning to mind. Learn *atypical,* for instance, to remind you that *a-* means *not, lacking,* or *without. Adhesive* literally means *sticking to or against,* once you know the root and prefix.

Prefix	Meaning	Examples
a, an (Gr)	*lacking, not, without*	atypical, anonymous, anarchy, apathy
a (AS)	*on, in, of, up, to*	aboard, astride, asleep
ab, abs (L)	*from, away*	absent, abstain, abdicate
ac, ad, af, ag, al,		
an, ap, as, at (L)	*to, toward, against*	adhere, attempt, appear
ambi (L), **amphi** (Gr)	*both, around*	ambidextrous, amphibian, amphitheater
ana (Gr)	*up, back, again*	anachronism, anagram, analogy
ante, anti (L)	*before, previous*	antecedent, antedate, anticipate
anti (Gr)	*against, opposing*	antithesis, antisocial, antiseptic
arch, archi (Gr)	*chief, first*	architect, archetype, archbishop
be (AS)	*to make (intensive)*	bemuse, bewhiskered, belabor, beset
bene (L)	*good, well*	beneficial, benevolent, benefactor
bon (L)	*good*	bonus, bona fide, bonny
circum (L)	*around*	circumference, circumnavigate
com, co, col, con, cor (L)	*with, together*	comply, coexist, collateral, condone, conciliate, correlate
contra, counter (L)	*against, opposing*	contraband, contradict, counterproductive
de (L)	*away, from, off, down*	destruct, deplore, demerit, degrade

Prefix	*Meaning*	*Examples*
dia (Gr)	*across, apart, through, between*	diagnose, dialogue, diameter
di, dif, dis (L)	*away, down, off, opposing*	digress, differ, disagree, dissent, diverse
en, em (Gr)	*in, among, within*	enliven, empathy – *caring*
epi (Gr)	*on, outside, over, outer*	epidermis, epitaph, epilogue
eu (Gr)	*good, well*	euphony, euphemism, eulogy
ex, e, ef (L)	*from, out, away*	expel, emit, efface, extol
ex (L)	*former*	ex-wife, ex-manager – *outgoing person*
extra, exter, extro (L)	*outside, beyond*	extraordinary, extrovert, external
for (AS)	*against, away*	forbid, forsake, forswear
fore (AS)	*before*	forecast, foreclose, forehead
hetero (Gr)	*other* ✓	heterogeneous, heterodox
homo (Gr)	*same* ✓	homogeneous, homonym, homograph
hyper (Gr)	*excessive, over* ✓	hyperactive, hyperbole, hypercritical
hyp, hypo (Gr)	*under, beneath*	hypodermic, hypotenuse, hypocrite
in, il, im, ir (Gr)	*in(to), within, not, opposing*	inspire, imprint, irradiate, infamy, inefficient, illegal, infidel
inter (L)	*among, between*	interregnum, intervene, interact
intro, intra (L)	*inwardly, within*	introvert, intramural, introduce
macr, macro (Gr)	*long, large, prominent*	macrocosm, macrobiotic, macroeconomics
mal, male (L)	*bad, badly*	malicious, malevolent, malformed
meta, met (Gr)	*change of, over, beyond*	metaphor, metabolism, metaphysics
micro (Gr)	*small*	microfilm, microscope, microbe
mis (AS)	*amiss, wrong(ly), bad*	misuse, misfortune, misnomer
neo (Gr)	*new, latest of a period*	neon, neologism, neophyte, neocene, Neo-Hebraic
non (L)	*not*	nondescript, nonsense, nonentity
ob, oc, of, op (L)	*over, against, toward*	object, obtuse, offend, oppose
orth (Gr)	*straight, right*	orthodonture, orthopedics, orthodox
para, par (Gr)	*beside, beyond, variation*	paradox, paraphrase, parenthesis
per (L)	*through, thoroughly*	permeate, perspire, permutation
peri (L)	*around, near*	perimeter, periscope, peristyle
post (L)	*after, following*	postmortem, posthumous, postpone
pre (L)	*before*	prepare, prevent, predict
pro (Gr)	*before, forward*	program, produce, provision, progress
pro (L)	*forward, forth, favoring*	
proto (Gr)	*first*	proton, protozoa, prototype
re (L)	*back, backward, again*	regression, retract, recurrent, redundant
retro (L)	*back, backward*	retroactive, retrogression, retrospect
se (L)	*away, aside*	secede, secret, secluded

top part
peak of something

Prefix	Meaning	Examples
sub, suc, suf, sug, sum, sup, sus (L)	under, beneath	subzero, supposition, suspend
super (L)	over, above, extra	superimpose, supervise, superstar
syn, sym, syl, sys (Gr)	together	synthesize, sympathy, synchronize
tele (Gr)	far, distant	telegraph, telepathy, telescope
tra, trans (L)	across, beyond	transfer, transform, travesty, transgress, transitive
ultra (L)	beyond, excessive	ultrasuede, ultraviolet, ultramodern
un (AS)	not, opposing	unhappy, unmitigated, uneven
with (AS)	against	withstand, withdraw, withhold
wri, wro (AS)	twist, wring; work	wrest, writhe, wreath, wrought, cartwright, playwright

PREFIXES QUIZ

Now that you know prefixes, here are some short questions to fix them in your mind for all time.

I.   **Fill-ins.** Fill in the blanks to complete the sentence and provide the meaning.

1. The prefix in *anachronism* and *analogy* is ____*ana*____, meaning *up, back, again*

2. The prefix in *contradictory* and *contravene* is ____*contra*____, meaning *against, opposing*

3. The prefix in *epitaph* and *epidermis* is _____, meaning _____.

4. In *homogeneous* and *homonym* the prefix is _____, and it means _____.

5. In *interscholastic* and *interplay* the prefix is _____, and it means _____.

6. The words *transfer* and *transgress* share the prefix _____, and it means _____.

7. The prefixes in *suspend, submerge, succumb,* and *supposition* are _____, and they mean _____.

8. The prefix _____ in *regression, redundant,* and *retract* means _____.

9. The words *orthopedic* and *orthodox* share the prefix _____, meaning _____.

10. The prefix _____ in *metamorphosis, metaphor,* and *metaphysics* means _____.

ANSWERS to all quizzes can be found in the back of the book, beginning on p. 417.

II. **Creating Words.** Use your knowledge of prefixes to make the words described. Each missing letter is represented by a dot.

1. bringing good; advantageous, profitable ....ficial
2. lacking shape or form Amorphous
3. against sepsis, putrefaction, or decay ANTiseptic
4. to sail around the earth (by water, of course) ......navigate
5. referring to an overactive thyroid .....thyroid
6. showing intense hatred or spite ....volent
7. to fail to concur ...agree
8. to predict ....tell
9. differing from acknowledged standards ......dox
10. inserted under or beneath the skin ....dermic
11. to force out ..pel
12. newcomer, beginner, tyro ...phyte
13. words given in advance, a foretelling ...diction
14. to lengthen in time ...long
15. backward movement .....gression
16. to change the shape .....form
17. verb that carries action over to a receiver .....itive
18. to coordinate time or action ...chronize
19. Elvis Presley .....star
20. under the earth ...terranean

III. **Matching.** Match prefixes with their meanings, writing the meaning on the line.

(B) small _____ 1. micro (a) straight, right
(G) large _____ 2. macro (b) small
H. after _____ 3. post (c) both
(J) through _____ 4. per (d) against, opposing
_____ 5. mis (e) first, chief
(C) both _____ 6. ambi (f) amiss, wrong, bad
_____ 7. contra (g) large, prominent
_____ 8. arch (h) after, following
_____ 9. eu (i) good, well
(A) straight _____ 10. orth (j) through, thoroughly

IV.   **Antonyms.** The words on the left are frequently tested on the SAT. Use your knowledge of prefixes to help you match them with their opposites. Write the correct antonym on the blank opposite each word.

Antonym

_____	1. indifferent	(a) sincere
_____	2. dissent	(b) vital, necessary
_____	3. anarchy	(c) nobility
_____	4. hypocritical	(d) zeal
_____	5. euphony	(e) condemn, castigate
_____	6. obtuse	(f) ill-tempered, cruel, miserly
_____	7. infamy	(g) biased
_____	8. apathy	(h) preserve
_____	9. conciliate	(i) rule, order
_____	10. diverse	(j) acute
_____	11. redundant	(k) good repute
_____	12. depravity	(l) uniform
_____	13. benevolent	(m) cacophony
_____	14. extol	(n) alienate
_____	15. efface	(o) agreement

ROOTS THAT REVEAL WORD MEANINGS

English is a blend of many languages. Knowing the sources of our words—their roots—is a powerful way to increase your vocabulary. Also, *roots help you to decode a mystery word.* It's been estimated that from 10 Latin and 2 Greek words have come over 2,500 English words. (Small drum roll, please.)

You'll be surprised by how easy roots are to learn. **Connect each root to a word you know well. Learning a list of roots all by themselves doesn't work,** but the combination of *word + root*-in-the-middle is a sure key to memory. Those 12 famous roots are starred for your special attention. Common roots that everyone knows, like *aqua ▬ water,* have been omitted. Why study what you already know?

Note that the root is a *part of a word* from our language's past. It may change its spelling slightly as it becomes part of an English word, and sometimes vowels are lost in the transfer, as in *acrid,* a word deriving from *acer,* meaning sharp or bitter.

You will know at least half of the English examples given, and you should *learn the meaning of any strangers.* They appear with dependable regularity on the SAT and PSAT.

Abbreviations are the same as in the section on prefixes: L means Latin; Gr means Greek; AS means Anglo-Saxon; and Fr means French.

Root	Meaning	English Examples
acer (L)	*sharp*	acrid—bitter, sharply noticeable to smell or taste acute—pointed; observant or keenly perceptive exacerbate—to make more severe, aggravate
aev or **ev** (L)	*age, era, time*	primeval—of earliest or ancient times medieval—of the Middle Ages
ag, act (L)	*do, drive, impel*	agitate—to stir up, keep in motion active—full of action
agog (Gr)	*lead, leader*	pedagogue—originally, a slave escorting children to school; now, sometimes a know-it-all demagogue—a popular (often false) leader

Root	*Meaning*	*English Examples*
agri (L)	*field, land, farm*	agriculture—science of land cultivation agronomy—theory of crops and soil management
am, amic (L)	*love, friend*	amity—accord, friendship amicable—friendly, easy to get along with
anim (L)	*mind, spirit, soul*	animated—lively, spirited, full of life magnanimity—generosity or greatness of spirit
annu, enni (L)	*year*	annuity—yearly pay; pay at regular intervals during the year biennial—occurring every two years
anthrop (Gr)	*man, mankind*	anthropology—the study of human beings misanthrope—one who dislikes people
arch (Gr)	*ancient, chief*	archaeology—study of artifacts patriarch—male leader of family or tribe
art (L)	*skill, art*	artisan—artist, creator artifice—ingenuity; guile or deceit artifact—result of human work; often a primitive product
aud, audit (L)	*hear, listen to*	auditory—of hearing inaudible—unable to be heard
auto (Gr)	*self*	automatic—self-acting, able to act autobiography—person's life story written by himself or herself
bel, bell (L)	*war*	belligerent—looking for a fight rebellious—warring against authority
bell (Fr)	*beautiful*	belle—much sought-after girl, a reigning beauty embellish—to decorate, adorn
ben, bon (L)	*well, good*	benefactor—person who does good bonus—an extra, added reward
bio (Gr)	*life*	biology—study of life systems biochemist—student of life chemistries
brev (L)	*short, brief*	brevity—briefness abbreviate—to make shorter
*cap, capt, cept, cip (L)	*take*	captive—someone or something taken precept—wise saying (orig., a command) anticipate—to foresee, to handle ahead of time
capit (L)	*head*	capital—major city or site; money stake; first-rate decapitate—to behead
ced, cede, cess (L)	*yield, go*	antecedent—something going before concede—to yield, agree with recession—act of receding or going back

Root	*Meaning*	*English Examples*
chrom (Gr)	*color*	monochromatic—of one color chromosome—small body in cells
chrono (Gr)	*time*	chronology—order in time synchronize—to cause to take place at the same time anachronism—a thing out of time sequence
cid, cis (L)	*cut, kill*	decisive—unmistakable, clear-cut; forceful homicide—killing of a human
clam (claim) (L)	*cry out*	clamor—great outcry or shouting acclaim—noisy approval
claus, clud, clus (L)	*close, shut*	claustrophobia—fear of closed places conclude—to end, finish; shut off seclusion—withdrawal from others
cogno, cognit (L)	*notice, become acquainted with*	cognizant—aware, conscious of recognize—to know from a previous time cognitive—known through awareness and judgment
corp (L)	*body*	corpse—dead body corpulent—fat (too much body)
cosm (Gr)	*world, order*	cosmology—study of the universe as an orderly system microcosm—little world, miniature, epitome
crac, crat (Gr)	*rule, power*	democracy—rule by the people autocrat—dictatorial ruler (makes own laws)
culp (L)	*fault, blame*	culpable—guilty of fault exculpate—to clear of blame, exonerate
cur, curr, curs (L)	*run, course*	excursion—journey, trip concurrent—occurring at the same time cursory—brief, haphazard run-through
cycl (Gr)	*circle, wheel*	cyclical—recurring regularly tricycle—three-wheeled vehicle
dem (Gr)	*people*	democracy—rule by the people demagogue—leader under false pretenses epidemic—widespread human illness
derm (Gr)	*skin*	dermatology—study of skin, its ailments epidermis—outer layer of skin
dict (L)	*speak, say, words*	diction—speech verdict—statement from a jury
doc, doct (L) and **dox** (Gr)	*teach, explain, show*	docile—meek, easily taught or led doctor—learned person (orig., a teacher) orthodox—according to teaching

Root	*Meaning*	*English Examples*
*duc, duct (L)	*lead, direct*	education—teaching, instruction aqueduct—waterway that directs flow abduct—to take or lead away (usually by force)
ego (L)	*I, self*	egoist (or egotist)—self-centered person ego trip—act satisfying one's ego or self
err (L)	*wander, mistake*	errant—wandering, maybe truant erroneous—full of mistakes
*fac, fict, fect,-fy (L)	*do, make*	manufacture—to make (orig., by hand) fiction—made-up story affect—to make a difference, influence testify—to make a statement of witness
fall, fals (L)	*false, untrue*	fallacious—faulty, erroneous falsify—to tell an untruth, lie infallible—without fault, perfect
*fer (L)	*carry, bear, yield*	transfer—to carry across inference—drawing a conclusion; assumption
fid (L)	*faith, trust*	Fido—faithful family hound affidavit—written statement as an oath perfidious—faithless, untrue
flect, flex (L)	*bend, turn, curve*	inflection—turns, "curves" of the voice flexible—changeable, bendable
flu, fluct (L)	*flow*	influx—that flowing or coming in effluvium—unpleasant emanation or smell fluctuate—to move up or down
gen (Gr and L)	*kind, origin, birth, race*	genus—group of species with similar characteristics engender—to found or foster, begin generic—characteristic of a class, universal
*graph, gram (Gr)	*write, writing*	graphic—delineated well, described exactly epigram—brief, meaningful statement
grav (L)	*weight, heavy*	gravid—pregnant (heavy with child) gravity—seriousness or weight (import)
greg (L)	*flock, group, herd*	gregarious—enjoying groups, sociable aggregate—group, total
hem (Gr)	*blood*	hemorrhage—to bleed (profusely) hematocrit—instrument for blood analysis
her, hes (L)	*cling, stick*	adhere—to stick fast, cleave; stay with coherence—consistency, sticking together; clear speech adhesive—sticking, clinging

Root	Meaning	English Examples
hom, homo (L)	*man*	homage—honor, tribute, deference Homo sapiens—literally thinking man
hydr (Gr)	*water*	hydrant—water discharge pipe with spout dehydrate—to deprive or to lose water
ign (L)	*fire*	igneous—referring to fire ignite—to kindle, set fire
ira (L)	*anger, rage*	ire—anger irritate—to annoy, make angry irascible—easily angered
it (L)	*go*	exit—way out; to go out circuit—that which goes around initiate—to start in, begin
jac, jact, ject (L)	*throw, cast, hurl*	ejaculation—impromptu, heartfelt remark projectile—something thrown (forward)
jud, jur, jus (L)	*trial, right, judgment, law, justice*	judge—arbiter jurisprudence—the science of law just—fair, equitable
leg, lect, lig (L)	*read, choose, select*	legumes—vegetables (beans) easily picked legible—able to be read election—choice negligible—not worthy of being singled out or noticed; unimportant
leg (L)	*law*	legislate—to make laws legitimate—within the law
lev (L)	*light*	levity—lightness, humor elevate—to raise, lift up
***log** (Gr) and **loqu, locut** (L)	*speech, study, word, talk*	theology—study of religion epilogue—words at end of book or play elocution—effective speech soliloquy—speech by one person
luc (L)	*light*	lucid—clear, easily understood translucent—allowing light to pass through elucidate—to make clear, enlighten
magn (L) and **mega** (Gr)	*large*	magnanimity—largeness or generosity of spirit megalomania—having grandiose ideas or delusions
mal (L)	*bad*	malignant—promising harm, virulent malediction—evil saying, curse dismal—gloomy, depressing
man, manu (L)	*hand*	manacle—restraint, handcuff manuscript—something written (orig., by hand)

Root	*Meaning*	*English Examples*
mar (L)	*sea*	marinate—to season, as in a salty brine maritime—connected with the sea
mater, matri (L)	*mother*	maternal—nurturing, motherly matriarch—female family head
medi (L)	*middle*	mediocre—only half, inferior mediate—to interpose, go between
min (L)	*small, less, little*	minuscule—tiny diminish—to reduce, make less
***mit, miss** (L)	*send*	transmit—to send across missile—something thrown, a projectile
mob, mot, mov (L)	*move*	mobility—ability to move remote—far removed, at a distance
mon, monit (L)	*warn*	admonish—to warn premonition—foreboding (usually of ill)
mor (L)	*custom, behavior*	morality—ethical principles or customs; virtue mores—customs, accepted behavior demoralizing—damaging to spirit or morale
mor, mort (L)	*die, death*	moribund—dying morbid—abnormally gloomy mortuary—a place for dead bodies prior to burial
morph (Gr)	*form*	metamorphosis—change of form amorphous—formless, without definite shape
mut, mutat (L)	*change*	immutable—changeless, eternal mutation—change, alteration of form or qualities
nom (Gr)	*law, order, rule*	economy—management of affairs; thrift autonomy—self-discipline; home rule
nomen, nomin (L) and **onym** (Gr)	*name*	nomenclature—any system of naming nominate—to specify by name; choose, select synonym—word with similar meaning pseudonym—pen name; literally false name
nov (L)	*new*	novel—fresh, new, original; book of fiction renovate—to make like new innovation—something new and different
ora (L)	*speak, pray*	oration—formal speech oral—referring to speech oracle—inspired prophet; a human intermediary for a god's voice
oss, oste (L)	*bone*	ossify—to change into or form bone osteopathy—branch of medicine concerned with spinal health and alignment

Root	*Meaning*	*English Examples*
pac (L)	*peace*	pacify—to soothe, calm pacifist—person opposed to war
pan (Gr)	*all, entire*	panacea—cure-all, perfect remedy pandemonium—a great commotion; literally all demons panorama—all-encompassing view
pater, patri (L)	*father*	paternal—fatherly, protective patrimony—inheritance from father patriotic—devotion to home country (fatherland)
path, pass (Gr)	*feeling, suffering*	apathy—lack of feeling empathy—feeling that is exactly like another's passionate—with deep feeling
ped (Gr)	*child*	pediatrician—children's doctor orthopedic—correcting/preventing deformities, especially in children
ped, pod (L)	*foot*	pedal—lever for foot, as on a bicycle quadruped—four-footed animal podium—speaking platform
pel, puls (L)	*drive*	impel—to drive or force compulsion—feeling of being forced or driven
pend, pens (L)	*hang, weigh*	depend—to be contingent upon, rely suspension—temporary stoppage
phon (Gr)	*sound*	phonograph—literally writing in sound; record player phonetics—speech sounds as elements of language
*plex, plic, ply (L)	*fold*	complex—difficult to understand replica—copy, likeness multiply—to increase in number; literally of many folds
*pon, pos (L)	*place, put*	postpone—to put off, delay interpose—to put in between, interject
port (L)	*carry*	portable—something that can be carried report—to carry information, inform, tell
pot (L)	*power*	potent—powerful omnipotent—all-powerful potential—possible, latent; something waiting to be developed
psych (Gr)	*mind*	psychiatry—science of healing the mind psychosomatic—relationship between the mind and body; caused by the mind
pyr (Gr)	*fire*	pyre—any pile to be burnt, often as a funeral rite pyrotechnics—fireworks pyromaniac—person who can't resist setting fires

Root	*Meaning*	*English Examples*
quer, quir, quis (L)	*ask, seek*	query—question inquire—to ask about quizzical—questioning (as a look) inquisition—usu., an official questioning or examination
reg, rig, rect (L)	*rule, right, straight*	regulation—rule incorrigible—unmanageable, delinquent rectify—to set right, correct
rog (L)	*ask*	interrogate—to question abrogate—to nullify or abolish derogatory—overly critical, disparaging
rupt (L)	*break*	rupture—a break; to break interrupt—to break into
sacr, sanct (L)	*sacred, holy*	sanctify—to make holy sacrosanct—holy, most sacred desecrate—to profane or foul something sacred
sci (L)	*know*	conscious—aware, knowing omniscient—knowing all
scrib, script (L)	*write*	scribble—to write carelessly transcript—letter; document; record
sent, sens (L)	*think, feel*	resent—to feel anger, indignation sensitive—showing feeling
solv, solu, solut (L)	*free, loosen*	absolve—to clear or free of blame soluble—capable of being dissolved dissolute—morally free, loose
somn (L)	*sleep*	somnolent—sleepy, lethargic insomnia—inability to fall asleep
soph (Gr)	*wise, wisdom*	sophist—one who sounds good, but whose reasoning is faulty philosophy—one's ethics; literally love of wisdom
*spec, spic, spect (L)	*see, look*	specimen—a sample, example perspicacious—cautious, observant spectator—one who watches, observes
string, strict (L)	*tie, bind tightly*	stringent—rigid, strict constrict—to constrain, bind together stricture—contracted part of the body; censure, adverse criticism
sum, sumpt (L)	*take*	assume—to take as one's own presumption—overconfidence; effrontery consumption—the using up of anything

Root	Meaning	English Examples
tang, ting, tact, tig (L)	*touch, border on*	tangible—touchable, perceptible contingent—dependent upon tactile—concerning the sense of touch contiguous—touching, adjacent
tempor (L)	*time*	temporize—to stall, delay extemporaneous—impromptu, immediate
*ten, tin, tain, tent (L)	*hold, contain*	tenacity—holding on like a bulldog, courage abstinence—holding back, refraining from detain—to hold back retention—holding on to something, keeping
*tend, tens, tent (L)	*stretch*	extend—to stretch out, lengthen pretense—sham, false show attention—notice, observation, applying mind or thought
terr (L)	*land, earth*	terrestrial—of the land subterranean—underground
the (Gr)	*god*	theism—belief in existence of a god or gods atheist—one who denies existence of god(s)
tort, tors (L)	*twist*	distort—to twist out of shape tortuous—winding, twisted torsion—wrenching or twisting
tract (L)	*pull, draw*	extract—to pull out; an essence (as vanilla) contraction—shortening, drawing in
turb (L)	*agitate*	turbulence—agitation, roiling (as of water or air) perturb—to annoy, irritate
urb (L)	*city*	urban—of the city urbane—(said of men) polished, citified
vad, vas (L)	*go*	invade—to go in (usually by force) pervasive—spreading throughout (as an attitude)
vert, vers (L)	*turn*	invert—to turn inside convert—to turn from one belief or course to another; person who changed aversion—turning against, dislike
via (L)	*road, way*	deviate—to alter or change course impervious—not penetrable; literally no way through
vinc, vict, vanqu (L)	*conquer*	invincible—unbeatable victory—winning, conquering vanquish—to conquer or defeat
vit, viv (L)	*life, lively*	vitamin—food element thought essential to life vitality—animation, liveliness vivacious—sprightly, lively

Root	Meaning	English Examples
voc, vok (L)	*call*	vocation—life's work, one's job
		invoke—to call upon (as a god)
volv, volut (L)	*roll, turn*	evolve—to develop over time, derive
		convolution—coiled state
zo (Gr)	*animal*	zodiac—the twelve divisions of the heavens, many symbolized by animals such as Leo the lion, who represents those born from July 23 to August 22
		protozoa—first animal, single-celled

QUIZ: OF COURSE YOU SPEAK LATIN AND GREEK

Use your knowledge of old roots from Latin, Greek, and Anglo-Saxon to explain modern English in these exercises.

I. **Underlining Roots.** In the following pairs of words, underline the common root. Then find its meaning in the choices in the right column and write in the correct word(s). Some have two roots.

_____	1. agitate, react	(a) to call
_____	2. artifact, artist	(b) guilt
_____	3. acrid, exacerbate	(c) to do, drive, impel
_____	4. audience, inaudible	(d) head
_____	5. evolve, convoluted	(e) well, good
_____	6. bonus, benevolent	(f) skill, art
_____	7. invincible, vanquish	(g) to wish, want
_____	8. invert, aversion	(h) sharp
_____	9. capital, captor	(i) god
_____	10. corpse, incorporate	(j) rule, power
_____	11. exclaim, clamor	(k) to roll or turn
_____	12. theocracy, autocrat	(l) to conquer
_____	13. education, ductile	(m) to hear
_____	14. vocation, invoke	(n) to lead, direct
_____	15. culprit, exculpate	(o) to turn
		(p) body
		(q) to cry out
		(r) self

II.   **Fill-ins.** Fill in the missing items in the roots chart below.

	Root	Meaning	Examples
1.	err		errant, aberration
2.		flow	
3.	fer		
4.			democracy, epidemic
5.	dic, dict		
6.		world, order	
7.	chrom		chromatic

III.   **Decoding Roots.** Old, literal translations of words and their modern meanings are often nearly identical—a helpful trait on the part of words. Be a translator to see how closely the old roots parallel modern definitions.

Word	Literal Translation	Modern Meaning
Example:		
graphology	writing study	study of handwriting
1. engender	_____	begin, found, foster
2. hydrophobia	_____	fear of water
3. pervade	_____	to spread or diffuse throughout
4. perspicacious	_____	cautious, observant
5. dismiss	_____	to send away or out
6. dismal	_____	gloomy, depressing
7. manuscript	_____	something written
8. premonition	_____	foreboding, warning
9. demoralizing	_____	damaging to spirit or morale
10. astronomy	_____	science of the heavens
11. renovate	_____	to remodel, make like new
12. osteopathy	_____	study of spinal health
13. patricide	_____	killing of father
14. dissonance	_____	discord, unpleasing sound
15. provoke	_____	to rouse anger

IV.   **Build-a-Word.** Put root parts together to create the word defined in parentheses.

Example: *before* + go + *ent* = ___antecedent___   (something that goes before)

1. *against* + *man* = _____   (one who dislikes people)

2. *to* + *stick* + *ive* = _____   (sticking together)

3. *before* + *run* + *or* = _____   (a forerunner, harbinger)

4. *between* + *place or put* = _____   (to insert)

5. *not* + *bend, twist* + *ible* = _____   (immovable)

V. **Mystery Words.** Once you might have called these mystery words. Probably they are easier for you now. See how many of the strangers below fall apart under your root analysis and give up their meanings.

1. reiterate _____
2. disclaimer _____
3. fictile _____
4. precognition _____
5. ideologue _____
6. pandemic _____
7. beneficence _____
8. rectitude _____

VI. **Antonyms.** Once again, some SAT and PSAT favorites that *won't* haunt you in the future if you learn them now. Write the correct antonym on the line provided.

Antonym

_____	1. exacerbate	(a)	philanthropic
_____	2. amity	(b)	to release
_____	3. magnanimous	(c)	peaceful, pacific
_____	4. artificial	(d)	praise
_____	5. misanthropic	(e)	fondness
_____	6. belligerent	(f)	straight, direct
_____	7. concede	(g)	to alleviate, soothe
_____	8. malediction	(h)	apart, separate
_____	9. corpulent	(i)	enmity
_____	10. aversion	(j)	contained
_____	11. convoluted	(k)	genuine
_____	12. conspicuous	(l)	petty, mean-spirited
_____	13. retain	(m)	hidden
_____	14. contiguous	(n)	to stand firm, be adamant
_____	15. pervasive	(o)	skinny, slender

NUMBER ROOTS

You will quickly recognize most of the roots in this list of number roots. Why? Because the derived English words closely resemble their parent roots. But did you know that the suffix *-ty* means *times ten*? Take a careful minute or two to read this list and see what bits of knowledge you can tuck away into your waiting brain cells. You never know when a root will unlock the meaning of a strange word on a test and thereby add golden points to your score!

Number	*Root(s)*	*English Words*
half	**hemi, demi, semi, med**	hemiplegia, demitasse, semicolon, medium
one	**uni, mono, sol**	unicycle, monotone, solo, solitaire
one and a half	**sesqui**	sesquicentennial (150 years)
two	**di, bi, du, duo, diplo**	diverge, binomial, duplicity, duodenal, diploma
three	**tri, ter**	trimester, tertiary
four	**quadr, tetra**	quadruped, tetragon

Number	Root(s)	English Words
five	quinque, quint, penta	quinquevalent, quintuplets, pentagon
six	sex, hexa	sextet, hexagon, hexameter
seven	sept, hepta	September, heptavalent
eight	oct, octa, octo	octagon, October, octopus, octave
nine	nona, novem, ennea	nonagon, November, ennead
ten	dec, deca	decimal, December, decathlon
twelve	duodec, dodeca	duodenary, dodecahedron
ten and	-teen	seventeen, nineteen
times ten	-ty	forty, eighty
hundred	cent, hecto, hecato	century, centennial, hectometer, hecatomb (in ancient Greece, a sacrifice of 100 oxen or cattle at a time; thus, a great slaughter)
thousand	milli, kilo	million, millimeter, kilowatt
ten thousand	myria	myriad (a large but unspecific number)
million	meg, mega	megaphone, megalomaniac
first	arch, prim, prin, proto	archaeology, primitive, principal, prototype
both	ambi, amphi	ambiguous, amphitheater
equal	equi, iso, par	equivalent, equivocal, isosceles, parity
few	oligo, pauci	oligarchy (rule by a very few); paucity (scarcity)
many	multi, myria, poly	multitude, myriagram (10 kilograms), polygamy
all	omni, pan, panto	omnivorous, pandemic, pantomime

QUIZ: FIGURE IT OUT

I.   **Underlining Roots.** *Underline the number root* in each word below and write the number it indicates.

1. decathlon _____
2. megaphone _____
3. seventeen _____
4. hexagon _____
5. trimester _____

6. binomial _____
7. tetragon _____
8. centennial _____
9. September _____
10. kilometer _____

II.   **Know Those Numbers.** Answer the questions by decoding the underlined words.

1. A <u>nonagenarian</u> is how old? _____

2. The ancient galley called the <u>quinquereme</u> had how many banks of oars or rowers to a bench? _____

3. When you tell me there's a <u>paucity</u> of chocolate chip cookies, why do I cry? _____

4. The building in Washington called the <u>Pentagon</u> has how many sides? _____

5. If the witches in *Macbeth* are called a terrible <u>triad</u>, how many witches are we worried about?_____

6. "That author is guilty of <u>sesquipedalian</u> words!" means what? _____

7. Why don't I like your <u>ambiguous</u> answer? _____

8. An elderly aunt once told us she had <u>sexagenarian</u> appeal, and we think she meant? _____

9. Are we surprised to learn that a monk living in a <u>monastery</u> lives basically alone? _____
   Do you suppose that's ever <u>monotonous</u>? _____

10. The number root in <u>protagonist</u> says what about that character in the play? _____

11. What kind of dance is a <u>quadrille</u>? _____

12. If a <u>trammel</u> is a net of <u>three</u> layers that could enmesh or entangle something or someone, what does <u>untrammeled</u> have to mean? _____

13. A notable translation of the Old Testament is called the <u>Septuagint</u> because _____ scholars produced it.

14. Why is the Russian sleigh called a <u>troika</u>? _____

15. The baby treat called <u>zwieback</u> is named that because? _____

WORDS FROM SPECIAL PLACES

Words come into everyday use in our language all the time. They come from a variety of places: from characters in literature, from myth and legend, from what people do and how they think, even from geographical place names.

These are special words—special because they enrich English, giving it specificity and color that it might otherwise lack. These are words to be enjoyed, and some of the hundreds we possess are offered here.

WORDS FROM CHARACTERS IN LITERATURE

Babbitt	George F. Babbitt was an American middle-class businessman who was vastly pleased with himself. He wasn't open-minded or tolerant, and you can meet him in Sinclair Lewis's satiric novel *Babbitt* (1922). Anyone like George is a *Babbitt*.
Brobdingnagian	In Jonathan Swift's *Gulliver's Travels* (1726), Gulliver met the Brobdingnagians, giants tall as steeples. This word is an interesting (and impressive) synonym for *gigantic*.
bumble	Mr. Bumble was the officious, puffed-up, and pompous orphanage official (a beadle) in Dickens's *Oliver Twist*. A modern-day bumble is someone to be avoided, just like the original.
Cinderella	Like her fairy-tale ancestor, a Cinderella is any girl who goes from *rags to riches*.
Don Juan	Don Juan is a lover, but very unsavory. The original character killed men and seduced women, and word of his behavior got around. Franciscan monks were finally forced to kill him to end his career. Nevertheless, in modern use, his name gives us the idea of a fellow who might be interesting to know.
Falstaffian	Sir John Falstaff is Shakespeare's bragging, bawdy, good-humored fat man introduced in the historical plays for comic relief. Something Falstaffian resembles the original character or his men.
Frankenstein	Mary Shelley was the creator of the book *Frankenstein,* which she wrote as a vacation entertainment in 1817. Her story still haunts us—the possibility that a living being might be created in a laboratory from dead human parts. Frankenstein was the name of the scientist who created the monster, but the word now refers to a monster that destroys its creator.
Friday	Like Robinson Crusoe's original, a helper who is dependable, cheerful, and hardworking is called a *man Friday*. A *girl Friday* is the same thing, only prettier.
Galahad	Most noble and pure of all knights was Launcelot's son, Sir Galahad. A male both good-looking *and* gallant is a Sir Galahad. (Also, remember the noble and pure part.)
Jekyll and Hyde	Someone described as a Jekyll and Hyde is a person who alternates between good and evil in startling contrast. Robert Louis Stevenson's story *The Strange Case of Dr. Jekyll and Mr. Hyde* ends with the kindly Dr. Jekyll trapped in the murderous Hyde personality. (There may be a lesson here for all of us.)
lilliputian	Opposite of the immense Brobdingnagians, the six-inch Lilliputians were also people in Swift's *Gulliver's Travels*. Anything *lilliputian* is miniature or tiny.
Little Lord Fauntleroy	Any little boy so good he isn't real is a Little Lord Fauntleroy. (I have never met one.) The original, in Frances Hodgson Burnett's book, is a poor New York child who inherits an earldom, zaps over to England to claim it, and endears himself to the entire Continent by his impeccable behavior. Sometimes this term means *sissy*.
lothario	One way to have your name become history, apparently, is to be a well-known lover. Lothario, a character in the play *The Fair Penitent,* was either a "cheerful seducer" or a "heartless libertine" depending on which dictionary you read. It is probably enough to say that a *lothario* gets around.

malapropism   Mrs. Malaprop, from Sheridan's play *The Rivals* (1775), gained immortality by her verbal mistakes. Among other gems, she said, "*Illiterate* him, I say, quite from your memory," and, "She's as headstrong as an *allegory* on the banks of the Nile." A *malapropism* is a *hilarious misuse of words.*

Milquetoast   Caspar Milquetoast was the detective hero of Webster's cartoon series *The Timid Soul.* Because milk toast is bland and soggy, a *milquetoast* is anyone who *can be pushed around—a wimp.*

Pickwickian   Another Dickens character is Mr. Pickwick of *Pickwick Papers.* In his club, comments were "not in accordance with their usual meaning, conveniently understood so as to avoid offense." Pickwickian words are thus ones used in an *esoteric, special sense.*

Pollyanna   Pollyanna is the female version of Little Lord Fauntleroy. She was a too-good-to-be-true kid from Eleanor Porter's 1913 novel, *Pollyanna.* Pollyanna practiced her piano for hours, always saw the good side of things, and I hated her. No matter how awful it may appear, a *Pollyanna finds something good about everything.* **Dr. Pangloss** behaves the same way in Voltaire's famous satire, *Candide.* He says things like "Everything's for the best in this best of all possible worlds." (Of course, he has a point, but blind acceptance is sometimes hard to take.)

pooh-bah   In Gilbert and Sullivan's light opera *The Mikado,* Pooh-Bah was the Lord-High-Everything-Else. Any politician who holds several offices or has many jobs is a *pooh-bah.* (Pooh Bear, created by A. A. Milne, sounds a lot like pooh-bah, and Milne was a Gilbert and Sullivan fan. Do you suppose???)

quixotic   Don Quixote was the lovable, idealistic, impractical old man who imagined himself a knight in Cervantes's novel *Don Quixote. The Man of La Mancha* is the musical based on this book, and both portray idealism contrasted with reality. *Quixotic* schemes or ideas are *noble, but unrealistic*—touched with glory, perhaps, but doomed. **Sancho Panza** was the faithful companion of Don Quixote, and Dulcinea was the queen of his heart. **Dulcinea** now means sweetheart.

robot   Czech playwright Karel Capek wrote a brilliant play titled *R.U.R.* (1923), the initials meaning Rossum's Universal Robots. As in *Frankenstein, Dr. Jekyll and Mr. Hyde,* and other works, the thing that was created rebels. The idea that our own inventions will destroy us is a compelling theme. A *robot* is anyone who exists and works without thought, who simply does what he or she is told.

rodomontade   One brave but boastful character in both *Orlando Innamorato* and *Orlando Furioso* is a Saracen king named Rodomonte. His courage forgotten, *rodomontade* now means "vain boasting; empty bluster." Roll this word off your tongue; it's more impressive than the word *bragging.*

scrooge   We all know Scrooge, the penny-pinching miser with a heart like the Grinch's—"two sizes too small." From Dickens's "A Christmas Carol" (1843), the name now refers to any *grasping, covetous person* seemingly without kindness, a *curmudgeon.*

Simon Legree   Roughly ten years before the Civil War, Harriet Beecher Stowe, who had never been south of Ohio, wrote an impassioned novel about slavery titled *Uncle Tom's Cabin.* Her slaver was Simon Legree, a brutal taskmaster and villain. Anyone who *works others mercilessly* is a Simon Legree.

Svengali   The musical hypnotic genius in Du Maurier's *Trilby* (1894) was Svengali. Anyone who *controls others by seemingly mysterious means* is a Svengali.

Tartuffe   Tartuffe was a complete moral hypocrite in Molière's play by that name. A *Tartuffe* is anyone who *pretends great devotion* to religion and its principles but lives a secretly immoral life.

Uncle Tom   In *Uncle Tom's Cabin,* the antislavery novel of the 1850s, Uncle Tom was the saintly old black man who understood (or tried to understand) both sides of the master-slave problem. (A sort of Pollyanna.) Today, a black called an *Uncle Tom* is seen by other blacks as being too quick to cooperate with white people.

Uriah Heep	From Dickens's *David Copperfield* comes Uriah Heep, a term to describe someone *hypocritical* and *holier-than-thou*, who needs careful watching when making a deal.
Walter Mitty	Humorist James Thurber's lovable character from "The Secret Life of Walter Mitty" is probably part of all of us. He's the *spirit* behind all good fantasy—the part of all of us that *dreams and fantasizes about what we'd like to be or do or have.*
yahoo	The Yahoos were another race in *Gulliver's Travels,* and a particularly unlovely lot. They were subjects of the *Houyhnhnms,* horses who could think and reason. That tells you how grungy they were. A *yahoo* is a crudball, a *stupid* person.

WORDS FROM MYTH AND LEGEND

Achilles' heel	*weak spot; place of vulnerability.* Achilles' mother dipped him in the river Styx as an infant to make him invulnerable to wounds. But she had to hold on to him somehow, and so she held his heel and it was unprotected. He died from an arrow in the heel, shot by Paris in the Trojan War. Despite the vulnerable heel, *Achilles* was *a mighty protagonist or hero.*
aeolian	*referring to winds.* Aeolus was god of the winds.
Apollo and **Adonis**	*An Apollo or Adonis is a handsome, desirable male.* Apollo was the sun god of the Greeks and Romans. Adonis was a mortal man beloved of Aphrodite (Venus).
Atlantean, Atlantic	from *Atlas; indicates strength.*
Atlas/atlas	*bearer of a significant burden/collection of maps.* Atlas was the Titan who supported the heavens on his head and hands.
aurora	*the dawn; half of aurora borealis.* Aurora was goddess of the dawn.
bacchanal	*an orgy;* a bacchant is *a reveler or carouser at parties.* Bacchus, also called Dionysus, was the god of wine.
bacchanalian	*like an orgy or wild party.*
calliope	*steam whistle or steam organ; anything making a similar shrill sound.* Calliope was the Muse of eloquence, and originally her name meant beautiful voice.
Cassandra	*one who prophesies trouble; doom prophet.* Apollo gave his beloved Cassandra (daughter of King Priam of Troy) the gift of prophecy, but when she didn't love him back, he changed the gift to a curse; none would believe her foresight. Thus, when she foretold the outcome of the Trojan War, everyone said, "Oh, ho hum, Cassie."
centaur	*a rider who seems part of his horse.* The centaurs were supposed to have the head, arms, and trunk of a man but the body and legs of a horse.
chimera	*imaginative creature; wild, scary dream or fancy.* The Chimera was a female monster who spouted flames and had a lion's head, goat's body, and dragon/serpent tail.
cupidity	*greed or avarice.* Cupid was the young god who embodied sexual desire.
erotic	*of or pertaining to sexual love.* Eros (Cupid) was the god of passionate love and the youngest of the gods. He was armed with arrows to inflame love in any heart.
furor	*frenzy, rage, excitement.* Called the Furiae in Latin, the Greek Erinyes were winged creatures with snakes for hair who pursued individuals who committed murders within their families.
fury	*an avenging spirit; virago; fierceness, vehemence.*
gorgon	*ugly, frightening person (usually a woman); repulsive creature.* Awful females, the Gorgons fixed their eyes on you and you turned to stone.
halcyon	*peaceful, tranquil.* Alcyon was a grieving widow who was metamorphosed by the gods into a kingfisher like her husband. To brood over a floating nest, she needed ten to fourteen days of peaceful ocean—the *halcyon* days.

harpy
grasping, greedy, scary female. Harpies were part woman, part bird, and they flew around snatching either the souls of the dead or food from anyone handy.

hector
to bully or pick on; to annoy exceedingly. At the time of the Trojan War, Hector (son of Trojan King Priam) was probably the noblest and stoutest fellow in the batch. He slew Patroclus, best friend of the Greek Achilles, and so Achilles slew him. (Storytellers always say *slew* in mythological tales.) The word changed its meaning because of a London street gang who called themselves "hectors," but it is a sad alteration when you think of the fine old Trojan hero.

Helen (of Troy)
a woman of incomparable beauty; a perfect 10. Because Helen (wife of Spartan King Menelaus) eloped to Troy with Paris, son of Trojan King Priam, we have all had to study the Trojan War. Helen's was "the face that launched a thousand ships."

Herculean
extraordinarily strong or large; difficult, dangerous. Hercules performed twelve great labors to atone for murdering his children. Work was easy for Herk. On the day of his birth he strangled two enormous serpents.

hydra-headed
an evil with many sources, difficult to control. The Hydra was a huge nine-headed serpent that Hercules had to kill. When one head was cut off, two grew in its place. (Sounds like the federal government.)

iridescent
having a rainbowlike play of colors, like a soap bubble. Iris, goddess of the rainbow, left a trail of colors as she carried the gods' messages to earth.

jovial
good-natured, jolly, expansive in nature. Jove, also called Jupiter, was king of the gods. (Zeus to the Greeks.) The *Ju* of Jupiter and the *Ze* of Zeus are an ancient root meaning shining sky.

Junoesque
queenly, statuesque, strikingly handsome (said of women). Juno, wife of Jupiter, was supposed to have been all of the above.

lethargy
sluggishness, torpor, languor, lassitude. The river Lethe ran through Hades (the underworld), and whoever drank of this river forgot his past.

martial
warlike; suited for army or military life. Mars, god of war, gave his name to the planet Mars and the month of March. (Ares is his Greek name.)

mentor
respected guide, teacher, or counselor. When Ulysses (Odysseus, hero of the Trojan War) left home to help out with the war, he left his respected, wise friend Mentor in charge of his son.

mercurial
volatile; as applied to mood, easily changeable. Messenger of the gods, Mercury also hid thieves from justice and guided souls to Hades—all very quickly. (Mercury also was the god of business, and so we have such words as **merchant, commerce,** and **merchandise.**)

mnemonics
the art of improving memory; a mnemonic device assists memory. Mnemosyne, one of Zeus's many wives, was goddess of memory.

morphine
an addictive narcotic. Morpheus was god of dreams and the son of Somnus, god of sleep. **Somnolent** means *sleepy.*

muse
source of inspiration or guiding genius; a poet. The nine Muses were daughters of Zeus and Mnemosyne, and they presided over the arts and sciences.

narcissism
self-love and admiration; extreme egotism. After the lovely nymph Echo faded into a faint sound because Narcissus didn't return her love, Nemesis punished the youth by causing him to fall in love with his own reflection in the fountain. Narcissus yearned for himself until he died and was metamorphosed into the trumpet-shaped white and yellow flowers we call by his name.

nemesis
relentless pursuer of evildoers; jinx, bane. Nemesis was goddess of retribution and punishment.

Neptune	*figuratively speaking, the ocean; a neptunist thinks the world emerged from water.* Neptune (Poseidon to the Greeks) was god of the sea and trainer of horses.
odyssey	*long wandering or voyage (often marked by change in fortunes).* Odysseus (Ulysses) was the hero of Homer's *Odyssey.* He spent ten adventure-filled years getting home after the Trojan War.
Olympian	*majestic, superior to others, regal or commanding.* Mount Olympus was the home of Zeus and his royal court.
paean	*hymn or song of praise or joy.* Paean was the physician of the gods, and his song invoked Apollo, god of healing.
Pandora's box	*source of ill or evil; a malign influence needing to be kept under control.* The myth that Pandora opened a sacred box that released all the evils into a perfect world is the Greek version of the Eve story, another old tale that blames all of the world's woes on a woman. (Now I ask you: is that logical?)
Parnassus	*having to do with poems; to climb Mount Parnassus is to write poetry.* Mount Parnassus, in Greece, was sacred to Apollo and the Muses.
pegasus	*extremely swift horse; poetic inspiration.* Pegasus was the winged steed of the Muses.
phoenix	*symbol of immortality; something that died and was reborn.* The phoenix was a fabulous bird that lived 500 years, perished in fire, and rose rejuvenated from its own ashes.
plutocracy	*government by the wealthy.* Pluto (Hades in Greek) was god of the underworld, a dark hideaway of valuable gems and gold (similar to today's "underworld").
Promethean	*unusually original and creative; life-giving.* Prometheus formed man from clay and stole fire from Mount Olympus for his use, giving mankind the potential to rival the gods. An eagle was sent to "persuade" Prometheus to tell Zeus which one of Zeus's sons would overthrow him.
protean	*assuming many shapes or forms; greatly adaptable.* Proteus, an old sea god, changed form and shape at will.
psyche	*the rational and spiritual in us; the soul or mind.* Psyche was the mortal girl beloved by Eros (Cupid). While he represented physical love, she embodied the spiritual side of love.
saturnalia	*wild party or orgy.* Saturn, god of sowing, was often a grim disciplinarian (from which we get **saturnine,** meaning *heavy, dour, dull*), but the festivals held in his honor were anything but grim. Saturnalias began on December 17, close to the winter solstice on the twenty-second, and continued riotously for days.
sibyl	*prophetess; fortune-teller.* The Sibyls were ancient Greek and Roman prophetesses.
Sisyphean	*needing to be redone, time and time again, unending.* After tattling on Zeus, Sisyphus, the king of Corinth, was condemned to Hades, forever to roll uphill a rock that always rolled right back down.
stentorian	*extremely loud, like a town crier's voice.* Stentor was the Greek herald whose voice was as loud as that of fifty men.
stygian	*gloomy, dark; hellish and frightening.* The river Styx carried the dead down into the Lower World on a ferry guided by Charon. Charon accepted only those souls who had received proper burial rites; other souls were doomed to wander.
tantalize	*to torment or tease.* Tantalus's punishment in Hades placed him in the center of a lake with water up to his chin—water that receded when he needed to drink—while overhead hung fruits forever out of reach.
terpsichorean	*referring to dance.* Terpsichore was the Muse of the Dance.

titanic   *gigantic in size, power, or both; awe-inspiring.* There were twelve Titans—six female and six male—of awesome size and strength. (Atlas was one.)

volcanoes   *erupting mountains, from the idea of Vulcan's steaming forges.*

vulcanize   *chemical treatment for rubber to enhance uses.* Vulcan was the Roman name of Hephaestus, master metalcraftsman of the gods. He created Achilles' armor, Apollo's chariot of the sun, and the first mortal woman, Pandora.

Zeus   *ruler, king.* Zeus, king of gods in Greek mythology, was Jove or Jupiter in Roman mythology. A Zeus has absolute power.

> **Note:** If these myths seem sexist to you, it's because they are. Old-time storytellers and scribes were nearly always men, and it's human nature to blame "the other team" for what went wrong. Human, but regrettable, because you can see that stories create and reinforce stereotypes.

WORDS FROM NAMES OF PEOPLE

Attila   Once, about A.D. 372, Attila the Hun was a ferocious and mangy-looking European conqueror. Anyone *now* known as Attila is *typically uncouth.* If you had a club, he'd be blackballed.

bacitracin   Marvelous for skin ailments, bacitracin is an antibiotic made from a bacillus that was found in the body of a girl named Margaret Tracy. *Bacitracin is an acronym: baci + Tracy + in.*

berserk   Berserk was an eighth-century Norse warrior, named after the bear skin (berserk) he'd had tailored for war. He fought like a crazy man, as did his twelve sons with him, and the group was known as Berserkers. (Good name for a rock group?)

bloomer   Amelia Bloomer, forerunner of women's liberation, was the suffragette from the late 1800s who urged women to give up their long, heavy skirts and wear her idea of trousers instead. Amelia's pants were baggy, tied tightly at the ankle, and worn under a knee-length outer skirt. They were never cute. Enlightened women of that day called themselves *bloomers;* now the word simply means *fullish pants, short or long.*

bowdlerize   Dr. Thomas Bowdler (1754–1825) decided that he should clean up literature, even Shakespeare's plays. He rewrote Lady Macbeth's famous cry, "Out, damned spot!" to read "Out, crimson spot!" To *bowdlerize* is *to rewrite to the detriment, not the improvement, of the original by removing or modifying offensive parts.* Supposedly, much of Chaucer and Mark Twain was bowdlerized.

    The following old, already carefully phrased little poem has been cited as a work that is probably safe from bowdlerization.

> No, no; for my Virginity,
>   When I lose that, says Rose, I'll die;
> Behind the elms, last Night, cry'd Dick,
>   Rose, were you not extremely sick?
>   —Matthew Prior (1664–1721)

boycott   Captain C. C. Boycott was an Irish land agent for an absentee owner in the late 1800s. Though people were starving, he refused to reduce rents. Everyone rebelled against him so totally that he was outcast; eventually he went home to England. His leaving meant a policy change for the boycotters. To *boycott* is to *refrain, as a group, from using or purchasing to force a change in policy.*

Casanova	The original Casanova was an eighteenth-century Italian hunk who must have been irresistible to women. He left memoirs, too, that cataloged just how wonderful he'd been and in how many countries. While *Romeo* conjures up the idea of a faithful lover, *Casanova* suggests a professional one.
chauvinist	Nicholas Chauvin was the soldier who worshiped Napoleon. His nauseating devotion irritated others, and after he was used as a character in a popular French play, his name caught on as a word. A *chauvinist* is *so devoted to a cause or opinion that judgment is affected—a blind patriot,* in other words.
derrick	Goodman Derrick was a hangman in England in the early 1600s. Now, any apparatus that hoists by means of a tackle at the end of a spar is termed a *derrick,* after the man and his noose.
Horatio Alger	Mr. Alger was the author of numerous books that always showed a poor boy making good in the end. The poor boy was loaded with sterling qualities and brains and lots of luck, which is still an unbeatable combination. Horatio Alger and Cinderella make a nice couple.
Machiavellian	A Renaissance Italian statesman, Niccolò Machiavelli thought that rulers could do whatever they wanted to keep a strong, central government. As a diplomat he was crafty and cunning. *Machiavellian* means *untrustworthy, conniving, and sneaky.*
McCarthyism	McCarthyism was born in the early fifties as a result of Joseph R. McCarthy's House Un-American Activities Committee, which investigated supposedly communistic citizens of the United States. His motives, his tactics, and his results have been shuddered over ever since. *McCarthyism suggests witch-hunting* and is a strongly negative term.
mesmerize	Anton Mesmer was the Austrian doctor who believed his hands held miraculous abilities to heal. He called it animal magnetism and he had great success, especially with hysterical patients. In the early 1800s, he was distrusted and feared by the medical community. Today, we call his "cure" hypnosis. A *mesmerist* is a *hypnotist.*
Nostradamus	Nostradamus was a physician-astrologer who made predictions famous for their accuracy back in 1555. His rhymed prophecies about our modern days are waiting for proof. Any *Nostradamus is a fortune-teller, a soothsayer.*
Pyrrhic	*describing a dubious victory, when more is lost than gained.* Pyrrhus, King of Epirus, was a brilliant military strategist living 200 years before Christ. One victory cost so many lives he admitted that he couldn't have any more similar "victories."
Rabelaisian	The French author François Rabelais, who wrote in the early 1500s, was known for his irreverence. He used embarrassingly descriptive language, and his satire was wildly broad. According to *Webster's Ninth New Collegiate Dictionary, Rabelaisian* means *"marked by gross robust humor, extravagance of caricature, or bold naturalism."* One of Rabelais's characters, the giant Gargantua, had a legendary appetite; as an infant he needed the milk of 17,913 cows. **Gargantuan** means *enormous, immense.* A *gourmand* probably has a gargantuan appetite.
stonewall	Meaning *not to yield an inch,* stonewalling grew out of General Stonewall Jackson's superb war tactics and bulldog tenacity. Thomas Jonathan Jackson, the Confederate genius of the Civil War, was accidentally but fatally wounded by his own men. His courageous name lives on.
Swiftian	Anything Swiftian, like Jonathan Swift's writing, is *strongly scornful* or mocking. His novel *Gulliver's Travels* and essay "A Modest Proposal" display the contempt Swift felt for mankind's stupid beliefs and behavior. *Swiftian satire* is biting and angry, not subtle.
thespian	Thespis was perhaps the first actor to speak lines separate from the Greek chorus. For this, he won a prize for tragedy in 534 B.C., thus laying the foundations for the Oscar award centuries later. *A thespian is an actor.*

Uncle Sam   The symbol we think of as Uncle Sam may have been named after Samuel Wilson, who helped to finance the Revolution. Uncle Sam represents the United States in the way that John Bull represents all Englishmen and Ivan represents the Russians.

Wagnerian   To say something is Wagnerian is to imply both *physical size* (as of Germanic opera divas) and *impressive power* like that of Richard Wagner's operas. His *Die Götterdämmerung (The Twilight of the Gods)* is music of unforgettable beauty and power. (It makes even boring jobs like waxing cars or cleaning rooms go better.)

WORDS FROM PLACE NAMES

bohemian   Bohemia was once believed to be the home of all the Gypsy tribes that roamed through Europe, and to be bohemian meant to be *nomadic or rootless.* Certain books and operas, and the roving artist-writers in them, were said to be bohemian, and now we have the concept of a poor artist or writer who lives a *free, nontraditional life.*

canopy   The Greek word *konops* means mosquito, and an Egyptian city named Canopus developed the canopy, *a cloth covering fixed or held above a person for protection, or sometimes for decoration.* Very early canopies were probably to keep out those danged mosquitoes.

donnybrook   The Irish fair at Donnybrook was, according to Bergen Evans, a scene of *"cheerful violence ... and sociable clouting of skulls by shillelaghs."* Any donnybrook is apt to be marked by fighting and brawling, and, if you want a **shillelagh,** look for a nearby oak tree to supply *a nice, stout club.*

dungaree   Dungarees or jeans date back to the strong cotton cloth woven in Dhungaree, India, and worn by gold miners in California in 1849. Levi Strauss, father of "Levi's," added the copper rivets. It has been estimated that more than half a billion yards of this fabric become salable products each year.

El Dorado   Indians in Colombia, South America, used to cover their king with gold dust as an annual ritual. He was *el dorado, the gold-covered one.* Eventually, this term meant the country where the king ruled, and later *a place of incredible wealth or good fortune.* Edgar Allan Poe's poem "Eldorado" ends:

> Ride, boldly ride,
> The shade replied,
> If you seek for Eldorado!

hackney   Hackney now means a horse; a special horse of English breed; a hired carriage; or a poor servant who does menial, tiring work. (Good ol' Charlie, he works like a horse.) Originally, this word was simply the name of Hackney, a region in Middlesex, England.

laconic   Laconia was the home of the Greek city Sparta. The Spartans were folk of few words because they were warriors and big-deed-doers. To be *laconic* is to be *brief and succinct of speech, to say as little as possible,* to be *pithy and terse.* Probably the most laconic exchange in writing was that between Victor Hugo and his publisher after *Les Misérables* was published. The author Hugo wrote: ? The reply he received read: !

limerick   The tiny town of Limerick, Ireland, gave its name to a most enjoyable verse form, the five-line limerick. Modern limericks are often suggestive, many unprintable, and extremely popular. An old anonymous, and memorable, limerick goes like this:

> There was a young lady of Kent
> Who said that she knew what it meant
>   When men asked her to dine
>   Gave her cocktails and wine,
> She knew what it meant—but she went!

marathon A marathon is anything that seems to go on forever—like school or a bad blind date. The original long-distance runner fell dead at the end of his run to Athens where he brought news of a victory at Marathon, in ancient Greece. Modern road races termed *marathons* are exactly 26 miles and 385 yards long.

meander The Asian river Meander, now called Menderes, winds and twists its way to the sea. If your speech or movements wend their way slowly, in twists and turns, you are said to *meander*.

sardonic An herb from Sardinia is so bitter that people who eat it go insane and, though sick, seem to be laughing. This laugh has been termed *rire sardonique* by the French and *sardonic* by the English. A *sardonic* expression is *superior, disdainful, scornful, and generally unpleasant.*

shanghai If you've been *fooled or coerced into a nasty job,* then you've been *shanghaied.* Originally this term referred to men kidnapped and shipped as sailors, often bound for Shanghai.

Spartan Spartans, from Sparta in Greece, were the original macho men. The story is told of the brave Spartan boy who, not wanting to admit theft, hid a stolen fox under his cloak. He was absolutely silent while the fox chomped on his vitals. (Some story.) To *suffer pain or unhappiness stoically* is to *be Spartan.* To live *without luxuries* is to follow a *Spartan* life.

sybaritic In contrast to the Spartans were the Sybarites, an old band of Greeks from southern Italy. Sybarites knew all about pleasure and were some of the first **hedonists,** people who seek pleasure as a way of life. A *sybaritic life* is *one of fun and luxuries* almost exclusively.

utopia The title of many books and imaginary places, utopia literally means "no place"; however, it stands as a symbol of our search for the perfect place. *Utopia, El Dorado, Erewhon* (*nowhere* almost spelled backwards), and *heaven* are similar—ideal locations that are probably unattainable.

Waterloo To meet one's Waterloo is to repeat Napoleon's dismal performance in his last battle and *lose.* If you're reading this now, you are working to see that college entrance exams are *not* your private Waterloo.

SUMMARY OF WORDS FROM SPECIAL PLACES

Consider these words as part of your basic word list, which comes later. Words appear with a capital letter if that is how they are most often used.

Babbitt	aeolian	* muse	boycott
Brobdingnagian	Apollo	* narcissism	Casanova
bumble	Atlantean	* nemesis	* chauvinist
Cinderella	Atlas/atlas	Neptune	derrick
Don Juan	* aurora	* odyssey	Horatio Alger
Dr. Pangloss	* bacchanal	Olympian	Machiavellian
Falstaffian	bacchanalian	paean	McCarthyism
Frankenstein	calliope	Pandora's box	mesmerize
Friday	Cassandra	Parnassus	Nostradamus
Galahad	centaur	pegasus	Pyrrhic
Jekyll and Hyde	* chimera	phoenix	Rabelaisian
* lilliputian	* cupidity	plutocracy	* stonewall
Little Lord Fauntleroy	erotic	Promethean	Swiftian
lothario	furor	protean	* thespian
* malapropism	fury	* psyche	Uncle Sam
Milquetoast	gorgon	saturnalia	Wagnerian
Pickwickian	* halcyon	* saturnine	* bohemian
Pollyanna	harpy	sibyl	canopy
pooh-bah	* hector	Sisyphean	donnybrook
* quixotic	Helen (of Troy)	* stentorian	dungaree
robot	Herculean	* stygian	El Dorado
rodomontade	* hydra-headed	* tantalize	hackney
scrooge	* iridescent	terpsichorean	* laconic
Simon Legree	* jovial	* titanic	limerick
Svengali	* Junoesque	volcanoes	marathon
Tartuffe	* lethargy	vulcanize	* meander
Uncle Tom	* martial	Zeus	* sardonic
Uriah Heep	* mentor	Attila	shanghai
Walter Mitty	merchant	bacitracin	* Spartan
yahoo	* mercurial	berserk	sybaritic
* Achilles' heel	mnemonics	bloomer	* utopia
Adonis	morphine	* bowdlerize	Waterloo

* These words are SAT and PSAT favorites, bound to reappear. Now that you know, wouldn't it be smart to learn them?

QUIZ: WHAT'S IN A NAME?

I.   **Giant Match-ups.** Match the word/name with the concept it represents.

_____ 1. bowdlerization	(a)	bully, torment
_____ 2. chauvinistic	(b)	oracle, soothsayer
_____ 3. hector	(c)	gross, robust humor
_____ 4. Machiavellian	(d)	wend your way slowly, with turns
_____ 5. Nostradamus	(e)	a clean rewrite
_____ 6. meander	(f)	all English people
_____ 7. bohemian	(g)	sneaky, deceitful
_____ 8. sardonic	(h)	men mow lawns; women are nurses
_____ 9. Sybarites	(i)	succinct, pithy, terse
_____ 10. stonewall	(j)	hedonists (pleasure lovers)
_____ 11. Spartan	(k)	free, nontraditional
_____ 12. Rabelaisian	(l)	Erewhon, El Dorado, heaven
_____ 13. John Bull	(m)	stoic, brave beyond belief
_____ 14. utopia	(n)	disdainful, scornful
_____ 15. laconic	(o)	refuse to budge

II. **Fill-ins.** Fill in the blanks to complete the sentences.

1. A rags-to-riches story is a _____ story.

2. "Rooty-ta-toot, rooty-ta-toot,
   We are the girls from the Institute.
   We don't smoke and we don't chew,
   And we don't go with boys who do."

   One of those girls might have been named _____.

3. Two classic lovers' names are _____ and
   _____.

4. When someone in the class said, "My aunt has bellicose veins," we couldn't help but laugh at his
   _____.

5. The sports team manager often has enough assorted duties to earn the title of
   _____.

6. If the dreams and hopes of people are _____, it's probably healthy; reality
   intrudes often enough to provide balance.

7. Sometimes the coach seems like _____. Still, if we survive training, we'll
   beat every team in our conference.

8. An object of _____ satire in our newspaper, the school cafeteria has shaped
   up and stopped serving mystery meat.

9. Two literary names that are synonyms for *hypocrite* are _____ and
   _____.

10. Most of us hope that our faults are _____ and our virtues more along
    _____ lines.

III. **Mythical Chaos.** The jumble below is like the Greek *chaos* before the world began and before the gods were created to bring order out of disorder and rule the universe. *You* create order by linking each word derived from a legendary figure with the idea he or she left behind. List the paired words in any order. There are twenty-one pairs.

mercurial   long journey   mentor   memory   inspiration   odyssey   jovial   jinx/bane   Adonis Cassandra   Achilles' heel   Third Kind encounter   Zeus   bacchanal   chimera   cupidity   frenzy demanding   male hunk   good-humored   loud   weak spot   scary hag   peaceful   doom prophet furor   lethargy   stentorian   life-giving   halcyon   torpor   Herculean   Mnemosyne   nemesis guide   volatile   muse   Jupiter   Promethean   saturnalia   avarice   omnipotent

1. _____
2. _____
3. _____
4. _____
5. _____
6. _____
7. _____
8. _____
9. _____
10. _____
11. _____
12. _____
13. _____
14. _____
15. _____
16. _____
17. _____
18. _____
19. _____
20. _____
21. _____

IV. **Names = Words to Remember.** For the following words, jot down a brief definition, and then select the best antonym for each word from the choices offered.

Word	*Definition*	*Antonym*
1. titan		
2. quixotic		
3. bacchanal (saturnalia)		
4. cupidity		
5. halcyon		
6. iridescent		
7. jovial		
8. lethargic		
9. mercurial		
10. saturnine		

Antonym Choices: unchangeable, jolly or jovial, active, funeral, midget, practical, gloomy, dull, generosity, chaotic.

FOREIGN WORDS AND PHRASES USED WITH ENGLISH

Some foreign words and phrases are used by English-speaking people in speech and writing because they give flavor to our language—sort of like salt in the soup. Other foreign expressions are used because there is no equally precise English expression. Whatever the reason, here are some words and phrases you will want to know and use. (L = Latin, F = French, It = Italian, Ger = German, Gr = Greek, Sp = Spanish)

Foreign word	*Meaning*
ad hoc (L)	with respect to this; for a particular purpose
alma mater (L)	one's old school; literally our fostering mother
aria (It)	fairly elaborate solo in operas, cantatas, etc.
bête noire (F)	your most hated thing; literally black beast
bona fide (L)	genuine; in good faith
bons mots (F)	clever, witty remarks; literally good words
bourgeois (F)	any person(s) of the middle class; implies tastelessness, so it's not a compliment
carte blanche (F)	full discretionary power; literally white paper
coup d'état (F)	decisive exercise of force or policy; stroke of state
cum laude (L)	with honor; *magna cum laude* = with great honor; *summa cum laude* = with highest honor
double entendre (F)	a word or expression allowing two interpretations, one often suggestive
e.g., exempli gratia (L)	for example
ersatz (Ger)	replacement or substitute, as *ersatz* coffee
et al., et alia (L)	and others
faux pas (F)	social blunder; literally false step
habeas corpus (L)	bring the person (before judge or court)
hasta luego (Sp)	until we meet again, as *adieu* and *au revoir* in French
ibid., ibidem (L)	in the same place (for footnotes)
i.e., id est (L)	that is, in other words (but *not* for example)
joie de vivre (F)	joy of living; joyous spirit
laissez-faire (F)	policy of noninterference; a letting alone
malfeasance (F)	illegal deed; often refers to official misconduct
N.B., nota bene (L)	note well; used for footnotes, reminders
non sequitur (L)	a phrase, concept, or reply that doesn't follow logically from what has gone before
quid pro quo (L)	this for that; a trade or barter
raison d'être (F)	reason for being or existence; e.g., dancing is Mikhail Baryshnikov's *raison d'être.*
subpoena (L)	A subpoena orders someone to appear at a specified time and place or face legal penalty.
tête-à-tête (F)	private conversation; literally head-to-head
touché (F)	a score, as in a contest or acknowledgment of a clever point; touched, as by a fencing weapon
tour de force (F)	a feat of power, strength, skill
vis-à-vis (F)	in relation to or as compared with; one thing as opposed to another; literally face to face

Unit 5: Basic Vocabulary

HOW TO LEARN NEW WORDS THROUGH USE, NOT MEMORIZATION

We have put the words in this unit of your book in the knowledge that you *can* learn them, not just *some* of them but *all of them*. Why? Because most of your brain cells go through life unused—empty. They just sit there waiting to be filled up with information. You have millions of them.

These words worth learning are divided into two categories: Plagued Pairs, a rather short list of homonyms and spellonyms, and the Basic Word Lists, composed of roughly 800 additional words. Another set of words selected for your study were presented in Unit 4 on roots and should be considered as part of the impressive vocabulary you are busy building.

If anyone tells you that you *can't* learn all these words, tell them, "Hogwash. I have brain cells I haven't even begun to use!" You know you can do it.

How to Do It

Take this book and get away somewhere by yourself where it's quiet. Read the list you plan to learn and read it slowly. (How many million times have you heard this advice? I tried not to say it, but I couldn't help myself, because *it works*.)

Flashcards? Yes!

Make flashcards of the words you find weird or difficult, hard to remember for some reason. **Flashcards are not babyish, and they work.** Keep the flashcards with you, like your lunch ticket. On the bus, in study hall, at night before you go to sleep, go over these stumpers.

Test Yourself

Take the quiz at the end of each list. It is designed to teach the words, not to be tricky. If you do fairly well, even though all words are not tested, chances are you know the list.

Occasionally, give the flashcards to your brother, sister, or parent and ask one of them to help you get ready for college entrance exams. Remind them that misery loves company. Moreover, when you have finished this book, say that you expect someone to *bake you a cake!*

PLAGUED PAIRS—AND THEN SOME

Homonyms you know. They're words that have different meanings and different spellings, but *sound the same. Two, too,* and *to,* for example.

Spellonyms (a made-up term) are words that have different meanings but are spelled so *nearly the same* that they mix people up—*torturous* and *tortuous,* for example, a sneaky pair if ever there was one.

STUDY THESE WORDS CAREFULLY

There is no easy way out. Sorry. These words must be learned.

---

to **abjure** ———➤ *to reject, renounce, or forswear*
　　　　　Charles *abjured* smoking when he went out for the cross-country team.
to **adjure** 　　　　　*to charge or command solemnly; to order*
　　　　　The three little kittens were *adjured* not to lose their mittens.

---

to **accept**	*to receive, take*

Most of us happily *accept* a compliment.

except (prep)	*but*

We all went ice-skating *except* Brian, who had a cold.

to **except** (v)	*to exclude, leave out*

I will *except* Brian from this exam, as he has been sick.

---

to **affect**	*to make a difference, to influence*

The weather *affects* my mood more than I'd like.

to **effect** (v)	*to bring about, cause to happen*

Our prisoner *effected* an escape by disguising himself.

effect (n)	*the result or outcome*

The *effects* of a drought are evident in the brown, dry countryside.

---

to **adapt**	*to modify; alter; adjust*

Our forebears *adapted* to new circumstances when they came to North America.

to **adopt**	*to take as one's own (a child, a puppy, a point of view, etc.)*

Our cat Fred *adopted* a superior air toward the puppy.

---

ascetic	*self-denying, austere* (like monks)

Ancient monks were extremely *ascetic*, denying themselves even basic comforts.

aesthetic	*referring to the sense of beauty*

A country drive in autumn, when the leaves are vividly colored, appeals to everyone's *aesthetic* sense.

---

averse	*strongly against, disinclined*

Like most cats, Fred is *averse* to shampooey baths.

adverse	*unfavorable, hostile, opposed*

The project was deferred because of *adverse* public opinion.

---

capitol (n)	*government building(s)*

The dome on our state *capitol* is covered in gold leaf.

capital (adj, n)	*all other uses, i.e., first-rate; a money stake; net worth; capital letter; seat of government (city)*

A gold-covered capitol is a *capital* idea! Of course, the citizens must have the *capital* needed to pay for such splendor.

---

censor (n)	*person judging/cutting offensive matter*

Film *censors* probably have interesting information to share at parties.

to **censor** (v)	*to edit or delete questionable material*

To *censor* or not to *censor*, that would be the question, wouldn't it?

censure (n)	*hostile criticism*

Private *censure* is difficult enough, but imagine the lives of those regularly criticized in newspapers.

to **censure** (v)	*to criticize harshly, find fault with*

Dad *censured* me at length when I rammed the car into the garage door.

---

complacent	*smug, self-satisfied* (like the Cheshire cat)

Everyone laughs at the *complacent* smile on Sylvester's face when he thinks he has outsmarted Tweety Bird.

complaisant	*amiable, docile, submissive*

Dogs are often obedient, *complaisant* pets, but cats do as they please most of the time.

---

complement (n)	*something that completes, goes well with*

The second algebra course acts as a *complement* to the first year's study.

to **complement** (v)	*to supply a lack, to complete*

His gregarious, convivial personality *complemented* her quiet, reflective temperament.

compliment (n)	*approving remark*

Your *compliments* are too generous, but they have often lifted my spirits.

to **compliment** (v)	*to speak approvingly*

How much more fun to *compliment* than to criticize!

contemptible   *hateful, deserving of contempt or scorn*
　　Nero is depicted as a *contemptible* Roman emperor.
contemptuous   *showing contempt or scorn*
　　Sophia, the stray pussycat, gave a *contemptuous* flick of ears and tail the first time we disciplined her.

---

credible   *believable, plausible*
　　His story was too slick to be *credible*.
creditable   *worthy of credit or merit*
　　The novice jumpers did not win ribbons but gave a *creditable* performance in their first horse show.
credulous   *gullible, innocent, naive*
　　Our Aunt Lilly is *credulous* enough to buy whatever a salesman touts.

---

to demur (v)   *to object, protest* (but not too strongly)
　　Mom *demurred* when I said I'd be out past midnight.
demure (adj)   *sedate, shy, modest, well-behaved*
　　In the 1800s, all girls were expected to be *demure* young ladies.

---

to deprecate   *to disapprove of with regret*
　　Mom sighs and shakes her head as she *deprecates* my use of "like" and "you know" in conversation.
to depreciate   *to go down in value, to undervalue*
　　No one expects his or her bank account to *depreciate*.

---

discrete   *separate, distinct*
　　We will study the *discrete* systems of the frog, beginning with its digestive system.
discreet   *showing good judgment, careful*
　　Any football player who's promised to be in early had better be *discreet* about late nights.

---

disinterested   *without prejudice or bias, neutral*
　　We expect a judge to render a *disinterested* verdict.
uninterested   *not interested*
　　At first Sophia kept to herself, *uninterested* in Fred's obvious feline charms.

---

diverse   *different, unlike, dissimilar*
　　After graduation, we'll go our *diverse* ways, some to work and others to schools far away.
divers   *several* (number)
　　Divers reasons persuade people to continue in school.

---

to elicit   *to draw forth* (information or a response), *to extract*
　　We could not *elicit* any further news from the doctor.
illicit   *illegal, against the law*
　　Illicit drug traffic terrifies any sensible person.

---

to elude   *to escape notice or apprehension*
　　Our cat Fred cleverly *eluded* the grasp of our sticky-fingered four-year-old cousin.
to allude   *to refer to indirectly, obliquely*
　　If you *allude* to his thinning hair, Tom strokes the remaining strands protectively.

---

to emend   *to correct by editing*
　　The playwright *emended* the scripts before rehearsals.
to amend   *to change slightly*
　　"I'd *amend* that to read 'Absolutely,'" Dad said as he suggested I change a word in my English paper.

---

equable   *even-tempered, steady, uniform*
　　Hal's *equable* nature makes him a class favorite.
equitable   *fair, just*
　　The lawyer recommended an *equitable* distribution of property among the heirs.

---

factious   *inclined to dispute* (to encourage factions), *seditious*
　　"One *factious* character among the crew has roused them all to mutiny," moaned the captain.
factitious   *artificial, sham*
　　Luckily for husbands, most wives are content with a *factitious* string of pearls.

formerly   *in times past, heretofore*
The new superintendent had *formerly* been principal of our high school.
formally   *following established form or custom*
We enjoyed seeing our classmates dressed *formally* for the prom.

---

gourmet   *lover of fine food* (e.g., Julia Child)
A *gourmet* particularly appreciates good cooking but may have no desire to do it.
gourmand   *lover of lots of fine food*
Confessing his fondness for food and wine, *gourmand* Orson Welles once said, "Gluttony is not a secret vice."

---

to hoard (v)   *to save for yourself; to keep safely*
A boy during World War II, my grampa *hoarded* bubble gum until it hardened into pink rocks in his bureau drawer.
horde (n)   *a swarm or teeming crowd*
Early American farmers dreaded a *horde* of locusts that could strip their grain crops in just a few hours.

---

to immigrate   *to move to another country or area*
Luckless farmers often *immigrate* to cities or towns.
to emigrate   *to leave your country and move elsewhere*
Many hungry families *emigrated* from Ireland during the great potato famine and settled in America.

---

indigenous   *native to an area, innate*
Cacti and lizards are *indigenous* to many deserts.
indigent   *poor, destitute, lacking necessities*
Desperate people in *indigent* countries are reduced to begging in order to survive.

---

ingenious   *inventive, clever*
We need an *ingenious* solution to this knotty problem.
ingenuous   *innocent, trusting, naive, gullible*
Dave's *ingenuous* smile reveals a trusting nature.

---

interment   *burial* (literally into earth)
The *interment* followed a brief graveside service.
internment   *imprisonment*
During her illness, Susan relieved the boredom of *internment* in the infirmary by playing solitaire.

---

later (adj, adv)   *occurring after something else in time*
(adj) Let's go at a *later* hour.
(adv) They left *later* than they had intended.
latter (adj)   *of two things, the one listed second; more recent*
"I didn't like your first suggestion," Dad said, "but the *latter* one has real merit."

---

to lie   *to recline, as on a bed*
Mom made me *lie* down for a nap after the slumber party.
to lay   *to put or place*
"Time is up. Please *lay* down your pens," said the instructor.

---

loath   *disinclined, reluctant* (to do something)
Loath to wade into the chilly water, Caroline gingerly tested the ocean with one toe.
to loathe   *to hate, detest, despise*
"Oh," she said, shivering, "I *loathe* cold water."

---

to lose (v)   *to misplace*
"Don't *lose* your mittens," adjured Mother Cat.
loose (adj)   *detached, free; not securely attached*
Loose, baggy pants have come back into style, as will all clothes if you hang onto them long enough.

---

marital   *of marriage*
Many churches offer *marital* counseling prior to the marriage ceremony.
martial   *warlike*
Judo and karate are only two of the *martial* arts.

nauseated *sick to the stomach*
That medication left him slightly *nauseated*.

nauseous *revolting or disgusting*
As kids, we made a *nauseous* mixture of red berries, mud, and dead bugs, which we called outdoor stew.

---

personable *pleasant, appealing*
Mac's *personable* nature wins him many friends.

personal *private, applying to oneself*
You didn't peek at my *personal* diary!

---

perspicacious *wise, shrewd, perceptive*
He chose the most *perspicacious* adviser on campus.

perspicuous *clear, easy to understand*
The law clerk rewrote the document to make it as *perspicuous* as possible.

---

principal (n) *the PAL in charge of the school*
Our student disciplinary board works closely with the *principal* of the school.

principal (adj) *main, chief, highest*
My *principal* reason for moving is to find a better job.

principle (n) *fundamental truth or ideal*
Shari won't compromise her *principles* by voting for someone she doesn't know.

---

to prophesy (v) *to foretell, predict*
Cassandra *prophesied* that the Greeks would destroy the city of Troy.

prophecy (n) *that which is foretold*
The Trojans failed to heed Cassandra's *prophecy* and opened their gates to the fatal Greek gift.

---

to prosecute *to bring legal action*
I decided to *prosecute* that firm in small claims court because their product was dangerously defective.

to persecute *to harass, annoy* (esp. for beliefs)
Sylvester *persecutes* Tweety Bird mercilessly.

---

to regale (v) *to entertain* (with food, jokes, etc.)
After their trip down the Colorado River, our neighbors *regaled* us with humorous anecdotes from their journey.

regal (adj) *referring to royalty*
Her naturally *regal* bearing made her perfect for the part of Elizabeth I.

---

social *referring to human society*
Anthropologists study *social* behavior in all the world's communities.

sociable *enjoying the company of people, friendly, amiable*
Rod's a *sociable* fellow who loves a big crowd.

---

tortuous *winding, twisted* (as a mountain road)
The *tortuous* path wound upward until it was lost in clouds and mist.

torturous *cruelly painful* (as torture is)
Wandering lost in the jungle was a *torturous* experience we'd like to forget.

---

urbane *sophisticated or polished* (of men)
David Niven was considered one of the screen's most *urbane* leading men.

urban *referring to cities*
The expression "*urban* blight" suggests the devastation wrought by careless use of property.

---

venal *open to bribery, corrupt*
Newspaper reporters feel it is their duty to expose *venal* public employees.

venial *excusable, minor*
Puritans were expected to avoid even the most *venial* sins if they hoped to save their souls.

---

vocation *job, career*
Brad has always planned on medicine as his *vocation*.

avocation *hobby*
Most writers feel they have combined vocation and *avocation* in the work they love.

QUIZ ON PLAGUED PAIRS

I.   **Words in Context.** Using the pairs below, select the word that fits correctly into each of the sentences. (Verbs may change tense and nouns may be either singular or plural, of course, depending on use.)

affect—effect	censor—censure	demur—demure
adapt—adopt	complement—compliment	elude—allude
emigrate—immigrate	contemptible—contemptuous	lose—loose

(handwritten: to get away; beat around bush)

1. Shirley stomped an angry foot, gave a(n) _____ toss of her head, and stormed out of the room.

2. The devastating __*affect*__ of the hurricane __*effected*__ every family and building in the tiny seacoast town.

3. The present of a matching green knit scarf and gloves was a fine __*complement*__ to my red and green Scotch plaid coat.

4. Hoping to __*elude*__ his tormentors, Norman squeezed under the old porch, where he would be hidden from view.

5. Grampa joked, "If I'm not careful, I'll __*lose*__ these pants, because they're too __*loose*__ around the waist."

6. Jean hadn't been in the dorm long before she _____ its philosophy; quiet hours were necessary after all.

7. Many of our relatives _____ from northern Europe and were then called _____ in the newly formed United States.

8. My boss's stiff _____ was hard to take, and I cringed under his verbal attack.

9. When we asked for the car keys, Dad _____ , saying that the car needed repair and was unsafe.

10. Aunt Myra is ill, but we never _____ to her sickness around her, since she asked us not to talk about it.

ANSWERS to all quizzes can be found in the back of the book, beginning on p. 417.

II.   **Analogies.** Analyze the relationship between the first two words. State it as simply and precisely as possible. Then look for a word from the Plagued Pairs list that accurately completes the relationship.

1. judgmental : censor :: _____ : monk

2. know-it-all : complacent :: Pollyanna : _____

3. Brobdingnagian : lilliputian :: _____ : lowercase

4. abjure : forswear :: bring about : _____

5. approve : deprecate :: _____ : prejudiced

6. Luke Skywalker : intrepid :: judge : _____

7. current : formerly :: _____ : wealthy

8. native : foreign :: _____ : alien

9. nauseous : stench :: _____ : dictionary

10. martial : marital :: discreet : _____ (Special trick—are you a linguist?)

III.   **Antonyms.** Select the best antonym or opposing phrase for each numbered word and write it on the line.

_____ 1. hoard	(a) peaceable
_____ 2. loath	(b) ingenuous
_____ 3. venal	(c) humble
_____ 4. personable	(d) of minor importance
_____ 5. discreet	(e) to squander, waste
_____ 6. urbane	(f) aloof
_____ 7. allude	(g) straight
_____ 8. deprecate	(h) inclinded, apt to
_____ 9. martial	(i) reckless
_____ 10. regal	(j) incorruptible
_____ 11. principal	(k) obtuse
_____ 12. tortuous	(l) disagreeable
_____ 13. sociable	(m) freedom
_____ 14. perspicacious	(n) to cite
_____ 15. internment	(o) to approve

IV.   **Quick Reminders.** Complete each sentence with the appropriate word from Plagued Pairs.

1. To reject, renounce, or forswear something is to _____ it.
2. _____ weather conditions are unfavorable or hostile, e.g., storms, freezing temperatures, high winds.
3. To criticize harshly is to _____ .
4. A believable, plausible story is _____ .
5. _____ persons seem to enjoy setting people at odds with one another.
6. A word meaning to bring legal action is _____ .
7. When you foretell or predict an event, you are _____ . (Use gerund form.)
8. Your _____ is that which you foretold.
9. _____ is to charge solemnly, to command or order.
10. The physician testing your reflexes hopes to _____ physical responses.

BASIC WORD LISTS

These words, which are divided into eighteen lists, were chosen with care and over a period of years. They are words that crop up repeatedly on college entrance exams and in advanced vocabulary lists. Words that you can puzzle through by knowing roots and prefixes have been omitted. Instead, those whose meanings are harder to figure out, whose clues are not obvious, were selected for study.

As a key to learning, let the sentences that illustrate each word do their jobs. Read each separate sentence several times to get a feel for the word in context. Check to see whether or not a word you're studying has a negative or positive connotation. Do the quiz at the end of each list, and the quiz itself will *fix* words in your mind. And don't worry about missing items on the quiz—what better place to learn?

Abbreviations

n = noun
v = verb
adj = adjective
adv = adverb

+ following a word means that its connotation is usually *positive*.
– following a word means that its connotation is usually *negative*.
* denotes which of several meanings is illustrated by the sentence.

List 1

abate (v)	*to become less in intensity; to subside, slacken, wane, or decrease* When the hurricane winds finally *abated*, we went outside to assess the damage to our house and garage.
abdicate (v)	*to give up, renounce, relinquish* (often formally) The king thundered at his daughter, "Would you *abdicate* your right to be queen by marrying that pipsqueak playwright?"
aberration (n) –	*straying from what is right, normal, or expected*; a mental straying that is strange or deviate* Uncle Harvey's humorous *aberrations* are understandable in a man who has always been a determined individualist.
abet (v) –	*to help or encourage a bad act; to egg on, foment, instigate* The law has penalties for those who aid and *abet* a criminal.
abeyance (n)	*a condition of suspended activity or development* (use after **in**) "We'll hold the plans for our class trip in *abeyance* until we have voted on the budget," said our class president.
abhor (v) –	*to hate or loathe; to dislike strongly, even to fear; to reject* Jill has *abhorred* snakes ever since she was scared by one in her sleeping bag last summer at camp.
aborigine (n)	*original person in a place* (as a native) The Australian *aborigine* has been the subject of many interesting TV programs.
abort (v) –	*to fail to go forward or develop as expected; to miscarry; to terminate early** The mission of *Columbia* had to be *aborted* for several reasons, one of which was bad weather.
abrasive (adj) –	*causing bad feelings of irritation or annoyance* The last thing a salesperson should have is an *abrasive* personality that sends customers hurrying away.
abscond (v) –	*to run off in secret* (usually because of bad actions or feelings/knowledge of guilt) Did you say that the French Club treasurer had *absconded* with our entire treasury and is now skiing in the Poconos?
absolve (v) +	*to free of guilt or blame; to exonerate, exculpate* The witness's testimony *absolved* Harold of any wrongdoing.
abstemious (adj)	*restrained in consuming strong drink or food; moderate, restrained* A deeply religious man, concerned about his health, Gregory has always been *abstemious* in his habits.
abstract (adj)	*not concrete or definite, thus hard to grasp or understand*; impersonal or detached in attitude* Brett had trouble as soon as he left the definite, concrete problems of math and moved on to *abstract* principles.
abstract (n)	*a written summary*
abstruse (adj)	*extremely difficult to understand; erudite, recondite* The *abstruse* calculations necessary to locate distant stars boggle my mind.
accolade (n) +	*verbal praise; award; or recognition of accomplishment* Merry bowed to the cheering audience and basked in their *accolades* backstage after her performance.
accrue (v)	*to accumulate, pile up, collect; to grow* (as a bank account) "I wish the interest on my bank account would *accrue* at a faster rate," sighed Carl.

acerbity (n) – | *bitterness, acrimony; having a biting, acidic nature, mood, or quality*
Scrooge's *acerbity* permeates his speech and actions, allowing readers to hear his sharp remarks cutting the air.

acme (n) | *the highest point or peak of achievement; zenith*
"I think," the mountain climber reflected, "that the *acme* of my career came when we conquered Everest."

acquiesce (v) | *to give in and agree without a fuss; to comply, assent*
Privately, we hated Grandfather's rules; publicly, we *acquiesced* to avoid awkward scenes that would have embarrassed our folks.

acronym (n) | *word formed from the initial letter(s) of a longer term*
The word *sonar* is an *acronym* for *so*und *na*vigation *r*anging.

acumen (n) + | *keen perception, shrewdness, and discernment*   [handwritten: your aware of your surroundings]
We studied industrial leaders who were famous for their business *acumen*.

adamant (adj) | *firm and unyielding; inflexible even when opposed*
Fred's *adamant* refusal to go out into the snowy weather demonstrates just how stubborn a cat can be.

adjudicate (v) | *to act as a judge or determiner*
"We will *adjudicate* the matter known as Andy's Missing Oreos as soon as we come in from recess," said my little brother's teacher.

admonish (v) | *to warn strongly or show disapproval; to reprove* / re   [handwritten: to criticize]
When I mistakenly left the car radio on all night and the car's battery was dead in the morning, Dad *admonished* me not to repeat my performance if I wished to continue enjoying my driving privileges.

adulation (n) + | *praise, flattery,* even *worship*
Hero worship is one form of *adulation*; yelling in appreciation at a rock concert is another.

advocate (n) | *a person who pleads a case* (as a lawyer)

advocate (v) | *to talk in favor of; to support, recommend*
Dwayne *advocates* swift justice and the availability of a professional *advocate* for needy people.

aesthetic (adj) | *referring to a sense of beauty*; artistic*
A visit to an art museum might awaken *aesthetic* senses you didn't know you had.

affable (adj) + | *easy to get along with; genial, friendly, warm*
You might have disagreed with Dwight Eisenhower's politics, but it was hard to resist his *affable* personality and innate dignity.

affinity (n) | *natural inclination or tendency; attraction to or kinship with*
Because they are nocturnal creatures, cats have a natural *affinity* with the night.

affluent (adj) + | *wealthy, rich*
Between the *affluent* "haves" and the indigent "have-nots" lies a gulf in understanding that makes communication difficult.

aggravate (v) – | *to make worse*; to exacerbate, burden, intensify, or irritate*
You will *aggravate* your swollen ankle if you go hiking.

aggregate (adj) | *total or combined amount of*
The *aggregate* earnings at our class flea market set a school record for fund-raisers.

agnostic (n) | *a person who thinks that God is unknown, probably unknowable; one who doubts and questions*

agnostic (adj) | *doubting or questioning regarding God and his nature*
If you want to hear a hot argument, just get my *agnostic* brother together with Frank, who is a devout Baptist.

[handwritten left margin: Atheist believes there is no god]

agrarian (adj)
referring to fields, lands, and their crops
Iowa State University in Ames has long been a Midwestern center for *agrarian* research.

alacrity (n) +
eagerness, willingness, or liveliness; celerity
Hal accepted Kim's invitation to the pool party with *alacrity* and said he'd try to borrow his dad's car for their date.

allay (v)
to lower in intensity or severity (as fears); *to assuage, relieve, calm, alleviate*
The veterinarian *allayed* our fears about our dog's sickness, saying that Chumley would be his old, spaniel self in a few days.

allegory (n)
a story using figurative language and characters*; a symbolic portrayal
Animal Farm, by George Orwell, is an *allegory* in which animals represent different human types and ideologies.

allocate (v)
to portion out or allot*; to distribute, designate
Jason *allocated* the west side of the barn to us for our 4-H project this spring.

allude (v)
to hint at or refer to indirectly, without specific mention
My sister and I *alluded* to Aunt Molly's dyed-orange hair, but Mom gave us a dirty look and sent us outside before we got into real trouble.

aloof (adj)
reserved or cool in manner; apart because of lack of involvement*, thus *removed*
Our older brother remained *aloof* as we planned how to turn the neighborhood empty lot into a health spa.

altercation (n) –
noisy fight or quarrel; angry dispute
The debate, which had started peaceably enough, soon turned into an *altercation* that left bitter feelings behind.

altruism (n) +
unselfish giving of time, money, interest, or support to others
Many revered saints lived lives of unusual *altruism*.

ambiguous (adj)
not clear or definite; obscure, uncertain
"His answer was *ambiguous,* and now I don't know any more than I did before," fumed Alicia.

ameliorate (v) +
to make better or to improve
Historically, we have tried to *ameliorate* the desperate conditions of developing countries.

QUIZ ON LIST 1

I.   **Words in Context.** From the words given, choose the ones that fit *best* into the sentences, using clues in context as your guide. Number and tense may be changed to fit context.

abate	agnostic — doubts believes in god	accrue — pile up
abeyance suspended activity	allegory	advocate (n and v) to support
accolade – award	altruism – unselfish	affinity -
acerbic – biterness	abet – egg on	alacrity eagerness
admonish to criticize	abort	allude to hint
aesthetic	abstruse difficult to understand	allay to relieve

1. It took Jeffrey more than two years to _____ *accrue* _____ sufficient vacation time for his trip to Europe.

2. My Uncle Harold was an _____ *agnostic* _____, forever in doubt about the nature of God. He asked me questions about the subject that I couldn't answer, since the subject seems so _____ *acerbic* _____ to me.

3. That painting, with its subtle blends of blues and purples, appeals to the ____aesthetic____ senses of everyone who sees it.

4. "Let me ____allay____ your fears," said the physician. "Your son will be out of danger and home before you know it."

5. If the enemy's siege does not ____abate____ soon, we will starve to death here inside the fort, where there is no more food.

6. When one thing after another went wrong, we were almost forced to ____abort____ our camping trip and set another date.

7. Bunyan's *Pilgrim's Progress* is one of the more famous pieces of figurative fiction in English. It is read as the perfect example of an ____allegory____.

8. Children and teenagers seem to have an ____affinity____ for malls, but as an adult I always avoid them.

9. Those familiar with the law know that it's a crime to _____ any person in a criminal act.

10. The _____ of your idea was never questioned, only your ability to carry through with such high ideals.

11. Because of threatening weather we'll have two plans, one held in ____abeyance____ to save the festival if it rains.

12. Parents or guardians who ____admonish____ too much may find themselves ignored as time goes on and lectures grow too frequent.

13. You'll need someone on your side in the debate, won't you, an ____advocate____ to plead your case with the administration?

14. There are some jobs that, even though they're work, people do with cheerful ____alacrity____, while other jobs cause all of us to drag our feet.

15. A good time to have ____accolade____ heaped upon your head is at graduation.

16. For the sake of friendship or good relationships, it's often better to ____allude____ to unpleasantness than to speak about it directly.

17. "In high school," said the teacher, "we ____abstruse____ a strong program of English, math, and science."

18. Mike made some ____abet____, nasty remark, and that's how we almost got in a fight with those lifeguards.

138   Basic Vocabulary/Unit 5

II.   Antonyms. From the list on the right, choose the best antonym for each vocabulary word.

_____ C _____	1. abrasive	(a) object
_____ E _____	2. abhor	(b) cite *quote*
P _____ A _____	3. acquiesce	(c) soothing
_____ G _____	4. abstract	(d) aggravate
_____ _____	5. acme	(e) love
_____ J _____	6. acrimony – sharp/severe	(f) nadir *Low point*
_____ K _____	7. alacrity	(g) concrete – firm
_____ I _____	8. adulation worship	(h) poor
_____ L _____	9. affable	(i) condemnation *damn*
_____ H _____	10. affluent	(j) sweetness, gentleness
_____ M _____	11. ambiguous	(k) reluctance – hesatant
_____ N _____	12. altercation	(l) irritable
_____ O _____	13. aloof	(m) definite
_____ B _____	14. allude	(n) accord, agreement
_____ D _____	15. ameliorate	(o) involved, caring

III.   Favorite SAT/PSAT Word Families. Certain roots are the basis of many words frequently found on the SAT and PSAT. Match these "repeat offenders" on the left with their synonyms or definitions on the right. Write your answers on the lines.

A. ACER = sharp, bitter

_____	1. exacerbate	(a) burning, stinging, pungent
_____	2. acrid	(b) pointed or keenly perceptive
_____	3. acrimony	(c) rancorous, biting, caustic
_____	4. acrimonious	(d) to aggravate, make worse
_____	5. acute	(e) acerbity, bitterness

B. LEV = light, to raise

_____	6. alleviate	(f) to lift up, raise
_____	7. levity	(g) to allay, relieve
_____	8. leverage	(h) power or effectiveness
_____	9. levitation	(i) lightness, humor
_____	10. elevate	(j) buoyancy; the illusion of the human body in air without support

IV.   Analogies. Choose the lettered pair that most nearly expresses the relationship of the given pair.

1. ABORIGINE : BUSH ::
   (A) thief : palace (B) explorer : ship (C) advocate : court (D) conductor : podium
   (E) postman : office

2. BEHAVIOR : ABERRANT ::
   (A) illness : contagious (B) response : ambiguous (C) retort : rapid (D) life-style : aesthetic
   (E) fear : allayed

3. SEATS : ASSIGN ::
   (A) awards : vote (B) candidates : elect (C) cookies : bake (D) portions : allocate
   (E) plans : design

4. FARM : AGRARIAN ::
   (A) cattle : docile (B) skyscraper : urban (C) museum : ancient (D) corporation : financial
   (E) apartment : efficient

5. MANAGER : ACUMEN ::
   (A) author : allegory (B) monk : abstemiousness (C) minister : agnosticism (D) clerk : adjudication
   (E) scientist : acronym

List 2

amiable (adj) +	*warm, friendly, easy to get along with; congenial, sociable* The words *amiable, amicable,* and *amity,* which come from the Latin word **amicus = friend,** all connote a friendly warmth and sociability.
amnesty (n) +	*pardon or acceptance (by government) of some group behavior* (as **amnesty** for refugees) Many veterans were filled with anger when the government granted *amnesty* to some draft dodgers.
anachronism (n)	*a thing out of place in time;* thus *a chronological error* A horse-drawn fruit and vegetable cart on suburban streets today would be a delightful and welcome *anachronism* for shoppers.
anarchy (n) –	*absence of government, often resulting in lawlessness and disorder* The tiny island was plunged into *anarchy* when its king fled north and took his ruling cabinet with him.
anathema (n) –	*curse* or formal ban; something or someone denounced in a strongly disapproving manner* To the werewolf, wolfsbane and a cross are *anathema.*
animosity (n) –	*strong dislike, even hate; enmity, hostility** We quarreled so much as children that some of the old *animosity* may still flare up when my sister and I get together.
animus (n)	*basic spirit, attitude, or intention*;* also *a spiteful feeling of ill will* Rob questioned the *animus* of his drill sergeant, wondering if Sergeant Jones meant all of the recruits to drop out of basic training.
annals (n)	*historical records; chronicles* In the *annals* of our town are accounts of early hand-to-hand combat with the native Indian tribes.
annihilate (v) –	*to wipe out, to destroy almost entirely; to vanquish, abolish* Speaking of Indians, wasn't Custer's troop *annihilated* by superior Indian forces?
anomaly (n)	*something different from the norm, irregularity or paradox* Our cat Fred is one of those lovable *anomalies,* a cat who cuddles, licks our hands, and follows us around like a puppy.
antipathy (n)	*extreme dislike or aversion; distaste, enmity* Fred likes people, but shows his *antipathy* for dogs by arching his back and glaring balefully at any canine.
antithesis (n)	*a direct opposite* That program is the *antithesis* of everything I enjoy watching and listening to, so I am turning off the TV set.
apathy (n) –	*lack of feeling; indifference, impassiveness* Uncle Bert's indifference to oatmeal is matched only by his *apathy* toward tapioca.
aphorism (n)	*short statement of principle, belief; adage, proverb* Ben Franklin wrote, "Experience keeps a dear school, but fools will learn in no other," and other *aphorisms* that have survived since the late 1700s.

aplomb (n) +

absolute cool; complete poise and self-confidence
Jenny's *aplomb* as she sang and danced in our school musical was envied by the rest of us in the cast.

apostate (n)

person who renounces a faith or a commitment to a previous loyalty
People who became *apostates* and left Jim Jones's weird cult were most fortunate, because many of the group subsequently died.

appalling (adj) –

shocking or dismaying; causing fear, disgust, or even horror
With his Golden Fleece award, Senator Proxmire attacked the grants and government programs he considered an *appalling* waste of money.

appease (v)

to quiet, calm, allay, soothe, pacify, or conciliate
His hunger and weariness somewhat *appeased* by a meal, the pony express rider leaped on a fresh horse and was gone.

apprehension (n) –

the fear of evil, thus a foreboding*; conception or comprehension of someone or something
The elderly couple viewed winter's approach with *apprehension*, dreading the ice storms and snow-covered streets.

arable (adj) +

suited to cultivation or the growing of crops; tillable
The price of *arable* land has gone up so much that would-be farmers need big money if they plan to buy a farm.

arbitrary (adj) –

according to wish or desire, decided by choice rather than merit; in a despotic or tyrannical way
Almost everyone respects a fair decision and loathes an *arbitrary* or capricious one.

arcane (adj)

known only to a select few people, therefore mysterious* or secret
Currently lost in the darkness of time, the *arcane* folklore of Stonehenge would be a fascinating discovery.

archives (n)

place for public records; the records themselves*
Establishment of a town as a national historic district requires researchers to spend many hours with local, county, and state *archives*.

arduous (adj)

demanding, difficult, and hard to achieve; strenuous, hard
Careful polishing of a car may be *arduous*, but the resulting shine is a terrific reward.

arrogance (n) –

the feeling of superiority shown by an overbearing manner*; excess pride
In olden times, serfs expected and accepted a certain *arrogance* in great landowners and noblemen, but today we rarely admire or tolerate an arrogant nature.

articulate (adj) +

*clearly spoken, intelligible and coherent (as an **articulate** person)*

articulate (v)

to speak distinctly and clearly; to enunciate; to put into a logical whole or group*
Melinda's school *articulated* a music program that began in kindergarten and continued through high school.

askance (adv) –

in a disapproving manner; scornfully
Wouldn't you suppose the townspeople looked *askance* at Lady Godiva perched upon her pony?

askew (adj) –

out of line or place; awry
For her part, Godiva probably hoped that her hair would remain carefully in place and not be blown *askew* in the breeze.

asperity (n) –

roughness or harshness of manner; acrimony
Whoever plays the part of Cinderella's irritable stepmother must speak with *asperity* to portray the character correctly.

assiduous (adj) +

marked by careful, diligent attention; persistent
Michael's *assiduous* attention to the harder math problems paid a big dividend last week when he helped the school math team score a major victory.

astute (adj) +

wise, shrewd, and perceptive; perspicacious
Making *astute* decisions about investments is a skill everyone would like to cultivate.

atavism (n)

harking back to a form of an earlier time (an individual exhibiting *atavism* would be termed a **throwback,** like Buck in *Call of the Wild*)
In *Planet of the Apes,* Charlton Heston played a man and was therefore an *atavistic* creature in the apes' culture since the apes believed they had progressed far beyond mankind.

atheist (n)

person who says there is no God
A powerful expression of *atheistic* philosophy is Mark Twain's "The Mysterious Stranger," in which Twain reveals his deeply pessimistic nature through a character who denies the Christian concept of God.

atrophy (v) –

to waste away (as muscles) *from a debilitating illness*; to degenerate, wither*
Betty was reluctantly put into a brace to support her left leg, which had *atrophied* as a result of polio.

attest (v)

to affirm or authenticate; to prove, testify, verify
We can *attest* to the raccoon's ingenuity; he figured out how to open the coonproof contraption Dad made for our garbage can.

audacious (adj) +

adventurous and bold; intrepid, daring, even rash
That same *audacious* coon has been christened Fearless by my sister.

augment (v)

to increase; to make something greater or larger
Every few months we *augment* the supplies in our meat freezer by going to the farmers' market and buying large, fresh cuts of beef and pork.

augur (v)

to foretell, presage (as from omens); *to predict*

augur (n)

person who foretells events
Those winds *augur* well for the sailing regatta today, and, if we were in ancient Greece, we would ask an *augur* to read birds' entrails and predict the winner of the race.

auspices (n)

sponsorship or patronage; also *favorable or prophetic signs* (as the **auspices** look good); **auspicious** (adj), *favorable, promising, of good omen*
My old summer camp still operates under the *auspices* of the YM-YWCA.

austere (adj)

reserved, somber, or grave in manner; unadorned;* also *abstemious or ascetic; restrained*
As children, we were put off by Aunt Dorothea's reserved, *austere* manner, but as adults we've learned to admire her strength.

autocratic (adj) –

*absolute in the sense of final; dictatorial, despotic**
A poor quality for a judge would be a tendency toward whimsical or *autocratic* decisions.

avid (adj)

*extremely eager or very greedy; fond of or devoted to**
Jim is an *avid* bread baker and spends every Saturday morning creating a variety of treats for his friends.

bailiwick (n)

distinct area; a person's normal territory or jurisdiction
Westside Preparatory School is educator Marva Collins's special *bailiwick.*

balm (n)

anything that soothes or makes you feel better
After running several miles, Tim reached the bridge where he'd hidden his water bottle, *balm* for his parched throat.

QUIZ ON LIST 2

I. **Matching.** Match words from the vocabulary list with their synonyms.

_____	1. amiable	intention
_____	2. animosity	congenial
_____	3. anomaly	curse
_____	4. antithesis	dislike
_____	5. apathy	indifference
_____	6. appalling	shocking
_____	7. arduous	diligent
_____	8. assiduous	abnormality
_____	9. anathema	opposite
_____	10. animus	demanding
_____	11. askance	soothsayer
_____	12. austere	reserved
_____	13. askew	scornfully
_____	14. audacious	awry
_____	15. augur	intrepid

II. **Synonyms.** Choose the word most nearly the same in meaning as the first word.

1. amnesty   (a) enmity   (b) government   (c) pardon   (d) anger
2. aphorism   (a) rule   (b) proverb   (c) an herb   (d) belief or creed
3. aplomb   (a) fruit   (b) poise   (c) straight line   (d) weapon
4. articulate   (a) intelligible   (b) map line   (c) thing or possession   (d) part of the eye
5. atrophy   (a) award   (b) moose head   (c) hatred   (d) degenerate

III. **Words in Context.** Read the phrase. Then select the vocabulary word that fits best into context.

balm	atavistic	anachronism
bailiwick	astute	annals
autocratic	augur	apostate
auspices	anarchy	apprehension
augment	attest	arable

1. can't help because it's out of my _____
2. the frightening _____ after the rebellion
3. sun that _____ well for my tanning program
4. a(n) _____ urge to return to the wilderness
5. wanting _____ for his aching muscles
6. fist thumped the table in a(n) _____ way
7. will _____ to my innocence by corroborating my story
8. enviably _____ decisions about crop planting
9. bazaar held under the _____ of the hospital guild
10. ought to _____ your allowance by mowing lawns
11. turned _____ after an acrimonious dispute with the church council
12. irrigation having converted the desert into _____ land
13. the clock in *Julius Caesar*, an obvious _____

14. faithfully recorded in the _____ of our town

15. understandable _____ on confronting her old enemy

IV. **Antonyms.** Select the best antonym or opposing phrase to write on each line.

_____	1. annihilate	(a) amity
_____	2. appease	(b) equitable, fair, just
_____	3. arcane	(c) humility
_____	4. antipathy	(d) timid
_____	5. asperity	(e) to mumble
_____	6. arbitrary	(f) to establish, found
_____	7. arrogance	(g) uninterested in, averse to
_____	8. audacious	(h) to exacerbate
_____	9. articulate	(i) well-known
_____	10. avid	(j) gentleness, kindness

List 3

banal (adj) – *stale from overuse; trite, insipid, commonplace*
"Any more of Harry's *banal*, century-old jokes, and I'm leaving this party," Sara told her roommate.

bane (n) – *source of bad luck or harm; curse, destruction*
The *bane* of John's college existence was Dr. Grindle, who insisted on correcting every tiny error in John's lab technique.

baroque (adj) *extravagant, elaborate style of decoration or presentation; ornate, as music or literature*
We are fascinated by Melissa's absolutely *baroque* life. Her huge Victorian house, complex career, and elaborate clothing intrigue us.

bellicose (adj) – *looking for a fight; aggressive, feisty, warlike*
Historians write that native tribes in England were *bellicose* and territorial, always contending for supremacy.

bellwether (n) *a leader, one who will take charge*

Surviving from the Middle Ages, the word *bellwether* once meant the leading sheep of the flock who wore a bell round his neck. Where he went, others followed, the sign of a true leader.

When someone told Bill he was the *bellwether* of the state senate, he replied, "Does that mean I'm an old ram or goat?"

benign (adj) + *gentle, gracious, kind*; mild or favorable, not malignant*
Once depicted as a god of wrath, the Christian Lord is now most often shown wearing a *benign* expression of love.

beset (v) – *to trouble, harass, or hem in*
The exhausted fox, *beset* by eager hounds, looked frantically for a way to escape pursuit or a place to hide.

bias (n) *diagonal line; prejudice or personal outlook*; bent, tendency*
Unfortunately, a person's *bias* on a given subject may prevent him from ever hearing the facts on that subject.

bicker (v) – *to quarrel over little things; quibble, argue*
One of the most amusing songs from *The Music Man* is about *bickering*. "Pick-a-little, talk-a-little, cheep, cheep, cheep. . . ."

bigot (n) –

hypocrite; intolerant person who thinks his way is the only way
It takes a talent like Carroll O'Connor's to make a *bigot* almost lovable, as the Archie Bunker character certainly was in the television series.

bilk (v) –

to cheat or defraud
The traveling magicians managed to *bilk* our townspeople thoroughly, absconding with several hundred dollars after a one-night stand.

blasphemy (n) –

profanity, as a lack of respect for God; swearing about something sacred
One thing that always riled our aunt was our cussing, which she termed *blasphemy* in a ringing voice as she punished us with mouthfuls of soapsuds.

blatant (adj) –

embarrassingly obvious, loud, or showy; brazen, tasteless
With *blatant* disregard of the club's rules, Rachel stomped noisily into the meeting, cracked her gum, and whispered repeatedly to her neighbor.

blithe (adj) +

cheerful, merry, and lighthearted*; casual, heedless
Once a popular name for girls, *Blithe* suggested someone who was cheerful and sunny in disposition.

boor (n) –

person lacking manners or sensitivity; clod, yokel
Millie said, "Jerry's fun, but he's always such a *boor* at my Gramma's house, and she's a stickler for manners."

bourgeois (adj)

middle class, thus *common* (said of things or persons in a capitalistic, i.e., business-oriented, society)

The *bourgeoisie*, or merchant class of people, emerged from the ranks of lower-class serfs as their small businesses or work guilds grew into money-making ventures. These folk were resented by the very poor, who hadn't made similar economic progress, and were hated as upstarts by the old rich, who weren't ready to share the pie with anyone. Thus, they were caught in the middle—the trade folk—truly accepted only by one another.

"Hmmph!" sniffed Clarice. "I abhor the summer people with their *bourgeois* clothes and manners." (But Clarice, no one loves a snob.)

bovine (adj)

cowlike; patient and slow-moving; dull or placid
There's a kind of *bovine* peace and relaxation that's a balm for weary minds each afternoon in the barn at milking time.

brackish (adj) –

rather salty; unappealing
Though the water in those marshes is *brackish* and foul-smelling to us, the birds all seem to like it.

brandish (v)

to wave about in a threatening way; to swing (a weapon) *back and forth; to flourish with a flair*
In *Raiders of the Lost Ark*, Harrison Ford *brandished* a cutlass with convincing menace.

brigand (n)

bandit or thief (used in a less negative sense than you might think)
Often in literature, a pirate or murderer is shown as a devil-may-care *brigand*, quite charming if you can overlook the murderous aspect.

brusque (adj) –

abrupt, short, or blunt*, usually unpleasant in effect; curt
The team was put off by the *brusque* manner of the new lacrosse coach, but after a few days we realized it was part of his dry, subtle humor.

bucolic (adj)

referring to the country; rustic, rural, pastoral

Bucolic poetry, which sometimes dwells on shepherds and imaginary pipes of Pan, is not our teacher's favorite.

bumptious (adj) –

egotistic, often irritatingly self-assured; pushy, arrogant
Often, the first impression Trevor makes is that of a *bumptious* teenager, but that's deceiving because he's really thoughtful and intelligent.

buoyant (adj)

lighthearted, cheerful, upbeat; also able to float (as, a **buoyant** raft)
The long trek westward to settle the plains and Western states of America required people of strong wills and *buoyant* spirits.

burlesque (n)

a literary or dramatic work making fun or ridiculing by comic exaggeration; a mockery or caricature
"The performance was a *burlesque*," our paper reported, "a mere mockery of what was originally a fine stage play."

buttress (n)

a support that gives stability and strength

buttress (v)

to shore up, support, or strengthen
A good report states its thesis clearly, then *buttresses* that thesis with examples and facts as proof.

cacophony (n) –

horrible sound; harsh, displeasing noise
Not all music strikes us as being worth listening to; some of it is *cacophony* making war on our eardrums.

cajole (v)

to beg, wheedle, or coax (Done right, may result in car keys.)
I practiced first in front of my mirror and then went downstairs to *cajole* my parents into letting me have a Halloween party.

caliber (n)

moral or mental worth*; quality; diameter of a projectile or bore of the gun
"The general *caliber* of our employees here at Lizard Lollipops is the envy of our competition," bragged Alonzo Lizard, president of the company.

calumny (n) –

malicious, damaging talk about another; slander
"Be thou as chaste as ice, as pure as snow, thou shalt not escape *calumny*," is Shakespeare's reminder that we are all subjects of gossip.

candid (adj) +

open and honest*; fair or free of bias; frank, even to bluntness
One of the joys, occasionally painful, of a close friendship is that you can depend on your friend's *candid* answers to your important questions.

cant (n) –

hypocritical talk*; dialect of a particular group; jargon; trite talk
The *cant* of careless tongues should be dismissed as gossip unworthy of you.

cant (v)

to tilt or slant at an angle
"I made that table in shop class, and I don't care if it *cants* off at a funny angle. It's my first big project," Wes said defensively.

cantankerous (adj) –

grumpy, testy, bad-tempered and quarrelsome
Don't you think it will be fun to be a *cantankerous* old person, insisting that things be done your way, maybe poking at people with an umbrella or cane?

canvass (v)

to do a survey; solicit votes, opinions, orders, etc.
Mother said we should *canvass* the neighborhood to see if all of the families want to share in our Fourth of July block picnic.

capitulate (v)

to give in, surrender, or acquiesce
Jess and I argued about our chem lab results until finally I *capitulated* before our differences could get us into trouble.

capricious (adj)

not steady or constant; changing at a whim
Darting in what seemed to be a *capricious* manner, the hummingbird flitted from flower to flower.

captious (adj) –

overly critical, thus *finding fault easily*
Teresa says that her boyfriend's mother is a *captious* person, always looking for faults in her son.

carnage (n) –

slaughter or massacre (as in a war)
"We'll kill 'em," the coach promised, carried away by enthusiasm. "It'll be a massacre—*carnage* at Keller High!"

carp (v) –	*to nitpick; find fault in a petty manner*
	Drama critics that can't view a play as a total presentation, who *carp* at all the minor flaws, usually are talking to hear themselves talk.
cathartic (n)	*something that cleans or purges**; a purifier*
	A brisk walk can be a *cathartic* that wakes and cheers you up after hours of desk work.
caustic (adj) –	*biting or corrosive; incisive, cutting*
	Ambrose Bierce, nicknamed "Bitter Bierce," was known for his *caustic* wit and revealing satire.
cavil (v) –	*to object in a trivial or unimportant way; to find fault in a captious way*
	"I know the cabin is pretty rustic," laughed Dad, "but let's not *cavil* at little things like holes in the floor, missing doors, and broken windows. We just need to put our backs into it for a week or two." (The whole family groaned.)
chagrin (n) –	*embarrassment; unhappiness brought on by humiliation*
	To Dad's *chagrin* and our sorry satisfaction, we all had to "put our backs into" cabin renovation for several months.

QUIZ ON LIST 3

I. ~~Antonyms.~~ Write an antonym on the line for each of the vocabulary words.

1. banal _stale from overuse_
2. baroque _elaborate way of decoration_
3. benign _not malignant_
4. bias _opinion_
5. blatant _obviously loud_
6. blithe _cheerful / happy_
7. brackish _salty taste_
8. bucolic _referring to the country_

9. buttress _to support_
10. cacophony _annoying sound_
11. blasphemy _profanity_
12. bumptious _pushy_
13. calumny _talk about another_
14. cantankerous _grummpy_
15. caustic _____

II. **Words in Context.** From the following words, select the best for each sentence. Number and tense may need to be changed.

brandish – _swing + threatening way_
beset – _to harass_
bourgeois – _middle class_
bilk – _to cheat / fraud_

chagrin – _embarrasing_
candid – _honest_
capitulate – _to give in, surrender_

capricious – _changing at a wim_
cathartic – _to purifiye_
bellwether – _a leader_

1. In *Sleeping Beauty*, the evil fairy Maleficent _____ long red fingernails and flaming ill will against Princess Aurora.

2. The camera is altogether too _____ for my liking, and I shudder when I've been caught in another unflattering snapshot.

3. Imagine our _____ when friends turned up on our doorstep all dressed for the party we had forgotten the date of—and at our house, too!

4. The paint-stained artist sniffed in a superior manner. "Those scratchings are not works of art; they are merely _____ attempts to daub paint on paper."

5. We pleaded for days, and at last our parents _____ and agreed to let us go with the youth group on their weeklong canoe trip.

6. "Have a good cry," the doctor told us. "Crying is natural and often _____. It may unburden you to some extent."

7. Rog admired his cousin, who always remained cheerful, even when he was _____ by troubles.

8. We discovered in time that the supposedly rare books were fakes, and luckily we weren't _____ of the several hundred dollars' cost.

9. The small town of Red Creek is like a _____; as it votes, so does the rest of the state.

10. If Scarlett O'Hara in *Gone with the Wind* had not been a flirtatious, alluring, but _____ heartbreaker, she would not have been so memorable a character.

III. **Favorite SAT/PSAT Word Families.** Match the words on the left with their meanings, and write your answer choices on the correct lines.

A. BENE = good, well

_____ B _____ 1. benign	(a) a blessing, literally *good words*
_____ 2. benevolent	(b) harmless or kindly
_____ C _____ 3. beneficent	(c) one who sponsors or supports you in some way
_____ 4. benediction	(d) kindly, generous
_____ 5. benefactor	(e) philanthropic, well-meaning, generous

B. CAP, CIP, CEIPT, CEPT = take

_____ 6. capitulate	(a) arrogance, pride; a whimsical idea or metaphor
_____ 7. perceptive	(b) to acquiesce, yield
_____ 8. susceptible	(c) to set free
_____ 9. emancipate	(d) astute, intuitive, acute
_____ 10. conceit	(e) liable, impressionable, responsive

IV. **Logical Connections.** Link each word in bold type to the person, word, or idea most suitable. Write your answers on the lines.

		(A)	(B)	(C)
_____ A _____	1. **bane**	swarm	undoing	awareness
_____	2. **bellicose**	sailor	instructor	pugilist
_____ A _____	3. **bicker**	quibble	refine	elucidate *to make clear*
_____	4. **bigot**	blasphemous	servile	pompous - *overbey*
_____	5. **bovine**	fortitude	patience	generosity
_____ A _____	6. **brigand**	pirate	insurgent	negotiator
_____	7. **cavil**	whimper	carp	bluster
_____	8. **carnage**	classification	archives	war
_____	9. **captious**	nationalism	criticism	deism
_____	10. **cant**	jargon	grammar	oratory
_____	11. **cajole**	demand	absolve	wheedle
_____	12. **burlesque**	costume	irony	caricature
_____	13. **brusque**	curt	effective	whimsical
_____	14. **caliber**	arrow	gun bore	lance
_____	15. **canvass**	tent	poll	material

List 4

chaos (n) –	*extreme disorder, confusion* The home stands were absolute *chaos* after the football game as we noisily celebrated our victory.
charlatan (n) –	*quack or fraud who pretends knowledge; cheat, impostor* At the time of the California gold rush, clever *charlatans* thrived by selling "secret" maps showing the way to mother lodes of gold.
	This word dates back to the 1300s in Italy, where some wily traders from *Cerreto,* a town north of Rome, became notorious for their sneaky practices. Over time, a *cerretano* blended with the Italian word *ciarlare* ("to chatter"), and the word *charlatan* was born.
chaste (adj) +	*pure and innocent; modest; clean or simple in design** The *chaste* designs of classic Greek architecture appeal to many people because of their simplicity and cleanness of line.
chastise (v) –	*to scold severely or punish*; to castigate, censure* Graduates of English boys' boarding schools used to tell hair-raising stories of how they were *chastised;* caning and missing meals were common punishments.
chicanery (n) –	*deceit, trickery, or deception by clever means* "I was a victim of *chicanery,*" Jeff sighed. "Dumb me. I believed them when they said that cat was too young to produce kittens."
circumspect (adj) +	*cautiously watchful, prudent, or careful* "Anyone who adopts a pussycat should be more *circumspect,*" Steve said, grinning, "and not let her go out on dates with neighborhood toms."
citadel (n)	*fortress; removed place of safety; stronghold* Above the town, on a high, steep peak, the *citadel* called Mountjoy looked out upon the world below.
cite (v)	*to refer to officially* (as **citing** a reference*); *to call to court; to commend in a formal manner* We're expected to *cite* two biographies, one live interview, and four other sources in our term paper for current events class.
civility (n) +	*good manners, politeness, or courtesy* The stereotype of an English butler includes a noticeably British accent, formal attire, and unfailing *civility* even in exasperating circumstances.
clandestine (adj)	*secret, surreptitious* Stacy wrote in her diary: I have four *clandestine* meetings planned with the football team captain, who's not supposed to date during football season.
clarity (n) +	*clearness, lucidity* The speech teacher said she'd judge our next speeches on *clarity* and organization, so I made a careful outline of my speech.
clement (adj) +	*lenient or merciful*; mild* (as **clement** weather) Hoping that the warlord would be *clement* and understanding, the captives fell to their knees and begged him for mercy.
coerce (v) –	*to force or compel* (someone or something) *Coercing* people to help you and having them volunteer to help are two different experiences indeed.
cogent (adj) +	*convincing, persuasive, or valid* (as reasons) The experienced lawyer warned his new associate to use only well-organized, *cogent* arguments when presenting a case in court for their law firm.

Paula Monette

cognate (n) — *relation*

cognate (adj) — *related, or alike generically*
English and French are *cognate* languages, and both derive much from their Latin and Greek heritage.

coherent (adj) + — *logically arranged or ordered (as a **coherent** speech)*
Frank's teacher smiled as she handed back his term paper, which was marked, "*Coherent*, interesting, and well-documented. Congratulations!"

cognizant (adj) — *aware, conscious (followed by **of**)*
Emily was not *cognizant* of the problems she might have gathering eggs in her aunt's henhouse, so she allowed only 5 minutes for the task on her first afternoon of vacation.

colloquy (n) — *fairly serious conversation, dialogue or conference*
Inside the henhouse, Emily saw a large red hen dozing on what appeared to be a full nest, plus many other hens in noisy *colloquy* over other nests.

comely (adj) + — *attractive to look at; pretty, appealing*
Emily approached the most *comely* of the cackling hens, a plump, well-groomed white one, who surely must be perched atop a freshly laid egg.

commensurate (adj) — *in proportion to; corresponding to size, type, abilities, etc.*
Comely only in appearance, the big hen gave Emily a rapid peck *commensurate* with the size of her large beak at the instant Emily reached under her to take the egg.

compassion (n) + — *awareness and caring for others; sympathy for others' misfortunes*
Appalled by the speed and viciousness of the hen's attack, Emily hastily withdrew her hand and ran for the *compassion* her aunt and uncle would provide.

compatible (adj) + — *well suited or fit*; adaptable, consonant, related*
As the vacation days went by, Emily wondered if she were *compatible* with chickens and cows and 5 a.m. milking appointments in the barn.

compunction (n) — *misgiving or guilt feeling; qualm, scruple*
With experience around hens came courage; Emily soon had no *compunction* about rapping hens sharply on their beaks to let them know who was boss.

conclave (n) — *private, secret meeting*; convention*
The cabinet spent most of the day deep in a *conclave*, debating who should be the next foreign minister of the new island republic.

concur (v) — *to agree, assent; approve; coincide*
After serious debate, all *concurred* that the most qualified candidate was a retired defense secretary.

condescend (v) − — *to come down in level; to unbend or stoop*
She Stoops to Conquer is an old, enjoyable play about a girl who *condescends* to play the part of a servant to learn the real character of a man.

condone (v) — *to overlook (an offense) or to pardon; to excuse*
"In the past," growled Father, "I have *condoned* your failure to come in on time, but I won't overlook your lateness any longer."

conducive (adj) — *promoting, furthering, or aiding; contributive*
The study carrels in the library are *conducive* to progress, since they are private and quiet places to work.

congenital (adj) — *occurring during pregnancy or at birth*; inherent, innate*
The speech therapist felt that a *congenital* defect of the patient's palate made formation of certain sounds very difficult.

conjecture (n) — *a guess or supposition; inference, conclusion*

conjecture (v) — *to guess or suppose; to infer or conclude*
I'd *conjecture* that those heavy clouds will bring us more snow by nightfall.

connive (v) –

*to conspire, intrigue, or plot secretly** (often followed by **at** or **with**)
Trapped behind the Berlin Wall, those who wished to leave East Germany often *connived* with others to plan their escape.

connoisseur (n)

expert or professional; a competent critic in an art, skill, or profession

Through Latin and French, we get *connoisseur* from *cognoscere*, meaning *to know*. A *connoisseur* is a person who honestly knows his subject, while a *dilettante* is a dabbler, maybe a pretender to extensive knowledge. Further down the scale is the *amateur*, a beginner just getting the hang of things.

An antiques *connoisseur* is always delighted to share her knowledge of antiquities with anyone who will listen.

connotation (n)

the various implied meanings of a word, act, or event; what is suggested rather than actually stated
The phrase "grubby job" has the *connotation* of dirty, tiring work, but probably not work full of real, live grubs, unless you're in the garden.

conscript (v)

to draft or enlist (a person) *by law or force*
Mother *conscripted* the entire family last fall to help her mulch the gardens for winter.

consort (n)

associate; your other half; conjunction or tandem* (as in **consort** with local groups)
Prince Charles's *consort* is the Princess Diana, whose frequent appearance on their covers sells many copies of the sensational weekly papers.

consort (v)

to run around with or associate with (followed by **with**)
In the musical *Oliver*, the boy Oliver learned to enjoy *consorting* with Fagin and his accomplished band of thieves and pickpockets.

consternation (n) –

worry or concern; dismay or astonishment
You could see how concerned Missy was about her brother's accident, because *consternation* and fear were written on her white face.

construe (v)

to interpret, analyze, decipher
"May I *construe* your remarks to mean that you haven't done your homework?" Miss Thompson asked Ricky.

consummate (adj) +

developed to a high degree; perfect, skilled, accomplished
His *consummate* skill in handling that quarter horse throughout the rodeo earned him applause and enough points to win first place.

consummate (v)

to bring to completion; perfect; or achieve
The two partners *consummated* a business deal with another firm that would augment their earnings considerably within the first year after signing the contract.

contaminate (v) –

to infect or in some way ruin; pollute, taint, defile
Businesses that *contaminate* their local streams with waste products will anger residents into petitioning local courts for restraint orders and fines.

contemplate (v)

to mull over, think about; meditate, consider
Jane *contemplated* the virtues and drawbacks of several colleges before she finally decided which ones she should apply to.

Notice this sentence ends in a *preposition*. Do this when it is awkward to follow the old rule of avoiding ending sentences with prepositions.

contiguous (adj)

bordering or adjacent; nearby as neighbors
Contiguous backyards often share things like swing sets, ball games, leaves, and crabgrass.

contingent (adj)

dependent on; by chance or accident (with **on** or **upon**)
My attendance at the office party was *contingent* upon my finishing the work due Friday by five o'clock.

contingent (n)   *group or body*
Bruce said that a *contingent* from the hospital staff would be joining our after-work party.

QUIZ ON LIST 4

I.   **Antonyms.** Match vocabulary words (or derived words) with their antonyms.

_____ 1. cognizant   (a) illogical
_____ 2. compassionate   (b) commend
_____ 3. chastise   (c) acquired
_____ 4. congenital   (d) encourage
_____ 5. conjecture   (e) unknowing
_____ 6. chicanery   (f) certainty
_____ 7. civility   (g) indifferent
_____ 8. clement   (h) honesty
_____ 9. coerce   (i) rudeness
_____ 10. coherent   (j) severe

II. **Words in Context.** Put the vocabulary words into the phrases where they fit according to the meaning and intention of the surrounding words.

colloquy	cognate	contingent
chaos	consternation	contemplate
condone	chaste	consummate
cite	commensurate	connive
consorting	citadel	conducive

1. a scene of _____, calamity, and crushed hopes
2. a Puritan girl of _____ reputation
3. know you must _____ authorities to buttress your argument
4. the office as a quiet _____, removed and safe
5. _____ peoples, joined by ages of shared culture
6. meeting in earnest _____, heads bent over the evidence
7. a salary _____ with his abilities
8. won't _____ this behavior another minute
9. joy in _____ with other neighborhood dogs
10. hear the _____ and apprehension in her voice
11. concentrated attention so _____ to progress
12. her _____ skill in all artistic endeavors
13. my participation, _____ as usual on my parents' permission
14. a reflective hour in which to _____ his situation
15. would never knowingly _____ at another person's downfall

III. **Favorite SAT/PSAT Word Families.** Bound to reappear on the tests as well as in college texts are the words below. Match them by writing the correct definitions or synonyms on the lines.

A. CIRCUM = around

_____ 1. circumvent   (a) to limit, constrict

_____ 2. circumscribe   (b) evasive in speech or excessively wordy

_____ 3. circumlocutory   (c) roundabout, indirect

_____ 4. circumspect   (d) prudent, cautious

_____ 5. circuitous   (e) to foil by intelligence; to frustrate or get around

B. SPEC, SPIC, SPECT = to see, look

_____ 6. speculate   (a) highly noticeable

_____ 7. perspicacious   (b) self-examination; looking inward

_____ 8. conspicuous   (c) promising, favorable in outlook

_____ 9. auspicious   (d) to conjecture, guess

_____ 10. introspection   (e) welcome rest or lull in activity

_____ 11. respite   (f) wise, shrewd, perceptive

IV. **Definitions.** Select two of the lettered choices to explain or define each word in bold type.

_____ 1. **contiguous**   (A) adjacent   (B) geometric   (C) nearby   (D) hardy (E) removed

_____ 2. **contaminate**   (A) water   (B) defile   (C) adjust   (D) substantiate (E) pollute

_____ 3. **consummate**   (A) tire   (B) weigh   (C) perfect   (D) achieve   (E) thwart

_____ 4. **construe**   (A) interpret   (B) obstruct   (C) offer   (D) decipher (E) flaunt

_____ 5. **connotation**   (A) suggestion   (B) imposition   (C) implication (D) conclusion   (E) value

_____ 6. **condescend**   (A) retreat   (B) stoop   (C) deceive   (D) revert   (E) unbend

_____ 7. **concur**   (A) halt   (B) agree   (C) assent   (D) share   (E) lead

_____ 8. **compunction**   (A) scruple   (B) excuse   (C) apology   (D) accord (E) qualm

_____ 9. **compatible**   (A) assorted   (B) correct   (C) well suited   (D) consonant (E) appealing

_____ 10. **comely**   (A) pretty   (B) homespun   (C) attractive   (D) repulsive (E) disagreeable

_____ 11. **cognate**   (A) foreign   (B) related   (C) alien   (D) alike   (E) known

_____ 12. **cogent**   (A) vague   (B) persuasive   (C) theoretical   (D) thoughtful (E) convincing

_____ 13. **inclement**   (A) harsh   (B) variable   (C) merciless   (D) unusual   (E) damp

_____ 14. **clarity**   (A) opacity   (B) lucidity   (C) clearness   (D) density (E) keenness

_____ 15. **clandestine**   (A) fated   (B) surreptitious   (C) intended   (D) partisan (E) secret

List 5

contrite (adj)	*sorrowful or repentant for some wrong; regretful* Her set, *contrite* face told him more about her misery than words could have expressed.
contumely (n) –	*rude talk or behavior resulting from feelings of superiority or contempt; disdain* In Hamlet's famous soliloquy, he says how terrible it is to "bear the whips and scorns of time, The oppressor's wrong, the proud man's *contumely*."
convivial (adj) +	*lively or spirited; congenial, sociable** My old Uncle Charlie is loved by many for his cheerful outlook and *convivial*, warmhearted ways.
copious (adj)	*superabundant; in plentiful supply* "For my birthday," Ted joked, "I want *copious* presents, piled up to the ceiling, spilling out the doors and windows."
corollary (n)	*the natural result or logical follow-up; a normal parallel* We tend to believe that success is the *corollary* to hard work, initiative, and stick-to-itiveness.
corporeal (adj)	*of the physical, not spiritual, body; material, substantial* "Scrooge's ghosts had more *corporeal* reality than any fears or ideas that ever haunted me," said Jane.
corroborate (v)	*to confirm or substantiate (by evidence or from an official position); to support* Scrooge's ghosts materialized to *corroborate* misgivings and regrets he had long suppressed.
coterie (n)	*a distinct group of people with common interests**; *a set, clique, faction*
	Synonyms for *coterie* can be misleading. A *clique* is an exclusive group of people being deliberately exclusive. A *faction* is a group often formed to disagree or stir up dissension. Both words have *negative* connotations that *coterie* and *set* lack.
	A distinguished *coterie* from the local art association represented our city at the state annual arts' convention.
covenant (n)	*a serious agreement, promise, or contract; pledge* In *Raiders of the Lost Ark*, Professor Indiana Jones helped to discover the lost Ark of the *Covenant*, a sacred vessel containing God's promise to His people.
cower (v) –	*to cringe in fear* When a normally friendly dog *cowers* before someone in terror, you can suppose that he's been hurt by that person in the past.
craven (adj) –	*cowardly to a strong degree; chickenhearted* Most of us hope we will be brave in tough circumstances, not *craven* with fear.
credence (n)	*believing acceptance**; *credentials* (letters of **credence**) "You don't expect me to give *credence* to such a wild story!" Mom exploded.
crony (n) +	*friend of long standing; pal, buddy, chum* Suspicious of each other to begin with, Luke Skywalker and Han Solo were old *cronies* by the end of *Star Wars*.
crux (n)	*central or pivotal point**; *essential or main item* The *crux* of the matter, said our play director, was whether or not we could afford the royalty payments on the play we had chosen.
culinary (adj)	*of the kitchen or cooking* The *Culinary* Institute of America, in Hyde Park, New York, educates tomorrow's superchefs and serves delicious meals to customers, too.

culmination (n) +

the highest point or summit; climax, zenith
Winning the school's spring decathlon was the *culmination* of Rob's dedicated training efforts.

culpable (adj) –

guilty (from L. **culpa = guilt**); *at fault*
Our society puts those *culpable* of serious crimes in jail, with the desperate hope that some may be rehabilitated.

cumbrous (adj) –

heavy, bulky, therefore often *unwieldy; cumbersome*
Down in the Grand Canyon one poetic donkey said to another, "I hate toting *cumbrous* loads up and down these rocky roads."

cursory (adj) –

sketchy, as opposed to thorough; hasty, superficial
After only *cursory* study, I took the algebra exam, and boy, was I sorry!

curtail (v)

to cut short, as an activity; to shorten, abbreviate
My sister, who always studies till midnight before an exam, was forced to *curtail* her studying when our lights went out in the ice storm.

cynic (n) –

a person who thinks others act only in self-interest

Named (oddly enough) for a dog (**dog = kyn** in Greek), the school of philosophers in Greece called *Cynics* believed virtue was the only good and held furthermore that the essence of virtue was in independence and self-discipline. Strangely changed, the word now means the opposite, since today's *cynics* think that everyone is motivated solely by greed or self-concern.

"Joel and his friends are such *cynics,*" Marty complained, "and they're always accusing me of being a starry-eyed idealist."

daunt (v) –

to dismay or take away the courage of; to cow or subdue
Although the power of the ring *daunted* the hobbits Bilbo and Frodo Baggins, they remained incorruptible.

dawdle (v) –

to waste time or spend it fruitlessly*; to delay
When his teacher said he was *dawdling* over *The Hobbit,* Jim answered, "It's so good I'm reading slowly to make it last longer."

dearth (n) –

scarcity or lack; paucity
For lovers of fantasy there's a *dearth* of good reading material, and only recently have publishers begun recognizing and responding to the demand.

debility (n) –

weakness, esp. after illness*; infirmity, lack of strength
The crippling *debility* in Larry's right leg after his auto accident made him grit his teeth in pain and frustration.

decorum (n) +

correct or expected behavior; politeness, propriety, fitness
Priscilla had always been known for her absolute *decorum.* Her sisters were astounded to hear that she'd called the principal an old windbag.

decrepit (adj) –

worn out from age or overuse; weak, dilapidated, run-down
All the kids on our block ride to school in Dan's *decrepit* Ford, but we think we'll end up pushing the car home one day soon.

deference (n)

honor or respect due an older or more experienced person; esteem
Priscilla's father said, "I wish you would show *deference* to older people and to those in positions of authority."

degenerate (v) –

to sink into a lower or less useful state; to "go to pot" morally
"Mom's worried I'll *degenerate* into a party-loving nonstudent when I go away to college," Sam told his friend Rip.

delineate (v)

to show, outline, portray accurately
We sat for hours with the architect as she *delineated* each aspect of our proposed office complex.

demeanor (n)   *manner of handling yourself; comportment, bearing*
Our cat Fred has a regal *demeanor* as he approaches any guest; then he sits down to survey the newcomer through slitted eyes.

denotation (n)   *the absolute literal meaning* (as opposed to what a word brings to mind)
The strict, biological *denotation* of the word "mother" is very different from its vast array of connotative meanings.

deplore (v) –   *to regret exceedingly; to lament, bemoan*
Dermatologists *deplore* our habit of cultivating a deep suntan, because the sun's rays are harmful to skin.

deploy (v)   *to arrange in an advantageous way* (as military troops are **deployed** in battle)
"If I ever learn how to *deploy* these chess pieces properly," Margo sighed, "I might have some hope of beating my sister."

depraved (adj) –   *sinful or evil*; perverted* (morals)
The Bible condemns the wicked cities of Sodom and Gomorrah as habitats of people living *depraved* lives.

derelict (n) –   *abandoned or neglected possession, often a ship; a person who cannot support himself, a bum**
The poorer streets of large cities are all too often strewn with human *derelicts*—people without place, without hope.

derision (n) –   *scorn or ridicule;* literally *"laughing down"*
After a "Ha!" of *derision*, Stacy put her hands on the table to steady herself and began her rebuttal calmly as the debate teacher had taught.

derogatory (adj) –   *negatively critical, disparaging;* literally *"talking down"*
Writers usually welcome helpful criticism, but *derogatory* remarks tend to put them on the defensive.

desecrate (v) –   *to defile or profane something sacred or very special*
The fear of a young Roman vestal virgin was that she might *desecrate* the temple and betray her vows if she let the sacred flame go out.

desiccate (v)   *to dry up, dehydrate; to wither away by dryness*
After an apple has *desiccated* and is no longer moist, you can apply fake hair, eyes, and ears to make it resemble a shrunken head.

desist (v)   *to cease or stop* (doing something)
"My father's always saying 'cease and *desist*' when he hears our arguments," Sharon said. "I don't think he enjoys a good fight."

desolate (adj) –   *alone or deserted*; downcast or sad; barren, lifeless*
The *desolate* stretches of seaside beach early in the morning offer a perfect place for walking and thinking.

despondent (adj) –   *downcast, dejected, depressed*
Many who write to Abby and Ann Landers are *despondent* about their love lives.

NOTE: Way over half of these words beginning with *de* are negative in meaning. If a mystery word begins with *de*, your safer guess is that it's negative, too.

QUIZ ON LIST 5

I.   **Synonyms.** Match the vocabulary words with appropriate synonyms.

_____	1. contrite	(a)	substantial
_____	2. contumely	(b)	pledge
_____	3. copious	(c)	wicked
_____	4. corporeal	(d)	repentant
_____	5. covenant	(e)	paucity
_____	6. daunt	(f)	congenial
_____	7. dearth	(g)	disdain
_____	8. convivial	(h)	profane
_____	9. depraved	(i)	dismay
_____	10. desecrate	(j)	plentiful

II. **Fill in the Blanks.** Choose the best word from the list below to complete each sentence.

despondent	corollary	coterie
culpable	derogatory	cower
corroborate	crux	dawdle
decrepit	debility	decorum
deference	cursory	culinary

1. That's a _____ old sofa, but it will be fine for our recreation room.

2. "We must know whether or not he was at the scene of the crime," said the inspector. "That's the _____ of our investigation at the moment."

3. I always enjoy figuring out who is _____ in a murder mystery before the author reveals the perpetrator of the crime.

4. After a long illness there may be some _____ as well as general listlessness.

5. _____, we watched our raft, our only hope of escape, sink below the waves.

6. With _____, the girl curtsied and asked the duchess if further service would be needed.

7. Most people avoided him, for he was a critical man, always ready with a _____ remark.

8. The _____ to your question is another question: How can a missing person best be located?

9. The fact that his suitcases are missing _____ your statement that he planned to leave and was not harmed in any way.

10. Inform the detectives that their investigations of this case should not be _____ but, instead, exceedingly thorough.

11. Get dressed and don't _____ with your packing. The bus leaves in a few minutes.

12. A _____ of members from the Arts Association called upon the museum director.

13. Fred _____ abjectly in his basket after the shampooing we gave him.

14. The _____ skills of Julia Child are shared through her TV show and many cookbooks.

15. To Mom's disgust, we did not behave with _____ during the lengthy lecture.

III. **Analogies.** Examine List 5 and complete the analogies with the best possible word from it.

1. hate : enemy :: friendship : _____

2. beginning : end :: start : _____

3. noble : depraved :: idealist : _____
4. damp : _____ :: desist : continue
5. _____ : barren :: derision : ridicule

IV. **Antonyms.** From the choices offered, select two antonyms or contrasting phrases for each vocabulary word. Write your choices on the lines.

_____	1. contrite	(a) favorable recognition	(k) to cloud
_____	2. craven	(b) failure to credit or believe	(l) intrepid
_____	3. credence	(c) expressing a high opinion	(m) to elongate
_____	4. cumbrous	(d) lacking remorse	(n) to confuse
_____	5. deplore	(e) revealing esteem	(o) lightweight
_____	6. curtail	(f) to commence	(p) applause
_____	7. derogatory	(g) to revel in	(q) to appreciate
_____	8. delineate	(h) unrepentant	(r) implausibility
_____	9. desist	(i) bold	(s) to begin
_____	10. derision	(j) to lengthen	(t) manageable

List 6

destitute (adj) – *experiencing extreme need* (of vital necessities); *indigent, poverty-stricken*
Pictures of *destitute*, pathetic children always tug at our heartstrings.

desultory (adj) *without set plan or purpose; random; haphazard, casual*
"A *desultory* approach to research is not what I call the scientific method," said the physics teacher.

deviate (v) *to vary from the normal or standard way; to digress, change course; swerve*
Made wary by the swollen river, we *deviated* from the original plan and paddled the canoes down a side stream instead.

deviate (n) – *someone who is noticeably different from the norm*
In a higher-level psychology course, we will study various *deviates* who have been unable to adjust to normal society.

devious (adj) – *at odds with the normal, accepted course*; *off the beaten path in the sense of remote; roundabout* (as a **devious** path)
One personality the instructor mentioned was a *devious* sort who approached all decision making in a roundabout way that complicated life immensely.

dexterous (adj) + *skilled with mind/hands; adroit, artful, expert, deft*

Dexter in Latin means *right*. *Sinister*, by contrast, means *left*. Custom was for the right hand to be held forth in greeting in order to show open friendliness and no concealed weapon. With your right hand extended, your left *could* conceal a weapon. Now, *sinister* suggests a dangerous, hidden menace.

"You need to be *dexterous* to build this model," advised the saleswoman. "We constructed it for display and it is quite difficult."

dichotomy (n) *division into two groups or ideas at odds with one another;* literally *"cut in two"*
Many women today are faced with a *dichotomy*; they want a demanding job and career yet feel an equally strong pull toward a traditional home and family life.

didactic (adj) *instructive, designed to teach; offering moral preachments; pedantic*
Unfortunately, *didactic* material is often boring and slow in pace; thus the word has acquired an unlovely connotation.

diffident (adj) –
lacking self-confidence; unassertive and shy
Connie's new employer was upset by Connie's *diffident* manner her first morning on the job, but by afternoon she was pleased to see her growing in self-confidence.

dilatory (adj) –
causing delay; tardy; "putting off" (as in procrastinating)
"A dillar, a dollar, A ten o'clock scholar" is the old nursery rhyme that chides a *dilatory* student.

dilemma (n) –
problem lacking a good solution; quandary in which the only two alternatives are equally unsatisfactory
"Caught on the horns of a *dilemma*" and "between a rock and a hard place" are synonymous phrases, both describing problems that lack good solutions.

dilettante (n) –
a dabbler of superficial knowledge/interest
The *dilettante* may wish he had the expertise of a professional, but just as often he lacks the dedication necessary to achieve greater status.

discernment (n) +
ability to fully understand; discrimination and penetrating insight*; acumen
His *discernment* in selecting young horses that would mature into winning racers gave Charles an edge over other trainers.

discomfiture (n) –
state of confusion and embarrassment; act of thwarting or state of being thwarted
Jeri's *discomfiture* was plain to see as she lost to her old chess rival from East High.

discord (n) –
tension, strife, or lack of agreement and harmony*; dissonance in music; conflict
Discord and social unrest seem to be the inevitable companions of revolution.

discrepancy (n) –
a difference
When I see a *discrepancy* between my checking account balance and the bank records, I hope that the error will be settled in my favor.

discriminate (v)
to notice differences; to distinguish between*; to differentiate; to treat differently
Joe loved being asked to *discriminate* between chocolate chip cookie recipes, tasting first one, then another, until he had found the best.

discursive (adj)
moving from one topic to another; digressive
Miss Wilson's presentation was *discursive*, yet highly interesting, and we enjoyed her digressions into humor.

disparage (v) –
to belittle, downgrade, or decry (desparagier; orig., to marry below one's class in old France)
"Sour grapes" is the Aesop's-fable expression to describe a person *disparaging* the virtues or accomplishments of another.

disparity (n)
difference in type or quality
Will and Troy are identical twins, even though the *disparity* in their interests might suggest otherwise.

disseminate (v)
to disperse or spread all over (knowledge, ideas) *almost as though sowing seeds*
The school paper was founded to *disseminate* information about students and school activities.

dissipate (v)
to thin out or to drive away to the point that almost nothing is left* (as a mob is **dissipated**); *to use up in a worthless, foolish way* (as an inheritance); *to waste*
By late spring, our fervent journalistic efforts are sadly *dissipated*, and the paper we put out in June is usually pretty embarrassing.

divulge (v)
to make known, reveal
My desk could *divulge* secrets about me that I'd prefer no one knew, such as my tendency to stuff unwanted papers into bottom drawers.

docile (adj)
easily managed; compliant, tractable, amenable, obedient
One kindergarten teacher said to another, "If I ever had a very *docile* student, I'd think he was ill and send him to the nurse!"

doctrinaire (adj)

dictatorial and autocratic in manner, usually *dogmatic and stubborn as well*
Since I discovered that that professor took such a *doctrinaire* approach to learning, I have advised my friends to avoid her class.

dogmatic (adj) –

strongly opinionated; dictatorial (from Gr. **dogma = opinion**)
Taking a *dogmatic* approach in human relations typically drives other people away, convincing them only that you are opinionated, not that you are right.

dormant (adj)

temporarily inactive, asleep; latent
One of the most exciting aspects of life is that each person has talents and abilities lying *dormant*, like gold, just waiting to be discovered.

dour (adj) –

harsh or stubborn; sometimes gloomy, even *sullen*
The idea that climate influences human personalities has given us the stereotypes of the relaxed Southerner and the *dour* Scot.

drastic (adj)

radical or severe
Drastic surgical procedures were necessary to save the boy's life after the accident.

drivel (n) –

foolish, witless talk*; as a verb, *to talk like an idiot*
"This poetry is absolute *drivel*," Mel complained. "If I wrote poetry, it would be profound and meaningful."

droll (adj) +

humorous; distinct in an appealing way*
Santa Claus has "a *droll* little mouth drawn up like a bow."

dubious (adj) –

doubtful or undecided; equivocal; questionable
Sara's tone was *dubious* as she said yes, and we reasoned that later on her answer could just as well be no.

duplicity (n) –

double-dealing in a contradictory way; deception
Shelley told us that she hadn't revealed our place in the woods, but when half of her friends marched into our hideout, we were sure of her *duplicity*.

duress (n) –

restraint by force; forcing by threat* (follows **under**)
Back home, under *duress*, Shelley finally confessed that she'd given away our secret.

dynamic (adj) +

energetic, forceful; unusually active
Our mother says that Shelley simply has a *dynamic* spirit and can't control her energies. We say that Shelley is a brat.

éclat (n) +

noticeable brilliance
The pianist performed with *éclat,* and the applause following each number was overwhelming.

eclectic (adj)

carefully selected; chosen from the best or from various sources
Marcia reads an *eclectic* array of books and can always suggest a good title.

edification (n)

act or process of instruction, enlightening, or improving
Gramma read us some poems that she said were for "our *edification*," and I suppose they were once her favorites, but they weren't ours.

efface (v)

to erase or obliterate*; to wear away (as by time)
Wise campers carefully *efface* all traces of their habitation in wilderness areas.

effete (adj) –

no longer useful, nonproductive*; outmoded (as a law)
Doom prophets warn us of what happens to *effete* cultures, pointing to the fall of Rome as a classic example.

efficacious (adj) +

capable of producing the effect wanted; effective, potent
We prayed that someone would discover an *efficacious* treatment for polio, and along came Dr. Salk with his lifesaving vaccine.

effigy (n)

likeness or image of a person (often a disliked person)
After we lost our tenth straight game, some clowns in the junior high hanged our coach in *effigy* in the doorway to the boys' locker room.

effluvium (n) –	*unpleasant odor or exhalation; waste by-products**
	Neighbors concerned about the *effluvium* in nearby streams and rivers have begun a clean-water campaign to help enforce our antipollution laws.
effrontery (n) –	*unlimited boldness; insolence, temerity; chutzpah*
	Did she have the *effrontery* to ask for a raise after working here only three days?
egregious (adj) –	*profoundly noticeable in a negative way; flagrant; outstandingly bad*
	Over the years, their *egregious* errors in management and public relations have cost that company the goodwill of everyone in town.
elicit (v)	*to draw forth* (as information is **elicited** from the witness)
	When newspaper reporters have tried to *elicit* the truth from company representatives, they have been given devious answers.
elixir (n) +	*liquid to give eternal life; a cure-all*
	In medieval days, alchemists searched for an *elixir* that would change ordinary metals into gold and would also prolong life indefinitely. Ponce de León searched Florida seeking the Fountain of Youth, which Indians had told him poured forth the precious *elixir*. Those Indians put one over on old Poncy.
	Kindly Dr. Jekyll created an *elixir* to restore his youth, but instead it transformed him into the evil Mr. Hyde.
eloquent (adj) +	*moving and forcefully phrased; memorable because of verbal skill*
	Making an *eloquent* speech that pleads the case of the defendant with consummate skill is one goal of trial lawyers.

QUIZ ON LIST 6

I.   **Words in Context.** Using a word puts it into your mind to stay. First, define in other words the phrases below; then use the phrases in sentences of your own.

1. desultory reading _____

_____

2. a dubious achievement _____

_____

3. sheer drivel _____

_____

4. dour Scot _____

_____

5. eclectic possessions _____

_____

6. egregious blunder _____

_____

7. effete society _____

_____

8. for my edification _____

_____

9. eloquent gesture _____

_____

10. hanged in effigy _____

_____

II. **Antonyms.** Match the vocabulary words with their antonyms.

_____ 1. devious
_____ 2. diffident
_____ 3. dilatory
_____ 4. dilettante
_____ 5. discord
_____ 6. discursive
_____ 7. divulge
_____ 8. duplicity
_____ 9. dynamic
_____ 10. elicit

(a) connoisseur
(b) conceal
(c) confident
(d) direct
(e) lifeless
(f) highly ordered, organized
(g) prompt
(h) straightforwardness
(i) draw in
(j) accord

III. **Synonyms.** Select the word or expression that best defines the vocabulary words on the left.

1. dilemma   (a) regret (b) harassment (c) quandary (d) worry
2. drastic   (a) radical (b) unknown (c) surgical (d) static
3. dexterous   (a) studious (b) maladroit (c) sinister (d) adept
4. dogmatic   (a) opinionated (b) canine (c) hard to train (d) automatic
5. didactic   (a) boring (b) instructive (c) interesting (d) uncanny
6. discomfiture (a) organization (b) inconvenience (c) pain (d) frustration
7. disparage   (a) criticize (b) belittle (c) talk about (d) off par
8. effigy   (a) kind of person (b) effort (c) treachery (d) likeness
9. docile   (a) tractable (b) cowlike (c) sorrowful (d) religious
10. effrontery (a) meanness (b) honesty (c) chutzpah (d) up front

IV. **Favorite SAT/PSAT Word Families.** Select the best definition of each numbered word to write on the lines.

A. FAC, FICT, FECT, –FY = do, make

_____ 1. efficacious
_____ 2. edify
_____ 3. effect
_____ 4. factious
_____ 5. exemplify

(a) to bring about, cause to happen
(b) potent, effective
(c) to act as an example of
(d) to teach, enlighten
(e) disputatious, quarrelsome

B. LOC, LOG, LOQU, LOCUT = speech, study; word, talk

_____ 6. loquacious
_____ 7. eloquent
_____ 8. colloquial
_____ 9. epilogue
_____ 10. monologue
_____ 11. elocution

(a) words at end of a book or play
(b) talk or speech for one person
(c) effective speech
(d) verbally skilled
(e) extremely talkative
(f) of conversation or speech of a distinct
time or place

V.   **Phrase Completion.** Select the best words to complete each of the phrases.

destitute	droll	discomfiture	discrepancy
deviate	éclat	disseminate	discriminated
dexterous	dichotomy	elixir	duress
disparage	discerning	didactic	dissipated

1. subjected designs to his _____ eye that so easily _____ between good and bad

2. unfortunately easy to _____ the _____ citizens of indigent Third World countries

3. his noticeable _____ when he saw the _____ between the actual bill and the quoted price

4. primary goal of his _____ lecture being to _____ as much information as possible

5. her digression to a modern topic, revealing an eagerness to _____ from the traditional

6. a sharp _____ between the adroit, _____ movements of the practiced weavers and the novices

7. the Prodigal Son, who _____ his inheritance

8. confessed under _____ that his secret attempt to create a magic _____ had failed

9. youth belies the _____ with which she performs that concerto

10. a(n) _____, amusing fellow welcome everywhere

List 7

emaciated (adj) –	*extremely thin; gaunt* A heart-wrenching story about a little match girl describes a destitute child whose *emaciated* body and face told a sad tale.
emanate (v)	*to seep forth* (as smells or ideas); *to emit* From the young match girl *emanated* an air of sorrow and abject poverty.
eminence (n) +	*importance or prominence; lofty station* It would be difficult for those in positions of *eminence* to comprehend the lives of those who lack life's most basic necessities.
emolument (n)	*salary, wages; compensation for work;* literally *"the miller's fee"*—what was due the miller who ground grain Hannah's *emolument* as a grocery store checkout clerk is generous, and she saves half of every paycheck for college expenses.
empirical (adj)	*experimental* (as data from experience or observation) The chemistry teacher described the difference between *empirical* evidence and that which is obtained by deductive reasoning.
emulate (v)	*to try to equal* (or even *exceed) an example; to imitate* My little brother is always *emulating* the older boys next door, trying to rival their feats on our backyard climber.
enervate (v)	*to diminish the strength of (either mind or body); to rob of energy* At the end of exam week, my friends and I were totally *enervated* physically and mentally.

engender (v)
to cause to exist*, sponsor; to beget (a child or an idea); to produce, originate
The record of our varsity basketball team *engenders* respect and envy in the younger junior varsity team.

enhance (v) +
to make better or more desirable in some way*; to intensify
The summer Brent spent at music camp *enhanced* his value to the orchestra, and now he plays the cello as well as the bass.

enigma (n)
a thing hard to understand or fathom; conundrum, riddle, mystery
"The wind instruments," Brent told us, "are still an *enigma*. Maybe I can work with them next summer at music camp."

enjoin (v)
to order or direct officially; to prohibit, forbid* (with **from**)
Our crowd was *enjoined* from loitering in front of the drug store after school.

enthralling (adj) +
charming; entrancing or spellbinding

A *thrall* was a slave or bondsman (woman, too) owned by a master. Anything *enthralling*, therefore, enslaves someone. By music, or beauty, or complexity, or any intriguing factor, it exerts power.

"The most *enthralling* performance I've ever seen," Roz said, "was Hal Holbrook in *Mark Twain Tonight*, and I'll go again if I ever get a chance."

ephemeral (adj)
of brief duration, therefore *fleeting, transient, short-lived* (from Gr **ephemeros = lasting one day,** or **daily**)
The life of a fly is *ephemeral,* which is the only good thing about flies.

epicure (n) +
person of discriminating taste; a perfectionist regarding food and drink; gourmet
Epicures and gourmets are typically persnickety eaters, but a gourmand usually eats lots of whatever is served.

epitaph (n)
writing on a tomb, or at the gravesite (in commemoration)
W. C. Fields wanted his *epitaph* to read: "On the whole I would rather be in Philadelphia," but unfortunately that wasn't inscribed on his tombstone.

epithet (n)
an expression representative of a person or place (as Rommel is referred to as "the Desert Fox"); also *a disparaging phrase about someone or something**
The little boys hurled cruel *epithets* at the awkward newcomer who had hoped to join their game.

epitome (n)
summary; a typical example representative of a type*
Ruth is the *epitome* of neatness. Her mother says she can't put anything down for a second, because Ruth will grab it and put it away somewhere.

equivocal (adj) –
open to two interpretations, therefore *unclear and often misleading*; undecided, obscure, evasive*
The witness was asked to answer the question a second time because his first answer was *equivocal* and might have misled the jury.

eradicate (v)
to wipe out, exterminate*; to pull up as if by the roots (because **radix = root** in Latin); also **extirpate,** *to eradicate, root out*
Through careful, persistent use of the smallpox vaccine, smallpox has been *eradicated* in the United States.

erratic (adj)
on no set course*; wandering or nomadic; devious
We had to laught at the *erratic* flight of the rabbit as he zigged and zagged ahead of us down the path.

erudite (adj) +
possessing great knowledge, therefore *learned*
After reading Winston Churchill, I concluded that he was one of the most *erudite,* profound men of this century.

esoteric (adj)	*of knowledge belonging to certain initiated people only* The old Druidic priests guarded their *esoteric* knowledge so carefully that archaeologists and historians fear that their information is lost forever.
essence (n)	*the very core or most vital aspect of a thing*; its very nature; essential, basic thing* The historian said, "We have only physical remains like Stonehenge to help us understand the *essence* of the ancient culture of Britain."
estrange (v) –	*to set apart or at odds that which had been closely attuned; to alienate* Sometimes new students in school feel *estranged* from society because they lack the close friendships they had in their former schools.
eulogy (n) +	*great praise* (often in a formal way as at a funeral); *encomium;* literally *"good words"* in Greek An apt *eulogy* for Mark Twain could have included his famous quote "When in doubt, tell the truth," since he always told it as he saw it.
euphemism (n)	*use of carefully chosen acceptable words in place of those that may insult, offend, or be too honest;* literally *"good speech"* in Greek

Our language is crammed with *euphemisms* that let us say in public what would otherwise be upsetting words or phrases, e.g., "unattractive" for "ugly"; "precocious" for "spoiled brat"; "terminated" for "fired" (from a job); and "passed on" for "died." It isn't hard to pick out the *euphemisms*, is it?

When Erin flunked her history test, she tried hard to think of a cheerful *euphemism* for "failing grade," but she couldn't, and her mother didn't mince any words in discussing Erin's study habits.

euphony (n) +	*pleasing, agreeable sound;* literally *"good sound"* in Greek Edgar Allan Poe, who wrote many horror stories and detective mysteries, is also remembered for the *euphony* of his poetry.
execration (n) –	*swear or curse*; the thing cursed or reviled* Jean spent the last 3 miles of the race muttering *execrations* at her injured knee, which threatened to give out at any minute.
exigency (n)	*an urgently demanding time or state of affairs; what is absolutely needed for a particular circumstance* (usually used in the plural: **exigencies**) "The *exigencies* of racing," Mickey explained, "are such that athletes must train carefully for marathons if they expect to finish and still be smiling."
exonerate (v) +	*to free from blame or guilt; to exculpate, absolve* A destitute man, Jean Valjean in *Les Misérables* stole bread to feed his family and was speedily imprisoned, where he aged with no hope of being *exonerated*.
exorcise (v)	*to get rid of something terrible* (as an evil spirit) *by formal prayer, order, etc.* A modern horror fantasy, *The Exorcist* tells the story of a girl possessed by the devil, which was finally *exorcised* by a courageous priest.
exotic (adj)	*foreign, strange, different* Many *exotic* horror tales not only stir the imagination but also foster nightmares galore.
expatiate (v)	*to write or speak lengthily, with detail; to expound* Old-time preachers *expatiated* each Sunday, often about hellfire and damnation, in the hope of convincing congregations that heaven was the place to aim for.
expatriate (n)	*one living outside his or her native country, often voluntarily*
expatriate (v)	*to order out of the country; to leave one's native country or renounce it;* literally *"out of the fatherland"* Certain crimes against the government call for the guilty to be *expatriated*, often for the rest of their lives.

expedient (adj)	*suitable, practical; advisable, opportunistic** Doing what is merely *expedient* rather than what is right can be a strong temptation, but it may lead to a regrettable end.
expedite (v) +	*to cause to move along at a desirable rate; facilitate* In order to *expedite* this shipment of oranges, we will send them with the fastest carrier available.
expiate (v)	*to make up for, in the sense of atoning; to make amends* Seeing the mouse in the trap made me feel so awful that I *expiated* part of my guilt by burying him in our backyard pet cemetery.
explicit (adj)	*absolutely clear and definite; precise; specific, express* Although the directions on the package of hair dye were *explicit*, Bonnie did it her own way, and the result was orange hair.
expunge (v)	*to obliterate, erase, efface totally; to destroy* Nat and Bob felt that their exemplary behavior throughout their senior year ought to encourage the guidance counselor to *expunge* notes of former mischief from their school records.
extant (adj)	*in actual experience; intact** (as opposed to lost or ruined) Many old, original manuscripts are *extant*, carefully preserved in the rare book rooms of libraries.
extemporize (v)	*to speak without formal preparation; to improvise on the spur of the moment* Using small note cards, with only a phrase on them for suggestions, each person in our speech class had to *extemporize* for 3 minutes.
extenuate (v)	*to reduce the severity or importance of; to mitigate* (a crime, an illness, etc.) Jill sat down after only 2 minutes of her extemporaneous speech, saying that her sore throat ought to *extenuate* her crime of being too brief.
extraneous (adj)	*of extra, nonessential parts; irrelevant;* **ex**trinsic as opposed to **in**trinsic "What is all this *extraneous* information about mice doing in a term paper on feline intelligence?" asked the biology teacher.

QUIZ ON LIST 7

I. **Words in Context.** Put the best possible word in each blank, using the clues in the phrases as your guide.

1. ideas _____ from his brain as naturally as piny smells from our forest

2. often _____ her older sister

3. awards that _____ respect

4. the _____ called Rubik's cube

5. _____ nature of perfect happiness

6. the _____ delights of fresh-baked bread

7. his thoughtless _____, yelled in anger

8. _____ scholars in advanced studies

9. nomadic caravans following their _____ course across our country

10. the _____ effects of the cross-country race against strong opponents

(a) engender
(b) epicurean
(c) enigma
(d) erudite
(e) emanated
(f) erratic
(g) epithets
(h) enervating
(i) emulates
(j) ephemeral

II.   **Antonyms or Synonyms.** Choose the best antonym *or* synonym from the choices offered. There will be one or the other, not both.

1. **extraneous**   (A) odorous (B) noisy (C) irrelevant (D) nasty
2. **exotic**   (A) common (B) exhausted (C) floral (D) democratic
3. **extant**   (A) stable (B) nonexistent (C) unstable (D) old
4. **expunge**   (A) type of sponge (B) wash (C) scrub (D) efface
5. **explicit**   (A) indefinite (B) folded (C) nice (D) split evenly
6. **expedite**   (A) journey (B) impede (C) on foot (D) retire
7. **expatiate**   (A) displaced person (B) home country (C) expound (D) fight
8. **exonerate**   (A) appall (B) desist (C) connect (D) absolve
9. **emaciated**   (A) wan (B) husky (C) prolonged (D) dire
10. **euphony**   (A) cacophony (B) noise (C) humor (D) poetry
11. **esoteric**   (A) vague (B) public (C) hand cream (D) of love
12. **extemporize**   (A) improvise (B) save time (C) dawdle (D) lengthen
13. **equivocal**   (A) loud (B) equitable (C) talk (D) evasive
14. **enthrall**   (A) entrance (B) unite (C) separate (D) cheer up
15. **enjoin**   (A) link (B) accrue (C) encourage (D) repeat

III. **Favorite SAT/PSAT Word Families.** Select the best definition of each numbered word to write on the lines.
A. GEN = kind, origin, birth, race

_____ 1. indigenous
_____ 2. degenerate
_____ 3. congenial
_____ 4. ingenuous
_____ 5. engender
_____ 6. ingenious
_____ 7. congenital

(a) warm, amicable, sociable
(b) inventive, clever
(c) to beget, produce, sponsor
(d) connected with birth
(e) native to an area
(f) innocent, trusting, naive
(g) to sink to a lower state

B. SACR, SANC, SECR = sacred, holy

_____ 8. desecrate
_____ 9. consecrate
_____ 10. sanctify
_____ 11. sacrosanct
_____ 12. execrable
_____ 13. execration
_____ 14. sacrilege

(a) to consecrate, set apart as holy
(b) gross lack of reverence
(c) a curse
(d) to profane, defile something sacred
(e) literally holy of holies, the most sacred
(f) to dedicate; note as sacred
(g) wretched, revolting

IV.   **Truth or Fiction?** Write T for statements that are true, F for those that are false.

_____ 1. If you can cite extenuating circumstances, you may get yourself out of a jam.
_____ 2. You can expiate your guilt by resolving to forget the whole nasty business.
_____ 3. People known for doing what is expedient have tons of friends.
_____ 4. Now living in France, John Schmatz of Wisconsin can be called an expatriate.
_____ 5. Michener's *Tales of the South Pacific* was properly termed an exotic story when it was published.
_____ 6. You should exorcise regularly to stay trim and healthy.
_____ 7. It is rarely acceptable to substitute a euphemism for the actual word you mean.
_____ 8. The exigencies of World War II demanded few sacrifices from involved nations.

_____ 9. Daffy Duck is the epitome of rational behavior.

_____ 10. A moving funeral eulogy may serve to reunite family members previously estranged.

_____ 11. The tourist appeal of old graveyards is greatly enhanced by eccentric epitaphs on some of the tombstones.

_____ 12. Empirical information is all that is required before marketing new medications.

_____ 13. One in an eminent position typically receives a limited emolument.

_____ 14. It's a good idea to extirpate perennials after they have bloomed in late autumn.

List 8

facade (n)	_front or outward appearance of a building or a person; the face you show to the world_ Huck Finn had a carefully preserved _facade_, an appearance of self-confidence and boldness that hid his lack of assurance and occasional fear.
facetious (adj)	_humorous, but sometimes awkwardly so; jocose, witty_

Word lovers have noted a few English words that have all their vowels in alphabetical order, e.g., **facetious** and **abstemious**. Can you think of any others—or maybe more fun, can you make up a word that has all the vowels in order and sounds like a "real" word? If so, _use_ your brand-new word and see if it catches on. New words come into our language all the time.

	If Huck were in your class, he might be known for _facetious_ remarks, nearly always made when a teacher would be unreceptive to humor.
facile (adj) –	_easily done, therefore maybe done superficially*; ready, fluent_ Joleen told our committee that a _facile_ solution would not suffice. She said that the administration wanted a carefully thought out plan.
fallacious (adj) –	_false or deceptive; tending to delude or mislead_ Scientific laboratories are aware that _fallacious_ results would be worthless, besides being damaging to their credibility.
fastidious (adj)	_demanding the utmost, persnickety; showing meticulous workmanship or care_ True science is exact, requiring that experiments be performed with _fastidious_ care under strict guidelines.
feasible (adj)	_capable of being accomplished; reasonable or possible; likely_ If it's _feasible_ to eat dinner early, we could go to the first movie showing and still be home by nine-thirty.
felicitous (adj) +	_fortunate or apt (as a remark); pleasant, fit, suitable_ The entire family enjoys Clare because her _felicitous_ comments and ever-pleasant manner put each one of us at ease.
feral (adj) –	_fierce, wild, savage_ (from L. **ferus = wild**); _returning to the wild after being domesticated_ _Feral_ dogs roam in packs throughout Africa, hunting for food, which is often hard to find.
fervent (adj)	_full of strong, sincere emotion; impassioned_ In some West Coast suburbs, occasional coyote raids on young children and pets have inspired _fervent_ pleas for action from local governments.
festoon (n)	_a draped garland_ (as crepe paper **festoons**)
festoon (v)	_to drape or hang into festoon shapes_ Steve's prom committee was allowed to _festoon_ the hotel ballroom with flower garlands before the dance.
fetid (adj) –	_stinking, malodorous_ As the water level dropped to lower and lower depths in the canal, nearby residents noticed a _fetid_ odor from that region.

fetish (n)	*something of personal—possibly irrational—significance; charm, talisman, or amulet* Fred, our crazy family cat, has an old piece of blanket that he carries about with him and curls up with at nap time. Dad says that old blanket is Fred's *fetish*.
fiasco (n) –	*a total flop, complete failure* "No more *fiascoes* like last time," my sister announced. "This time we'll plan the party so that people don't sit around and yawn."
filch (v) –	*to steal in a sneaky way* (usually something of minor value) Our cat Fred tried to *filch* one of my brother's gerbils as a tasty lunch, but luckily we heard the clink of the cage cover just in time.
flaccid (adj) –	*without customary firmness, flabby, limp* Fred has become a *flaccid* old tomcat from too many naps on the sofa and no mice to goad him into action.
flagrant (adj) –	*conspicuous in a highly negative way; glaring, gross* In *flagrant* disobedience of house rules, Fred crouches atop the television set and gazes longingly down into the gerbils' cage.
flaunt (v) –	*to show off; display in a superior, objectionable manner* Safe inside their dry aquarium, the gerbils *flaunt* themselves in front of Fred and carry on as though he weren't a threat.
florid (adj)	*very flowery* (as writing style*); *high-colored, ruddy* (of complexion) Modern editors generally avoid a *florid* literary style, deleting extraneous words and sentences whenever feasible.
fluctuate (v)	*to come and go, as waves; to shift up and down** (as the stock market **fluctuates** daily) Temperatures in a Florida winter may *fluctuate* greatly, a fact that gives citrus growers many headaches.
foible (n) –	*a minor fault or shortcoming; weakness* It's strangely comforting to know that others are as full of *foibles* as we are, perfection seeming forever beyond human reach.
forensic (adj)	*of law or public debate; argumentative** (as in a case in court) For a kid, Andy's *forensic* skills are considerable. He succeeded in convincing our parents that Fred belonged outdoors unless Andy was home to guard the gerbils.
formidable (adj)	*arousing fear or worry; fostering respect or awe** Fred's *formidable* meowing echoed in our ears as the disgruntled cat begged to be let inside.
forte (n) +	*special strength or skill; what you're known for* Loud meows had always been Fred's *forte,* and as time passed it looked as though the family was weakening in its resolve to keep him outside.
fortnight (n)	*two weeks* (from Old English **feowertyne niht = fourteen nights**) After a long and vocal *fortnight,* Fred won and was allowed back in the house, much to my relief.
fortuitous (adj)	*happening by chance*; accidental* Fred's temporary exile led to several *fortuitous* meetings with unlucky neighborhood mice.
fractious (adj) –	*difficult to discipline; unruly, troublesome* When Fred took up his watch on the gerbils once more, my brother Andy resumed his *fractious* ways until Mom threatened to put *him* outside for a fortnight.
frugal (adj)	*careful about how money or goods are used; carefully economical; sparing* Cara says she has enough money to last through the month, but only if she is *frugal* in her spending.

fulsome (adj) –
overabundant; flattering to the point of annoyance or embarrassment*; overdone; obsequious or servile
The professional golfer was embarrassed to read the newspaper's *fulsome* praise of his achievements on the tour.

furtive (adj) –
of sly or secretive behavior*; surreptitious, even *stolen* (as **furtive** goods)
The *furtive* movements of the fox in the henhouse went unnoticed until it was too late for one sleepy hen.

futile (adj) –
without use or purpose; ineffectual; vain, fruitless
The noisy and *futile* efforts of the hen to escape the fox aroused all of the other chickens and eventually the entire farm.

gambol (v) +
to frolic about like lambs in a pasture; to frisk about
In *All Creatures Great and Small*, James Herriot affectionately describes young animals *gamboling* across the hillsides of spring in England.

gamut (n)
a range (as scales run the **gamut** from high to low notes)
As he watched the birth of his first child, the father's emotions ran the *gamut* from fear to excitement to awe.

garrulous (adj) –
extremely talkative; loquacious, gabby, verbose
After his daughter's birth, the new father was *garrulous* in the extreme, telling everyone he saw about his new and perfect child.

gelid (adj)
very cold; icy (said of people's attitudes as well as of substances)
The haughty old queen gave her subjects a brief, *gelid* smile as she informed them that their audience was over.

generic (adj)
of a type or class (not a brand name, for example)*; *universal*
Generic products appear regularly as merchants try to offer lower prices and a variety of products to their customers.

gentility (n)
referring to the upper class or gentry*; courtesy
Staring at pictures of my cousin's run-down commune, our aunt shuddered. "It's obvious they're not concerned with *gentility*," she snapped.

germane (adj)
fitting and appropriate; pertinent, relevant
My cousin snapped back. "We were experimenting with community life, and outdated mannerisms weren't *germane* to our experiment."

gibe (v) –
to make fun of or tease with rude remarks; to scoff, deride
Feeling self-conscious, I listened as my aunt and cousin *gibed* at each other, each determined to express her own opinions.

girth (n)
a measurement around (as the dog's **girth** was large even for a Saint Bernard); *strap or band that encircles* (as the **girth** that helps to hold a saddle in place on a horse)
Derived from the European Saint Nicholas, our Santa Claus is usually depicted as a round fellow of rather noticeable *girth*.

goad (n)
an instrument or prod used to stimulate action

goad (v)
to urge onward; to spur (from Old English **gad = spear**)
My cousin *goaded* my normally considerate, polite aunt into remarks that I was sure she would later regret.

gossamer (n)
anything delicate, as a spider's web

gossamer (adj)
filmy, insubstantial

Legends tell different tales of the origin of the word **gossamer.** One story says that it was the threads of the Virgin Mary's shroud, which drifted down to earth as she ascended to heaven. That tale says it was "god's seam." Another version suggests derivation from "god's summer" and another from *gaze à Marie,* Mary's thread. Still another possible source is the Middle English word *gossomer = goose summer,* a time when geese and their feathery down are in full supply (early November).

According to Cole Porter, "a trip to the moon" could be made "on *gossamer* wings." (How do you suppose the astronauts would feel about that?)

gratuitous (adj) –　*offered freely; not necessary under the circumstances,* and therefore *unwanted; unasked for; unwarranted*
Ever ready with *gratuitous* advice, my uncle spent hours telling me how to handle myself the first year away at college.

gregarious (adj) +　*fond of groups; social and sociable, convivial*
Like people, elephants are *gregarious* and enjoy the company of family groups.

gremlin (n) –　*a tiny person* (like a gnome) *blamed for equipment problems*
When I baby-sat with Harold, a six-year-old, I told him he was a *gremlin* who would always be in trouble if he couldn't keep his hands off other people's things.

grueling (adj) –　*demanding, exhausting, tiring; punishing*
Sitting for Harold is a *grueling* job, his mother admitted, because you have to keep your eyes on him every minute.

guile (n) –　*trickery or cunning; duplicity*
The use of *guile* is not respected in humans, but in the wild a *guileless* coyote would be a hungry coyote.

gullible (adj)　*easy to fool or deceive; ingenuous*
The cartoon cat Garfield loves to play tricks on the *gullible* dog Odie, who is the butt of Garfield's jokes.

QUIZ ON LIST 8

I.　**Words in Context.** Put the best possible words in the sentences below, choosing from the list given. Number and tense may need to be changed.

generic	fetish	filch
formidable	fallacious	girth
fortuitous	facetious	foible
forensic	germane	fulsome
gamut	futile	gentility

1. "As a lawyer who ought to possess fine _____ skills, he leaves much to be desired," grumbled the client.

2. Mark Twain's _____ skill with words is evident in the novella *The Mysterious Stranger.*

3. Your _____ early arrival will allow us to go ahead and do great things before the day gets away from us.

4. He's a seasoned performer, with dramatic talent running the _____ from Shakespeare to musical comedy.

5. Druggists stock _____ drugs, which are often less expensive than brand-name products and are just as efficacious.

6. Trying to scale that mountain without proper equipment will be a _____, senseless task.

7. "Telling me that 'everyone does it' is an example of _____ reasoning," Mom said, "and it makes me mad besides!"

8. The lawyer dredged up every bit of corroborative evidence that he felt was _____ to the case and might be used as evidence in court.

9. No longer a legend for his monumental _____, the now-slender old elephant searched hungrily throughout the game reserve for food.

10. The young Indian boy's _____ bag contained a precious blue stone, an eagle feather, and other objects that he kept hidden.

11. Andy's _____ comment was hilarious to us, but not to Mom or Dad.

12. When Mom's not in the kitchen, I quietly _____ a few cookies to stave off hunger pangs before dinner.

13. Jane Austen's female characters manage to combine English _____ with universally feminine traits.

14. Most pets have a fault or two, but our Fred was endowed with more than his share of _____.

15. Much eighteenth- and nineteenth-century writing appears _____ when compared with today's leaner, more concise prose.

II. **Antonyms.** Match the vocabulary words with their antonyms.

_____	1. facade	(a) complex
_____	2. facile	(b) unfortunate
_____	3. fastidious	(c) to compliment
_____	4. gibe	(d) fragrant
_____	5. felicitous	(e) casual
_____	6. feral	(f) warranted
_____	7. fetid	(g) rear
_____	8. guile	(h) hide
_____	9. flaccid	(i) discerning
_____	10. flaunt	(j) civilized
_____	11. gullible	(k) honesty
_____	12. gratuitous	(l) muscular

III. **Favorite SAT/PSAT Word Families.** Select the best definition for each numbered word and write it on the line.

A. FRA, FRAG, FRACT = break

_____	1. fragmentary	(a) unmanageable, literally breaking back or away
_____	2. fractious	(b) weak, slight; easily destroyed or broken
_____	3. frail	(c) a violation of rules
_____	4. refractory	(d) to encroach on, trespass
_____	5. infraction	(e) incomplete, in parts
_____	6. infringe	(f) unruly, troublesome

B. GREG = group, herd, flock

_____	7. gregarious	(a) to set aside or apart
_____	8. segregate	(b) outstandingly bad
_____	9. congregate	(c) the total, combined amount
_____	10. aggregate	(d) convivial, sociable
_____	11. egregious	(e) to gather together

IV.   **Analogies.** Select the lettered pair that best reflects the relationship of the given pair.

1. COMPLEXION : FLORID ::
   (A) decoration : fruitless (B) error : flagrant (C) ideas : gossamer (D) water : liquid
   (E) physique : fastidious

2. GARRULOUS : FRUGAL ::
   (A) formidable : awesome (B) felicitous : flaccid (C) fallacious : prone (D) fortuitous : chancy
   (E) fervent : apathetic

3. FLUCTUATE : STATIC ::
   (A) festoon : decorative (B) flaunt : aggressive (C) gambol : fixed (D) gibe : taunting
   (E) goad : successful

4. THIEF : FURTIVE ::
   (A) artist : formidable (B) chef : frugal (C) impostor : grueling (D) charlatan : facile
   (E) brigand : facetious

5. REMEDY : DRASTIC ::
   (A) task : grueling (B) overcoat : gossamer (C) gremlin : derisive (D) purchase : flagrant
   (E) speech : flaccid

V.   **Remembering Definitions.** Without looking back (at least until you're totally stumped), write a brief definition or explanation—maybe synonyms—for the following:

1. facetious ___
2. feasible ___
3. festoon (v) ___
4. fiasco ___
5. forte ___
6. fortnight ___
7. gelid ___
8. goad ___
9. gratuitous ___
10. gullible ___

List 9

hackneyed (adj) –	*without originality; trite, banal, overused*
	The hackney was a breed of horse that pulled the large, public coaches in England—especially popular in London, near the place where the horses were bred. Like the dull, repetitive routine of a hackney coach, a hackneyed phrase is boring, all-too-common, overused.
	The book reviewer criticized the author for his use of *hackneyed* phrases such as "dry as dust" and "comfortable as an old shoe."
haggard (adj) –	*appearing drawn, gaunt, and exhausted* After hours of dragging the river for bodies from the capsized boat, the rescuers were *haggard* and distraught.
hapless (adj) –	*unlucky, unfortunate* The *hapless* boat crew, unused to the whims of the river, had run aground and capsized their craft in the night.
harass (v) –	*to irritate or annoy repeatedly; to worry (someone)* Lollipop, a young and frisky poodle, delights in *harassing* our old tomcat, Fred. To *harass* Lollipop, Fred leaps to a branch just out of the dog's reach.

harbinger (n)

forerunner; something that foreshadows the future; precursor
If robins are the *harbingers* of spring, then dandelions are never far behind as precursors of summer.

haughty (adj) –

unbecomingly proud, disdainful (from L. **haut = high**)
Normally a laughing, friendly girl, Ellen had to act *haughty* and reserved for her role in the school play.

hedonist (n)

someone who lives for pleasure or happiness
Ann warned us, "For that one summer before college, I plan to live a *hedonist's* life and play all day long, every day."

heed (v)

to pay attention to or notice; be mindful of
Physicians caution patients to *heed* the advice printed on all medicine bottles.

heinous (adj) –

absolutely hateful; abominable, outrageous
Newspapers seem to concentrate on reporting *heinous* crimes, knowing that gory news sells papers.

heresy (n) –

belief that is against church teachings; any strong dissent from accepted belief or theory*
It would be *heresy* to the news media to suggest that reporters spend their time covering life's finer, better moments.

heyday (n) +

the best period in performance, prosperity, health, etc.
In his *heyday*, Fred Astaire was film's most polished dancer.

hiatus (n)

a gap or lapse in action; a break (from L. **hiatus = yawn**)
The Christmas vacation provides a welcome *hiatus* for students who need a holiday from books.

hirsute (adj)

noticeably hairy; bristly
An orangutan has a special *hirsute* appeal dressed in human clothes and clowning happily before an audience.

histrionic (adj)

of acting or drama; sometimes, overly dramatic; theatrical
The *histrionic* abilities of chimps and orangutans have been developed to high levels by trainers who understand the intelligence of those animals.

hoax (v) –

to deceive, dupe

hoax (n) –

a trick or deception
My Aunt Betty dressed as a witch for Halloween, but her *hoax* was almost too good: the younger trick-or-treaters were scared silly.

homily (n)

a lecture or sermon on being good
Mr. Tillson delivers little *homilies* on the slightest provocation, but we like him, so we all nod and say, "Yes, sir," at the end of each speech.

hoodwink (v) –

to fool by false appearances; to dupe or hoax
Hoping to *hoodwink* our cat Fred, Lollipop the poodle lay very still, all bunched up, pretending to be a black rock until Fred came close.

humane (adj) +

demonstrating kindness, understanding, and compassion for other human beings or for animals
Humane zookeepers interested in promoting a species and keeping their animals contented create the most natural environments possible for their inmates.

husbandry (n)

careful use of resources; conservation; also the care and growth of plants and animals*; agriculture
The bounty of their vegetable garden and the beauty of their property testify to the careful *husbandry* that Jan and Frank have practiced over the years.

hyperbole (n)

wild exaggeration, often deliberate (for effect)

Legend has it that a fourth-century B.C. Athenian named Hyperbolus ("far-throwing") was known for his great exaggerations. But experts suspect that the word **hyperbole** actually predated the Athenian. "I'm so hot I could die," is *hyperbole*, also "hungry as a bear" and "mile-high pie."

As a major technique of satirists, *hyperbole* is used to good effect in books such as *Huckleberry Finn, Gulliver's Travels,* and *Vile Bodies.*

hypocrite (n) –	*someone who pretends to hold beliefs or virtues that he or she really doesn't have; a dissembler; a fake* (in a sense) ". . . the *hypocrite's* crime is that he bears false witness against himself."—Hannah Arendt, *On Revolution,* 1963
hypothetical (adj)	*depending on conditions; based on a hypothesis or supposition** "Our premise is purely *hypothetical* so far," said the director of our student poll. "Now we must test our theory by taking an actual poll."
iconoclast (n) –	*a person who criticizes established ideas or traditions;* literally *"image destroyer"* in Greek Besides being something of an *iconoclast,* John Lennon is remembered for his very special musical talents.
idiom (n)	*a language (or phrases) distinct for a locale or set of people; dialect; a common, well-known expression of a specific person, place, or time* (as "redd up the house" = to clean house in regional dialect) *Idioms* from the 1950s were revived and made popular again by the hit musical *Grease.*
idiosyncrasy (n)	*a peculiarity that sets someone apart; eccentricity* My grampa had many lovable *idiosyncrasies,* one being his insistence that dessert be served after every meal, even after breakfast.
ignominy (n) –	*profound disgrace or humiliation; dishonor; infamy* Lucifer's *ignominy* caused him to set up shop as Satan, master of the bleak realms severely south of heaven.
imbroglio (n) –	*an awkward, embarrassing, often confusing situation; embroilment or altercation* As usual, Andy's free-for-all variety of football ended up in an *imbroglio* that forced Dad to step in as umpire.
immutable (adj)	*unchangeable, unalterable; eternal* "Survival of the fittest" is one of nature's *immutable* laws.
impale (v) –	*to stab with a pointed instrument* (often a form of torture, almost always leading to death); also used metaphorically, as *she impaled him with her stare* The wild animal, pathetically *impaled* on a sharp stake, died a slow and painful death.
impalpable (adj)	*not able to be felt, therefore intangible;* also *not easily discernible to the mind* Certain feelings, like lifting of the spirits, are nearly *impalpable,* yet highly significant to each of us.
impart (v)	*to give information, communicate; to give as from an abundance* (e.g., for **imparting** flavor, Parmesan cheese is marvelous in soups) The beginning writer felt that, if the instructor could *impart* only a portion of her knowledge, then the course would be worthwhile.
impasse (n) –	*point at which no way out can be seen*; a dead end or cul-de-sac; a deadlock* "Negotiations have reached an *impasse,*" reported the mediator, "with both sides refusing to budge an inch."
impeccable (adj) +	*flawless or perfect; free from blame or sin; immaculate* Although our French instructor was English, his French accent was *impeccable.*
impecunious (adj)	*without money; penniless; poor; indigent* (from L. **pecunia** = **money**) While it is common for novice writers and actors to live *impecunious* lives, none appreciate it very much.

impediment (n) –   *something that gets in your way and impedes progress or speech; a hindrance*
Railing at his leg cast in exasperation, Todd complained that it was more of an *impediment* than he had ever believed possible.

imperturbable (adj) +   *being unusually calm and serene; cool or unflappable*
Todd told us how he respected the *imperturbable* attitudes of nurses he had met in the emergency room after his accident on the soccer field.

impervious (adj)   *not capable of being penetrated or harmed; impenetrable; unaffected*
"It's not that the nurses were *impervious* to pain or suffering," Todd explained, "because they weren't."

impetus (n)   *the stimulus that gets something going; impulse, incentive*
Don's salutatorian address at commencement was titled "The *Impetus* to Achieve."

implacable (adj) –   *not able to be appeased or soothed;* literally *"not peaceful"* in Latin
By her youthful beauty, Snow White incurred the *implacable* hatred of the evil queen, her stepmother.

implicit (adj)   *implied though not stated; suggested; potential* (as a musician may hear new melodies **implicit** in old ones)
Dad didn't actually say we had to be home by 12, but it was *implicit* when he urged us to "be in on time," which has always meant midnight in our family.

importunate (adj) –   *being persistent and pesty in demands or requests; troublesome*
Our cat Fred drove us berserk with his *importunate* demands for attention after he broke his hip in a fall from the roof.

imprecation (n) –   *curse; denunciation; execration*
After Fred had been in his hip cast for only a few days, everyone in the family was mumbling *imprecations* in the direction of our demanding cat.

impunity (n)   *freedom from punishment or penalty*
The Latin motto of the Scottish crown and all Scottish regiments is "Nemo me *impune* lacessit," which translates, "No one provokes me with *impunity*," a noble way of saying, "Don't bug me if you know what's good for you."

inadvertent (adj)   *not on purpose; unintentional; accidental*
My *inadvertent* gesture knocked my glass of Coke to the floor.

inane (adj) –   *empty, silly, and foolish; insipid, fatuous*
Those without a fund of small talk tend to regard party chatter as *inane* and boring.

QUIZ ON LIST 9

I.　**Synonyms.** Write the best synonym beside each vocabulary word.

_____	1. haughty	(a) bigot
_____	2. hoodwink	(b) lapse
_____	3. idiom	(c) embroilment
_____	4. imprecation	(d) intangible
_____	5. hypocrite	(e) abominable
_____	6. immutable	(f) troublesome
_____	7. hiatus	(g) hoax
_____	8. humane	(h) compassionate
_____	9. impalpable	(i) execration
_____	10. importunate	(j) dialect
_____	11. heinous	(k) disdainful
_____	12. imbroglio	(l) eternal
_____	13. inane	(m) serene
_____	14. imperturbable	(n) hindrance
_____	15. impediment	(o) fatuous

II.　**Words in Context.** Choose the most appropriate word to fit each phrase.

1. an _____ slip of the tongue　　　impecunious
2. _____ remarks that drive us crazy　　　implicit
3. deeper meanings _____ in her phrases　　　imparting
4. necessary _____ to go ahead with this project　　　inane
5. raincoat _____ to moisture　　　impervious
6. _____ beggars on the church steps　　　inadvertent
7. a skeleton _____ deep mystery to the cave　　　immutable
8. the _____ march of time　　　impetus
9. an _____ determination to seek revenge　　　idiosyncrasies
10. understandable _____ of one who is old and　　　implacable
   has always lived alone

III.　**Antonyms.** Find the two words that are antonyms in each set of words.

1. (A) impasse　(B) indigent　(C) cul-de-sac　(D) affluent
2. (A) clean　(B) flawed　(C) impeccable　(D) nice
3. (A) honor　(B) hate　(C) ignominy　(D) grace
4. (A) faith　(B) belief　(C) iconoclast　(D) traditionalist
5. (A) fact　(B) studious　(C) hypothesis　(D) earnest
6. (A) ascetic　(B) hedonist　(C) hypocrite　(D) demagogue
7. (A) undervalued　(B) ingenious　(C) histrionic　(D) understated
8. (A) bird　(B) follower　(C) harbinger　(D) robin
9. (A) foolish　(B) fortunate　(C) hapless　(D) happy
10. (A) fresh　(B) airy　(C) carriage　(D) hackneyed

IV.   **Truth or Fiction?** Circle T for statements that are true, F for those that are false.

T F   1. You can pinch your little brother with impunity.

T F   2. Answers to SAT/PSAT reading comprehension questions are often implicit in the written passages and not stated directly.

T F   3. You have reached an impasse when you want to borrow the car and your folks say, "No dice."

T F   4. Metaphorically speaking, your debating opponents can impale themselves on an emotional, insupportable statement.

T F   5. "A number of Northern and Southern soldiers died in the Civil War," is a comment exemplifying hyperbole.

T F   6. If you husband your resources while in high school, you'll have a bigger nest egg to deposit in your college bank account.

T F   7. When you supervise young children, you're apt to find yourself repeating homilies learned from those who guided you.

T F   8. A good chess player would never resort to a hoax.

T F   9. Abraham Lincoln eschewed (shunned, avoided) a hirsute appearance.

T F 10. Vaudeville is currently in its heyday.

T F 11. The Salem "witches" were accused of heresy.

T F 12. Those heedless of the wind and weather will have wet feet some day.

T F 13. Wile E. Coyote wouldn't dream of harassing the Roadrunner.

T F 14. After days of pounding westward with the mails, a pony express rider had the right to appear haggard.

T F 15. *Fresh* or *novel* or *original* might appear on an SAT as an antonym for *hackneyed*.

List 10

incandescence (n)	*from* **candere = to glow;** *noticeable brightness or clarity; glowing* (as a light or candle) Mary's *incandescence* on stage lights up not only her performance but that of the other cast members too.
incantation (n)	*a written or spoken spell with the hope of invoking magic; any special group of repeated words* My usual *incantation* before a Latin test is, "O Minerva, goddess of wisdom, visit me during this test!"
incarcerate (v)	*to lock up or confine against a person's will; to imprison* The baby I cared for last weekend was so naughty that I had to *incarcerate* him in his playpen in order to keep track of him.
incendiary (n)	*a person who sets fires; a bomb*
incendiary (adj)	*of deliberate burning* (of property); *tending to start fires, either literally or figuratively*; inflammatory** The rebel's *incendiary* pamphlets were circulated among the people, who were then inflamed by the revolutionary words and ideas.
incessant (adj)	*going on without interruption; ceaseless, continuous* Our science field trip had to be canceled because the *incessant* spring rains had flooded many roads that led to the wildlife refuge.
inchoate (adj)	*not well formed or formulated; embryonic, in a sense; vague* The principal's *inchoate* suspicions that the seniors were up to another prank were proved accurate when a mooing cow met him at the door to the gym on Monday morning.

incipient (adj)

just beginning or apparent; commencing, burgeoning
"I think," Kay said as she scratched discreetly, "that these little bumps are an *incipient* case of poison ivy."

incite (v) –

to stir or spur on to action; to foment, instigate, abet
People are restless in internment camps; it never takes much to *incite* a full-scale riot.

incognito (adj or adv)

with a hidden identity
Famous stars prefer traveling *incognito* to avoid being mobbed for autographs.

incongruous (adj)

seeming out of place or unsuited; incompatible
The formal waistcoat looked *incongruous* on Sid, who was also wearing jeans and basketball shoes.

incorrigible (adj) –

extremely difficult to manage or control (of people or animals)*; *delinquent, recalcitrant*
"That's an absolutely *incorrigible* beast," my older brother John said, as he watched our cat Fred stare hungrily down into the gerbils' cage.

increment (n)

an increase, as in salary or worth; one of a series of regular enlargements
A regular cost-of-living pay raise provides salary *increments* based on rising costs, a debatable practice believed by some to fuel inflation.

incriminate (v) –

to accuse of blame or implicate as blameworthy
We suspected that Fred the cat had been fishing in our goldfish bowl. When we felt his paw, its dampness *incriminated* Fred and confirmed our suspicions.

incubus (n) –

evil spirit; any depressing weight (as worry) or burden

From Latin, for *nightmare*, in the Middle Ages, this word came to mean a male demon, *incubus,* that took advantage of women while they slept. The opposite number was a female demon, *succubus,* who was attracted to men.

The decision of whether or not to move pressed upon our family like an *incubus* as the days wore on without a conclusion.

indifferent (adj)

neutral or unbiased*; impartial; sometimes apathetic
Molly said she was *indifferent* to where we pitched camp at Lake Wannawanna, since she planned to stay near the tent and read every day.

indolent (adj) –

naturally lazy or idle
We accused Molly of being basically *indolent,* but she retorted that vacations were supposed to be a change and relaxation was the change she had in mind.

indomitable (adj)

unconquerable; dauntless
Molly proved *indomitable* as our vacation days slid by and she continued to read contentedly near the tent.

ineffable (adj)

indescribable; difficult to express in words
As we tired of the constant swimming, boating, and hiking, we noticed the *ineffable* expression of peace that had settled on Molly's face—she who had never left camp.

inept (adj) –

lacking competence or fitness; not suited to the place, time, or job; awkward, bungling
We had to laugh with Molly over her dedicated yet *inept* attempts to build a campfire.

inert (adj)

exceedingly slow to move or act; sluggish, inactive
One late afternoon we returned to camp to find Molly *inert,* dozing on her air mattress. "Reading's too strenuous," she joked.

inevitable (adj)

not avoidable by any means
I suppose it was *inevitable* that the end of our camping trip found everyone in a state of sun-burned exhaustion—all except Molly, of course, who had mastered the art of relaxation.

inexorable (adj)

not movable by any means; relentless, inflexible
Romeo's *inexorable* path to suicide takes him to the apothecary (druggist), and he says,

> The time and my intents are savage-wild,
> More fierce and more *inexorable* far
> Than empty tigers or the roaring sea.—Act V, *Romeo and Juliet*

inference (n)

something deduced or concluded from evidence*; a proposition gained from available data; a conclusion
Even though the dancer did not tell us she was from Mexico, we made that *inference* from her clothing, style of dance, and strongly accented English.

infidel (n)

a religious unbeliever in respect to a particular religion; a disbeliever in some specific sense*
"*Infidel!*" roared the editor. "Anyone who thinks he can publish without careful research and editing will never write for me!"

ingratiate (v)

to work your way into someone's good graces (use with **with**)
Cowed by the editor's anger, the new writer spent the rest of the week *ingratiating* himself with all of the other editors on the staff.

inherent (adj)

natural, inborn*; of essential nature, given the subject; innate
"We hold these truths to be sacred and undeniable; that all men are created equal and independent, that from that equal creation they derive rights *inherent* and inalienable, among which are the preservation of life, and liberty, and the pursuit of happiness."
—Thomas Jefferson, from the original draft of the Declaration of Independence

iniquity (n) –

wickedness, sin*; also grave injustice
Commonly termed "original sin," mankind's inherent *iniquity* is a tenet of many religions.

innocuous (adj)

not offensive or harmful*; also dull or insipid
Cedric had thought Constance was annoyed with him, but her *innocuous* letter gave no hint of anger.

inordinate (adj)

beyond normal limits; unreasonable, excessive, immoderate*
When our cat Fred broke his hip and had to wear a cast, he made *inordinate* demands on the family in the classic style of the terrible patient.

inscrutable (adj)

difficult to understand or interpret; mysterious
During Fred's convalescence he became a master of *inscrutable* stares designed to set us all worrying about how we could make him happy.

insidious (adj) –

alluring but dangerous; treacherous or deceitfully damaging*
Even though Ben's roommate was sick with flu, Ben had thought he was safe until the *insidious* virus sent him to bed too.

insipid (adj) –

lacking interest or stimulation; flat, dull
"Hours of *insipid* conversation and dull games are not my idea of a good date," Nan said with exasperation.

insolvent (adj) –

lacking money; impoverished, "broke"; the opposite is **solvent**
In a typical cartoon gesture, Wally pulled out his pants pockets to illustrate that he was *insolvent* after buying Christmas gifts.

insular (adj)

set apart; isolated (as an island) (from L. **insula = island**)
"The students at our school lead rather *insular* lives," explained the headmaster, "because we are so far outside the town."

interpolate (v)

to add by insertion (words or ideas); *to insert* (something) *between other things*
As Jessie explained how to care for her horse, her sister Meg *interpolated* for my benefit, since I was overwhelmed by all of the instructions.

intone (v)

to say something in a ritualistic or singsong way; to chant
Marni invokes the gods and goddesses at our Latin banquets, but she *intones* her litany in a voice we can barely hear.

intrinsic (adj)

referring to the essential nature of a thing; innate
We all like to be judged for our *intrinsic* worth and not for extrinsic things like money or position.

intuition (n)

natural, quick understanding or perception
Most new parents hesitate to rely on their *intuition* about infants and readily consult a variety of helpful books.

inundate (v)

to overwhelm or flow over, as with a flood
Near the end of the year, the seniors were *inundated* with commitments and work at school.

inure (v)

to adjust to something basically unpleasant; to habituate or accustom
After basic training, recruits are *inured* to long hours and inclement weather—the harsh demands of army life.

invective (n) –

verbal abuse or insult; vituperation
The legendary *invective* that characterizes a drill sergeant's speech serves to goad recruits to achievements they hadn't believed possible.

inveigh (v) –

to object with bitterness; to complain forcefully, maybe lengthily; to rail
The lawyer *inveighed* against the unnecessarily strict sentence given to his client.

inveigle (v)

to convince or persuade by cleverness or flattery; to entice, cajole, wheedle

---

Some words can partially substitute for *inveigle*, but over time each of these synonyms has acquired special shades of meaning.
   1. **Entice** means to allure in a clever, imaginative manner.
   2. **Cajole** means to persuade through flattery and sweet talk.
   3. **Wheedle** means to persuade by repeated begging.

We at last *inveigled* Dad into lending us the car keys by promising to drive carefully and to call home as soon as we got to the party.

inveterate (adj)

well established over time (as a habit); *confirmed; chronic*
Huck Finn's father was an *inveterate* drinker and eventually died from his fatal habit.

irascible (adj) –

easily angered; testy, touchy; cross, choleric, splenetic (from L. **ira = anger**)
Pa Finn was an *irascible* old coot whose ready anger made him a parent Huck was almost unable to mourn after death.

irony (n)

the unexpected, when it is the opposite of what you expected; humor based on incongruity; deliberate use of words so that the meaning construed is the opposite of what was actually said*
At the end of his life, Napoleon was imprisoned ignominiously on an island; that was *irony* for one who envisioned himself a glorious conqueror to be admired by all the world.

iterate (v)

to repeat over and over; to reiterate
Gramma thinks we don't pay attention to her, and so she *iterates* her favorite injunctions on a regular basis.

itinerary (n)

travel route or guide; guidebook
We planned an *itinerary* for our trip that takes us through seven Southern states.

QUIZ ON LIST 10

I.   **Word Meanings.** Choose the word or expression that best matches the word at the left.

1. **incipient**   (A) without a chief (B) beginning (C) final (D) taking over
2. **incantation**   (A) fetish (B) decoration (C) jargon (D) spell
3. **inert**   (A) foolish (B) fast moving (C) inactive (D) inborn
4. **incongruous**   (A) unpleasant (B) not agreeing with (C) not together (D) raucous
5. **incessant**   (A) off and on (B) intermittent (C) entering (D) without pause
6. **incorrigible**   (A) unbreakable (B) tough (C) unmanageable (D) impervious
7. **indomitable**   (A) invincible (B) flat, not domed (C) unrealistic (D) homeless
8. **incubus**   (A) depressing burden (B) embryo (C) beginning (D) evil
9. **incarcerate**   (A) liberate (B) imprison (C) pack up (D) wound
10. **inexorable**   (A) final (B) blameworthy (C) fatal (D) relentless
11. **irony**   (A) hilarity (B) the unexpected (C) the unknown (D) tragedy
12. **inveterate**   (A) aged (B) aggressive (C) habitual (D) erratic
13. **intuition**   (A) eager quickness (B) natural skill (C) uncanny mastery (D) ready perception
14. **intone**   (A) harmonize (B) declaim (C) deliver (D) chant
15. **insidious**   (A) treacherous (B) enticing (C) thoughtful (D) inexorable

II. **Analogies.** Add the word from List 10 that most accurately completes each analogy.

1. splenetic : _____ :: inveigle : cajole
2. _____ : stimulating :: insidious : obvious
3. chandelier : incandescent :: bomb : _____
4. prejudiced : _____ :: inchoate : definite
5. _____ : riot :: foment : dispute

III. **Antonyms.** From the choices offered, select two antonyms to write on the lines for each word in bold type.

dynamic	innocuous	decrease	energetic
alienate	competent	skillful	absolve
harmful	believer	stimulating	divorce
reduction	acquired	devotee	harmless
learned	exculpate	moderate	reasonable

_____   1. **increment**   _____   6. **ingratiate**

_____   2. **incriminate**   _____   7. **inherent**

_____   3. **indolent**   _____   8. **innocuous**

_____   4. **inept**   _____   9. **inordinate**

_____   5. **infidel**   _____   10. **insidious**

IV.   **Favorite SAT/PSAT Word Families.** Write a brief definition or a synonym for each of these test veterans.

    A. COGN = to know

      1. incognito _____

      2. cognizant _____

      3. cognitive _____

      4. connoisseur _____

      5. recognition _____

    B. FER = to carry, bear, yield

      6. inference _____

      7. confer _____

      8. defer _____ deference _____

      9. indifferent _____

    10. coniferous _____

V.   **Words in Context.** Complete each phrase with the most appropriate word from the choices offered.

interpolate	ineffable	innate
inevitably	indolent	inundate
incipient	incantation	innocuous
		insolvent

      1. natural congeniality an _____ and appealing trait

      2. the _____ bliss of doing exactly as she chose on vacation

      3. an _____ but unmistakable case of senioritis

      4. chills that _____ accompany a cold or the flu

      5. urged to bestir his _____ bones after a long, housebound winter

      6. generosity belies the _____ state of her purse

      7. a mumbled _____ over the brew in her pot

      8. can _____ between the lines and know how contented she is

      9. an _____ idea that was fun without being harmful

    10. seasonal rains that swelled the river and _____ nearby lowlands

List 11

jargon (n)	*special language or terminology*; a dialect or hybrid language*

One of the more interesting jargons is that of the computer industry. Computer jargon uses English words in new ways besides developing words of its own. *Up* means that a computer system is running; *down* means it is not. A *byte* is 8 bits of information, while a *nybble* is half a byte. *Hardware* refers to the computer itself, but *software* means the programs that tell the computer what to do. A computer program with problems (*bugs*) must be *debugged*, unless, of course, there is a *glitch*, which is electrical interference with the circuits.

The advertising *jargon* confused Suzanne for days until she learned all the terms in her new profession.

jaundice (n) –	*disease characterized by yellowness of skin; an attitude of unfriendliness, envy, or boredom*
jaundiced (adj) –	*revealing an attitude of unpleasantness or distaste*

The neighbors regarded our noisy, late party with *jaundiced* eyes, saying that they'd had quite enough of our cacophony for one evening.

jaunty (adj) +

lively and cheerful in manner; sprightly
Our mountain guide had a *jaunty* air about him as we set off on our trek up the slopes of White Mountain.

jeopardize (v) –

to put in danger; to risk, imperil
Mike's guidance counselor warned him not to *jeopardize* his high standing in his class by giving in to senioritis.

jingoism (n) –

strongly partisan nationalism, usually accompanied by an aggressive, chauvinistic foreign policy; a **jingoist** *may be termed a "hawk" in modern slang*
Because it appears to lack rational balance, *jingoism* is not favored by moderates.

jocular (adj) +

naturally cheerful and playful*; witty, jocose
Tom Sawyer was a normally *jocular* character in contrast to Huck, whose hard life had made him serious in outlook.

judicious (adj) +

showing sound judgment; wise, discreet
At my first job interview, I was very nervous and hoped my prospective employer would give my résumé a *judicious* appraisal.

juxtapose (v)

to arrange side by side, one thing next to another
We watched as the artist skillfully *juxtaposed* colors and shapes on his canvas.

kaleidoscopic (adj)

like a kaleidoscope, in a variety of different patterns
Watching the seasons change around the lakeshore is viewing a *kaleidoscopic* array of shifting colors and moods as the seasons pass by.

karma (n)

destiny (from Sanskrit, literally **work**) (Hindus and Buddhists believe a person's deeds in one life determine his or her fate in the next); also **kismet** (Turkish), *fate or destiny*
"It must be *karma*," Jenny exclaimed as she rushed toward Brent. "I knew we'd meet again."

ken (n)

sight or range of sight; knowledge, understanding

ken (v)

to know or recognize
An old Scottish song goes, "Do ye *ken* John Peel when he's far away, Do ye *ken* John Peel at the break of day?"

labyrinth (n)

any maze or complex arrangement difficult to figure out; intricacy; perplexity

The *Labyrinth* was built by the skillful Daedalus, an Athenian who had to hide after he murdered his nephew. He hid in his maze on the island of Crete, where he also confined the Minotaur, which was half man, half bull.

One portion of the human ear is so intricate that it has been termed the *labyrinth*, and *labyrinthitis* is an inflammation of that area.

Trying to find our way around the corridors and rooms in the ancient castle was like puzzling through a *labyrinth*.

lacerate (v) –

to rip, rend, or tear in a harsh way*; to distress emotionally
As a result of his serious car accident, Phil was *lacerated* and bruised but fortunately escaped more serious injury.

laconic (adj)

sparing or terse in speech; concise almost to the point of rudeness (from the Spartans, also known as **Laconians**)
A naturally *laconic* man, President Calvin Coolidge was sometimes thought to be cold and abrupt.

laity (n)

church congregation, not the ministers (clergy)*; the masses, as opposed to those with special skills
Our minister believes in involving the *laity* in as many important church decisions and issues as possible.

lampoon (n)

satire aimed at a person or persons

lampoon (v)

to ridicule or make fun of, to satirize
In *My Family and Other Animals*, the witty naturalist Gerald Durrell gently *lampoons* his family as he tells of their years on the Greek island Corfu.

languor (n)

tiredness or weakness of body or mind; indolence, dreaminess*; lassitude
Pat was so used to the snapping cold of the far north that she was surprised by her *languor* when she first moved to New Orleans.

lascivious (adj) –

wanton, lustful, lewd
In the 1950s, *Forever Amber* was thought to be a *lascivious* book, but it is almost dull in comparison with many frank books recently published.

latent (adj)

hidden or submerged, waiting to be aroused; dormant, quiescent
Since my uncle retired from law, his *latent* abilities as a chef have blossomed, and he now makes delicious soups and stews.

laudable (adj) +

deserving of praise; commendable
Natalie is counting on her *laudable* gymnastic ability to help her earn a college scholarship.

levity (n) +

lightness of approach or treatment; humor
Students recognize that a little *levity* in the classroom helps rather than hinders learning.

levy (n)

an assessment or tax

levy (v)

to take or require by legal means
The city council had to *levy* higher taxes to pay for road repairs.

lexicon (n)

a dictionary*; vocabulary particular to a language or topic
Try browsing through a Greek *lexicon* sometime to see how many words you recognize as parents of today's English words.

linguistics (n)

study of speech; philology
College *linguistics* majors are having difficulty finding jobs at a time when colleges are reducing staff and trimming curricula.

litany (n)

a chant, either musical or repetitive* (or both); a prayer of entreaty with responses
Andy's *litany* of complaints about our cat Fred seems to have no end.

litigation (n)

a lawsuit or legal dispute
We thought we held clear title to that land, but since another claim has been filed against it we will be in *litigation* for months.

lithe (adj) +

flexible and graceful
We sat watching the *lithe*, beautiful motions of the dancers and were impressed with their outstanding physical condition as well as their grace.

livid (adj) –

discolored, as by bruises*; pale or ashen; also extremely angry, enraged
Jane wore a long-sleeved shirt and scarf to hide the *livid* bruises that resulted from her fall off the horse.

loquacious (adj)

extremely talkative; gabby, garrulous
Dad has dubbed one of our aunts *Loquacious* Lill because Aunt Lilly so loves to talk.

lucid (adj)

clear and distinct*; being sane, in full possession of intelligence; intelligible
The salesman's forceful, *lucid* delivery convinced Carrie that he knew his product and the competitor's products well enough to be trusted.

lucrative (adj) +

earning money or something valuable; profitable
My little brother Andy says that, although weeding the neighbors' flower beds may be *lucrative*, it is also a rotten job.

ludicrous (adj)

appearing ridiculous or laughable; absurd
For the holidays we dressed our cat Fred in a Santa suit and floppy red cap. Fred knew he looked *ludicrous*, and he was mortified.

lugubrious (adj) –	*looking or sounding profoundly sad, maybe for effect* (from Gr. **lygros = mournful**) In *The Book of the Dun Cow*, Mundo Cani Dog gives vent to repeated and *lugubrious* howls, wailing in sorrow for his overly large nose. (Great book! No people, only animals in charge of the world.)
lurid (adj) –	*excessively pale-looking; red, as fire seen through smoke; provoking horror, gruesome** My brother insisted on relating the *lurid* details of a car accident he had witnessed.
machinations (n) –	*schemes or artful plots* (usually toward bad ends) The wily *machinations* of some government officials engender distrust of all who are in government.
magnanimous (adj) +	*noble and generous in victory as well as defeat; forgiving* Our class president is respected for her intelligence, but she is loved for her *magnanimous* nature and ready laughter.
malevolent (adj) –	*exuding evil or intense hatred* Who could forget the *malevolent* cackle of the wicked witch in *The Wizard of Oz*?
malign (v) –	*to speak of in an evil, ill-willed manner; to defame or slander* People in high political positions realize that unscrupulous opponents may *malign* them in an effort to gain advantages.
manifest (adj)	*readily understood or perceived; obvious, evident*
manifest (v)	*to show; to make certain and clear* Mozart *manifested* his incredible talents at the early age of 4, when he composed five piano pieces that are still performed by the world's great musicians.
manipulate (v)	*to use skillfully or appropriately*; to manage to your own benefit; to doctor* (as he **manipulated** the results) After Art had *manipulated* the puzzle pieces for a time, he perceived the solution.
marauder (n) –	*seeker of foods, goods, or whatever; raider, pillager** The raccoon is a masked nighttime *marauder* who's hard to hate, unless you wake up and find he's taken all the food from your camp supplies.
maudlin (adj) –	*overly sentimental*, even *weepy with sentiment* "Don't talk to me," warned Jillian. "I'm caught up in the *maudlin* miseries of this soap opera, and I want to enjoy every minute of it."
maxim (n)	*a proverb or repeated saying of truth* My dad's favorite *maxim* is "Early to bed, early to rise, Makes a man healthy, wealthy, and wise."
melancholy (n) –	*abnormal depression; excessively low spirits; dejection*
melancholy (adj)	*depressed, blue*; sorrowful; downcast* To your sorrowful sweetheart you can hum, "Come to me my *melancholy* baby, Cuddle up and don't be blue." (An oldie. Maybe your folks or grandparents will hum it for you.)
mendacious (adj) –	*lying, deceptive, dishonest* We howled with laughter at the quack's obviously *mendacious* claims for his cure-all.

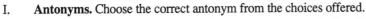

QUIZ ON LIST 11

I.   **Antonyms.** Choose the correct antonym from the choices offered.
1. **jaunty**   (A) cheery (B) jocular (C) melancholic (D) on a trip
2. **judicious**   (A) indiscreet (B) wise (C) like a judge (D) legal
3. **juxtapose**   (A) join (B) separate (C) juncture (D) position

4. **ken**   (A) Barbie's friend (B) see (C) failure to understand (D) recognize

5. **lacerate**   (A) mend (B) rend (C) capture (D) wound

6. **laconic**   (A) terse (B) blunt (C) loquacious (D) indolent

7. **languor**   (A) sleepiness (B) weakness (C) lassitude (D) dynamism

8. **latent**   (A) obvious (B) dormant (C) tardy (D) truant

9. **levity**   (A) humor (B) sobriety (C) haste (D) gruesomeness

10. **lithe**   (A) woodworking tool (B) stone (C) graceful (D) inflexible

11. **mendacious**   (A) trustworthy (B) inexpensive (C) opulent (D) grave

12. **maudlin**   (A) dogmatic (B) uplifting (C) dispassionate (D) educational

13. **malign**   (A) grovel (B) behoove (C) straighten (D) laud

14. **magnanimous**   (A) gainsaying a point (B) harboring a grudge (C) belying the truth
                      (D) negating the issue

15. **lugubrious**   (A) preoccupied (B) discreet (C) blithe (D) bluff

II.   **Words in Context.** Put the appropriate word into each phrase, using the clues in the phrases as your guide.

livid	lucid	jeopardize
loquacious	ludicrous	lampoon
lucrative	lexicon	linguistics
litany	malevolent	jaundiced
manifest	lurid	laity

1. familiar, comforting _____ of prayers

2. handy _____ of German phrases

3. face red, she was _____ with anger and frustration

4. drowned in his _____ flow of words

5. recovered from concussion, therefore _____ in thought

6. important and _____ position with the bank

7. Dad, _____ in his getup as Baby New Year

8. _____ glow of flames in the night

9. their abilities, readily _____ on the job

10. the _____ glare of the trapped tiger

11. an understandably _____ view of excessive drinking

12. careful not to _____ his life on the risky climb

13. bulletin to inform the _____ of the bishops' decisions

14. hilarious _____ highlighting the principal's foibles

15. _____ text that traced the development of the English language

III.   **Analogies.** Choose the lettered pair that expresses the same relationship as the given pair.

1. ADAGE : MOTTO ::
   (A) melancholy : derisiveness (B) proverb : maxim (C) machinations : awards (D) litany : linguistics
   (E) languor : buoyancy

2. KARMA : LIFE ::
   (A) race : goal (B) concert : finale (C) design : building (D) dawn : day (E) painting : canvas

3. LAWYER : LITIGATION ::
   (A) harbinger : mask (B) charlatan : closure (C) director : board (D) lexicographer : copy
   (E) marauder : pillage

4. LANGUAGE : JARGON ::
   (A) path : labyrinth   (B) bed : languor   (C) speech : loquacity   (D) knowledge : ken
   (E) humor : lampoon

5. GESTURE : MAGNANIMOUS ::
   (A) hat : jaunty   (B) film : lascivious   (C) decision : laconic   (D) achievement : laudable
   (E) address : loquacious

IV. **Favorite SAT/PSAT Word Families.** Match the perennial SAT and "good writer" favorites with their meanings.

   A. MAL = bad, badly

   _____ 1. malign   (a) illness, ailment

   _____ 2. malevolent   (b) literally *maker of bad;* one who creates trouble

   _____ 3. malcontent   (c) curse, execration

   _____ 4. malefactor   (d) exuding evil or hatred

   _____ 5. malady   (e) to slander, defame

   _____ 6. malediction   (f) perennial complainer or discontented person

   B. JOC = joke (Hint: Each answer used more than once.)

   _____ 7. jocular

   _____ 8. jocund   (a) fond of joking, witty, merry

   _____ 9. jocose   (b) merriment, joy

   _____10. jocularity

   _____11. jocundity

   (No joke . . . or **joc.** Some positive words for a change!)

List 12

mendicant (adj)	*begging*
mendicant (n)	*beggar; occasionally, a monk or friar* One of the most beautiful songs from the movie *Mary Poppins* is about a bird woman, a *mendicant* who sold food for the birds on the steps of a cathedral.
menial (adj) –	*lowly or servile*; humble, subservient* It's difficult to get excited about *menial* household tasks such as dishwashing, dusting, and vacuuming.
mercenary (adj) –	*working only with money or reward in mind; greedy*
mercenary (n) –	*a person working only for money;* also *a hired soldier** Noblemen were accustomed to hiring *mercenaries,* who fulfilled their military obligations for them.
meretricious (adj) –	*glamorous in a cheap, showy way; gaudy;* also *rooted in bigotry or hypocritical views,* therefore *specious** The *meretricious* arguments of certain lobbyists were discounted by the more thoughtful legislators, who tried to examine proposals fairly.
metamorphosis (n)	*unexplainable but usually very noticeable change of form or character* (from L. and Gr. **meta = change**)

Legend tells that the laurel tree was once a beautiful maiden, Daphne. She ran from Apollo's ardent pursuit until she was exhausted, then fell to her knees begging her father, a river god, to save her. In an instant she was metamorphosed into bark and leaves. When Apollo finally held her, she was a laurel tree, or daphne. After that, the laurel leaves were sacred to Apollo and worn as a crown of victory by nobles or winners in games and contests.

Alan's *metamorphosis* from playboy to serious student was greeted with relief by his parents, astonishment by his friends.

meticulous (adj) +	*showing extreme care in all respects* A copy editor must correct written materials with *meticulous* care so that published writing is as nearly perfect as possible.
mien (n)	*manner of comporting yourself; demeanor; appearance that reveals your personality* Daughters of an English minister, the Brontë sisters were girls of sober *mien* in public, but women of artistic, passionate bent in the private lives of their minds.
mince (v)	*to cut into tiny sections; to talk or walk in an affected or overly dainty manner; to hold back words discreetly** "Do not *mince* words with me, young man!" snapped the librarian. "Did you or did you not lose the book?"
minion (n)	*a minor official, sometimes a dependent servant* Jesse James and others of his ilk had little use for the *minions* of the law.
mitigate (v)	*to relieve or lighten or lessen* (as pain is **mitigated** by medication); *to mollify* (as anger is **mitigated**); *to alleviate* The knowledge that Joel's surgery had been successful *mitigated* his classmates' fears.
mollify (v) +	*to calm someone's temper or appease bad feelings, placate* We *mollified* Mom by promising to clean our rooms when we got home from school.
moot (adj)	*something debatable or in dispute; also plainly abstract, strictly academic* (in the sense that the outcome will not be affected)* Since we'd been told we absolutely could not go on a skiing trip to Vermont, my brother's report of beautiful new powder snow was *moot*.
morass (n) –	*a thing that entraps or restricts* (as a marsh or swamp) Bob felt he was drowning in the *morass* of legal questions he needed to answer before he could claim his inheritance.
mordant (adj)	*biting or stinging in approach; cutting to the heart of the matter*; incisive* (from L. **mordere = to bite**) From the outset as a reporter at the famous "monkey trial," H. L. Mencken displayed a *mordant* wit and insightful approach on every issue.
motley (n)	*typical, multicolored garments of a court fool*
motley (adj)	*of different, oddly grouped parts* Captain Hook's *motley* crew lent interest to the tale of Peter Pan.
mundane (adj)	*earthly as opposed to heavenly; worldly; ordinary or run-of-the-mill*; also menial* (as **mundane** chores) The easiest time to let your imagination roam is when you're doing *mundane* jobs like mowing the lawn or cleaning up the kitchen.
munificent (adj) +	*very liberal; generous in giving; lavish* *Munificent* contributions from some corporations make it possible for excellent programs to appear on public television.
murky (adj)	*heavy, foggy dark* (as air); *obscure or vague in approach* (as **murky** prose) (from Middle English **mirke = darkness, gloom**) Lloyd's bike light was a feeble glow in the *murky* night air and fog that enveloped the lane leading to his house.
nadir (n) –	*exact opposite of zenith; the lowest point or absolute bottom** "Yes, I remember physics," Jean said morosely. "It was the absolute *nadir* of my college career, and the labs were at eight in the morning."

naive (adj)

unworldly, unsophisticated, unaffected; ingenuous, innocent, natural
"The part of our ingenue must be played by a girl who is natural and artless—completely *naive*," stressed the play director.

nebulous (adj)

vague and unformed (as a **nebulous** idea); *indistinct*
Our plan for touring the West had been so *nebulous* that every night on the trip we had to pore over guidebooks, deciding where to go next.

nefarious (adj) –

noticeably wicked, evil; vicious (from L. **nefas = crime**)
The *nefarious* villain in the musical *Oliver* led such an evil life that audiences cheered when he died.

negligible (adj)

of little or no importance; *inconsequential, trifling*
I tried to tell Andy that Fred's sins were *negligible* when you considered how affectionate and personable he was as a pet.

negligence (n) –

lack of proper care and attention
Andy is afraid that, through someone's *negligence*, the lid to his precious gerbil cage will be left off, and Fred will feast on gerbils.

neophyte (n)

a convert or beginner; novice, tyro, proselyte
"We have several *neophytes* in our sales organization," the manager noted, "but their enthusiasm and zeal more than make up for their lack of experience."

niggardly (adj) –

very tight with money or means; stingy, penurious, parsimonious
The stereotypical miser is Scrooge, who was *niggardly* when it came to salaries and equally stingy with kindliness of any sort.

nocturnal (adj)

referring to night (from L. **nox = night**)
Lise asked her music teacher if a nocturne were a musical piece to be practiced only during *nocturnal* hours or if she had to practice it during afternoons, too.

noisome (adj) –

extremely unpleasant to the senses, especially the sense of smell; malodorous, noxious
As we drove by the sewer plant, we rolled up our car windows to block out the *noisome* vapors.

nominal (adj)

referring to nouns; in name only (as a **nominal** fee for a job); *trifling, insignificant*
Although Rising Sun was the *nominal* head of his tribe, the younger, more educated men took care of most tribal affairs.

nuance (n)

a shade of difference or variation; subtlety, hint, trace
Professor Higgins, the linguistics tutor to Eliza in *My Fair Lady*, worked to erase every *nuance* of cockney accent from Eliza's speech.

nurture (n)

training or upbringing; education

nurture (v)

to feed, nourish, raise (from L. **nutrire = suckle, nourish**)
When Fred brings us a young rabbit, we *nurture* it carefully, intent on returning it to the wild as a healthy adult.

obdurate (adj) –

rigid or set in feelings or behavior; unyielding, inflexible, adamant
When you meet with *obdurate* resistance to your suggestions, even persuasive argument is usually wasted speech.

obese (adj) –

uncommonly fat
The *obese* person often has a psychological reason for being overweight rather than a physical one.

obliterate (v)

to erase completely or wipe out; to efface, remove, cancel
A sandstorm swiftly *obliterates* any evidence of human or animal movement on the desert.

obloquy (n) –

strong verbal abuse; *the state of being discredited* (as a bad reputation)
Listening to the *obloquy* one candidate heaped upon the head of the other persuaded me not to vote for either one of them.

obsequious (adj) –	*unusually servile or subservient; overly compliant, fawning* Lady Jane distrusted the *obsequious* attitude of her new servant and requested an investigation into his past.
obsolete (adj)	*out of style or no longer used*; old, outmoded* The Model A Ford is *obsolete* for today's roads and driving conditions, but many people own restored vehicles for pure enjoyment.
obtuse (adj) –	*slow to catch on; insensible or rather dull mentally* "Don't be deliberately *obtuse*," my brother John grumbled. "You know which ones are weeds and which are flowers, so lend a hand."
odious (adj) –	*arousing hatred or disgust* (as an **odious** job) Remember the pesty dog named Odie in the Garfield cartoons? Do you suppose the cartoonist named him that because a dog is an *odious* object to a cat?
officious (adj) –	*butting in with advice where none is wanted; meddlesome* "I can't take my roommate's *officious* attitude," Ron said. "He's a freshman, too, so why does he think he knows everything?"
oligarchy (n)	*government by a very few, often ruling for selfish reasons; the ruling group itself or group being ruled*

Arch- words are found all over the place in English. A *monarchy* has a sole (usually royal) leader, as in England. A *matriarchy* is any society ruled by a woman (matriarch), just as a *patriarchy* is governed by a man. The *archangel* Gabriel is the head angel in the celestial *hierarchy,* their order of things. Being an *archbishop* is a post of great honor within the church. An *archetype* is the model on which others of the same type are patterned. And you know more. . . .

At one time, Rome was governed by a triumvirate, an *oligarchy* of three.

ominous (adj) –	*promising or foreshadowing something bad; inauspicious, portentous* The storm in the distance sounded *ominous,* causing us to worry about exposed livestock and young crops.
omniscient (adj)	*possessing complete awareness and understanding;* literally *"all-knowing"* in Latin As children we think that our parents are *omniscient,* a belief that gives both comfort and stability.

QUIZ ON LIST 12

I.   **Puddle of Words.** Sort through the words below to discover ten sets of synonyms.

mendicant   specious   servile   demeanor

alleviate   moot   mitigate   incisive   murky   meretricious

mundane   menial   beggar   mordant   gloomy   munificent

worldly   mien   lavish   debatable

1. _____   6. _____

2. _____   7. _____

3. _____   8. _____

4. _____   9. _____

5. _____   10. _____

II. **Words in Context.** Put the appropriate word (from the choices offered) into each of the sentences.

nadir	negligence	obdurate
nebulous	noisome	obloquy
nefarious	nuance	officious
negligible		

1. Although the summer rains were heavy, they had a(n) _____ effect on our hilltop campsite.

2. Unlike the rains, the local skunks did have their customary _____ effect, and they also had frequent fights in horrible proximity to our tents.

3. The _____ of our skunk experiences came the night that several of them had a smelly altercation directly behind our main tent.

4. The morning after the big skunk fight we sat gloomily around the campfire heaping _____ on one another, everyone saying that *someone else* had chosen a dumb campsite.

5. "Well, I'm staying put," our fearless leader announced as she tried not to breathe the air. "I'm just _____ enough to refuse to budge."

6. Shelley wrinkled her nose. "A(n) _____ of skunk is one thing, but this overpowering stench is something I've never smelled before!"

7. "I can't see why we don't all agree to pack up and leave!" Dan said in a(n) _____ manner, as if he alone had the answer.

8. "This is where we told our families we'd camp," our leader protested. "We can't notify everyone of a move. It would be _____ on my part to move since I'm the one responsible."

9. "Maybe the skunks are part of some _____ plot to drive us out of North Woods Campgrounds," Carol said with a grin. "I hate to see them win."

10. In the end we agreed with Carol. Although the skunks had rendered North Woods' charm rather _____, we decided to stay and show the animals who was boss.

III. **Favorite SAT/PSAT Word Families.** Select the best definition to write on the line for each numbered word.

A. NOM, NOMEN, NOMIN, ONYM = name, rule, order

_____ 1. nominal	(a)	paradox, irregularity
_____ 2. ignominy	(b)	a naming system for classification purposes
_____ 3. renown	(c)	in name only
_____ 4. physiognomy	(d)	utter shame, disgrace
_____ 5. anomaly	(e)	incorrect or misleading name
_____ 6. nomenclature	(f)	facial features; general character or makeup
_____ 7. misnomer	(g)	fame; wide acclaim or high honor

B. SEQU, SECUT = follow

_____ 8. obsequious	(a)	insignificant, negligible
_____ 9. sequel	(b)	following, successive
_____ 10. inconsequential	(c)	fawning, servile
_____ 11. execute	(d)	to carry out
_____ 12. subsequent	(e)	that which follows or comes after

IV.   **One More Time.** For each word in bold type, write first a definition or synonym in the appropriate column, then the best antonym you can think of.

	Definition/Synonym	*Antonym*
1. **nadir**	the absolute bottom	zenith
2. **mercenary** (adj)		
3. **meticulous**		
4. **mollify**		
5. **motley** (adj)		
6. **naive**		
7. **adamant**		
8. **neophyte**		
9. **nocturnal**		
10. **nurture**		
11. **obese**		
12. **obliterate**		
13. **obtuse**		
14. **obsolete**		
15. **odious**		
16. **ominous**		
17. **omniscient**		

V.   **A Need for Words?** Certain concepts must be integral to human society because we have coined so many words to express the same idea. How many blanks can you fill?

Extremely Careful with Money

s _____
n _____
p _____
p _____
t _____

Lacking Worldly Knowledge

n _____
i _____
n _____
un _____
i _____

Rigidly Set in Feelings or Behavior

o _____
a _____
un _____
in _____
s _____

List 13

onus (n) –	*any (disliked) chore, necessity, burden, or obligation* "The *onus* of proving this man's guilt lies with the prosecution," reiterated the judge. "We don't presume guilt."
opprobrium (n) –	*public shame following bad conduct; disgrace, infamy* The politician's latest scandal brought on the *opprobrium* of his own party as well as that of the opposition.
opulence (n)	*wealth* A display of *opulence* is considered bad taste by many.

oracular (adj)	*as from the mouth of an oracle, therefore solemn; sometimes, dictatorial* Insistence upon *oracular* pronouncements is one of the shorter roads to unpopularity.
orifice (n)	*a mouth or opening* *Jaws* is a much catchier title for a book or movie than *The Toothy Orifice*.
ossify (v)	(from Gr. **os = bone**) *to become bone or like bone; to turn hardened and callous; set in one's ways, rigid** An elderly volunteer at the hospital told us she preferred activity and meeting people. "I didn't want to *ossify* like so many old people do," she said.
ostentatious (adj) –	*noticeably showy in display; pretentious* "Having five cars seems *ostentatious*," Diane observed, "when you consider that he can drive only one of them at a time."
ostracize (v) –	*to exclude someone from society or from a group*

It was Greek custom to banish from the state any politically dangerous people. The banishment was voted on by the people, who simply used an **ostrakon** *(a tile or broken piece of pot)* lying about the marketplace to cast a vote in favor of expulsion. Enough votes, and the undesirable was forced to leave town for anywhere from five to ten years. The root **os** *(bone or shell)* is interesting because many of the tiles contained bone ash, as does today's fine bone china.

Modern jails and reformatories provide one way to *ostracize* individuals who cannot live acceptably in society. Fraternities and sororities practice their own forms of *ostracism*.

overt (adj)	*easily seen because of being open to view; manifest* "An act of kindness, whether *overt* or covert," Aunt Sal promised, "will help you feel good about yourself all day long."
pacify (v) +	*to soothe or appease; to settle or calm down* (from L. **pac = peace**) One of the more difficult jobs a baby-sitter has is to *pacify* a fretful, crying infant.
palatable (adj) +	*agreeing with your taste buds or your mind; appetizing, pleasing, agreeable* "Craig's food is more than palatable," Leigh remarked. "It's absolutely five-star delicious!
pall (n)	*a coffin drapery*
pall (v)	*to lessen in interest; to become boring; to grow weary because of overexposure* "Perhaps I'm old and jaded, but TV has *palled* as far as I'm concerned, and I rarely watch it anymore," Mrs. Timmons told us.
panacea (n) +	*a cure-all; the perfect remedy* Keeping Fred outside was not the *panacea* we had hoped for; although Andy's gerbils were safe, Fred clawed persistently at the door.
panache (n) +	*flair or flamboyance in style, behavior, speech, etc.; dash or verve* Although the French word *panache* came into our language over 450 years ago, it has only recently been used with great frequency.
parable (n)	*short tale pointing out a moral idea* The authors of the Bible often favored *parables* as a method of illustrating Christian ethics.
paradigm (n)	*an extremely fine model or example of a type; archetype* Modern journalists and speechwriters have pounced on the word *paradigm* as a synonym for the more commonplace words *model* and *example*.
paradox (n)	*a statement that appears to contradict itself but, even so, may be true; anything with apparent contradictions* Oscar Wilde, known for his ability to compose a memorable *paradox*, wrote: "One's real life is so often the life that one does not lead." And, "Life is too important to be taken seriously."

paragon (n) +

a model, or anything that is perfect; the ideal
After hearing repeatedly that our cousin Amy was a *paragon* of virtue, we lost all interest in meeting her.

paraphrase (v)

to reword written material in your own way to aid understanding or clarity; a free translation
Caedmon, an Anglo-Saxon monk, *paraphrased* certain parts of the Bible in poetic form.

pariah (n) –

an outcast of society
The word *pariah* refers to a member of a low caste in Indian society and also to dogs that roam as wild scavengers in southern Asia and North Africa.

pastoral (adj)

of the country*; rural, rustic, bucolic; also referring to a member of the clergy and his or her job
Robert Burns is remembered for his *pastoral* poems, such as "To a Mouse":

> Wee, sleekit, cow'rin', tim'rous beastie,
> O what a panic's in thy breastie!
> Thou need na start awa sae hasty,
> Wi'bickering brattle!
> I wad be laith to rin an' chase thee,
> Wi'murdering pattle!

patent (n)

referring to legal claim (as a **patent** on an invention)

patently (adv)

evidently; obviously
It is *patently* clear that Joe doesn't want to be disturbed, since he's locked his door and posted a "Keep Away" sign.

pathos (n)

stirrings of pity; poignancy
The *pathos* in an animal story such as *Watership Down* arouses feelings of kinship with animals.

paucity (n)

lack or scarcity; dearth
The *paucity* of bilingual people in government jobs ought to be an encouragement to those who want to major in a foreign language.

peccadillo (n) –

a minor fault or flaw; small offense
My older brother John told Mom that his inability to keep his room clean was "a *peccadillo*, really, when you consider all my good points." (He had to clean it anyhow.)

pedant (n) –

someone who shows off his knowledge; a nitpicking type
In college, where students can often choose their professors, *pedants* may find their classrooms rather empty.

pejorative (adj) –

making something worse; disparaging (as **pejorative** remarks)
Receiving a term paper marked in red with only *pejorative* comments makes the writer less willing to write the next paper.

perceptive (adj)

observant and aware; keenly discerning
"You don't need to be *perceptive* to see that Fred is hungry for a bite of gerbil," Dad said as he eyed our cat, who was eyeing the gerbils again.

peremptory (adj)

not allowing contradiction; showing need or urgency; haughty, masterful, dictatorial*, autocratic
With a *peremptory* wave of his hand, the coach called all of the team into his office for a meeting.

perfidy (n) –

faithlessness, disloyalty, treachery
"Boys," Maria said sadly, "are full of *perfidy*. Rob and I were supposed to have had a date, but his coach told him to be in bed by ten, and he listens only to his coach."

perfunctory (adj)

mechanical or routine, therefore not careful; without enthusiasm; apathetic
We could tell by his *perfunctory* nod that he did not wish to renew our acquaintance.

pernicious (adj) –

very destructive, even deadly; deleterious, noxious, baneful (from L. **nec = violent death**)
Now outdated, but still amusing, is an old William Cowper poem about tobacco:

> *Pernicious* weed! whose scent the fair annoys,
> Unfriendly to society's chief joys,
> The worst effect is banishing for hours
> The sex whose presence civilizes ours. [Females, of course.]

perquisite (n) +

an extra, other than salary, that may accompany a job*; special privilege; now called *"perks"*
"The best *perquisite* I have in my job, other than my big office window," Dad told us, "is the freedom to set my own hours."

perspicacious (adj) +

acutely shrewd or keen in understanding and perception, discerning
We think of the owl as a wise, *perspicacious* bird, one of many stereotypes in the animal world.

pertinacity (n)

a stubborn persistence, sticking with ideas or purposes; obstinacy
Watching a well-trained Labrador retriever at work, I had to admire his *pertinacity* as he repeatedly located birds.

perturb (v) –

to bother greatly or annoy; to disquiet, discompose
Andy's insistence upon dessert *perturbs* Mom; she worries that he'll eat more desserts than other foods when he's off on his own.

pervade (v)

to become part of something else; to permeate (as smoke **pervaded** the air)
An air of expectation and holiday spirits *pervaded* the halls of our school the week before Christmas vacation.

petulant (adj) –

ill-humored and peevish; occasionally *rude and ill-mannered*
As she is normally warm and polite, her *petulant* reply to my question caught me off guard.

philanthropy (n) +

monetary or volunteer promotion of mankind's welfare; generous giving of self or resources

---

The Greek root **anthropos = human being** has many English spin-offs. A werewolf is a victim of *lycanthropy*, while someone who hates people is caught by *misanthropy*. *Anthropology* is the study of human cultures, but, curiously enough, an *anthropoid* is only manlike and can be either a man *or* an ape. Calling your last date an *anthropoid* is definitely not a compliment.

The Art Museum in Toledo, Ohio, acquired many of its fine art objects through the *philanthropy* of Edward Drummond Libby, founder of Libby Glass Company.

phlegmatic (adj) –

sluggish, slow, showing little emotion; impassive, stolid
My uncle's workhorses were *phlegmatic* types, plodding through the long day's routine without resistance.

placate (v) +

to calm, appease, particularly by offering to "be good" or to do a favor for someone
After we made gingersnaps and covered the floor with sugar, we *placated* Mom by giving her enough cookies for her party.

platitude (n) –

an old, stale comment lacking originality or freshness; banality, trite remark
Guest speakers who mouth *platitudes* usually aren't invited to speak again.

plausible (adj)

superficially believable, whether actually true or not
I told Andy it was perfectly *plausible* that our cat Fred just wanted to be friends with the gerbils, but Andy said that was nonsense.

plebeian (adj, n)	*concerning the common folk or masses* (often used in a derogatory way); also **plebiscite** (n), *a vote by the entire population* (from L. **plebs = common people**) After a year abroad at a fancy boarding school, our cousin Buffy was impossible. She kept referring to ordinary people as "mere *plebeians*" and said everyone had "*plebeian* tastes."
plethora (n)	*a vast amount*; great excess* Our neighboring physician owns a *plethora* of books on tropical diseases, which he lent me as references for my term paper on malaria.
poignant (adj)	*profoundly affecting feelings*; highly emotional in effect; piercing* An old, unbearably *poignant* story titled *Beautiful Joe* tells the tale of a pathetically mistreated dog who wanted only to love someone.

QUIZ ON LIST 13

I. **Puddle of Synonyms.** Search the puddle for *two* synonyms to write on the line for each word in bold type.

example annoy flaw common scarcity
remedy evidently rural pity noxious dearth verve
infamy ordinary disgrace poignancy discompose deleterious
flamboyance obviously fault bucolic cure-all archetype

Synonyms

1. plebeian   _____
2. perturb   _____
3. pernicious   _____
4. peccadillo   _____
5. paucity   _____
6. pathos   _____
7. patently   _____
8. pastoral   _____
9. panacea   _____
10. opprobrium   _____
11. panache   _____
12. paradigm   _____

II. **Antonyms.** Match vocabulary words with their antonyms.

_____ 1. opulence	(a) flippant or lighthearted
_____ 2. oracular	(b) irritate
_____ 3. overt	(c) excite
_____ 4. pacify	(d) include
_____ 5. palatable	(e) obscure
_____ 6. pall	(f) indigence
_____ 7. ostracize	(g) praising
_____ 8. patent	(h) obtuse
_____ 9. pejorative	(i) covert
_____ 10. perceptive	(j) disagreeable

III. **Words in Context.** Fit words into phrases where they make good sense. Select words from the list given. Word form or tense may need changing.

onus   phlegmatic   pariah
peremptory   platitude   pedant
perfidy   plausible   paraphrase
pernicious   orifice   philanthropy
perquisite   parable   plethora
pervade   ossified   pertinacity
perfunctory   paradox

1. handy parking space, a _____ of his position
2. _____ glance through the book before he rushed on
3. beckoned imperiously with a _____ finger
4. a _____, although highly unlikely, story
5. his _____ tendency to try anything once
6. fresh odor of pine _____ the forest
7. same old remark, a _____ we've all heard
8. the _____ of Aaron Burr
9. the _____ of her responsibility weighing heavily
10. _____ reaction, which gave us no clue whatsoever
11. generous _____ that made the library possible
12. life a puzzling series of contradictions, making him a veritable human _____
13. roar of the lion, which revealed an awesome _____
14. on the job till dawn with admirable _____
15. a _____, ousted and doomed to roam for the rest of his days
16. boring lectures of our school _____
17. her brief story, a _____ to guide us in the coming months
18. prolonged hardship that _____ her previously gentle nature
19. needing someone to _____ that abstruse passage for me
20. prefer a(n) _____ of solutions, not just one

IV. **Favorite SAT/PSAT Word Families.** Choose the best definition to write on the line beside each numbered word. (One synonym used twice in A.)

A. TEND, TENS, TENT = stretch, thin

_____ 1. ostentatious
_____ 2. attenuate
_____ 3. contend
_____ 4. pretentious
_____ 5. contention
_____ 6. tenuous
_____ 7. portent
_____ 8. ostensible

(a) opinion; rivalry
(b) omen, warning sign
(c) flimsy, weak, thin
(d) showy
(e) to weaken; reduce strength or vitality
(f) to hold, maintain, believe
(g) apparent, plausible; in appearance only

B. TEN, TIN, TAIN, TENT = hold, contain

_____ 9. pertinacity	(a) ability to hold on, to persist no matter what
_____ 10. tenacity	(b) refraining from indulgence
_____ 11. abstain	(c) persistence, obstinacy
_____ 12. abstinence	(d) to keep or hold in place
_____ 13. retain	(e) to refrain from

V.   **A Need for Words?** Here are a few more ideas so universal to human nature that we have many words for each. Again, how many blanks can you fill?

Soothing Injured Feelings

p _____

m _____

a _____

c _____

p _____

For Plodding, Unemotional Types

p _____

i _____

s _____

b _____

s _____

Describing Smart Folk

k _____

p _____

d _____

p _____

a _____

List 14

portly (adj)	*round in shape, but not grossly fat*; also dignified in manner* The old stereotype of a banker calls for a rather *portly* man, sober of mien, wearing a dark, pin-striped suit, whereas today's banker may just as well be a woman in tweeds.
posthumous (adj)	*occurring after death* (as **posthumously** published manuscripts) The government awarded several soldiers *posthumous* medals; the wives and families of the men received the awards.
postulate (n)	*an axiom or assumed truth; a hypothesis, presupposition*
postulate (v)	*to accept as truth or to offer as truth; to presume** The thieves were first thought to be in the city. "But now we're *postulating* that they escaped our dragnet," said the policeman.
potent (adj) +	*possessing strength or power; effective** (as a **potent** remedy) "These medicines have been around so long that I doubt if they're still *potent*," Mom said as she sorted through the old bottles.
pragmatic (adj)	*useful and practical*; down-to-earth, sometimes excluding artistic or intellectual endeavors* I suggested taking my cat and her kittens to college with me to ward off loneliness, but Dad said that wasn't a *pragmatic* solution.
precarious (adj) –	*subject to chance or circumstances beyond control, therefore risky or hazardous* "No boring moments on that mountain!" Drew exclaimed. "We crept from one *precarious* position to another all day."

precedent (n)	*something occurring before that may serve as a model for subsequent, similar acts*; antecedent* Before sentencing the convicted offender, the judge considered *precedents* set by similar cases in her state.
precipitate (adj)	*unusually (maybe unwisely) fast; headlong, impetuous*
precipitate (v)	*to bring about in an abrupt manner*; to fall suddenly or move unexpectedly* Steve and Otis had a loud argument with the band director, which *precipitated* first Otis's departure, then Steve's.
preclude (v)	*to make impossible or ineffectual by planning or acting in advance; to forestall, hinder, avert, prevent** Hoping to *preclude* any chance of failure when he folded his first parachute, Jesse memorized every step of the procedure until he thought he could fold a chute in his sleep.
precocious (adj)	*having unusually early mental development;* literally *"precooked"* or *"prematurely ripe"* in Latin "Aunt Flora's always telling me how amazingly *precocious* her children are," Mom said, "but if you ask me they're amazingly naughty!"
predatory (adj)	*of plundering and preying* (as a **predatory** wolf) Some anthropologists regard war as a legacy of man's *predatory* ancestors.
predilection (n)	*positive feelings or opinion held beforehand; natural preference, prejudice* Our old tomcat Fred doesn't see why he should respect our caged gerbils. Fred's *predilection* for small, furry creatures is ingrained.
prelude (n)	*introduction to the main work, performance, or musical movement* Mr. Morrison said to his doctor, "I hope that all these bloodlettings, patient histories, thumpings, and examinations are necessary as a *prelude* to my operation, as they certainly have been uncomfortable."
prerogative (n)	*special right or privilege* "It's your *prerogative* to refuse to eat dinner," Mom told Andy, "and it's mine to say no when you ask for dessert."
presumptuous (adj) –	*presuming or assuming too much in an overbearing way; overweening, overstepping* "*Presumptuous* female," muttered old Mr. Dudley. "Just because I offered her a look through the opera glasses didn't mean I was giving them to her for the whole performance!"
prevaricate (v) –	*to stray from the truth; to lie or equivocate*

A *prevaricator* in ancient Rome was a prosecuting attorney who presented his case in court so poorly that the defendant was acquitted. The Roman *prevaricator* straddled the case, it seemed, with one foot on either side of it. You are prevaricating today when you give an equivocal answer, or say yes when you really mean no, anytime you want to avoid the truth.

If I say that I *prevaricated* about the time I got in after the party, that sounds better than saying I lied about the time.

probity (n)	*sticking to noble ideals; uncorruptibility; uprightness* Millicent Fenwick, former Congresswoman from New Jersey, has always been respected for her absolute *probity* and sincerity of purpose.
proclivity (n)	*natural inclination or tendency toward; inherent leaning toward something objectionable** The *proclivity* of these mountain roads to turn icy every winter keeps most tourists away.

procrastinate (v)

to put off or delay until another time; literally *"for tomorrow"* in Latin
"Don't do today what you can put off till tomorrow" seems to be the motto of those who *procrastinate*.

prodigal (adj)

wildly extravagant or lavish in spending
The biblical story of the *prodigal* son tells about a boy who recklessly spent his inheritance and returned home to a warm welcome anyway.

prodigious (adj)

*arousing awe; extremely large; enormous, monstrous**
Rabelais's giants, Pantagruel and Gargantua, were noted for their *prodigious* appetites.

profess (v)

to declare or affirm (as to **profess** faith in a religion); *also to pretend, to feign**
"Howard *professes* to enjoy skiing," Rhonda told us, "but I notice he spends most of the day sipping cocoa by the lodge fire."

proficient (adj) +

skillful and advanced in knowledge, ability, performance; adept
Brad spent many hours behind the motorboat, perfecting his skill on water skis; by summer's end he felt *proficient* enough to audition for a ski team.

prolific (adj)

extremely fruitful or productive; fertile, fecund*
Flannery O'Connor was not as *prolific* as some writers who turn out reams of material, but her stories are gems that live on after her early and tragic death.

propensity (n)

distinct, and sometimes strong, natural tendency or inclination; leaning*
Amphibians have a *propensity* for water when nesting time arrives.

propinquity (n)

proximity or nearness of relationship; contiguity
The *propinquity* of China to Japan has led to some interesting comparisons in cultures, as well as to contrasts worth noting.

propitiate (v)

to get into someone's good graces or to earn someone's goodwill; to appease, to gain favor; also **propitious** (adj), *favorable, auspicious, of good omen*
In ancient Greece and Rome, small and large animals were sacrificed to *propitiate* the gods.

propriety (n) +

what is proper or customary; decorum; polite manners
Molly said that her children were holy terrors everywhere but in church, where they became models of *propriety*.

prosaic (adj)

of facts, therefore *not imaginative or original; everyday, ordinary;* also *dull, banal*
Josie's account of our trip to Mexico was a carefully *prosaic* recital tailored for our grandmother, who would have been appalled by some of our adventures there.

proscribe (v)

to outlaw, forbid, prohibit
Knowing that *proscribed* drugs can cause permanent damage to their children's minds and bodies, most parents would like the dealers to be vigorously prosecuted by the law.

protuberant (adj)

swelling or bulging out; obtrusive (from L. **tuber = a swelling**)
Jimmy Durante, a comic actor known as "The Schnozz," used his *protuberant* nose to good advantage in show business.

provident (adj) +

providing for times ahead; saving, thrifty; prudent, frugal
An aptly named bank in Philadelphia is The Provident©.

provoke (v)

to arouse, stir up, spark; to pique; literally *"to call forth"* in Latin
"I wanted to pet the twin bear cubs," Raoul said, "but their mother was marching toward our car and I was afraid to *provoke* any mama that big and furry."

prowess (n) +

unusual skill or ability; military bravery and skills*
If our cat Fred could talk, he would boast of his mousing *prowess*.

prurient (adj) –

fostering lewd ideas or desires; lascivious
The old corner drugstore catered to customers' *prurient* interests with "girly magazines" that the druggist said we kids weren't allowed to read.

pseudonym (n)	*a pen name; any assumed name*

Anytime you see *pseudo* in front of a word, you know it's a false something-or-other. A *pseudoclassic* is only masquerading as a classic, just as a *pseudoscience* attempts to pass for the real thing. *Pseudosophistication* is pretend cool and like other "pseudos" is usually pretty obvious.

Saki, one of the more interesting *pseudonyms* in literature, was the name used by author Hector Hugh Munro.

puerile (adj) –	*juvenile or immature; silly, inane* (from L. **puer = child, boy**) The assembly speaker bored all of us with his *puerile* remarks, which were an insult to our intelligence.
pugnacious (adj) –	*spoiling for a fight; combative, belligerent, truculent* (from L. **pugnare = to fight**) Aunt Helen's banty rooster Willard led a vocal and *pugnacious* life, which is surprising when you think that he weighed only 2 pounds.
punctilious (adj)	*precise* (or *careful*) *about observing customs and rules*; conventional, scrupulously exact* Indian lore of early American tribes tells of people who were *punctilious* about honoring their gods, their ancestors, and their living elders.
pungent (adj)	*extremely painful or poignant* (said of odors, tastes, or words); *biting** (of remarks); *apropos or fitting** (as **pungent** lines in a play); *acrid, caustic* Although a bit petty at times, the critics' *pungent* movie reviews are refreshing compared with the daily doleful litany called television news.
purge (n)	*an elimination*
purge (v)	*to cleanse or rid yourself of something unwanted*; to eliminate or free* "It takes the north woods only a week or so to *purge* you of unimportant, citified notions," our trail guide said with a grin.
purport (n)	*meaning that is open or suggested; the substance, gist, import*
purport (v)	*to appear to be something*; to profess, intend* Our cat Fred is a good actor. All the time he's *purporting* to be a model cat gazing out the window, he's actually keeping watch on my brother's caged gerbils nearby.
pusillanimous (adj) –	*very timid, cowardly*; lacking forcefulness* Tweety Bird has often infuriated Sylvester the cat by calling him a "*pusillanimous* pussycat."

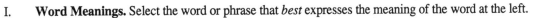

QUIZ ON LIST 14

I. **Word Meanings.** Select the word or phrase that *best* expresses the meaning of the word at the left.

1. **precocious**   (A) unruly (B) prompt (C) juvenile (D) prematurely bright
2. **propitiate**   (A) exonerate (B) offer (C) fight for (D) appease
3. **prerogative**   (A) expected right (B) calling forth (C) calling ahead (D) royal demand
4. **prolific**   (A) in favor of fighting (B) in favor of life (C) eloquent (D) fecund
5. **pungent**   (A) smelly (B) insipid (C) sharp (D) gassy
6. **protuberant**   (A) a potato (B) bulging (C) noisy (D) having a large nose
7. **puerile**   (A) childish (B) nasty (C) boring (D) flawless
8. **prelude**   (A) delusion (B) conclusion (C) preliminary (D) new moon
9. **prowess**   (A) a vow (B) bow of a ship (C) skill (D) female lion

10. **propinquity** (A) in favor of color (B) enmity (C) kinship (D) warfare
11. **pusillanimous** (A) animated (B) cowardly (C) poverty-stricken (D) feebleminded
12. **predilection** (A) forecast (B) command (C) omen (D) preference known in advance
13. **punctilious** (A) scrupulously exact (B) on time (C) tardy (D) imprecise
14. **procrastinate** (A) to be grumpy (B) to put off (C) to argue (D) to favor rules
15. **preclude** (A) forestall (B) introduce (C) go before (D) shut in
16. **posthumous** (A) delayed humor (B) after death (C) compost (D) postlude
17. **pragmatic** (A) boring (B) useful (C) mentally slow (D) direct
18. **predatory** (A) wolflike (B) of plundering (C) dated ahead (D) preservative
19. **prevaricate** (A) be evasive (B) be truthful (C) difficult to manage (D) be on time
20. **pseudonym** (A) error (B) arrangement (C) byline (D) pen name

II. **Antonyms.** Match vocabulary words with their antonyms.

_____	1. portly	secure
_____	2. potent	meager
_____	3. precarious	moral laxness
_____	4. precedent	dislike
_____	5. presumptuous	stingy
_____	6. probity	emaciated
_____	7. proclivity	maladroit
_____	8. prodigal	unassuming
_____	9. prodigious	weak
_____	10. proficient	following act

III. **Favorite SAT/PSAT Word Families.** Bonanza this time. See how many of these old veterans you can match with their definitions.

A. SCRIB, SCRIPT = write

_____	1. proscribe	(a) to impute, attribute, assign
_____	2. postscript	(b) to write down, record
_____	3. ascribe	(c) what follows other writing
_____	4. transcribe	(d) to forbid, prohibit
_____	5. circumscribe	(e) to define, limit, or surround with limitations

B. PRO = for, in favor of, much

_____	6. profess	(a) decorum, good manners
_____	7. propitious	(b) prudent, providing for the future
_____	8. propriety	(c) favorable, auspicious
_____	9. propensity	(d) extraordinary thing; highly gifted child
_____	10. provident	(e) wildly extravagant, prodigal
_____	11. profligate	(f) to declare, affirm
_____	12. prodigy	(g) strong natural tendency or inclination

C. VOC, VOKE = to call

_____ 13. provoke	(a) to prevaricate; evade by responding indirectly
_____ 14. evoke	(b) unchangeable, unable to be called back or undone
_____ 15. irrevocable	(c) to be in favor of, promote
_____ 16. advocate	(d) noisily demanding
_____ 17. vociferous	(e) to pique, annoy
_____ 18. equivocate	(f) to call forth subtly

IV. **Sentence Completion.** From the choices offered, complete each sentence with the most appropriate word or words.

purporting	prurient	prosaic
pugnacious	purged	precipitate
postulate	pragmatic	precluded

1. "That movie _____ to be for adults is just trash, appealing only to someone's base, _____ interests," Dad said with disgust.

2. "No pie in the sky ideas," Sally warned our committee. "We need _____ suggestions."

3. Jeff's _____ nature _____ any idea of an amicable discussion.

4. If we _____ that more people will appear later on, we should prepare for them in advance.

5. The instructor _____ most of the trite and _____ sentences from my paper.

6. "I hope that my red pencil won't _____ any hasty corrections on your part," said my writing instructor. "Rewrite slowly and carefully, please."

List 15

quaff (v)	_to take a long, deep drink_ After football practice, my brother races home to _quaff_ every cold drink in the house.
quell (v)	_to put down completely or overwhelm_ (as **quell** an insurrection); _to crush, squash;_ also _to pacify or soothe_ (from Old English **cwellan = to kill**) Military troops were ordered to _quell_ the rioting workers in strife-torn Poland.
querulous (adj) –	_complaining, faultfinding, and fretful_ (usually applied to tone of voice); _petulant, captious_ _Querulous_ by nature, the ballet master seldom praised his students but instead complained about their performances in whining tones.
quiescent (adj)	_resting, quiet; giving no trouble*; inactive_ Normally _quiescent_ Mount Saint Helens erupted violently and caught many area residents off guard.
quietus (n)	_permanent settlement_ (as of an obligation); _end of any activity*_ (as in death); _anything that quiets or holds down in a repressive manner_ The president's statement put the _quietus_ on all rumors about her impending resignation.
quintessence (n) +	_the core of a thing in its purest state; its essential part;_ also _the model or typical example_

Literally "the fifth essence," _quintessence_ comes to us from ancient and medieval philosophy. Old philosophers believed that the fifth was the highest element in all the world, that it not only permeated all things but was the substance of heavenly bodies.

Perhaps our concept of a soul derives from this idea of a perfect essence, a thing most pure.

One look at Nate astride a horse reveals that he is the *quintessence* of a knowledgeable equestrian.

quizzical (adj)	*teasing, yet often questioning at the same time; puzzled, yet with humor* Alain's face had a *quizzical* look as he exclaimed, "You've got to be kidding! You don't seriously expect to go to dinner at the White House in jeans?"
rabid (adj)	*incredibly furious; pursuing at length some opinion or interest*; also referring to the disease rabies* Dr. Frankenstein's *rabid* enthusiasm for human experimentation led him to create in his laboratory the monster we now call Frankenstein.
raconteur (n) +	*a fine storyteller* Oscar Wilde, known for his plays, was also in demand as a gifted *raconteur* around the turn of the century.
ramifications (n)	*offshoots or outgrowths; also the implications or consequences* (as of an act)* We need to consider all the *ramifications* of your problem before we can decide how to solve it.
rancid (adj) –	*smelling or tasting strong, perhaps spoiled; malodorous and offensive to taste or smell** "Just walking in the door of that restaurant makes me sick," Antoine said. "The odor of *rancid* fat has permeated even the tables!"
rancor (n) –	*enmity or hatred built up over time; bitterness* As he denounced the government, we could hear the *rancor* behind every word.
rant (v) –	*to denounce in an angry way or to rave against noisily; also to talk pretentiously, in a dominating manner* When someone *rants* at length about a subject, I find myself ignoring the actual words and watching the display instead.
rapport (n)	*a closeness (usually positive) of beliefs, interests; a good relationship of understanding and sympathy* Anyone watching Brian Boitano skate can sense the *rapport* between him and his element, which translates into fluid beauty on ice.
rational (adj)	*open to logical reason or being reasonable; of sane mind** "If the patient is now *rational*, we need to talk to her to see if she knows anything about the crime," the police sergeant said.
raucous (adj) –	*sounding annoyingly loud or disagreeable; disorderly in a noisy way* Fans of Western movies revel in the *raucous* barroom brawls featuring hurled chairs, broken mirrors, and random gunshots.
ravenous (adj)	*extremely hungry, for food or other satisfaction* "My goal is to develop *ravenous* readers," the librarian said with a smile. "To have lines outside the doors every morning would be heaven."
raze (v)	*to destroy totally, right down to the ground; demolish* Crowds of curious onlookers gathered to watch as a professional wrecking crew *razed* the old Paramount Theatre.
rebuttal (n)	*denial or opposition to an argument*; refutation; disproving response* Our debate team was demoralized by the strong *rebuttal* of their opponents at the state debate contest.
recalcitrant (adj) –	*tough to manage or control*; strongly against authority; unruly, refractory;* literally *"kicking back with your heels"* in Latin Cancer is a stubbornly *recalcitrant* disease, defying research, money, and all efforts to bring it under control.

recant (v)

to renounce (an opinion, belief, position); *to confess error or wrongdoing*
Salem "witches" were sternly advised to *recant* and to admit that they had performed evil deeds under Satan's influence.

recapitulate (v)

to "recap" or restate the main points in discussions, papers, proposals, etc.
Before we continue, let's *recapitulate* our reasons for reading this book so that the main goals are kept in mind for discussion later.

reciprocal (adj)

analogous, complementary, evident on both sides; referring to a this-for-that arrangement, often mutually beneficial
Reciprocal trade agreements are often canceled when two countries differ over foreign policy.

recluse (n)

anyone who lives mostly alone, or mainly secluded from others; a hermit
Thoreau lived as a *recluse* at Walden Pond in order to think about what he believed and why.

recollect (v)

to call back to mind in remembrance
Our favorite grandfather stories were those he began with, "I *recollect* one time when I was a boy. . . ."

redoubtable (adj)

inspiring fear or awe or both; formidable
William the Conqueror landed in England with a *redoubtable* force that won him control of the lands he coveted.

refute (v)

to show as wrong by giving evidence to the contrary; to disprove, rebut; to deny
One by one, the young chief *refuted* rival chieftains' claims to his territory, overcoming their attempts to rule by his intelligence and superior abilities in war.

relegate (v)

to put away or aside; to classify in a definite place or position by rank; to commit
Our cat Fred liked to sharpen his claws on an old chair, making such a pathetic object of it that we had to *relegate* it to the basement to await reupholstery.

relevant (adj)

important, significant (to whatever is being considered)
"Whether or not Fred has a lovable personality isn't one bit *relevant*," Mom snapped. "Just look at what he's done to our chair."

remiss (adj) –

failing to give care or attention, therefore *negligent or neglectful; careless, lax*
"We'd be *remiss* in our duty as good cat parents if we didn't get Fred a scratching post to replace his old chair," I told Mom.

remonstrate (v)

to speak out strongly against something; to object or expostulate with feeling
Before he turned me loose with his car, Dad *remonstrated* at length about the price of cars, the dangers of driving, and the many worries parents have when kids begin to drive.

remorse (n)

an uneasy feeling derived from real or imagined guilt; self-reproach or regret*
Wouldn't you think that people who kill animals for trophy or sport would be tormented by feelings of *remorse*?

remuneration (n)

payment for goods or services; recompense
I told Andy that his *remuneration* for walking the neighbors' dogs was generous, and I'd take the job anytime he didn't want it.

reprehensible (adj) –

earning disapproval or blame; blameworthy

Words from Latin **prehendere** are close in meaning to the root, which means **to grasp**. A monkey's **prehensile** tail helps him to grasp branches. If you **apprehend** a criminal, you are somehow holding onto him. To **comprehend** information is to understand it, thereby laying claim to it. To feel **apprehensive** is to shrink away from something in a reluctance to take hold.

"I don't think," Mom said angrily, "that giving Fred an expensive scratching post is the way to show him how we feel about his *reprehensible* treatment of our chair."

reprisal (n)	*retaliation for wrongs suffered*; taking something back; a reaction to another's behavior causing you to act* (usually in a negative way) Since the settlers didn't expect a reaction to their theft of Indian ponies, they were shocked by the swift Indian raid that took livestock in *reprisal*.
requisite (adj)	*required, essential* As soon as all the *requisite* forms have been filled out, we will process your application.
rescind (v)	*to cancel, annul* (as **rescind** a command); *to repeal or call back* Mom didn't give up easily in her opposition to Fred's behavior. "I think we ought to *rescind* his right to come into the house if he's going to destroy furniture," she decided.
resonant (adj)	*echoing, as sound; vibrating* (as rich sound) From outdoors, Fred emitted *resonant* and mournful meows, which grated on our nerves and somehow made us all feel guilty.
resourceful (adj) +	*showing intelligence and skill at meeting situations and dealing with them; capable* As Mom opened the door to Fred, she had to admit that he was a *resourceful* cat, even though he was also a refractory one.
respite (n)	*a time of relief; a pause, rest from activity, lull* After his punishment, Fred was a paragon of virtue, giving us a welcome *respite* from his normally trying ways.
reticent (adj)	*not talkative by nature*; naturally silent or reserved;* also *simple and restrained in manner* Normally *reticent* about our pets, Dad finally said that he "got a kick out of Fred," because he never knew what the beast would do next.
retribution (n)	*the payment of either reward or punishment* In *retribution* for the capture of one of their ships, the pirate band attacked and sank two valuable cargo ships.
revere (v)	*to respect and honor; venerate, worship* Qualities that cause us to *revere* a person's memory include honesty, intelligence, and bravery.
rhetoric (n)	*the skill of fine, meaningful speaking and writing*;* also *pompous and hypocritical language; discourse* (from Gr. **rhetorike = art of oratory**) Listening to recordings of Franklin Delano Roosevelt's speeches and "Fireside Chats" is a lesson in effective *rhetoric*.

QUIZ ON LIST 15

I. **Synonyms.** Select two words that are synonyms from each of the four-word groups.

1. (A) drink (B) overwhelm (C) raze (D) quell
2. (A) petulant (B) querulous (C) inquisitive (D) affectionate
3. (A) angry (B) inactive (C) quiescent (D) dull
4. (A) flower (B) fragrant (C) rancid (D) offensive
5. (A) rational (B) argument (C) rabid (D) reasonable
6. (A) please (B) enervate (C) revere (D) venerate
7. (A) vibrating (B) jerky (C) recalcitrant (D) resonant
8. (A) rejection (B) retaliation (C) resignation (D) reprisal

9. (A) recompense (B) recourse (C) remuneration (D) defection

10. (A) object (B) repair (C) unmask (D) remonstrate

11. (A) delegate (B) set aside (C) relegate (D) reissue

12. (A) quell (B) urge (C) drink (D) quaff

13. (A) raconteur (B) storyteller (C) lecturer (D) pedant

14. (A) implications (B) adjustments (C) ramifications (D) desecrations

15. (A) tastelessness (B) bitterness (C) deceit (D) rancor

II. **Sentence Completion.** Complete each sentence with the best word possible from List 15.

1. The art of effective speaking or writing is known as _____.

2. When someone pays you back, it can be called _____.

3. A naturally shy, untalkative person is said to be _____.

4. _____ is what you'd say of someone who can deal with almost any situation.

5. A cat's paw on a mouse may be anything but gentle—a primeval, instinctive _____, and the mouse is no more.

6. Acts that deserve blame are termed _____.

7. A strong feeling of regret for something you did is _____.

8. Giving evidence to deny something is termed _____. (Use noun form.)

9. Failure to do what you're expected to do means you've been _____ in your duty.

10. _____ (noun form) is what you're doing when you review the significant points in your talk or presentation.

III. **Find the Oddball.** In each group of words below, one does *not* belong. Find the oddball word.

1. (A) raze (B) rectify (C) destroy (D) demolish

2. (A) debate (B) rebuttal (C) refutation (D) denial

3. (A) recant (B) confess (C) elect (D) renounce

4. (A) awesome (B) redoubtable (C) formidable (D) decisive

5. (A) refractory (B) broken (C) recalcitrant (D) stubborn

6. (A) known (B) relevant (C) significant (D) applicable

7. (A) remiss (B) message (C) careless (D) lax

8. (A) necessary (B) requisite (C) preliminary (D) essential

9. (A) annul (B) repeal (C) rescind (D) pronounce

10. (A) hiatus (B) respite (C) break (D) action

IV. **Antonyms.** Choose the best antonym or opposing phrase for each word in bold type.

1. **quintessence** (A) interesting addenda (B) extraneous material (C) strange amusement (D) misshapen form (E) misplaced object

2. **rabid** (A) vital (B) carefree (C) lukewarm (D) candid (E) dormant

3. **quizzical** (A) according to form (B) vibrantly alive (C) comfortably stolid (D) quiescently waiting (E) patently uninterested

4. **rant** (A) move softly (B) act warily (C) speak peaceably (D) listen patiently (E) chatter lengthily

5. **rapport** (A) juxtaposition (B) retirement (C) depravity (D) discord (E) conjunction

6. **reclusive** (A) convivial (B) jocund (C) introspective (D) diffident (E) boisterous

7. **ravenous** (A) pacific (B) irritated (C) pompous (D) satiated (E) querulous

8. **raucous** (A) acute (B) subtle (C) perspicacious (D) amusing (E) decadent

9. **recollect** (A) dismay (B) distribute (C) forget (D) allot (E) forestall

10. **reciprocate** (A) accede to demands (B) bow to precedent (C) deny entrance (D) forget to honor (E) refuse to barter

V.   **Favorite SAT/PSAT Word Family.** For these words that are bound to reappear, write a brief definition or synonym. Consult a friend, your parents, or Webster if you need help.

QUER, QUIR, QUIS = ask, seek

1. query _____

2. querulous _____

3. required _____ requisite _____

4. inquisitive _____

5. inquisition _____

6. acquire _____ acquisition _____

List 16

ribald (adj) –	*offensive, often because of crudeness* (language or behavior); *indecent or coarse* (as **ribald** humor); also **risqué** (adj), *indecent, improper, lewdly suggestive* Boys and girls in grade school derive great pleasure from *ribald* jokes and expressions that often embarrass their parents.
rococo (adj)	*referring to elaborately detailed artistic or musical style; intricately ornate* The old painting was dull when compared to its gilt, *rococo* frame, which drew our immediate attention.
rostrum (n)	*a raised dais, stage, or platform for speaking or performing*
	The old Roman *rostra* was a public platform located in the Forum. Its edges were adorned with the beaks of captured ships (*rostra = beak or ship's beak*). A Roman orator gained authority merely by speaking from this prestigious location. Today anyone speaking from a raised position (as on a *rostrum)* is presumed to have authority. Think about the old game "King of the Hill."
	The speaker on the *rostrum* is the man who spoke to us last year about animals that are nearly extinct.
rotund (adj)	*referring to any sound with notable rhythm or richness* (as a **rotund** phrase); *plump or chubby of body** I wouldn't describe my French teacher as fat, but he is *rotund*, maybe because he loves to cook gourmet meals based on old family recipes.
rue (n) –	*regret or sorrow*
rue (v) –	*to regret exceedingly; to feel remorse or sorrow* "I *rue* the day we bought those shoes," Mom moaned as she eyed the diamond-shaped mud globs left by Andy's sneakers.
ruse (n)	*a clever trick or deception; subterfuge* When Fred sits by the door and meows, we assume he wants to go outdoors, but that is only a *ruse*. He merely wants to look outside to see if anything interesting is happening.
sacrilegious (adj) –	*lack of deference, respect, or reverence for anything sacred or special* "I suppose," Dad joked, "it would be *sacrilegious* to suggest that you play some of my classical music tonight at your party."
sagacity (n) +	*wisdom and discernment; keen perception, shrewdness* (from L. **sagire = to perceive keenly**) When we had to write a poem for English class, I began, "His enviable, cool *sagacity,* / His admirable perspicacity. . . ." Then I couldn't go any further and had to start over.

salient (adj)	*very noticeable or conspicuous; prominent* Unpredictability is a *salient* feature of Fred's personality and the one our dad finds most intriguing.
salubrious (adj) +	*giving a feeling of well-being or aiding in well-being; favorable to health;* also **salutary** (adj), *promoting good health* (from L. **salut = health**) Members of the Polar Bear Club have tried to convince me that it's *salubrious* to plunge into icy winter waters, but I'm skeptical.
sanguine (adj) +	*high-colored* (as of complexion), therefore *healthily optimistic or cheerful; confident* (from L. **sanguin- = blood**) After the attempt on his life, President Reagan was admirably *sanguine*, displaying enviable composure.
satiate (v)	*to give complete satisfaction; surfeit* "When I waddled out of Mama Leone's restaurant," Dad told us, "I was so *satiated* with good Italian food that I walked to the office instead of taking the bus as usual."
scathing (adj) –	*harsh or severe to an extreme; strongly critical** José wrote a *scathing* editorial for our school newspaper attacking those who pollute our local streams and waterways.
scourge (v) –	*to lash, whip, or flog; to make miserable*
scourge (n) –	*any instrument—person or thing—used to punish*; whip or lash; affliction* Attila the Hun was a skillful king, plunderer, and conqueror later nicknamed "the *Scourge* of God."
scrupulous (adj) +	*being punctilious and precisely correct*; showing painstaking care and adherence to scruples or morals* Jackie said with exasperation, "I paid *scrupulous* attention to the recipe and just look at this disaster of a cake!"
sedulous (adj) +	*done with care and diligence; particular* Every day, several times a day, our cat Fred washes his fur and paws with *sedulous* attention.
senile (adj) –	*showing advanced age or mental deterioration that may accompany old age* (from L. **senex = old**) Yesterday Dad stomped into the house complaining about an erratic driver, whom he called "a *senile* old bat," who had forced him off the road.
serendipity (n) +	*the finding of luck or good fortune when you're not even looking for it*
	Serendipity comes to us from a fairy tale titled "The Three Princes of Serendip." The princes were travelers who repeatedly came upon rewards they weren't seeking.
	"I found several marvelous things at an aptly named little shop called *Serendipity*," Mom said.
serene (adj) +	*calm, tranquil, peaceful; free from stress;* also part of a title as Her **Serene** Majesty In order to attain a *serene* outlook on life, many people practice yoga or meditation.
servile (adj) –	*subservient* (as a slave or menial worker); *overly submissive in an off-putting way* Only insecure or threatened people find it necessary to keep others in a *servile* state.
shibboleth (n)	*a commonly accepted word or phrase that has become a byword or slogan;* also *old doctrine or beliefs of a group*
	A Hebrew word meaning *stream, shibboleth* was used as a word test to separate Gileadites from Ephraimites, who said the word in a distinctive way. Today, any *shibboleth* is apt to be an overused catchphrase.
	The *shibboleths* of the militant sixties seem generally inadequate to the problems of today.

simulate (v) — *to approximate*; to appear to be like something else in a superficial way* (as **simulated** pearls in a necklace); *to assume or feign*
"We can *simulate* flying conditions here on the ground in our trainer," the flying instructor told his class.

sinecure (n) – *any job or position that yields an income but demands little work, maybe none at all*
"This job ought to be a *sinecure*," Mom told the baby-sitter, "because our children are older and the freezer is packed with prepared meals you can serve quickly."

sinuous (adj) — *showing flexibility in the form of undulating, wavy motion* (as a snake moves in a **sinuous** manner)
"The *sinuous* movements of those dancers certainly are entertaining," my brother John said, with his eyes glued to the TV set.

skeptic (n) — *someone inclined to doubt or suspend judgment, to be disbelieving, uncertain, or frankly critical*
Uncle Bart is such a *skeptic* that he won't believe anything until he's read it in several places.

slavish (adj) – *behaving as a slave; servile; also reproducing exactly in a manner lacking freshness or originality, therefore imitative**

The word *slave* has historically bad connotations. It derives from the *Slavs* of eastern Europe, who were conquered many times and repeatedly forced into bondage as a result.

My earliest attempts at drawing cartoons were *slavish* imitations of my favorite cartoonists, but when I realized what I was doing, I tore up the drawings.

slovenly (adj) – *sloppy and unkempt* (in appearance); *lazy and haphazard* (in workmanship)
The store manager lectured his employees on the importance of neatness, warning them that a *slovenly* appearance was cause for dismissal.

solicitous (adj) + *concerned or worried; anxious; showing thoughtfulness or care; also very careful, meticulous*
Mother cats tend their kittens in a *solicitous* way, washing them frequently and teaching them how to care for themselves.

somber (adj) — *of dark or gloomy aspect; sober or grave in manner*
What had been merely an overcast sky turned *somber* and forbidding as the storm approached our city.

sophisticated (adj) — *removed from original, natural simplicity, therefore complex** (as **sophisticated** machinery); *of persons, knowledgeable and often polished* (mentally or socially); *worldly, informed, highly aware*

Sophisticated dates back to the Greek school of philosopher-educators known as *Sophists* in the fifth century B.C. Their name meant "skilled" or "clever." The Sophists were among the most highly educated men of their time, and the first to offer a system of education that went beyond the basics. In time, they were disparaged because of their too-subtle, often specious arguments, and today a **sophist** is regarded as *someone whose reasoning is faulty and conclusions erroneous.*

Our school band has progressed to several *sophisticated* musical arrangements, which we're practicing for the winter concert.

Note: A sophomore is wise (**soph**) plus **moronic,** according to word derivation. *Sophomores are wise fools.*

specious (adj) – *appearing legitimate on the surface but lacking truth or validity; plausible, but false underneath*
Our debate coach warned us to be on the lookout for *specious* reasoning so that our rebuttal could poke holes in the argument of the opposition.

spectral (adj)

referring to a specter or ghost; ghostly*; also of a spectrum
In the dimness of nighttime hospital corridors, patients flapping down the halls in white gowns assume a *spectral* appearance.

speculate (v)

to think or wonder about something; to guess or suppose*; also to risk in business, hoping for profit
In current events class, we were asked to *speculate* on the future of the world twenty-five years from now.

splenetic (adj) –

easily irritated and grouchy; ill-tempered, spiteful

The spleen used to be considered the seat of emotion and passion, especially the darker emotions. Someone who "vented his spleen" was behaving in a splenetic way and was therefore cross and thoroughly unpleasant.

"The *splenetic* nature of her prose turns me off," said the book reviewer.

sporadic (adj) –

not regular or predictable; infrequent, random
Our cat Fred makes *sporadic* attempts to present us with tasty mole or mouse carcasses as gifts.

spurious (adj) –

false or fake, though outwardly legitimate*; forged (as **spurious** credentials)
After a famous millionaire died, several people submitted *spurious* inheritance claims that were easily disproved.

squalor (n) –

the dirt and abject neglect associated with poverty
The colonists heading for North America didn't expect to travel in *squalor*, but as the days wore on conditions belowdecks deteriorated alarmingly.

squander (v) –

to use in a silly or extravagant way*; to waste or dissipate
Andy *squandered* an entire month's allowance on a giant paperweight to keep the lid safely on his gerbil cage. "Just in case Fred gets too clever," he said to me.

stagnate (v)

to be without movement or inactive; to be out of use, therefore *stale*
The saying "A mind is a terrible thing to waste" tells us that we shouldn't let our brains *stagnate*.

static (adj)

lacking change or movement; being quiet, at rest (as a **static** pattern); *fixed or stationary*; of electronic noise,* as radio **static** (n); colloquially: *negative noises or disagreement*
The population in our town has remained relatively *static* for a decade but now shows signs of declining.

status (n)

the state or condition of someone or something; rank relative to others; a position in any hierarchy; situation
Confident of his *status* in the family, Fred brought home a lady friend—a homeless calico pussycat.

strident (adj) –

unpleasantly harsh; getting attention through persistence and loudness
The pleasure of public television is twofold: intelligent programming combined with the absence of *strident,* insensitive commercials.

stringent (adj)

showing strict and rigid compliance with accepted standards*; also lacking money or credit
In spite of the rather *stringent* rules at camp, we enjoyed the activities, the other campers, and the counselors.

stupefy (v)

to astonish or astound*; to cause someone to be slow-witted or insensible
Stupefied by the number of items required for a lengthy canoe trip, I gritted my teeth and set about collecting the supplies.

QUIZ ON LIST 16

I.   **Antonyms.** Match vocabulary words with their antonyms.

_____	1. ribald	svelte
_____	2. salient	pessimistic
_____	3. sacrilegious	slovenly
_____	4. rococo	proper
_____	5. sanguine	respectful
_____	6. rotund	overt act
_____	7. scrupulous	obscure
_____	8. ruse	haughty
_____	9. serene	splenetic
_____	10. servile	simple
_____	11. spectral	dynamic
_____	12. specious	flexible
_____	13. static	mundane, worldly
_____	14. stringent	naive
_____	15. sophisticated	genuine

II.   **Fill-ins.** From the choices given, select the best word to complete each phrase.

1. enough books to _____ me for an entire year   salubrious
2. bitter, _____ remarks that made my ears burn   scathing
3. the _____ to look ahead and choose intelligently   satiate
4. _____ effects of walking and bicycling   sedulous
5. grooming each feather with _____ care   sagacity
6. used his work like a _____, to punish himself for imagined sins   serendipity
7. unbelievable _____ that led to the discovery of the treasure   simulation
8. discarded that old _____ as an outmoded slogan   sinecure
9. admirable _____ of serenity even when she was disturbed   scourge
10. job in his dad's office, a rather obvious _____   shibboleth

III. **Analogies.** Complete each analogy with the pair that expresses the same relationship as the original pair.

1. RUNG : LADDER ::
   (A) static : radio   (B) raincoat : umbrella   (C) status : hierarchy   (D) size : shoe
   (E) speculation : guess

2. RAUCOUS : SOUND ::
   (A) salutary : exercise   (B) strident : voice   (C) splenetic : health   (D) servile : government
   (E) noisome : music

3. RECANT : ADHERE ::
   (A) quell : observe   (B) rant : rave   (C) debate : rebut   (D) flow : stagnate   (E) mete : attribute

4. MINISTER : PULPIT ::
   (A) speaker : rostrum   (B) actor : dressing room   (C) doctor : office   (D) conductor : baton
   (E) politician : headquarters

5. CRIME : PUNISH ::
   (A) misdemeanor : relegate   (B) faux pas : dismiss   (C) character : denigrate   (D) lampoon : bemoan
   (E) error : rue

IV.   **Truth or Fiction?** Mark T for true statements, F for those that are false.

_____ 1.   A sophisticated traveler would assume he could use American money in any European country.

_____ 2.   Avoiding salutary exercise may help you to become senile sooner.

_____ 3.   The mental stimulation provided by any sinecure will satisfy most enthusiastic employees.

_____ 4.   Somber apparel should never be worn to a funeral.

_____ 5.   Someone will accuse you of levity if you describe a hummingbird as a sinuous creature.

_____ 6.   A nurse who is rarely solicitous toward her patients may incur dislike, even dismissal.

_____ 7.   Skeptical Sam would be an appropriate name for Doubting Thomas's alter ego.

_____ 8.   Museums are eager to acquire slavish imitations of the great works of art owned by other museums.

_____ 9.   The best housekeepers are slovenly by nature.

_____ 10.   You would be wise to examine the arguments of a sophist carefully.

List 17

subsistence (n)	*minimal standard of living; the necessities of existing or the minimum required to permit life*; the source that allows life to exist* "We're managing a bare *subsistence* on this poor land," admitted the farmer, "but we plan to stick it out and maybe buy better acreage next year.
succinct (adj)	*brief and to the point; concise, pithy, terse, economical* (word use) Some words defy *succinct* definition and require a fairly lengthy explanation for understanding.
succulent (n)	*a type of fleshy plant* (from L. **sucus** = **juice**)
succulent (adj) +	*juicy and very appealing to the taste** Fred regards a fresh mouse as a *succulent* morsel, but he hasn't managed to convince our family yet.
sully (v) –	*to make less appealing*; to soil or defile* (usually refers to persons' names, reputations, standing in the community) "No," said the model sadly, "I don't dare work in the garden, because if I *sully* my hands I'll have to forgo this afternoon's photography session."
supercilious (adj) –	*excessively proud; disdainfully superior* (from L. **supercilium** = **eyebrow**) The actress threw a brief, *supercilious* glance at her audience, then disappeared— actions that hardly endeared her to the crowd.
superficial (adj)	*on the surface** (as a **superficial** cut); *interested mainly in appearances, hence shallow in nature* Todd's interest in ice hockey is mainly *superficial;* he prefers the intricacies of figure skating.
surfeit (v)	*to feed too much; to cloy, satiate*
surfeit (n)	*an extra amount or excess*; a kind of gluttony regarding food and drink; the revulsion brought on by overindulgence* "A *surfeit* of rich foods over the holidays has made me look like a fire hydrant—short and squat," Ginny moaned.
surpass (v)	*to reach beyond or exceed expectations*; to overstep* "Each year he *surpasses* his past year's performance," Mom said with pride as she watched my brother John score another soccer goal.
surreptitious (adj) –	*in a secretive, underhanded, or deceptive way; clandestine* Hidden in Anna's drawer, under her socks, was a rather trashy novel, which she read in a *surreptitious* way at night.
tacit (adj)	*understood or suggested but not actually stated* (from L. **tacitus** = **silent**) Craig and Leigh Ann have had a *tacit* agreement not to date anyone else, but today Craig's ring is on Leigh Ann's finger, so they must have decided to go public.

taciturn (adj)   *untalkative by nature; silent, reticent*
A naturally *taciturn* man, Whittier's Quaker father said little and encouraged his son to do likewise.

tactile (adj)   *felt, touchable; tangible* (from L. **tangere = to touch**)
Learning how to read Braille, which uses a series of raised dots for letters, is a *tactile* skill taught in schools for the blind.

talisman (n) +   *a special, meaningful object thought to be lucky; an amulet, fetish*
Swashbucklers, such as D'Artagnan in *The Three Musketeers*, often carried scarves of their sweethearts as *talismans* to protect them when they fought duels.

tautology (n)   *needless repetition of words or ideas; redundancy*

Examples of *tautology* fill our speech and writing, perhaps arising from an effort to be absolutely clear in communication. But it isn't necessary to say *young kitten* or *young foal*, because kittens and foals have to be young—otherwise they'd be cats or horses. All *tautologies*, like *visible to the eye*, are funny, and when you think about it, obviously redundant. Consider the phrases *but yet, close proximity, each and every one, first and foremost, my personal opinion*, and *past history*. History wouldn't be history unless it's past, right? Avoid using these phrases, most of which are also clichés. Whenever *one word* will do the job, let it.

"I have to edit all my work for *tautological* expressions," the writer confessed. "I get carried away in my first drafts and repeat myself for emphasis."

tedious (adj) –   *going on at length, often boring; tiresome*
Poet William Cowper (who must have been married) understood a wife's feelings when he wrote, in "John Gilpin":

> John Gilpin's spouse said to her dear—
>   Though wedded we have been
> These twice ten *tedious* years, yet we
>   No holiday have seen.

temerity (n) –   *unwise boldness; reckless or rash behavior in the face of danger; effrontery*
Fred's new calico friend, whom we named Sophia, had the *temerity* to sleep on our living room couch, a resting place forbidden to cats.

tenet (n)   *a basic belief or truth for a group of people* (e.g., a church congregation); *doctrine*
When Mom put Sophia the cat outdoors, she told her formally, "One of the *tenets* of our household is that people sit on sofas, cats sit on floors."

tentative (adj)   *incomplete or lacking development; hesitant or uncertain** (as a **tentative** smile)
Allowed back in the house, beautiful Sophia looked mournfully at the couch and gave a *tentative* meow, waiting for Mom's response.

tenuous (adj)   *slim or slender; flimsy; weak, barely perceptible* (as a **tenuous** grasp of the idea)
(from L. **tenuis = thin, slight**)
My grasp of the new algebra material was so *tenuous* I stayed after school for help.

terse (adj)   *stripped of all but the essentials*; concise, succinct* (said of written or spoken words)
Willa had hoped for a comment about her term paper, but all she received was the mark "B"—a *terse* response to all her hard work.

theology (n)   *religion and its accompanying theory; a set body of beliefs* (as *Christian theology*);
literally *"study of god"*
Many aspects of Russian and Greek Orthodox *theology* are illuminated by various icons, small paintings of exquisite beauty and deep significance.

thwart (v)   *to foil, baffle, or frustrate* (someone's attempts)
Mom successfully *thwarted* our cat Sophia's attempts to sleep on the sofa, and now Sophia has picked Dad's chair as a satisfactory alternative.

tolerance (n)

ability to withstand adverse conditions; understanding or acknowledgment of another's viewpoint or beliefs*
"My *tolerance* for animals does not extend to having my chair used as a cat's bed," Dad told Sophia as he set that disgruntled cat firmly on the floor.

tome (n)

usually refers to a large volume or set of volumes*; a weighty book, very scholarly or heavy or both
Carl Sandburg's masterly biography of Lincoln can rightfully be called a *tome*.

torpid (adj)

motionless or lacking feeling (as numb); *slow or sluggish in action*; lethargic*
The sloth is a *torpid* animal, asleep much of the time.

toxic (adj) –

poisonous (as snake's venom may be **toxic**)
Across the country, we are building plants to treat *toxic* wastes safely in response to citizens' demands.

tractable (adj)

obedient and docile; easy to teach, train, control*
Killer whales, once presumed dangerous, are now known as *tractable* mammals who enjoy performing for an audience.

transcend (v)

to go above or beyond the known or accepted limits*; to exceed expectations
For Saint Francis of Assisi, founder of the Franciscan Order, love of God, man, and animals *transcended* all else.

transient (adj)

of extremely brief duration; short-lived, transitory, fleeting, ephemeral, evanescent
When I was a high school senior, I thought the year would never end. As a college sophomore, I realized the *transient* nature of my days in high school.

trenchant (adj)

highly effective and well-spoken, hence keenly perceptive; penetrating, even biting or caustic (of comments)**; incisive*
Many times Mark Twain abandoned his lighter satire for the *trenchant* commentary of a bitterly disappointed idealist.

trepidation (n)

fear, worry, or apprehension (from L. **trepidare** = to tremble)
Frequently found in writing, the phrase "in fear and *trepidation*" is a tautology since *trepidation* always suggests some amount of fear.

trite (adj) –

worn out and ineffective from over-use; hackneyed, banal, stale (applies to expressions and words)
Anything written in haste is apt to be marked by *trite* expressions, which are so fixed in the mind that they crop up easily and repeatedly.

truculent (adj) –

showing a belligerent or cruel attitude; harsh or destructive (from L. **truc-** = fierce)
"Don't go near that sow," my uncle warned us. "She's a *truculent* old pig when she's just had a litter."

truncate (v)

to cut short (something that might normally be longer, anything from an interview to a dog's tail); *curtail*
If anyone had dared to tell Napoleon he had a *truncated* body, Napoleon might have *truncated* that person's life.

tumid (adj)

swollen or protuberant; enlarged, bulging; also bombastic or wordy, verbose (said of prose)
Bed rest proved a miserable experience for Ken, whose body felt *tumid* and sluggish from enforced idleness.

turgid (adj)

distended by swelling; also ornate or verbose in language use*; tumid
Readers fond of Hemingway's succinct style have accused earlier authors of writing *turgid* prose.

ubiquitous (adj)

being everywhere at once; widespread
"I can't stand these *ubiquitous* commercials," Mom said. "I find them on every station, every place I turn the dial."

unbridled (adj)	*without restraint or confinement* (like a horse minus its bridle); *uncontrolled* A temper tantrum is a display of *unbridled* rage, not calculated to win friends or influence people.
undulate (v)	*to move in a wavy, rhythmic motion*; to move sinuously; to swing* The Snake River *undulates* for a thousand miles through the Northwest from Idaho to Washington.
unremitting (adj)	*without pause or letting up; constant, incessant* *Unremitting* attention to detail is one mark of a thorough laboratory scientist.
untenable (adj)	*not possible to defend or uphold* (as an **untenable** position) "We have an *untenable* location in this remote outpost," reported the army captain, "and we must have additional troops."
upbraid (v) –	*to scold in a severe manner; to criticize harshly for faults* The angry basketball coach *upbraided* his team after the game, listing each of the errors that had led to their defeat.
usurp (v)	*to take* (a position or authority) *forcefully and often without the right to do so* Although he loves her company, we often see Fred eyeing the luscious Sophia as if he feared she might *usurp* his position as Head Cat in the family.
usury (n) –	*lending money at abnormally high (or illegal) interest rates* Andy said he would lend me five dollars if I paid him six dollars back and in one week. "That's *usury!*" I hollered.

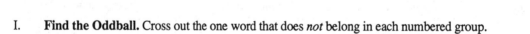

QUIZ ON LIST 17

I.   **Find the Oddball.** Cross out the one word that does *not* belong in each numbered group.

1. (A) scold (B) chastise (C) upbraid (D) warn
2. (A) lengthy (B) unremitting (C) ceaseless (D) incessant
3. (A) tumid (B) turgid (C) big (D) swollen
4. (A) minister (B) religion (C) theology (D) beliefs
5. (A) caustic (B) acid (C) tractable (D) trenchant
6. (A) scholarly book (B) heavy volume (C) pocket book (D) tome
7. (A) turgid (B) torpid (C) sluggish (D) lethargic
8. (A) docile (B) well-behaved (C) servile (D) tractable
9. (A) baffle (B) fool (C) thwart (D) frustrate
10. (A) identity (B) belief (C) tenet (D) doctrine

II. **Synonyms and Definitions.** Write the best synonym or definition on the line after each numbered word.

1. tentative _____   clandestine
2. terse _____   redundancy
3. temerity _____   curtail
4. tactile _____   unrestrained
5. talisman _____   amulet, fetish
6. tautology _____   juicy, appealing
7. surreptitious _____   tiresome
8. truncate _____   succinct
9. tedious _____   hesitant
10. tacit _____   unspoken
11. supercilious _____   sway rhythmically
12. unbridled _____   effrontery
13. undulate _____   indefensible
14. succulent _____   disdainfully superior
15. untenable _____   tangible

III. **Words in Context.** Put the best possible word from List 17 into each sentence, selecting from the words given.

sully   surpass   usurped
tolerance   taciturn   trepidation
surfeit   tenuous   truculent
transcends

1. "She's holding on by that skinny little tail," Jack said, staring at the monkey. "It seems like a _____ hold on security."

2. I agreed with Jack and commented on the remarkable _____ monkeys have for zoo life. "They seem to adapt extremely well," I said.

3. A large monkey wearing a _____ expression thumped his chest, shoved the first little monkey aside, and _____ her place on the branch.

4. The first monkey dusted her little hands together and stalked to the corner of the cage, as if to say, "Humph. I wouldn't _____ my hands with the likes of *him*."

5. Seeing he'd been dismissed, the larger monkey dropped to the ground and began to _____ himself at the food trough. He stuffed the food into his mouth rapidly, seemingly without much pleasure.

6. Animal behaviorists have learned that the intelligence level of certain animal species may _____ former estimates of their capabilities.

7. A _____ animal trainer who rarely speaks to his animals typically has less success than a talkative trainer who makes a close friend of each animal he's teaching.

8. It's probably wise to approach the larger apes with some healthy _____ until you're sure they feel that humans are nice folks.

9. Stories written by animal lovers often portray their subjects in a way that _____ traditional attitudes.

IV.   **Favorite SAT/PSAT Word Families.** Two prefixes appear repeatedly on standardized tests and in all written material. Choose the best definition or synonym to write on the lines beside the numbered words.

A. TRA, TRANS = across, beyond

_____ 1. transient	(a) mockery, caricature
_____ 2. transcend	(b) change
_____ 3. travesty	(c) ephemeral, fleeting
_____ 4. transgress	(d) to alter position, shift, reverse
_____ 5. transpose	(e) to go beyond certain limits
_____ 6. transition	(f) to go beyond a legal or moral boundary, to sin

B. SUPER, SUR = over, above, extra

_____ 7. superficial	(a) to take precedence over
_____ 8. supercilious	(b) on the surface, shallow
_____ 9. surpass	(c) extra, unneeded, unimportant
_____ 10. supersede	(d) to go beyond expectations
_____ 11. superfluous	(e) haughty, proud

V.   **In Need of a Word?** Here are a few more ideas for which we have many words. How many synonyms can you remember?

For Those Dull, Overused Expressions

c _____   (noun)

t _____   (all the rest adjectives)

h _____

b _____

s _____

To Describe Someone Spoiling for a Fight

b _____

t _____

a _____

b _____

f _____

p _____

To Describe the Exceedingly Economical Use of Words

t _____

c _____

s _____

p _____

List 18

vacillate (v)	*to move or sway back and forth; to fluctuate; to change from one opinion to another*; also to hesitate* Dad *vacillated* from one day to the next, first saying we could go with the youth group on a canoe trip, then saying no.
vacuous (adj)	*without content, empty; minus ideas or intelligence* (as looks, words, the mind) When Dad finally said yes to the canoe trip, I was so stunned that everyone laughed at the *vacuous* expression on my face.
vagary (n)	*a whimsical, erratic, or unexpected occurrence or idea; caprice* (from L. **vagari = to wander**) "Let's leave as little as possible to the *vagaries* of chance," Dad said as we made exhaustive lists in preparation for the canoe trip.

validate (v)   *to declare or make legally true or valid; to authenticate; to support, corroborate, affirm*
Before Ralph could board his flight for Holland, he had to have his passport *validated* by airport officials.

vanguard (n)   *the forward or first army troops; any forerunner*
Jeb found himself almost paralyzed with fear in the *vanguard* of the troops that advanced into enemy territory.

vehement (adj)   *fervent or strongly emotional; impassioned*
Andy's *vehement* pleas to go along on our canoe trip fell on deaf ears. Our folks said he was too young.

venerate (v)   *to revere or admire deeply; to worship*

Venerate derives from **Venus,** goddess of love—from the Latin root **ven = to desire or to hunt.** The Russian word for war is *voina,* a close relative of Venus. Thus, we get love and war and hunting all mixed up in the derived words. While *veneration* is a positive notion, *venereal* disease is a loud negative. And *venom,* which started out to mean love potion, now means a bitter brew, even a poison. Of course, love turned sour *is* a bitter drink.

"If there are any river gods you *venerate,*" Dad joked to our canoe group leader, "you'd better seek their favors for the next two weeks of your trip."

veracity (n) +   *truthfulness or accuracy; honesty*
A boy in our group professed to be an expert canoeist, but one look at his canoeing form made us doubt his *veracity.*

verbatim (adv)   *repeated word for word, exactly*
Our canoeing leader made us repeat *verbatim* the description of our first stop until he was sure everyone knew where to meet for that first lunch.

verbose (adj) –   *using more words than necessary; wordy*
My partner on the first leg of our canoe trip was a *verbose* type who talked nonstop and illustrated with gestures.

verify (v)   *to confirm or make certain, leaving no doubt; to establish in a definite way*
By noon I had *verified* my suspicion that Wade, my canoeing partner, wanted to talk and not canoe, and I decided to trade him off.

vernal (adj)   *of the springtime*; also *fresh, like spring; youthful*
My voluble canoeing partner babbled all through lunch about the *vernal* beauties of the Michigan north woods until I wanted to clonk him with my paddle.

vestige (n)   *the barest trace or amount*
"You know, I haven't a *vestige* of interest in what you're saying," I finally told Wade. "Besides, other people like to talk, too, now and then."

vicarious (adj)   *felt or experienced through another person*; in place of someone or something*
"For now, I prefer to know Wade *vicariously,*" my brother John told me. "Maybe later in the trip I'll work up to some firsthand experience."

vicissitudes (n)   *changeability; mutability; movement or change in circumstances; fluctuations or difficulties**
I thought I'd planned for the *vicissitudes* of life on a canoe trip, but I hadn't counted on getting Wade as a partner.

vilify (v) –   *to slander, malign, defame, or reduce someone's name or community standing*
I decided it wouldn't do to go around *vilifying* Wade. I would just have to civilize him instead.

vindicate (v)   *to free, clear of blame; to absolve, exonerate, or exculpate; to prove right, to justify**
By nightfall of our first day on the river, I felt *vindicated* in my decision to reform Wade. He was paddling more and talking less.

vindictive (adj)
seeking revenge; spiteful
Lucky for me, Wade was not a *vindictive* person and didn't resent my attempts to make him over into the ideal canoeing partner.

virile (adj) +
manly, masculine (from L. **vir = man**)
Around the campfire that night, I noticed several girls eyeing Wade's *virile* charms and decided I ought to reappraise what Fate had sent me.

virtuoso (n) +
any highly skilled person in the arts and sciences (from L., *a skilled performer**, as a violin **virtuoso**)
To everyone's surprise, Wade turned out to be an absolute *virtuoso* on the guitar.

virulent (adj) –
*with fast, powerful, and often fatal progress** (as a **virulent** disease); *highly poisonous; noted for malignancy or evil intent* (from L. **virus = poison**)
Later, as we sat telling stories around the dying campfire, I told about the time I went camping and developed such a *virulent* case of poison ivy that I landed in the hospital.

visage (n)
the appearance (often the face) *of a person, animal, or place; aspect*
Kyle, a city boy, admitted that in the woods he imagined a frightful *visage* carved on the trees in the darkness. "Remember Snow White in the forest? That's the way I feel," he said sheepishly.

viscera (n)
the vital organs of the body; the guts
"Yes," Len agreed, remembering Snow White's desperate flight. "It gets you in the gut." "Surely you mean your *viscera*," our youth group leader added, grinning.

viscous (adj)
slow-flowing, like heavy oil, honey, or syrup
"Did somebody say this was oatmeal?" Becky asked at breakfast, as she watched a large, *viscous* blob drop from her spoon.

vitiate (v) –
*to cause imperfections or errors, sometimes by adding a substance that harms**; to lower in status (esp. moral status); to debase or cause to lack effectiveness*
"I added lots of honey to the oatmeal," the camp cook said, to which our leader replied, "Well, it *vitiated* the entire batch, and I'm switching to good ol' Cheerios."

vitriolic (adj) –
of words or emotions akin to the biting effect of vitriol (a sulfate), therefore *caustic, corrosive*
Claude, who loathed even well-made oatmeal, made a short but *vitriolic* speech about this breakfast and said he'd cook the next one.

vociferous (adj)
loudly vocal, and usually insistent; clamorous, boisterous (from L. **voc = voice**)
Claude's offer was greeted with *vociferous* cries of approval from everyone who had poured oatmeal into the river.

volatile (adj)
easily triggered or exploded (as a **volatile** chemical); *quick to express emotion; explosive, changeable; easy to "set off"*
We wanted a fireworks display for July Fourth but were told that all *volatile* and most flammable materials were prohibited in the woods.

voluble (adj)
extremely talkative; loquacious, garrulous, glib, fluent
Wade proved nearly as *voluble* the second day of the canoe trip as he had the first, but at least he remembered to keep paddling.

voracious (adj)
incredibly hungry; ravenous; also *showing a large appetite* (as a **voracious** student who devours subjects)
By noon we were *voracious*, since we'd canoed for 5 hours on almost no breakfast.

votary (n)
a devout admirer, a devotee; someone who worships, venerates; a believer, advocate, enthusiast
"I am a true *votary* of the wilderness," our leader said, as he gazed appreciatively at the vast pine woods.

vulnerable (adj)
open to harm or physical or emotional hurt; assailable, indefensible
"I guess I like the wilderness," Alicia said, "but I feel *vulnerable* somehow, because I'm not used to being away from civilization."

wan (adj)

pale in appearance or sickly*; also weak or feeble; faint, slight
"I know what you mean," Jan replied. "And if I looked a little *wan* this morning, it was because I dreamed about mountain lions all night!"

wane (v)

to dwindle or grow less (as the moon **wanes**); *to dim, be less noticeable; to decline in power or influence*
"Okay, the day is *waning* while we dawdle over lunch," our leader said. "Let's go. We have 10 miles to paddle before supper."

wanton (adj)

sexually loose or arousing sexual desire; lacking human kindness (as **wanton** cruelty to animals); *malicious;* also *unchecked** (as **wanton** growth)
In the afternoon, we canoed a byway of the river that led to a lagoon where water lilies grew in *wanton* profusion.

wary (adj)

being aware and cautious regarding danger; prudent (from Old English **waer = careful, aware**)
"Be *wary* of putting your hands in the water here," Peter warned us. "Looks like good snake territory to me."

willful (adj) –

showing a strong will to do as you like; headstrong, intentional; also *stubborn, unruly*
Paddling back upstream, we had to cope with a *willful* canoe that wanted to turn and head downstream.

winsome (adj) +

very appealing and winning of personality; cheerful, in a childlike or innocent way; sweet (from Old English **wynn = joy**)
We became very good friends with our group leader's wife, a woman whose *winsome* personality and ready laugh made her popular with everyone.

wistful (adj)

showing much longing or desire; yearning; also *sad, pensive, thoughtful*
With a *wistful* look at the beautiful river and woods, Abby said she wished that our canoe trip could go on forever.

wizened (adj)

dried up, wrinkled, and shrunken; withered
"You say this was once a real apple?" Wade asked as he held up a *wizened,* cream-colored piece of dried fruit.

wont (n)

custom, use, habit (as her **wont** to shop on Fridays)

wont (adj)

used or accustomed; apt, inclined
"We should stop canoeing early tonight as we've been *wont* to do," said our leader, who enjoys using interesting words like *wont.*

wraith (n) –

a ghost or apparition of a person; shadow or vague human form
We told ghost stories around the campfire one night. The one called "The *Wraith* of Locksburne Hall" scared us silly.

wreak (v) –

to inflict misery upon, punish, or avenge; to allow ill feelings free rein; to cause, bring about* (from Old English **wrecan = to drive, punish**)
Those ghost stories *wreaked* havoc with my night's sleep, and I had one nightmare after another.

wrest (v)

to bring about by forceful action or hard work; also *to distort* (from Old English **writhan = to twist, wring**)
Finally, hoping to *wrest* a few hours' sleep out of the night, I began reciting old bits of poetry to myself in an effort to forget the ghost stories.

zealous (adj)

eager or determined in the pursuit of something*; fervent, passionate

Zealous derives from the Greek root **zelous** meaning **fervor** or **tremendous eagerness**. As *Zealot,* it became the name for a Jewish sect that rebelled against the Romans in the first century A.D. They were a group that stopped at nothing. *Zealotry* is way too much zeal—an unwise extreme.

My *zealous* efforts to get to know Wade paid a good dividend, as we became close friends by the end of the canoe trip.

zephyr (n)   *a typically gentle breeze, often from the west* (from L. **Zephyrus = god of the west wind**)

Memories of any good experience, like *zephyrs,* return and drift through our minds.

QUIZ ON LIST 18

I.   **Synonyms.** Choose the two words that are the best synonyms in each of the four-word groups.

1. (A) vacillate (B) move (C) fluctuate (D) jump
2. (A) vagrant (B) caprice (C) luck (D) vagary
3. (A) authenticate (B) ascertain (C) certain (D) validate
4. (A) glad (B) vehement (C) zealous (D) vacuous
5. (A) veracity (B) hungry (C) truthfulness (D) meanness
6. (A) civilize (B) vilify (C) malign (D) approve
7. (A) wreath (B) wraith (C) apparition (D) corpse
8. (A) enhance (B) debase (C) vitiate (D) to give life
9. (A) oily (B) volatile (C) vitriolic (D) corrosive
10. (A) voluble (B) noisy (C) glib (D) reticent

II. **Legacy from England.** When you see words beginning with **w,** especially **wr,** you can be fairly sure they are English in origin. Using these words from Old or Middle English—still favorites today—complete the following phrases.

wanton	waned	wan
wary	winsome	wont
wreaked	wrest	wistful
wizened	willful	wraith (orig. obscure)

1. the artifact, a _____ human head impaled on a stick
2. appearing _____ and weak after a long illness
3. timid puppy, ever _____ of strangers
4. headstrong child with a _____ disposition
5. an engaging person known for her _____ smile
6. begging and giving a _____ glance at the cotton candy
7. was his _____ to rise early every morning
8. storm that _____ disaster along the coastline
9. laws that attempt to prevent _____ cruelty to animals
10. worked to _____ the last drop of moisture from the tuberous root
11. a mere _____ after being a prisoner of war
12. waxed fat for days, then _____ slowly to nothing

III.   **Antonyms.** Choose two antonyms to write on the lines beside each word in bold type.

benign	agnostic	terse	beneficent	impregnable
skeptic	stolid	tyro	disparage	scorn
aged	succinct	invincible	impassive	soft-spoken
deny	negate	understated	novice	decaying

_____   1. **vulnerable**   _____   6. **virtuoso**

_____   _____

_____   2. **votary**   _____   7. **vernal**

_____   _____

_____   3. **volatile**   _____   8. **verify**

_____   _____

_____   4. **vociferous**   _____   9. **verbose**

_____   _____

_____   5. **virulent**   _____   10. **venerate**

_____   _____

IV.   **Remembering Definitions.** See how many study words you can match with their definitions before looking back for help.

Study Word

1. gentle, westerly breeze   _____

2. empty of ideas or intelligence   _____

3. ravenous, incredibly hungry   _____

4. forerunner, harbinger   _____

5. slow-flowing   _____

6. manly, masculine   _____

7. repeated exactly, word for word   _____

8. facial appearance or aspect   _____

9. the barest trace or amount   _____

10. vital bodily organs   _____

11. fluctuations, changes; difficulties   _____

12. felt or experienced through others   _____

V.   **Favorite SAT/PSAT Word Family.** Words from **DIC, DICT** (*speak, say, words*) pop up frequently on standardized tests and in all writing. Using the process of elimination, prefixes, and your own good brain, make the correct matches.

_____   1. vindicate   (a) to order, pronounce absolutely

_____   2. vindictive   (b) to renounce, give up

_____   3. dictate   (c) to speak against or in opposition

_____   4. predicament   (d) order, edict

_____   5. abdicate   (e) adjudicated result

_____   6. dictum   (f) curse

_____   7. indict   (g) to exculpate; to justify

_____   8. verdict   (h) to surrender an alleged criminal to
                                                       another authority with jurisdiction
_____   9. benediction
                                                  (i) spiteful
_____   10. malediction
                                                  (j) literally *"good words"*; blessing
_____   11. extradite
                                                  (k) complex problem
_____   12. contradict
                                                  (l) to charge with an offense

RESPECT FOR THE LANGUAGE: CORRECT WORD USAGE

Like Eliza Doolittle of stage and movie fame, we announce who we are every time we open our mouths. Educated people like to be thought of as intelligent, and so they're careful to sound intelligent when speaking and writing. You, too, can avoid the more common errors in diction (choice of words) and idiom (accepted American English expressions).

Problem Words	*Standard Usage*
aggravate	The hike *aggravated* her swollen ankle.
agree *to*	The board has *agreed to* that amendment.
all ready	Our choir is *all ready* to sing.
already	We have *already* taken our places. (adverb)
all right	His answers on the test were *all right*. Or: Would it be *all right* for me to borrow these books?
a lot	Tonight I have *a lot* of math homework.
all together	Sing *all together*, please, on cue.
altogether	Sal was *altogether* too weary to keep singing. (adverb)
among	We shared the pie *among* the six of us. (Must be more than two.)
amount	There's a large *amount* of water in the pool. (Refers to quantity that *can't* be counted.)
anxious	I'll be *anxious* until I hear the doctor's report on those tests. (nervous, worried)
bad	Sam feels *bad* about his brother's illness.
badly	Is his brother *badly* hurt? (Adverb tells *how*.)
between	We'll share the cake *between* the two of us.
can hardly	I *can hardly* see the stars for the clouds. (never *can't hardly,* a double negative)
contrast *to*	In *contrast to* the sky, the clouds appear pure white.
concerned *with*	The study of English is *concerned with* a variety of language-related topics.
could *have*	We *could have* studied French this year. (*Of* is never a helping verb.)
device	Alliteration is a common *device* in poetry.
devise	We need to *devise* a better plan. (verb)
different *from*	His gloves are *different from* mine.
done	Cakes are *done;* people are *finished.*
every one	Please do *every one* of those jobs.
everyone	Is *everyone* ready to get in the bus?
few	*Few* cookies are left. (Use *few* with things that *can* be counted.)
good	He looks *good* on the basketball court.
hanged	People are *hanged;* jackets are *hung.*
healthy	I walk several miles daily to keep *healthy.*
healthful	*Healthful* foods aid in promoting health.
human	*Human* beings may be called Homo sapiens.
humane	Rescuing the drowning cat was a *humane* act.
I	Never shift from *I* to *you* in sentences like this bad example: I like going to rock concerts because you can always count on having a good time. **Stay with the pronoun you select.**
	I like going to rock concerts because *I* can always count on having a good time.
idol	The religion of Baal was *idol* worship.
idle	The car's *idle* seems a bit too slow.
	They say that the devil finds mischief for *idle* hands. (unbusy ones)
imply	Are you *implying* that I'm late? (suggesting)
infer	From your comments, I *inferred* that I should try to arrive early. (deduced or concluded)
instance	In this *instance*, I'd say you were right.

instants	It was several *instants* before the team came on the field. (unit of time)
its	The cat was wet; *its* fur was soggy. (possession)
it's	*It's* too cold to go skating today. (contraction of the pronoun *it* and the verb *is*)
kind of—sort of	*Kind of a* and *sort of a* do not exist!
lead	*Lead* us to the treasure. (guide or direct)
lead	Is that a *lead* pencil? (soft gray metal)
led	Luckily, they *led* us to the right spot. (past tense of *lead*)
lend	I'll *lend* you some money. (*Loan* is a noun.)
less	There's *less* water in the pool today. (Use *less* with quantities that *can't* be counted.)
metal	The symbol for the *metal* lead is *Pb*.
mettle	He was on his *mettle* for the fight. (spirit or courage)
might *have*	He *might have* left already. (Not might of; *of* can never be a helping verb.)
moral	Parables often teach a *moral*.
morale	Our team's *morale* is at a low ebb.
number	We have a large *number* of tumbling mats. (Use *number* with things that *can* be counted.)
past	In *past* times we kept a herd of goats. (adjective)
passed	The troops *passed* in review. (verb)
percent	Butch gave 10 *percent* of his allowance.
percentage	What *percentage* did you give?
precede	Did ice or sleet *precede* the snow? (come before)
proceed	Please *proceed* down the aisle, single file. (move forward)
precedents	Earlier court decisions have set *precedents*.
precedence	That matter takes *precedence* over this one.
presence	The king is known for a royal *presence*.
	Her *presence* in the room is desirable.
presents	Under the Christmas tree is a pile of *presents*.
raise	*Raise* your head up off the pillow.
rise	Please set the bread out to *rise*.
	I loathe *rising* early in the morning.
reason . . . is that	The *reason* we agreed *is that* I gave up the fight! (After the *be* verb, do not use *because* to begin a clause.)
regardless	I plan to go, *regardless* of what you say. (The term *irregardless* is not acceptable in standard English.)
reign	The queen's *reign* has been a long one.
rein	My horse's left *rein* is broken.
respectably	Please dress *respectably* for the wedding. (Make yourself look respectable.)
respectfully	She sat *respectfully* during the long memorial service. (manner showing respect)
respectively	Awards for highest average and best attendance were given to Martha and Britt, *respectively*. (Martha had the highest average; Britt had the best attendance.)
see that	We *see that* your team is in first place. (*See where* is slang.)
surely	Margaret *surely* is a fine soccer player.
than	Dwight is older *than* Whitney. (comparison)
then	We should plan to leave *then*. (adverb)
their	*Their* hats are on hooks. (possessive pronoun)
they're	I know *they're* planning to go. (pronoun *they* + verb *are*)
there	*There* are their coats. (adverb telling *where*)
to	Would you turn *to* the right? (preposition)

too	That is *too* wide a turn! (adverb)
two	I wish we had *two* steering wheels. (number)
unique	*Unique* is an absolute, meaning "the only one of its kind." Things cannot be "very" or "quite" unique, and ordinary things should not be called unique.
used to	We *used to* go to the beach every summer.
way	He lives a long *way* from us. (not *ways*)
well	Try to draw that as *well* as you can.
who's	*Who's* planning to go to the library? (pronoun *who* + verb *is*)
whose	*Whose* books are these? (possessive pronoun)
your	*Your* books are on the shelf. (possessive pronoun)
you're	Do you think *you're* ready to leave? (pronoun *you* + verb *are*)

RED ALERT
RED ALERT
RED ALERT
RED ALERT
RED ALERT
RED ALERT

RED ALERT
PRACTICE WITH THE REAL THING

This mini-SAT is composed of actual SAT questions from recent tests, published by ETS and reprinted here with their permission.

> **First, answer these 24 verbal and 25 math questions** as carefully as you can. The directions are exactly what you will see on Test Day as you take your SAT or PSAT exam.
>
> **Second, check the answers** to each question.
>
> **Third, and Most Important, read the detailed explanations for all questions you missed or found difficult.** These explanations show the step-by-step thought processes that lead to right answers. This "picture" of correct logic and reasoning COULD BE the most helpful thing you read as you get ready for your own exam.

Do not set a timer as you work these questions. Instead, concentrate on how the questions are framed or designed.

VERBAL QUESTIONS

> Each sentence below has one or two blanks, each blank indicating that something has been omitted.
>
> Beneath the sentence are five lettered words or sets of words. Choose the word or set of words that best completes the meaning of the sentence as a whole.

1. By nature he was ----, usually confining his remarks to ---- expression.

   (A) acerbic. .friendly
   (B) laconic. .concise
   (C) garrulous. .voluminous
   (D) shrill. .complimentary
   (E) vague. .emphatic

2. Many contemporary novelists have forsaken a traditional intricacy of plot and detailed depiction of character for a distinctly ---- presentation of both.

   (A) convoluted
   (B) derivative
   (C) conventional
   (D) conservative
   (E) unadorned

3. The film star conveys the wit and charm of the character she portrays, but unfortunately many of her most ---- lines have been cut.

   (A) tactless   (B) sober   (C) ingenious
    (D) unintelligible   (E) unnecessary

4. His ---- maintained that Mr. Frank was constantly at odds with the corporate officers; the truth, on the contrary, was that his ideas were not at all ---- with the officers' reasonable goals.

   (A) detractors. .in accord
   (B) supporters. .at variance
   (C) advocates. .harmonious
   (D) disparagers. .incompatible
   (E) apologists. .in conflict

5. The short story, with its ----, its pointed movement toward a single moment of discovery, can economically reveal the ---- of the illusions that somehow sustain most people's lives.

   (A) casualness. .destructiveness
   (B) optimism. .barrenness
   (C) capriciousness. .rigidity
   (D) digressiveness. .poignancy
   (E) compression. .precariousness

6. The speaker asserted that humans have such a strong natural tendency toward self-deception that the moral imperative to ---- this drive with respect for ---- is becoming more critical than ever.

   (A) dignify. .individuality
   (B) intensify. .integrity
   (C) invalidate. .treachery
   (D) counterbalance. .truth
   (E) rationalize. .privacy

7. Robert was the embodiment of amorality, capable of committing the most odious acts without ever ---- even a hint of ----.

   (A) suppressing. .revulsion
   (B) betraying. .reproof
   (C) inspiring. .malice
   (D) evincing. .compunction
   (E) condoning. .indelicacy

Each question below consists of a related pair of words or phrases, followed by five lettered pairs of words or phrases. Select the lettered pair that best expresses a relationship similar to that expressed in the original pair.

---

8. EXPOSITION : CLARIFY ::
   (A) rebuttal : humiliate   (B) refutation : disprove
   (C) illumination : darken   (D) allegation : verify
   (E) summary : end

9. PARODY : IMITATION ::   (A) farce : laughter
   (B) caricature : likeness   (C) mask : disguise
   (D) deviation : similarity
   (E) gem : embellishment

10. BULKY : VOLUME ::   (A) straight : curvature
   (B) hollow : vastness   (C) gouged : surface
   (D) hefty : weight   (E) grisly : appearance

11. FORD : RIVER ::   (A) basement : edifice
   (B) terminal : airport   (C) dam : reservoir
   (D) crosswalk : road   (E) gangplank : boat

12. PRECIPITATE : HASTE ::
   (A) withdrawn : interaction
   (B) preposterous : belief
   (C) vindictive : motive
   (D) hesitant : speed
   (E) overwrought : excitement

13. ASK : IMPORTUNE ::   (A) begin : recommence
   (B) damage : restore   (C) pursue : hound
   (D) misbehave : displease
   (E) stimulate : motivate

14. CONVALESCENCE : HEALTHY ::
   (A) contamination : purified
   (B) renovation : dilapidated
   (C) validation : unproven
   (D) isolation : uninhabited
   (E) reclamation : useful

Each passage below is followed by questions based on its content. Answer all questions following a passage on the basis of what is stated or implied in that passage.

Natural history, to a large extent, is a tale of different adaptations to avoid predation. Some individuals hide, others taste bad, others grow
Line spines or thick shells, still others evolve to look
(5) conspicuously like a noxious relative; the list is nearly endless, a stunning tribute to nature's variety. The periodical cicada, or 17-year locust, follows an uncommon strategy: it is eminently and conspicuously available, but so rarely and in such
(10) great numbers that predators cannot possibly consume the entire bounty. Among evolutionary biologists, this defense goes by the name of "predator satiation."

An effective strategy of predator satiation
(15) involves two adaptations. First, the synchrony of emergence or reproduction must be very precise, thus assuring that the market is truly flooded with goods, and only for a short time. Second, this flooding cannot occur very often, lest predators
(20) simply adjust their own life cycle to predictable times of superfluity.

The story of periodical cicadas is more amazing than most people realize: for 17 years, the nymphs of periodical cicadas live underground, sucking
(25) juices from the roots of forest trees all over the eastern half of the United States (except for the southern states, where a very similar or identical group of species emerges every 13 years). Then, within just a few weeks, millions of mature
(30) nymphs emerge from the ground, become adults, mate, lay their eggs, and die.

Most remarkable is the fact that three separate species of periodical cicadas follow precisely the same schedule, emerging together in strict
(35) synchrony. Different areas may be out of the phase—populations around Chicago do not emerge in the same year as forms from New

England. But the 17-year cycle (13 years in the South) is invariant for each "brood"—the three *(40)* species always emerge together in the same place.

I am most impressed by the timing of the cycles themselves. Why do we have 13- and 17-year cicadas, but no cycles of 12, 14, 16, or 18 years? The numbers 13 and 17 share a common property. *(45)* They indicate time periods long enough to exceed the life cycles of most predators, and they are also prime numbers (divisible by 1 and themselves only). Many potential predators have 2- to 5-year life cycles. Such cycles are not set by the *(50)* availability of periodical cicadas (for such predators peak too often in years of nonemergence), but cicadas might eagerly be harvested when the cycles coincide. Consider a predator with a cycle of five years: if cicadas *(55)* emerged every 15 years, each bloom would be hit by the predator. By cycling at a large prime number, cicadas minimize the frequency of coincidences with predators—in this example, every 85 (5 x 17) years.

15. Which of the following is the most appropriate title for the passage?

  (A) The Cicada's Persistent Predators
  (B) Adaptations for Survival Among Predators of the Cicada
  (C) Three Species of the Cicada
  (D) The Amazing Life Cycle of the Cicada
  (E) The Origin of the 17-Year Locust

16. The statement that cicadas are "eminently and conspicuously available" (lines 8–9) is used to illustrate which of the following assertions?

  (A) The cicada's strategy for survival is an unusual adaptation.
  (B) Cicadas do not have any relatives that are noxious to predators.
  (C) Predators of cicadas do not have many different kinds of prey.
  (D) The cicada is rarely available to its predators.
  (E) The timing of the cicada's life cycle is amazing.

17. It can be inferred that the strategy referred to in line 14 is dependent on which of the following principles?

  (A) Predators can eat only so many of their prey.
  (B) Predators seldom eat what they find distasteful.
  (C) An increased population of predators reduces the number of prey in a given environment.
  (D) Few organisms have life spans that extend beyond three years.
  (E) What one generation of a species learns is transmitted to the following generation through conditioning.

18. All of the following questions are answered in the passage EXCEPT:

  (A) How do cicadas in the Northeast differ from those in the South?
  (B) What is a prime number?
  (C) What are various means that animals use to evade predators?
  (D) What do cicada nymphs eat?
  (E) How do cicadas detect the passage of time?

19. The author's tone in presenting the information in the passage can best be described as

  (A) skeptical (B) cautious (C) detached
  (D) tolerant (E) enthusiastic

Turkey was a short man, of about my own age—that is, somewhere not far from sixty. In the morning, one might say, his face was of a fine *Line* florid hue, but after twelve o'clock, meridian—his *(5)* lunch hour—it blazed like a grate of Christmas coals; and continued blazing—but, as it were, with a gradual wane—till six o'clock p.m., or thereabouts; after which, I saw no more of the proprietor of the face, which, gaining its meridian *(10)* with the sun, seemed to set with it, to rise, culminate, and decline the following day, with the like regularity and undiminished glory. There are many singular coincidences I have known in the course of my life, not the least among which was *(15)* the fact, that, exactly when Turkey displayed his fullest beams from his red and radiant countenance, just then, too, at that critical moment, began the daily period when I considered his business capacities as seriously disturbed for the *(20)* remainder of the day. There was then a strange, inflamed, flighty recklessness of activity about him. He would be incautious in dipping his pen into his inkstand. All his blots upon my documents were dropped there after twelve o'clock, meridian. *(25)* Indeed, not only would he be reckless and sadly given to making blots in the afternoon, but, some days, he went further, and was rather noisy. He made an unpleasant racket with his chair; stood up, and leaned over his desk, filing his papers in a *(30)* most indecorous manner, very sad to behold in an elderly man like him. Nevertheless, as he was in many ways a most invaluable person to my business, and all the time before twelve o'clock, meridian, was the quickest, steadiest creature, too, *(35)* accomplishing a great deal of work in a style not

GO ON TO THE NEXT PAGE →

easily matched—for these reasons, I was willing to overlook his eccentricities, though, indeed, as his employer, occasionally, I remonstrated with him. I did this very gently, however, because, though the

(40) civilest, nay, the blandest and most reverential of men in the morning, yet, in the afternoon, he was disposed, upon provocation, to be slightly rash with his tongue—in fact, insolent. Now, valuing his morning services as I did, and resolved not to

(45) lose them—yet, at the same time, made uncomfortable by his inflamed ways after twelve o'clock—and being a man of peace, unwilling by my admonitions to call forth unseemly retorts from him, I took upon me, one noon, to hint to him,

(50) very kindly, that perhaps, now that he was growing old, it might be well to abridge his labors; in short, he need not come to my chambers after twelve o'clock, but, lunch over, had best go home to his lodgings, and rest himself. But no; he

(55) insisted upon his afternoon devotions. He assured me that if his services in the morning were useful, how indispensable, then, in the afternoon?

20. It can be inferred from the passage that the narrator would describe Turkey's work at 11 a.m. as

(A) occasionally sloppy and inaccurate
(B) characterized by inexplicable interruptions
(C) requiring constant correction
(D) uniformly excellent and exemplary
(E) excessively neurotic and intense

21. The narrator's primary motive for asking Turkey not to return to work in the afternoon was

(A) a need to save money
(B) a predilection for solitude

(C) a concern for Turkey's health
(D) an aversion to unseemly behavior
(E) a fear of physical violence

22. Turkey apparently believed that his efforts in the office during the afternoon were

(A) pathetic   (B) suspicious   (C) annoying
 (D) erratic   (E) productive

23. The narrator can appropriately be described as all of the following EXCEPT

(A) reasonable   (B) elderly   (C) compassionate
 (D) unobservant   (E) nonaggressive

24. With which of the following statements concerning his office would the narrator be most likely to agree?

(A) Turkey's presence enlivened an otherwise tedious workday.
(B) If Turkey had not returned after lunch, the office would have run more efficiently.
(C) If Turkey had acted in the mornings as he did in the afternoons, all concerned would have been happier.
(D) If the narrator had demanded a better performance from Turkey, the situation would have improved.
(E) The narrator himself was in part responsible for provoking Turkey's eccentric behavior.

MATH QUESTIONS

The following information is for your reference in solving some of the problems.

Circle of radius r: Area $= \pi r^2$; Circumference $= 2\pi r$
   The number of degrees of arc in a circle is 360.
The measure in degrees of a straight angle is 180.

Definitions of symbols:

$=$ is equal to $\leq$ is less than or equal to
$\neq$ is unequal to $\geq$ is greater than or equal to
$<$ is less than $\parallel$ is parallel to
$>$ is greater than $\perp$ is perpendicular to

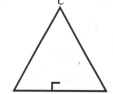

Triangle: The sum of the measures in degrees of the angles of a triangle is 180.
If $\angle CDA$ is a right angle, then

(1) area of $\triangle ABC = \dfrac{AB \times CD}{2}$
(2) $AC^2 = AD^2 + DC^2$

Note: Figures that accompany problems in this test are intended to provide information useful in solving the problems. They are drawn as accurately as possible EXCEPT when it is stated in a specific problem that its figure is not drawn to scale. All figures lie in a plane unless otherwise indicated. All numbers used are real numbers.

1. A right triangle has one leg of length 16 and a hypotenuse of length 20. What is its perimeter?

    (A) 36 (B) 40 (C) 44 (D) 48 (E) 52

2. In the figure above, $x + y = 110$. What is the value of $w + x + y + z$?

    (A) 220 (B) 235 (C) 250 (D) 290
    (E) It cannot be determined from the information given.

3. At most, how many $1\frac{1}{4}$-foot pieces of string can be cut from a string that is 20 feet long?

    (A) 15 (B) 16 (C) 18 (D) 20 (E) 25

Questions 4–5 refer to the following definition.

    A rating number R_n can be assigned to any four-digit whole number n in the following manner.

    $R_n =$ (thousands' digit $\times 3$) +
    (hundreds' digit $\times 2$) + (tens' digit $\times 1$) +
    (ones' digit $\times 0$)

For example,
$R_{7985} = (7 \times 3) + (9 \times 2) + (8 \times 1) + (5 \times 0) = 47$

---

4. $R_{1234} =$

    (A) 10 (B) 14 (C) 17 (D) 20 (E) 30

5. If H represents an unknown digit, for which of the following numbers n can the value of R_n always be determined?

    (A) $H652$ (B) $6H64$ (C) $65H6$ (D) $652H$
    (E) $6HH8$

6. If $n = -1,000$, which of the following is a negative number?

    (A) $\dfrac{n}{3} - \dfrac{n}{2}$

    (B) $\dfrac{n}{3} - \dfrac{n}{4}$

    (C) $-\dfrac{n}{3} - \dfrac{n}{2}$

    (D) $-2(n - 1)$

    (E) $n(n + 1)$

---

7. If $2x = 3y = 4w$, what is $5x + 6w$ in terms of y?

    (A) $8y$ (B) $9y$ (C) $10y$ (D) $12y$ (E) $15y$

---

8. If x is an odd integer and if y is an even integer, then $x^2 - y^2$ is always which of the following?

    I. An odd integer
    II. An even integer
    III. The square of an integer

    (A) I only (B) II only (C) III only (D) I and III
    (E) II and III

Questions 9–15 each consist of two quantities, one in Column A and one in Column B. You are to compare the two quantities and on the answer sheet blacken space

   A   if the quantity in Column A is greater;
   B   if the quantity in Column B is greater;
   C   if the two quantities are equal;
   D   if the relationship cannot be determined from the information given.

Notes: 1. In certain questions, information concerning one or both of the quantities to be compared is centered above the two columns.

2. In a given question, a symbol that appears in both columns represents the same thing in Column A as it does in Column B.

3. Letters such as x, n, and k stand for real numbers.

GO ON TO THE
NEXT PAGE

Column A | Column B

$$
\begin{array}{cc}
S & T \\
\underline{\times R} & \underline{\times S} \\
24 & 32
\end{array}
$$

R and T are positive.

9. R T

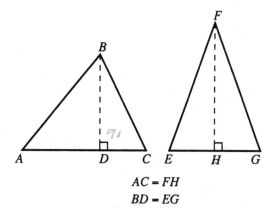

$$AC = FH$$
$$BD = EG$$

10. The area of $\triangle ABC$ The area of $\triangle EFG$

The sequence 1, –2, 3, –4, 5, . . . is formed by taking all positive integers in increasing order and changing each even integer to its opposite.

11. The sum of the 100th   The sum of the 101st
     and 101st terms   and 102nd terms

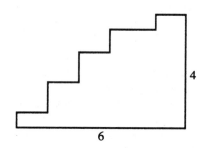

All line segments in the figure above are either horizontal or vertical.

12. The perimeter of the figure   22

For all nonzero values of a let $\boxed{a} = a^2$ and $@ = -a$.

13. $\boxed{a} + \boxed{a}$ $@ + @$

Column A   Column B

$$x > 0$$

14. The volume of a   The volume of a rectan-
     cube with edge of   gular solid with edges
     length $x + 1$ of length x, $x + 1$,
                      and $x + 2$, respectively

On a certain trip, a car averaged 40 miles per hour. If it had traveled 10 miles farther in the same amount of time, its average speed would have been x miles per hour.

15. x 50

> Solve the remaining problems and select the response that best answers the question.

16. B dozen oranges costs a total of C cents. At this rate, how many oranges can be bought for E cents?

   (A) $\dfrac{CE}{12B}$

   (B) $\dfrac{BE}{12C}$

   (C) $\dfrac{12BC}{E}$

   (D) $\dfrac{12BE}{C}$

   (E) $\dfrac{12CE}{B}$

17. In the last 5 years, the price of a new Brand X car has increased 30 percent. If it is assumed that the percent increase in the next 5-year period will be the same, then the percent increase in the price of a new Brand X car over the <u>entire</u> 10-year period will be

   (A) 15%
   (B) 30%
   (C) 39%
   (D) 60%
   (E) 69%

18. If $x^2 + y^2 = 18$ and $xy = 6$, then $(x - y)^2 =$

   (A) 12
   (B) 6
   (C) 0
   (D) –6
   (E) –12

19. If $2 \leq y \leq 3$ and $4 \leq z \leq 5$, then the least possible average (arithmetic mean) of $\frac{1}{y}$ and $\frac{1}{z}$ is

(A) $\frac{3}{8}$

(B) $\frac{4}{15}$

(C) $\frac{1}{4}$

(D) $\frac{1}{6}$

(E) $\frac{1}{16}$

20. A circle has the same area as a square with side of length $\frac{1}{\pi}$. What is the <u>diameter</u> of the circle?

(A) $\frac{1}{\sqrt{\pi}}$

(B) $\frac{2}{\sqrt{\pi}}$

(C) $\frac{1}{\pi\sqrt{\pi}}$

(D) $\frac{2}{\pi\sqrt{\pi}}$

(E) $\frac{1}{\pi^3}$

21. There are between 60 and 70 eggs in a basket. If they are counted out 3 at a time there are 2 left over, but if they are counted out 4 at a time there is 1 left over. How many eggs are in the basket?

(A) 61
(B) 62
(C) 65
(D) 68
(E) 69

22. In $\triangle MNP$, $\angle M$ is 65° and $\angle P$ is 40°. Q is a point on side MP such that $NQ \perp MP$. Of the following line segments, which is shortest?

(A) MN
(B) NP
(C) PQ
(D) NQ
(E) MQ

23. Tom is t years old, which is 3 times Becky's age. In terms of t, after how many years will Tom be just twice as old as Becky?

(A) $\frac{t}{3}$

(B) $\frac{t}{2}$

(C) $\frac{2t}{3}$

(D) t

(E) $\frac{3t}{2}$

24. If $x = \frac{2}{5}y$ and $x \neq 0$, then y is what percent of x?

(A) 2.5%
(B) 4%
(C) 25%
(D) 40%
(E) 250%

25. Of the 400 students at a certain college, $\frac{3}{4}$ have automobiles and 120 live on campus. Of the students living on campus, 65 have automobiles. How many students do <u>not</u> live on campus and do <u>not</u> have automobiles?

(A) 45
(B) 98
(C) 129
(D) 215
(E) 335

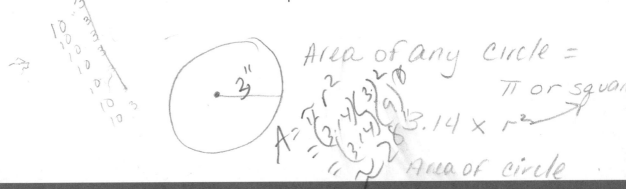

ANSWERS TO AND ANALYSES OF VERBAL QUESTIONS

FILL-IN-THE-BLANK QUESTIONS

1. **(B) laconic . . concise**

   Sentence: **By nature he was ----, usually confining his remarks to ---- expression.**

   Step 1. Read for meaning, and type of sentence, noting the key word *confining*. If you *confine your remarks*, what does that mean?

   Step 2. *You think:* this sentence needs words with similar meanings. Put any word in the first blank and boom—the rest of the sentence ends up defining that word!

   Step 3. Sentence type? *A definition sentence.* Go immediately to the answer choices, remembering that the word in the second blank must define or explain the word in the first blank.

   Step 4. Get your own answer in mind if you're sure of what this sentence is saying. But I can't be sure until I see the answer choices here. Let's go to Step 5 and eliminate answers.

   Step 5. Eliminate answers, choosing from:

   (A) acerbic . . friendly   (B) laconic . . concise   (C) garrulous . . voluminous
   (D) shrill . . complimentary   (E) vague . . emphatic

   Starting with *(A)*, does *friendly* define *acerbic*? No way. Acerbic means bitter or caustic—almost the opposite of friendly. We need closely related words, remember?

   (B) Does *concise* explain/define *laconic*? You bet. A laconic person (one sparing of speech) is concise (brief of speech) by definition.

   RIGHT NOW, TEST THIS ANSWER IN THE SENTENCE: *By nature he was laconic, usually confining his remarks to concise expression. Beautiful. This answer is a keeper.*

   (C) Does *voluminous* explain *garrulous*? Not really. Voluminous describes full skirts, billowing sails—maybe voluminous notes for a term paper, but it doesn't describe speech. Garrulous means very talkative. A garrulous soul never "confines" his or her remarks. Bad choice. Cross out.

   (D) Shrill and *complimentary* don't go together well either; in fact, this is a totally wacko choice.

   (E) And *vague* and *emphatic* are opposites! All wrong for this sentence which demands words that explain and complement (fill out or complete) each other's meanings.

   Therefore only *answer (B)* will work.

2. **(E) unadorned**

   Sentence: **Many contemporary novelists have forsaken a traditional intricacy of plot and detailed depiction of character for a distinctly ---- presentation of both.**

   Step 1. Read for sentence sense. What have today's authors done? What did they give up (forsake)?

   Step 2. Cleaning up the sentence, we have: *Today's writers gave up intricate plots and tons of character details and chose a ---- presentation* **instead.** (Word inserted to clarify meaning)

   Step 3. Sentence type? Note key words that tell us what writers gave up: *traditional intricacy of plot* and *detailed depiction of character*. INSTEAD, they're giving us a **distinctly ---- presentation.** Sounds like a sentence of contrast, right?

   Step 4. A brave trial of our own word in that blank: Authors forsook all that fancy, detailed, traditional plot and character stuff for a distinctly SIMPLE or CLEAN or maybe even STARK presentation of both.

   Step 5. Eliminate answers, one by one, choosing from:

   (A) convoluted   (B) derivative   (C) conventional   (D) conservative   (E) unadorned

   Answer (A), convoluted, means indirect, roundabout—the opposite of straightforward and clear. That's off the mark as sentence topic here. Cross out.

   (B) is the wacko answer. Nowhere does the given sentence bring up the topic of *original* material, for which *derivative* would be the contrast.

   (C) Conventional is similar to traditional, but the authors forsook all that, remember? Cross out this obvious bad choice.

(D) Conservative would contrast with liberal or freethinking or risk-taking—ideas NOT present in this sentence. The word you need must be the opposite of detailed and traditional, remember?

(E) Unadorned means simple, clean (in the sense of clean prose), not fancy, NOT adorned—a perfect contrast to the traditional, more detailed style that the authors gave up.

Only *(E)* offers the contrast demanded by the logic of this sentence.

3. **(C) ingenious**

   Sentence: **The film star conveys the wit and charm of the character she portrays, but unfortunately many of her most ---- lines have been cut.**

   Step 1.   Read for meaning, noting key words here: **wit and charm** tell us what kind of character is being portrayed. **Unfortunately** something happened to her best lines in the film.

   Step 2.   This sentence really says: *She's a great actress in spite of losing her best lines.*

   Step 3.   Sentence type? Not clearly cause and effect or definition, but a combination of the two. This question calls for your logic and common sense.

   Step 4.   Getting your own word in mind, try: *unfortunately her* **cleverest** *lines have been cut* (those that revealed her wit and charm)

      The word you need must be positive or else the word *unfortunately* wouldn't be used.

   Step 5.   Eliminate answers, choosing from:

      (A) tactless   (B) sober   (C) ingenious   (D) unintelligible   (E) unnecessary

      Answers (A), (D), and *(E)* can be eliminated as they are negative and don't refer to wit and charm.

      Answer (B) is the wacko answer, another howler.

      Answer (C) is just right; it refers to wit and charm. Ingenious lines are the ones we would be sorry to have cut from the film, right?

4. **(D) disparagers . . incompatible**

   Sentence: **His ---- maintained that Mr. Frank was constantly at odds with the corporate officers; the truth, on the contrary, was that his ideas were not at all ---- with the officers' reasonable goals.**

   Step 1.   Read for sentence sense, noting these key words; **at odds with + truth, on the contrary + ideas not at all** blank **with the officers**

   Step 2.   Making it simple, this sentence really says: *Folks picking on Frank say he disagrees with the biggies in the corporate office, but,* **on the contrary,** *his ideas are just like theirs!*

   Step 3.   This is a sentence of contrast. Contrary to what people think, Frank and the officers have similar ideas.

   Step 4.   *First blank* must be the people criticizing Frank; *second blank* must mean "at odds with"—which Frank certainly is not.

   Step 5.   Eliminate answers, choosing from:

      (A) detractors . . in accord   (B) supporters . . at variance   (C) advocates . . harmonious (D) disparagers . . incompatible   (E) apologists . . in conflict

      Only *(A)* and *(D)* show people criticizing Frank. If we choose *(B) supporters* or *(C) advocates* or *(E) apologists,* the sentence makes no sense.

        IGNORE these 3 answer choices.

      Answer (A) is good for the first blank, bad for the second. The second blank must mean "at odds with."

      Only *answer (D)* fills our needs stated in Step 4.

5. **(E) compression . . precariousness**

   Sentence: **The short story, with its ----, its pointed movement toward a single moment of discovery, can economically reveal the ---- of the illusions that somehow sustain most people's lives.**

   Step 1.   Read for sentence meaning, noting these key words:

      Pointed movement + *economically* nearly *define* the word needed for the first blank.

      Illusions + somehow sustain most people's lives require us to find a word that fits *illusions.*

Step 2. Making it simpler, this sentence really says: *Even a very short story can show us the (fragile ?) illusions on which we base our lives.*

Step 3. Eliminate answers, choosing from:

(A) casualness .. destructiveness **(B) optimism .. barrenness** **(C) capriciousness .. rigidity** **(D) digressiveness .. poignancy** **(E) compression .. precariousness**

Step 4. Wow. You may understand the sentence, but here are some tough words as answer choices.

Still, remember what that first blank has to do? It must be the word that *pointed movement* and *economically* refer to.

Only *answer (E) compression* works in the first blank. A short story is indeed compressed or reduced in size.

Thus . . . IGNORE ALL OTHER CHOICES.

Step 5. Read both words of *(E)* in the sentence. Yes, illusions are very *precarious* things. Don't waste your time reading any of the other choices or testing them because their words for the first blank are wrong.

6. **(D) counterbalance .. truth**

Sentence: **The speaker asserted that humans have such a strong natural tendency toward self-deception that the moral imperative to ---- this drive with respect for ---- is becoming more critical than ever.**

Step 1. Whoa. A thirty-word sentence. Right away, read it two or three times until you see what it means.

Step 2. Before noting key words, SIMPLIFY THIS MONSTER.

Try: *People naturally deceive themselves, so we have a moral need to counteract this tendency with something better (probably honesty).*

Step 3. Check those key words now to be sure you have the true sense of this sentence.

Note: **self-deception**

That's it, folks. This thirty-word sentence is about our lying and how we'd better do something about it.

Step 4. Kind of sentence? *Contrast. Self-deception vs. the word in the second blank.*

Step 5. Eliminate answers, choosing from:

(A) dignify .. individuality **(B) intensify .. integrity** **(C) invalidate .. treachery** **(D) counterbalance .. truth** **(E) rationalize .. privacy**

Do you want to *(A) dignify* or *(B) intensify* or *(C) invalidate* or *(D) rationalize* our natural tendency for self-deception??? NO, OF COURSE NOT. But we could *(D) counterbalance* this lying with *respect for truth,* couldn't we?

Step 6. Read both words from *answer (D)* in the sentence, and it is completely logical. Don't bother to check the words in the second blanks in other answer choices, because their first-blank words were nonsense.

7. **(D) evincing .. compunction**

Sentence: **Robert was the embodiment of amorality, capable of committing the most odious acts without ever ---- even a hint of ----.**

Step 1. Read for sentence sense. Here, you must know that an *amoral person has no sense whatever of right and wrong.* And you must know that *odious means hateful.* (This sentence is a pure vocabulary problem. Grrr.)

Step 2. Suppose you sense that Robert is a total turkey because you noted that

amorality = **a** (not) + **moral** + **ity** = **no morality**

Step 3. So. Robert lacks morality. He really stinks.

Step 4. This is like a definition sentence as it proceeds to explain just how amoral Robert is.

Step 5. Thinking logically. If Robert has no moral sense, is he ever sorry about anything he does? Or proud of doing something very noble?

You think: Nah. He probably doesn't care one way or the other. *Right and wrong mean nothing to him.*

Step 6. Eliminate answers, choosing from:
(A) suppressing . . revulsion   **(B)** betraying . . reproof   **(C)** inspiring . . malice
(D) evincing . . compunction   **(E)** condoning . . indelicacy
(Now you *know* it's a pure vocabulary problem, just in case you missed that earlier.)

**Skip this problem altogether if you cannot eliminate at least 1 or 2 answer choices.

Step 7. *After any elimination, read both words in the remaining choices in the entire sentence. Listen carefully.* Only one choice works, of course, *answer (D).*
You could eliminate *(A)* for lack of logic, and *(B)* because *reproof* makes no sense. *(C)* makes no logical sense, given the word choices, and *(E)* is wacko.

**Questions like this one should send you scurrying to Vocabulary Lists 1 through 18 in this book, plus your list of roots and prefixes. The verbal questions mainly test vocabulary knowledge.

ANALOGY QUESTIONS

8. **(B) refutation : disprove**
The question asks: *"What pair of words is related in the same way as* **EXPOSITION : CLARIFY?"**

Step 1. How does clarify affect exposition? Or is it exposition that clarifies?? Ah. If you have no clue as to the meaning of exposition, you could guess intelligently here.

Step 2. *Use ROOTS for intelligent deduction/guessing.* **Expose** means to make visible, to reveal. The noun exposition logically means an exposure, or something made very visible.

Step 3. Now, back to the problem. *If exposition reveals something, it makes it clear or open—visible or understandable.* AHA!

Step 4. *Make a sentence* to express the original relationship. Try: *The purpose of exposition is to clarify something, to make it clear.*

Step 5. So . . . **for type of analogy, we have an Implied Comparison,** where one word defines or explains the other. The "job" of the noun (1st slot) is defined by the verb (2nd slot).
[Phew! Remember that your mental computer (brain) does all this reasoning in seconds.]

Step 6. Examine answers, choosing from:
(A) rebuttal : humiliate   **(B) refutation : disprove**   **(c) illumination : darken**
(D) allegation : verify   **(E) summary : end**
Testing each pair in our trial sentence:
(A) The purpose of rebuttal is to humiliate . . . Well, no. A rebuttal is a reply that gives the other side, adds information, or corrects a wrong idea. Only rarely would its purpose be to humiliate. Off the mark, so cross out.
(B) The purpose of refutation is to disprove . . . You betcha! To refute anything is to disprove it. **Stop!**
Say the whole analogy:
The purpose of exposition is to clarify just as the purpose of refutation is to disprove.
KEEP. Probably right. Read the others quickly, remembering that you never grab the first good-looking answer.
(C) The purpose of illumination is to darken . . . Har, har. Love those wacko answers.
(D) The purpose of allegation is to verify . . . Well, both words are used in law, but to allege that someone has done something is NOT to verify (prove) it beyond question.
Or: You could say that *an allegation needs to be verified.* But that's muddy thinking. Cross out this weak answer.
(E) The purpose of a summary is to end . . . This one is a trap for sloppy thinkers. A summary appears at the end, yes, but its purpose is not to END something. Its purpose is recapitulation of main points, remember?

** I suppose you noticed the vocabulary here. Knowing the meanings of words in the answers is SUPER-critical.

9. **(D) caricature : likeness**
The question asks: *"What pair of words is related in the same way as* **PARODY : IMITATION?"**

Step 1. This question tests your language arts knowledge. Remember that a parody imitates another work in a funny way, to ridicule it perhaps, but always to arouse laughter.

You think: **This analogy is a "definition" analogy.** [Note: This type is common on the new SATs, as it's a good way to test the size of your vocabulary.]

Step 2.   A clear sentence stating the relationship begins

A parody is a humorous imitation just as . . .

Step 3.   Check answers, choosing from:

(A) farce : laughter   (B) caricature : likeness   (C) mask : disguise   (D) deviation : similarity (E) gem : embellishment

Beginning with *(A), A farce is a humorous laughter* . . . Oh, my. Farce (exaggerated comedy) arouses laughter, or results in laughter. They're related, but one doesn't define the other.

(B) A caricature is a humorous likeness. YES! STOP! Say the entire analogy:

A parody is a humorous imitation, just as a caricature is a humorous likeness.

KEEP—SO PERFECT—BUT YOU ARE TOO BRIGHT TO POUNCE. CHECK REMAINING ANSWER CHOICES.

(C) A mask is a humorous disguise . . . Sometimes, but not always. One doesn't define the other. Weak choice, so cross out.

(D) A deviation is a humorous similarity . . . Another brilliantly wacko answer. Chuckle time.

(E) A gem is a humorous embellishment . . . Not unless the gem is in your belly button. More yuks here. (Wondering about *embellish?* See *bell* in the Roots Section.)

In the end, (B) is the only possible choice.

10.   **(D) hefty : weight**

The question asks: *"What pair of words is related in the same way as* **BULKY : VOLUME?"**

Step 1.   What does bulky SAY about volume? Just HOW are these two words related? **What KIND of analogy is this?**

You think: Bulky refers to the volume of something. It's a measurement of size in other words. If we say something's bulky, we know it's pretty big and maybe awkward to lug around, too.

Conclusion: **The real topic is SIZE.**

Step 2.   A clear sentence stating the relationship begins

Something bulky has a lot of volume . . .

or *Bulky refers to volume (or size)* . . .

Step 3.   Check answers, choosing from:

(A) straight : curvature   (B) hollow : vastness   (C) gouged : surface   (D) hefty : weight (E) grisly : appearance

Plugging each answer pair into our growing sentence:

(A) Something straight has a lot of curvature.

      (Yuk, yuk—no way.)

(B) Something hollow has a lot of vastness . . . or hollow refers to vastness? Again, no way.

(C) Something gouged has a lot of surface . . . or gouged refers to surface. No relationship here at all—a wacko answer.

(D) Something hefty has a lot of weight—yahoo!

Stop! Say the entire analogy.

Something bulky has a lot of volume just as something hefty has a lot of weight.

KEEP—PROBABLY IT—CHECK LAST CHOICE QUICKLY

(E) Something grisly has a lot of appearance??

Wrong relationship altogether. Grisly refers to bad appearance, not to the amount of appearance. The question here is one of SIZE.

Only *answer (D)* completes the basic idea in the given pair, an idea of SIZE.

11.   **(D) crosswalk : road**

The question asks: *What pair of words is related in the same way as* **FORD : RIVER?**

Step 1.   Analyze the given pair to determine HOW ford is related to river. Here, ford is the name of the place where you cross the river.

NOTE that answer pairs are all nouns.

Step 2. A clear sentence stating the relationship begins
The ford (a place) is where you cross the river . . . or *At the ford, you can cross the river . . .*

Step 3. Check answers, choosing from:
(A) basement : edifice **(B) terminal : airport** **(C) dam : reservoir** **(D) crosswalk : road**
(E) gangplank : boat
Plugging each answer pair into our sentence:
(A) Basement and edifice have no clear relationship; this is a wacko answer.
(B) The terminal is where you cross the airport . . . no. (A terminal is *located* at an airport.)
(C) A dam is where you cross the reservoir . . . Again, this is a different relationship. (A dam may *create* a reservoir—*cause and effect*.)
(D) A crosswalk is where you cross the road—AHA!
STOP! Say the entire analogy.
A ford is where you may safely cross the river, just as a crosswalk is where you safely cross the road.
(Note adding *safely;* it makes the analogy even truer.)
(E) A gangplank is a safe way to cross the boat . . .
Wrong. You get *onto* the boat via a gangplank. This expresses a different relationship.
Only *answer (D)* gives us perfectly balanced pairs on either side of the double colon.

12. **(E) overwrought : excitement**
The question asks: *"What pair has the same relationship as* **PRECIPITATE : HASTE?"**

Step 1. Tough vocabulary question here. If you have no idea, see if you can eliminate some answers that do not show a clear relationship to each other.
Guess what? All answer choices are good pairs, exhibiting a relationship of some kind to each other. None should be dismissed out of hand. **DECISION:** If you have no clue here, skip this question, as no answer pairs can be eliminated and guessing would be exceedingly iffy.

Step 2. If you think you know the given pair, decide on the Real Question: *"HOW is precipitate related to haste?"*
You think: Precipitate signifies a great deal of haste. *The idea of haste (hurrying) is inherent in the word precipitate.*

Step 3. Making a sentence, try:
To be precipitate is to act in haste . . .
or *Anything done in a precipitate manner is done in haste . . .*
or *Precipitate refers to lots of haste . . .*

Step 4. Check answers, choosing from:
(A) withdrawn : interaction **(B) preposterous : belief** **(C) vindictive : motive**
(D) hesitant : speed **(E) overwrought : excitement**
Plugging these pairs into the growing sentence:
(A) Withdrawn refers to lots of interaction . . . no. Wrong relationship.
(B) Preposterous refers to lots of belief . . . no. Something preposterous is *beyond belief.*
(C) Vindictive refers to lots of motive . . . no again. You could say that a vindictive person has revenge as a motive.
(D) Hesitant refers to lots of speed . . . wrong. If you're hesitant, you probably *lack* speed.
(E) Overwrought refers to lots of excitement. YES! **STOP! Say the entire analogy,** refining the sentence if you can.
Precipitate always refers to haste, just as overwrought always refers to excitement.

13. **(C) pursue : hound**
The question asks: *"What pair has the same relationship as* **ASK : IMPORTUNE?"**

Step 1. Again, a tough word. If you don't know importune, you may have to skip this one. (Checking for a root or prefix usually helps, but this root is uncommon.)

HOWEVER . . . how many answers can we brilliantly eliminate???

Step 2. Inspect the answer choices, hoping to eliminate some bad pairs.
(A) begin : recommence **(B) damage : restore** **(C) pursue : hound** **(D) misbehave : displease**
(E) stimulate : motivate

(A)   Begin is to recommence (or re-begin)??? No. Lucky you. A wacko answer to eliminate.

(B)   Damage is to restore . . . Opposites. Be brave and eliminate this answer as *opposites RARELY occur in analogy questions.*

(C)   Pursue is to hound . . . A relationship of degree. *Pursuing is just plain following, but hounding is very determined following, a major step up in pursuit.* Clear relationship here. A KEEPER.

(D)   How can misbehave relate to displease? If you misbehave you'll displease someone? Maybe, but weak. Keep, for now.

(E)   Stimulate and motivate are nearly synonyms. Like antonyms, *synonyms rarely if ever occur in analogy questions.* Be brave and cross this out.

Step 3.   You are now down to 2 choices, *answers (C) and (D),* even without knowing the word importune. **ALWAYS GUESS WHEN YOU'RE DOWN TO 2 CHOICES.**

Step 4.   Pick the answer with a clear and logical relationship, here *answer (C),* an analogy of degree. Say the entire analogy.

To ask is less pressing than to importune, just as to pursue is less demanding than to hound.

Of course, this is correct. *Importune means to beg or plead,* and importuning is much more demanding than merely asking.

**Moral:*   Don't give up on a question until you inspect the answers to see how many can be eliminated.

14.   **(E) reclamation : useful**
The question asks: *"What pair has the same relationship as* **CONVALESCENCE : HEALTHY?"**

Step 1.   What kind of analogy is this? How do these two words relate to one another?
You think: This is cause and effect, basically. The result of convalescence is a healthy person.
Conclusion: The matching pair must show a cause and effect relationship—some action (like convalescence) *leading to a good result* (like the healthy person).

Step 2.   A sentence to express this idea could read: *The result of convalescence is a healthy person . . .* or *Convalescence leads to being healthy again . . .*

Step 3.   Check answers, choosing from:

(A) contamination : purified   (B) renovation : dilapidated   (C) validation : unproven
(D) isolation : uninhabited   (E) reclamation : useful

(A)   Contamination results in being purified again? No.

(B)   Renovation leads to or results in being dilapidated again? Nope.

(C)   Validation leads to or results in being unproven again? Hardly. Like *(A)* and *(B),* no good at all.

(D)   Isolation leads to or results in being uninhabited? Yes, but that's not a *good* result, like health.

(E)   Reclamation results in something useful once again.

Hallelujah! Say the entire analogy.

Convalescence results in a healthy person, just as reclamation gives us something useful.

Note: Approaches to analogies vary with the pairs given. You will develop a variety of flexible approaches as you work analogy questions. The more you can do, the better.

READING COMPREHENSION QUESTIONS

15.   **(D)   The Amazing Life Cycle of the Cicada**

Step 1.   Examine the question: *"Which of the following is the* **most** *appropriate title for the passage?"*

Step 2.   If you have a good grasp of the passage and read through it looking for this answer (as our book advises), examine the answer choices now.
OR   If you did not read questions before the passage, read again, thinking up your own good title.

Step 3.   *Get your own good title in mind before checking these answer choices:*

(A)   The Cicada's Persistent Predators
(B)   Adaptations for Survival Among Predators of the Cicada
(C)   Three Species of the Cicada
(D)   The Amazing Life Cycle of the Cicada
(E)   The Origin of the 17-Year Locust

Step 4.   Elimination of answers.

Answers (A), (B), and *(E)* are all too limited in scope. The hero of this passage is the cicada—not his predators—not the *origin* of one cicada type.

Answer (C) is truly narrow in scope—discussed in only the fourth paragraph.

Answer (D) is the only title that captures the enthusiasm that this author feels for his subject.

16.   **(A)   The cicada's strategy for survival is an unusual adaptation.**

Step 1.   Examine the question: *"The statement that cicadas are 'eminently and conspicuously available' (lines 8–9) is used to illustrate which of the following assertions?"*

Step 2.   Check all the material around lines 8 and 9. *Start several sentences ahead of these lines and read a few sentences after this quoted bit.*

Step 3.   As you read, ask what point there is in having so dang many cicadas all over the place?

Step 4.   When ready, examine the answer choices:

   (A)   The cicada's strategy for survival is an unusual adaptation.
   (B)   Cicadas do not have any relatives that are noxious to predators.
   (C)   Predators of cicadas do not have many different kinds of prey.
   (D)   The cicada is rarely available to its predators.
   (E)   The timing of the cicada's life cycle is amazing.

Step 5.   Using your head, look at the first two paragraphs. *The entire topic is adapting to avoid predators. The 17-year locust is cited as having "an uncommon strategy."* This strategy is then described in the exact lines on which this question is based.

Conclusion: Since we have had only one topic presented at this point in the passage, we can only choose *(A),* which gives us adaptation as its topic.

Answers (B) and *(C)* weren't discussed, and *(D)* and *(E)* were treated much later in the passage.

17.   **(A)   Predators can eat only so many of their prey.**

Step 1.   Consider the question carefully: *"It can be inferred that the strategy referred to in line 14 is dependent on which of the following principles?"*

Step 2.   **Read everything around line 14.** Be clear about which strategy is referred to. Here it is *predator satiation* (fat, satisfied hunters)—see lines 12–13.

   FOCUS on lines 9–11, where the passage states that the cicada is around only rarely but in such enormous numbers that **"predators cannot possibly consume the entire bounty."** Bingo.

Step 3.   Remind yourself that the question is "Which principle is predator satiation dependent on?"

Step 4.   Examine answers, choosing from:

   (A)   Predators can eat only so many of their prey.
   (B)   Predators seldom eat what they find distasteful.
   (C)   An increased population of predators reduces the number of prey in a given environment.
   (D)   Few organisms have life spans that extend beyond three years.
   (E)   What one generation of a species learns is transmitted to the following generations through conditioning.

Step 5.   Eliminating answers.

   (A)   is clearly outstanding and the first keeper.
   (B)   is off the subject, as we're talking about enormous numbers of prey (lines 8–11).
   (C)   Increasing the predator population is not discussed, only the cicada's adaptations that ensure its survival.
   (D)   Life span is off subject, as is transmitted learning, *answer (E).*

   Thus, only *(A)* can be supported logically and by information actually given in the passage.

18.   **(E)   How do cicadas detect the passage of time?**

Step 1.   Examine the question: *"All of the following questions are answered in the passage EXCEPT:"*

   Groan. You must be absolutely sure of what *was discussed* in order to find the one topic *not discussed.*

Step 2.   These roundup questions requiring mastery of facts in the passage are easy IF YOU HAVE MARKED THE FACTS AS YOU READ THROUGH THE PASSAGE.

Step 3.   Right now, you must check answers so you can begin eliminating as quickly as possible.

(A) **How do cicadas in the Northeast differ from those in the South?**

(B) **What is a prime number?**

(C) **What are various means that animals use to evade predators?**

(D) **What do cicada nymphs eat?**

(E) **How do cicadas detect the passage of time?**

Step 4.   Fact-check the passage in order to eliminate choices.

(A)   The 13-year cycle of the southern cicada is mentioned in lines 26 and 28 and lines 38 and 39, so this question IS answered.

(B)   A prime number is defined clearly in lines 47 and 48.

(C)   is answered in the first paragraph.

(D)   is answered in the third paragraph.

(E)   is the puzzler *not answered anywhere.*

19.   **(E)   enthusiastic**

Step 1.   Examine the question: *"The **author's tone** in presenting the information can best be described as"*

Step 2.   Remember that the tone or mood of a piece is revealed by the author's choice of words.

When reading, you should have circled these words:

lines 22 and 23 "the story of periodical cicadas is more amazing than most people realize"

line 32 "most remarkable is . . . "

line 41 "I am most impressed by the timing . . . "

Step 3.   You could and probably should have decided after only one quick reading that *this author loves cicadas*. The foregoing comments are obvious, not subtle.

Step 4.   Thus, *any negative or lukewarm answer choices will be wrong and can be quickly eliminated.*

Step 5.   Eliminate choices, selecting from:

(A) **skeptical**   (B) **cautious**   (C) **detached**   (D) **tolerant**   (E) **enthusiastic**

Answers (A), (B), (C), and *(D)* are all blah or way too negative.

Here, only *(E)* could apply to this author, who is so clearly impressed by the cicada.

20.   **(D) uniformly excellent and exemplary**

Step 1.   Examine the question: *"It can be inferred from the passage that the narrator would describe Turkey's work at 11 a.m. as"*

Step 2.   Read again to be absolutely clear. It is the *narrator's opinion* we're seeking.

Step 3.   All significant lines about Turkey's character and work habits should be marked. Questions should be read BEFORE READING THE PASSAGE, remember???

Focus on line 4, "BUT after twelve o'clock . . ."

(Clearly, something changed after noon!)

lines 15–20—narrator says that after Turkey's face reached its full redness he wasn't much good the rest of the day

line 21 "flighty recklessness of activity"

lines 23 and 24 "all his blots . . . after twelve o'clock"

lines 33 and 34 "all the time before twelve o'clock [he] was the quickest, steadiest creature"

lines 35 and 36 "a great deal of work in a style not easily matched" (before noon only)

Conclusion: Turkey was terrific before noon, after which he went sorely awry.

Step 4.   Examine answers, having your own in mind first:

(A) **occasionally sloppy and inaccurate**

(B) **characterized by inexplicable interruptions**

(C) **requiring constant correction**

(D) **uniformly excellent and exemplary**

(E) **excessively neurotic and intense**

Step 5.   Elimination. Since we know that Turkey was terrific before noon, *only good answers can be considered.*

Eliminate *(A), (B), (C),* and *(E)* on this basis.

Select *(D)* as the only possible choice.

21. **(D) an aversion to unseemly behavior**

Step 1. Consider the question: *"The narrator's primary motive for asking Turkey not to return to work in the afternoon was"*

Clarify: **Why didn't the narrator want Turkey back in the office after noon?**

Step 2. If you don't know, reread the last half of the passage, where the narrator discusses this topic.

Ideally, you should have marked:

lines 45–47 "made uncomfortable by his inflamed ways after twelve o'clock"

lines 47–49 "being a man of peace, unwilling by my admonitions to call forth unseemly retorts from him"

Step 3. After reading the relevant portions, consider:

(A) **a need to save money**
(B) **a predilection for solitude**
(C) **a concern for Turkey's health**
(D) **an aversion to unseemly behavior**
(E) **a fear of physical violence**

Step 4. Eliminate carefully, one by one.

Answer (A) was not discussed—not anywhere.

Answer (B) wasn't discussed either, but aren't those words impressive? Never fall into this trap!

Answer (C) makes us pause. Think. Is the narrator really worried about Turkey's health or is he just using his concern as a blind? *Keep for now.*

(D) Yes, and *the word unseemly is repeated.* Also, the *entire last half of this passage reveals the narrator's distaste for Turkey's p.m. behavior.*

(E) Maybe. Insolence, for sure. See line 43. But mainly, the narrator doesn't wish to call forth "unseemly retorts," line 48.

Of the keepers, *(C)* and *(D)*, the *passage gives most support for answer (D).* The narrator tried to ease Turkey out of his chambers after noon, citing Turkey's age as an excuse, but the question of health is only vaguely implied.

22. **(E) productive**

Step 1. Consider the question: *"Turkey apparently believed that his efforts in the office during the afternoon were"*

Clarify: **What did Turkey think of himself in the p.m.?**

Step 2. Turkey's view contrasts with the narrator's—a major point at the end of this piece. If you missed it, return to the last four lines and reread.

line 54 "But no; he insisted upon his afternoon devotions. He assured me that *if his services in the morning were useful, how indispensable, then, in the afternoon?"*

FOCUS on line 54. Note that critical word *But*.

Step 3. Conclusion: Turkey was convinced he was as great in the p.m. as he was in the a.m.—a real contrast to the narrator's viewpoint.

Step 4. The right answer will be *very positive to reflect Turkey's opinion of himself.*

Step 5. Eliminate answers, choosing from

(A) **pathetic** (B) **suspicious** (C) **annoying** (D) **erratic** (E) **productive**

Eliminate any negative answers, including *(A), (B), (C),* and *(D).* Quick, huh?

Only *answer (E)* gives us Turkey's view of himself in the afternoon.

23. **(D) unobservant**

Step 1. Consider the question: *"The narrator can appropriately be described as all of the following EXCEPT"*

Clarify: All the answer choices BUT ONE will apply to the NARRATOR, not to Turkey.

What one choice is wrong?

Step 2. See if you can quickly eliminate a few choices, based on your memory of the passage.

(A) **reasonable** (B) **elderly** (C) **compassionate** (D) **unobservant** (E) **nonaggressive**

Step 3. *Early Elimination.*

Even a quick read tells you that this narrator is *(A) reasonable, (C) compassionate* (or he wouldn't have kept such a tricky employee), and *(E) nonaggressive,* as we noted in line 47 earlier.

Step 4.   *Final Elimination.* Where does it say that the narrator is old, *answer (B) elderly,* the only competitor for *answer (D)*?
Note lines 1 and 2, where the narrator says that both he and Turkey were *"not far from sixty."*
Answer (D) unobservant is clearly NOT a characteristic of our narrator, who has closely observed and faithfully recorded Turkey's behavior.

** Keep mumbling **"not a characteristic"** to yourself as you work problems of this nature on PSATs and SATs. Remembering what you're REALLY LOOKING FOR is vital.

24.   **(B)   If Turkey had not returned after lunch, the office would have run more efficiently.**

Step 1.   The question asks: *"With which of the following statements concerning his office would the narrator be most likely to agree?"*
Step 2.   Another form of the roundup question, this one requires that you understand every bit of the passage. Answers must be eliminated one by one.
Step 3.   By now you are probably very familiar with this passage, having answered four questions on it already. So . . . *try early elimination:*
(A)   Turkey's presence enlivened an otherwise tedious workday.
(B)   If Turkey had not returned after lunch, the office would have run more efficiently.
(C)   If Turkey had acted in the mornings as he did in the afternoons, all concerned would have been happier.
(D)   If the narrator had demanded a better performance from Turkey, the situation would have improved.
(E)   The narrator himself was in part responsible for provoking Turkey's eccentric behavior.
Answer (C)—wrong immediately; you know that Turkey's p.m. behavior is hopeless.
Answer (E)—dismiss quickly, as no evidence supports it.
Step 4.   Zip through the passage searching for any evidence that says the day was tedious *(A)*, or *(D)*, that the narrator should have been more demanding.
Step 5.   *Final Elimination:* The passage cannot support either *(A)* or *(D)*, so *answer (B)*, tempting from the beginning, and supported by the last half of the passage, is right.

ANSWERS TO AND ANALYSES OF MATH QUESTIONS

1. (D) The problem asks you to find the perimeter of a right triangle given the lengths of two of its sides. (The SAT loves to use problems that involve the Pythagorean theorem: $a^2 + b^2 = c^2$.) Memorize this formula and the Pythagorean triplets on p. 335.
We first solve for the missing leg. Call it x.

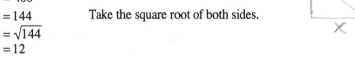

$$x^2 + 16^2 = 20^2$$
$$x^2 + 256 = 400$$
$$x^2 = 144$$ Take the square root of both sides.
$$x = \sqrt{144}$$
$$x = 12$$

We want the perimeter, so we now add the lengths of the three sides.
$12 + 16 + 20 = 48$.
Answer choice (D)
Look at Lesson 12 for more of these types of problems.

2. (D) The sum of the three angles of ANY triangle is always 180°, so $z = 70°$. $w° + z° = 180°$ because they are supplementary angles. Therefore, $x + y + w = 110 + 70 + 110 = 290$. Answer choice (D).

You could also find the value of w by recognizing that w is an exterior angle of the triangle, which is equal to the sum of the two remote interior angles (p. 349). Therefore, $w = x + y = 110$.

3. (B) This problem asks you to divide 20 by $1\frac{1}{4}$. First convert $1\frac{1}{4}$ into an improper fraction. $1\frac{1}{4} = \frac{5}{4}$.

Remember that dividing by a fraction is the same as multiplying by the reciprocal.

$$\frac{20}{\frac{5}{4}} = 20 \cdot \frac{4}{5} = \frac{80}{5} = 16.$$

Answer choice (B).

4. (A) Do not panic when you encounter these problems. They are really quite simple. The problem asks you to find the rating number for 1234 by multiplying the thousands digit by 3, the hundreds digit by 2, the units digit by 1, and the ones digit by 0, and then to find their sum.

$$1234 = (1 \times 3) + (2 \times 2) + (3 \times 1) + (4 \times 0) = 3 + 4 + 3 + 0 = 10$$

Answer choice (A).

5. (D) In this problem you are asked to select the number whose R_n can always be determined. In other words, in which number does the value of H not affect the answer. Clearly, when H is in the units place it will not affect the total because it is to be multiplied by 0.

$652H = (6 \times 3) + (5 \times 2) + (2 \times 1) + (H \times 0) = 30$

Answer choice (D).

For more problems dealing with these "funny functions" refer to Lesson 17.

6. (B) This is a plug and chug problem. Put (−1,000) in for each n until you get the correct answer.

(A) $\frac{-1,000}{3} - \frac{-1,000}{2} = -333\frac{1}{3} + 500 = +166\frac{2}{3} = $ NO!

(B) $\frac{-1,000}{3} - \frac{-1,000}{4} = -333\frac{1}{3} + 250 = -83\frac{1}{3} = $ YES!

Stop here.

Answer choice (B).

If you scan the answer choices quickly, you can eliminate (C), (D), and (E) because a negative times a negative gives you a positive.

7. (D) Given $2x = 3y = 4w$, you are asked to solve for the value of $5x + 6w$ in terms of y. The least common multiple for $2x$ and $5x$ is $10x$. So

$$5(2x) = 5(3y)$$
$$\frac{10x}{2} = \frac{15y}{2}$$
$$5x = \frac{15y}{2}$$

The least common multiple for $4w$ and $6w$ is $12w$. So

$$3(4w) = 3(3y)$$

$$\frac{12w}{2} = \frac{9y}{2}$$

$$6w = \frac{9y}{2}$$

Therefore, $5x + 6w = \frac{15y}{2} + \frac{9y}{2} = \frac{24y}{2} = 12y.$

8. (A) In these problems you *must* test items I, II, and III for their validity. If x is odd, then x^2 is odd. If y is even, then y^2 is even. An odd number minus an even number gives you an odd number. Choose a number for x and y. For instance, let $x = 3$ and $y = 4$. Then $3^2 - 4^2 = 9 - 16 = -7$, which is odd but not the square of an integer. The only correct choice is I.

The following tables are useful for the solution of problems of this type.

Addition Table for Odd and Even Integers

+	Odd	Even
Odd	Even	Odd
Even	Odd	Even

Multiplication Table for Odd and Even Integers

×	Odd	Even
Odd	Odd	Even
Even	Even	Even

Answer choice (A).
Be careful when choosing values for the variables. In the above problem, if you had chosen $x = 5$ and $y = 4$, then $x^2 - y^2 = 5^2 - 4^2 = 25 - 16 = 9$, which would have made I and III be correct. The problem asks which answer is ALWAYS correct. Clearly I is, but III is not.

9. (B) Since R and T are positive, S is positive, and S is a factor of both 24 and 32. You can find the common factors, which are 2, 4, and 8. Plug those in for S, and solve for R and T. You quickly find that since $32 > 24$, then $T > R$.

If $32 > 24$, then $\frac{32}{S} > \frac{24}{S}$, provided S is a positive number.

Answer choice (B).
Refer to Lesson 4 for more problems dealing with inequalities.

10. (C) The formula for the area of a triangle is $A = \frac{1}{2}(\text{base}) \times (\text{height})$.

Area of $\triangle ABC = \frac{1}{2}(AC) \times (BD)$. Area of $\triangle EFG = \frac{1}{2}(EG) \times (FH)$.

Since $AC = FH$ and $BD = EG$, the two triangles must have the same area.
Another method would be to substitute numbers for AC and BD and calculate the area of each triangle.

Example: If $AC = FH = 4$ and $BD = EG = 6$, then the area of $\triangle ABC = \frac{1}{2}(4) \times (6) = 12$ and the area of

$\triangle EFG = \frac{1}{2}(6) \times (4) = 12$. This is a quick and easy solution to a reasonably difficult problem.

Answer choice (C).

11. (A) Looking at the given sequence 1, –2, 3, –4, 5, . . . , you should recognize that each odd-numbered term is positive and each even-numbered term is negative. The 100th term would be (–100) and the 101st term would be (+101).
101 + (–100) = 1   would be the sum of the 100th and 101st terms.

The 102nd term would be (–102).
$101 + (-102) = -1$ would be the sum of the 101st and 102nd terms.
Answer choice (A).

12. (B) If you think of the diagram as stairs, then the distance traveled vertically would be 4 units and the distance traveled horizontally would be 6 units. The perimeter would be $6 + 6 + 4 + 4 = 20$; therefore, Column B, (22), is greater than Column A, (20).
Answer choice (B).

13. (D) $\boxed{a} + \boxed{a} = a^2 + a^2 = 2a^2$

$\textcircled{a} + \textcircled{a} = (-a) + (-a) = -2a$
We want to compare $2a^2$ with $(-2a)$.
If $2a^2 = -2a$, then solving for a gives $a = -1$.
But if you were to choose any other value for a, say $+3$, then $2(3)^2 > -2(3)$.
Since Column A = Column B when $a = -1$ and Column A > Column B when a is different from 1, we mark answer choice (D).
This problem shows the importance of plugging in more than one number to compare quantities, especially the values 1 and –1.

14. (A) The volume of a cube is Volume = (side)^3.
The volume of a rectangular solid is Volume = (length)(width)(height).
We want to compare $(x + 1)^3$ with $(x)(x + 1)(x + 2)$.
A simple solution to this problem would be to plug in a couple of numbers for x and evaluate. For instance, if $x = 1$, then $(x + 1)^3 = (1 + 1)^3 = (2)^3 = 8$.
$(x)(x + 1)(x + 2) = (1)(1 + 1)(1 + 2) = (1)(2)(3) = 6$.
If $x = 2$, then $(x + 1)^3 = (2 + 1)^3 = 3^3 = 27$.
$(x)(x + 1)(x + 2) = (2)(2 + 1)(2 + 2) = 2(3)(4) = 24$.
In both cases Column A > Column B.
Answer choice (A).
The algebraic solution would be to expand both quantities using the distributive property and the FOIL method.
$(x + 1)^3 = (x + 1)(x + 1)(x + 1) = x^3 + 3x^2 + 3x + 1$
$(x)(x + 1)(x + 2) = x^3 + 3x^2 + 2x$.
Comparing both quantities, Column A is $(x + 1)$ more than Column B. This method would obviously take more time.

15. (D) This is a Rate × Time = Distance problem. The easiest way to solve the problem is to set up an equation and plug in a couple of values in the equation for the Time. Since $R \times T = D$, then $R = \dfrac{D}{T}$.

In this problem, $D = 40T$ and, if we let x equal the New Rate, then $x = \dfrac{40T + 10}{T} = \dfrac{\text{New Distance}}{\text{Same Time}}$.

Plug in $T = 1$. $x = \dfrac{40 \cdot (1) + 10}{1} = 50$
In this case, Column A = Column B. But DO NOT jump to hasty conclusions.

If $T = 2$, then $x = \dfrac{(40) \cdot (2) + 10}{2} = \dfrac{90}{2} = 45$ When you divide by a fraction, invert the fraction and multiply.

When $T = 1$, Column A = Column B.
When $T = 2$, Column B > Column A.
The correct answer choice must then be (D).

16. (D) We first want to calculate the cost of each orange. If B dozen oranges costs C cents, then each orange would

cost $\dfrac{C}{12B}$ cents. (Remember, you must multiply B by 12 to get the total number of oranges.) Next, divide E

cents by $\dfrac{C}{12B}$ to get the number of oranges you could buy with E cents if each orange costs $\dfrac{C}{12B}$ cents.

$$\dfrac{E}{\dfrac{C}{12B}} = E \cdot \dfrac{12B}{C}$$

$$= \dfrac{12BE}{C}$$

Answer choice (D).

17. (E) Percent means $\dfrac{x}{100}$ so 30 percent would be $\dfrac{30}{100}$. If the car originally cost y dollars, it would cost $y + \dfrac{30}{100}y$

after 5 years.

Simplify: $y + \dfrac{30}{100}y = 1y + \dfrac{3}{10}y = 1.3y$. The car will increase in cost another 30 percent over the next 5 years.

Its cost then would be:

$(1.3y) + \dfrac{30}{100}(1.3y) = 1.3y + \dfrac{3}{10}(1.3y) = 1.3y$

$+ (.3)(1.3y) = 1.3y + .39y = 1.69y$.

If the car originally cost y dollars and after 10 years costs $1.69y$ dollars, the increase was $.69y$ or $\dfrac{69}{100}y$. This is

an increase of 69 percent.

Fractions, decimals, and percents generally give students heartburn. I would strongly suggest reviewing
Lessons 7 and 8.

Answer choice (E).

18. (B) The SAT loves to include problems involving either $(x + y)^2$ or $(x - y)^2$. Memorize these binomial expansions
in order to save time on your test.

$(x - y)^2 = x^2 - 2xy + y^2$.

You are given that $x^2 + y^2 = 18$ and that $xy = 6$. From the above equation you know that $(x - y)^2 = x^2 - 2xy + y^2$;

so $(x - y)^2 = (x^2 + y^2) - 2(xy) = 18 - 2(6) = 18 - 12 = 6$.

Answer choice (B).

This problem was classified as one of the most difficult on a recent SAT. You can see that by knowing the

expansion of $(x - y)^2$ you can quickly and easily obtain the correct answer.

19. (B) The key concept behind this problem is that a number $\dfrac{1}{x}$ gets smaller as x gets larger.

If $2 \le y \le 3$, then the least value of $\dfrac{1}{y}$ would be $\dfrac{1}{3}$.

If $4 \le z \le 5$, the least value of $\dfrac{1}{z}$ would be $\dfrac{1}{5}$. We obtain the average by using the equation:

$$\text{Average} = \frac{\text{Sum of parts}}{\text{Number of parts}}$$

Our answer would be: $\text{Average} = \dfrac{\dfrac{1}{3} + \dfrac{1}{5}}{2} =$

$$\frac{\dfrac{1}{3} + \dfrac{1}{5}}{\dfrac{2}{1}} = \frac{\dfrac{5+3}{15}}{\dfrac{2}{1}} = \frac{\dfrac{8}{15}}{\dfrac{2}{1}} = \frac{8}{15} \cdot \frac{1}{2} = \frac{8}{30} = \frac{4}{15}$$

Remember, dividing by 2 is the same as multiplying by $\dfrac{1}{2}$.

Answer choice (B).
To review averages, refer to Lesson 7.

20. (D) The formulas to use in this problem are:

Divide both sides by π^3.

Area of a square $= s^2$
Area of a circle $= \pi r^2$
Diameter $= 2r$

Area of a square of side $\left(\dfrac{1}{\pi}\right) = \left(\dfrac{1}{\pi}\right)^2 = \dfrac{1}{\pi^2}$

We want to find the radius of the circle whose area equals $\dfrac{1}{\pi^2}$.

Substitute πr^2 for the area of the circle.
Area of circle = Area of square

$\pi r^2 = \dfrac{1}{\pi^2}$ Solve for r. Multiply both sides by π^2.

$\pi^2\left(\pi r^2\right) = \pi^2\left(\dfrac{1}{\pi^2}\right) = \pi^3 r^2 = 1$

$r^2 = \dfrac{1}{\pi^3}$

$\sqrt{r^2} = \sqrt{\dfrac{1}{\pi^3}}$ Take the square root of both sides.

$r = \dfrac{\sqrt{1}}{\sqrt{\pi^3}} = \dfrac{1}{\sqrt{\pi^2 \cdot \pi}} = \dfrac{1}{\pi\sqrt{\pi}}$ Simplify the radical.

$D = 2r;\ D = \dfrac{2}{\pi\sqrt{\pi}}$

Answer choice (D).
Knowing area formulas and being able to simplify radicals will make a difficult problem easy.

21. (C) The integers between 60 and 70 that have a remainder of 2 when divided by 3 can be found as follows:

$61 \div 3 = 20$ R1
$62 \div 3 = 20$ R2
$63 \div 3 = 21$ R0
$64 \div 3 = 21$ R1

$$65 \div 3 = 21 \quad R2$$
$$66 \div 3 = 22 \quad R0$$
$$67 \div 3 = 22 \quad R1$$
$$68 \div 3 = 22 \quad R2$$
$$69 \div 3 = 23 \quad R0$$

Notice that remainders for a divisor of 3 can only be 0, 1, or 2.
So when 4 is the divisor, the remainders can only be 0, 1, 2, or 3.

$$60 \div 4 = 15 \quad R0$$
$$61 \div 4 = 15 \quad R1$$
$$62 \div 4 = 15 \quad R2$$
$$63 \div 4 = 15 \quad R3$$
$$64 \div 4 = 16 \quad R0$$
$$65 \div 4 = 16 \quad R1$$

65 satisfies both conditions.
Answer choice (C).

22. (E) Draw a quick sketch. Label the important information.

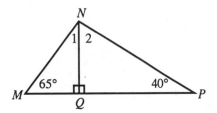

MN and NP are the hypotenuses of $\triangle QNM$ and $\triangle QNP$. Therefore, these are greater than MQ, NQ, and QP (the hypotenuse is the longest side of a right triangle). So eliminate MN and NP

$NQ > MQ$, since $\angle QMN$ (65°) $> \angle MNQ$ (25°) (the longest side is opposite the greatest angle in a triangle).

Eliminate NQ. Similarly, since $\angle QNP$ (50°) $> \angle NPQ$ (40°), $QP > NQ$. Eliminate QP.

Therefore, the answer is MQ, the only remaining line.
Answer choice (E).

23. (A) Set up a chart.

	Now	In x years
Tom	t	$t + x$
Becky	$\dfrac{t}{3}$	$\dfrac{t}{3} + x$

Let x = the number of years from now.

If Tom is t years old and he is 3 times as old as Becky, then Becky must be $\dfrac{t}{3}$ years old. In x years, Tom will be

$t + x$ years old and Becky will be $\dfrac{t}{3} + x$ years old.

Set up an equation based upon your chart.
In how many years will Tom be twice as old as Becky?

$$t + x = 2\left(\frac{t}{3} + x\right) \quad \text{Distribute.}$$

$$t + x = \frac{2t}{3} + 2x \quad \text{Solve for } x.$$

$$\frac{t}{3} = x$$

Answer choice (A).
For more practice on word problems, review Lesson 10.

24. (E) "y is what percent of x" translates to $y = \frac{p}{100}x$. We want to solve for y in terms of x.

If $x = \frac{2}{5}y$, then multiply both sides by $\frac{5}{2}$.

$$\frac{5}{2}x = \left(\frac{5}{2}\right)\left(\frac{2}{5}\right)y; \quad y = \frac{5}{2}x.$$

Now you have y in terms of x. Convert $\frac{5}{2}$ to a percent to get your answer.

$$\frac{5}{2} = \frac{p}{100} \quad \text{Cross multiply.}$$
$$500 = 2p \quad \text{Solve for } p.$$
$$p = 250$$
Answer choice (E).
Percentage problems are always on the SAT. Master Lesson 8.

25. (A) If $\frac{3}{4}$ of the students have automobiles, then $\frac{1}{4}$ do not have automobiles. $\frac{1}{4}$ of $400 = 100$ total students who do not have a car. 120 students live on campus. If 65 of those students have automobiles, then $120 - 65$, or 55, students who live on campus do not have automobiles. The question asks how many students do not live on campus and do not have an automobile?
So the answer is $100 - 55 = 45$ students off campus who do not have a car.
Answer choice (A).
In more difficult problems such as this one, DO NOT PANIC. Read the question carefully before trying to solve it. Determine exactly what you are looking for, and try to find an easy solution. Most SAT questions do not require a great deal of pencil pushing. A few extra seconds analyzing the problem can save you minutes.

The twenty-five questions in this section were chosen from two of the most recent tests and, in general, they were the more difficult problems. By analyzing your mistakes and the solutions, you should be able to recognize areas of strength and areas of weakness. The more practice problems you do, the higher your score will be.

Unit 6: Math for SATs and PSATs

Preparation for the math segments of an SAT or PSAT has always meant reviewing basic arithmetic, algebra I, and geometry. This study should not change in any way. The same knowledge will continue to be tested by the College Board because it is the essential math knowledge you need for college and beyond.

But of course you have heard that changes are in the air. Calculators . . . and grids. What's that all about? We discuss the changes in our Introduction, pages 1–4. Read those pages now, if you haven't read them before.

Basically, though, you need to grip your handy calculator and spend time practicing with a few of the new grids for student-produced answers. Grids are easy as soon as you understand the concept, and coming up with your own answers for 10 questions on a PSAT or SAT is the same as working 10 problems for a math assignment.

USING THE NEW ANSWER GRIDS

You know how to blacken in little spaces with your #2 pencil, right? Well, that's it mainly . . . HOWEVER, since machines—not people—score these tests, **you must learn how to use the new grids properly.** On both the new PSAT and the SAT I, you will have 10 questions for which you will be required to "grid in" your answers. Read the directions below for "gridding-in" tips; then consult Appendix A on page 461 for samples of grids that have already been filled in.

The first step is, of course, to obtain an answer to the question. (Remember—on the new tests, you'll be able to use a calculator to do this.)

After you have calculated your answer, it is VERY IMPORTANT for you to **enter the answer you have obtained in the boxes directly above the grid;** doing this will keep the answer in front of you at all times. This way, you'll have the answer right there as you grid in.

Remember the following when gridding in your answer:

- Mark no more than one space in any column; because answers are machine-scored, you will receive credit only if you fill in the spaces correctly.
- No question will have a negative answer.
- If your answer is a *fraction*, remember that the fraction line (which you **must grid in**) will **ALWAYS** be located at the very top of the grid in the middle two positions.
- If your answer contains a *decimal point* (which must **also be gridded in**), blacken it in using the spaces found directly below fraction lines.
- **VERY IMPORTANT:** *Mixed numbers* (such as 3 1/2) **must be** gridded in using *decimals* (i.e., as 3.5) or as *improper fractions* (i.e., as 7/2). **If you enter your answer as a mixed number, it will be scored as INCORRECT.** (For instance, the machine will read 3 1/2 as 31/2.)
- If you obtain a *decimal* answer, enter the most accurate value that the grid can accommodate. For instance, if your answer is .8888, you may record it as either .888 or .889. **Less accurate values** (such as .88 or .89) **will be scored as INCORRECT.**

When gridding in answers to practice questions, follow the techniques used in the sample grids with answers in Appendix A (page 461) just to be sure you're on the right track.

ABOUT THOSE CALCULATORS . . .

You may now use a calculator (no hand-held computers) on the new PSAT or on SAT I. The College Board has offered some helpful suggestions about how to use your calculator to your best advantage, and we summarize their hints here:

1. *Take your calculator to the exam,* even if you're not sure you will use it.
2. *Take your "old buddy" calculator* that you know how to use accurately, not a hot-shot new model that you bought hoping to ace the SAT.
3. Think on every question: *Do I need to use the calculator here or not?* If not, set it aside.
4. Many problems shouldn't be worked with a calculator; often, problems on SATs and PSATs demand careful logic and reasoning—THINKING—but no computation to speak of.
5. *Get "Taking the SAT" from your guidance counselor,* and take the sample test using your calculator.

To that we add #6, and MOST IMPORTANT: *Work these practice SAT problems with your calculator, too.* Also, *practice gridding-in your answers to some of the practice problems.* (**Grids for practice appear in Appendix B on pages 462-464 for you to use whenever you wish, however you wish.**)

Early trials of the new tests showed that scores rose slightly for students using calculators, about 10-20 points. That's one or two questions better than test-takers score without a calculator, but hardly an earth-shaking difference.

Best Advice Says: Practice with some pretty tough questions, just in case the difficulty level has risen.

Lesson 1

Goal: To review skills of addition, subtraction, multiplication, and division.

THE BASICS OF ARITHMETIC

You will never see a problem $5 \times 3 = ?$ on a college entrance exam. First of all, it is too straightforward. It's the twists that make the SAT a challenge. Second, arithmetic is considered a tool at the college level. You are expected to know it, and to know it well enough to be able to do it quickly. Mastery of arithmetic skills and knowledge of basic terms will enable you to do well on the SAT.

Remember These Terms?

Sum—Indicates the result obtained by adding two or more numbers.

Example: The sum of 157 and 43 is the same as $157 + 43$.

Difference—Indicates the result obtained by subtracting one number from another.

Example: The difference between 2,149 and 1,562 is the same as $2,149 - 1,562$.

Product—Indicates the result obtained by multiplying two numbers.

Example: The product of 27 and 42 is written $27 \cdot 42$ or 27×42.

Factors—When two or more numbers are multiplied together, each is called a *factor* of the product.

Example: 7 and 9 are factors of 63 because $7 \cdot 9 = 63$.

Quotient—Indicates the result obtained when one number called the *dividend* is divided by another number called the *divisor.*

Example: The quotient of 144 and 8 is written $144 \div 8$ or $\frac{144}{8}$.

Digits—Are the set of numbers 0, 1, 2, 3, 4, 5, 6, 7, 8, 9.

Example: 53 is a two-digit number.

For practice, try to do the following problems as *accurately* and *quickly* as you can.

ADDITION

1.	852	2.	656	3.	206	4.	989
	257		868		417		768
	547		349		638		476
	362		237		751		554
	+187		+611		+459		+707

5.	1,248	6.	9,548	7.	440	8.	1,574
	4,357		9,735		8,553		1,982
	941		4,373		1,216		532
	3,284		1,625		1,832		8,111
	+4,618		+3,649		+6,513		+6,789

9.	4,323	10.	3,426
	8,060		7,153
	6,512		6,832
	148		222
	+436		+4,132

ANSWERS to all practice problems can be found in the back of the book, beginning on p. 417.

SUBTRACTION

11.	91	12.	148	13.	285	14.	1,080
	−63		−95		−98		−868

15.	703
	−289

16. From 2,185 take 1,790.
17. Subtract 1,778 from 1,887.
18. What is the difference between 8,324 and 7,219?
19. $9,045 - 4,412 - 2,945 - 936 =$
20. $225 - 97 - 49 - 23 - 17 =$
21. Take 89 from 311.
22. Subtract 1,964 from 2,965.
23. From 896 subtract 397.
24. From 833 take 528.
25. Find the difference between 4,173 and 7,882.

Are you making silly, grade school errors? *Most mistakes on math tests are simple arithmetic errors.* That's really dumb, when you think about it, because you *do* know how to work these problems. Let's get serious now about eliminating the simple errors.

MULTIPLICATION

26. $\begin{array}{r} 1,864 \\ \times\,847 \\ \hline \end{array}$

27. $623 \times 8,451 =$
28. $8,113 \times 924 =$
29. 3,112 and 192 are the factors of what product?
30. What is the product of 1,982 and 1,020?
31. $4 \times 18 \times 36 = ?$
32. What is the product of 764 and 168?
33. Find the product of 517 and 205.
34. What is 617 multiplied by 668?
35. What is 692 multiplied by 921?

DIVISION

36. $23,403 \div 29 =$
37. $4,620 \div 66 =$
38. $1,053 \div 13 =$
39. $35,808 \div 96 =$
40. Find the quotient of 1,024 and 32.

41. $4\overline{)2,836}$

42. $7\overline{)504}$

43. Divide 3,185 by 65.
44. Find the quotient of 8,427 and 53.
45. Divide 0 by 7,642.

A quick note: You can never *divide by 0*. That is, 85 divided by 0 does not exist. You may, however, divide 0 by another number. The quotient in this case will always be 0.

For practice with grid-in boxes, enter your answers to problems 36 through 45 in the grids on the following page.

36.

	/	/	
.	.	.	.
	0	0	0
1	1	1	1
2	2	2	2
3	3	3	3
4	4	4	4
5	5	5	5
6	6	6	6
7	7	7	7
8	8	8	8
9	9	9	9

37.

	/	/	
.	.	.	.
	0	0	0
1	1	1	1
2	2	2	2
3	3	3	3
4	4	4	4
5	5	5	5
6	6	6	6
7	7	7	7
8	8	8	8
9	9	9	9

38.

	/	/	
.	.	.	.
	0	0	0
1	1	1	1
2	2	2	2
3	3	3	3
4	4	4	4
5	5	5	5
6	6	6	6
7	7	7	7
8	8	8	8
9	9	9	9

39.

	/	/	
.	.	.	.
	0	0	0
1	1	1	1
2	2	2	2
3	3	3	3
4	4	4	4
5	5	5	5
6	6	6	6
7	7	7	7
8	8	8	8
9	9	9	9

40.

	/	/	
.	.	.	.
	0	0	0
1	1	1	1
2	2	2	2
3	3	3	3
4	4	4	4
5	5	5	5
6	6	6	6
7	7	7	7
8	8	8	8
9	9	9	9

41.

	/	/	
.	.	.	.
	0	0	0
1	1	1	1
2	2	2	2
3	3	3	3
4	4	4	4
5	5	5	5
6	6	6	6
7	7	7	7
8	8	8	8
9	9	9	9

42.

	/	/	
.	.	.	.
	0	0	0
1	1	1	1
2	2	2	2
3	3	3	3
4	4	4	4
5	5	5	5
6	6	6	6
7	7	7	7
8	8	8	8
9	9	9	9

43.

	/	/	
.	.	.	.
	0	0	0
1	1	1	1
2	2	2	2
3	3	3	3
4	4	4	4
5	5	5	5
6	6	6	6
7	7	7	7
8	8	8	8
9	9	9	9

44.

	/	/	
.	.	.	.
	0	0	0
1	1	1	1
2	2	2	2
3	3	3	3
4	4	4	4
5	5	5	5
6	6	6	6
7	7	7	7
8	8	8	8
9	9	9	9

45.

	/	/	
.	.	.	.
	0	0	0
1	1	1	1
2	2	2	2
3	3	3	3
4	4	4	4
5	5	5	5
6	6	6	6
7	7	7	7
8	8	8	8
9	9	9	9

Quick Tests for Divisibility

Sometimes you do not need to go through the whole process of dividing one number by another to see if it goes in evenly. Being able to determine divisibility by inspection, or with simpler arithmetic such as addition, can save a lot of time and trouble.

A number is
divisible by:

2   if the number ends in 0, 2, 4, 6, or 8. Example: 3,248 is divisible by 2 since it ends in 8; 7,639 is not divisible by 2 since it ends in 9. Any number divisible by 2 is called an *even number*. (If the last digit of a number is 1, 3, 5, 7, or 9, the number is called an *odd number*.)

3   if the sum of the digits of the number is divisible by 3. Example: 1,245 is divisible by 3 since (1) + (2) + (4) + (5) = 12, which is divisible by 3; 175 is not divisible by 3 since (1) + (7) + (5) = 13, which is not divisible by 3.

4   if the last two digits of the number name a number divisible by 4. Example: 23,736 is divisible by 4 since the last two digits (36) name a number divisible by 4 (36 ÷ 4 = 9).

5   if the number ends in 0 or 5. Example: 3,250 is divisible by 5 since it ends in 0; 4,567 is not divisible by 5 since it ends in 7.

6   if the number is divisible by both 3 and 2. Example: 96 is divisible by 2 since it ends in 6, and it is divisible by 3 since (9) + (6) = 15, which is divisible by 3. Since it is divisible by both 3 and 2, it is divisible by 6.

7   No quick rule.

8   if the last three digits of the number name a number divisible by 8. Example: 5,144 is divisible by 8 since the last three digits (144) name a number divisible by 8 (144 ÷ 8 = 18).

9   if the sum of the digits of the number is divisible by 9. Example: 23,571 is divisible by 9 since (2) + (3) + (5) + (7) + (1) = 18, and 18 is divisible by 9.

10   if the last digit is 0.

PRACTICE PROBLEMS

1. Is 114 divisible by 6? How many times?
2. Is 456 divisible by 24?
   Since you don't have a quick rule for 24, factor it into 8 × 3. *If 456 is divisible by 8 and it is divisible by 3, then it is divisible by 8 × 3, which is 24.*
3. Is there a remainder when 112 is divided by 5?
   If there is a remainder, this means one number doesn't go into the other number evenly.
4. Can 718 be divided by 3 evenly?
5. Does 12 divide 204 evenly?
6. Is 69.92 divisible by 8?
7. Is there a remainder when 1,800,091 is divided by 9?
8. Is there a remainder when 7,930 is divided by 20?
9. Is 62,622 divisible by 3?
10. Is 10,848 divisible by 4?

SIGNED NUMBERS

In math we deal with *signed numbers*. A signed number is one with a plus or minus sign in front of it. A *positive* number is one that is greater than zero. It can be preceded by a + sign, but normally the sign is omitted. +3 and 3 name the same number.

A number that is less than zero is a *negative* number. It is always preceded by a – sign. 3 and –3 are sometimes called opposites, or *additive inverses*. The sum of additive inverses is always 0.

Zero is neither positive nor negative.

The *absolute value* of a number *is that number without* a sign in front of it. Using symbols, the absolute value of a number is written $|\,x\,|$ and is read: *The absolute value of x.*

Absolute values are useful when defining how to add, subtract, multiply, or divide signed numbers.

Examples

$$|+4|=4$$
$$|-4|=4$$
$$|0|=0$$

Addition of Signed Numbers

If the signs of the two numbers are the same, *add* their absolute values and keep the sign that is common to them both.

Examples

$(-13)+(-8)\ =\ -21$ (add 13 and 8 and keep the minus sign)
$(+7)+(+11)\ =\ 18$ (add 7 and 11 and keep the plus sign)

If the signs of the two numbers are different, find the difference between the two numbers and *keep the sign of the number with the larger absolute value.*

Examples

Simplify $-12+8$.

Ignoring the signs and finding the difference between the two numbers gives you $12-8$, or 4. Since 12 is greater than 8 and has a negative sign, the answer must have a negative sign. The answer is –4.

Simplify $14+(-6)$.

Ignoring the signs and finding the difference gives you $14-6$, or 8. The greater number is 14, and it is positive, so the answer is positive. The answer is 8.

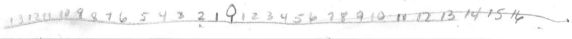

PRACTICE PROBLEMS

1. $(-32)+(-14)=$ -46
2. $26+(-9)=$ $+15$
3. $17+(-28)=$ -11
4. $(-8)+19=$ $+11$
5. $(-137)+(-42)=$ -279

6. $127+(-54)=$ $+73$
7. $(-95)+44=$ -51
8. $(-26)+(-89)=$ -115
9. $144+(-144)=$ 0
10. $(-32)+46+(-53)=$ -39

A good way to add long strings of signed numbers is to first add the positive numbers, then the negative numbers. Then find the difference between the sums of the positive numbers and the negative numbers.

$-85+46$

Example

Add: −15 + 53 − 38 + 73 − 74 − 81 + 13

1. Find the sum of the positive terms.

   53 + 73 + 13 = 139

2. Find the sum of the negative terms.

   (−15) + (−38) + (−74) + (−81) = −208

3. Find the difference between the sums.

   a. 208 − 139 = 69

   b. 208 is the bigger number and 208 is negative, so the answer is −69.

Subtraction of Signed Numbers

Since $x − y$ means $x + (−y)$, subtraction of signed numbers can be defined in terms of addition. To subtract one number (the subtrahend) from another number, change the sign of the subtrahend and proceed using the rules for addition of signed numbers.

Examples

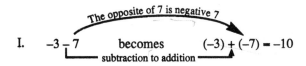

I.   −3 − 7   becomes   (−3) + (−7) = −10

II. (−4) − (−9) is the same as (−4) + (+9) = 5

   (−4) − (+9) is the same as (−4) + (−9) = −13

   (4) − (−9) is the same as (+4) + (+9) = 13

   (4) − (9) is the same as (+4) + (−9) = −5

PRACTICE PROBLEMS

1. 38 − (−76) = ⁺114
2. −17 − (−59) = ⁺42
3. −14 − 32 = ⁺46
4. 73 − (−26) = ⁻99
5. −10 + (+53) = ⁻43

6. −127 − 58 = ⁻185
7. 54 − (−97) = ⁺151
8. 723 − 469 = 254
9. −356 − 227 = ⁻583
10. −445 − (−188) = ⁻257

Multiplication of Signed Numbers

The rules for multiplication of signed numbers are easy to remember. If the signs are the *same*, the product is *positive* and takes a + sign. This rule holds even when two negatives are multiplied, because a *negative times a negative equals a positive*.

   If the signs of the numbers are *different*, then the product is *negative* and takes a − sign.

Examples

3 • 2 = 6	*(Both numbers are positive, so the answer is positive.)*
−4 • 5 = −20	*(One number is negative and one is positive, so the answer is negative.)*
5 • −7 = −35	*(One number is positive and one is negative, so the answer is negative.)*
−6 • −3 = 18	*(Both numbers are negative, so the answer is positive.)*

Division of Signed Numbers

The rules for division of signed numbers are the same as the rules for multiplication. If the numbers have the same sign, the quotient will be positive. If the numbers have different signs, then the quotient will be negative.

Examples

$18 \div 9 = 2$	*(Both numbers are positive, so the answer is positive.)*
$-9 \div 3 = -3$	*(One number is negative and one is positive, so the answer is negative.)*
$24 \div -6 = -4$	*(One number is positive and one is negative, so the answer is negative.)*
$-16 \div -4 = 4$	*(Both numbers are negative, so the answer is positive.)*

PRACTICE PROBLEMS

1. $12 \div (-3) =$ −4
2. $-144 \div 16 =$ −9
3. $-225 \div 15 =$ −15
4. $-484 \div (-4) =$ +121
5. $5,144 \div 8 =$ +643

6. $18 \cdot (-4) =$ −72
7. $-28 \times 3 =$ −84
8. $-16 \times (-15) =$ +240
9. $38 \cdot 14 =$ +532
10. $-17 \cdot (-13) =$ +221

ORDER OF OPERATIONS

To evaluate a numerical expression that involves powers, two or more operations such as addition and multiplication, *or* one or more sets of grouping symbols, you must follow what is called *the order of operations*.

Grouping symbols are used to determine the order of the operation that you are to use when solving a problem.

The grouping symbols that are used in math are parentheses ( ), braces { }, the division symbol or bar ——, and brackets [ ].

The order of operations is as follows:

1.   Simplify any powers.

2.   Simplify the terms within any grouping symbols, starting with the innermost symbols.

3.   Multiply or divide as you move from left to right.

4.   Add or subtract as you move from left to right.

Remember: *My Dear Aunt Sally*
This means that you *m*ultiply or *d*ivide before you do any *a*ddition or *s*ubtraction.

Hot Tip: Remember that terms are separated by + or – signs, and you must simplify each term using the above rules. Always work from left to right. Remember that grouping symbols form *one* term.

Examples

I.	$6 - [28 - (4+2)^2] =$	$6 - [28 - (6)^2]$	*Simplify within the innermost grouping symbol.*
		$= 6 - [28 - 36]$	*Do all powers before addition or subtraction.*
		$= 6 - [-8]$	*Simplify within the brackets.*
		$= 6 + 8 = 14$	*Follow rules for subtraction.*
II.	$-4[12 - 2(8-5)] =$	$-4[12 - 2(3)]$	*Simplify within the innermost grouping symbol.*
		$= -4[12 - 6]$	*Multiply before subtracting.*
		$= -4[6]$	*Simplify within the brackets before multiplying.*
		$= -24$	*Multiply using the rules for signed numbers.*

$11(xy + 3xy + y^2 + 4 + 16 = 4xy + z^2 + 20$

III. $\dfrac{(9+6)\cdot(7-4)}{-7\cdot-3-6} = \dfrac{(15)\cdot(3)}{-7\cdot-3-6}$ *Simplify within parentheses first.*

$= \dfrac{(15)\cdot(3)}{21-6}$ *Multiply before you subtract in the denominator, going from left to right.*

$= \dfrac{45}{15}$ *Multiply the numerator; subtract in the denominator. Divide, using the rules for signed numbers.*

$= 3$

FOIL $(x+1)(y+2) = xy + 2x + 1y + 2$ Answer

PRACTICE PROBLEMS

Use this short problem set to polish your "gridding-in" skills. Practice grids are in Appendix B on pages 462–464.

1. $4(32 - 4) + 6(5 - 22) =$ $112 + 6(-17) = 10$
2. $3 \cdot 4 - 5 + 4 \div 2 =$ 9
3. $32 - [8 - (20 - 42)] =$ 12
4. $3(7 - 4)^2 =$ 27
5. $6(7 - 3[5 - 2 \cdot (6 - 4)]) =$ 144

6. $\dfrac{42 - 4^2}{5 - 3} =$ 13
7. $12 + 4 \div 4 - 2 \div (3 - 5) =$ 14
8. $[4 - (3 - 22)][42 - 3 \cdot 2 + 1] =$
9. $24 - [3 \cdot 32 - (2 + 4)^2] =$
10. $3 \times 8 - 4 \div 2 + 3 =$ 19

$[4 - (3 - 22)][42 - 3 \cdot 2 + 1] =$
$4 - (-19)][42 - 6 + 1]$
$[4 + 19]$ 37
$(23)(37) = 851$

$\dfrac{34\frac{2}{6}}{36}$

$\dfrac{1\frac{22}{3}}{19}$

Lesson 2

Goal: To review basic operations with polynomials.

0

POLYNOMIALS

$\dfrac{32}{\frac{41}{32}}$ MOAS $\dfrac{19\frac{2}{5}}{17}$ $\dfrac{32}{\times 4}$ 128

Remember These Terms?

Variable—A letter or symbol that can represent any number from a specified set.

Monomial—A single number, a variable, or a product of factors consisting of numbers and variables. Monomial means one term.

Examples of monomials: 4, x, $3xy$, $[2x + 1]$, $(4y + 3)$.

Binomial—Two monomials separated by a plus or minus sign.

Examples of binomials: $x + 3$, $x^2 - 4$, $(x + 1)^2 + y^3$.

Trinomial—Three terms, or monomials, separated by plus or minus signs.

Examples of trinomials: $x + y + z$, $x - 2xy + y^2$.

Monomials, binomials, and trinomials fall under the general heading of *polynomials*.

Numerical coefficient—The number in front of the variable.

Base—That which is being raised to a power.

Exponent—The power. It tells you how many times the base is to be used as a factor.

Example: $x^3 = x \cdot x \cdot x$.

$4(32 - 4) + 6(5 - 22) =$
$4(32) + 6(-17) =$
$128 + 6(-17)$

262   Math for SATs and PSATs/Unit 6

Example of numerical coefficient, base, and exponent combined:

$$3x^5 \begin{cases} 3 \text{ is the numerical coefficient.} \\ x \text{ is the base.} \\ 5 \text{ is the exponent.} \end{cases}$$

One of the most important laws in dealing with polynomials is the distributive law. It allows you to get rid of parentheses and convert messy equations into polynomials. The distributive law says that:

(1) $a(b + c) = ab + ac$ and

(2) $a(b - c) = ab - ac$

Examples

Using the distributive law, get rid of the parentheses and then simplify these expressions.

I. $3t(x + 2yz) = 3tx + 6tyz$ *Distribute the 3t over each monomial inside the parentheses.*

II. $-4(2xy - 5t)$

     1. $(-4 \cdot 2xy) - (-4 \cdot 5t)$ *Distribute the –4 over each monomial inside the parentheses.*

     2. $-8xy - (-20t)$ *Do the multiplication.*

     3. $-8xy + 20t$ *Follow the rules for subtracting signed numbers.*

ADDITION AND SUBTRACTION OF POLYNOMIALS

The key to addition and subtraction of two polynomials is remembering that only monomials with *identical variables and exponents*—usually referred to as "like" or "similar" terms—may be combined. To combine similar monomials, you need to *combine only their numerical coefficients. The variables and exponents remain unchanged.*

Examples

I. Find the sum of $(4z + 3xy)$ and $(7z + 4xy)$.

     1. $(4z + 3xy) + (7z + 4xy)$ *Write out the expression.*

     2. $4z + 7z + 3xy + 4xy$ *Get rid of the parentheses and rearrange.*

     3. $11z + 7xy$ *Add the numerical coefficients of the like terms.*

II. Find the difference between $(26r^2st^3)$ and $(7r^2st^3)$.

     1. $26r^2st^3 - 7r^2st^3$ *Write out the expression.*

     2. $26(r^2st^3) - 7(r^2st^3)$ *Sometimes adding parentheses will simplify a complex-looking problem.*

     3. $19r^2st^3$ *Combine like terms.*

III. Find the difference between $(2x^2 - 2x - 5)$ and $(x^2 + 8x + 12)$.

     1. $(2x^2 - 2x - 5) - (x^2 + 8x + 12)$ *Write out the expression.*

     2. $2x^2 - 2x - 5 - x^2 - 8x - 12$ *Get rid of the parentheses. Remember that a subtraction sign in front of parentheses will change the signs of all of the terms inside the parentheses, which must then be added to the other terms in the polynomial.*
$(2x^2 - 2x - 5) - (x^2 + 8x + 12)$ *becomes*
$(2x^2 - 2x - 5) + (-x^2 - 8x - 12)$.

     3. $2x^2 - x^2 - 2x - 8x - 5 - 12$ *Rearrange the equation so like terms are next to one another.*

     4. $x^2 - 10x - 17$ *Combine like terms.*

Note: When you get rid of the parentheses, you must change the sign of every term within the parentheses if the parentheses have a minus sign in front. Example: $x - (5 - x)$ becomes $x - 5 + x = 2x - 5$.

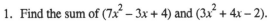

PRACTICE PROBLEMS

1. Find the sum of $(7x^2 - 3x + 4)$ and $(3x^2 + 4x - 2)$.
2. Add $(3rp + 4rs + 8ps)$ to $3(5rp - 6rs - 6ps)$.
3. Subtract $-4(5ab + 6a^2)$ from $-6(2ab - b^2)$.
4. Find the sum of $-4(2xy + 4x^2)$ and $-6(-2x^2 - 3xy)$.
5. Simplify $3(x^2 + 2xy + y^2) - 2(x^2 - y^2) + (x^2 - 2xy + y^2)$.
6. Simplify $10x - 2[3x - (x - 2) + 3(x + 3)]$.

7. Simplify $(4x - 5y + 8) + (3 - 2x - 4y)$.
8. Simplify $(x^3y - 2xy^2 + 3xy) - (4xy^2 - 3x^3y + 2xy)$.
9. Simplify $(p^4 - 2p^3 - 3p^2 + 7p + 1) + 2(p^3 - 3p^2 - 4p + 6)$.
10. Simplify $-3(x^2 - 5x) - 2(3x - 2x^2 + 5)$.

MULTIPLICATION OF POLYNOMIALS

Multiplication of polynomials is also done monomial by monomial, but each term *does not need to be similar*. To multiply one polynomial by another, *multiply each term of the one polynomial by each term of the other.*

Remember when multiplying terms to multiply the numerical coefficients, and, if the bases are the same, you add the exponents.

Examples

I. $x^5 \bullet x^3 = x^{5+3} = x^8$

II. $2x^3y \bullet 3xy^5 = (2 \bullet 3)(x^3x^1)(y^1y^5) = 6x^4y^6$

III. $6ab^2 \bullet 3xy = (6 \bullet 3)(ab^2)(xy) = 18ab^2xy$

To multiply a polynomial by a monomial, simply multiply each term of the polynomial by the monomial.

Examples

I. $3x(2x + 4) = (3x \bullet 2x) + (3x \bullet 4) = 6x^2 + 12x$

II. $-5a^2b(3a + 4b - 2) = (-5a^2b)(3a) + (-5a^2b)(4b) + (-5a^2b)(-2) = -15a^3b - 20a^2b^2 + 10a^2b$

You are not likely to be asked to multiply anything more difficult than two binomials (polynomials with two terms) together on the SAT. A way of making sure you do not skip any of the terms while doing the multiplication is to set the binomials side by side and "FOIL" (an acronym meaning *F*irst, *O*uter, *I*nner, *L*ast) them. That is, multiply the *first* two terms of each binomial together, the *outer* two, the *inner* two, and the *last* two. Then combine any similar terms.

Examples

I. Find the product of $(n + 5)$ and $(n + 3)$.

$(n + 5)\ (n + 3)$ *Set up the two polynomials side by side and FOIL.*

$n^2 + 3n + 5n + 15$ *Add the four partial products.*
$n^2 + 8n + 15$ *Add the like terms.*

II. Multiply $(y - 3)$ by $(y + 6)$.

$(y + 3)\ (y + 6)$ *FOIL the polynomials.*

$y^2 + 6y - 3y - 18$ *List the four partial products.*
$y^2 + 3y - 18$ *Combine the similar terms: $(6y - 3y) = 3y$.*

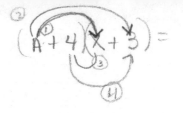

III. Find the product of $(3a + b)$ and $(c - d)$.

FOIL

$(3a + b)(c - d)$ *Write the binomials side by side and FOIL.*

$3ac + (-3ad) + bc + (-bd)$ *Add the partial products, making sure to treat d as a negative.*

$3ac - 3ad + bc - bd$ *Get rid of the parentheses and change the appropriate signs. Notice that there are no similar terms so you cannot combine any terms.*

FOIL

PRACTICE PROBLEMS

1. $3a(5a + 4) =$ $15A^2 + 12A$
2. $-2x^2(3x^3 - 2x^2 - 4x + 3) =$
3. $-8xy^2(2x - 3y - 4) =$
4. $3x^2yz^3(2xy - yz + 5x^2z^2) =$ Don't try
5. $(x^3y^4z^5)(3x^8yz^3) =$ SKIP

6. $(x + 3)(x + 3) =$ $x^2 + 3x + 3x + 9$
7. $(2x - 1)(3x + 4) =$ $6x^2 + 8x - 3x - 4$
8. $(3xy + 2z)(2xy - z) =$ $6x^2y^2 - 3xyz + 4xyz - 2z^2$
9. $(6x - 4)(3x^2 - 5x + 2) =$
10. $(5x - 2y)(3x + 8y) =$ $15x^2 + 40xy - 6xy - 16y^2$

$15x^2 + 34xy - 16y^2$

DIVISION OF POLYNOMIALS

To divide a monomial by a monomial, you divide the numerical coefficients, and, if the bases are the same, you subtract the exponents.

Examples

I. $\dfrac{6x^3}{2x^2} = \dfrac{6x^{3-2}}{2} = 3x$

II. $\dfrac{7x^5y^7}{3x^2y^4} = \dfrac{7x^{5-2}y^{7-4}}{3} = \dfrac{7x^3y^3}{3}$

III. $\dfrac{12x^2}{3y^3} = \dfrac{4x^2}{y^3}$

$3A(5A + 4)$

$15A^2 + 12A$

$3A(5A + 4)$ $15A^2 + 12A$

To divide a polynomial by a monomial, divide each term of the polynomial by the monomial.

Examples

I. $\dfrac{3x^3 + 9x^2 - 27x}{3x} = \dfrac{3x^3}{3x} + \dfrac{9x^2}{3x} - \dfrac{27x}{3x} = x^2 + 3x - 9$

II. $\dfrac{16x^4y^3 - 32x^2y^5}{4xy^3} = \dfrac{16x^4y^3}{4xy^3} - \dfrac{32x^2y^5}{4xy^3} = 4x^3 - 8xy^2$

PRACTICE PROBLEMS

1. $81x^6y^5 + -27x^3y =$
2. $-144a^3b^2c^5 + 30ac^4 =$
3. $18x^2 + 3x =$
4. $12x^3y^2 + 4xy =$
5. Divide $4x^2y^3$ into $(-12x^5y^8 + 8x^3y^6)$.

6. Find the quotient of $(36a^3b^4 - 24a^4b^3 + 8a^2b^2) \div 2ab^2$.
7. Divide r^2s into $(r^4s^2 - 2rs)$.
8. Divide $(54a^7b^9 - 27a^6b^5)$ by $3a^3b^3$.
9. Find the quotient of $(12a^8b - 8ab^2) \div 4ab$.
10. $(6xy + 9y^2) + 3xy =$

PRACTICE SAT PROBLEMS

1. Simplify $-4 + 16 + (-17)$.
   (A) -35 (B) 1 (C) -5 (D) -1 (E) 5

2. Simplify $-(35 + 16) + 40$.
   (A) 11 (B) 16 (C) -11 (D) 21 (E) 59

3. Simplify $-3(4 - 8)$.
   (A) -12 (B) -36 (C) 36 (D) 12 (E) 18

4. Simplify $-24 \div -6 - 2$.
   (A) -2 (B) 3 (C) -3 (D) 2 (E) 4

5. Simplify $|-6| + |6|$.
   (A) 0 (B) -36 (C) 36 (D) 12 (E) -12

6. Simplify $10\left(4 + \dfrac{10 - 4}{2}\right)$.

   (A) 50 (B) 56 (C) 70 (D) 54 (E) 100

7. Simplify $5xy^2 \cdot 2x^3y^0$.
   (A) $7x^3y^0$ (B) $7x^4y$ (C) $10x^3y^2$ (D) 10^4y (E) $10x^4y^2$

8. Simplify $(x - 2)(2x + 3)$.
   (A) $2x^2 + x - 6$ (B) $2x^2 - 6$ (C) $2x^2 - x - 6$ (D) $2x^2 + 6$ (E) $2x^2 - 5x - 6$

9. Simplify $2x^2 - x + 5 - (x^2 + 3x - 3)$.
   (A) $x^2 + 2x + 8$ (B) $x^2 + 4x - 4$ (C) $x^2 - 4x + 4$ (D) $x^2 - 2x + 4$ (E) $x^2 - 4x + 8$

10. Find the sum of $4x^2 - 6x + 3$ and $4x^2 - 2x - 6$.
    (A) $8x^2 - 8x + 7$ (B) $8x^2 - 8x - 3$ (C) $8x^2 - 6x - 3$ (D) $8x^2 + 6x + 3$ (E) $8x^2 + 8x + 7$

11. $(18x^2y^3 - 48x^4y^2 + 27x^3y^4) \div (-3xy^2) =$
    (A) $6xy^2 + 16x^3 - 9x^2y^2$ (B) $-6xy + 16x^3y - 9x^2y^2$ (C) $-6xy + 16x^3 - 9x^2y^2$ (D) $6xy + 16x^3 + 9x^2y^2$
    (E) $-6xy + 16x^3 + 9x^2y^2$

12. Simplify $\dfrac{.2 + .2 + .2 + .2 + .2}{5}$.

    (A) .02 (B) .125 (C) .1 (D) 1 (E) .2

13. Subtract $(2x^2 - 3x - 4)$ from $(6x^2 - 4x + 7)$.
    (A) $8x^2 - x + 3$ (B) $4x^2 - x + 11$ (C) $-4x^2 + x - 11$ (D) $4x^2 - 7x + 3$ (E) $4x^2 - x + 3$

14. Find the quotient of $(15p^2q^2 - 5pq^3 + 10p) \div (5pq)$.
    (A) $3pq - pq^2 + 2q$ (B) $3pq - q^2 + 2q$ (C) $3pq - q^2 + \dfrac{2}{q}$ (D) $3pq + q^2 + \dfrac{2}{pq}$ (E) $3pq - q^2 + \dfrac{2}{pq}$

15. Simplify $2(3A - 4B + C) - 3(A - 2B - 3C)$.
    (A) $-3A - 14B + 11C$ (B) $3A - 2B - 7C$ (C) $3A - 2B - 2C$ (D) $3A - 2B + 11C$ (E) $3A - 2B + 9C$

Lesson 3

Goal: To be able to solve linear equations and set up and solve word problems.

SOLVING LINEAR EQUATIONS

SUBSTITUTION

There are two methods of solving linear equations. The first is substitution, and the second is juggling.

Substitution consists of being given *two equal quantities and replacing one by the other every time the equal quantity appears.* After having done this, you will have one less quantity and a much simpler equation to deal with.

Example

If $a = b$ and $(a + b) = 36$, then $a =$

1.	$(a + b) = 36$	*Given*
2.	$(a + a) = 36$	*Since $a = b$, every time you see b, you may put a in for it.*
3.	$(2a) = 36$	*$a + a = 2a$*
4.	$a = 18$	*Divide both sides by 2.*

JUGGLING EQUATIONS

An equation rarely starts out the way you want it, so most of the time you will need to juggle the different terms of each equation around until you get it into the form you need.

An equal sign is like a balance. As long as you do the *same thing to both sides of the equation, the equation remains the same.* The seven types of juggling you may need to do are to divide both sides by the same number, multiply both sides by the same number, add the same number to both sides, subtract the same number from both sides, square both sides, take the square root of both sides, and invert both sides.

> The steps to use in solving a linear equation are:
> 1. Eliminate any parentheses, brackets, or braces.
> 2. Collect like terms.
> 3. Transform the equation into an equivalent equation by moving the variable that you are solving for to one side of the equation and everything else to the other side.
> 4. Divide both sides by the coefficient of the variable that you are solving for.

Examples

1. Solve for x in the problem $4x - 5 = 7$.

$4x = 12$	*Add 5 to both sides.*
$x = 13$	*Divide both sides by 4.*

2. Solve for x in the problem $\frac{1}{3}x - 5 = \frac{1}{4}x - 2$.

$4x - 60 = 3x - 24$	*Multiply every term on both sides by 12 (the common denominator).*
$x - 60 = -24$	*Subtract 3x from both sides.*
$x = 36$	*Add 60 to both sides.*

3. Solve for z in the problem $\dfrac{z}{2}+\dfrac{z}{5}=\dfrac{7}{10}$.

$$10\left(\dfrac{z}{2}\right)+10\left(\dfrac{z}{5}\right)=10\left(\dfrac{7}{10}\right)$$ *Multiply both sides by the common denominator 10.*

$\quad\quad 5z+2z=7$ *Do the multiplication.*

$\quad\quad\quad\; 7z=7$ *Combine the similar terms.*

$\quad\quad\quad\;\; z=1$ *Divide both sides by 7.*

4. Solve for p in the problem $\dfrac{p}{3}+\dfrac{p}{5}+\dfrac{p}{6}=7$.

$10p+6p+5p=210$ *Multiply both sides by the common denominator 30.*

$\quad\quad 21p=210$ *Combine similar terms.*

$\quad\quad\quad p=10$ *Divide both sides by 21.*

5. Solve for z in the problem $\dfrac{7z+5}{4z}=8$.

$7z+5=32z$ *Multiply both sides by 4z.*

$\quad\; 5=25z$ *Subtract 7z from both sides.*

$\dfrac{1}{5}=z$ *Divide both sides by 25.*

6. Solve for w in the problem $\dfrac{5}{w-6}+\dfrac{7}{6-w}=2$.

$\dfrac{5}{w-6}+\dfrac{-7}{w-6}=2$ *Multiply the numerator and denominator of the second fraction by –1. (Remember: multiplying the numerator and denominator of a fraction by the same number does not change the value of the fraction.)*

$\dfrac{-2}{w-6}=2$ *Add the fractions.*

$-2=2w-12$ *Multiply both sides by (w – 6).*

$\;\; 10=2w$ *Add 12 to both sides.*

$\quad\; 5=w$ *Divide both sides by 2.*

7. Solve for x in the problem $6(x+1)=3(x+10)$.

$6x+6=3x+30$ *Eliminate the parentheses by multiplying.*

$3x+6=30$ *Subtract 3x from both sides.*

$\quad 3x=24$ *Subtract 6 from both sides.*

$\quad\; x=8$ *Divide both sides by 3.*

8. Solve for y in the problem $6(2y+3)-3(y+1)=3(y+1)+3$.

$12y+18-3y-3=3y+3+3$ *Eliminate the parentheses.*

$9y+15=3y+6$ *Collect like terms on both sides of the equation.*

$6y+15=6$ *Subtract 3y from both sides.*

$\quad 6y=-9$ *Subtract 15 from both sides.*

$y=\dfrac{-9}{6}=\dfrac{-3}{2}$ *Divide by 6 and reduce the fraction to lowest terms.*

9. Solve for m in the problem $\dfrac{1}{m}+\dfrac{1}{n}=\dfrac{1}{p}$.

$np+mp=mn$ *Multiply both sides by the common denominator mnp.*

$np=mn-mp$ *Get all of the m's on the same side by subtracting mp from both sides.*

$np=m(n-p)$ *Use the distributive law.*

$\dfrac{np}{n-p}=m$ *Divide both sides by (n – p).*

Note: You cannot just invert every element of both sides if the elements are separated by a + or – sign. That is, the equation does *not* imply $m+n=p$.

Remember that an answer can be represented in more than one way. If you're fairly sure you did a problem correctly, check to see if the answer you got is the same as one of the answer choices given for the problem, *but in a different form.*

For example, you may have solved a problem and gotten $\dfrac{2m}{a} - L$ as an answer and you're sure it is correct. On the test, however, the correct answer is given as $\dfrac{2m - aL}{a}$. Who's correct? You both are. $\dfrac{2m}{a} - L$ and $\dfrac{2m - aL}{a}$ are the same value written in different forms.

Don't forget the "working backward" technique:
If you're stumped on one of these problems, pick one of the answers and plug it in.

PRACTICE PROBLEMS

1. Solve for x: $\dfrac{2x}{3} + \dfrac{5}{6} = \dfrac{x}{6}$

   (A) $\dfrac{5}{3}$ (B) -1 (C) $\dfrac{-5}{3}$ (D) 1 (E) -5

2. Solve for x: $4x - 6\left(3 - \dfrac{1}{2}x\right) = 10$

   (A) 28 (B) 4 (C) 18 (D) 2 (E) 6

3. Solve for y: $4(y - 3) + 1 = 2(y + 4) - 3$
   (A) -5 (B) 2 (C) 8 (D) 12 (E) -8

4. If $\dfrac{1}{x+y} = 2$, then $y =$

   (A) $\dfrac{1}{2} - x$ (B) $-x$ (C) $1 - 2x$ (D) $\dfrac{1}{2} + x$ (E) $1 + 2x$

5. If $E = IR$, then $R =$

   (A) EI (B) $E - I$ (C) $E + I$ (D) $\dfrac{I}{E}$ (E) $\dfrac{E}{I}$

6. If $\dfrac{p + q + r}{3} = \dfrac{p + q}{2}$, then $r =$

   (A) $q + p$ (B) $2p + 2q$ (C) $\dfrac{1}{2}(p + q)$ (D) 1 (E) 3

7. If $a + b = 3$, then $a + b - 6 =$
   (A) -3 (B) 0 (C) 3 (D) 6 (E) 1

8. If $a = b - c$ and $d = c - b$, what is the value of $d - a$ when $b = 4$ and $c = -4$?
   (A) 0 (B) 8 (C) -8 (D) 16 (E) -16

9. Solve for v if $\dfrac{3}{u} + \dfrac{4}{v} = 1$.

   (A) $\dfrac{4u}{u - 3}$ (B) $\dfrac{12 - 4u}{3}$ (C) $7 - u$ (D) $\dfrac{1 - 4u}{3}$

   (E) $\dfrac{3u}{u - 4}$

10. If $7x - 4y = 7$ and $x = \dfrac{3}{7}y$, then $x =$
   (A) -7 (B) -5 (C) -3 (D) 5 (E) 7

WORD PROBLEMS

Just the phrase "word problem" seems to make more people run and stick their heads in the sand than any other phrase in math. But a word problem translates into an equation, and you can get very good at turning words into equations by working this section of the text. It is *practice,* yes, but it's practice that works!

There is no *one* kind of word problem because they deal with anything from basic arithmetic to working with two equations in two unknowns. But there *is* one factor common to all word problems: it's your job to *rewrite the problem in algebraic symbols.* To do this, you must look for key words that clue you in—words that tell you what operations will be used and how the equation must be set up.

The most important key words are those that represent the $=$ sign. Remember, to have an equation, you *must have* an equal sign.

Example

The sum of 3 and an unknown number represented by x is 5. ☐

Rewritten algebraically this becomes: $3 + x$ 5

Translating Words and Phrases into Algebraic Symbols

Word or Phrase	Symbol	Written Example	Algebraic Result
is	=	The sum of unknown number and 3 $\boxed{\text{is}}$ 5.	$x + 3 = 5$
is the same as	=	$\frac{1}{4}$ of one number $\boxed{\text{is the same as}}$ $\frac{1}{5}$ of another.	$\frac{1}{4}x = \frac{1}{5}y$
is equal to	=	4 $\boxed{\text{is equal to}}$ $\frac{1}{10}$ of what number?	$4 = \frac{1}{10}x$
sum	+	The $\boxed{\text{sum}}$ of two numbers is 5.	$x + y = 5$
increase	+	By what must I $\boxed{\text{increase}}$ 5 to equal 7?	$5 + x = 7$
added	+	What must be $\boxed{\text{added}}$ to 9 to equal 14?	$9 + x = 14$
received	+	John $\boxed{\text{received}}$ 5 apples to give him a total of 10. How many did he start with?	$5 + x = 10$
more	+	How much $\boxed{\text{more}}$ is 7 than –3?	$-3 + ? = 7$
decreased	–	A budget of \$10.00 is $\boxed{\text{decreased}}$ by 5%.	$10 - \frac{5}{100}(10) = ?$
subtracted	–	–6 is $\boxed{\text{subtracted}}$ from 7	$7 - (-6) = ?$
of	× or •	5% $\boxed{\text{of}}$ z	$\frac{5}{100}(z) = ?$
product	× or •	What is the $\boxed{\text{product}}$ of 5 and 4?	$5 \times 4 = ?$
idea of containment	÷	How many 4-cubic-inch boxes $\boxed{\text{can fit into}}$ a 16-cubic-inch box?	$16 \div 4 = ?$
divided	÷	What is 6 $\boxed{\text{divided}}$ by 2?	$6 \div 2 = ?$

Note: This list is not complete, and probably no list could be. In each problem you do, words can have different meanings. That is why you should read carefully to see what each question is asking.

Another key word that comes up often is *consecutive,* meaning *in order. Three consecutive integers* are any three numbers that occur naturally in a row. For example, 3, 4, and 5 are three consecutive integers.

Consecutive odd or *consecutive even integers* are taken in jumps of two.

Examples

> 1, 3, and 5 are three consecutive odd integers.
> 4, 6, and 8 are three consecutive even integers.

Once you have spotted the key words, figure out exactly what you're solving for. Give this value a variable name, such as x. If it's height you're solving for, you might want to use an h instead. It doesn't matter what variable you use as long as you use the *same one* throughout the problem.

Next, set up the equation. Break the problem up into as many small phrases as you find necessary. Each phrase should have you doing only *one step.* Rewrite each phrase algebraically, *one at a time.*

Finally, check yourself—plug the answer back into the problem—does it work? If not, did you set your equations up correctly? Is what you solved for what you were asked to solve for?

Summary of Word Problem Steps

(1) Define what you are solving for.

(2) Set up the equation.

(3) Solve the equation.

(4) Check your answer.

Examples

I. A storage tank is $\frac{1}{4}$ full. When 5 gallons are removed, the tank will be $\frac{1}{5}$ full. How many gallons does the tank hold when it is full?

1. Call the capacity of the tank c (for capacity).

2. Set up the equation: Think:

    a. $\frac{1}{4} c$ A storage tank is $\frac{1}{4}$ full

    b. $\frac{1}{4} c - 5$ When 5 gallons *are removed* . . .

    c. $\frac{1}{4} c - 5 =$ *will be* (a phrase that is the same as *is*) . . .

    d. $\frac{1}{4} c - 5 = \frac{1}{5} c$ $\frac{1}{5}$ *full.*

3. Solve the equation:

    a. $5c - 100 = 4c$ *Multiply both sides by 20 (a common denominator).*

    b. $c - 100 = 0$ *Subtract 4c from both sides.*

    c. $c = 100$ *Add 100 to both sides.*

4. Check the answer:

    A storage tank is $\frac{1}{4}$ full: $\frac{1}{4} \times 100 = 25$ gallons. When 5 gallons are removed (or $25 - 5 = 20$ gallons)

    the tank will be $\frac{1}{5}$ full: $\frac{1}{5} \times 100 = 20$ gallons.

    20 gallons = 20 gallons (the answer's right!)

II. Three consecutive odd numbers have a sum of 99. What is the largest of the numbers?

1. Call the first number n.
    This means that the three consecutive odd numbers are n, $(n + 2)$, and $(n + 4)$. Notice that even though the numbers are odd they are still taken in jumps of two.

2. Write the equation: Think:

    a. $n, n + 2, n + 4$ Three consecutive odd numbers . . .

    b. $(n) + (n + 2) + (n + 4) =$ have a sum of . . .

    c. $(n) + (n + 2) + (n + 4) = 99$ 99.

3. Solve for n:

    a. $3n + 6 = 99$ *Get rid of the parentheses.*

    b. $3n = 93$ *Subtract 6 from both sides.*

    c. $n = 31$ *Divide both sides by 3.*

4. The three consecutive odd integers are 31, 33, and 35. Adding them does indeed give 99. The *largest* is 35, so 35 is the correct answer. (Putting 31 is a common mistake! Make sure you always answer what is asked.)

III. $72 is to be divided among Michael, Paul, and Susan in such a way that Michael receives 5 times as much as Susan and Paul receives 3 times as much as Susan. How much does Paul receive?

    1. Define the variables:

       a. Call S the amount Susan receives

       b. Michael receives $5S$

       c. Paul receives $3S$

    2. Set up the equation: Think:

       a. $72 =$ 72 is . . .

       b. $72 = S + 3S + 5S$ among Michael, Paul, and Susan

    3. Solve the equation:

       a. $72 = 9S$ *Combine terms.*

       b. $8 = S$ *Divide both sides by 9.*

    4. Since Paul receives 3 times as much as Susan, and Susan receives $8, Paul receives $24. Again, be sure not to put $8 as your answer. Also note that no one asked how much money Michael would get, even though you now know that he got $5S$ or $40.

IV. Six years ago I was half the age I will be in six years. How old am I?

    1. Define the variables.

       a. Call my age *now x*.

       b. Six years ago my age was $x - 6$.

       c. In 6 years my age will be $x + 6$.

    2. Set up the equation: Think:

       a. $(x - 6) =$ Six years ago I was . . .

       b. $(x - 6) = \dfrac{1}{2}$ half . . .

       c. $(x - 6) = \dfrac{1}{2}(x + 6)$ the age I will be in 6 years.

    3. Solve the equation $(x - 6) = \dfrac{1}{2}(x + 6)$:

       a. $2(x - 6) = (x + 6)$ *Multiply both sides by 2.*

       b. $2x - 12 = x + 6$ *Get rid of the parentheses.*

       c. $x - 12 = 6$ *Subtract x from both sides.*

       d. $x = 18$ *Add 12 to both sides.*

    4. Thus 6 years ago I was 12, which is half of what I will be in 6 years—24—and I am now 18.

Usually the last few (maybe only two?) problems on the SAT are complicated. Sometimes it is because of the ideas involved, but often they are word problems with many little twists. By *breaking up the problems* into steps as shown, you should have a much easier time.

PRACTICE PROBLEMS

1. If a woman is paid c dollars per hour for every hour she works up to 8 hours and is paid double for every hour she works after 8 hours, how many dollars will she be paid for working 13 hours?

    (A) $13c$ (B) $\dfrac{13}{c}$ (C) $\dfrac{c}{18}$ (D) $18c$ (E) $\dfrac{18}{c}$

2. A number is multiplied by another number. The product is then divided by the difference between the two numbers. What is the result?

    (A) $\dfrac{xy}{x-y}$ (B) $\dfrac{x+y}{x-y}$ (C) $\dfrac{x-y}{xy}$ (D) $\dfrac{xy}{x+y}$ (E) $\dfrac{x-y}{x+y}$

3. Bill had x dollars and he bought y apples for 16 cents each and z pears for 12 cents each. How many cents did he have left?
    (A) $x - 16y + 12z$ (B) $100x - 6y + 12z$ (C) $x - 16y - 12z$ (D) $x - (y+z)$ (E) $100x - 16y - 12z$

4. If 3 is subtracted from a certain number, then the result is 6 more than twice the number. Find the number.

    (A) -3 (B) -9 (C) 3 (D) $\dfrac{9}{7}$ (E) $\dfrac{-9}{7}$

5. How many 29-cent stamps can be purchased for d dollars?

    (A) $29d$ (B) $\dfrac{d}{29}$ (C) $\dfrac{29}{d}$ (D) $\dfrac{100d}{29}$ (E) $\dfrac{29}{100d}$

For problems 6–20 enter your solutions into the grids that follow the questions.

---

6. On a given day in February, the temperature in a town ranged from –12 to 19 degrees. What is the difference between the high and the low temperature for the day?

7. Four years ago my age was half of what it will be in eight years. How old am I?

8. Chris and Andrea have $100.00 together. If Chris gives Andrea $10.00, she will have 20 more dollars than he will. How many dollars did Chris start with?

9. One quarter of the students at a high school take algebra. One fifth of the students take geometry. The remaining 110 students do not take any math. How many students are there at the school?

10. The sum of five consecutive integers is equal to 3 times the largest. What is the largest of the integers?

11. A man goes to a bank with $4.00 and asks for change. He is given an equal number of nickels, dimes, and quarters. How many of each is he given?

12. The difference between the squares of two numbers is 9. The difference between the two numbers is 1. What is their sum?

13. The volume of a box is 24 cubic inches. If its length is 3 inches and its width is 8 inches, what is its depth?

14. One third the sum of 13 and a certain number is the same as one more than twice the number. Find the number.

15. Tom has a brother one third his age and a sister three times his age. If the combined ages of all three children is five less than twice the oldest, how old is Tom?

16. A woman leaves one fourth of her estate to her son and one third of her estate to her daughter. If she leaves the balance of $1,000 to charity, how large was her estate in dollars?

17. A woman buys a pound of steak for $3.00. If the meat loses one fourth of its weight when cooked, what is the cost in dollars per pound when it is served at the table?

18. A gas tank that is $\dfrac{1}{3}$ full requires 6 gallons to make it $\dfrac{5}{6}$ full. What is the capacity of the tank in gallons?

19. The sum of five consecutive odd integers exceeds three times the largest by 6. Find the sum of the integers.

20. Ten houses line one side of a street. The average space between houses is 60 feet more than the average width of each house. A sidewalk starts 60 feet before the first house and ends 60 feet after the last house. If the total length of the sidewalk is 3,206 feet, find the average width of each house in feet.

6.

	/	/	
.	.	.	.
	0	0	0
1	1	1	1
2	2	2	2
3	3	3	3
4	4	4	4
5	5	5	5
6	6	6	6
7	7	7	7
8	8	8	8
9	9	9	9

7.

	/	/	
.	.	.	.
	0	0	0
1	1	1	1
2	2	2	2
3	3	3	3
4	4	4	4
5	5	5	5
6	6	6	6
7	7	7	7
8	8	8	8
9	9	9	9

8.

	/	/	
.	.	.	.
	0	0	0
1	1	1	1
2	2	2	2
3	3	3	3
4	4	4	4
5	5	5	5
6	6	6	6
7	7	7	7
8	8	8	8
9	9	9	9

9.

	/	/	
.	.	.	.
	0	0	0
1	1	1	1
2	2	2	2
3	3	3	3
4	4	4	4
5	5	5	5
6	6	6	6
7	7	7	7
8	8	8	8
9	9	9	9

10.

	/	/	
.	.	.	.
	0	0	0
1	1	1	1
2	2	2	2
3	3	3	3
4	4	4	4
5	5	5	5
6	6	6	6
7	7	7	7
8	8	8	8
9	9	9	9

11.

	/	/	
.	.	.	.
	0	0	0
1	1	1	1
2	2	2	2
3	3	3	3
4	4	4	4
5	5	5	5
6	6	6	6
7	7	7	7
8	8	8	8
9	9	9	9

12.

	/	/	
.	.	.	.
	0	0	0
1	1	1	1
2	2	2	2
3	3	3	3
4	4	4	4
5	5	5	5
6	6	6	6
7	7	7	7
8	8	8	8
9	9	9	9

13.

	/	/	
.	.	.	.
	0	0	0
1	1	1	1
2	2	2	2
3	3	3	3
4	4	4	4
5	5	5	5
6	6	6	6
7	7	7	7
8	8	8	8
9	9	9	9

14.

	/	/	
.	.	.	.
	0	0	0
1	1	1	1
2	2	2	2
3	3	3	3
4	4	4	4
5	5	5	5
6	6	6	6
7	7	7	7
8	8	8	8
9	9	9	9

15.

	/	/	
.	.	.	.
	0	0	0
1	1	1	1
2	2	2	2
3	3	3	3
4	4	4	4
5	5	5	5
6	6	6	6
7	7	7	7
8	8	8	8
9	9	9	9

16.

	/	/	
.	.	.	.
	0	0	0
1	1	1	1
2	2	2	2
3	3	3	3
4	4	4	4
5	5	5	5
6	6	6	6
7	7	7	7
8	8	8	8
9	9	9	9

17.

	/	/	
.	.	.	.
	0	0	0
1	1	1	1
2	2	2	2
3	3	3	3
4	4	4	4
5	5	5	5
6	6	6	6
7	7	7	7
8	8	8	8
9	9	9	9

18.

19.

20.

Lesson 4

Goal: To be able to solve inequalities.

SOLVING INEQUALITIES

An equality or equation is shown by an = sign. An *inequality* is shown by a *less than* sign or a *greater than* sign.

Examples

$3 < 5$ Three is *less than* five.
$6 > 0$ Six is *greater than* zero.

If you have trouble remembering in which direction the sign points, notice that the smaller end points to the smaller number and the bigger end is open to the bigger number.

Just as with equalities, you may meet problems dealing with inequalities that you must juggle before you can solve them. The six basic manipulations are the same as those for equalities, but certain manipulations require you to change the direction of the inequality sign. The additional rules are:

1. Adding or subtracting a number from both sides of an inequality, whether the number is negative or positive, does *not* change the direction of the sign.

    Example
    $$-4 < 2 \; so$$
    $$-4 + 5 < 2 + 5$$
    $$1 < 7$$

2. Multiplication or division by a positive number does *not* affect the direction of the inequality sign.

    Example
    $$1 < 3$$
    $$4 \cdot 1 < 4 \cdot 3$$
    $$4 < 12$$

3. Taking the square roots of both sides does *not* affect the direction of the sign, but remember you may *only take the square root of a positive number.*

    Example
    $$4 < 5 \; so$$
    $$2 < \sqrt{5}$$

4. Squaring both sides of an inequality does *not* change the direction of the inequality sign if both numbers are positive.

    Example
    $$4 > 3 \; and$$
    $$4^2 > 3^2 \; because \; 16 > 9$$

5. Squaring both sides of an inequality *will* change the direction of the inequality sign if both numbers are negative.

    Example
    $$-3 > -4 \; but$$
    $$(-3)^2 < (-4)^2 \; because \; 9 < 16$$

6. Squaring both sides of an inequality may or may not change the direction of the inequality sign if one number is negative and the other number is positive.

   Examples

   $-3 < 1$ *but*   Here, the inequality sign changes.
   $(-3)^2 > (1)^2$
   $9 > 1$

                                     but . . .

   $-3 < 4$ *and*   Here it stays the same.
   $(-3)^2 < 4^2$
   $9 < 16$

7. If you multiply or divide both sides of an inequality by a *negative* number you *must* switch the direction of the inequality sign.

   Example

   $3 < 4$ *but*
   $3 \cdot (-2) > 4 \cdot (-2)$
   $-6 > -8$

8. Inverting both sides of an inequality *will* change the direction of the inequality sign if both sides are positive or both sides are negative.

   Examples

   $$\frac{1}{3} < \frac{3}{4} \ but$$

   $$3 > \frac{4}{3}$$

   $$-\frac{1}{5} > -\frac{2}{3} \ but$$

   $$-5 < -\frac{3}{2}$$

9. If x is any real number and $a > 0$ for which $|x| > a$, then $x > a$ or $x < -a$.

   Example

   If the $|x| > 5$ then $x > 5$ or $x < -5$

10. If x is any real number and $a > 0$ for which $|x| < a$, then $-a < x < a$.

    Example

    If the $|x| < 7$ then $-7 < x < 7$

Two other ideas that come in handy in solving certain problems are:

1. If $a < b$ and $x < y$ then $a + x < b + y$

   Example

   $1 > -1$ *and* $3 > 2$ *so*
   $1 + 3 > -1 + 2$
   $4 > 1$

2. If $x > t$ and $t > y$ then $x > y$

   Example

   If $x > 3$ and $3 > y$
   then $x > y$

As you can see, it is very important to keep the + and − signs straight when working with inequalities. You should review the multiplication and division rules for signed numbers from Lesson 1:

(positive) • (positive) = (positive)
(positive) • (negative) = (negative)
(negative) • (positive) = (negative)
(negative) • (negative) = (positive)

The same rules hold for division.

(positive) ÷ (positive) = (positive)
(positive) ÷ (negative) = (negative)
(negative) ÷ (positive) = (negative)
(negative) ÷ (negative) = (positive)

Example

If $abc < 0$ and $c < 0$ then which is larger, c or the product of a and b?

1. $c < 0$ *Given in problem.*
2. $abc < 0$ *Given in problem.*
3. $\dfrac{abc}{c} > \dfrac{0}{c}$ *Divide both sides by c.*
                     Since c is negative, you must change the direction of the inequality sign.
4. $ab > 0$ *Do the division out.*
                     Since ab is greater than 0 and c is less than 0, ab is greater than c.

The symbols ≤ and ≥ mean: *less than or equal to* and *greater than or equal to*. When working with inequalities of this type, you should follow the same rules as when you work with inequalities.

Examples

I. If $x \leq 3$ and $x \geq 3$, x can equal 3 and both statements will still be true. But if $x < 3$ and $x > 3$, there is no x that can fulfill both statements; therefore there is no solution to this problem.

II. $2 \leq 2$ is a true statement, while $2 < 2$ is a false statement.

Example Problems

I. Solve for x in the problem $5x - 3 < 12$.

     $5x - 3 < 12$ *Given.*
     $5x < 15$ *Add 3 to both sides.*
     $x < 3$ *Divide both sides by 5.*

II. If $x + y = z$ and $y > 0$, which of the following statements *cannot* be true?
     (A) $x > z$ (B) $x + y > -z$ (C) $y = z$ (D) $x + z > 1$ (E) $z > x + 1$

You can do this problem from two directions, forward and backward. To do it forward:

1. $y > 0$ *Given.*
2. $-y < 0$ *Multiply both sides by negative one and change the direction of the inequality sign.*
3. $z + (-y) < z + (0)$ *Add z to both sides.*
4. $x + y - (y) < z$ *Substitute x + y for z.*
5. $x < z$ *Do the addition.*

Since this answer and answer (A) are exclusive—that is, they both can't be true at the same time—answer (A) must be false.

To go in the other direction, start with the answers.

1. $x > z$ *Answer (A).*
2. $x + y > z + y$ *Add y to both sides.*
3. $x + y - z > z + y - z$ *Subtract z from both sides.*
4. $(x + y) - (x + y) > y$ *Substitute x + y for z.*
5. $0 > y$ *Do the subtraction.*

But we know this is false because the initial given was $y > 0$.

One common mistake is to read too much into a statement. An example is $a < b$. This says nothing about the signs of a or b. They could both be negative, both positive, or b could be positive while a is negative. The inequality definitely *does not imply that a is negative and b is positive*, although it could be true.

PRACTICE PROBLEMS

1. If $x - 3y > x + 3y$, then which of the following must be *false*?

   (A) $y > 0$ (B) $x > 0$ (C) $x = y$ (D) $y < x$ (E) $x < y$

2. If $a^2 - 2ab + b^2 > a^2 + 2ab + b^2$ and $b < 0$, then which of the following describes a?

   (A) $a = b$ (B) $a = 0$ (C) $a < 0$ (D) $a > 0$ (E) $a < b$

3. If $p \geq 0$, then:

   (A) $-p < -3p$ (B) $-2p > 0$ (C) $7p \leq 4p$ (D) $6p \geq 2p$ (E) None of the above

4. If $a > b$ and $b > c$, then:

   (A) $a > 0$ (B) $c < 0$ (C) $a - b > b - c$ (D) $abc < 0$ (E) None of the above

5. If $a > b$, then:

   (A) $4a > 3b$ (B) $2a > 0$ (C) $a - b > 0$ (D) $ab < 0$ (E) $a^2 > b^2$

6. If $a < -1$, then which statement is *not* true?

   (A) $a + 4 < 3$ (B) $-3a < 3$ (C) $a - 5 < -6$ (D) $5a < -5$ (E) $-4a > 4$

7. If $x < y$ and $y < -4$, then which statement is *not* true?

   (A) $-4 < x$ (B) $x - 2 < y - 2$ (C) $x < -4$ (D) $2x < -8$ (E) $x + y < -4$

8. Solve for x: $-1 - 5x \geq 14$

   (A) $x < 3$ (B) $x > -3$ (C) $x \geq 3$ (D) $x \leq -3$ (E) $x > 3$

9. Solve for y: $3y + 5 \leq -10$

   (A) $y \leq 5$ (B) $y \leq 9$ (C) $y \leq -5$ (D) $y \leq -1$ (E) $y < 9$

10. If $\dfrac{1}{x} > \dfrac{1}{5}$, then:

    (A) $x < 5$ (B) $x > 5$ (C) $x \leq 5$ (D) $0 < x < 5$ (E) $0 \leq x \leq 5$

11. If $y > 4$, which of the following has the least value?

    (A) $\dfrac{4}{y+1}$ (B) $\dfrac{4}{y-1}$ (C) $\dfrac{4}{y}$ (D) $\dfrac{y}{4}$ (E) $\dfrac{y+1}{4}$

12. Solve for x: $2 - 2x \leq 10 + 2x$

    (A) $x \geq -8$ (B) $x \leq -2$ (C) $x > -2$ (D) $x \geq 8$ (E) $x \geq -2$

13. If $x > 2$, then:

    (A) $x + \dfrac{2}{x} < 2$ (B) $x + \dfrac{2}{x} > 2$ (C) $x + \dfrac{2}{x} = 2$ (D) $2x < 2$ (E) $x - 2 < 0$

14. Point B is on the line segment AC. Which of the following is always true?

    (A) $AB > BC$ (B) $BC > AB$ (C) $BC = AB$ (D) $AC > AB$ (E) $AB + AC > AC + BC$

15. In the inequality $3x + 4 < 6x + 10$, all of the following may be a value of x except:

    (A) -1 (B) 10 (C) 0 (D) -2 (E) 1

16. If $x < y < z$ and $x < 0$, which of the following is always true?

    (A) $y > 0$ (B) $z > 0$ (C) $y < 0$ (D) $z - y > 0$ (E) $x - y > 0$

17. If a and b are positive and $a > b$, then which of the following is always true?

    (A) $\dfrac{b^2}{a^2} > \dfrac{b}{a}$ (B) $\dfrac{a}{b} > \dfrac{a^2}{b^2}$ (C) $\dfrac{b^2}{a^2} > 1$ (D) $\dfrac{b^2}{a^2} > \dfrac{a^2}{b^2}$ (E) $\dfrac{a^2}{b^2} > \dfrac{a}{b}$

18. If $|2x - 1| > 3$, then which of the following could *not* be a value of x?

    (A) 5 (B) 3 (C) -3.5 (D) -1 (E) $2^{\frac{1}{4}}$

19. The solution set of $\dfrac{x}{3} + 2 > \dfrac{x}{2}$ is

    $\dfrac{x}{3} + 2 > \dfrac{x}{2}$ is

    (A) $x > 12$ (B) $x < -12$ (C) $x > -12$ (D) $x < 12$ (E) $x < \dfrac{2}{3}$

20. If p and q are both positive and $q < p$, which of the following is false?

    (A) $-4q > -4p$ (B) $\dfrac{q}{2} < \dfrac{p}{2}$ (C) $5 - q < 5 - p$ (D) $\dfrac{-p}{3} < \dfrac{-q}{3}$ (E) $\dfrac{1}{q} > \dfrac{1}{p}$

Lesson 5

Goal: To review the skills of factoring.

FACTORING

Factoring is the process of finding two or more expressions whose product is equal to a given expression.

There are really only three types of factoring problems that you will encounter on the SAT. These are taking out the common monomial factor, factoring a binomial, and factoring a trinomial.

COMMON MONOMIAL FACTORS

These are one-term expressions that can be divided into each term of a given expression. Always look first for the *greatest* common factor.

Example

Factor $12xy^2 + 16x^2y = 4xy\,(3y + 4x)$

$4xy$ is the greatest common factor. Note that we could have factored out $2xy$, but $2xy$ is not the *greatest* common factor.

When the terms of the given expression contain the same variables, take out the smallest power of each variable that is common to each term.

Example

The greatest common factor of $x^3y^5z^7 + x^2y^6z^4$ is $x^2y^5z^4$.

PRACTICE PROBLEMS

1. Factor $3x^2 + 6x + 12$
2. Factor $4p^2q^3 + 24p^3q - 16p^4q^2$
3. Factor $-7xy^2z^4 + 21x^2y^3z^2 - 84x^3z^3$
4. Factor $75p^5q^2 - 225p^2q^5 + 375p^3q^3$
5. Factor $x(x-3) + 5(x-3)$
6. Factor $4(x+5)^2 - 3(x+5)$
7. Factor $p(p^2-1) + 4(p^2-1)$
8. Factor $15a^3b^2 - 18a^4b^3 + 24ab^5$

9. Factor $2r^2 - 2rh$
10. Factor $3x(3x+y) - 4(3x+y)$
11. Factor $(12 \times 33) + (12 \times 67)$
12. Factor $(129 \times 51) + [51 \times (-29)]$
13. Factor $5x^7y^3z^4 + 10x^4y^5z^3 - 5x^2y^8z^3$
14. Factor $4x^2 + 36x$
15. Factor $3(2x+y)^3 + 12(2x+y)^2$

BINOMIALS

The most common binomial that is to be factored on the SAT is called the difference of two perfect squares. The rule you *must* learn is:

$$x^2 - a^2 = (x+a)(x-a)$$

Examples

I. $x^2 - 36$ factors to $(x+6)(x-6)$.

II. $p^4 - 225$ factors to $(p^2 - 15)(p^2 + 15)$.

III. $(x+3)^2 - 1$ factors to $[(x+3)-1][(x+3)+1]$.

To be able to factor, you must know your multiplication tables and the table of squares.
You should memorize the following table of squares:

$2^2 = 4$	$6^2 = 36$	$10^2 = 100$	$14^2 = 196$	$20^2 = 400$
$3^2 = 9$	$7^2 = 49$	$11^2 = 121$	$15^2 = 225$	$24^2 = 576$
$4^2 = 16$	$8^2 = 64$	$12^2 = 144$	$16^2 = 256$	$25^2 = 625$
$5^2 = 25$	$9^2 = 81$	$13^2 = 169$	$17^2 = 289$	

To take the square root of a power divide the power by two.

Example

$$\sqrt{x^{10}} = x^{\frac{10}{2}} = x^5$$

PRACTICE PROBLEMS

1. Factor $y^2 - 81$
2. Factor $64 - p^2$
3. Factor $169x^2 - 25y^2$
4. Factor $121A^6 - 144B^4$
5. Factor $36x^2 - 225$
6. Factor $(x-y)^2 - z^2$
7. Factor $x^{2n} - 4$
8. Factor $a^{4n} - 9b^{6n}$

9. Factor $32x^2 - 18$ (Look for the common factor first.)
10. Factor $75z^2 - 147b^2$
11. Factor $256 - 81x^2$
12. Factor $(2x+3)^2 - 16$
13. Factor $49A^8 - 225B^4$
14. Factor $289A^2 - 625$
15. Factor $50x^6 - 98y^2$

TRINOMIALS

The rules for factoring two of the more frequently seen trinomials are:

1. $a^2 + 2ab + b^2 = (a + b)(a + b) = (a + b)^2$
2. $a^2 - 2ab + b^2 = (a - b)(a - b) = (a - b)^2$

Examples

I. $x^2 + 6x + 9 = (x + 3)(x + 3) = (x + 3)^2$

II. $y^2 - 16y + 64 = (y - 8)(y - 8) = (y - 8)^2$

The SAT loves these trinomials, so learn how to factor them and how to unfactor them quickly.

Example

If $(x + 5)^2 = (x - 5)^2$, then $x = ?$

Squaring both binomials you get:

$$x^2 + 10x + 25 = x^2 - 10x + 25$$
$$10x = -10x$$
$$20x = 0$$
$$x = 0$$

When you encounter a trinomial that cannot be factored by using the above rules, you must resort to the trial-and-error method. That means you have to guess the factors. There are some rules that will help you though.

Rule 1: If the last sign is positive, then the signs of your two factors will be the same as the sign of the middle term.

Examples

I. $x^2 - 4x + 3 = (x - 3)(x - 1)$ Last sign is positive.

   middle term   factors   The signs of the two factors (–) are the same as the
      (–)   (–)   sign of the middle term.

II. $a^2 + 6a + 5 = (a + 5)(a + 1)$ Last sign is positive.

   middle term   factors   The signs of the two factors (+) are the same as the
      (+)   (+)   sign of the middle term.

Rule 2: If the last sign is negative, the signs of your two factors will be different.

Example

                           Last sign is negative.

$$x^2 - 7x - 8 = (x - 8)(x + 1)$$

                           Signs of the factors are different.

Notice that factoring is the opposite of FOILing. The clues about what to use as factors come from the *factors of the first and last terms*.

Rule 3: If the coefficient of the first term is 1 and the last sign is positive, look for factors of the last term that *add up* to the middle term.

Example

$x^2 + 10x + 24 = (x + 6)(x + 4)$ because the last sign is positive and the factors of 24 that add up to 10 are 6 and 4.

Factors of 24	Sum
1 and 24	25
2 and 12	14
3 and 8	11
4 and 6	10 Bingo!

Rule 4: If the coefficient of the first term is 1 and the last sign is negative, then look for factors of the last term whose difference equals the middle term.

Example

$x^2 - 5x - 36 = (x-9)(x+4)$ because the factors of 36 that differ by 5 are 9 and 4.

Factors of 36	Difference
1 and 36	35
2 and 18	16
3 and 12	9
4 and 9	5 Bingo!
6 and 6	0

Remember that you check your factoring by FOILing. *Always* check your answer, especially when the last sign is negative. If you are careful and learn your rules, you will conquer these problems.

Rule 5: In solving equations involving factors, if $A \cdot B = 0$, then either A is zero, B is zero, or both are zero. To solve an equation of this type, set each factor equal to zero and then solve for the variable.

Example

$(x+2)(x-4) = 0$ *if*
$(x+2) = 0$ *or*
$(x-4) = 0$

Solve for x in each equation.
$x = -2$ or $x = 4$

Example

Solve for x by factoring.

$2x^2 - 3x + 1 = 0$ Notice that the last sign is positive.
$(2x-1)(x-1) = 0$ Signs of the factors are the same.
$(2x-1) = 0 \quad (x-1) = 0$ Set each factor equal to 0.
$2x = 1$ or $x = 1$ Solve for x.

$x = \dfrac{1}{2}$ or $x = 1$

PRACTICE PROBLEMS

Lowest Terms

1. Factor $p^2 - 9p - 10$
2. Factor $x^2 + 16x + 15$ $x(x + 16) + 15$
3. Factor $a^2 - 3a - 4$ $a(a - 3) - 4$
4. Factor $x^2 + 12x + 27$ $x(x + 12) + 27$
5. Factor $x^2 - 7x - 144$ $x(x - 7) - 144$

6. Factor $x^2 - x + \dfrac{1}{4}$ $x(x - 1) + \dfrac{1}{4}$

7. Factor $x^2 + 4x + 4$ $x(x + 4) + 4$

8. Factor $y^2 + 32y + 256$ $y(y + 32) + 256$

9. Factor $p^2 + \dfrac{1}{2}p + \dfrac{1}{16}$ $p(p + \dfrac{1}{2}) + \dfrac{1}{16}$

SKIP 10. Factor $x^{2n} - 4x^n + 4$ $x^n(x^2 - 4) + 4$

11. Solve for x if: $(x-5)(x+7) = 0$

$X^2 + 7x - 5x - 35$
$X^2 - 12x + 35$

12. Solve for y if: $3y(2y - 5) = 0$
13. Solve for p if: $p^2 - 3p - 4 = 0$ (Factor first.)
14. Solve for x if: $x^2 - 16 = 0$
15. Solve for y if: $y^2 - 9y = 0$
16. Simplify $(23)^2 + (2)(23)(27) + (27)^2$ (Did you remember the rule for factoring $a^2 + 2ab + b^2$?)
17. Simplify $(38)^2 - 2(38)(18) + (18)^2$
18. Simplify $(.52)^2 - 2(.52)(.5) + (.5)^2$
19. Simplify $(48)^2 - (2)^2$
20. Simplify $(.25)^2 - (.24)^2$

Lesson 6

Goal: To review radicals and exponents.

SQUARE ROOTS (RADICALS)

DEFINITION AND USE OF SQUARE ROOTS

If $a^2 = b$, then a is the square root of b. For the purposes of the SAT, the symbol $\sqrt{}$ is used to denote the *positive* square root of a number.

Example

$2^2 = 4$ implies that $2 = \sqrt{4}$; that is, 2 is the square root of 4.

The expression under the radical sign is called the *radicand*. The *coefficient* is the number in front of the radical.

Example

$3\sqrt{2}$ $\begin{cases} 3 \text{ is the coefficient} \\ 2 \text{ is the radicand} \end{cases}$

Another way of defining the square root of a number n is asking the question "What number multiplied by itself equals n?" This number is called the square root of n.

Example

$4 \cdot 4 = 16$, so 4 is the square root of 16.

When working with square roots you should remember:

(1) You cannot take the square root of a negative number. For example $\sqrt{-9}$ does not exist, since there is no real number that when multiplied by itself equals -9.

(2) $\sqrt{x}$ is <u>never</u> negative on the SAT.

Key Point: Two of the most important concepts when dealing with square roots are:

(1) The square root of the product is the product of the square roots:

$$\sqrt{xy} = \sqrt{x} \cdot \sqrt{y}$$

(2) The square root of the quotient is the quotient of the square roots:

$$\sqrt{\frac{x}{y}} = \sqrt{x} \div \sqrt{y} = \frac{\sqrt{x}}{\sqrt{y}}$$

Examples

I. $\sqrt{24 \cdot 6}$

$= \sqrt{24} \cdot \sqrt{6}$

II. $\sqrt{24 \div 6}$

$= \sqrt{\dfrac{24}{6}}$

$= \dfrac{\sqrt{24}}{\sqrt{6}}$

A very important consequence of these rules is that they provide a method of *simplification*. To simplify a radical means to reduce the radical to its lowest terms by factoring the radicand into two factors, one of which is a perfect square, and extracting the square root of the perfect square.

Example

$$\sqrt{24} = \sqrt{4 \cdot 6}$$
$$= \sqrt{4} \cdot \sqrt{6}$$
$$= 2\sqrt{6}$$

$2\sqrt{6}$ is $\sqrt{24}$ simplified.

Example

$$\frac{\sqrt{48}}{\sqrt{6}} = \sqrt{\frac{48}{6}}$$
$$= \sqrt{8}$$
$$= \sqrt{4 \cdot 2}$$
$$= \sqrt{4} \cdot \sqrt{2}$$
$$= 2\sqrt{2}$$

$2\sqrt{2}$ is $\dfrac{\sqrt{48}}{\sqrt{6}}$ simplified.

MULTIPLICATION AND DIVISION OF SQUARE ROOTS

Multiplication and division of square roots are done by using the product and quotient rules from above.

$$\left(\sqrt{x}\right)\left(\sqrt{y}\right) = \sqrt{xy} \ and \ \frac{\sqrt{x}}{\sqrt{y}} = \sqrt{\frac{x}{y}}$$

Example

$$\sqrt{27} \cdot \sqrt{12}$$
$$= \sqrt{27 \cdot 12}$$
$$= \sqrt{324}$$
$$= 18$$

Almost always, however, it is easier to simplify the radical first. Doing the same example this way reads:

$$\sqrt{27} \cdot \sqrt{12}$$
$$= \sqrt{9}\sqrt{3} \cdot \sqrt{4}\sqrt{3}$$
$$= 3\sqrt{3} \cdot 2\sqrt{3}$$
$$= 3 \cdot 2 \cdot \sqrt{3} \cdot \sqrt{3}$$
$$= 6 \cdot 3$$
$$= 18$$

Example

Simplify $\dfrac{\sqrt{180}}{\sqrt{245}}$

$= \dfrac{\sqrt{5} \cdot \sqrt{36}}{\sqrt{5} \cdot \sqrt{49}}$ Notice how the simplification gets around a lot of division with large numbers.

$= \dfrac{\sqrt{36}}{\sqrt{49}}$

$= \dfrac{6}{7}$

An extension of the rule for multiplication of radicals is

$a\sqrt{x} \cdot b\sqrt{y} = ab\sqrt{xy}$

Example

$3\sqrt{12} \cdot 5\sqrt{6} = (3 \cdot 5)\sqrt{12 \cdot 6}$
$\qquad\qquad = 15\sqrt{72}$
$\qquad\qquad = 15\sqrt{36} \cdot \sqrt{2}$
$\qquad\qquad = 15 \cdot 6\sqrt{2}$
$\qquad\qquad = 90\sqrt{2}$

8.7   PRACTICE PROBLEMS

1. Simplify $2\sqrt{75}$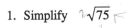

2. Simplify $\sqrt{162}$

3. Simplify $\sqrt{450}$

4. Simplify $\sqrt{294y^2}$

5. Simplify $\sqrt{242x^6}$

6. Simplify $\sqrt{12} \cdot \sqrt{32}$

7. Simplify $\sqrt{98} \cdot \sqrt{8}$

8. Simplify $\dfrac{\sqrt{196}}{\sqrt{4}}$

9. Simplify $\sqrt{\dfrac{150}{3}}$

10. Simplify $\dfrac{\sqrt{112}}{\sqrt{175}}$

11. Simplify $\sqrt{32} \cdot 4\sqrt{6}$

12. Simplify $2\sqrt{18} \cdot 7\sqrt{98}$

13. Simplify $16\sqrt{\dfrac{50}{16}}$

14. Simplify $\dfrac{8\sqrt{50}}{5\sqrt{2}}$

15. Simplify $2\sqrt{3} \cdot 4\sqrt{8} \cdot \sqrt{54}$

ADDITION AND SUBTRACTION OF SQUARE ROOTS

Addition and subtraction of square roots may be done only if the radicals are like (or "similar"), meaning that square roots can only be added to or subtracted from other square roots and cube roots can only be added to or subtracted from other cube roots. Like radicals are radicals that have the same radicand and the same root index. (Don't worry about the root index because you will be working only with square roots.) To add or subtract like radicals, combine the coefficients, leaving the radicand unchanged. (Just as $2x + 3x$ can be combined to give $5x$ but $2x + 3y$ cannot be combined, $3\sqrt{2} + 2\sqrt{2}$ can be added to give $5\sqrt{2}$, while $3\sqrt{2} + 2\sqrt{5}$ cannot be combined.)

$$a\sqrt{x} + b\sqrt{x} = (a+b)\sqrt{x}$$
$$a\sqrt{x} - b\sqrt{x} = (a-b)\sqrt{x}$$

More often than not, you will have to simplify the square root before the radicands are equal.

Example

Find the sum of $\sqrt{45}$ and $\sqrt{125}$.

$\sqrt{45} + \sqrt{125}$	*Write out the expression described in the problem.*
$= \sqrt{9}\sqrt{5} + \sqrt{25}\sqrt{5}$	*Break 45 up into 9 times 5 and 125 up into 25 times 5.*
$= 3\sqrt{5} + 5\sqrt{5}$	*Replace $\sqrt{9}$ with 3 and $\sqrt{25}$ with 5.*
$= 8\sqrt{5}$	*Do the addition.*

Example

Find the sum of $\sqrt{\dfrac{3}{4}}$ and $\sqrt{\dfrac{25}{3}}$.

$\sqrt{\dfrac{3}{4}} + \sqrt{\dfrac{25}{3}}$	*Write out the expression described in the problem.*
$= \dfrac{\sqrt{3}}{\sqrt{4}} + \dfrac{\sqrt{25}}{\sqrt{3}}$	*Use the quotient rule:* $\sqrt{\left(\dfrac{x}{y}\right)} = \dfrac{\sqrt{x}}{\sqrt{y}}$
$= \dfrac{\sqrt{3}}{\sqrt{3}} \cdot \dfrac{\sqrt{3}}{\sqrt{4}} + \dfrac{\sqrt{4}}{\sqrt{4}} \cdot \dfrac{\sqrt{25}}{\sqrt{3}}$	*Rename each fraction to have a common denominator.*
$= \dfrac{\sqrt{3}\sqrt{3} + \sqrt{4}\sqrt{25}}{\sqrt{3}\sqrt{4}}$	*Apply the rules for addition of fractions.*
$= \dfrac{3+10}{2\sqrt{3}}$	*Do the multiplication.*
$= \dfrac{13}{2\sqrt{3}}$	*Do the addition.*
$= \dfrac{13}{2\sqrt{3}} \cdot \dfrac{\sqrt{3}}{\sqrt{3}}$	*Multiply the top and bottom by $\sqrt{3}$.*
$= \dfrac{13\sqrt{3}}{6}$	*Do the multiplication.*

RATIONALIZING THE DENOMINATOR

Notice how the *radical was moved from the denominator to the numerator* in the preceding problem by multiplying by $\sqrt{3}$, the radical in the denominator. This is called *rationalizing the denominator* and is done to put the fraction in its simplest form by removing all radicals from the denominator.

In general, to rationalize a denominator involving a square root multiply the numerator and the denominator of the fraction by the radical that appears in the denominator.

Example

Rationalize the denominator of the fraction $\dfrac{1}{\sqrt{3}}$.

$$= \frac{1}{\sqrt{3}} \cdot \frac{\sqrt{3}}{\sqrt{3}} \qquad \textit{Multiply the numerator and denominator by } \sqrt{3}.$$

$$= \frac{\sqrt{3}}{3} \qquad \textit{Do the multiplication.}$$

Rationalize the denominator of the fraction $\dfrac{12}{5\sqrt{6}}$.

$$= \frac{12}{5\sqrt{6}} \cdot \frac{\sqrt{6}}{\sqrt{6}} \qquad \textit{Multiply the numerator and denominator by } \sqrt{6}.$$

$$= \frac{12\sqrt{6}}{5 \cdot 6} \qquad \textit{Do the multiplication.}$$

$$= \frac{2\sqrt{6}}{5} \qquad \textit{Divide a 6 out of the numerator and the denominator.}$$

If there is a decimal under the radical sign, convert it to a fraction, then follow your rules for simplifying $\sqrt{\dfrac{x}{y}}$.

Example

Simplify $\sqrt{.27}$.

$$= \sqrt{\frac{27}{100}} \qquad \textit{Convert to a fraction.}$$

$$= \frac{\sqrt{27}}{\sqrt{100}} \qquad \textit{Use the quotient rule.}$$

$$= \frac{\sqrt{9} \cdot \sqrt{3}}{10} \qquad \textit{Break down and simplify.}$$

$$= \frac{3\sqrt{3}}{10} \qquad \textit{Simplify.}$$

Important Fact

A radical sign is a grouping symbol, so you must simplify under the radical sign before extracting any square roots.

Example

$$\sqrt{16+9} = \sqrt{(16+9)} = \sqrt{25} = 5$$

$\sqrt{16+9}$ *is not equal to* $\sqrt{16} + \sqrt{9}$.

If you have not already done so, memorize the chart of perfect squares on p. 280, as it will save you a great deal of time on the test.

PRACTICE PROBLEMS

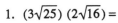

1. $(3\sqrt{25})\,(2\sqrt{16}) =$

2. $\sqrt{(3\sqrt{25})\,(5\sqrt{9})} =$

3. If $7x = \sqrt{625} - \sqrt{576}$, what is x?

4. $\sqrt{98} + \sqrt{2} =$

5. $\sqrt{1.96} =$

6. $(\sqrt{3} - 2)\,(\sqrt{3} + 2) =$

7. $(2\sqrt{3} - \sqrt{6})(3\sqrt{3} - \sqrt{8}) =$

8. $\sqrt{72} + \sqrt{75} =$

9. $\dfrac{4 - \sqrt{56}}{4} =$

10. $\sqrt{40} - \sqrt{50} =$

11. $\sqrt{.042} =$

12. $\dfrac{7}{\sqrt{14}} =$

13. $\dfrac{\sqrt{6}}{\sqrt{108}} =$

14. $\sqrt{\dfrac{8}{75}} =$

15. $\dfrac{3}{\sqrt{27}} =$

16. $\sqrt{3} \cdot \sqrt{5} \cdot \sqrt{7} \cdot \sqrt{35} =$

17. $\sqrt{6} \cdot \sqrt{75} =$

18. $(2\sqrt{2} - 3)^2 =$

19. $\dfrac{(\sqrt{6})^2 - (\sqrt{2})^2}{\sqrt{8}} =$

20. $\dfrac{\sqrt{75}}{\sqrt{3}} =$

PRACTICE SAT PROBLEMS

1. If $2^{x+2} = 32$, then x equals
   (A) 0   (B) 2   (C) 3   (D) 4   (E) 5

2. If $\dfrac{1}{y} = \sqrt{.25}$, then y equals

   (A) $\dfrac{1}{4}$ (B) $\dfrac{1}{2}$ (C) 1   (D) 2   (E) 4

3. $4\sqrt{48} - 3\sqrt{12} =$

   (A) 5   (B) 10   (C) $\sqrt{3}$ (D) $2\sqrt{3}$ (E) $10\sqrt{3}$

4. $\left(\dfrac{1}{2}x^6\right)^2 =$

   (A) x^8 (B) x^{12} (C) $\dfrac{1}{4}x^8$ (D) $\dfrac{1}{4}x^{12}$ (E) $\dfrac{1}{4}x^{36}$

5. 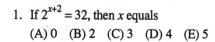 $\sqrt{\dfrac{x^2}{4} + \dfrac{4x^2}{9}} =$

   (A) $\dfrac{x}{2} + \dfrac{2x}{3}$ (B) $\dfrac{3x}{5}$ (C) $\dfrac{x\sqrt{5}}{36}$ (D) $\dfrac{5x}{36}$

   (E) $\dfrac{5x}{6}$

6. If $x + y = 6$ and $x^2 - y^2 = 48$, then $x - y =$
   (A) 4   (B) 6   (C) 8   (D) .6   (E) –8

7. If $3x - .3x = 54$, then $x =$

   (A) .2   (B) $\dfrac{1}{2}$ (C) 2   (D) 20   (E) 200

8. If $x^2 - y^2 = 100$ and $x - y = 100$, then $x + y =$

   (A) $\dfrac{1}{10}$ (B) 1   (C) 10   (D) 100   (E) 0

9. If $7x - 7y = 20$, then $x - y =$

   (A) $\dfrac{20}{7}$ (B) –2   (C) $\dfrac{-20}{7}$ (D) 2   (E) 20

10. Simplify $\sqrt{.0121}$
    (A) .011   (B) .11   (C) 1.01   (D) 1.11   (E) 1.1

11. $2\sqrt{2} \cdot 3\sqrt{32} =$
    (A) 48   (B) 64   (C) 96   (D) 112   (E) 320

12. If $2x = 6$, then $(2x + 4)^2 - 5^2 =$
    (A) 41   (B) 36   (C) 75   (D) 95   (E) 100

13. If $2x + 3y = 17$ and $x + 2y = 7$, then $\dfrac{3x + 5y}{2} =$

    (A) 24   (B) 14   (C) 12   (D) 10   (E) 5

14. If $5A - 3B = 12$ and $7A + 15B = 36$, then $A + B =$
    (A) 4   (B) 12   (C) 24   (D) 36   (E) 48

15. If $A^2 - B^2 = 16$, then $2(A - B)(A + B) =$
    (A) 8   (B) 14   (C) 16   (D) 32   (E) 256

16. If $x = -2$ and $y = 1$, then $3y^2 - 2x =$
    (A) –1   (B) 1   (C) 5   (D) 7   (E) 13

17. If $A = \dfrac{B}{5}$ and $10A = 14$, then $B =$

    (A) 2   (B) 5   (C) 7   (D) 14   (E) 28

18. If $xy \neq 0$, then $\left(\dfrac{2x^6 y^5}{3x^3 y^2}\right)^2 =$

(A) $\dfrac{2}{3}x^9 y^9$ (B) $\dfrac{4}{9}x^9 y^9$ (C) $\dfrac{4}{9}x^6 y^6$

(D) $\dfrac{4}{9}x^5 y^5$ (E) $\dfrac{4}{9}x^4 y^6$

19. $3(a)(-b)(-c)(-d) + 3abcd =$

(A) $6abcd$ (B) $-6abcd$ (C) $-6a^2 b^2 c^2 d^2$
(D) $6a^2 b^2 c^2 d^2$ (E) 0

20. If $p - 7 = 5 - p$, then $p =$

(A) -6 (B) -2 (C) 1 (D) 6 (E) 12

21. If $(x - 4)^2 = (x + 4)^2$, then $x =$

(A) 0 (B) 1 (C) 4 (D) -4 (E) 16

22. If $\dfrac{(2+5)+(3+x)}{2} = 7$, then $x =$

(A) 3 (B) 4 (C) 5 (D) 6 (E) 7

23. $4^2 \cdot 4^4 =$

(A) 4^2 (B) 4^6 (C) 4^8 (D) 16^6 (E) 16^8

24. $\dfrac{4}{5} \cdot \dfrac{5}{6} \cdot \dfrac{6}{7} \cdot \dfrac{7}{8} \cdot \dfrac{8}{9} \cdot \dfrac{9}{10} \cdot \dfrac{10}{11} \cdot \dfrac{11}{12} =$

(A) $\dfrac{15}{17}$ (B) $\dfrac{11}{15}$ (C) $\dfrac{11}{60}$ (D) $\dfrac{1}{4}$ (E) $\dfrac{1}{3}$

25. If $3x - 2 = 13$ and $x + y = 4$, then $y =$

(A) 1 (B) -1 (C) $\dfrac{1}{3}$ (D) $\dfrac{-1}{3}$ (E) $\dfrac{23}{3}$

Good work! You have now completed one third of the lessons in the math section. Do not pat yourself on the back just yet though, because some major areas are still ahead of us. Catch a breather, get yourself a snack, and relax before we move on.

Remember that practice does *not* make perfect. *Perfect* practice makes perfect, so always correct your problems and rework any that you did incorrectly. If you are having problems in one area, refer to your algebra book or see your teacher for some extra help.

Lesson 7

Goal: To review the rules for fractions, decimals, and averages.

FRACTIONS

Fractions, decimals, and averages are stressed heavily on the SAT, so let's gear up for this section.

A fraction is a way of writing a *division* problem. The top number, the *numerator,* is being divided by the bottom number, the *denominator.* Since you can never divide by zero, the denominator can *never* be zero.

$$\frac{a}{b} \text{ means } a \div b \; (b \neq 0)$$

Example

$$\frac{3}{4} = 3 \div 4$$

Another way to visualize a fraction is to call it "a part over the whole." A proper fraction is always less than one; the value of its numerator is *always* less than the value of its denominator.

Example

If I take 11 cards from a deck of 52, what fraction of the cards will I have taken?

The part = 11
The whole = 52

Part over whole: $\dfrac{11}{52}$

If you want to represent a whole number by a fraction, all you have to do is put it over 1.

Example

$$4 = \frac{4}{1}$$

Every fraction has three signs: the one in front of the numerator, the one in front of the denominator, and the one in front of the fraction as a whole. A sign's position may be shifted without changing the value of the fraction.

Example

$$\frac{-4}{7} = -\frac{4}{7} = \frac{4}{-7}$$

Just as with division, where a negative divided by a negative gives a positive, when two minus signs are present in a fraction they cancel each other out and combine to become a *plus* sign.

Example

$$\frac{-4}{-7} = \frac{4}{7}$$

$$-\frac{-3}{2} = \frac{3}{2}$$

THE EQUIVALENCE RULE

One of the most important rules of fractions is the *equivalence rule:* If you multiply or divide the numerator and the denominator of a fraction by the same number, the *value of the fraction remains the same.* Algebraically this can be stated:

$$\frac{a}{b} = \frac{a \cdot c}{b \cdot c} \ or \ \frac{a}{b} = \frac{a \div c}{b \div c}$$

Example

$$\frac{2}{3} = \frac{2 \cdot 2}{3 \cdot 2} = \frac{4}{6}, \ or \ \frac{9}{12} = \frac{9 \div 3}{12 \div 3} = \frac{3}{4}$$

A result of applying the equivalence rule is *simplification*. When you simplify fractions you are looking for common factors. A fraction is in its simplest form when there is *no number that divides both the numerator and the denominator evenly.*

Example

$\frac{3}{5}$ is in simplest form.

$\frac{4}{6}$ is not, since 2 goes into 4 and 6 evenly. However, dividing the numerator and denominator by 2 leaves $\frac{2}{3}$, which is in simplest form.

Usually it is good to simplify fractions *before* starting a problem. It's a lot nicer to work with $\frac{5}{7}$ than with $\frac{105}{147}$.

(Divide top and bottom by 21; you'll see that the two fractions are equal by the equivalence rule.) Simplification becomes more and more important as problems become more complicated. To be able to simplify fractions you must be able to factor. If you are still a little shaky on factoring, review your multiplication tables and the rules for factoring that were presented in Lesson 5.

Example

If $\dfrac{a^2-1}{a+1} = 3$, then $a = $?

1. $\dfrac{(a-1)(a+1)}{(a+1)} = 3$ *Factor $a^2 - 1$ into $(a-1)(a+1)$.*

2. $\dfrac{(a-1)}{1} = 3$ *Simplify the fraction by dividing top and bottom by $(a+1)$.*

3. $a-1 = 3$ *Multiply both sides by 1.*

4. $a = 4$ *Add 1 to both sides.*

THE BASIC OPERATIONS WITH FRACTIONS

I. To multiply two fractions:

 1. Multiply the two numerators to get the numerator of the product.

 2. Multiply the two denominators to get the denominator of the product.

$$\frac{a}{b} \cdot \frac{c}{d} = \frac{ac}{bd}$$

Example

$$\frac{3}{4} \cdot \frac{5}{7} = \frac{3 \cdot 5}{4 \cdot 7} = \frac{15}{28}$$

II. To divide one fraction by another:

 1. Invert the divisor (the second fraction).

 2. Multiply the first fraction and the "flipped" second fraction.

$$\frac{a}{b} \div \frac{c}{d} = \frac{a}{b} \cdot \frac{d}{c} = \frac{ad}{bc}$$

Example

$$\frac{4}{3} \div \frac{5}{7} = \frac{4}{3} \cdot \frac{7}{5} = \frac{4 \cdot 7}{3 \cdot 5} = \frac{28}{15}$$

As a result of the way division is done, you can make the generalization: $\dfrac{1}{\frac{a}{b}} = \dfrac{b}{a}$

Since $\dfrac{1}{\frac{a}{b}}$ means $1 \div \dfrac{a}{b}$ and using the rule for dividing fractions: $1 \div \dfrac{a}{b} = 1 \cdot \dfrac{b}{a} = \dfrac{b}{a}$

Example

$$\frac{1}{\frac{3}{5}} = \frac{5}{3}$$

III. To add two fractions:

1. If the denominators are the same, simply add the numerators to get the numerator of the sum. Carry the denominator over.

$$\frac{a}{c}+\frac{b}{c}=\frac{a+b}{c}$$

2. If the denominators are different, things become a bit hairier. You have to find a common denominator. To do this, you use the equivalence rule. (Remember, we said it was important.) Multiply the numerator and denominator of the first fraction by the denominator of the second fraction. Multiply the numerator and denominator of the second fraction by the denominator of the first. Now the denominators are the same. (A mouthful wasn't it?) Algebraically it looks like this:

Given:

$$\frac{a}{b}+\frac{c}{d}$$

Result

Step 1:   Multiply the numerator (*a*) and denominator (*b*) of the first fraction by the denominator of the second (*d*).

$$\frac{ad}{bd}+\frac{c}{d}$$

Step 2:   Multiply the numerator (*c*) and denominator (*d*) of the second fraction by the denominator of the first (*b*).

$$\frac{ad}{bd}+\frac{cb}{db}$$

Now that the denominators are the same, you can go ahead with the addition. In the generalized example above, the sum is $\frac{ad+bc}{bd}$. *bd* is the *common denominator* of the two fractions. We normally look for the least common denominator, but if you are in a hurry *any* common denominator will do. Remember to reduce your *answer* to lowest terms.

Example

Simplify $\frac{3}{4}+\frac{2}{3}$

$$=\frac{(3)\cdot 3}{(4)\cdot 3}+\frac{(2)\cdot 4}{(3)\cdot 4}$$ *Find a common denominator.*

$$=\frac{9}{12}+\frac{8}{12}$$ *Do the multiplication.*

$$=\frac{17}{12}$$ *Do the addition.*

IV. To subtract one fraction from another:

Subtraction of fractions will be carried out almost exactly like addition.

If the denominators are the same, subtract the second numerator from the first, and *keep* the denominator.

$$\frac{a}{c}-\frac{b}{c}=\frac{a-b}{c}$$

If the denominators are different, find a common denominator by using the same method as was used in addition.

Example

Simplify $\dfrac{5}{8} - \dfrac{1}{3}$

$= \dfrac{(5)\cdot 3}{(8)\cdot 3} - \dfrac{(1)\cdot 8}{(3)\cdot 8}$ *Find a common denominator.*

$= \dfrac{15}{24} - \dfrac{8}{24}$ *Do the multiplication.*

$= \dfrac{7}{24}$ *Do the subtraction.*

A quick trick that you may want to use for addition and subtraction of fractions looks like:

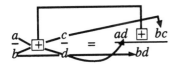   or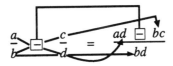

Example

$\dfrac{5}{7} \;-\; \dfrac{2}{3} \;=\; \dfrac{1}{21}$

Remember!

In addition and subtraction the denominator stays the same, while in multiplication and division the denominator *changes.*

Example

$\dfrac{3}{4} + \dfrac{2}{4} = \dfrac{5}{4}$ $\dfrac{5}{8} - \dfrac{2}{8} = \dfrac{3}{8}$

$\dfrac{3}{4} \cdot \dfrac{3}{4} = \dfrac{9}{16}$ $\dfrac{5}{8} \div \dfrac{2}{8} = \dfrac{5}{8} \cdot \dfrac{8}{2} = \dfrac{5}{2}$

PRACTICE PROBLEMS

1. Simplify $\dfrac{9}{8} \cdot \dfrac{16}{27}$

2. Simplify $\dfrac{15}{24} \cdot \dfrac{72}{50}$

3. Simplify $\dfrac{5}{9} \cdot \dfrac{12}{25} \cdot \dfrac{45}{24}$

4. Simplify $\dfrac{x^2 - 25}{x^2 + 10x + 25}$

5. Simplify $\dfrac{A^2 - 16}{A^2 - 3A - 4}$

6. Simplify $\dfrac{9}{8} \div \dfrac{3}{4}$

7. Simplify $\dfrac{2}{3} + \dfrac{4}{9} + \dfrac{1}{2}$

8. Simplify $\dfrac{\dfrac{9}{16}}{\dfrac{5}{48}}$

9. Simplify $\dfrac{1}{3} + \dfrac{3}{4}$

10. Simplify $\dfrac{1}{2} + \dfrac{1}{3} + \dfrac{1}{4}$

11. Simplify $\dfrac{2}{3} - \dfrac{3}{4}$

12. Simplify $\dfrac{7}{24} - \dfrac{3}{16}$

13. Simplify $\dfrac{3}{8} - \dfrac{2}{3} + \dfrac{1}{2}$

14. Simplify $\dfrac{3}{5} \cdot \dfrac{4}{9} - \dfrac{8}{15} + \dfrac{2}{3}$

15. Simplify $\dfrac{3}{4} + \dfrac{2}{3} + \dfrac{5}{6} + \dfrac{3}{8}$

MIXED NUMBERS AND COMPLEX FRACTIONS

For the most part, that's the arithmetic of fractions. There are only a few other terms and manipulations you should know, such as *mixed number* and *complex fraction*.

A *mixed number* is a whole number and a fraction together. It indicates *addition*.

Example

$$4\dfrac{1}{4} \text{ means } 4 + \dfrac{1}{4}$$

$$= \dfrac{4}{1} + \dfrac{1}{4}$$

$$= \dfrac{(4) \cdot 4}{(1) \cdot 4} + \dfrac{(1) \cdot 1}{(4) \cdot 1}$$

$$= \dfrac{16}{4} + \dfrac{1}{4}$$

$$= \dfrac{17}{4}$$

A quick way to convert mixed numbers into fractions is to multiply the whole number by the denominator and add the result to the numerator. Then put this number over the denominator to get the new fraction.

Example

$$2\dfrac{2}{3} = \dfrac{(2 \cdot 3) + 2}{3} = \dfrac{8}{3}$$

A *complex fraction* is one in which the numerator or denominator or both are fractions themselves, such as $\dfrac{\dfrac{3}{4}}{\dfrac{5}{6}}$.

The most important thing to remember here is that a fraction indicates division. This means that $\dfrac{\dfrac{3}{4}}{\dfrac{5}{6}}$ is equal to $\dfrac{3}{4} \div \dfrac{5}{6}$.

Carrying the arithmetic through gives:

$$\frac{3}{4} \cdot \frac{6}{5}$$ *Inversion for division.*

$$= \frac{3 \cdot 6}{4 \cdot 5}$$ *Rule for multiplication.*

$$= \frac{18}{20}$$ *Do the multiplication.*

$$= \frac{9}{10}$$ *Divide both the numerator and denominator by 2.*

If there is more than one term in the numerator or denominator, simplify first before inverting and multiplying.

Example

$$\frac{3 + \frac{5}{2}}{2 - \frac{1}{6}} = \frac{\frac{11}{2}}{\frac{11}{6}} = \frac{11}{2} \cdot \frac{6}{11} = \frac{3}{1} = 3$$

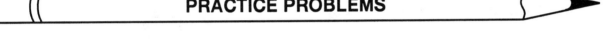

PRACTICE PROBLEMS

1. Simplify $\dfrac{2\frac{1}{3}}{3\frac{1}{4}}$

2. Simplify $\dfrac{\frac{1}{4} + \frac{1}{2}}{\frac{1}{3} + \frac{1}{4}}$

3. Simplify $\dfrac{3\frac{1}{6} - 2\frac{1}{2}}{1\frac{5}{8}}$

4. Simplify $\dfrac{4\frac{1}{2} + 1\frac{2}{3}}{2\frac{1}{4} - 1\frac{1}{8}}$

5. Simplify $\dfrac{\frac{3}{5} - 2\frac{1}{3}}{1\frac{2}{15} - \frac{3}{5}}$

An application of the equivalence rule is called *cancellation*. Suppose you have a row of numbers that you must *multiply* and *divide*, such as,

$$\frac{3}{4} \cdot \frac{5}{6} \div \frac{7}{3} \div \frac{6}{2} \cdot \frac{8}{3} \cdot \frac{1}{4}$$

First, you flip over all of the fractions that follow a division sign, and proceed with multiplication. This gives you:

$$\frac{3}{4} \cdot \frac{5}{6} \cdot \frac{3}{7} \cdot \frac{2}{6} \cdot \frac{8}{3} \cdot \frac{1}{4}$$

or, by the rules for multiplication:

$$\frac{3 \cdot 5 \cdot 3 \cdot 2 \cdot 8 \cdot 1}{4 \cdot 6 \cdot 7 \cdot 6 \cdot 3 \cdot 4}$$

Since you may divide the top and bottom by the same number, you can divide out common factors of the numerator and the denominator to eliminate them before doing the multiplication. The first common factor is an obvious one, 3.

$$\frac{\cancel{3} \cdot 5 \cdot 3 \cdot 2 \cdot 8 \cdot 1}{4 \cdot 6 \cdot 7 \cdot 6 \cdot \cancel{3} \cdot 4}$$

That's one less multiplication step you have to do and about 15 seconds of time saved. Other cancellations include:

1. Divide the top and bottom by 4. Notice how a 2 is left after the 8 is divided by 4.

$$\frac{5 \cdot 3 \cdot 2 \cdot \overset{2}{\cancel{8}}}{\cancel{4} \cdot 6 \cdot 7 \cdot 6 \cdot 4}$$

2. Divide the top and bottom by 6.

$$\frac{5 \cdot \cancel{3} \cdot \cancel{2} \cdot 2}{\cancel{6} \cdot 7 \cdot 6 \cdot 4}$$

3. Divide the numerator and denominator by 2.

$$\frac{5 \cdot \cancel{2}}{7 \cdot 6 \cdot \underset{2}{\cancel{4}}}$$

What's left after all of the possible cancellations are done is:

$$\frac{5}{7 \cdot 6 \cdot 2} \text{ or } \frac{5}{84}$$

You can see how much better this route is than multiplying everything out first and then trying to simplify. But remember that you can cancel out only the common factors, not terms.

Example

$$\frac{15}{5} + \frac{6}{3} = 3 + 2 \text{ or } 5$$

Example

Simplify $\dfrac{10}{21} \div \dfrac{6}{35} \cdot \dfrac{3}{25}$

$= \dfrac{10 \cdot 35 \cdot 3}{21 \cdot 6 \cdot 25}$ *Invert and use the multiplication rules.*

$= \dfrac{\overset{2}{\cancel{10}} \cdot 35 \cdot 3}{21 \cdot 6 \cdot \underset{5}{\cancel{25}}}$ *Divide the top and bottom by 5.*

$= \dfrac{\cancel{2} \cdot 35 \cdot 3}{21 \cdot \underset{3}{\cancel{6}} \cdot 5}$ *Divide the top and bottom by 2.*

$= \dfrac{35 \cdot \cancel{3}}{21 \cdot \cancel{3} \cdot 5}$ *Divide the top and bottom by 3.*

$$= \frac{\overset{7}{\cancel{35}}}{21 \cdot \cancel{5}}$$ *Divide the top and bottom by 5.*

$$= \frac{\cancel{7}}{\underset{3}{\cancel{21}}}$$ *Divide the top and bottom by 7.*
(Notice that 7 divided by 7 leaves 1 and not 0.)

$$= \frac{1}{3}$$ *The answer in its simplest form.*

INEQUALITIES INVOLVING FRACTIONS

Solving inequalities uses cross multiplication. To determine which fraction is greater, $\frac{3}{5}$ or $\frac{2}{3}$, *start from the bottom and work up.*

Example

Cross multiply. The bigger number will always come up on the side of the bigger fraction. In the above, since $10 > 9, \frac{2}{3} > \frac{3}{5}$ is a true statement.

Example

Since both multiplications give 72, the ? must stand for an = sign. And indeed, by simplification you can see $\frac{6}{8} = \frac{9}{12} = \frac{3}{4}$.

Sometimes you will be able to work inequalities without doing the cross multiplication by remembering the following rule:

Key Point:
1. If there is an increase only in the *numerator* of a fraction, the value of the fraction will *increase*.
2. If there is an increase only in the *denominator* of a fraction, the value of the fraction will *decrease*.

Example

$\frac{2}{7} < \frac{4}{7}$ since $4 > 2$ and they are in the *numerator*.

$\frac{2}{7} > \frac{2}{10}$ since $10 > 7$ and they are in the *denominator*.

FRACTIONS IN WORD PROBLEMS

A word problem involving fractions should be dealt with the same way you would deal with any other word problem, step by step. Some of the key words you should look for which indicate the use of fractions are:

part	"What part of 7 is 5?"	$\dfrac{5}{7}$
per	"Sugar costs 59¢ per pound."	$\dfrac{59 \text{ cents}}{1 \text{ pound}}$
fraction of	"What fraction of a dollar is a nickel?"	$\dfrac{5}{100} = \dfrac{1}{20}$

Example

Peter earned E dollars and spent S dollars. What fractional part of his earnings did he save?

1. part saved $=$ amount earned – part spent
    $= E - S$
2. whole $=$ amount earned
    $= E$
3. $\dfrac{\text{part}}{\text{whole}} = \dfrac{E - S}{E}$

UNIT FRACTIONS

If you are given a question in one set of units, such as inches, and are asked to convert the answer to another set, such as feet, you use *unit fractions*. A unit fraction is a fraction equal to 1, since the denominator and numerator are equal; however, the units in the denominator and numerator are different.

Example

$\dfrac{12 \text{ inches}}{1 \text{ foot}}$ is a unit fraction since 12 inches = 1 foot

Since multiplication or division by 1 does not change the value of a fraction, you can multiply or divide by unit fractions without changing your answer.

Example

3 blips = 1 blap
4 blaps = 1 blop

If you have 5 blops how many blips do you have?

$= \dfrac{5 \text{ blops}}{1} \cdot \dfrac{4 \text{ blaps}}{1 \text{ blop}} \cdot \dfrac{3 \text{ blips}}{1 \text{ blap}}$

$= \dfrac{5 \text{ blops}}{1} \cdot \dfrac{4 \text{ blaps}}{1 \text{ blop}} \cdot \dfrac{3 \text{ blips}}{1 \text{ blap}}$ *Cancel the units just as you would cancel common factors.*

$= 5 \cdot 4 \cdot 3 \text{ blips}$ *Use the multiplication rule.*

$= 60 \text{ blips}$ *Do the multiplication.*

PRACTICE PROBLEMS

1. Add $\dfrac{3}{4}, \dfrac{7}{4}, \dfrac{8}{4}$

2. Add $2\dfrac{1}{3}, 3\dfrac{1}{6}, 4\dfrac{1}{2}, 1\dfrac{1}{4}$

3. Add $26.2, 5\dfrac{3}{4}, \dfrac{17}{2}$

4. Subtract $\dfrac{1}{3}$ from $\dfrac{3}{4}$

5. Subtract $6\frac{2}{5}$ from $12\frac{3}{4}$

6. From $5\frac{1}{2}$ take $4\frac{2}{3}$

7. Multiply $5\frac{1}{2}$ by $6\frac{3}{4}$

8. Multiply $2\frac{1}{2} \times 3\frac{1}{3} \times \frac{3}{4}$

9. Divide $13\frac{7}{3}$ by $2\frac{5}{6}$

10. Divide $14\frac{3}{8}$ by $16\frac{1}{4}$

11. Divide 12.3 by .006

12. Simplify $\dfrac{3}{5} \div \dfrac{4}{10} \div 2\dfrac{1}{2} \cdot \dfrac{10}{3}$

13. Simplify $\dfrac{\dfrac{5}{3}}{4+\dfrac{1}{6}}$

14. Simplify $\dfrac{\dfrac{7}{6}-\dfrac{1}{3}}{2+\dfrac{1}{2}}$

15. Simplify $\dfrac{1\dfrac{2}{3}-\dfrac{5}{6}}{3\dfrac{1}{4}+1\dfrac{1}{8}}$

DECIMALS

Problems involving decimals usually won't have a lot of messy arithmetic. It is extremely important to *keep track of the decimal point*. A decimal is a fraction with a power of ten in the denominator.

Examples

$$.3 = \frac{3}{10}$$

$$.467 = \frac{467}{1,000}$$

CONVERTING FRACTIONS INTO DECIMALS

To convert a fraction into a decimal, divide the denominator into the numerator.

Example

Convert $\frac{1}{8}$ to a decimal numeral.

$$
\begin{array}{r}
.125 \\
8\overline{)1.00000} \\
\underline{8} \\
20 \\
\underline{16} \\
40 \\
\underline{40} \\
0
\end{array}
$$

Notice how the decimal point moves "straight up."

$$\frac{1}{8} = .125$$

CONVERTING DECIMALS INTO FRACTIONS

To convert a decimal to a fraction:

(1)   Count the number of digits following the decimal point. Call this number n.

(2)   The denominator of the fraction is a 1 followed by n zeros.

(3)   The numerator of the fraction is the decimal number without its decimal point.

(4)   Simplify the fraction using the equivalence rule.

Example

Write .016 as a fraction.

1. n is 3 since there are three numerals following the decimal point.

2. The denominator is 1,000 (a 1 with 3 zeros after it).

3. The numerator is 016 or just 16 (.016 without the decimal point).

4. To simplify $\dfrac{16}{1,000}$, divide top and bottom by 8 to get $\dfrac{2}{125}$.

When working with decimals, a good rule to remember is that *multiplication by 10 moves the decimal point to the right one place*, and *division by 10 moves the decimal point to the left one place*.

Examples

I. $.016 \cdot 10 = .16$

II. $.016 \div 100 = .00016$ *Since $100 = 10^2$, you must move the decimal point two places to the left.*

III.   If $d_1 = .007 \cdot 9.2$ and $d_2 = .7 \cdot .92$, which of the following is true?

(A) $d_1 < d_2$ (B) $d_1 + d_2 = 10$ (C) $d_1 = d_2$ (D) $d_1 > 9.5$ (E) $d_1 > d_2$

Instead of doing the multiplication out rewrite d_1 and d_2 as:

$d_1 = (7 \div 1,000) \cdot (9.2) = (7 \cdot 9.2) \div 1,000$

$d_2 = (7 \div 10) \cdot (9.2 \div 10) = (7 \cdot 9.2) \div (10 \cdot 10) = (7 \cdot 9.2) \div 100$

In its new form the problem is a lot simpler. d_1 is some positive quantity divided by 1,000 and d_2 is the same positive quantity divided by 100. d_2 is obviously bigger, so answer (A) is the correct answer.

BASIC MATHEMATICAL OPERATIONS WITH DECIMALS

Addition and subtraction of decimals are just like addition and subtraction of whole numbers except that you must line the numbers up so that all of the decimal points are in the same place.

Example

Find the sum of 42.5, .333, 999, 5.67, 4.025

```
     42.5
      .333
   999.
      5.67
 +   4.025
 1,051.528
```

Multiplication of decimals is also a lot like multiplication of whole numbers. Set the problem up and work it as you would any multiplication problem. To determine where the decimal point goes, add the number of digits to the right of the decimal point of the first number to the number of digits to the right of the decimal point of the second number. The sum gives the number of digits which must be to the right of the decimal point in the product.

Example

Find the product of 25.4 and 3.1.

$$
\begin{array}{rl}
25.4 & \text{(one digit to the right of the decimal point)} \\
\times\ \underline{3.1} & \text{(one digit to the right of the decimal point)} \\
254 & \\
\underline{762} & \\
78.74 & \text{(one + one = two digits to the right of the decimal point)}
\end{array}
$$

In a case where there are not enough digits, you must add zeros to the left of the number before putting in the decimal point.

Example

What is the product of .05 and .06?

$$
\begin{array}{rl}
.05 & \text{(two digits to the right of the decimal)} \\
\times \underline{.06} & \text{(two digits to the right of the decimal)} \\
30 & \\
\underline{00} & \\
030 & \text{(two + two = four digits needed to the right of the decimal point)}
\end{array}
$$

Adding a zero to the left of the number gives .0030 or, more simply, .003.

To divide two decimal numbers, it is usually easiest to convert them first to fractions and then do the division according to the rules for fractions. Then, if the answer is given in decimals or a mixture of decimals and fractions, you can convert back.

Example

If $28.4 \div .04 = x$, then $x =$

1. $28.4 = \dfrac{284}{10}$ and $.04 = \dfrac{04}{100} = \dfrac{4}{100}$ *Write the decimals in their fractional forms.*

2. $28.4 \div .04 = \dfrac{284}{10} \div \dfrac{4}{100}$ *Convert the decimals to fractions.*

3. $= \dfrac{284}{10} \cdot \dfrac{100}{4}$ *Use the rules for dividing fractions.*

4. $= \dfrac{284}{1} \cdot \dfrac{10}{4}$ *Cancel a 10 out from the numerator and denominator of the two fractions.*

5. $= \dfrac{71}{1} \cdot \dfrac{10}{1}$ *Cancel a 4 from the denominator of the second fraction and the numerator of the first.*

6. $= 710$ *Do the multiplication.*

Key Point: In general, fractions are easier to use than decimals, so when given a problem with *both fractions and decimals*—go with the fractions.

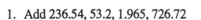

PRACTICE PROBLEMS

1. Add 236.54, 53.2, 1.965, 726.72
2. Add .004, 55.81, 82.26, 6.709
3. Add .56, .071, .0063, 2.00035
4. From 87.63 take 29.7
5. From 119.015 take 89.54
6. Subtract 63.915 from 100
7. Multiply 7.62 by 3.4

8. Multiply 18.6 by 9.72
9. Multiply 1.29 by 0.764
10. Divide 34.56 by 14.4
11. Divide 1.536 by .16
12. Divide 248 by .03
13. Divide 216.4 by the sum of 5.3 and 1.9
14. Multiply 6.42 by the quotient of 14.4 and 2.4

15. From 110.7 take the product of 12.3 and 3.42
16. Convert .0125 to a fraction
17. Convert 2.34 to a fraction
18. Convert 34.215 to a fraction

19. Convert $\frac{84}{5}$ to a decimal

20. Convert $\frac{36.34}{1.2}$ to a decimal

AVERAGES

The average or mean value of a group of quantities is defined by the equation:

$$\text{Average} = \frac{\text{Sum of the quantities}}{\text{Number of quantities}}$$

Any problem dealing with averages uses this equation. Consequently there are only three types of average problems. Find the average, find the sum, or find the number of quantities.

Example I

If the average cost of five books is $2.30, what would it cost to buy all five books?

$$\text{Average} = \frac{\text{Sum}}{\text{Number}}$$

$$\$2.30 = \frac{x}{5}$$

$$x = 5 \cdot \$2.30$$

$$x = \$11.50$$

Example II

What is the average of .6, 6, and 60?

$$\text{Average} = \frac{\text{Sum}}{\text{Number}}$$

$$= \frac{60 + 6 + .6}{3}$$

$$= \frac{66.6}{3}$$

$$= 22.2$$

Example III

If the total time it takes Jim to paint a house is 20 hours and Jim can paint an average room in 2.5 hours, how many rooms are there in the house?

$$\text{Average} = \frac{\text{Sum}}{\text{Number}}$$

$$2.5 = \frac{20}{\text{Number of rooms}}$$

$$\text{Number of rooms} = 20 \div 2.5$$

$$= 8$$

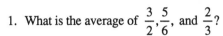

PRACTICE PROBLEMS

1. What is the average of $\frac{3}{2}, \frac{5}{6}$, and $\frac{2}{3}$?

2. What number must be added to 6, 16, and 8 to attain an average of 13?

3. After taking his fourth quiz, Bill's average dropped from 78 to 75. What was Bill's last quiz grade?

4. A piece of rope 18 feet 4 inches long is to be cut into four equal pieces. What will be the length of each piece?

5. What is the average of $\frac{3}{4}$, .64, and .87?

6. Find the average of $x, x-3, 2x-5, 2x+2$, and $1-x$.

7. The lowest temperatures recorded each day during a week were $-7°, 5°, 1°, -10°, -8°, 2°$, and $0°$. To the nearest degree, what was the average minimum temperature?

8. The average of $2x-1, 4, 6, 12$, and 13 is 9. What is the value of x?

9. The average of x and y is 4. If $x = 5y$, what is the value of y?

10. Three sisters weigh $108\frac{1}{2}$ pounds, $97\frac{1}{4}$ pounds, and $121\frac{3}{4}$ pounds. What is their average weight?

PRACTICE SAT PROBLEMS

1. If $\frac{4}{5} = \frac{x}{4}$, then $x =$

   (A) $\frac{5}{16}$ (B) $\frac{5}{4}$ (C) $\frac{16}{5}$ (D) 5   (E) 16

2. Juan's quiz scores in math were 95, 87, 84, 84, and 60. What was the average of these scores?
   (A) 80.2   (B) 81   (C) 81.5   (D) 82   (E) 84

3. A woman's bill at the food store was $15.00. She had coupons worth $3.50. If she handed the clerk $20.00, how much change did she get back?
   (A) $3.50   (B) $5.00   (C) $6.50   (D) $7.50   (E) $8.50

4. If $\frac{1}{3}$ of a number is 6 more than $\frac{1}{4}$ of the number, what is the number?

   (A) 72   (B) 60   (C) 48   (D) 24   (E) 18

5. If $x = \frac{3}{4}$ and $y = \frac{9}{8}$, what is the value of $\frac{x}{y}$?

   (A) 1   (B) $\frac{2}{9}$ (C) $\frac{2}{3}$ (D) $\frac{1}{3}$ (E) $\frac{27}{32}$

6. $(.53)^2 - (.52)^2 =$
   (A) .0105   (B) .105   (C) 1.05   (D) 10.5   (E) 105

7. What fraction of 8 hours is 120 seconds?

   (A) $\frac{1}{60}$ (B) $\frac{1}{120}$ (C) $\frac{1}{240}$ (D) $\frac{1}{1,200}$ (E) $\frac{1}{2,400}$

8. The average of Sandy's scores on four tests was 82. If she received a score of 78 on each of her first two tests and a 92 on the third test, what was her score on the fourth test?

    (A) 74   (B) 78   (C) 80   (D) 82   (E) 88

9. $\dfrac{23}{1,000} + \dfrac{6}{100} + \dfrac{7}{10} =$

    (A) .7623   (B) .0042   (C) .783   (D) .2367   (E) .327

10. If $8x + 8y = 64$, what is the average of x and y?

    (A) 16   (B) 4   (C) 8   (D) 2   (E) It cannot be determined from the information given.

11. If 8 and 36 each divide N without remainder, what must be the value of N?

    (A) 64   (B) 72   (C) 108   (D) 288   (E) It cannot be determined from the information given.

12. The number of boys attending Union High School is twice the number of girls. If $\dfrac{1}{6}$ of the girls and $\dfrac{1}{4}$ of the boys play soccer, what fraction of the students at Union play soccer?

    (A) $\dfrac{5}{12}$ (B) $\dfrac{1}{3}$ (C) $\dfrac{1}{4}$ (D) $\dfrac{2}{9}$ (E) $\dfrac{1}{6}$

13. What is the thickness in inches of three sheets of paper if the thickness of a uniform pack of 250 sheets is 2.0 inches?

    (A) 0.008   (B) 0.024   (C) 0.04   (D) 0.4   (E) 0.8

14. If the average (arithmetic mean) of 5, 6, 8, x, and 12 is 12, then x is

    (A) 17   (B) 25   (C) 29   (D) 39   (E) 60

15. Which of the following is a pair of numbers that are NOT equal?

    (A) $\dfrac{1}{25}$, .04   (B) $\dfrac{14}{5}$, 2.8   (C) $\dfrac{5}{9}$, $\dfrac{55}{99}$ (D) $\dfrac{8}{12}$, $\dfrac{32}{42}$ (E) $\dfrac{84}{16}$, $5\dfrac{1}{4}$

Lesson 8

Goal: To review the rules for percentages, ratios, and proportions.

PERCENTAGE

Percent is an implied fraction. It means "divided by 100." The fraction represented by x percent is $\dfrac{x}{100}$.

Example

Write 60% as a fraction

$= \dfrac{60}{100}$ *Write the quantity over 100.*

$= \dfrac{3}{5}$ *Then reduce to lowest terms.*

Almost every percentage problem can be reduced to the phrase *"the part is some percent of the whole."*

Algebraically, this can be written: $\boxed{P = \dfrac{c}{100} \cdot W}$, where P stands for the part, W stands for the whole, and c is the percent. Notice how the word *of* indicates multiplication and *is* is represented by an equal sign.

Percents are easy to master once you do a few of them. Pay attention to the key words.

Is and *are* mean *equals* and are represented by an equal sign.
Of means multiplication.

What percent? means $\dfrac{x}{100}$.

It is helpful to know these fractions and their equivalent percents.

$\dfrac{1}{3} = 33\dfrac{1}{3}\%$ $\qquad \dfrac{1}{4} = 25\%$ $\qquad \dfrac{1}{5} = 20\%$ $\qquad \dfrac{1}{6} = 16\dfrac{2}{3}\%$ $\qquad \dfrac{1}{8} = 12\dfrac{1}{2}\%$

$\dfrac{2}{3} = 66\dfrac{2}{3}\%$ $\qquad \dfrac{1}{2} = 50\%$ $\qquad \dfrac{2}{5} = 40\%$ $\qquad \dfrac{5}{6} = 83\dfrac{1}{3}\%$ $\qquad \dfrac{3}{8} = 37\dfrac{1}{2}\%$

$\dfrac{3}{4} = 75\%$ $\qquad \dfrac{3}{5} = 60\%$ $\qquad \dfrac{5}{8} = 62\dfrac{1}{2}\%$

$\dfrac{4}{5} = 80\%$ $\qquad \dfrac{7}{8} = 87\dfrac{1}{2}\%$

Key Point: To convert a fraction to a percent, divide the numerator by the denominator and then move the decimal point *two* places to the *right*.

Example

$\dfrac{3}{5} = .6$ $\qquad$ *Divide to make a decimal.*

$.6 = 60\%$ $\qquad$ *Move the decimal two places to the right.*

Key Point: To convert a percent to a decimal, move the decimal point *two* places to the *left*.

Example
$27\% = .27$ $\qquad$ *Move the decimal point two places to the left.*

THE THREE TYPES OF PERCENTAGE PROBLEMS

Consequently, there are three types of percentage problems:

I. Problems that ask you to find the part, P.

Example
What is 25% of 80?

$P = \dfrac{25}{100} \cdot 80$

$P = 20$

II. Problems that ask you to find the whole, W.

Example
50 is 40% of what number?

$$50 = \frac{40}{100} \cdot W$$

$$W = \frac{50 \cdot 100}{40}$$

$$W = 125$$

III. Problems that ask you to find the percent, c, one quantity is of another.

Example
What percent of 165 is 33?

$$33 = \frac{c}{100} \cdot 165$$

$$c = \frac{33 \cdot 100}{165}$$

$$c = 20$$

Example
Given that there are 100 people in a football stadium, if 25% more people come and then 20% of the new total leave, how many people remain?

1. Translate the word problem to an algebraic expression.

   a. $(100) + \dfrac{25}{100}(100)$ *"25% more people come."*

   b. $100 + 25$ *Do the multiplication.*

   c. 125 *Do the addition.*

   d. $125 - \dfrac{20}{100}(125)$ *"20% of the new total leave."*

   e. $125 - \dfrac{20}{100}(125) =$ *"How many people remain?"*

2. Do the math.

   a. $125 - \dfrac{20 \cdot 125}{100} =$ *Do the multiplication.*

   b. $125 - \dfrac{20 \cdot 5}{4} =$ *Divide the top and bottom of the fraction by 25.*

   c. $125 - 25 =$ *Divide the top and bottom of the fraction by 4.*

   d. 100 *Do the subtraction.*

The same amount is there! Even though 25% and 20% do not represent the same fraction, they can represent the same part of two different wholes. When doing this problem, it is crucial to *add 25% more* to the original and not just put the value that is 25% *of* the original, because the problem asks the question "how many *more?*"

PRACTICE PROBLEMS

1. What is 40% of 72?
2. What is 125% of 24?
3. What is .05% of 150?

4. 16 is what percent of 40?
5. 9 is what percent of 2.25?
6. 12 is what percent of 75?

7. 4.4 is 16% of what number?

8. 42 is what percent of 120?

9. $\frac{5}{4}$ is what percent of $3\frac{1}{8}$?

10. What is 101% of 3?

11. If 8 people share a lottery prize, what percent of the prize is owned by 3 of the people?

12. After a 25% discount a can of tennis balls costs $2.00. What was the original price of the can of tennis balls?

13. 15% of 300 is what percent of 50?

14. After driving for 2 hours, Carlos had completed $12\frac{1}{2}$% of his trip. How many more hours did he have to drive before reaching his destination?

15. In a class of 1,025 students, 44% were boys. How many girls were there?

RATIO

A ratio is a comparison between the number of elements in one group and the number of elements in another group. Ratios may be represented in several ways:

With words	three *to* two
With ratio signs	3:2
With fractions	$\frac{3}{2}$
With percents	150%

In most problems, converting the problem to its fractional form makes it easier to work with.

Example

What is the ratio of 12 minutes to 1 hour?

12 minutes to 1 hour

$= \dfrac{12 \text{ minutes}}{1 \text{ hour}}$ *Convert to a fraction.*

$= \dfrac{12 \text{ minutes}}{1 \text{ hour}} \times \dfrac{1 \text{ hour}}{60 \text{ minutes}}$ *Multiply by the unit fraction.*

$= \dfrac{12 \,\cancel{\text{minutes}}}{1 \,\cancel{\text{hour}}} \times \dfrac{1 \,\cancel{\text{hour}}}{60 \,\cancel{\text{minutes}}}$ *Cancel the units.*

$= \dfrac{1}{5}$ *Divide top and bottom by 12.*

$= 1:5$ *Convert to a ratio sign.*

It is important to notice that a ratio *compares the different parts* of a group *to each other;* it does *not* compare them to the group as a whole. A fraction compares the part to the whole.

Example

In a math class the ratio of the number of boys to the number of girls is 3:2. What percent of the class consists of girls?

1. The *part* of the class that is girls *is 2 parts* and the *part* of the class that is boys *is 3 parts,* so the *total class* is made up of *5 parts.*

2. The fraction of the class that is girls is $\dfrac{2 \text{ parts}}{5 \text{ parts}}$.

3. Canceling the units leaves $\dfrac{2}{5}$, the part of the class that is girls.

4. To change this to a percent, set up the equation

$$\frac{2}{5} = \frac{x}{100}$$ and solve for x.

5. In this case x is 40, so the percent of the class that is girls is 40%.

Notice how you add 2 and 3 from 3:2 to get 5, the whole, which you use as the denominator of the fraction. Putting 2 or 3 in the denominator of the fraction would be a grave mistake.

PROPORTION

A proportion is two ratios set equal to each other.

Example

$$\frac{2}{3} = \frac{8}{12}$$

An important point about proportions is that the cross products are equal. We use this fact to solve many equations.

Example

If $\frac{x}{8} = \frac{21}{12}$, solve for x.

$$\frac{x}{8} = \frac{21}{12} \qquad 12 \cdot x = 8 \cdot 21 \qquad \textit{Cross multiply.}$$

$$12x = 168 \textit{Multiply.}$$
$$x = 14 \qquad \textit{Divide by 12.}$$

 **PRACTICE PROBLEMS**

1. A room is 15 feet 8 inches long and 9 feet 8 inches wide. What is the ratio of the length to the width?
2. What is the ratio of 3 pounds to 6 ounces?
3. The ratio of two numbers is 3 to 5. If the larger number is 165, what is the smaller?
4. If a school has 124 boys and 176 girls, what is the ratio of girls to the total number of students in the school?
5. If x baseballs cost d dollars, how much will y baseballs cost?
6. If 8 men can paint a house in 12 hours, how long would it take 6 men to paint the same house?
7. If $\frac{18}{5x} = \frac{9}{25}$, solve for x.
8. On a certain map 1 inch is equal to 32 miles. How many miles would 5.2 inches equal?
9. If 3 teaspoons equals 1 tablespoon and 2 tablespoons equals 1 ounce, how many ounces are there in 30 teaspoons?
10. If snow is falling at the rate of $\frac{1}{3}$ inch per 24 minutes, how much snow will fall in 2 hours?

PRACTICE SAT PROBLEMS

1. $1 - \dfrac{1}{1 - \dfrac{1}{2}} =$

   (A) –2   (B) –1   (C) 0   (D) 1   (E) 2

2. If $\dfrac{5}{x} = \dfrac{15}{9}$, then $x =$

   (A) 1   (B) 3   (C) 9   (D) 18   (E) 27

3.

   A: X / 0 0 / X X X

   B: 0 / 0 0 / 0 0 0

   How many X cards would have to be taken from pile A and put into pile B for the fractional part of X cards to be the same in both piles?

   (A) None   (B) 1   (C) 2   (D) 3   (E) 4

4. In a race, runner B falls x inches farther behind runner A every y minutes. At this rate how far in feet will runner B be behind runner A after 1 hour?

   (A) $12xy$ (B) $\dfrac{x}{12y}$ (C) $\dfrac{12y}{x}$ (D) $\dfrac{y}{5x}$ (E) $\dfrac{5x}{y}$

5. The difference between $7\dfrac{3}{4}$ feet and $5\dfrac{5}{6}$ feet in *inches* is

   (A) 12   (B) 12.5   (C) 18   (D) 23   (E) 25

6. Simplify $\dfrac{1}{\dfrac{1}{a} - \dfrac{1}{b}}$ $(a \neq 0, b \neq 0, a \neq b)$

   (A) $\dfrac{ab}{a-b}$ (B) $\dfrac{a-b}{ab}$ (C) $b - a$ (D) $\dfrac{ab}{b-a}$ (E) $\dfrac{b-a}{ab}$

7. $8 \cdot .125 =$

   (A) 0   (B) 1   (C) .1   (D) 8.125   (E) .825

8. If $.2^2 = \sqrt{x}$, then $x =$

   (A) .2   (B) .02   (C) .04   (D) 0.016   (E) .0016

9. If $-0.6(0.4 - p) = 1.2(.8p + .7p)$, then $p =$

   (A) –5   (B) –.2   (C) .2   (D) .5   (E) None of the above

10. If $10N = 3.33333\ldots$ and $N = .33333\ldots$, then N can be rewritten as

    (A) $\dfrac{1}{3}$ (B) $.3^2$ (C) $\dfrac{3}{10}$ (D) $\dfrac{1}{.3}$ (E) None of the above

11. What is the average of $2x + 1, x + 5, 1 - 4x, 3x + 1$?

    (A) $2x + 1$ (B) $2x + 4$ (C) $\dfrac{1}{2}x + 2$ (D) $\dfrac{x+4}{4}$ (E) $\dfrac{2x+4}{4}$

12. Three members of a basketball team have weights that range from 150 to 175 pounds. Which of the following cannot possibly be the average weight of the three players?

    (A) 159   (B) 161   (C) 163   (D) 165   (E) 167

13. The average of A and another number is P. The other number must be

    (A) $P - A$ (B) $\dfrac{PA}{2}$ (C) $2A - P$ (D) $2P - A$ (E) $\dfrac{2P + A}{2}$

14. The average grade of 10 students is x. If 5 other students each earned a grade of 84, what would be the average grade of the entire group?

    (A) $\dfrac{x + 84}{2}$ (B) $\dfrac{x + 420}{5}$ (C) $\dfrac{10x + 84}{15}$ (D) $\dfrac{10x + 420}{15}$ (E) None of the above

15. After picking 120 peaches, a woman eats 12 of them. What percent remains?

    (A) 10   (B) 30   (C) 50   (D) 70   (E) 90

16. If a boy must walk 12 miles to school and he has completed 75% of the trip, how many miles does he have left to go?

    (A) 3   (B) 4   (C) 6   (D) 8   (E) 9

17. A 60-gallon tank is 40% full of water. If the water is then poured into a 40-gallon tank, what percent of the 40-gallon tank has been filled?

    (A) 24   (B) 40   (C) 60   (D) 96   (E) 100

18. If 30% of a class consists of boys and there are 21 girls in the class, how many boys are there in the class?

    (A) 30   (B) 9   (C) 60   (D) 42   (E) 10

19. After taking 30 socks out of the dryer, Debbie noticed that the ratio of blue socks to brown socks to black socks was 2:3:5. How many black socks were in the dryer?

    (A) 21   (B) 15   (C) 9   (D) 6   (E) 3

20. It costs $6y$ dollars to fence three sides of a square field. How much will it cost to fence the fourth side?

    (A) $\dfrac{3y}{4}$ (B) y (C) $\dfrac{4y}{3}$ (D) $2y$ (E) $24y$

21. If 3:4 is equivalent to a:12, then $a =$

    (A) 1   (B) 9   (C) 11   (D) 12   (E) 14

22. In a class of 25 students, 44% are boys. What is the ratio of boys to girls in the class?

    (A) 11:1   (B) 11:25   (C) 11:14   (D) 14:11   (E) 25:14

23. In 15 years the ratio of my age to my father's age will be 1:2. Five years ago, the ratio of my age to his was 1:4. How old am I?

    (A) 10   (B) 15   (C) 30   (D) 40   (E) 60

24. A machine can copy 6 pages in 9 seconds. How many pages can it copy in 24 *minutes?*

    (A) 12   (B) 16   (C) 36   (D) 960   (E) 2,160

25. The ratio of the length of a side of an equilateral triangle to the perimeter of the triangle is

    (A) $\dfrac{1}{6}$ (B) $\dfrac{1}{3}$ (C) 1   (D) $\dfrac{3}{1}$ (E) $\dfrac{60}{1}$

For problems 26–35 enter your solutions into the grids that follow the questions.

26. One half of the socks in a drawer are brown, $\frac{1}{4}$ of them are black, and $\frac{1}{5}$ of them are blue. If the rest of them are white, what fractional part of the socks are white?

27. If a $\frac{1}{4}$-inch piece of ribbon costs a nickel, then 1 foot of ribbon costs how much in dollars?

28. How much more is $\frac{1}{2}$ of $\frac{2}{3}$ than $\frac{3}{4}$ of $\frac{1}{3}$?

29. Jim paints $\frac{1}{3}$ of a fence, Joan paints $\frac{1}{2}$ of what is left. What fraction of the fence is left unpainted?

30. How many $\frac{1}{10}$-inch pieces of string can be cut from a 16.3-inch string?

31. Frank can cut a lawn in $2\frac{1}{2}$ hours; Tom cuts the same lawn in $1\frac{3}{4}$ hours. What is the average length of time it takes, in hours, to cut the lawn?

32. 30% of 80 is what percent of 24?

33. If the cost of a 4-minute telephone call is $0.24, then what is the cost in dollars of a 15-minute call at the same rate?

34. In a scale drawing, 3 inches represents 9 feet. How many inches represents 1 foot 6 inches? (1 foot = 12 inches)

35. Michele, Ned, and Owen split the award for a contest in the ratio of 6:2:1, respectively. If the total award was worth $72.00, then Ned received how many dollars?

26.

27.

28.

29.

30.

31.

32.

33.

34.

35.

Way to go! You are almost halfway through the math review. By now you should be feeling a lot more comfortable with the problems that involve arithmetic and algebra.

In Lesson 9, we will look at how to solve two equations in two unknowns and how to set up and solve different types of word problems.

Have you been noticing the similarity of the problems? If you master the concepts covered in this book and work on correcting your mistakes, you should do quite well on the SAT.

Remember to analyze your mistakes, and, if you find yourself making mistakes on problems related to one specific area, such as fractions or percentages, then go back over that section or see your math teacher for some extra help.

Don't give up! Your hard work will pay off!

Lesson 9

Goal: To review solving two equations in two unknowns.

TWO EQUATIONS IN TWO UNKNOWNS

In Lesson 2 you were given an equation and asked to solve for some variable (unknown) in it. A simple example of this is $3x = 9$. This type of problem is called a linear equation in one unknown (x).

An example of *two equations in two unknowns* is:

$3x + 2y = 12$
$4x + y = 11$

The two unknowns are x and y. Since there are two equal signs, there are two equations.

There are two methods of solving these equations. Sometimes one is easier than the other but *both work all of the time*. If you like one method better, after having tried both, just use that one.

METHOD I: THE SUBSTITUTION METHOD

1. Solve one equation for one of the variables (unknowns).
2. Substitute the value found for the variable from one equation for that variable in the second equation.
3. Now the new equation can be solved with the rules for juggling equations having only one variable.

Examples

I. Solve the following two equations for x and y.

> (1) $3x + 2y = 12$
>
> (2) $4x + y = 11$

1. Using the rules for juggling equations, solve equation (2) for y. (It does not make a difference whether you solve equation (1) or equation (2) for x or y. Solve whichever is easier.)

    $4x + y = 11$ becomes $y = 11 - 4x$

2. Take the value found for y in the second equation and substitute it for the y in the first equation.

    $3x + 2y = 12$ becomes $3x + 2(11 - 4x) = 12$

3. Solve the equation with rules for juggling equations.

    $$3x + 2(11 - 4x) = 12$$
    $$3x + 22 - 8x = 12 \qquad \textit{Use the distributive property.}$$
    $$-5x = -10 \qquad \textit{Combine similar terms.}$$
    $$x = 2 \qquad \textit{Divide both sides by } -5.$$

This is only half of the answer! To solve for *y*, you must now substitute the value you found for *x* in one of the original equations.

From the above you would get:

$$3(2) + 2y = 12$$
$$2y = 6$$
$$y = 3$$

It does not matter which equation you use. In fact, a way to test whether or not you have the correct values for *x* and *y* is to plug the values back into both equations. If the values you found make both equations true statements (that is, you don't get something like $3 = 4$), then you have found the *one and only* solution.

II.   Solve the following two equations for *x* and *y*.

  (1) $4x + 2y = 0$
  (2) $5x + 2y = 1$

 1. Solving equation (1) for *y* gives:

   $$4x + 2y = \ 0$$
$2y = \ -4x$	*Subtract 4x from both sides.*
$y = \ -2x$	*Divide both sides by 2.*

 2. Take the value found for *y* in the first equation and substitute it for the *y* in the second equation.

   $5x + 2y = 1$ becomes $5x + 2(-2x) = 1$

 3. Solve for *x*:

   $$5x + 2(-2x) = \ 1$$
$5x + (-4x) = \ 1$	*Multiply the 2 by what is inside the parentheses.*
$x = \ 1$	*Do the addition.*

 4. Plugging back into the original equations gives:

   $$4(1) + 2y = 0 \ or$$
   $$5(1) + 2y = 1$$

   Solving either equation for *y* gives:

   $$y = -2$$

 5. Check your results by plugging *x* and *y* into the original equations:

   $$4(1) + 2(-2) = 0 \ and$$
   $$5(1) + 2(-2) = 1$$

Since *both are true statements,* the values found for *x* and *y* are the correct values.

Notice that in this problem we could have solved either equation (1) or equation (2) for $2y$ and then substituted that value into the other equation. This would have saved some time. Look for these shortcuts on your SAT.

METHOD II: THE LINEAR COMBINATION METHOD

Go back to the original two equations:

  $$3x + 2y = 12 \ and$$
  $$4x + y = 11$$

You are going to combine the two equations to "get rid of" either the *x*'s or the *y*'s so that only *one* variable remains. To do this you must make the numerical coefficients in front of one of the variables the same in both equations. Then you add the two equations or subtract one from the other in order to eliminate that variable. To solve the example from above:

 1. Multiply the first equation by the numerical coefficient of *x* from the second equation, 4, and multiply the second equation by the numerical coefficient of *x* from the first equation, 3.

   $$12x + 8y = 48$$
   $$12x + 3y = 33$$

2. Subtract the second equation from the first. Remember to change the signs of all of the terms.

$$12x + 8y = 48$$
$$\underline{-12x - 3y = -33}$$
$$0x + 5y = 15$$

3. Solve for y by juggling:

$$5y = 15$$
$$y = 3 \qquad \textit{Divide both sides by 5.}$$

4. Plug y back into the original equation to get x:

$$3x + 2(3) = 12$$
$$3x + 6 = 12$$
$$3x = 6$$
$$x = 2$$

Hot Tip:

Sometimes it is not necessary to solve for x and y directly. When the problem asks you to solve for the value of an expression, you may be able to add the two equations or subtract one from the other to get the desired results.

Example

If $2x + y = 7$ and $3x - y = 5$, find the value of $x - 2y$. Subtracting the first equation from the second gives the answer.

$$3x - y = 5$$
$$\underline{-(2x + y) = -7}$$
$$x - 2y = -2$$

(Remember to change the signs of all the terms when you subtract.)

You will see problems like this example frequently on SATs. Again, look for this shortcut before you solve for x and y. Remember that not every problem on the SAT is designed to gobble time, so if you're spending several minutes solving an equation or doing long computations, *look for an easier way*.

Always keep in sight what is being asked for. After you've solved for the variables, there may be one more step—*the one that gives the correct answer*.

In the following problems try each of the two methods. If they *both* come easily to you, use the one that fits the problem best. If one is decidedly easier for you, use it to save your sanity.

PRACTICE PROBLEMS

1. Solve for x and y:

$$y = 2x - 1$$
$$3x + 2y = 12$$

2. Solve for a and b:

$$a = 6 - b$$
$$-3a + b = -2$$

3. Give the value of $y - x$ if:

$$3y - 4x = 5$$
$$2y - 3x = 10$$

4. Solve for p and q:

$$3p - 2q = 6$$
$$-2p - q = 10$$

5. Find the value of $a - b$ if:

$$-2a - 5b = -15$$
$$3a + 4b = 19$$

6. Solve for x and y:

$$\frac{1}{x} + \frac{1}{y} = 3$$
$$\frac{1}{x} - \frac{1}{y} = 2$$

7. Solve for the value of $3a - 2b$:

$$12 = 4a - 3b$$
$$7a = 5b - 2$$

8. Solve for x and y:

$$\frac{2}{x} + \frac{1}{y} = 2$$
$$\frac{3}{x} - \frac{1}{y} = 8$$

9. Solve for p and q:

$$\frac{p}{3} + q = 1$$

$$p - q = 2$$

10. Solve for x and y:

$$x = 2(2y + 2)$$

$$3(x - 3y) = 15$$

Lesson 10

Goal: To review setting up and solving different types of word problems.

WORD PROBLEMS

In this section we are going to review how to set up and solve various types of word problems.

Just the thought of word problems produces anxiety in many students. We hope to overcome that fear and learn how to master these problems in this section.

MOTION PROBLEMS

In order to solve motion problems, you must understand the equation

$$(Rate)\ (Time) = (Distance)\ \text{or}\ R \cdot T = D$$

This formula tells us that the distance that an object travels is equal to the product of its rate (speed) and the amount of time that it is traveling.

Two other useful formulas are derived from $R \cdot T = D$.

If you divide both sides of the equation by R, you get $T = \dfrac{D}{R}$. The time that it takes to travel a certain distance is equal to the total distance traveled divided by the rate (speed).

If you divide $R \cdot T = D$ by T, you get the equation $R = \dfrac{D}{T}$. The rate that one travels is equal to the total distance traveled divided by the amount of time.

Examples

I. If a car travels at a rate of 30 mph for $5\frac{1}{2}$ hours, how many miles will the car travel?

Solution $R = 30$; $T = 5\frac{1}{2}$. We solve for D.

Using the formula $R \cdot T = D$, we get:

$$(30)\left(5\frac{1}{2}\right) = D \qquad \textit{Substitute the values for R and T.}$$

$$(30)\left(\frac{11}{2}\right) = D \qquad \textit{Now, multiply.}$$

$$\frac{330}{2} = D \qquad \textit{Next, divide.}$$

$$165 \text{ miles} = D$$

II. If a plane travels 720 miles in $2\frac{1}{4}$ hours, what is its average speed?

Solution $D = 720$; $T = 2\frac{1}{4}$. We solve for R.

Using the formula $R = \dfrac{D}{T}$, we get:

$R = \dfrac{720}{2\frac{1}{4}}$ *Substitute the values for D and T.*

$R = \dfrac{720}{\frac{9}{4}}$ *Convert $2\frac{1}{4}$ to an improper fraction.*

$R = 720 \cdot \dfrac{4}{9}$ *Invert and multiply.*

$R = 320$

III. How long will it take a car to travel 420 miles at an average speed of 48 mph?
   Solution $D = 420$; $R = 48$. We solve for T.

Using the formula $T = \dfrac{D}{R}$, we get:

$T = \dfrac{420}{48}$

$T = \dfrac{35}{4}$ *Reduce to lowest terms (divide the numerator and denominator by 12).*

$T = 8\dfrac{3}{4}$ hours   *Convert to a mixed numeral.*

Those weren't too bad, were they? They do get a little trickier though. Here are some other examples.

Example
   Two cars traveling in opposite directions pass each other at 1:00 p.m. One of the cars travels at a rate of 60 mph, while the other car travels at a rate of 45 mph. At what time will the cars be 455 miles apart?

Solution
   Since the cars are traveling in opposite directions, we will have to add the distance traveled by the first car to the distance traveled by the second car and let the sum equal 455. Expressed as a formula, $d_1 + d_2 = 455$. The important fact in this problem is that both cars will travel for the same amount of *time*.
   A useful aid in motion problems is a chart.

	R	• T	= D
Car 1	60	x	$60x$
Car 2	45	x	$45x$

We let x = number of hours that each car will travel. Using our equation $d_1 + d_2 = 455$, we get:

$60x + 45x = 455$
$105x = 455$ *Combine like terms.*

$x = \dfrac{455}{105}$ *Divide by 105.*

$x = \dfrac{13}{3} = 4\dfrac{1}{3}$ hours   *Reduce to lowest terms (divide by 35).*

This is *not* the answer. Remember that the problem asked: *when* will the cars be 455 miles apart? Add $4\dfrac{1}{3}$ hours

to 1:00 p.m. and you get 5:20 p.m. $\left(\dfrac{1}{3} \text{ of an hour is } \dfrac{1}{3}(60) \text{ minutes, or 20 minutes} \right)$.

PRACTICE PROBLEMS

1. What is the distance a plane can travel from 1:45 a.m. to 8:00 a.m. flying at a rate of 120 mph?

2. At what speed must a car travel in order to go 940 miles in $15\frac{2}{3}$ hours?

3. What is the rate of a boat that travels pq kilometers in p hours?

4. Mr. Smith left his house at 7:30 a.m. and drove at a rate of 50 mph until 10:00 a.m. He then stopped for half an hour. At what rate must he travel in order to get to work by noon if he still has 105 miles to go?

5. A boy can pedal his bicycle $\frac{3}{4}$ mile in 6 minutes. What is his rate in mph?

6. A boy walks at a rate of 5 mph for 2 hours and then rides his bike at a rate of 12 mph for 3 hours. What is his average rate for the entire trip?

7. A plane travels x miles during the first 2 hours of a trip and y miles during the last 3 hours of the trip. What was the average rate for the entire trip?

8. Two cars travel in opposite directions starting from the same point. One car travels at a rate of 40 mph, and the other car travels at a rate of 54 mph. How long will it take for the two cars to be 188 miles apart?

9. How many minutes would it take for a fire engine to get to a fire x miles away if it travels at a rate of y mph?

10. How much farther can a boat traveling at a rate of 15 kilometers per hour for x hours travel than a second boat traveling at a rate of 18 kilometers per hour for $x - 3$ hours?

ANSWERS to all practice problems can be found in the back of the book, beginning on p. 417.

MIXTURE PROBLEMS

The basic idea behind mixture problems is that the sum of the values of the component parts of the mixture is equal to the total value of the mixture.

For this type of problem, a chart can be a handy tool to help visualize the problem and set up an equation.

Example
How many pounds of peanuts, costing 70 cents per pound, should be mixed with 30 pounds of cashews, worth $1.20 per pound, to obtain a mixture worth $1.00 per pound?

Solution

First, determine what you are solving for and represent that quantity with a variable, say x.
Second, fill in the chart with the known and unknown quantities.

Component	Unit Value (dollars) •	Amount (pounds) =	Value (dollars)
Peanuts	.70	x	$.70x$
Cashews	1.20	30	$(1.20)\,(30)$
Mixture	1.00	$x + 30$	$(1.00)\,(x + 30)$

Use the rule that the unit value (which is the cost per pound) times the amount (number of pounds) equals the value of the mixture.

Set up your equation.

$(.70)\,(x) + (1.20)\,(30) = (1.00)\,(x + 30)$

$.70x + 36 = x + 30$	*Subtract .70x and 30 from both sides.*
$6 = .3x$	*Multiply both sides by 10.*
$60 = 3x$	*Divide by 3.*
$x = 20$ pounds	

Example

How many pints of a 30% acid solution must be added to 5 pints of a 40% acid solution to produce a solution that is 36% acid?

Solution

We are solving for the number of pints of a 30% acid solution. Call it x.

Fill in the chart.

Component	Unit Value (%) •	Amount (pints) =	Value (pints in mixture)
30% Acid Solution	.30	x	$.30x$
40% Acid Solution	.40	5	2
Mixture	.36	$x + 5$	$.36(x + 5)$

Set up the equation.

$$.30x + .40(5) = .36(x + 5)$$

Solve for x. Multiply by 100 to eliminate the decimals:

$$30x + 200 = 36x + 180$$

$$20 = 6x \qquad \textit{Get your numbers on one side, variables on the other side.}$$

$$\frac{20}{6} = x \qquad \textit{Divide by 6.}$$

$$x = 3\frac{1}{3} \text{ pints} \qquad \textit{Convert to a mixed numeral.}$$

Example

Tickets to a baseball game cost $4.00 for reserved seats and $3.00 for general admission. In all, 500 tickets were sold for a total of $1,760. How many reserved seats were sold?

Solution

We are solving for the number of reserved seats sold. Call this x.

Fill in the chart.

Component	Unit Value (dollars) •	Amount (no. of tickets) =	Value (dollars)
Reserved Tickets	4.00	x	$(4.00)(x)$
General Admission	3.00	$500 - x$	$(3.00)(500 - x)$
Mixture		500	1,760

Set up the equation.

$$4x + 3(500 - x) = 1,760 \qquad \textit{Remove parentheses and solve for x.}$$

$$4x + 1,500 - 3x = 1,760 \qquad \textit{Collect like terms and subtract 1,500 from both sides.}$$

$$x = 260 \text{ reserved seats}$$

Notice that you were given the *total* number of tickets that were sold (500), not the number of *each type*. Since x reserved tickets were sold, $(500 - x)$ general admission tickets must have been sold.

PRACTICE PROBLEMS

1. How much silver valued at $4.00 per gram must be mixed with gold valued at $24.00 per gram to obtain 30 grams of an alloy worth $12.00 per gram?

2. A 200-gram solution is 25% acid. How much pure acid must be added to produce a solution that is 40% acid?

3. A 30-gallon solution is 80% salt. How much pure water must be added to produce a solution that is 60% salt?

4. How many quarts of grape juice worth $1.20 a quart should be mixed with 3 quarts of apple juice worth 90 cents a quart to produce a punch worth $1.00 a quart?

5. Tickets to a concert cost $15.00 for the balcony and $20.00 for an orchestra seat. If 540 tickets were sold for a total price of $9,750, how many balcony tickets were sold?

6. How many pounds of cashews valued at $2.00 per pound must be mixed with 30 pounds of peanuts valued at 80 cents per pound to produce a mixture worth $1.25 per pound?

7. How many ounces of water must be added to 20 ounces of a 10% salt solution to produce a 6% salt solution?

8. In a container there are 60 ounces of a solution that is 20% acid. How many ounces of pure acid must be added to produce a solution that is 25% acid?

9. One type of candy costs 60 cents a pound while a second type costs 80 cents a pound. How many pounds of each type must be combined in order to produce 20 pounds of a mixture worth 75 cents a pound?

10. A boy has 34 coins in his pocket consisting of nickels and dimes. If the total value of the coins is $2.20, how many nickels does he have?

WORK PROBLEMS

The main idea behind work problems is that if x equals the amount of time that it takes to complete a certain job, then $\frac{1}{x}$ is the rate at which the job is done.

Example

If a boy can cut a lawn in 4 hours, he would be able to cut $\frac{1}{4}$ of the lawn *per hour*.

Another important fact to know about work problems is that the total work that is done is equal to the sum of the component parts.

Example

If one pipe can fill a pool in 8 hours while a second pipe can fill the same pool in 6 hours, then both pipes working together could fill the pool at a rate of $\left(\frac{1}{8}+\frac{1}{6}\right)$ per hour.

Also, when the total job is completed, the amount of work done is equal to 1. This means that you want to complete 1 job.

Example

How many hours would it take the two pipes in the previous example to fill the pool if both pipes work together?

Solution

We are solving for the number of hours that both pipes would work. Call this x. The rate of the first pipe is $\frac{1}{8}$, meaning that it alone can fill $\frac{1}{8}$ of the pool per hour. In x hours it fills $\frac{x}{8}$ of the pool. The second pipe alone fills $\frac{1}{6}$ of the pool per hour. Working for x hours, the second pipe would fill $\frac{x}{6}$ of the pool.

The total work that is done is equal to the sum of the two components. Set up the equation:

$$\frac{x}{8}+\frac{x}{6}=1$$
$$3x+4x=24 \qquad \textit{Multiply each term by 24, the least common denominator.}$$
$$7x=24 \qquad \textit{Combine like terms.}$$
$$x=\frac{24}{7}=3\frac{3}{7} \text{ hours}$$

We set the equation equal to 1 because we want to fill 1 pool. If the problem had said fill 3 pools at the same rate, we would set the equation equal to 3 because we would want to complete 3 jobs.

Example

John can polish his car in 45 minutes, while Jim can polish the same car in 30 minutes. How long would it take to polish the car if both boys worked together?

Solution

Let x = number of minutes that John and Jim would work together.

John's rate $\dfrac{1}{45}$; Jim's rate is $\dfrac{1}{30}$.

In x minutes, John will do $\dfrac{x}{45}$ of the job.

In x minutes, Jim will do $\dfrac{x}{30}$ of the job.

Working together indicates the *sum* of their rates.

They want to complete 1 job; therefore the equation to solve is

$$\frac{x}{45} + \frac{x}{30} = 1$$

Clear of fractions:

$$90\left(\frac{x}{45}\right) + 90\left(\frac{x}{30}\right) = 90(1) \qquad \textit{Multiply each term by 90.}$$

$$2x + 3x = 90 \qquad \textit{Solve for x; collect like terms.}$$

$$5x = 90 \qquad \textit{Divide by 5.}$$

$$x = 18 \text{ minutes} \qquad \textit{It would take 18 minutes to wax the car if both boys worked together.}$$

PRACTICE PROBLEMS

1. If one pipe can fill a pool in 12 hours, how much of the pool is filled after 8 hours?

2. If Brutus can eat 16 hamburgers in 1 hour, how many can he eat in 3 hours?

3. One machine can dig a ditch in 128 minutes. How much of the ditch can be dug in 40 minutes?

4. One machine can process a payroll in 2 hours. A second machine can process the same payroll in 90 minutes. How long would it take to process the payroll if both machines worked together?

5. One pipe can drain a pool in 4 hours. A second pipe can drain the same pool in 3 hours. How many hours would it take to drain the pool if both pipes worked together?

6. Frank can cut his lawn in $4\frac{1}{2}$ hours, his wife Mary can cut the same lawn in 4 hours, while their son Tom can cut the lawn in $3\frac{1}{2}$ hours. How long would it take to cut the lawn if all three worked together?

NUMBER PROBLEMS

Remember these terms?

Integers   Positive and negative counting numbers and zero.
   Examples: $\{ \ldots -3, -2, -1, 0, 1, 2, 3, \ldots \}$

Consecutive Integers   Integers that differ by 1.
   Examples: 7, 8, 9, 10 or $x, x + 1, x + 2$ where x is any integer.

Consecutive Odd Integers   Odd integers that differ by 2.
   Examples: 15, 17, 19, 21 or $x, x + 2, x + 4$ where x is any odd integer.

Consecutive Even Integers   Even integers that differ by 2.
  Examples: 0, 2, 4, 6, 8 or $x, x + 2, x + 4$ where x is any even integer.

  To solve number problems you must be able to translate the question into an equation. Go back over your list of key words on p. 283–84.
  Remember that the steps to solving word problems are:
    1. Define your variable.
    2. Set up your equation.
    3. Solve the equation.
    4. Check your answer.

Examples

 I. Two less than six times a certain number equals five times the number plus 2. What is the number?

  Solution
    Define your variable. Let $x =$ the number.
    Set up your equation, noting the key words: *less than, times, equals, plus:*
     $6x - 2 = 5x + 2$
    Solve the equation by subtracting $5x$ and adding 2 to both sides:
     $6x - 2 = 5x + 2$
       $x = 4$
    Check your answer:
     $6(4) - 2 = 5(4) + 2$
     $24 - 2 = 20 + 2$
      $22 = 22$

 II. Find three consecutive integers whose sum is 84.

  Solution
    Let x represent the first integer.
    The second integer would be $x + 1$.
    The third consecutive integer would be $x + 2$.
    Set up your equation remembering the key words, *sum* and *is.*
     $x + (x + 1) + (x + 2) = 84$
         $3x + 3 = 84$ *Collect like terms.*
          $3x = 81$ *Subtract 3 from both sides.*
           $x = 27$ *Divide by 3.*
    The three consecutive integers whose sum is 84 would then be 27, 28, and 29.

 III. Find three consecutive even integers such that the sum of the first and twice the third is 134.

  Solution
    Define your terms.
     Let $x =$ the first even integer. Then
     $x + 2 =$ the second even integer.
     $x + 4 =$ the third even integer.

    Set up your equation, remembering that *twice the third* means multiplication.
      $x + 2(x + 4) = 134$
        $x + 2x + 8 = 134$ *Eliminate the parentheses.*
          $3x + 8 = 134$ *Collect like terms.*
           $3x = 126$ *Subtract 8 from both sides.*
            $x = 42$ *Divide by 3.*
    The three consecutive even integers would then be 42, 44, 46. The sum of the first (42) plus twice the third (46) = 134.

IV. Find four consecutive odd integers such that the sum of three times the first and twice the third is 11 more than twice the sum of the second and fourth integers.

Solution

Define your variables.

Let x = first odd integer. Then

$x + 2$ = second odd integer.

$x + 4$ = third odd integer.

$x + 6$ = fourth odd integer.

Set up your equation. Watch for the key words.

$$3(x) + 2(x + 4) = 2[(x + 2) + (x + 6)] + 11$$

$3x + 2x + 8 = 2[2x + 8] + 11$	*Eliminate the parentheses and collect like terms.*
$3x + 2x + 8 = 4x + 16 + 11$	*Eliminate the brackets by multiplying by 2.*
$5x + 8 = 4x + 27$	*Combine like terms on both sides.*
$x = 19$	*Juggle the equations.*

The four consecutive odd integers are 19, 21, 23, and 25. The sum of 3 times the first (19) and twice the third (23) = 11 plus twice the sum of the second (21) and the fourth (25).

PRACTICE PROBLEMS

1. Find six consecutive integers whose sum is 513.
2. Find five consecutive odd integers whose sum is 225.
3. Four times one odd integer is 14 less than three times the next even integer. Find the integers.
4. The largest of five consecutive integers is twice the smallest. Find the smallest integer.
5. The average of four consecutive odd integers is 16. Find the largest integer.
6. When the sum of three consecutive integers is divided by 9 the result is 7. Find the three integers.
7. If each of three consecutive integers is divided by 3, the sum of the quotients is 84. Find the smallest integer.
8. The sum of three numbers is 65. The first is twice the second, and the third is twice the result obtained by subtracting 5 from the second. Find the largest number.
9. A baseball team played 150 games and won 32 more than it lost. How many did it lose?
10. One number exceeds another number by 12, and the sum of the smaller number and twice the larger number is 93. Find the numbers.

AGE PROBLEMS

Age problems are easy to solve if one realizes that if a person is now x years old, then 8 years ago that person was $(x - 8)$ years old, and in 10 years the person will be $(x + 10)$ years old.

A chart is very useful in visualizing and solving problems involving ages.

Examples

I. Sally is half her father's age. In 2 years the sum of their ages will be 67. How old is each now?

Solution

1. Set up a chart and define the variables. Let x = Sally's age now. Therefore $2x$ = her father's age now.

	Age Now	Age in 2 Years
Sally	x	$x + 2$
Father	$2x$	$2x + 2$

2. Set up your equation:
$$(x + 2) + (2x + 2) = 67$$

3. Solve the equation:

$(x + 2) + (2x + 2) =$	67	
$3x + 4 =$	67	*Eliminate the parentheses and collect like terms.*
$3x =$	63	*Juggle the equation.*
$x =$	21	*Divide by 3.*

Sally is now 21 and her father is 42.

4. Check your answer:

$$(21 + 2) + (42 + 2) = 67$$
$$23 + 44 = 67$$
$$67 = 67$$

II. Katie is 2 years older than Sue. In 8 years the sum of their ages will be 48. How old is each now?

Solution

1. Set up a chart and define the variables. Let $x =$ Sue's age now. Therefore Katie now is $(x + 2)$ years old.

	Age Now	Age in 8 Years
Sue	x	$x + 8$
Katie	$x + 2$	$x + 10$

2. Set up the equation:
$$(x + 8) + (x + 10) = 48$$

3. Solve the equation:

$(x + 8) + (x + 10) =$	48	
$2x + 18 =$	48	*Collect like terms.*
$2x =$	30	*Subtract 18.*
$x =$	15	*Divide by 2.*

Sue is now 15 and Katie is 17.

4. Check your answer:

$$(15 + 8) + (15 + 10) = 48$$
$$23 + 25 = 48$$
$$48 = 48$$

III. A father is 30 years older than his daughter. Half the present age of the father will equal the age of the daughter in 9 years. How old is the daughter?

Solution

1. Set up a chart and define the variables. Let $x =$ the daughter's age; then $(x + 30)$ is the father's present age.

	Age Now	Age in 9 Years
Daughter	x	$x + 9$
Father	$x + 30$	$x + 39$

2. Set up the equation:
$$\frac{1}{2}(x + 30) = x + 9$$

3. Solve the equation:

$$\frac{1}{2}(x+30) = x + 9$$
$$x + 30 = 2x + 18 \qquad \textit{Multiply both sides by 2.}$$
$$12 = x \qquad \textit{Juggle the equation.}$$

The daughter is 12.

4. Check the answer:

$$\frac{1}{2}(42) = 12 + 9$$
$$21 = 21$$

PRACTICE PROBLEMS

1. If Roger were 32 years older, he would be three times as old as he is now. How old is Roger?

2. Brad is 12 years older than Sam. If Brad were 8 years older than he is now, he would be twice as old as Sam. How old is Sam now?

3. Barrie is now 2 years older than Krista. In 15 years Barrie's age will be 2 years more than twice Krista's age now. How old will Barrie be in 6 years?

4. John is now 10 years older than Marcus. Three times John's age 5 years from now will be the same as five times Marcus's age 5 years ago. How old is John now?

5. In 1 year Kristen will be four times as old as Danielle. Ten years from then Kristen will only be twice as old as Danielle. How old is Kristen now?

6. A woman was 30 years old when her daughter was born. Her age is now 6 years more than three times her daughter's age. How old will the daughter be in 5 years?

7. Ralph's age is currently 3 years more than twice Joe's age. But, 3 years go Ralph was four times as old as Joe was then. How old will Joe be in 10 years?

8. Lisa is 15 years old and her father is 40. How many years ago was the father six times as old as Lisa?

9. Joel is one third the age of Bob. In 7 years the combined ages of the boys will be 58. How old is each now?

10. Tom is three times as old as Leigh Ann. In 7 years, the sum of half of Tom's present age and a third of Leigh Ann's age will be the same as Tom's age now. How old will Tom be in 7 years?

Aren't you glad this section is over? Still, by reading each question carefully and noting the key words, you *should* be able to set up and solve the equations.

We have now completed our units on arithmetic and algebra.

PRACTICE SAT PROBLEMS

1. If the price of grass seed has increased from 5 pounds for $10.00 to 3 pounds for $10.00, how many fewer pounds can now be bought for $6.00 then could be bought before?

   (A) .2   (B) .3   (C) .8   (D) 1.2   (E) 1.5

2. Jasmin was M years of age 4 years ago. In terms of M, how old will Jasmin be 4 years from now?

   (A) $M + 4$ (B) M (C) $M + 8$ (D) $2M$ (E) $\frac{M}{2}$

3. Rocky is p years old, and he is 5 years older than Apollo. In terms of p, how old was Apollo 3 years ago?

    (A) $p-8$ (B) $p-5$ (C) $p-3$ (D) $p-1$ (E) $p+1$

4. Lumpy now weighs 18 pounds more than he did 1 year ago. If his weight 1 year ago was 90 percent of his present weight, what is his present weight?

    (A) 144 pounds   (B) 162 pounds   (C) 180 pounds   (D) 190 pounds   (E) 216 pounds

5. One number is 20 less than another number. Two thirds of the lesser number is equal to one fourth of the greater number. Find the greater number.

    (A) -20 (B) 12   (C) 20   (D) 24   (E) 32

6. One pipe can fill a pool in 8 hours, and a second pipe can fill the same pool in 12 hours. If both pipes work together, how long will it take to fill the pool?

    (A) $4\frac{1}{5}$ hours   (B) $4\frac{2}{5}$ hours   (C) $4\frac{3}{5}$ hours   (D) $4\frac{4}{5}$ hours   (E) 5 hours

7. Twin A leaves New York City, heading north at 35 miles per hour. At the same time, Twin B leaves New York City, heading south at 45 miles per hour. In how many hours will they be 640 miles apart?

    (A) 6   (B) 7   (C) 8   (D) 12   (E) 16

8. How many ounces of a 40 percent salt solution must be added to 20 ounces of a 12 percent salt solution to produce a mixture that is 28 percent salt?

    (A) 26   (B) $26\frac{1}{3}$ (C) $26\frac{2}{3}$ (D) 28   (E) 32

9. How many gallons of gas with an octane rating of 94 and gas with an octane rating of 89 mixed together will yield 100 gallons of 92-octane gas?

    (A) 60 gallons at 94 with 40 gallons at 89   (B) 70 gallons at 94 with 30 gallons at 89

    (C) 80 gallons at 94 with 20 gallons at 89   (D) 90 gallons at 94 with 10 gallons at 89

    (E) 75 gallons at 94 with 25 gallons at 89

10. One brother is 5 years older than the other. One third of the older brother's age now is equal to the age of the younger brother 1 year ago. How old will the younger brother be in 4 years?

    (A) 4   (B) 6   (C) 8   (D) 9   (E) 13

11. Solve for the value of $3x - y$ if $2x + 3y = 7$ and $x - 4y = 12$.

    (A) 5   (B) 7   (C) 19   (D) 84   (E) 144

12. If $6p - 5q = 12$ and $2p + 7q = 10$, what is the value of $2p + \frac{1}{2}q$?

    (A) 22   (B) 11   (C) 6   (D) 5.5   (E) 5

13. If $2x - 6 = y$ and $3x + y = 4$, what is the value of $3y$?

    (A) 6   (B) 2   (C) 0   (D) -2 (E) -6

14. If $\frac{7}{x} = 1$ and $\frac{y}{4} = 6$, then $\frac{3+x}{3+y} =$

    (A) $\frac{10}{27}$ (B) $\frac{7}{24}$ (C) $1\frac{7}{24}$ (D) $2\frac{7}{10}$ (E) $\frac{90}{23}$

15. If $x + y = 12$, what is the value of $x^2 + 2xy + y^2$?

    (A) 1   (B) 12   (C) 24   (D) 144   (E) It cannot be determined from the information given.

Lesson 11

Goal: To review the basic theorems and definitions relating to the geometry of angles.

GEOMETRY OF ANGLES

Approximately one third of your questions will involve geometry, so it is important to master the material in the next four lessons. The geometry problems will involve angle relationships, area and perimeter, properties of triangles and other polygons, volume, and coordinate geometry.

Many students are a little rusty on geometry, so take some time to memorize and understand the material in these lessons.

In solving any geometry problem, the illustration that has been drawn for you (or that you will draw) is the path to the answer. Use it. First fill in all of the given information from the problem, such as lengths of segments and measures of angles (often this information will already be drawn in for you). Then, using the theorems and definitions that are reviewed here, solve for the different unknown quantities, step by step, until you find the one asked for.

Diagrams that are already drawn for you are drawn to scale unless otherwise stated. Do not hesitate to write in your booklet or draw new diagrams. Use whatever resources you have: your pencil, your watchband, your answer sheet—the wires from your braces?—to measure angles or compare the lengths of line segments. Problems that relate to a diagram are usually easier to solve, so try not to omit any of them.

BASIC DEFINITIONS AND THEOREMS

Two pairs of *vertical* (or opposite) *angles* are formed when two lines intersect.

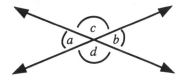

Vertical angles are *equal: a=b, c=d.*

A *ray* is half a line. A ray has an endpoint and extends in one direction. $\overrightarrow{AB}$ denotes ray *AB* with its endpoint at *A*. A ray has an arrow extending in only one direction.

Two rays sharing a common endpoint form an angle.

Example

$\overrightarrow{AB}$ and $\overrightarrow{AC}$ form $\angle BAC$. *A* is the common endpoint, called the vertex of the angle.

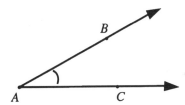

Note when an angle is named using three letters, the middle letter is the vertex of the angle.

A *straight angle* equals 180°.

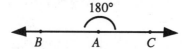

Two angles are *supplementary* if their sum is 180°.

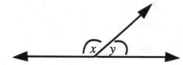

$\angle x$ and $\angle y$ are supplementary: $\angle x + \angle y = 180°$.

Two lines are *perpendicular* (denoted by $\perp$) if they form a 90° angle where they cross.

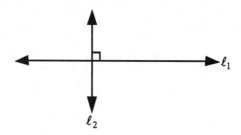

Note that $\neg$ indicates an angle of 90°. $\ell_1 \perp \ell_2$ means line 1 is perpendicular to line 2.

Two angles are *complementary* if their sum is 90°.

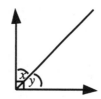

$\angle x$ and $\angle y$ are complementary: $\angle x + \angle y = 90°$.

A *right angle* is an angle whose measure is 90°.

An *acute angle* is an angle whose measure is less than 90°.

An *obtuse angle* is an angle whose measure is more than 90° but less than 180°.

With some practice you should be able to estimate the degree measure of many of the angles given on the SAT. This could save you some time, especially when you work backward.

Two lines are *parallel* (denoted $\parallel$) if they never intersect and are in the same plane.

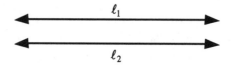

$\ell_1 \parallel \ell_2$ means line 1 is parallel to line 2.

If two parallel lines are intersected by a third line, called a *transversal*, eight angles are formed and certain pairs are related.

Example

Given $\ell_1 \parallel \ell_2$, ℓ_3 intersects ℓ_1 and ℓ_2.

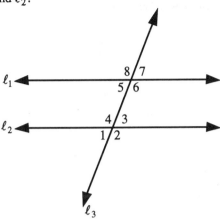

Angles 3 and 5, 4 and 6 are called *alternate interior angles.*

Angles 3 and 7, 4 and 8⎫
$\quad\quad$ 2 and 6, 1 and 5⎭ are called *corresponding angles.*

Angles 3 and 6, 4 and 5 are called *same side interior angles.*

Rule 1. If two parallel lines are cut by a transversal, the alternate interior angles are *equal.*

Rule 2. If two parallel lines are cut by a transversal, the corresponding angles are *equal.*

Rule 3. If two parallel lines are cut by a transversal, the same side interior angles are *supplementary.*

Example

Given $\ell_1 \parallel \ell_2$, ℓ_3 is a transversal.

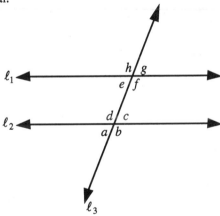

If $\angle c = 60°$, how many degrees are in

1. $\angle a$? $a = 60°$ because a and c are vertical angles, and vertical angles are equal.

2. $\angle e$? $e = 60°$ because c and e are alternate interior angles, and alternate interior angles are equal.

3. $\angle g$? $g = 60°$ because c and g are corresponding angles, and corresponding angles are equal.

4. $\angle f$? $f = 120°$ because c and f are same side interior angles, and same side interior angles are
        supplementary.

$\quad\quad$ Notice that if you have two parallel lines and a transversal, and, if you are given the measure of any one angle, you can find the measures of the *other seven angles.*

$\quad\quad$ Remember that Rules 1, 2, and 3 apply *only* if the lines are *parallel.*

$\quad\quad$ An *angle bisector* is a ray that divides an angle into two equal parts.

$\quad\quad$ A *perpendicular bisector* is a line or line segment that is $\perp$ to a segment, passing through the *midpoint* of the segment.

Example

Given $\overrightarrow{AD}$ bisects $\angle BAC$. If $\angle BAC = 50°$, then $\angle BAD = \angle DAC = 25°$.

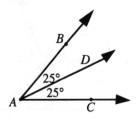

PRACTICE PROBLEMS

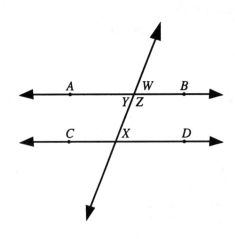

1. $\overleftrightarrow{AB} \parallel \overleftrightarrow{CD}$, $\angle X = 62°$. Find the measures of angles

   Y, Z, and W.

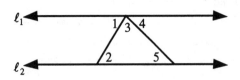

2. $\ell_1 \parallel \ell_2$, $\angle 1 = 50°$, $\angle 5 = 39°$. Find the measures of angles 2, 3, and 4.

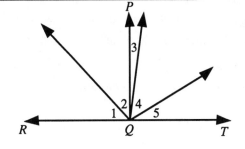

3. RQT is a straight line and $\angle PQR$ is a right angle, $\angle 1 = 42°$, $\angle 3 = 17°$, and $\angle 2 = \angle 4$. Find the measure of $\angle 5$.

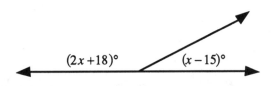

4. Solve for x.

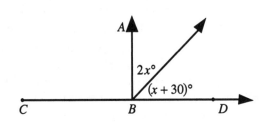

5. Given that $\overrightarrow{BA} \perp \overrightarrow{CD}$, solve for x.

6. Find the measure of an angle if its measure is 40°
more than that of its supplement.

7. Two angles are complementary. Three times one
angle is 30° more than twice the other. Find the
measure of the angles.

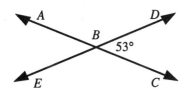

8. In the diagram, find the measures of
∠*ABE* and ∠*EBC*.

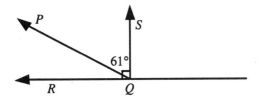

9. In the diagram, find the measure of ∠*PQR*.

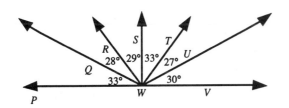

10. In the diagram, which pairs of rays are
perpendicular?

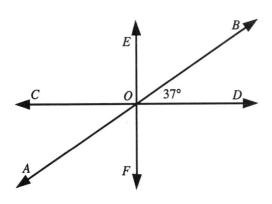

11. Lines *AB*, *CD*, and *EF* meet at *O*. ∠*EOC* is a right
angle; ∠*BOD* = 37°. Find the measure of
∠*AOF*.

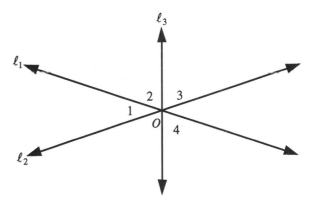

12. ℓ_1, ℓ_2, and ℓ_3 intersect at *O*. If ∠2 is twice the
measure of ∠1 and ∠1 is half the measure of ∠3,
find the measure of ∠4.

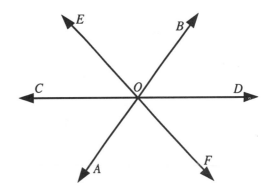

13. Lines *AB*, *CD*, and *EF* intersect at *O*. If
∠*COF* = 120° and ∠*COA* = 47°, find the
measure of ∠*EOB*.

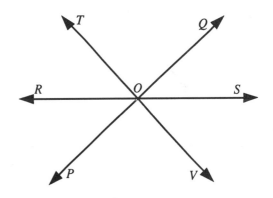

14. Lines *PQ*, *RS*, and *TV* intersect at *O*. If
∠*ROQ* = 142° and ∠*TOS* = 129°, find the
measures of ∠*ROT* and ∠*POV*.

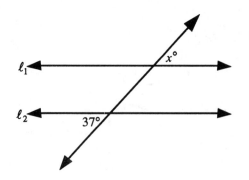

15. If $\ell_1 \parallel \ell_2$, solve for x.

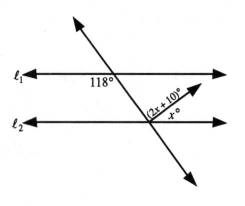

16. If $\ell_1 \parallel \ell_2$, solve for x.

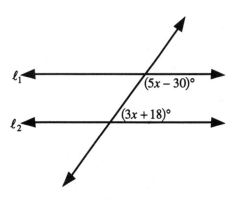

17. If $\ell_1 \parallel \ell_2$, solve for x.

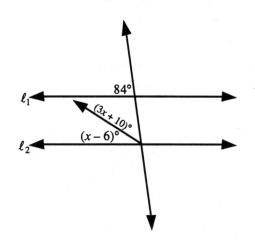

18. If $\ell_1 \parallel \ell_2$, solve for x.

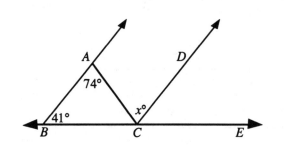

19. If $AB \parallel CD$, solve for x.

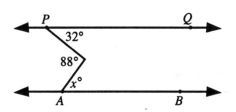

20. If $PQ \parallel AB$, solve for x.

Lesson 12

Goal: To master the theorems and definitions related to polygons and polyhedrons.

GEOMETRY OF POLYGONS AND POLYHEDRONS

A *polygon* is a closed plane figure with three or more straight sides.

We will first review triangles.

A *triangle* is a three-angled and three-sided figure that appears often on the SAT because it is basic to geometry.

As with any other geometry problem on a test, you will be given some basic information and asked to solve for a given value using the theorems and definitions reviewed here.

BASIC DEFINITIONS AND THEOREMS FOR TRIANGLES

The sum of the angles of a triangle is 180°.

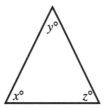

$\angle x + \angle y + \angle z = 180°$

The perimeter of a triangle, or any polygon, is equal to the sum of the lengths of its sides.

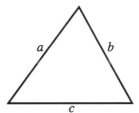

Perimeter $= a + b + c$

An *equilateral* triangle has three equal sides and three 60° angles.

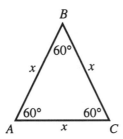

$\triangle ABC$ is equilateral.

An *isosceles* triangle has two equal sides and two equal angles. The two equal angles are called the base angles and the third angle is called the vertex angle.

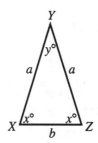

Δ *XYZ* is isosceles.
∠*YXZ* and ∠*YZX* are the base angles.
∠*XYZ* is the vertex angle.
In a triangle, opposite sides of equal angles are equal.

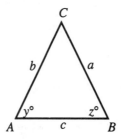

If $y = z$ then $a = b$. Conversely, if $a = b$ then $y = z$.
If ∠*A* is greater than ∠*B*, then the side opposite ∠*A* is greater than the side opposite ∠*B*.

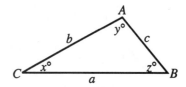

If $y > z$ then $a > b$, or, conversely, if $a > b$ then $y > z$.

A *right* triangle has a right (90°) angle.

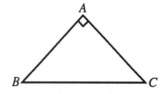

BAC is a right triangle.
An *obtuse* triangle has one obtuse angle.
An *acute* triangle has three acute angles.

Pythagorean Theorem

In a right triangle the length of the side opposite the right angle (the *hypotenuse*) squared equals the sum of the squares of the other two sides, called the legs.

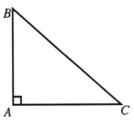

$(AB)^2 + (AC)^2 = (BC)^2$

This theorem is one of the most useful theorems in geometry. The SAT makes good use of it.

Example

Given $\triangle ABC$ with $AB = 6$, $BC = 8$. Find the length of AC, if $AB \perp BC$.

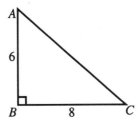

Solution

The Pythagorean theorem tells us that

$$6^2 + 8^2 = (AC)^2$$
$$36 + 64 = (AC)^2$$
$$100 = AC^2$$
$$\sqrt{100} = AC$$
$$10 = AC$$

The Pythagorean theorem works only for right triangles.

Helpful Hint: Certain sets of Pythagorean numbers are commonly used on the SAT. These triplets are

$3 - 4 - 5$ $8 - 15 - 17$

$5 - 12 - 13$ $7 - 24 - 25$

and any multiples of them.

Example

Solve for x in the given diagram.

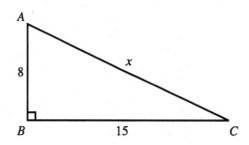

Solution

Using the Pythagorean theorem,
$$8^2 + 15^2 = x^2$$
$$64 + 225 = x^2$$
$$289 = x^2$$
$$\sqrt{289} = x$$
$$17 = x$$

Or recognize that the triangle is an $8 - 15 - 17$ right triangle.

Example

Solve for x in the given diagram.

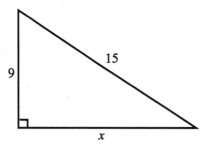

Solution

Using the Pythagorean theorem,
$$9^2 + x^2 = 15^2$$
$$81 + x^2 = 225$$
$$x^2 = 144$$
$$x = \sqrt{144}$$
$$x = 12$$

Or notice that $9 = 3 \cdot 3$ and $15 = 3 \cdot 5$, so $x = 3 \cdot 4$, since the lengths of the sides are multiples of $3 - 4 - 5$.

The *area* of a triangle equals one half the base times the height: $A = \dfrac{1}{2}bh$.

(a) Every triangle has 3 bases, as each of its sides is a base.

(b) The height, or the altitude, of a triangle is the distance (or length) from the base to the vertex opposite it.

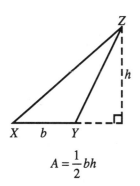

$$A = \frac{1}{2}bh$$

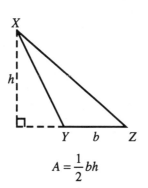

$$A = \frac{1}{2}bh$$

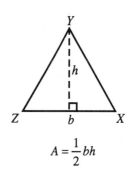

$$A = \frac{1}{2}bh$$

Note that the base is always perpendicular to the height.

A *45-45-90 triangle* is one with angles of 45°, 45°, and 90°.

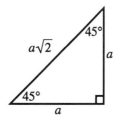

If the length of a leg of this triangle is *a*, then the hypotenuse is $a\sqrt{2}$.

Notice that this triangle is a *half of a square*.

A *30-60-90 triangle* is one with a 30°, a 60°, and a 90° angle.

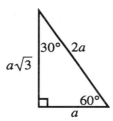

If the length of the side opposite the 30° angle is *a*, then the length of the side opposite the 60° angle is $a\sqrt{3}$, and the side opposite the right angle is 2*a*.

Conversely, if the sides of a triangle are *a*, 2*a*, and $a\sqrt{3}$, then the triangle is a 30-60-90 triangle.

An exterior angle of a triangle is formed by extending one of the sides.

Key Point: The sum of the measures of the two remote interior angles (the angles *opposite* the exterior angle) of a triangle is equal to the measure of the exterior angle.

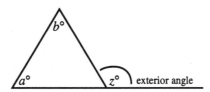

$$z = a + b$$

Similar triangles are triangles with equal angles and proportional sides.

Key Point: If two triangles or polygons are similar, then the ratio of their perimeters is equal to the ratio of their corresponding sides, and the ratio of their areas is equal to the square of the ratio of their corresponding sides.

Example

$\triangle ABC$ is similar to $\triangle XYZ$ because the angles are equal and their sides are in the same ratio.

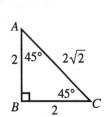

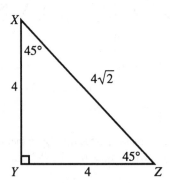

The ratio of the sides is $= \dfrac{1}{2}$.

The area of $\triangle ABC = 2$.
The area of $\triangle XYZ = 8$.

The ratio of the area of $\triangle ABC$ to the area of $\triangle XYZ = \dfrac{1}{4}$.

Perimeter of $\triangle ABC = 4 + 2\sqrt{2}$
Perimeter of $\triangle XYZ = 8 + 4\sqrt{2}$

Ratio of their perimeters is $\dfrac{4 + 2\sqrt{2}}{8 + 4\sqrt{2}} = \dfrac{1(4 + 2\sqrt{2})}{2(4 + 2\sqrt{2})} = \dfrac{1}{2}$

Notice that the ratio of the areas is equal to the square of the ratio of the sides, and that the ratio of their perimeters is equal to the ratio of their sides.

PRACTICE PROBLEMS

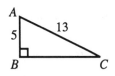

1. The area of $\triangle ABC =$

_____

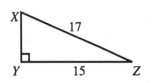

2. The area of $\triangle XYZ =$

_____

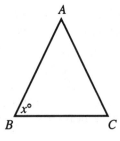

3. In $\triangle ABC$, $AB = AC$, $\angle ABC = x°$. In terms of x, how many degrees are in $\angle BAC$?

_____

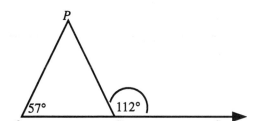

4. In △ *PQR*, how many degrees are in ∠*QPR*?

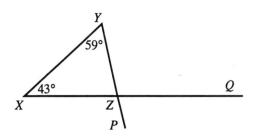

5. In the diagram, ∠*QZP* =

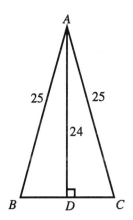

6. △ *ABC* is isosceles with *AB* = *AC* = 25, *AD* ⊥ *BC*, and *AD* = 24. Find the area of △ *ABC*.

7. *ABC* is an equilateral triangle. *AB* = 6. What is the area of △ *ABC*?

8. Triangle *XYZ* is similar to △ *ABC*. The area of △ *XYZ* = 64, and the area of △ *ABC* = 16. What is the ratio of their sides?

9. Triangle *ABC* is similar to △ *PQR*. If the ratio of their corresponding sides is $\frac{3}{5}$, what is the ratio of their areas?

10. What is the perimeter of a right triangle whose legs are 16 and 30?

11. The angles of a triangle are in the ratio of 2:3:4. Find the number of degrees in the smallest angle.

12. Triangle *ABC* has a right angle at *B*, angle *C* = 30°, and *BC* = 6. Find the area of △ *ABC*.

13. Triangle *PQR* is obtuse. Angle *QPR* = 120°, *PQ* = 10, *PR* = 10. Find the area of △ *QPR*.

14. What is the perimeter of a right triangle of which the hypotenuse is 20 inches and one leg is 12 inches?

15. The areas of two similar triangles are in the ratio of 49:16. What is the ratio of their sides?

QUADRILATERALS

Quadrilaterals are four-sided polygons such as parallelograms and trapezoids.
A *parallelogram* is a quadrilateral with both pairs of opposite sides parallel.
Properties of all parallelograms:
1. The opposite sides are equal.
2. The opposite angles are equal.
3. The diagonals bisect each other. (Remember that bisect means to cut in half.)

Example

$ABCD$ is a parallelogram $\left(AB \parallel CD,\ AD \parallel BC\right)$. The diagonals meet at O. Name the equal angles and equal segments:

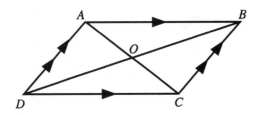

$$\left. \begin{array}{l} \angle DAB = \angle BCD \\ \angle ADC = \angle ABC \end{array} \right\}$$ The opposite angles are equal.

$$\left. \begin{array}{l} AB = CD \\ AD = BC \end{array} \right\}$$ The opposite sides are equal.

$$\left. \begin{array}{l} AO = OC \\ BO = OD \end{array} \right\}$$ These segments are equal because the diagonals bisect each other.

A *square* is a parallelogram with four equal sides and four 90° angles.

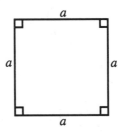

If a is the length of a side of a square:
  (1)   The *perimeter* of the square equals $4a$.
  (2)   The *area* of the square equals the length of one side squared, or a^2.
  (3)   The *diagonal* of the square has a length of $a\sqrt{2}$.

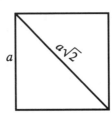

A *rectangle* is a parallelogram that has four 90° angles and two pairs of equal sides.

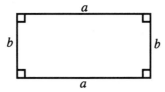

The *perimeter* of a rectangle = $2a + 2b$.
The *area* of a rectangle is the length times the width, or $a \cdot b$, or ab.

The *sum of the angles* of a *quadrilateral* (a figure with four sides) is 360°.

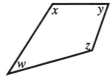

$\angle w + \angle x + \angle y + \angle z = 360°$

A *cube* is a three-dimensional figure, or polyhedron, with all sides equal.
The *volume* of a cube that has a side with length s is s^3.

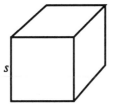

Volume = s^3

The *volume* of a *rectangular solid* (a box) is its length times its width times its height.

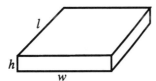

Volume = $l \cdot w \cdot h$ or lwh

Example I

Find the volume of a cube that has a face with a diagonal of length 2.

1. Draw the picture.

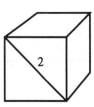

2. The face of a cube is a square, and the diagonal of a square equals $\sqrt{2}$ times the length of a side. Calling s the length of a side:

$$2 = \text{diagonal length} = s\sqrt{2}$$

$$s\sqrt{2} = 2$$

$$\frac{s\sqrt{2}}{\sqrt{2}} = \frac{2}{\sqrt{2}}$$

$$s = \frac{2}{\sqrt{2}}$$

$$s = \frac{2}{\sqrt{2}} \cdot \frac{\sqrt{2}}{\sqrt{2}}$$

$$s = \frac{2\sqrt{2}}{2}$$

$$s = \sqrt{2}$$

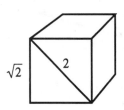

3. Volume is s^3.

$$s^3 = \sqrt{2} \cdot \sqrt{2} \cdot \sqrt{2} = \sqrt{8}$$

$$= 2\sqrt{2}$$

Example II

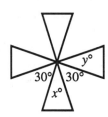

From the figure above, if $y \geq 10°$, then what is the maximum x could be?

1. $30° + x° + 30° + y° = $ a straight angle $= 180°$; therefore $x + y = 120$.

2. The larger y is, the smaller x will have to be; so to find the maximum x, you should use the minimum y. The minimum y can be is 10. Substitute it into the equation to get $x + 10 = 120$, or $x = 110$.

A *rhombus* is a parallelogram with four equal sides. The diagonals of a rhombus are perpendicular.

Example

ABCD is a rhombus. $AB = BC = CD = DA$. $AC \perp BD$.

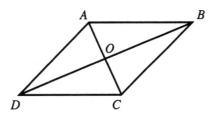

Remember that the diagonals of a rhombus meet and form right angles. As a result, four right triangles of equal area are formed.

A *trapezoid* is a quadrilateral that has one pair of opposite sides parallel. The parallel sides are called the bases, and the nonparallel sides (*AD* and *BC*) are called the legs. *ABCD* is a trapezoid. $AB \parallel CD$. *AB* and *CD* are the bases. *AD* and *BC* are the legs.

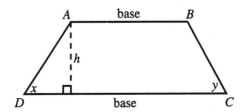

If the legs of a trapezoid are equal, the trapezoid is called *isosceles* and the base angles (*x* and *y*) are equal.

Since $AB \parallel CD$, $\angle A + \angle D = 180$, $\angle B + \angle C = 180$. The area of a trapezoid is $\frac{1}{2}h(b_1 + b_2)$, where h = height (altitude), and b_1 and b_2 are the bases.

Example

Find the area of the trapezoid *ABCD*. $AB = 8$, $CD = 12$. $AE \perp CD$, $AE = 6$.

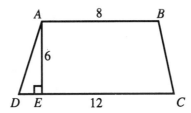

Using the formula $A_{\text{(trapezoid)}} = \frac{1}{2}h(b_1 + b_2)$, we get

$$A = \frac{1}{2}(6)(8+12)$$
$$= 3(20)$$
$$= 60 \text{ square units}$$

Example

Find the area of the isosceles trapezoid *PQRS* if ∠*S* = 60°, *PS* = 16, *PQ* = 12.

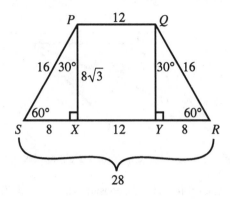

In problems like these, you have to add an auxiliary line or two. Drop perpendiculars from *P* and *Q* to *SR*. What figure is *PQYX*? You're right if you said, "rectangle." Triangles *PXS* and *QYR* are 30-60-90 triangles. Side *PQ* = *XY* = 12. Angle *PSX* = 60°, side *SX* = 8, *YR* = 8, *PX* = $8\sqrt{3}$.

Now you have solved for the missing pieces of the formula $A = \dfrac{1}{2}h(b_1 + b_2)$.

Plug in the values to get $A = \dfrac{1}{2}(8\sqrt{3})(12 + 28)$

$A = 4\sqrt{3}(40)$

$A = 160\sqrt{3}$ square units

PRACTICE PROBLEMS

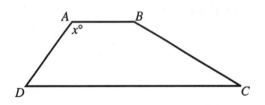

1. *AB* is parallel to *DC*. Angle *A* = *x*°. Angle *D* equals?

2. Find the area of a rectangle if the base is 4 inches and the height is 12 inches.

3. A cross is formed by cutting equal squares from the corners of a square piece of paper with a side of 9 inches. If each segment is 3 inches long, what is the perimeter of the cross?

4. What is the area of the cross in problem 3?

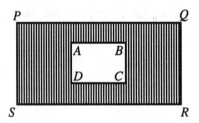

5. *PQRS* is a rectangle.   *PQ* = 12, *QR* = 6.
   ABCD is a rectangle.   *AB* = 4, *BC* = 3.
   Find the area of the shaded region.

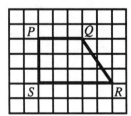

6. What is the area of *PQRS*?

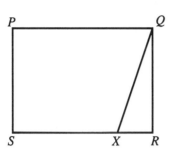

7. The area of each square is 16. What is the perimeter of the figure?

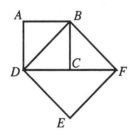

8. *PQRS* is a rectangle. *RX* is $\frac{1}{4}$ of *SR*. The area of $\triangle RQX = 16$. What is the area of *PQXS*?

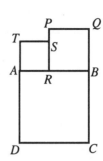

9. *ABCD* is a square whose area is 100. *PQBR* is a square of area 36. What is the area of square *TSRA*?

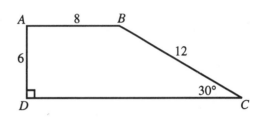

10. *ABCD* is a trapezoid. $AB \parallel CD$, $AD = 6$, $AB = 8$, $BC = 12$. Angle $C = 30°$. Find the area of *ABCD*.

PRACTICE SAT PROBLEMS

1. *ABCD* and *BFED* are both squares. If square *ABCD* has side 4, then $CF =$

(A) 2   (B) $2\sqrt{2}$ (C) 4   (D) $4\sqrt{2}$ (E) 8

2. Four square pieces are cut out of a square sheet of metal. If the original area of the metal sheet was $x^2 + 24x$, then the area of the sheet without the four pieces is

(A) 1   (B) 4   (C) 6   (D) 9   (E) 15

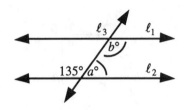

3. If, from above, $\ell_1 \parallel \ell_2$, then $b - 2a =$
   (A) 45   (B) 85   (C) 90   (D) 105   (E) 135

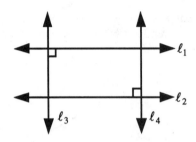

4. In the figure above, if $\ell_1 \perp \ell_3$ and $\ell_2 \perp \ell_4$, then which of the following statements must be true?
   I. $\ell_1 \parallel \ell_2$
   II. $\ell_3 \parallel \ell_4$
   III. $\ell_2 \parallel \ell_3$
   (A) None   (B) I, II, and III   (C) I and II
   (D) I and III   (E) II and III

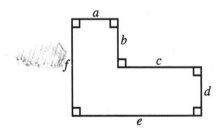

5. The area of the above figure is all of the following EXCEPT
   (A) $ab + de$ (B) $af + cd$ (C) $fe - bc$
   (D) $af + ed$ (E) $ab + ad + cd$

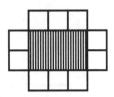

6. From the figure above, if each of the equally sized square tabs is folded up and a lid is put on to form a box, then the volume of the box in terms of s, the side of one of the squares, is:
   (A) $10s^2$ (B) $6s^3$ (C) $6s$ (D) $10s^3$
   (E) It cannot be determined from the information given.

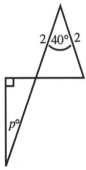

7. From the figure above find p.
   (A) 20   (B) 40   (C) 45   (d) 70
   (E) It cannot be determined from the information given.

8. What is the average degree measure of the angles of a triangle?
   (A) 30   (B) 45   (C) 60   (D) 90
   (E) It cannot be determined from the information given.

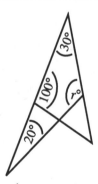

9. From the figure above, $r =$
   (A) 50°   (B) 70°   (C) 100°   (D) 130°   (E) 150°

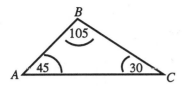

10. If AB equals $\sqrt{2}$, then the area of triangle ABC is

(A) $\dfrac{1}{2} + \dfrac{\sqrt{3}}{2}$ (B) $2\sqrt{2}$ (C) $1 + \sqrt{3}$

(D) $\dfrac{1}{2} + \dfrac{\sqrt{6}}{2}$ (E) $\dfrac{\sqrt{2}}{2} + \sqrt{3}$

> For problems 11–15 enter your solutions into the grids that follow the questions.

11. What is the measure of one of the acute angles of the triangle that is both a right triangle and an isosceles triangle?

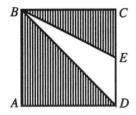

12. $ABCD$ is a square, and E is the midpoint of CD. Find the percentage of the square that is shaded.

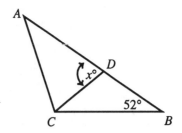

13. If in $\triangle ABC$ $CD = DB$, then $x =$ how many degrees?

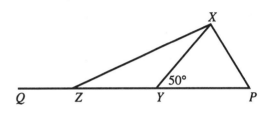

14. In $\triangle XYZ$, $XY = YZ$. If the measure of $\angle XYP = 50$, how many degrees are in $\angle QZX$?

15. The two triangles shown above are equilateral with sides as shown. What is the ratio of the perimeter of the larger triangle to that of the smaller?

11.

12.

13.

14.

15.

Aren't you glad you bought this book? You have now completed two thirds of the math review. Some major sections lie ahead, such as quantitative comparisons, but for now put this book down (I know that is hard to do), and do something different, like SAT verbal exercises (only kidding), before we work on circles.

Lesson 13

Goal: To memorize and understand the geometric theorems and their applications to circles.

GEOMETRY OF CIRCLES

A *circle* is the set of all points in a plane a given distance from a fixed point called the center.

BASIC DEFINITIONS AND THEOREMS

The distance from the center to any point on the circle is defined as *r*, the *radius*.

A *chord* of a circle is a line segment whose end points are on the circle.

The *diameter* (D) is defined as a chord that passes through the center.

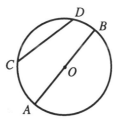

CD is a chord of the circle.
AB is a diameter. Its length is twice the radius.
The diameter is the longest segment that can be drawn inside a circle.

The Greek letter π (pi) stands for an irrational number that is approximately $\frac{22}{7}$, or a bit more than 3. It is the ratio of a circle's circumference (*perimeter*) to its diameter. Knowing the approximate value of π can be useful when estimating your answer.

Concentric circles are circles that have the same center. The distance between concentric circles is the difference of their radii.

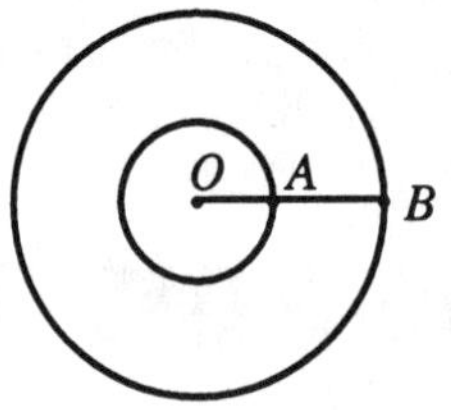

If O is the center of both circles and $OA = 3$ and $OB = 8$, then the distance between the two circles would equal $OB - OA$, or 5.

The *circumference* equals π times the diameter, D.

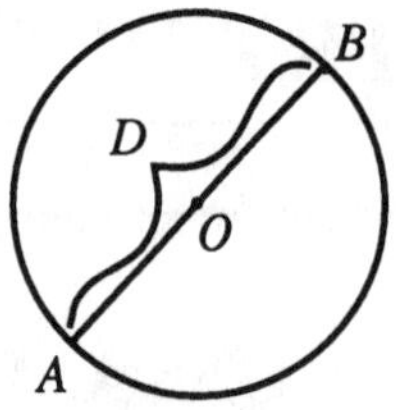

$C = \pi D$

Since $D = 2r$, $C = \pi(2r) = 2\pi r$.

The *area* of a circle is equal to πr^2.

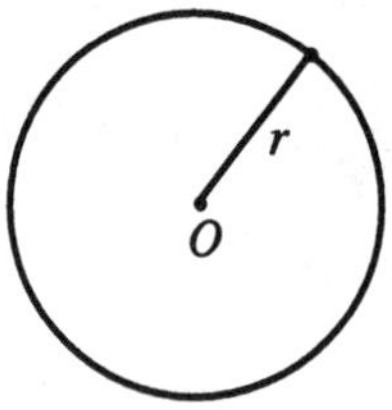

$A = \pi r^2$

Notice that if the *radius is doubled* you have $A = \pi(2r)^2 = 4\pi r^2$; thus the area is *quadrupled.*

The *volume* of a cylinder equals π times the radius squared times the height of the cylinder.

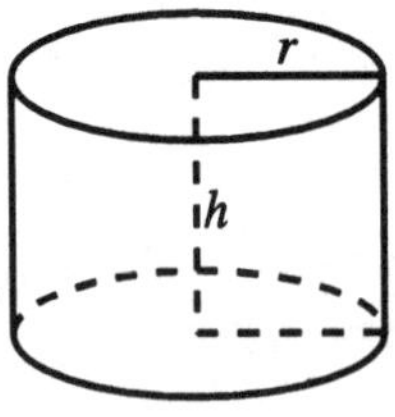

$V = \pi r^2 h$

A circle is defined to have 360°.

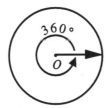

An *arc* is a section of a circle. The *number of degrees in an arc* is equal to the number of degrees in the angle formed by the radii drawn to the ends of the arc. An angle whose vertex is at the center of the circle is called a *central* angle.

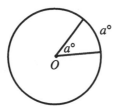

An angle whose vertex is on the circle is called an *inscribed* angle. The number of degrees in an inscribed angle is equal to half the arc that it intercepts.

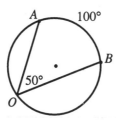

$\angle AOB$ is an inscribed angle. If arc $AB = 100°$, then $\angle AOB = \frac{1}{2}(100°)$ or 50°.

A *semicircle* is half a circle (180°) and is formed by a diameter.
An angle that is inscribed in a semicircle is a *right angle*.

AB is a diameter of the circle with center O.

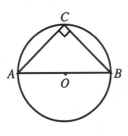

$\angle ACB = 90°$

The *ratio* of the number of *degrees in an arc* to the number of *degrees in a circle*, 360, is equal to the *ratio* of the *length of the arc* to the *circumference of the circle*.

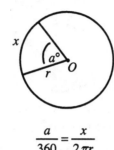

$$\frac{a}{360} = \frac{x}{2\pi r}$$

Circumference of circle $= 2\pi r$

The *ratio* of the number of *degrees in an arc* to the number of *degrees in a circle*, 360, is equal to the *ratio* of the *area of the sector* (the shaded area below) to the *area of the circle*, πr^2. A *sector* of a circle is like a piece of pie.

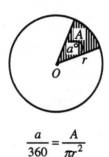

$$\frac{a}{360} = \frac{A}{\pi r^2}$$

Area of circle $= \pi r^2$

A segment of a circle is like the crust on a piece of pie. It is the area between the arc and the chord.

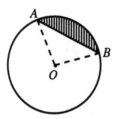

The shaded region would be the segment between arc *AB* and chord *AB*.

To find the area of a segment of a circle, first find the area of the sector $\frac{t}{360}\pi r^2$, where $t =$ the number of degrees in the central angle. Then subtract the area of the triangle.

Area of a segment = (area of the sector) − (area of the triangle)

Example I

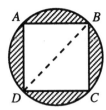

From the figure above, *ABCD* is a square whose sides each have a length of 1. Find the area of the shaded region.

1. Notice that the area of the shaded region is the area of the circle *minus* the area of the square.
2. The area of the square is 1 since the length of each side is 1.
3. The area of a circle is πr^2, so you must first solve for r to find the area.
4. *BD* is *both the diameter of the circle and a diagonal of ABCD*. The length of a diagonal of a square is $\sqrt{2}$ times the length of a side: $BD = \sqrt{2}(1) = \sqrt{2}.$
5. The radius is half the diameter: $r = \dfrac{1}{2}\sqrt{2}.$
6. Going back to the equation for the area of a circle you plug in $\dfrac{1}{2}\sqrt{2}$ for r to get:

$$A = \pi \left(\frac{1}{2}\sqrt{2}\right)^2 = \pi \left(\frac{1}{4} \times 2\right) = \pi \frac{1}{2} = \frac{\pi}{2}$$

7. The area of the shaded region is the area of the circle minus the area of the square, which is $\dfrac{\pi}{2} - 1.$

Example II

What is the area of the largest circle that may be inscribed in a square whose sides have length 2?

1. Draw the picture.

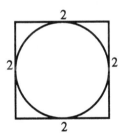

2. Draw in a diameter of the circle that is parallel to one of the sides of the square.

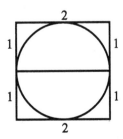

  Notice that it forms a rectangle with this side and half of two other sides.
  It must therefore have the same length as the side opposite it, 2.
3. The diameter is 2 so the radius, being half the diameter, is 1.
$$A = \pi r^2 = \pi (1)^2 = \pi$$

PRACTICE PROBLEMS

1. What are the area and circumference of a circle with a radius of 3 inches?

2. The areas of two circles are in the ratio of 1:16. If the radius of the smaller circle is 2, what is the radius of the larger circle?

3. If the radius of a circle is multiplied by 3, the circumference is _____.

4. If the radius of a circle is multiplied by 3, the area is _____.

5. Find the circumference of a circle whose diameter is 18 inches.

6. The circumference of a circle is 48π. Find the length of the radius.

7. Find the number of inches in the diagonal of a square that is inscribed in a circle whose circumference is 40π inches.

8. Find the thickness of a pipe whose outer radius is 4.2 inches and whose inner radius is 3.75 inches.

9. How far will a wheel of radius 28 inches travel if it makes 240 revolutions? (Use $\pi = \dfrac{22}{7}$.)

10. If a tire has a radius of 14 inches, how many revolutions does it make in covering a distance of 1 mile? (Use $\pi = \dfrac{22}{7}$.)

11. In a circle of radius 10 inches, find the length in inches of an arc of 144°.

12. In a circle whose radius is 12 inches, find the number of degrees in the central angle of an arc whose length is 8π inches.

13. The circumference of a circle is 36π. If a central angle of 60° intercepts arc AB, find the length of arc AB. (A problem of this type asks for the length of minor arc AB, which is an arc measuring less than 180°.)

14. $ABCD$ is a square with sides 2 inches in length. If semicircles surround each side of the square, what is the perimeter of the figure?

15. The area of a circle is 169π square inches. Find the diameter.

16. The circumference of a circle is 36π. Find the area.

17. Find the area between two concentric circles with radii of 6 and 9 inches.

18. Find the radius of a circle whose area is the sum of the areas of two circles having radii of 8 and 15 units.

19. Find the area of a sector of a circle with a radius of 5 inches if the central angle measures 72°.

20. The area of a circle is 64π square inches. If there are 240° in the central angle XOY, what is the area of the sector XOY?

21. The radius of a circle is 12. Find the number of degrees in the central angle of a sector that has an area of 8π.

22. If the angle of a sector of a circle is 45° and the area of the sector is 24π, find the radius of the circle.

23. A dog is tied to a post in a corner where two fences meet at an angle of 120°. If the length of the rope is 8 feet, over how many square feet can the dog roam?

24. In the diagram below, if $OX = 2$, find the area of the shaded region.

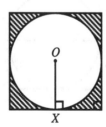

25. Two circles of radius 6 inches are tangent (touch at one point) externally to each other and to the sides of a rectangle. Find the area of the shaded region.

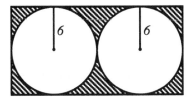

26. Find the volume of a cylinder if the base has a diameter of 8 inches and the height of the cylinder is 12 inches.

27. If the radius of a cylinder is increased from 4 to 6 inches and if the height is increased from 12 to 15 inches, how many more cubic inches of volume will it have?

28. A rectangle has dimensions of 8 inches by 12 inches. Using the corners of the rectangle as the centers, circles of radii 2 inches are constructed at each corner. Find the total area of the figure.

29. A circular pool of radius 12 feet has 3 feet of water in it. How many cubic feet of water are in the pool?

30. A sector of a circle with a radius of 6 inches has an angle of 120°. Find the area of the segment of the circle formed by the sector.

If this were a baseball game, we would now be going into the bottom of the seventh inning. It is customary to take a seventh-inning stretch at this time, so get up and get a soda, hot dog, or whatever and unwind a bit before we move on to coordinate geometry.

Lesson 14

Goal: To review the concepts of coordinate geometry.

COORDINATE GEOMETRY

QUICK REVIEW OF BASIC CONCEPTS

Coordinate geometry deals with sets of points and how they are represented on the coordinate axes.

The coordinate axes are formed by a horizontal number line, called the *x*-axis, and a vertical number line, called the *y*-axis. The point at which they intersect is called the origin.

Points are located by their *x* and *y* coordinates. The *x* coordinate, called the *abscissa*, is the first number in the ordered pair, and the *y* coordinate, called the *ordinate*, is the second number. Positive is to the right on the *x*-axis and up on the *y*-axis. Negative is to the left on the *x*-axis and down on the *y*-axis.

Example

(2,3) 2 is the abscissa, the *x*-coordinate
      3 is the ordinate, the *y*-coordinate

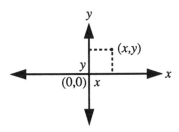

The point (*x*,*y*) is *x* units away from the *origin* (0,0) along the *x*-axis, and *y* units away from the origin along the *y*-axis.

The coordinate axes (the graph itself) is divided into four quadrants. The quadrants are numbered counterclockwise, starting with the upper right-hand quadrant.

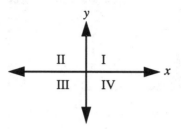

When:

x is	and	y is	
positive		positive	(x,y) is in Quadrant I
negative		positive	(x,y) is in Quadrant II
negative		negative	(x,y) is in Quadrant III
positive		negative	(x,y) is in Quadrant IV
0		—	(x,y) is on the y-axis
—		0	(x,y) is on the x-axis

All points on a horizontal line that is parallel to the x-axis have the same y-coordinate.
All points on a vertical line that is parallel to the y-axis have the same x-coordinate.

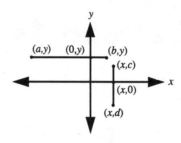

THREE IMPORTANT FORMULAS

Midpoint   If (x_1,y_1) and (x_2,y_2) are two points, then their *midpoint* is given by the point:

$$\left(\frac{x_1 + x_2}{2}, \frac{y_1 + y_2}{2} \right)$$

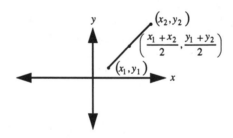

Notice that this is just the average of the x-values and the y-values.

Distance   The *distance* between two points (x_1,y_1) and (x_2,y_2) is given by the equation:

$$D = \sqrt{(x_2 - x_1)^2 + (y_2 - y_1)^2}$$

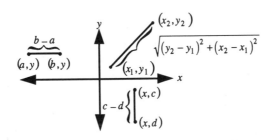

Notice that if $y_1 = y_2$ or $x_1 = x_2$, one of the terms being squared becomes 0, and the equation is simplified to either $y_2 - y_1$ or $x_2 - x_1$.

Slope   The slope of a line is defined to be the

$$\frac{\text{rise}}{\text{run}} \text{ or } \frac{\text{vertical change}}{\text{horizontal change}}$$

The formula for finding the slope of the line between two points (x_1,y_1) and (x_2,y_2) is

$$\text{slope} = \frac{y_2 - y_1}{x_2 - x_1}$$

Example

What is the slope of the line joining the points (2,3) and (–1,4)?

Using the formula, we get:

$$\text{slope} = \frac{(4) - (3)}{(-1) - (2)} = \frac{1}{-3} = -\frac{1}{3}$$

Notice that you would get the same answer if you reverse the order.

$$\frac{(3) - (4)}{2 - (-1)} = \frac{-1}{3} = -\frac{1}{3}$$

The slope of a horizontal line is zero.

The slope of a vertical line is infinite.

An equation of a line in slope-intercept form is

$$y = mx + b$$

  m is the slope of the line.

  b is the y-intercept (the y-intercept is where the line crosses the y-axis).

Example

$y = 3x - 5$

  3 is the slope

  –5 is the y-intercept

To find the equation of a line you need to know the slope and the y-intercept.

Examples

I. Find the equation of a line having a slope of 2 and a y-intercept of 5.

Solution

  $m = 2$

  $b = 5$

  Substitute these values directly into the equation $y = mx + b$ to get $y = 2x + 5$.

II. Find the equation of the line passing through the point (3,4) having a slope of –2.

   Solution

   You know the slope, so $m = -2$. You do not know the y-intercept, b, but you know a point that the line goes through. In the equation $y = mx + b$, substitute -2 for m, 3 for x, 4 for y, and solve for b.

$y = mx + b$	
$(4) = (-2)(3) + b$	*Substitute the given values for m , x, and y.*
$4 = -6 + b$	*Simplify.*
$10 = b$	*Solve for b.*
$y = -2x + 10$	*Substitute back into the equation for the value of b.*

III. Find the equation of the line passing through the points (1,2) and (5,6).

   Solution

   To use the equation $y = mx + b$, you need to know the slope and the y-intercept. First use the slope formula,

   $\dfrac{y_2 - y_1}{x_2 - x_1}$, to find the slope, m.

$$\frac{(6)-(2)}{(5)-(1)} = \frac{4}{4} = 1 = m$$

   Use the slope, 1, and either point to solve for b.
   We will use the point (1,2)

$y = mx + b$	*Use the slope-intercept equation.*
$(2) = (1)(1) + b$	*Substitute the values for m, x, and y.*
$2 = 1 + b$	*Simplify and solve for b.*
$1 = b$	

   $y = 1x + 1$ is the equation of the line passing through (1,2) and (5,6).

Example

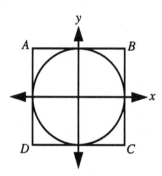

If the circle pictured above has area 16π and is centered at (0,0) and *ABCD* is a square, find the x-coordinate of point *B*.

1.   The area of a circle is given by the equation $A = \pi r^2$. Substituting 16π in for A and solving for r you get $r = 4$. Now you know that every point on the circle is 4 units from the origin.

2.   Where the circle crosses the positive x-axis it must have coordinates (4,0). The circle must cross the positive y-axis at the point (0,4).

3.   *B* is on the same line parallel to the y-axis as (4,0), so its x-coordinate is 4. *B* is on the same line parallel to the x-axis as (0,4), so its y-coordinate is also 4.

4.   Putting these together, you have that the coordinates of point *B* are (4,4).

PRACTICE PROBLEMS

1. Find the distance between (3,5) and (–1, –2).
2. Find the midpoint of the line segment joining (2,2) to (8,6).
3. Find the slope of the line joining (3,7) to (–1,2).
4. If (2,3) is the midpoint of the segment joining (7,6) to (x,y), solve for x and y.
5. If $(-4, K)$ is a point on the graph of $3x - 2y = 0$, find K.
6. What are the coordinates of the point on the graph of $y = 2x + 6$ that has equal coordinates?
7. A line has an x-intercept of 3 and a y-intercept of –2. What is the slope of the line passing through these two points?

8. Find the distance between the points $\left(\frac{8}{3}, \frac{1}{2}\right)$ and $\left(\frac{2}{3}, -\frac{3}{2}\right)$.

9. Find the midpoint of the segment joining $\left(\frac{5}{3}, \frac{1}{6}\right)$ and $\left(\frac{3}{2}, \frac{2}{3}\right)$.

10. Find the slope of the line joining $\left(1\frac{3}{4}, 2\frac{1}{3}\right)$ and $\left(-1\frac{1}{6}, 3\frac{1}{4}\right)$.

11. Find the equation of the line having a slope of –2 and a y-intercept of 1.
12. Find the equation of the line having a slope of 5 passing through the point (6, –2).
13. Find the equation of the line passing through the points (–2, –3) and (3,5).
14. Find the equation of the line passing through the points (0,3) and (4,3).
15. What is the slope of the line $3x - 4y = 6$?

PRACTICE SAT PROBLEMS

1. If the circumference of a circle is doubled, then how many times as large is the area of the circle?
   (A) 1   (B) 1.5   (C) 2   (D) 3   (E) 4

2. The radius of the largest ball that can fit in a 5-inch-tall cylinder with volume 20 cubic inches is

   (A) 2   (B) $\frac{2}{\sqrt{\pi}}$ (C) 4   (D) 4π (E) 5

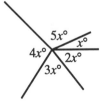

Note: Figure not drawn to scale.

3. From above, $x =$
   (A) 24   (B) 48   (C) 72   (D) 96   (E) 120

4. The length of AB is 3 and the length of BC is 4. Find the area of the shaded semicircle if AB is perpendicular to BC.

   (A) $\frac{5}{2}\pi$ (B) 5π (C) $\frac{25}{2}\pi$ (D) $\frac{25}{4}\pi$ (E) $\frac{25}{8}\pi$

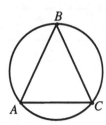

5. *ABC* is an equilateral triangle. What is the number of degrees in minor arc *AB*?

    (A) 60   (B) 90   (C) 120   (D) 240   (E) 300

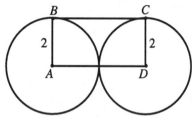

6. From the figure above, *A* and *D* are the centers of two equivalent circles. Find the area of rectangle *ABCD* if *AB* and *CD* are both radii of the circles and have length 2.

    (A) 1   (B) 2   (C) 4   (D) 6   (E) 8

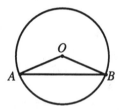

Note: Figure not drawn to scale.

7. The measure of angle *OAB* is 20°. If O is the center of the circle, then the number of degrees in angle *AOB* is

    (A) 40   (B) 70   (C) 80   (D) 140   (E) 160

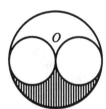

8. As shown in the figure above, two equivalent circles are drawn inside a third circle in such a way that they each intersect the third circle at only one point, and they share a common point at the center of the third circle. Find the area of the shaded region if the radius of the larger circle is 4.

    (A) π (B) 2π (C) 4π (D) $2\pi - 2$ (E) $\frac{1}{2}(4\pi - 2)$

9. A cylindrical roller is dipped in paint and then rolled for one complete revolution over a piece of paper. If the line of paint is 4 inches long, what is the radius, in inches, of the roller?

    (A) $\dfrac{2}{\pi}$ (B) 2   (C) π (D) 2π

    (E) It cannot be determined from the information given.

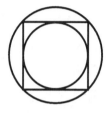

10. One circle is circumscribed around a square with side of length 2, and another circle is inscribed in the same square. Find the ratio of the area of the larger circle to the smaller circle.

    (A) 4:1   (B) $\sqrt{3}$:1   (C) 1.5:1   (D) $\sqrt{2}$:1   (E) 2:1

11. The distance between points (3,4) and (*a*,*b*) is 5. Point (*a*,*b*) could be any of the following EXCEPT

    (A) (0,0)   (B) (3,1)   (C) (–2,4)   (D) (3,9)   (E) (6,0)

12. If $x > y$, then point (*x*,*y*) can be in all of the following EXCEPT

    (A) quadrant I   (B) quadrant II   (C) quadrant III
    (D) quadrant IV   (E) the *x*- or *y*-axis

13. If the midpoint of *AB* is (0,0) and the coordinates of point *A* are (*x*,*y*), then the coordinates of point *B* are

    (A) (–*x*, –*y*)   (B) (–*x*,*y*)   (C) (*x*, –*y*)   (D) (*x*,*y*)
    (E) None of the preceding answers

14. If the distance between (*a*,3) and (*b*,9) is 10, then $b - a =$

    (A) 4   (B) 12   (C) 8   (D) 64
    (E) It cannot be determined from the information given.

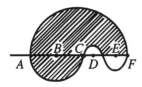

15. If the area of $\triangle ABC$ is 12, then the y-coordinate $C(x,y)$ is

(A) –4 (B) 4 (C) –2 (D) 2
(E) It cannot be determined from the information given.

16. Points B, C, D, and E are the midpoints of the diameters of the 4 semicircles in the figure above. AF is a segment containing the diameters of the four semicircles. If $CF = 6$ inches and $CD = EF$, what is the area of the shaded region?

(A) 16π (B) $\dfrac{161\pi}{8}$ (C) $\dfrac{171\pi}{8}$ (D) $\dfrac{181\pi}{8}$
(E) 30π

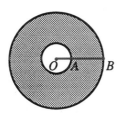

17. In the figure above, the radius of the smaller circle is $\dfrac{1}{3}$ the radius of the larger circle. If the circles have the same center O, what is the ratio of the area of the shaded region to the area of the larger circle?

(A) $\dfrac{1}{9}$ (B) $\dfrac{2}{9}$ (C) $\dfrac{2}{3}$ (D) $\dfrac{3}{4}$ (E) $\dfrac{8}{9}$

18. Which of the following points will be twice as far from (5,6) as from (4,5)?

(A) (3,5) (B) (3,4) (C) (1,6) (D) (2,5) (E) (1,5)

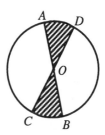

19. The circle above has center O and radius 3. If the total area of the shaded region is π, then $\angle AOD =$

(A) 10 (B) 20 (C) 30 (D) 40 (E) 60

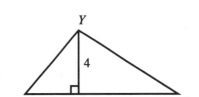

20. In the figure above, if the area of $\triangle XYZ$ is 28 and $XR = 3$ and $YR = 4$, then $RZ =$

(A) 5 (B) 7 (C) 8 (D) 11 (E) 12

That takes care of geometry. I cannot stress enough the importance of knowing the definitions and formulas that were given in the last two sections.

Lesson 15

Goal: To study quantitative comparison problems—in arithmetic and algebra.

QUANTITATIVE COMPARISONS: ARITHMETIC AND ALGEBRA

Quantitative comparisons constitute one third of the math section on the SAT. That's 15 questions of the 60 total questions. It normally takes less time to solve these questions, but watch out, because questions that appear to be easy can be tricky. The trend on these problems, as with the other math problems, is to progress from easy to quite difficult.

To solve quantitative comparison problems, use all of the facts that we have reviewed so far, plus some common sense. Many problems that appear easy are just that; so do not make the problems more difficult than they really are.

In order to do well on this section you must fully understand the directions. Below are the directions that you will see in your test booklet. Take a few minutes to *memorize them now.*

<u>Questions A-Z</u> each consist of two quantities, one in Column A and one in Column B. You are to compare the two quantities and on the answer sheet blacken space

    A   if the quantity in Column A is greater;

    B   if the quantity in Column B is greater;

    C   if the two quantities are equal;

    D   if the relationship cannot be determined from the information given.

<u>Notes:</u>   1.   In certain questions, information concerning one or both of the quantities to be compared is centered above the two columns.

          2.   In a given question, a symbol that appears in both columns represents the same thing in Column A as it does in Column B.

          3.   Letters such as x, n, and k stand for real numbers.

EXAMPLES			
	<u>Column A</u>	<u>Column B</u>	<u>Answers</u>
E1.	2×6	$2 + 6$	A ● B ○ C ○ D ○

$x°$ $y°$

E2.	$180 - x$	y	A ○ B ○ C ● D ○
E3.	$p - q$	$q - p$	A ○ B ○ C ○ D ●

SPECIAL NOTES FOR QUANTITATIVE COMPARISON PROBLEMS

1. Never mark space E on your answer sheet; there are only four possible answers in this section.

2. Figures are drawn as close to scale as possible unless stated otherwise. This fact can be beneficial when you are estimating answers.

3. Figures are often marked to give you added information. For example . The little box tells you that line 1 and line 2 are perpendicular; that is, the angle between them is 90°.

4. Since you are comparing quantities, the concepts of *equalities and inequalities* are used often in helping you determine the relationships between the quantities in the two columns.

Point 4 is perhaps the most important. It provides shortcuts to problems that could otherwise take up large amounts of valuable time.

For example, if in Column A you saw $\frac{1}{3}+\frac{1}{7}$ and in Column B you saw $\frac{1}{5}+\frac{1}{9}$, adding the fractions could take a minute's worth of work and introduce the possibility of arithmetic error. But by noticing that $\frac{1}{3}>\frac{1}{5}$ and $\frac{1}{7}>\frac{1}{9}$, you can complete a two-minute problem in 15 seconds.

Another example of this type of problem is being asked to multiply long strings of numbers and to determine which product is bigger. By subtracting quantities from both sides or by dividing out common factors, you can work with smaller numbers *without having disturbed the relationship between the two quantities.*

Go back now and review the rules for working with equalities and inequalities that were given in Lesson 2.

Example

Column A	Column B
$28 \times 34 \times 16$	$28 \times 32 \times 16$

By dividing out the 28 and 16 from both columns, you are left with a 34 in Column A and a 32 in Column B; a relationship is easily determined. Doing the multiplication out and getting 15,232 in Column A and 14,336 in Column B wouldn't have been quite as simple, although if you didn't spot the shortcut it would definitely have worked.

In doing the following problems, *look for tricks that save you time,* such as factoring first or determining relationships *before* doing the math.

5. Special numbers to remember to use in this section are 1, −1, 0, and fractions. This means, would your answer have changed if any of these were substituted for the variable?

6. Information that is centered is to be used for both columns.

Example

Column A		Column B	
	$z \neq 0$		A ○
$2z$		$3z$	B ○
			C ○
			D ○

This problem shows the importance of trying *both* positive and negative numbers. If you try a positive number, for example (1), then Column B is greater than Column A. But, if you choose a negative number, for example (−1), then Column A is greater than Column B. Therefore, the correct answer is D.

7. Look for shortcuts. Try not to spend a great deal of time doing long calculations.

Quantitative comparison problems are actually exercises in reasoning and logic. Extensive computation or mindless pencil pushing is altogether wrong. Examine each problem and *think.* Then you will find that minimal figuring is needed.

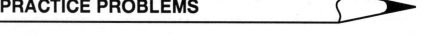

PRACTICE PROBLEMS

<u>Questions 1–60</u> each consist of two quantities, one in Column A and one in Column B. You are to compare the two quantities and on the answer sheet blacken space

A   if the quantity in Column A is greater;
B   if the quantity in Column B is greater;
C   if the two quantities are equal;
D   if the relationship cannot be determined from the information given.

<u>Notes:</u>   1.   In certain questions, information concerning one or both of the quantities to be compared is centered above the two columns.
2.   In a given question, a symbol that appears in both columns represents the same thing in Column A as it does in Column B.
3.   Letters such as x, n, and k stand for real numbers.

<u>Column A</u>	<u>Column B</u>	

1. $2 - 0.002$ $2 - 0.0022$ A ○ B ○ C ○ D ○

2. $44{,}544$ 100×445 A ○ B ○ C ○ D ○

$$x^2 + y^2 = 30$$
$$xy = 12$$

3. $(x - y)^2$ 6 A ○ B ○ C ○ D ○

4. $A(B - 4) + B(B - 4)$ $(A + B)(B - 4)$ A ○ B ○ C ○ D ○

$$\frac{1}{A} > 1$$

5. A 1 A ○ B ○ C ○ D ○

$$AB \neq 0$$

6. AB^3 $-A^3 B$ A ○ B ○ C ○ D ○

$$3x - y = 7$$
$$3x + y = 11$$

7. x y A ○ B ○ C ○ D ○

	Column A		Column B	

$$4x - 2y = 6$$
$$y + 3 = x$$

8. Column A: x Column B: y

A ○
B ○
C ○
D ○

$$3x - 6y = 9$$
$$2x - 6 = 4y$$

9. Column A: x Column B: y

A ○
B ○
C ○
D ○

10. Column A: $\dfrac{1}{2} + \dfrac{1}{3}$ Column B: $\dfrac{1}{2} \bullet \dfrac{1}{3}$

A ○
B ○
C ○
D ○

11. Column A: $\dfrac{\sqrt{5}}{3}$ Column B: $\dfrac{\sqrt{5}}{6}$

A ○
B ○
C ○
D ○

12. Column A: $\dfrac{48}{24 - 6}$ Column B: $\dfrac{48}{24} - \dfrac{48}{6}$

A ○
B ○
C ○
D ○

13. Column A: $\dfrac{1,001 - 26}{13}$ Column B: $\dfrac{1,001}{13} - 26$

A ○
B ○
C ○
D ○

$$x > y$$
$$xy \neq 0$$

14. Column A: $\dfrac{x}{y}$ Column B: $\dfrac{y}{x}$

A ○
B ○
C ○
D ○

15. Column A: $0.63 \bullet 2.9$ Column B: $0.029 \bullet 6.3$

A ○
B ○
C ○
D ○

16. Column A: $\sqrt{.036}$ Column B: $.06$

A ○
B ○
C ○
D ○

17. Column A: 4 Column B: $\dfrac{1}{.25}$

A ○
B ○
C ○
D ○

18. Column A: $-.026$ Column B: $-.017$

A ○
B ○
C ○
D ○

	Column A		Column B	

19. $\dfrac{49.92}{1.6}$ .... $\dfrac{4{,}992}{16}$ A ○ B ○ C ○ D ○

20. $a+b=10$, $a-b=20$; b .... 0 A ○ B ○ C ○ D ○

21. $x+y=7$, $x-y=7$; 0 .... y A ○ B ○ C ○ D ○

22. $x>0$; $\sqrt{x}$ .... x A ○ B ○ C ○ D ○

23. $2-\sqrt{2}$ .... $2-\sqrt{3}$ A ○ B ○ C ○ D ○

24. $\sqrt{a^2}$ .... a A ○ B ○ C ○ D ○

25. $\sqrt{\dfrac{3}{2}}$ .... 1 A ○ B ○ C ○ D ○

26. $x\neq 0$; $2x^2$ .... $(2x)^2$ A ○ B ○ C ○ D ○

27. $6+5^2$ .... 30 A ○ B ○ C ○ D ○

28. $n>0$; $(-1)^n$ .... 1^n A ○ B ○ C ○ D ○

29. $8^{4a}=4^{6b}$; a .... b A ○ B ○ C ○ D ○

	Column A	Column B	

30.

$$x + 4 > 3$$

Column A	Column B	
$x + 2$	1	A ○ B ○ C ○ D ○

31.

$$a > b + 1$$

Column A	Column B	
a	b	A ○ B ○ C ○ D ○

32.

$$z \neq 0$$

Column A	Column B	
z	$2z$	A ○ B ○ C ○ D ○

33.

$$b \neq 0$$
$$b^2 - 4ac < 0$$
$$a < 0$$

Column A	Column B	
c	0	A ○ B ○ C ○ D ○

34.

$$p < 4$$
$$q < 5$$

Column A	Column B	
p	q	A ○ B ○ C ○ D ○

35.

$$x > y > 1$$

Column A	Column B	
$x^2 - y^2$	$x - y$	A ○ B ○ C ○ D ○

36.

A jacket that costs $63.90 is sold
at a 30% discount.

Column A	Column B	
Price of the jacket after the discount	$19.17	A ○ B ○ C ○ D ○

37.

$$0 \leq X < Y \leq 100$$

Column A	Column B	
X% of Y	Y% of X	A ○ B ○ C ○ D ○

38.

Column A	Column B	
.005	$\dfrac{1}{2}$%	A ○ B ○ C ○ D ○

39.

Column A	Column B	
80%	The percent of 80 that 100 is	A ○ B ○ C ○ D ○

40.

Column A	Column B	
$16 \times 2 \times 13$	$4 \times 8 \times 15$	A ○ B ○ C ○ D ○

	Column A	Column B

41. $5 + .003$ $3 + .005$
A ○ B ○ C ○ D ○

42. $\dfrac{1,058}{23}$ $\dfrac{1,058}{46}$
A ○ B ○ C ○ D ○

$$x < y < -1$$

43. x $-3y$
A ○ B ○ C ○ D ○

$$p > 0$$

44. 1^p $[(-2) + 2]^p$
A ○ B ○ C ○ D ○

45. $a + b$ ab
A ○ B ○ C ○ D ○

46. $\dfrac{1}{3} \times \dfrac{1}{7} \times \dfrac{1}{11}$ $\dfrac{1}{3} \times \dfrac{1}{5} \times \dfrac{1}{7}$
A ○ B ○ C ○ D ○

$$\dfrac{y}{-3} > 0$$

47. y $\dfrac{-3}{y}$
A ○ B ○ C ○ D ○

$$-2 \le a \le 5$$
$$5 \le b \le 7$$

48. a b
A ○ B ○ C ○ D ○

Each figure is made up
of 4 equal-size squares.

49. Perimeter of
figure A   Perimeter of
figure B
A ○ B ○ C ○ D ○

$$\dfrac{1}{x} + \dfrac{1}{y} = \dfrac{1}{z} \text{ and } xy = z$$

50. $y + x$ 1
A ○ B ○ C ○ D ○

$$a = b = c$$

51. $a + b$ $b + c$
A ○ B ○ C ○ D ○

$$x + 2 = y \text{ and } y - 1 = t$$

52. x t
A ○ B ○ C ○ D ○

	Column A	Column B	

$$y = 2x$$

A ○
B ○
C ○
53. x y D ○

A ○
B ○
54.   40% $\frac{2}{\frac{5}{2}}$ C ○
D ○

$$\boxed{x} = 2^x$$

A ○
B ○
C ○
55. $\boxed{3}$ $\boxed{9}$ D ○

After she has been at school three
quarters, Shannon's average is 80%.

A ○
The average she will need   B ○
to have during the fourth quarter   C ○
56. to have an 85% average overall   100%   D ○

$$n > 0$$

A ○
The sum of n numbers   B ○
divided by the average   C ○
57.   of the n numbers. n D ○

$$[a, b, c] = \frac{abc}{3}$$

A ○
B ○
The average of 3,   C ○
58.   [3,3,3]   3, and 3   D ○

$$y^2 = 36$$
$$x^2 = 25$$

A ○
B ○
C ○
59. x y D ○

$$xy = 50$$

A ○
B ○
C ○
60. $x + y$ 15   D ○

Lesson 16

Goal: To study quantitative comparison problems—in geometry.

QUANTITATIVE COMPARISONS: GEOMETRY

By now you should feel more comfortable with the format of the quantitative comparison questions. In this section we will work on quantitative comparison questions that relate to geometry and "funny functions"—those denoted by unusual symbols.

Special Notes for Quantitative Comparison Problems Dealing with Geometry

1. Memorize the formulas for area, volume, and perimeter that were given in Lessons 6 and 7. Knowing the formulas will save you a great deal of time on the test.

2. When working with right triangles, remember the common Pythagorean triplets: 3-4-5, 5-12-13, 8-15-17, 7-24-25.

3. Diagrams not drawn to scale can be resketched in the booklet. *Mark any important facts on your diagram.* Mark on your diagram any sides or angles that are equal.

4. Do not hesitate to *write in your booklet.* You paid for it, and it is the only scrap paper that you have.

5. *Never mark E on your answer sheet.*

PRACTICE PROBLEMS

Questions 1–60 each consist of two quantities, one in Column A and one in Column B. You are to compare the two quantities and on the answer sheet blacken space

     A   if the quantity in Column A is greater;
     B   if the quantity in Column B is greater;
     C   if the two quantities are equal;
     D   if the relationship cannot be determined from the information given.

Notes: 1.   In certain questions, information concerning one or both of the quantities to be compared is centered above the two columns.

            2.   In a given question, a symbol that appears in both columns represents the same thing in Column A as it does in Column B.

            3.   Letters such as *x*, *n*, and *k* stand for real numbers.

	Column A	Column B	
1.	The length of the hypotenuse of a right triangle with legs of 12 and 16	The length of the hypotenuse of a right triangle with legs of 8 and 15	A ○ B ○ C ○ D ○
2.	Volume of a rectangular box with dimensions 4 yards by 3 yards by 15 yards	Volume of a rectangular box with dimensions 1 yard by 12 yards by 2 yards	A ○ B ○ C ○ D ○

Column A   Column B

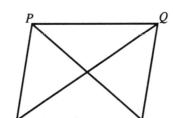

Parallelogram $PQRS$ $\angle SPQ > \angle PQR$.

3.   Length of PR Length of QS

A ○
B ○
C ○
D ○

---

4.   Circumference of a circle with a radius   Circumference of a circle with a diameter
      of r of $3r$

A ○
B ○
C ○
D ○

---

5.   Area of a circle with a diameter of x^2 Area of a circle with a radius of x

A ○
B ○
C ○
D ○

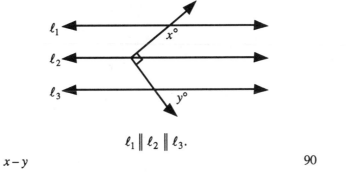

$\ell_1 \parallel \ell_2 \parallel \ell_3.$

6. $x - y$ 90

A ○
B ○
C ○
D ○

---

7.   The area of $\triangle XYZ$ 8

A ○
B ○
C ○
D ○

<u>Column A</u>   <u>Column B</u>

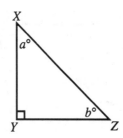

$$XY = 2$$
$$XZ = 2\sqrt{2}$$

8. $a°$ $b°$

A ○
B ○
C ○
D ○

[*x*] is defined
to be the greatest integer
less than or equal to the number.

9.   [−1.5]   [−2]

A ○
B ○
C ○
D ○

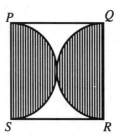

PQRS is a square, and the two
shaded regions are semicircles.
PQ = 4

10.   Area of the unshaded region   4 square units

A ○
B ○
C ○
D ○

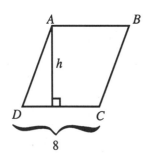

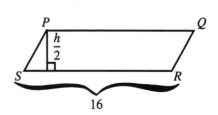

Note: Figures not drawn to scale.

ABCD and *PQRS* are parallelograms.

11.   Area of *ABCD*   Area of *PQRS*

A ○
B ○
C ○
D ○

Column A	Column B

$48°$

$x°$ $41°$

Note: Figure not drawn to scale.

12. x 89

A ○   B ○   C ○   D ○

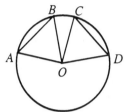

Circle with center O

Segment AB = Segment CD

13. $\angle AOB$ $\angle COD$

A ○   B ○   C ○   D ○

14. The sum of the interior angles of an isosceles triangle   The sum of the exterior angles of a parallelogram

A ○   B ○   C ○   D ○

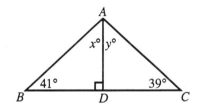

Note: Figure not drawn to scale.

$AD \perp BC$

15. x y

A ○   B ○   C ○   D ○

Let $\triangle\!\!\!\!x = \dfrac{1}{3}x$ if x is odd.

Let $\triangle\!\!\!\!x = \dfrac{1}{x}$ if x is even.

16. $\triangle\!\!\!\!7 \cdot \triangle\!\!\!\!4$ $\triangle\!\!\!\!2$

A ○   B ○   C ○   D ○

<u>Column A</u>   <u>Column B</u>

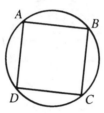

A ○
B ○
C ○
D ○

17.   6   *x*

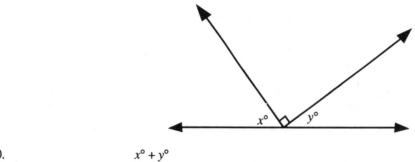

ABCD are points equally spaced
on a circle. The diameter
of the circle is 2.

A ○
B ○
C ○
D ○

18.   Perimeter of quadrilateral *ABCD* $4\sqrt{2}$

For all positive numbers *x* and *y*,

$$x \ O \ y = \frac{x-y}{x+y}$$

A ○
B ○
C ○
D ○

19. $\frac{3}{4} O \frac{1}{2}$ $\frac{3}{8} O \frac{1}{8}$

A ○
B ○
C ○
D ○

20. $x° + y°$ 90°

Column A   Column B

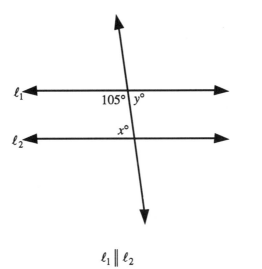

$\ell_1 \parallel \ell_2$

A ○
B ○
C ○
D ○

21. $105° - x°$ $y°$

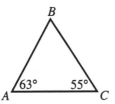

Note: Figure not drawn to scale.

A ○
B ○
C ○
D ○

22.   Length of AC Length of BC

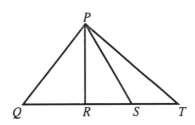

Note: Figure not drawn to scale.
$PR \perp QT$

A ○
B ○
C ○
D ○

23. PS PQ

<u>Column A</u>   <u>Column B</u>

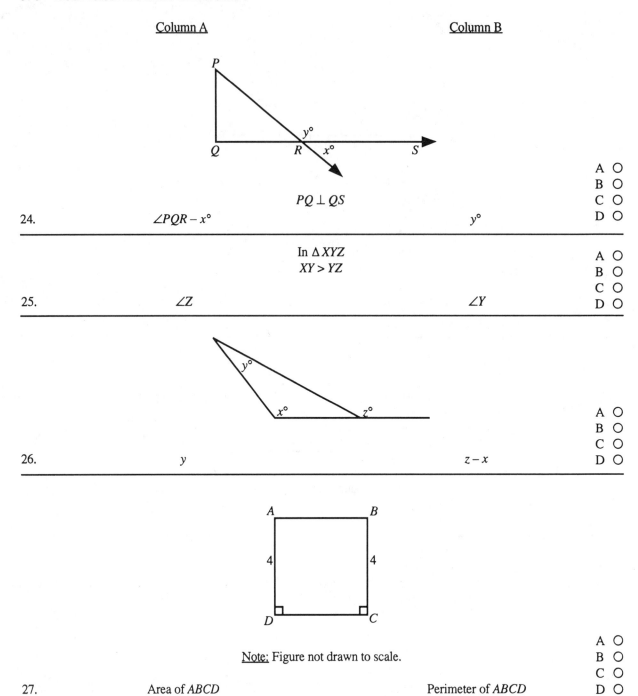

$PQ \perp QS$

A ○
B ○
C ○
24. $\angle PQR - x°$ $y°$ D ○

In $\triangle XYZ$

$XY > YZ$

A ○
B ○
C ○
25. $\angle Z$ $\angle Y$ D ○

A ○
B ○
C ○
26. y $z - x$ D ○

Note: Figure not drawn to scale.

A ○
B ○
C ○
27.   Area of $ABCD$ Perimeter of $ABCD$ D ○

	Column A	Column B	

A   30°   *B*

80°

y°

x°

C   *D*

Note: Figure not drawn to scale.

$AB \parallel CD$

A ○
B ○
C ○
D ○

28.   *y*   *x*

R

44°

P   *Q*

Note: Figure not drawn to scale.

A ○
B ○
C ○
D ○

29.   *PR*   *PQ*

X

Y   *Z*

Area of $\triangle XYZ = 48$
$XY = 12$

A ○
B ○
C ○
D ○

30.   8   *YZ*

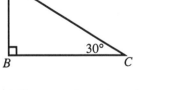

A

30°

B   *C*

Note: Figure not drawn to scale.
$BC = 4$

A ○
B ○
C ○
D ○

31.   *AB*   3

	Column A	Column B

$AB \perp BC$

32.   The average of x, y, z y

A ○
B ○
C ○
D ○

Perimeter of square $ABCD = 12$
Perimeter of equilateral triangle $XYZ = 18$

33.   Area of $ABCD$ Area of $\triangle XYZ$

A ○
B ○
C ○
D ○

Perimeter of $\triangle ABC = 27$

34. a 2

A ○
B ○
C ○
D ○

Area of $\triangle XYZ = 16\sqrt{3}$

35. XY 4

A ○
B ○
C ○
D ○

D and E are the midpoints of AB
and AC, respectively. $DE \parallel BC$.

36.   Area of $\triangle ADE$ $\dfrac{1}{3}$ area of $\triangle ABC$

A ○
B ○
C ○
D ○

Column A	Column B

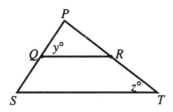

<u>Note:</u> Figure not drawn to scale.

$QR \parallel ST$

$PQ = PR$

37. y z

A ○ B ○ C ○ D ○

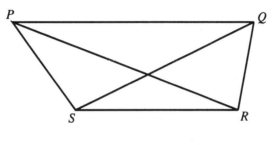

$PQ \parallel SR$

38.   Area of $\triangle PSR$ Area of $\triangle QRS$

A ○ B ○ C ○ D ○

$B(a,3)$ $C(b,3)$

$A(0,0)$ $D(d,0)$

$b > a$

39.   Area of triangle   Area of triangle
                 ACD ABD

A ○ B ○ C ○ D ○

The point (a,b) is on the x-axis.

40. a b

A ○ B ○ C ○ D ○

<u>Column A</u>   <u>Column B</u>

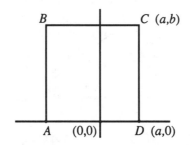

ABCD is a square.
D has coordinates (a,0).
C has coordinates (a,b).

41.   a   b

A ○
B ○
C ○
D ○

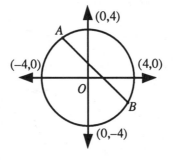

42.   The length of segment AB   8

A ○
B ○
C ○
D ○

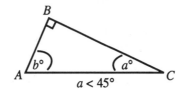

43.   The length of   The length of
                AB   CB

A ○
B ○
C ○
D ○

44.   The length of the third
       side of a right triangle
       having two sides of
       length 1 and $\sqrt{2}$ $\sqrt{3}$

A ○
B ○
C ○
D ○

Column A   Column B

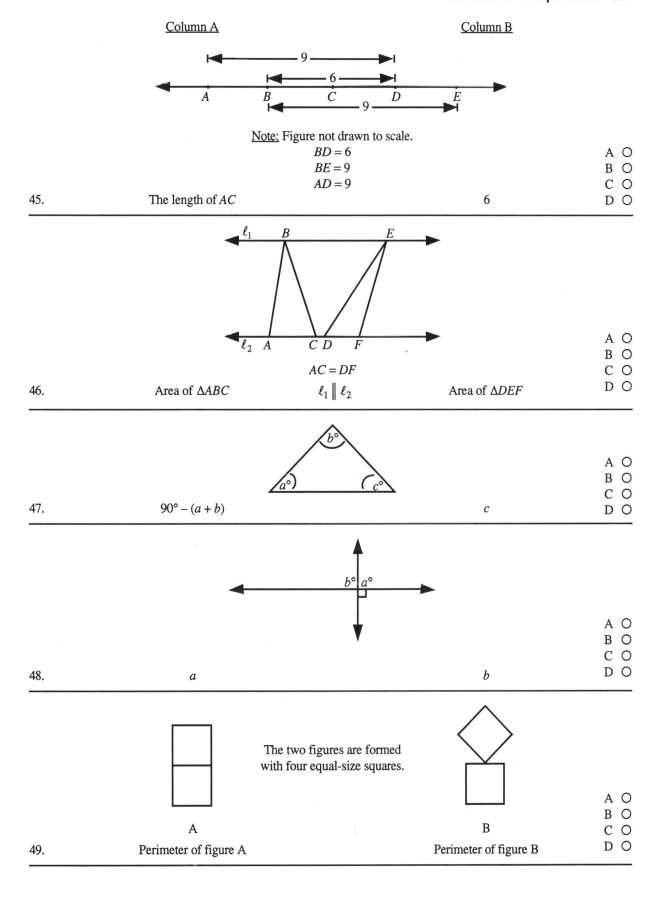

Note: Figure not drawn to scale.

$BD = 6$
$BE = 9$
$AD = 9$

45.   The length of AC 6

	A ○
	B ○
	C ○
	D ○

$AC = DF$

46.   Area of $\triangle ABC$ $\ell_1 \parallel \ell_2$ Area of $\triangle DEF$

	A ○
	B ○
	C ○
	D ○

47. $90° - (a + b)$ c

	A ○
	B ○
	C ○
	D ○

48. a b

	A ○
	B ○
	C ○
	D ○

The two figures are formed
with four equal-size squares.

A   B

49.   Perimeter of figure A   Perimeter of figure B

	A ○
	B ○
	C ○
	D ○

Column A   Column B

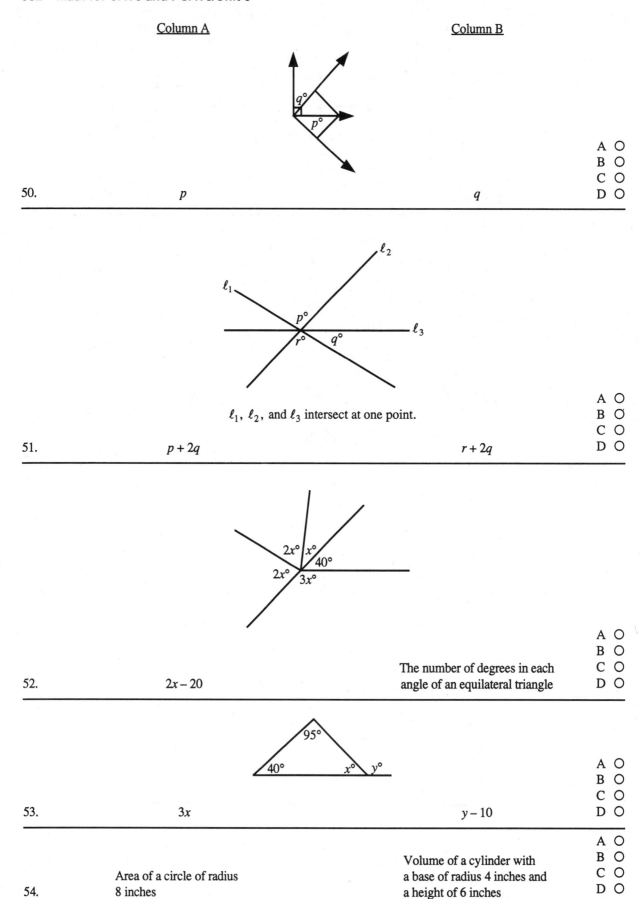

			A ○
			B ○
			C ○
50.	p	q	D ○

ℓ_1, ℓ_2, and ℓ_3 intersect at one point.

			A ○
			B ○
			C ○
51.	$p + 2q$	$r + 2q$	D ○

			A ○
		The number of degrees in each	B ○
		angle of an equilateral triangle	C ○
52.	$2x - 20$		D ○

			A ○
			B ○
			C ○
53.	$3x$	$y - 10$	D ○

			A ○
	Area of a circle of radius	Volume of a cylinder with	B ○
	8 inches	a base of radius 4 inches and	C ○
54.		a height of 6 inches	D ○

Column A   Column B

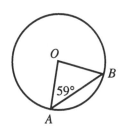

A and B are points on the
circle with center O

A ○
B ○
C ○
D ○

55.   OA   AB

A ○
B ○
C ○
D ○

56.   Circumference of a circle   Perimeter of a square
        of radius 3   of side 3.5

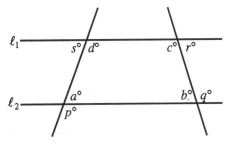

$\ell_1 \parallel \ell_2$

A ○
B ○
C ○
D ○

57. $a + b + c + d$ $p + q + r + s$

A ○
B ○
C ○
D ○

58.   Surface area of a cube with   Area of a square of side
        an edge of length 4 inches $6\sqrt{3}$ inches

$\triangle XYZ$ is equilateral

A ○
B ○
C ○
D ○

59.   Length of the altitude $\frac{1}{2}$ of length XY
        to the side XY

Column A		Column B	
	Area of the triangle		A ○
	formed by the *x*-axis, the		B ○
	y-axis, and the line		C ○
60.	$2x - 3y + 12 = 0$	12	D ○

Thank heavens!

Sixteen lessons down, two to go.

Lesson 17

Goal: To review data interpretation, sequences, and funny functions.

SPECIAL TOPICS

DATA INTERPRETATION

Every SAT contains a couple of questions relating to a graph or a pictorial representation of data. The graph, diagram, or chart can represent any type of problem. Read the problem carefully, try to understand the units of measurement used in the graph, and answer the question.

When working with data interpretation problems, make sure that you understand what the problem is asking for. Avoid lengthy computations, and do not add any information that you may know about the material.

Bar graphs, line graphs, and circle graphs commonly represent data.

Bar graphs can be horizontal or vertical. Relationships between quantities are determined by comparing the lengths of the bars.

Line graphs show the continuous change of an item or quantity.

Circle graphs look like pieces of a pie and express percentages of a whole. (Remember that there are 360 degrees in any circle.)

Problems involving arithmetic, algebra, and geometry often appear as graphs, so your efforts in Lessons 1–16 should be helpful.

Examples

I.

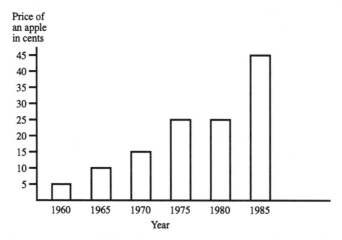

In the figure above, the five years over which the percent increase was the greatest were
(A) 1960–65   (B) 1965–70   (C) 1970–75   (D) 1975–80   (E) 1980–85

Solution

The percent increase is defined as the increase over the starting value times 100.

From 1960 to 1965 the percent increase is $\dfrac{10-5}{5} \cdot 100 = 100\%$

From 1965 to 1970 the percent increase is $\dfrac{15-10}{10} \cdot 100 = 50\%$

From 1970 to 1975 the percent increase is $\dfrac{25-15}{15} \cdot 100 = 66\dfrac{2}{3}\%$

From 1975 to 1980 the percent increase is $\dfrac{25-25}{25} \cdot 100 = 0\%$

From 1980 to 1985 the percent increase is $\dfrac{45-25}{25} \cdot 100 = 80\%$

The greatest percent increase occurred from 1960 to 1965, 100%. Do not make the mistake of marking answer (E) because it has the greatest increase in value; percent increase and value increase *are different.*

II.

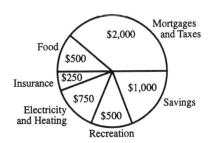

The circle graph shows the monthly outlays of the Jones family as percentages. If their monthly income is $5,000, how much money would the Joneses save each month if the electric and heating bills were reduced by 20%?

Solution

15% of $5,000 is $750; 20% of $750 equals $150.

III.

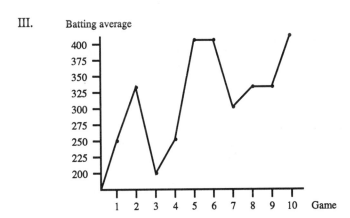

The line graph above shows the batting average of Nick Marino over a ten-game stretch.
In which game did Nick's batting average drop the most?

Solution

In game 3 Nick's batting average dropped 133 points.

SEQUENCES

Sequences are numbers arranged in a certain pattern. Some of these problems are quite easy, while others require a bit of thought and ingenuity.

All sequence problems are characterized by a listing of a few of the elements. You are required to give the next number.

Examples

I. Find the next number in the sequence 1, 1, 3, 3, 6, 6, 10, 10 . . .

Solution

Notice the successive differences between

	difference
1 and 3	2
3 and 6	3
6 and 10	4

The difference increases by 1 each time. Therefore, the next difference will be 5. (2, 3, 4, 5, etc.) Adding 5 to 10, the last number in the sequence, gives 15, your answer.

II. Find the next number in the sequence 64, 32, 16 . . .

Solution

Each successive number is $\frac{1}{2}$ of the preceding number, so the answer is 8.

III. Find the next number in the sequence 2, 5, 26 . . .

Solution

No clear pattern is suggested, but notice how the numbers jumped quickly from 5 to 26. This suggests multiplication or the use of exponents.
$2^2 + 1 = 5, 5^2 + 1 = 26$ This suggests that the next term would be $26^2 + 1$, or 677.

PATTERN REPETITION

A decoration is made by hanging colored streamers from a rope. The colors form the pattern red, orange, yellow, green, blue, violet, red, orange . . . What is the color of the 100th flag in the pattern?

To do this *type* of problem take the last member of the original pattern and determine what place it is in. From above, *violet* is the last color and it is the sixth flag. If you were to continue the pattern you would notice it is also the twelfth and the eighteenth flag. In fact, *violet occupies all the places that are divisible by 6.*

Now find a number divisible by 6 that is near 100, 102 let's say. The 102nd flag is violet so the 101st must be the color before it, blue, and the 100th flag must be green.

All repetition problems are done this way:
1. Isolate the pattern.
2. Find the number of the *last* element of the pattern; call it *n*.
3. Any place number divisible by *n* has that element.
4. Find a place number divisible by *n* near the one you are asked to find.
5. Count off to the place number you are asked to find and determine its element.

PRACTICE PROBLEMS

Find the next number in each of the following sequences.

1. $3, 5, 8, 12 \ldots$

2. $15, 21, 16, 20 \ldots$

3. $-2, 4, -6 \ldots$

4. $-9, 17, -35, 69 \ldots$

5. $32, -16, 8, -4 \ldots$

6. $\dfrac{1}{2}, \dfrac{1}{3}, \dfrac{2}{9} \ldots$

7. $3, 1, 3, 4, 3, 7, 3 \ldots$

8. $4, 10, 22, 46 \ldots$

9. $4, 9, 16, 25 \ldots$

10. $2, 4, 8, 16 \ldots$

11. $15.4, 11.7, 8 \ldots$

12. $81, 9, 3 \ldots$

13. $324, 289, 256, 225 \ldots$

14. $3, 9, 4, 8, 5, 7 \ldots$

15. $-2, 8, -32, 128 \ldots$

16. $15, 18, 18, 22, 22, 27, 27 \ldots$

17. $35, 24, 15, 8 \ldots$

18. When dresses are made at a certain factory they are made in the following colors: red, black, blue, and white. If the dresses are made in that order, what color is the 115th dress?

19. At Burger World, as the burgers come off the conveyor belt they are made into cheeseburgers; bacon, lettuce, and tomato burgers; and chiliburgers. If they are made in that order, what type is the 76th burger?

20. In a certain gym class the coach has the students line up and count off by fours. All of the ones are on Team A, the twos are on Team B, the threes are on Team C, and the fours are on Team D. On which team will the 53rd student be?

FUNNY FUNCTIONS

These problems test your problem-solving ability. Different symbols are used to tell you how to evaluate the problem. Do not get hung up on this type of problem. Read the problem, determine the relationship between the variables, and then plug in any known values to evaluate the problem.

Example

The symbol $\begin{vmatrix} p & q \\ r & s \end{vmatrix}$ means $ps - rq$.

What is the value of $\begin{vmatrix} 2 & 3 \\ 5 & 4 \end{vmatrix}$?

Solution

Those of you who have taken Algebra II should recognize this problem as a determinant. If you've never seen this type of problem, read on.

Using the rule that was given to evaluate the problem, you get

$$\begin{vmatrix} 2 & 3 \\ 5 & 4 \end{vmatrix} = \overset{p}{(2)} \cdot \overset{s}{(4)} - \overset{r}{(5)} \cdot \overset{q}{(3)} = 8 - 15 = -7$$

PRACTICE SAT PROBLEMS

For the following 10 problems enter your solutions in the grids provided.

1. If $A \star B \star C = \dfrac{A}{\dfrac{B}{C}}$ for all positive integers, what

   is the value of $3 \star 4 \star 6$?

2. If $\triangle\!\!\!\!{\scriptstyle y} = (y+1)^2 - (y-1)^2 + 1$, what is the value of

   $\triangle\!\!\!\!{\scriptstyle 3}$?

3. For all positive integers, if $(p, q \uparrow x, y) = py - qx$,

   then what is the value of $(4, 6 \uparrow 2, 8)$?

4. For all positive numbers x, if $\downarrow x = (x-1)^2$,

   then what is the value of $\downarrow \dfrac{3}{4}$?

5. If $x \bigcirc y$ means $y^2 - 2x^2$, then what is the value of $2 \bigcirc (-3)$?

6. If $p \,\square\, q = \left(\dfrac{p-1}{q+1}\right)^2$, then what is the value of

   $\dfrac{3}{2} \,\square\, \dfrac{2}{3}$?

7. If $x\!\uparrow = 3x$ and $x\!\downarrow = \dfrac{1}{3}x$, and

   $x\!\uparrow \,\bullet\, x\!\downarrow = ax^b$, what is

   $a + b$?

8. If $\bigcirc\!\!\!\!{\scriptstyle p} = \dfrac{p}{4}$, for what value of p does $\bigcirc\!\!\!\!{\scriptstyle p}$ equal 3?

9. Let $[x]$ denote the greatest integer less than or equal to x. For example, $[3.4] = 3$ and $[-.4] = -1$. What is the value of $[2.3] - [-2.3]$?

10. If $a \star b = a^2 b^3$, then what is the value of $(-2) \star 3 ? =$

1.

2.

3.

4.

5.

6.

7.

8.

9.

10.

Lesson 18

Goal: To focus on the last three math problems on a typical SAT.

THE LAST THREE PROBLEMS ON A TYPICAL SAT

Congratulations! You've finally reached the last section. By now you should have done a big chunk of the problems.

This last section, instead of teaching a topic, gives examples of the tougher types of problems. These are the ones that usually make up the last three problems of the math sections on the SAT.

If you find that you are having too much trouble with this section, it is better that you go back and do the regular problems. If you aren't shooting for an 800 score, you probably will not, and should not, get to these problems. More time spent on the easier problems will be more beneficial to your score than rushing through the test. Remember, it is better to get a few problems correct than many wrong. If these problems aren't too hard for you, you're in good shape—they're as hard as any you'll ever see on an SAT.

PRACTICE SAT PROBLEMS

1. The average of the remainders when 5 is divided into 5 consecutive positive integers is

   (A) 1   (B) 2   (C) 1.2   (D) 4
   (E) It cannot be determined from the information given.

2. The function * is defined by the equation:

   $$x * y = \frac{x+y}{xy} \quad (xy \neq 0)$$

   I. $a * b = b * a$

   II. $(a * b) * c = a * (b * c)$

   III. $a * (b + c) = a * b + a * c$

   Of the properties listed, the ones that are true for all nonzero a, b, and c are

   (A) I only   (B) I and II   (C) II and III
   (D) I and III   (E) I, II, and III

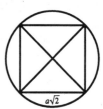

3. A square is drawn inside a circle in such a way that the diagonals of the square pass through the center of the circle, and the vertices of the square touch the circle's edge. If the square has side $a\sqrt{2}$, then the area of the circle is

   (A) $\frac{1}{4}\pi a^2$ (B) $\frac{1}{2}\pi a^2$ (C) πa^2 (D) $\sqrt{2}\pi a^2$

   (E) $2\pi a^2$

4. At a movie the cost of an adult's ticket is $1.50 and the cost of a student's ticket is $0.75. If 500 people see the show and spend a total of $450, how many of the people who saw the show were students?

   (A) 100   (B) 200   (C) 300   (D) 400
   (E) It cannot be determined from the information given.

5. In a town there are fewer than 30 unlicensed dogs. If $\frac{2}{5}$ of the unlicensed dogs are males and $\frac{3}{8}$ of the unlicensed male dogs are beagles, then how many unlicensed dogs are there in the town?

    (A) 20   (B) 25   (C) 30   (D) 40
    (E) It cannot be determined from the information given.

6. After the first two quarters at school, Buffy had an 87% average. What is the lowest average Buffy can have during the third quarter and still be able to have a 90% average for the year?

    (A) 83   (B) 86   (C) 87   (D) 93   (E) 96

7. G girls share the cost of buying P pizzas at D dollars per pizza. B boys decide to join the girls. If no new pizzas are ordered and all of the boys and girls pay an equal share of the total cost of the pizzas, then how much less is each girl's share of the cost than it would have been if the boys hadn't come?

    (A) $\dfrac{PDB}{G(B+G)}$ (B) $\dfrac{PD}{B+G}$ (C) $\dfrac{PD}{G}$

    (D) $\dfrac{PD(B+G)}{BG}$ (E) $\dfrac{PD}{B}$

8. At a carnival a booth is set up with a chance game that costs 15 cents to play. The first person to play wins a penny, the second person a nickel, the third person a dime, and the fourth a quarter. The cycle is repeated infinitely with the fifth person winning a penny and so on. After 43 people have played the game how much money has the booth made as a net profit?

    (A) $2.06   (B) $2.19   (C) $3.00   (D) $4.30
    (E) $6.45

9. If $x^2 + y^2 = 25$ and $xy = -5$, then $(x - y)^2 =$
    (A) 15   (B) 20   (C) 25   (D) 30   (E) 35

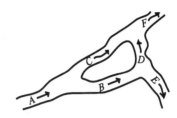

10. The river Paix flows in the directions indicated by the arrows on the map above. If $\frac{5}{8}$ of the water flowing from channel A takes channel B, and $\frac{3}{5}$ of the water from channel B takes channel D, then what percentage of the water takes channel F?

    (A) 25%   (B) 33.3%   (C) 37.5%   (D) 62.5%
    (E) 75%

Congratulations! Now you can pat yourself on the back. Having completed the eighteen lessons, you should be familiar with the types of questions that will be asked. You should have enough knowledge to do well on the SAT or PSAT.

If you have time after the completion of this unit, go back and review any difficult areas. You have been analyzing your mistakes on the actual SATs and should know your major problem areas.

The next unit contains one practice SAT. Use it for additional review work. And do not hesitate to ask your math teacher for some additional help.

Above all, relax. If you work hard on the material covered in this book, you will be prepared to take the PSAT or SAT.

GLOSSARY OF FORMULAS AND RELATIONSHIPS

AREA OF POLYGONS

Area of a parallelogram $= bh$

Area of a rectangle $= bh$

Area of a trapezoid $= \frac{1}{2}h \cdot (b_1 + b_2)$

Area of a square of side $s = s^2$

Area of a triangle $= \frac{1}{2}bh$

Area of a right triangle $= \frac{1}{2}(\text{leg}) \cdot (\text{leg})$

Area of an equilateral triangle of side $s = \frac{1}{4}s^2\sqrt{3}$

CIRCLES

Area of a circle of radius $r = \pi r^2$

Circumference of a circle of radius $r = 2\pi r$ or πD, where D = diameter of the circle

Length of an arc of a circle $= \frac{t}{360}(2\pi r)$, where t equals the number of degrees in the central angle

Area of a sector of a circle $= \frac{t}{360} \cdot \pi r^2$, where t equals the number of degrees in the central angle

VOLUME

Volume of a cube of side $s = s^3$

Volume of a rectangular solid $= lwh =$ (length)(width)(height)

Volume of a right circular cylinder $= \pi r^2 h$, where r is the radius of the base and h is the height of the cylinder

COORDINATE GEOMETRY

Distance between two points =

$\sqrt{(x_2 - x_1)^2 + (y_2 - y_1)^2}$, where (x_1, y_1) and (x_2, y_2) are the coordinates of the two points

Midpoint formula $= \dfrac{x_1 + x_2}{2}, \dfrac{y_1 + y_2}{2}$

Slope formula $= \dfrac{y_2 - y_1}{x_2 - x_1} = m$

IMPORTANT RIGHT TRIANGLES

In any 30–60–90 triangle the side opposite the 30° angle is $\frac{1}{2}$ of the hypotenuse. The side opposite the 60° angle is $\frac{1}{2}$ the hypotenuse times $\sqrt{3}$.

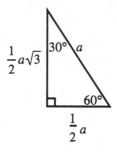

In any 45–45–90 triangle the hypotenuse is always $\sqrt{2}$ times either leg. Either leg is $\frac{1}{2}$ the hypotenuse times $\sqrt{2}$.

PYTHAGOREAN THEOREM

$a^2 + b^2 = c^2$, or $(\text{leg})^2 + (\text{leg})^2 = (\text{hypotenuse})^2$

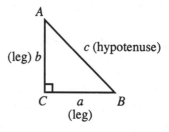

COMMON RIGHT TRIANGLES

3–4–5   5–12–13   8–15–17   7–24–25

<u>Note:</u> Any multiple of these triples will also be a right triangle, e.g., 6–8–10.

OTHER IMPORTANT RELATIONSHIPS

(Rate) • (Time) = Distance, or $RT = D$

$Time = \dfrac{\text{Distance}}{\text{Rate}}$, or $T = \dfrac{D}{R}$

$Rate = \dfrac{\text{Distance}}{\text{Time}}$, or $R = \dfrac{D}{T}$

$Average = \dfrac{\text{Sum of the component parts}}{\text{Number of parts}}$

EXPONENTS

$x^a \cdot x^b = x^{(a+b)}$

$(x^a)^b = x^{ab}$

$\dfrac{x^a}{x^b} = x^{a-b}$

$x^0 = 1$

$x^{-b} = \dfrac{1}{x^b}$

SIMILARITY

If two polygons are similar, the ratio of their areas is equal to the square of the ratio of their corresponding sides.

If two polyhedrons are similar, the ratio of their volumes is equal to the cube of the ratio of their corresponding edges.

IMPORTANT BINOMIAL EXPANSIONS

$(a+b)^2 = a^2 + 2ab + b^2$

$(a-b)^2 = a^2 - 2ab + b^2$

IMPORTANT SYMBOLS

> greater than
< less than
≥ greater than or equal to
≤ less than or equal to

⊥ perpendicular to
∥ parallel to
≅ congruent to
≈ similar to

Unit 7: The Practice Test

The practice test is as nearly like an actual SAT as possible, with the exception of the experimental set of questions, which is omitted. When you finish taking the practice test, score your results, and make the conversion to an approximate SAT score. Then—and most important—ANALYZE YOUR RESULTS, using the analysis pages that follow the exam.

PSAT test takers, you will find the test every bit as helpful as an actual PSAT because the questions are the same. Preparing for both tests is the same process. Just remember that on Test Day, you will have only four segments, each 30 minutes long.

Problems? If you find certain question types causing you repeated problems, please seek out a helpful teacher or brilliant friend who can spend time with you to make life easier.

PRACTICE SAT

Before starting each timed section, you should prenumber an answer sheet for the exact number of questions in that section. This preparation is not counted as part of the timed test, of course. When ready, set a timer and begin.

SECTION **1**	Time — 30 minutes	30 Questions

The following sentences need a word or words to complete their meaning. Choose the word or words that <u>best</u> fit the meaning of each sentence.

1. Although we've seen considerable ---- in the various media about political realignments and power shifts, no one has professed certain knowledge on these complex topics.

   (A) articles   (B) coverage   (C) essays
   (D) journalism   (E) speculation

2. Most people are willing to accept just and well-
   ⋯⋯ it is the ---- ones that provoke

   ⋯ negative

   ⋯mp counselor,
   ⋯less offenses, felt
   ⋯he rule.

   ⋯(C) unusual

4. Appalled by the nearly ---- conditions in the run-down tenement, the social worker wrote a(n) ---- letter to the newspapers hoping to focus attention on the problem.

   (A) awful. .entrancing
   (B) intolerable. .impassioned
   (C) indescribable. .upbeat
   (D) unique. .irritable
   (E) unpleasant. .furious

5. Unlike his early figures with ---- proportions that disturbed most viewers' sensibilities, Claude's later sculptures revealed an agreeable symmetry.

   (A) skewed   (B) uneven   (C) offbeat
   (D) surprising   (E) astounding

6. Fans of Gabriel García Márquez believe that the atypical ---- of fantasy and reality in his novels is a deliberate attempt to ---- the bizarre juxtaposition of those elements in real life.

   (A) mixture. .repudiate
   (B) exposition. .highlight
   (C) blend. .mirror
   (D) occurrence. .explain
   (E) complexity. .justify

7. As genetic research and data grow in respect and amount, the old question of ---- vs. environment, or nature vs. ----, is painfully resolving itself, with the geneticists currently in command.

   (A) genes. .culture
   (B) personality. .modernity
   (C) upbringing. .civilization
   (D) heredity. .nurture
   (E) family. .community

8. *The Autocrat of the Breakfast Table*, by Oliver Wendell Holmes, reflects not the ---- attitude suggested by its title but rather the ---- of an educated, witty man.

   (A) lighthearted. .novel insights
   (B) frivolous. .profound contemplations
   (C) serious. .jocularities
   (D) doctrinaire. .enlightened humor
   (E) cavalier. .sharp observations

9. Plowing through some extraordinarily wordy nineteenth-century prose is a tedious job, because it is often both ---- and ----.

   (A) boring. .dull
   (B) annoying. .enervating
   (C) terse. .intensely profound
   (D) formal. .depressing
   (E) verbose. .convoluted

The following questions are based on analogous relationships. Choose the lettered pair that best expresses a relationship similar to the pair in capital letters.

10. TIRED : EXHAUSTED ::   (A) free : democratic
    (B) tidy : haphazard   (C) hungry : famished
    (D) hesitant : weak   (E) innocent : savvy

11. CINNAMON : SPICE ::   (A) batter : cake
    (B) lace : braid   (C) cider : beverage
    (D) broccoli : condiment
    (E) decoration : furniture

12. CHUCKLE : AMUSEMENT ::
    (A) sorrow : misery   (B) comment : opinion
    (C) tremor : glee   (D) whimper : fear
    (E) titter : giggle

13. STRENGTH : STEEL ::   (A) reflection : mirror
    (B) clarity : prose   (C) density : water
    (D) energy : motor   (E) firmness : attitude

14. FALLACIOUS : TRUTH ::   (A) erroneous : fault
    (B) anxious : perception   (C) ornery : scorn
    (D) distraught : thought   (E) diminutive : bulk

15. JEOPARDIZE : DANGER ::   (A) legalize : threat
    (B) lampoon : ridicule   (C) undermine : faith
    (D) compose : harmony   (E) hypothesize : theory

Questions on the following reading passages should be answered based on what is <u>stated</u> or <u>implied</u> in the passage.

There has been very little research on the relationship between economics and sociology. But even if many single pieces of knowledge are
Line still missing, the main structure of the relationship
(5) can be discerned without too much difficulty. There are only a few different ways in which economics and sociology can be related to each other. One of the two disciplines can try to take over the subject matter of the other, which would
(10) constitute a case of "economic imperialism" or "sociological imperialism." Alternatively, they can each have their own distinct subject areas and ignore the other, as has been the case during the twentieth century. And finally, there can be open
(15) borders and free communication between economics and sociology, which it is hoped represents the direction in which things are currently moving.

The early economists, such as Adam Smith,
(20) Karl Marx, and John Stuart Mill, are generally considered to have struck a happy balance between economics and sociology. They wrote about economic theory as well as social institutions with both ease and insight. It is true that "economics"
(25) and "sociology" did not exist as two distinct academic disciplines at that time, but it was of course perfectly clear to these economists when they were dealing with economic topics as opposed to social topics.

(30) What distinguished Smith, Marx, and Mill from many later sociologists and economists was their ambition to define economics in a broad manner and to be interested in the insights of the other social sciences. Mill said, "A person is not likely
(35) to be a good economist who is nothing else. Social phenomena acting and reacting on one another, they cannot rightly be understood apart."

Mill's pragmatic attitude toward economic science was not popular in all circles, least of all
(40) with his colleague and one-time friend Auguste Comte. The thrust of Comte's argument (in *Cours de Philosophie Positive*) was that knowledge and society are going through an evolutionary development from lower to higher stages, and that
(45) "sociology" represents the highest stage of human knowledge. In Comte's scheme, "economics" had no independent place and his book actually contained a vitriolic attack on economics—that "alleged science" as he repeatedly referred to it.
(50) Apart from the work of Adam Smith, which Comte for some idiosyncratic reason exempted from his attack, he considered economics a thoroughly useless and metaphysical enterprise. The best one could do was give it up and replace it
(55) with sociology, the "queen of all sciences."

16. With which of the following statements about economics and sociology would the author of the passage be most likely to agree?

   (A) Very little is understood about the difference between economics and sociology.
   (B) One discipline should simply blend with the other for the sake of unity.
   (C) Economics and sociology are separate but equal disciplines.
   (D) Economics is best understood separate from sociology altogether.
   (E) The metaphysical aspects of economics render it impossible to quantify.

17. The views of the author of the passage most closely correspond to the views of which of the following?

   (A) John Stuart Mill
   (B) Karl Marx
   (C) Almost any economic imperialist
   (D) Auguste Comte
   (E) Almost any sociological imperialist

18. The passage presents Auguste Comte as

   (A) a close former associate of Adam Smith
   (B) a thoughtful, if argumentative, scientist
   (C) the only former economist who understood the new discipline of sociology
   (D) a bitter and prejudicial sociologist
   (E) the most respectable sociologist since John Stuart Mill

19. According to the passage, John Stuart Mill was

   (A) regrettably in opposition to Auguste Comte
   (B) the only sensible economist of the early group
   (C) the only early economist worth quoting
   (D) more interested in sociology than in economics
   (E) both practical and broad-minded

20. The author of the passage believes that the difficulty with more recent professionals in economics and sociology is

   (A) their inattentiveness to earlier colleagues
   (B) their parochial interests
   (C) their absolute lack of pragmatism
   (D) an ignorance of the current global state
   (E) a lack of awareness of the historic contributions of colleagues even in their own fields

21. In line 30, "distinguished" most nearly means

   (A) eminent
   (B) set apart
   (C) dignified
   (D) discriminated
   (E) recognized

22. The primary purpose of the passage as a whole is to

   (A) suggest that the fields of economics and sociology should interact more closely than they do now
   (B) support Auguste Comte's assertion that sociology is the "queen of all sciences"

   (C) describe the primary differences between the disciplines of economics and sociology
   (D) trace the historical development of the fields of economics and sociology
   (E) contrast the views of Adam Smith, Karl Marx, and John Stuart Mill with those of Auguste Comte

Several years ago Ralph Nader sailed through our town knocking everyone flat with fear. His pronouncement? Hot dogs contain only 12 percent
Line protein!
(5)   What did this mean to a nation of weiner eaters? Was it much too little? How much harm does a 12 percent hot dog do? The panic eventually subsided and we are now able to place the weiner in perspective. From a nutritional point
(10) of view we should calculate protein as a proportion of the calories, rather than of the weight, in the food. In weiners, 16 percent of the calories are protein. The real reason for concern is not that hot dogs contain 16 percent protein calories, but that
(15) they contain 80 percent fat calories.
       The protein content of a hot dog is actually quite respectable. There is no such thing as a 100 percent protein food. All protein sources contain large amounts of fats, carbohydrates, and water
(20) and probably quite a bit less protein than you have been led to believe. People on so-called high protein diets are advised to eat steak and cheddar cheese, for example. The proportion of calories from protein in round or T-bone steak is at most 50
(25) percent (and 50 percent fat), cheddar cheese is 25 percent protein and 75 percent fat, while fillet of sole is almost 80 percent protein (with 20 percent fat). While all these foods are rich in protein, they (except for the sole) are even richer in fat. They
(30) contain no carbohydrates.
       There are rich sources of protein that contain no fat, but are high in carbohydrates. Take, for example, skim milk, with 40 percent of calories from protein and 60 percent from carbohydrates;
(35) cooked red kidney beans with 25 percent protein calories and 70 percent carbohydrate calories; whole wheat bread with 16 percent protein and almost 80 percent carbohydrate calories; and oatmeal porridge with 15 percent protein and 70
(40) percent carbohydrate calories. This is why we need to eat a variety of sources of protein to ensure the right balance of fat and carbohydrates. Remember, we want our diets to have no less than 10 percent of the calories from protein, no more
(45) than 30 percent from fat and the remaining 60 percent from carbohydrates.
       Protein is necessary for the constant building and rebuilding of every cell in our bodies. It and other nutrients are used in the performance of the
(50) various functions of the body. Proteins produce enzymes that cause life-sustaining reactions in the body. There are enzymes to handle every nutrient

in our food. For example, there are enzymes called amylases in the mouth and intestines that convert
(55) the starch in our foods to the sugar maltose. The enzyme maltase in the intestine converts it to glucose (blood sugar) which passes through the intestine wall into the blood to be distributed to various tissues such as muscle, brain, and liver. In
(60) every cell of these tissues there are about thirty enzymes involved in breaking down glucose to give the cell the energy it contains; about four calories for each gram of glucose. Without these enzymes, the body can't use the food it receives.
(65)   We must have amino acids to make protein. Amino acids look like beads, and proteins are like long bead chains twisted together. The body breaks down the protein it receives from foods into amino acids, reorganizes them, and then forms its
(70) own protein. Of about twenty amino acids in all protein foods, only nine cannot be formed or transformed by our bodies and must be in the diet in the right amounts. These are called essential amino acids.

23. The passage suggests that one reason for not eating hot dogs is that

(A) Ralph Nader finds them objectionable
(B) 80 percent of their calories are fat calories
(C) they are low in protein
(D) their caloric value is unknown
(E) our diets don't require fats

24. According to the passage, the calories in a T-bone steak are

(A) half protein, half fat
(B) mainly protein calories
(C) mainly fat calories
(D) the same as in cheddar cheese
(E) less than those in broiled sole

25. According to the passage, amino acids

(A) produce enzymes that sustain life
(B) manufacture maltase and convert it to glucose
(C) are derived from carbohydrates
(D) are used by the body to form proteins
(E) are the source of our calories from protein

26. The primary purpose of the passage is to

(A) arouse concern
(B) promote dissension about proteins
(C) inform
(D) discourage people from eating carbohydrates
(E) amuse

27. It can be inferred from the passage that a relatively low-fat meal that is relatively high in both protein and carbohydrates could consist of

(A) skim milk, broiled sole, and whole wheat toast
(B) whole wheat toast, cheddar cheese, and milk
(C) oatmeal, whole wheat toast, and steak
(D) steak, cheddar cheese, and red kidney beans
(E) steak, cheddar cheese, and broiled sole

28. The questions in lines 5-7 serve primarily to

(A) highlight the author's doubt about the role of protein in the human diet
(B) express the confusion with which the public greeted Ralph Nader's pronouncement about the protein in hot dogs
(C) condemn Ralph Nader's inability to explain the significance of his finding about the protein content of hot dogs
(D) outline the main points that the author will discuss in the rest of the passage
(E) introduce the distinction between protein content as a proportion of weight and protein content as a proportion of calories

29. The passage suggests that the primary role proteins play in the body is to

(A) convert sugars into starches
(B) strengthen the muscles and bones
(C) break down and rearrange amino acids
(D) enable the body to convert food into energy
(E) rebuild the tissues of the liver and brain

30. The reference to "beads" in line 66 provides an analogy for the

(A) difference between amino acids and enzymes
(B) purposes for which the body uses amino acids
(C) importance of certain amino acids in the body
(D) functions of amino acids in the body
(E) way in which amino acids form proteins

STOP Do not go on to the next section of the test until you have numbered an answer sheet and set your timer.

SECTION 2   Time — 30 minutes   25 Questions

In this section, solve each problem and then choose the most appropriate answer from the choices given.

1. The cost of a 25-cent candy bar is raised 20 percent. What is the new cost of the candy bar?

   (A) 45¢ (B) 40¢ (C) 30¢ (D) 25¢ (E) 20¢

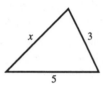

Note: Figure not drawn to scale.

2. Which of the following best describes x?

   (A) $3 < x < 5$ (B) $x = 2$ (C) $x = 4$
   (D) $2 < x < 8$ (E) $2 < x < 5$

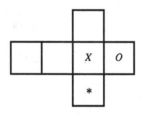

3. The above pattern can be folded into all of the following cubes EXCEPT

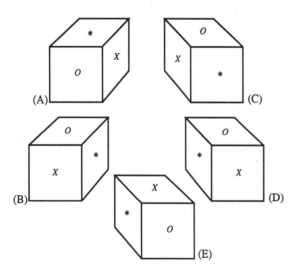

4. If $\frac{1}{2} + \frac{1}{8} - \frac{1}{4} - \frac{1}{6} = \frac{1}{x}$, then $x =$

   (A) 0 (B) 1 (C) $1\frac{1}{2}$ (D) $\frac{5}{24}$ (E) $4\frac{4}{5}$

5. A $50,000 inheritance has been left after a man has died. Before the money may be divided up, $10,000 must be paid on outstanding debts. Of what is left, half is to be given to charity and the remainder is to be split evenly among 4 cousins. The amount each cousin receives is expressed by which of the following?

   (A) $\frac{1}{2}(50,000 - 10,000) \div 4$

   (B) $\left(\frac{1}{2}(50,000) - 10,000\right) \div 4$

   (C) $\frac{1}{2}(50,000) - 10,000 \div 4$

   (D) $\left(\frac{1}{2}\right)(4)(50,000 - 10,000)$

   (E) $50,000 - \frac{1}{2}(50,000 - 10,000) \div 4$

6. A desk-chair set costs $9.89. If a dozen sets are purchased at once, the cost is reduced to $9.14 per set. A school needs to buy 1 gross (12 dozen) sets. How much does it save by buying the sets by the dozen instead of singly?

   (A) $9.00 (B) $18.00 (C) $19.03 (D) $24.00
   (E) $108.00

7. How many times between 12 noon and 12 midnight do the minute and hour hands of a clock line up exactly?

   (A) 10 (B) 11 (C) 12 (D) 23 (E) 24

8. If one is added to each of the digits of 3,642, then the resulting number is

   (A) 1 more than 3,642

   (B) 4 more than 3,642

   (C) 1,000 more than 3,642

   (D) 1,111 more than 3,642

   (E) 4,753 more than 3,642

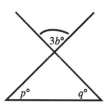

9. From the diagram above, the sum of p and q, in terms of b, equals

(A) $2b$ (B) $3b$ (C) $180 - b$ (D) $180 - 2b$
(E) $180 - 3b$

10. Over what interval(s) is the statement $x^3 > x^2$ true?

(A) All x (B) $x > 0$ (C) $x > 1$ or $x < -1$
(D) $-1 < x < 1$ (E) $x > 1$

11. If $y = \dfrac{1}{x+1}$, then what is x in terms of y?

(A) $\dfrac{1}{1+y}$ (B) $\dfrac{1}{y-1}$ (C) $\dfrac{1}{y}$

(D) $\dfrac{1-y}{y}$ (E) $\dfrac{1}{y} - y$

12. The instructions on a can of orange juice concentrate state that the water should be mixed with the concentrate in the ratio of 3 to 1. If 12 liters of orange juice are needed, how many liters of concentrate need to be bought?

(A) 3   (B) 4   (C) 6   (D) 36   (E) 48

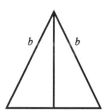

13. The area of the above isosceles triangle, with altitude $2\dfrac{2}{3}$, is 2. What is the base of the triangle?

A $\dfrac{2}{3}$ (B) $\dfrac{3}{2}$ (C) $\dfrac{3}{4}$ (D) $\dfrac{8}{3}$ (E) $\dfrac{3}{8}$

14. $(a-b)(b-a) =$

(A) $a^2 - 2ab + b^2$ (B) $a^2 - b^2$
(C) $a^2 + 2ab + b^2$ (D) $a^2 + 2ab - b^2$
(E) $-a^2 + 2ab - b^2$

15. The solution set of the equation $\sqrt{x} = x$ is

I. -1

II. 0

III. 1

(A) II only   (B) III only   (C) I and III only
(D) II and III only   (E) I, II, and III

16. A cylinder is formed in such a way that a sphere of radius 2 can just fit inside. What is the volume of the cylinder?

(A) π (B) 2π (C) 4π (D) 8π (E) 16π

17. In a certain state one must pay a state income tax of 5%. The federal income tax instructions say that one may deduct 75% of the amount of one's state income tax. If a man was able to deduct $900 from his federal income tax because of his state income tax, what was his income?

(A) $3,375   (B) $6,000   (C) $7,200
(D) $13,500   (E) $24,000

18. Margaret has d dimes and n nickels totaling $3.00. If she has 40 coins altogether, which of the pairs of equations could be used to solve for the number of nickels and dimes Margaret has?

(A) $\begin{cases} x(d) + (40 - x)n = 300 \\ n + d = 40 \end{cases}$

(B) $\begin{cases} 300 - d = n \\ n + d = 40 \end{cases}$

(C) $\begin{cases} 5n + 10d = 300 \\ n + d = 40 \end{cases}$

(D) $\begin{cases} 40 - (n + d) = 300 \\ n + d = 40 \end{cases}$

(E) $\begin{cases} 2n + d = 300 \\ n + d = 40 \end{cases}$

19. In a prehistoric village, rocks, stones, and pebbles were used as money. The relative values of the "coins" were:

   1 rock = 7 stones
   1 rock = 49 pebbles

If a man used 6 rocks to purchase a hide that cost 5 rocks, 2 stones, and 3 pebbles, how much change was he owed?

(A) 1 rock, 5 stones, 4 pebbles
(B) 5 stones, 4 pebbles
(C) 4 stones, 4 pebbles
(D) 5 stones, 5 pebbles
(E) 6 stones, 5 pebbles

20. All of the following are implied by the equation

    $\dfrac{a}{b} = \dfrac{c}{d}$ EXCEPT

    (A) $ad = bc$ (B) $\dfrac{a}{c} = \dfrac{b}{d}$ (C) $\dfrac{a-b}{b} = \dfrac{c-d}{d}$

    (D) $\dfrac{a+b}{a-b} = \dfrac{c+d}{c-d}$ (E) $\dfrac{ad}{c} = \dfrac{bc}{d}$

21. The sum of three consecutive odd numbers is how many times as large as the middle number?

    (A) 1   (B) $1\dfrac{1}{2}$ (C) 2   (D) 3   (E) 5

22. The set S contains the integers 1 through 9 inclusive. What is the value of the number of even numbers in S minus the number of odd numbers in S?

    (A) –2   (B) –1   (C) 0   (D) 1   (E) 2

23. Four equilateral triangles are placed so they form one big equilateral triangle. How many times greater than the perimeter of a small equilateral triangle is the perimeter of the big equilateral triangle?

    (A) 2   (B) $2\dfrac{1}{2}$ (C) 3   (D) $3\dfrac{1}{2}$ (E) 4

24. A 21-inch by 56-inch piece of material is to be cut up into equal squares. What is the largest length that the sides of the squares may be so that there is no extra material?

    (A) 1   (B) 3   (C) 7   (D) 14   (E) 21

25. A job can be done in 25 hours by 6 people. How many people would be needed to do the same job in 8 or fewer hours?

    (A) 16   (B) 17   (C) 18   (D) 19   (E) 20

STOP   Do not go on to the next section of the test until you have numbered an answer sheet and set your timer.

SECTION 3

Time — 30 minutes   **35 Questions**

The following sentences need a word or words to complete their meaning. Choose the word or words that <u>best</u> fit the meaning of each sentence.

1. Ancient Greek art is frequently described as timeless, partly because of its mathematically precise, ---- proportions.

    (A) even   (B) desirable   (C) inventive
    (D) classic   (E) historic

2. Long terms in prison foster an odd duality for prisoners who regard their release date with both ---- and ----.

    (A) eagerness. .excitement
    (B) fear. .trepidation
    (C) anticipation. .apprehension
    (D) antipathy. .fear
    (E) pleasure. .confusion

3. While the ancient Greek artists valued beauty, they were ultimately ----, who felt that function dictated form.

    (A) craftspeople   (B) pragmatists
    (C) goal-oriented   (D) aesthetes
    (E) traditionalists

4. Doctors frequently warn dedicated runners that a(n) ---- return to training will only serve to ---- an injury.

    (A) failure to. .prolong
    (B) hurried. .exacerbate
    (C) impulsive. .expedite
    (D) inevitable. .extenuate
    (E) prompt. .coddle

5. He was a truly ---- man, insistent upon ---- pronouncements at inopportune times, so that his family tended to leave the scene if his lips so much as parted.

    (A) misunderstood. .deliberate
    (B) maligned. .historic
    (C) loquacious. .hearty
    (D) irascible. .placid
    (E) tedious. .oracular

6. Escaping a stormy, ---- career as head coach at a state university, Jeff gratefully accepted a more private position at a small college.

    (A) blustering   (B) public   (C) exciting
    (D) recent   (E) impressive

7. The director allowed her young dance troupe to embark on a world tour, yet ---- committing them to a breakneck pace and ---- the right to cancel engagements if the toll of traveling proved too great.

    (A) wisely forbade. .anticipated
    (B) was unaware of. .ignored
    (C) refrained from. .reserved

    (D) eschewed. .observed
    (E) thought nothing of. .embraced

8. Lawmakers eager to promote a piece of legislation no doubt feel ---- whenever their bill ---- committee.

    (A) exhilaration. .is studied in
    (B) exasperation. .races through
    (C) uplifted. .bogs down in
    (D) thwarted. .languishes in
    (E) satisfaction. .is deposited in

9. In a typical autocracy, ---- is held by one individual, frequently oblivious to the public will and bent on following his own ---- course.

    (A) control. .arbitrary
    (B) rule. .sophisticated
    (C) the economy. .monetary
    (D) power. .mandated
    (E) management. .abstract

10. The Berlin Wall, constructed between East and West Berlin after World War II, formed a visible political ----; still, on either side of it, people thought and celebrated and dreamed as ---- nation.

    (A) barrier. .a conquered
    (B) boundary. .a divided
    (C) statement. .a separated
    (D) partition. .a democratic
    (E) demarcation. .one

The following questions are based on analogous relationships. Choose the lettered pair that <u>best</u> expresses a relationship similar to the pair in capital letters.

11. PILOT : JET ::   (A) pharmacist : drugs
    (B) chef : assistant   (C) director : firm
    (D) guide : museum   (E) teacher : colleague

12. FURNACE : WARMTH ::   (A) vessel : space
    (B) coffee : caffeine   (C) bicycle : trip
    (D) thread : cloth   (E) tube : conduction

13. SYLLABUS : COURSE ::
    (A) condensation : novel   (B) nave : church
    (C) outback : territory   (D) introduction : lesson
    (E) history : nation

14. REFEREE : GAME ::   (A) manager : sales
    (B) dancer : technique   (C) arbiter : dispute
    (D) coach : team
    (E) consultant : recommendation

15. REASON : PLAUSIBLE ::   (A) welcome : cordial
    (B) desire : fervent   (C) pursuit : vain
    (D) defense : lackluster   (E) argument : cogent

16. PHARMACIST : PRESCRIPTION ::
    (A) dancer : pirouette   (B) baker : salad
    (C) author : novel   (D) builder : blueprint
    (E) cartwright : shed

17. CANISTER : STORAGE ::   (A) barn : insulation
    (B) safe : security   (C) wine : cask
    (D) yoke : partner   (E) train : travel

18. DAINTY : BITE ::   (A) puny : effort
    (B) artless : glance   (C) massive : shoulders
    (D) small : petite   (E) fanciful : idea

19. DOUR : OUTLOOK ::   (A) sage : counsel
    (B) prolonged : life   (C) unique : approach
    (D) inclement : weather   (E) esoteric : design

20. VISION : MYOPIC ::   (A) hearing : audible
    (B) movement : symbolic   (C) knowledge : arcane
    (D) reasoning : fallible   (E) growth : rapid

21. ATTITUDE : BROAD-MINDED ::
    (A) education : catholic   (B) goal : elusive
    (C) opinion : hidebound
      (D) behavior : uninhibited
       (E) business : international

22. SPREAD : PROLIFERATE ::
    (A) plead : remonstrate   (B) goal : prod
    (C) seep : pour   (D) preach : promote
      (E) desist : commence

23. INDIFFERENT: PREJUDICE ::
    (A) explicit : clarity   (B) timid : effrontery
    (C) alluring : apparel   (D) elaborate : detail
      (E) articulate : presentation

> For the following reading passage, answer the questions based on what is <u>stated</u> or <u>implied</u> in the passage.

The following passage is adapted from a short story, published in 1891.

Suddenly Lady Windermere looked eagerly round the room, and said, in her clear contralto voice, "Where is my chiromantist?"

Line
(5) "Your what, Gladys?" exclaimed the Duchess, trying to remember what a chiromantist really was, and hoping it was not the same as a chiropodist.

"My chiromantist, Duchess; I can't live without him at present. I must certainly introduce him to you."

(10) "Introduce him!" cried the Duchess. "You don't mean to say he is here?" She began looking about for a small tortoise-shell fan and a very tattered lace shawl so as to be ready to go at a moment's notice.

(15) "Of course he is here; I would not dream of giving a party without him. He tells me I have a pure psychic hand."

"Oh, I see!" said the Duchess, feeling very much relieved. "He tells fortunes, I suppose?"

(20) "And misfortunes, too," answered Lady Windermere. "Any amount of them. Next year, for instance, I am in great danger, both by land and sea, so I am going to live in a balloon, and draw up my dinner in a basket every evening. It is all (25) written down on my little finger, or on the palm of my hand. I forget which."

"But surely that is tempting Providence, Gladys."

"My dear Duchess, surely Providence can resist (30) temptation by this time. Everyone should have their hands told once a month, so as to know what not to do. Of course, one does it all the same, but it is so pleasant to be warned. Ah, here is Mr. Podgers! Now, Mr. Podgers, I want you to tell the (35) Duchess of Paisley's hand."

"Dear Gladys, I really don't think it is quite right," said the Duchess, feebly unbuttoning a rather soiled kid glove.

"Nothing interesting ever is," said Lady (40) Windermere. "But I must introduce you. Duchess, this is Mr. Podgers, my pet chiromantist. Mr. Podgers, this is the Duchess of Paisley, and if you say that she has a larger mountain of the moon than I have, I will never believe in you again."

(45) "I am sure, Gladys, there is nothing of the kind in my hand," said the Duchess gravely.

"Your Grace is quite right," said Mr. Podgers, glancing at the little fat hand. "The mountain of the moon is not developed. The line of life, (50) however, is excellent. You will live to a great age, Duchess, and be extremely happy. Ambition— very moderate, line of intellect not exaggerated, line of heart—"

"Now, do be indiscreet, Mr. Podgers," cried (55) Lady Windermere.

"Nothing would give me greater pleasure," said Mr. Podgers, bowing, "if the Duchess ever had been, but I am sorry to say that I see great permanence of affection, combined with a strong (60) sense of duty."

"Pray go on, Mr. Podgers," said the Duchess, looking quite pleased.

"Economy is not the least of your Grace's virtues," continued Mr. Podgers, and Lady (65) Windermere went off into fits of laughter.

"Economy is a very good thing," remarked the Duchess complacently. "When I married Paisley he had eleven castles, and not a single house fit to live in."

(70) "And now he has twelve houses, and not a single castle," cried Lady Windermere. "You have told the Duchess's character admirably, Mr. Podgers, and now you must tell Lady Flora's." In answer to a nod, a tall girl stepped awkwardly (75) from behind the sofa and held out a long, bony hand.

"Ah, a pianist!" said Mr. Podgers. "Very reserved, very honest, and with a great love of animals."

(80) "Quite true!" exclaimed the Duchess, turning to Lady Windermere. "Flora keeps two dozen collie dogs at Macloskie, and would turn our town house into a menagerie if her father would let her."

"Well, that is just what I do with my house
(85) every Thursday evening," cried Lady Windermere,
laughing. "Only I like lions better than collie dogs.
But Mr. Podgers must read some more hands for
us. Come, Lady Marvel, show him yours."
    But Lady Marvel entirely declined to have her
(90) past or her future exposed. In fact, many people
seemed afraid to face the odd little man with his
stereotyped smile and his bright, beady eyes; and
when he told poor Lady Fermor right out before
everyone that she did not care a bit for music, but
(95) was extremely fond of musicians, it was generally
felt that chiromancy was a most dangerous
science, and one that ought not to be encouraged,
except in private.
    Lord Arthur Savile, however, who did not
(100) know anything about Lady Fermor's unfortunate
story, was filled with curiosity to have his own
hand read, and feeling somewhat shy about putting
himself forward, crossed to where Lady
Windermere was sitting and asked her if she
(105) thought Mr. Podgers would mind.
    "Of course he won't mind," said Lady
Windermere. "That is what he is here for. All my
lions, Lord Arthur, are performing lions, and jump
through hoops whenever I ask them."

24. Lady Windermere's statement that she "can't live
without" (lines 7–8) her chiromantist is an example
of

    (A) wit
    (B) parody
    (C) satire
    (D) exaggeration
    (E) generalization

25. The Duchess wants to "be ready to go at a
moment's notice" (lines 13–14) because she

    (A) is afraid of chiropodists
    (B) is tired of Lady Windermere
    (C) is embarrassed at not being able to remember
        the difference between a chiropodist and a
        chiromantist
    (D) thinks having her fortune told would be
        tempting Providence
    (E) does not want to meet Mr. Podgers

26. The passage suggests that the Duchess wears a
tattered shawl (line 13) and soiled gloves (line 38)
because she

    (A) likes to save money
    (B) cannot afford to buy nicer ones
    (C) cares little about her appearance
    (D) prefers to buy nice things for her homes
    (E) knew that this party would not require fancy
        dress

27. Lady Windermere's plan to live in a balloon and
draw up her dinner in a basket (lines 23–24)
indicates her

    (A) desire to impress the Duchess

(B) inability to separate reality from fantasy
(C) whimsical attitude toward fortunetelling
(D) fear of the danger Mr. Podgers has predicted
(E) respect for the accuracy of Mr. Podger's
    fortunes

28. Lady Windermere's speech in lines 29–33 shows
that she

    (A) likes to give advice to others
    (B) dislikes knowing what is going to happen to her
    (C) believes that Mr. Podgers has amazing and
        uncanny powers
    (D) does not take either Providence or chiromancy
        very seriously
    (E) makes a point of disagreeing with the Duchess
        whenever possible

29. The Duchess says, "I really don't think it is quite
right" in lines 36–37 because she

    (A) has philosophical and moral objections to
        fortunetelling
    (B) thinks that trying to discern the future could be
        dangerous
    (C) does not like to do what Lady Windermere tells
        her to do
    (D) believes that Mr. Podgers is likely to predict
        bad events in her future
    (E) is afraid that Mr. Podgers will reveal her secrets
        in front of Lady Windermere

30. Lady Windermere's use of the phrase "my pet
chiromantist" (line 41) suggests that Lady
Windermere

    (A) provides for Mr. Podgers's needs
    (B) desires Mr. Podgers's companionship
    (C) perceives Mr. Podgers's devotion to her
    (D) feels possessive toward Mr. Podgers
    (E) likes to belittle Mr. Podgers in front of her
        friends

31. By characterizing the Duchess's line of intellect as
"not exaggerated" (line 52), Mr. Podgers shows
himself to be

    (A) tactful
    (B) disdainful
    (C) imaginative
    (D) indifferent
    (E) suspicious

32. The Duchess looks "quite pleased" (line 62) because

    (A) her future is brighter than is Lady
        Windermere's
    (B) she is relieved that Mr. Podgers is not a
        chiropodist
    (C) her fears about tempting Providence have been
        allayed
    (D) Mr. Podgers has not suggested any danger in
        her immediate future
    (E) Mr. Podgers has described her characteristics
        positively

33. The word "reserved" in line 78 most nearly means

    (A) limited in scope
    (B) retained for oneself
    (C) characterized by reticence
    (D) set aside for a particular purpose
    (E) marked by lack of enthusiasm

34. In addition to telling people's fortunes, Mr. Podgers

    (A) describes their characteristics
    (B) describes their past endeavors
    (C) describes their present occupations
    (D) encourages their unspoken plans
    (E) tells them how to avoid the difficulties he foresees

35. In line 89, the word "declined" most nearly means

    (A) failed
    (B) drooped
    (C) refused
    (D) descended
    (E) deteriorated

STOP Do not go on to the next section of the test until you have numbered an answer sheet and set your timer.

| SECTION **4** | Time — 30 minutes | 25 Questions |

Questions 1–15 each consist of two quantities. Determine their relationship and write

    A   if the quantity in Column A is greater;
    B   if the quantity in Column B is greater;
    C   if the two quantities are equal;
    D   if the relationship between the two quantities cannot be determined.

Information that may help you in determining the relationship between the two quantities is centered above the two columns.

	Column A	Column B
1.	$\dfrac{32 \times 10^6}{8 \times 10^4}$	10^2
2.	$x\%$ of y	$y\%$ of x
3.	32	8.2×4.3

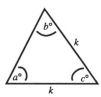

4.	$a + c$	$b + c$

$$z \neq 0$$

5.	$4z$	$(2z)^2$

	Column A	Column B
6.	$3^2 \cdot 2^3$	$2^2 \cdot 3^3$

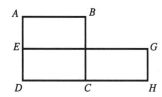

The area of square $ABCD$ is equal to the area of rectangle $EGHD$.

7.	The perimeter of square $ABCD$	The perimeter of rectangle $EGHD$

A coat on sale costs x dollars, which is 25% less than the normal cost of the coat.

8.	The normal cost of the coat	$.75x$

9.	Volume of a cylinder with diameter 2 and height 4	Volume of a rectangular solid with dimensions $2 \times 2 \times 4$

Column A Column B

Questions 10 and 11 refer to the following definition:

$$a!b = \frac{1}{a} + \frac{1}{b} \qquad (ab \neq 0)$$

10. $a!b$ $\dfrac{a+b}{ab}$

$x!y + 9 = 0$

11. $x!y$ 9

---

12. The distance from the point (a,a) to the point (p,q) on the coordinate axes The distance from the point (a,a) to the point (q,p) on the coordinate axes

---

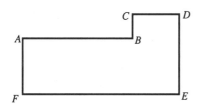

In the figure above all segments intersect at right angles.

13. $FA + AB + BC + CD$ $FB + BD$

---

14. $(x+y)^2 - (x-y)^2$ $4xy$

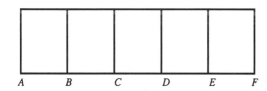

Note: Figure not drawn to scale.

A row of apartments is represented by the boxes above. A surveyor wants to measure the width of each apartment. He finds that:

$AD = CF = 12$ and

$BD = CE = 8$

15. CD 4

On the following page are a set of blank grids. For each problem, 16–25, write the solution in the first row of the corresponding grid. For each box from the first row with a number, slash, or decimal point in it, fill in the corresponding box below it.

16. All of the following are equal to 368 except one; what is its value?

$300 + 60 + 8$
$10(30 + 6) + 8$
$100(3) + 10(6) + 1(8)$
$10(30) + 68$
$300 + 10(60 + 8)$

---

17. If Kelvin eats $\dfrac{1}{4}$ of a pie, Kirsty eats $\dfrac{1}{3}$ of what's left after Kelvin is done, and Kitty eats $\dfrac{1}{2}$ of what's left after Kirsty is done, then what part of the pie is left?

---

1 pound of turkey costs $0.79
2 pounds of chicken costs $1.49

18. What is the difference, in dollars, of the price per pound for chicken and turkey?

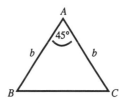

19. How many degrees greater is the measure of $\angle B$ than the measure of $\angle A$?

---

20. The average of three numbers is 67. The average of two of the numbers is 65. What is the third number?

While walking from town A to town B, a man meets another man who has 12 siblings, each of whom is carrying 10 sacks, each of which contains 4 cats.

21. How many cats are being carried?

$4 \leq a \leq 14$
$7 \leq b \leq 12$

22. Find the maximum value of $\dfrac{b}{a}$

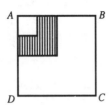

23. Each of the three squares pictured above share a common vertex at *A*. The interior squares each have another vertex at the center of another one of the squares. What is the ratio of the area of the shaded region to the area of the unshaded region?

24. On a long street the houses are numbered in jumps of 6. That is, the first house has a street number 6, the second 12, and so on. What is the sum of the last digits of the street numbers of the 83rd, 84th, 85th, 86th, and 87th houses?

25. On a street corner there are two flashing lights, a red one and a blue one. The red one flashes three times per minute, and the blue one flashes two times per minute. If the lights start off flashing at the same time, once every how many seconds do they flash together?

STOP Do not go on to the next section of the test until you have numbered an answer sheet and set your timer.

16.

17.

18.

19.

20.

21.

22.

23.

24.

25.

| SECTION **5** | Time — 15 minutes | 13 Questions |

Questions on the following reading passages should be answered based on what is <u>stated</u> or <u>implied</u> in the passages.

These passages are adapted from opinions of the United States Supreme Court on a case in which the "petitioner" appealed his conviction on a charge of carrying a concealed weapon on the grounds that the search that revealed the weapon was unconstitutional. The Fourth Amendment to the U.S. Constitution holds that "the right of the people to be secure . . . against unreasonable searches and seizures, shall not be violated" and that search warrants may not be issued except on "probable cause." Passage 1 is the majority opinion, Passage 2 a dissenting opinion.

Passage 1

We must first establish at what point in this encounter the Fourth Amendment becomes relevant: whether the police officer "seized"
Line petitioner and conducted a "search" before placing
(5) him under arrest. Using the terms "stop" and "frisk" may suggest that these police actions are outside the purview of the Fourth Amendment because neither action rises to the level of a "search" or "seizure." We emphatically reject this
(10) notion. The Fourth Amendment clearly governs "seizures" of a person that do not result in arrest. Whenever a police officer restrains an individual's freedom to walk away, the officer has "seized" that person. And it is sheer torture of the English
(15) language to suggest that a careful exploration of a person's clothing in order to find weapons is not a "search."

The main governmental interest involved here is crime prevention; this interest authorizes police
(20) officers to approach individuals to investigate possibly criminal behavior even though there is no "probable cause" for arrest. The arresting officer was discharging this legitimate function when he approached petitioner and his companions. He had
(25) observed them go through a series of acts, each perhaps innocent in itself, but which taken together warranted investigation. There is nothing unusual in two men standing on a street corner, perhaps waiting for someone. Nor is there anything
(30) suspicious about people strolling up and down the street. Store windows, moreover, are made to be looked in. But the story is quite different where, as here, two men hover about a street corner for an extended time, obviously not waiting for anyone;
(35) where these men pace along an identical route, pausing to stare in the same store window numerous times; where they confer on the corner after each completion of this route; and where they

are joined in one such conference by a third man
(40) who leaves swiftly. For the officer to have failed to investigate would have been poor police work indeed.

At the time he seized and searched petitioner, the officer had reasonable suspicion that petitioner
(45) was armed and dangerous. Such a search is a reasonable search under the Fourth Amendment, and any weapons seized may properly be introduced in evidence against the person who carried them.

Passage 2

(50) I agree that petitioner was "seized" within the meaning of the Fourth Amendment, and that frisking petitioner for guns was clearly a "search." But it is a mystery how that "search" and that "seizure" can be constitutional by Fourth
(55) Amendment standards, unless there was "probable cause" to believe that a crime had been, was about to be, or was in the process of being committed.

The majority opinion does not claim the existence of "probable cause." If loitering were the
(60) offense charged, there would be "probable cause" shown. But the crime here is carrying concealed weapons; the officer had no "probable cause" for believing that this crime was being committed. Had a search warrant been sought, a judge would,
(65) therefore, have been unauthorized to issue one, for judges can act only if "probable cause" is shown. The Court holds today that the police have greater authority to make a "seizure" and conduct a "search" than a judge has to authorize such action.

(70) To give the police greater power than judges have is to take a long step down the totalitarian path. Perhaps such a step is desirable to cope with modern forms of lawlessness. But it should be taken only as the deliberate choice of the people
(75) through a constitutional amendment. Until the Fourth Amendment is rewritten, the person and his or her effects are beyond the reach of all governmental agencies until there are reasonable grounds to believe ("probable cause") that a
(80) criminal venture has been or is about to be launched.

There have been powerful pressures throughout our history that bear heavily on the Court to water down constitutional guarantees and give the police
(85) the upper hand. That pressure has probably never been greater than it is today.

Yet if the individual is no longer to be sovereign, if the police can pick someone up whenever they do not like the cut of his or her jib,
(90) if they can "seize" and "search" an individual in their discretion, we enter a new regime. The decision to enter it should be made only after a full debate by the people of this country.

1. The author of Passage 1 implies that the "point in this encounter" at which "the Fourth Amendment becomes relevant" (lines 1–3) is the point at which the police officer

   (A) noticed the suspicious behavior of petitioner
   (B) stopped petitioner and frisked him
   (C) found the concealed weapon in petitioner's clothing
   (D) arrested petitioner
   (E) placed the weapon he had found in evidence against petitioner

2. With which of the following interpretations of the Fourth Amendment is the author of Passage 1 most likely to agree?

   (A) The Fourth Amendment applies to "stop and frisk" actions only when there is "probable cause" to believe that a crime is taking place.
   (B) The police may momentarily stop a person whose behavior seems suspicious without having engaged in a "seizure" as defined by the Fourth Amendment.
   (C) Searches that result from a well-founded suspicion of criminal activity are not "unreasonable searches" under the Fourth Amendment.
   (D) The requirement for "probable cause" applies only to judges issuing search warrants and not to police officers conducting a search at the scene of a possible crime.
   (E) Fourth Amendment guarantees of individual rights must take second place to the duty of the police to protect public safety.

3. The word "discharging" in line 23 most nearly means

   (A) performing
   (B) unloading
   (C) releasing
   (D) dismissing
   (E) setting aside

4. In concluding that the police officer had reason to believe petitioner was "armed and dangerous" (lines 44–45), the author of Passage 1 assumes that

   (A) a person who carries a concealed weapon should be considered armed and dangerous
   (B) a person whose actions seem to indicate an intention to rob a store is likely to be carrying a weapon
   (C) the police officer conducted an unreasonable search under the Fourth Amendment
   (D) actions that might otherwise seem innocent become suspicious when someone engages in them repeatedly
   (E) police officers have the duty to investigate all unusual behavior

5. The word "properly" in line 47 most nearly means

   (A) strictly
   (B) suitably
   (C) validly
   (D) decorously
   (E) characteristically

6. In line 59, "loitering" is presented as an example of the crime

   (A) that is less likely to endanger public safety than is the crime of carrying a concealed weapon
   (B) that requires grounds of "probable cause" before a search can be conducted
   (C) for which the police officer in the case should have arrested petitioner
   (D) in which petitioner appeared to be engaged at the time he was accosted by the police officer
   (E) to which "probable cause" applies more directly than it does to the crime of carrying a concealed weapon

7. The author of Passage 2 believes that the police

   (A) may stop and frisk a person only if they have a search warrant issued by a judge
   (B) should not be allowed to conduct searches that a judge would be unable to authorize
   (C) should have proof that a crime is under way or being planned before they can search or seize an individual
   (D) have as their primary responsibility the protection of individuals' Fourth Amendment rights
   (E) must be given considerable leeway in investigating possible criminal behavior

8. In Passage 2, the author's attitude toward the ruling allowing a police officer to frisk an individual whose behavior the officer finds suspicious is most clearly indicated in which of the following phrases?

   (A) "a long step down the totalitarian path" (lines 71–72)
   (B) "desirable to cope with modern forms of lawlessness" (lines 72–73)
   (C) "the deliberate choice of the people" (line 74)
   (D) "beyond the reach of all governmental agencies" (lines 77–78)
   (E) "powerful pressures throughout our history" (lines 82–83)

9. The author mentions "modern forms of lawlessness" (line 73) primarily in order to provide

   (A) a reason for accepting his argument
   (B) an illustration to support his argument
   (C) a rebuttal of a point made against his argument
   (D) a modification of the position taken earlier
   (E) a concession to the opposing viewpoint

10. By insisting that this Fourth Amendment issue should be put before the people of the United States, the author of Passage 2 suggests that

(A) public trust in the police would increase if the people were allowed to decide the limits of police power
(B) a guarantee of Fourth Amendment rights is no longer necessary in modern society
(C) the interpretation of the Constitution should be determined by the public rather than by the courts
(D) the people are not likely to choose to rewrite the Fourth Amendment because recent increases in crime rates have made them fearful of criminal activity
(E) the majority opinion has taken over a right reserved to the people by effectively overthrowing the Fourth Amendment

11. The author of Passage 2 believes that the majority opinion in Passage 1 does not meet Fourth Amendment standards because the majority opinion

(A) replaces the term "unreasonable searches" with the term "probable cause"
(B) holds that frisking a person before arresting that person is a "search"
(C) ignores the need to show "probable cause" before conducting a search
(D) places too much emphasis on the "governmental interest" (line 18) of preventing crime
(E) rejects the necessity of obtaining a warrant from a judge before conducting a search

12. The basic disagreement between the author of Passage 1 and the author of Passage 2 is over the issue of whether

(A) the Fourth Amendment should be rewritten
(B) Fourth Amendment standards are relevant to this case
(C) the Fourth Amendment required the police officer to obtain a warrant for the arrest of petitioner before searching him
(D) the search and seizure of petitioner was a reasonable search as required by the Fourth Amendment
(E) a search and seizure, as defined in the Fourth Amendment, had occurred prior to petitioner's arrest by the police officer

13. The author of Passage 2 uses the phrase "it is a mystery" in line 53 to express which of the following reactions to the majority opinion in Passage 1?

(A) His admission that defining the terms "search" and "seizure" can be difficult
(B) His doubt that the Fourth Amendment applies to this particular search and seizure
(C) His disapproval of the way the majority opinion defined "search" and "seizure"
(D) His rejection of the assertion that this particular search and seizure meets Fourth Amendment standards
(E) His opposing argument that the Fourth Amendment should be revised

---

STOP   Do not go on to the next section of the test until you have numbered an answer sheet and set your timer.

| SECTION **6** | Time — 15 minutes | 10 Questions |

In this section, solve each problem, and then choose the most appropriate answer from the choices given.

1. If $1 + 2 + 3 + 4 + 5 + 6 = x + 7 + 11$, then $x =$
   (A) 1   (B) 2   (C) 3   (D) 4   (E) 5

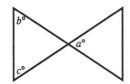

2. In the figure above, $\angle a$ equals the sum of $\angle s\ b$ and c
   (A) always
   (B) never
   (C) only when $\angle a$ has a measure of 45°
   (D) only when $\angle a$ has a measure of 90°
   (E) None of the above

3. At a dairy it takes 90 seconds to fill 30 one-gallon jugs of milk. How many minutes does it take to fill 90 jugs of milk?
   (A) 1   (B) 3   (C) 3.5   (D) 4   (E) 4.5

4. If the ratio of the altitude of ΔA to the altitude of ΔB is 2:1, then the ratio of the area of ΔA to the area of ΔB is
   (A) 1:1   (B) 2:1   (C) 4:1   (D) 8:1   (E) It cannot be determined from the information given.

5. A number that is divisible by both 6 and 8 is also divisible by
   (A) 5   (B) 9   (C) 11   (D) 16   (E) 24

6. On a certain island there are liars and truth-tellers. Liars must always lie and truth-tellers must always tell the truth. A visitor comes across a native and asks him if he always tells the truth. The native responds, "I always tell the truth." The native could be
   (A) a truth-teller
   (B) a liar
   (C) either a truth-teller or a liar
   (D) neither a truth-teller nor a liar
   (E) None of the above answers is correct.

7. A man can paint m meters of fence in h hours and 15 minutes. What is his average speed in meters per hour?
   (A) $h(1 + \frac{1}{4})m$ (B) $\dfrac{m}{h + 15}$
   (C) $\dfrac{m}{h + \frac{1}{4}}$ (D) $\dfrac{h + 15}{m}$ (E) $\dfrac{h + \frac{1}{4}}{m}$

8. A car is driven 2 miles across town. If the radius of a wheel on the car is 1 foot, how many revolutions has the wheel made? (5,280 feet = 1 mile)
   (A) $\dfrac{5,280}{\pi}$ (B) $\dfrac{10,560}{\pi}$ (C) $\dfrac{2,640}{\pi}$
   (D) 5,280   (E) 10,560

9. The operation $\boxed{x}$ indicates that one should subtract 2 from x and then multiply the result by 2. The operation $\textcircled{x}$ indicates that one should multiply x by 2 and then subtract 2 from the product.
   $\textcircled{x} - \boxed{x} =$
   (A) –2   (B) 0   (C) 2   (D) 4
   (E) It cannot be determined from the information given.

10. $\left(x - \dfrac{1}{x}\right)^2 + 4 =$
   (A) 4   (B) 5   (C) $x^2 - \left(\dfrac{1}{x}\right)^2 + 4$
   (D) $x^2 + \left(\dfrac{1}{x}\right)^2$ (E) $\left(x + \dfrac{1}{x}\right)^2$

SCORING THE PRACTICE SAT

Verbal Sections 1, 3, and 5

1. Write the total number of questions answered correctly in space ① .
2. Multiply this correct answer total by 7.7 and write that product in space ② .
3. Add 200 and put the sum in space ③ .
4. Now, count the number of questions answered incorrectly—the number of wrong answers—and write this total in space ④ .
5. Multiply the value in space ④ by 2.5 and put this product in space ⑤ .
6. Subtract the value in space ⑤ from the total in space ③ (your right answer total) and put the result in space ⑥ . This number in space ⑥ is your *approximate* score.

Verbal Score Sheet

Total # Correct: ① _____   × 7.7 =   ② _____

                                                  +   200
                                                       _____

                                  Positive Score   ③ _____

Total # Incorrect: ④_____   × 2.5 –   ⑤ _____
     except the grid-in problems

                              Approximate SAT score: ⑥ _____

Math Sections 2, 4, and 6

Write the total number of questions you answered correctly in space ① . Multiply this by 10 and put the product in space ② . Add 200 and put the sum in space ③ . Write the *total* number of questions you answered incorrectly, except the grid-in problems (i.e. #16 – #25 in section 2), in space ④ . Multiply the value in space ④ by 4 and put the product in space ⑤ . Subtract the value in space ⑤ from the value in space ③ and put the result in space ⑥ . This is your *approximate* score.

   This is only an approximate score because your actual score not only depends on how well you do, but also on how well everyone else does who is taking the test with you. For example, if you make 20 mistakes but a lot of people only made 10 mistakes, your score will be lower than if you make 20 mistakes, and everyone else makes 30 mistakes.

Math Score Sheet

Total # Correct: ① _____   × 10 =   ② _____

                                                  +   200
                                                       _____

                                  Positive Score   ③ _____

Total # Incorrect: ④_____   × 4 –   ⑤ _____
     except the grid-in problems

                              Approximate SAT score: ⑥ _____

About Your Score

If you scored somewhat lower than you expected, fret not. This diagnostic SAT is often harder for students than real SATs, and most people score a bit lower. A *real* test will be a treat, then, won't it? Also, now you can analyze what caused you to lose points and do something about the problem before the actual test day.

Take a look at the evaluation sheet that follows. It will help to guide your study during further test preparation. And don't look at the columns that show what you did *wrong* as your sole evaluation. What did you do *right?* If you do certain things well, you know you can learn to do *other* things well, too.

EVALUATION OF THE PRACTICE SAT

Sentence Completions

_____ right   _____ wrong   (19 total questions)

Difficulty encountered:
_____ 1st half of question set (easy to medium)
_____ 2nd half of question set (more difficult)

Unknown words include _____

_____

Analogies

_____ right   _____ wrong   (19 total questions)

Difficulty encountered:
_____ 1st half of question set (easy to medium)
_____ 2nd half of question set (more difficult)

Unknown words include _____

_____

Relationships misunderstood or puzzling are _____

_____

_____

Were you always able to express the given relationship in a sentence or phrase? _____ If not, please look at the answers now and create a sentence or phrase that correctly states the given relationships. (Now, of course, these problems will seem much easier.)

Reading Comprehension Questions

_____ right   _____ wrong   (40 total questions)

Unknown words include _____

_____

Question type(s) that gave trouble? _____

_____

Conclusions

My best kinds of questions are _____

My worst question types are _____

Areas for serious review are _____

_____

Timing Problems?

If you ran out of time on any segments, remember that practice will make you faster. It will also give you a feel for a 30-minute test period—part of the "test smarts" you want to perfect.

Vocabulary Alert

If you couldn't answer several questions because you didn't know words in the question or in the answers, then your problem is really VOCABULARY. Half (or more) of your review time should be spent learning the words in Unit 5, the vocabulary unit, pp. 127–226.

MATH QUESTIONS

Total number of problems worked correctly _____

Total missed _____

Total omitted problems _____

Any missed in problems numbered 1–12 in section 2? (These are normally simpler problems.) _____

If any missed, list why: (Carelessness, moving too fast, unknown formula, etc.) _____

_____

_____

Other problems missed were in the areas of _____

_____

_____

Quantitative comparison problems worked correctly _____

Quantitative comparison problems missed _____

Do you need to study Math Lessons 15 and 16 to improve performance in this area? _____

Problems worked correctly tested which concepts? (These can be considered areas of strength.) _____

_____

_____

Conclusions

Best kinds of problems include _____

_____

(Merely skim over these topics in the Lessons as a refresher.)

I need to review and work practice problems in the areas of _____

_____

_____

Lessons I plan to STUDY include _____

_____

Timing Problems?

Folks who run out of time on PSAT and SAT math segments can get faster with practice, but only up to a point. Work too fast and you may begin to make errors. The only way to time yourself intelligently on these exams is by practicing at home, with a timer, until you find what works best for you. Racing madly through problems is a lousy idea.

Unit 8: The Answer Section

UNIT 3: REASONING SKILLS FOR VERBAL QUESTIONS

Practice Analogies 1, from p. 56

1. **(D)** **bicuspid : teeth** Part of whole.
2. **(B)** **worry : frown** Cause and effect or result. Answer (D) shows too strong an emotion to balance equally with *good news : smile;* terror and fright may also be thought of as synonyms.
3. **(C)** **geese : gaggle** Part of whole.
4. **(E)** **water : thirst** Implied comparison; lacking water, you have thirst, just as you have hunger if you go without food.
5. **(A)** **conservatory : music** Implied comparison; first the place, then the subject that is studied or practiced there.
6. **(E)** **plow : furrow** Implied comparison; a scalpel makes an incision or cut in the skin, just as a plow makes a furrow (incision) in the soil.
7. **(B)** **government : laws** Cause and effect or result. The media provide news as one of their major functions, just as the government provides laws.
8. **(C)** **chapeau : head** Implied comparison. The item of clothing and what it covers or adorns.
9. **(D)** **gentility : coarseness** Both sides show antonyms; also a lack of accord or agreement may result in dissension, just as a lack of gentility or politeness may result in rude or coarse behavior.
10. **(C)** **convoluted : prose** Implied comparison. A tortuous path is winding and twisted, just as convoluted writing is winding and twisted—not direct and straightforward.

Practice Analogies 2, from p. 57

1. **(C)** **walk : cement** This is an analogy of substance to end product; just as *rafters* are typically constructed of *wood,* so is a *sidewalk* normally made of *cement.* The other answers do not show this same relationship. A *harness* is used to guide an animal that pulls a *cart* (A); you can put a *peg* into a *hole* (B); you may fertilize a *garden* with *manure* (D); and the outside of a *horse* is his *hide.*
2. **(B)** **linguist : language** A pediatrician's specialty is children, just as a linguist's specialty is language. Answer (A) is erroneous, because a numismatist is a collector of coins, not a therapist. A podiatrist is a foot doctor, answer (C), and doesn't specialize in bones per se. Answer (D) features a lawyer, who does more than institute suits in court. Answer (E) gives us unrelated nouns.
3. **(B)** **cup : quart** This analogy is a relationship of quantity or volume. A peck is $\frac{1}{4}$ of a bushel, just as a cup is $\frac{1}{4}$ of a quart. All of the other answer choices are factually incorrect.
4. **(B)** **harmony : dissonance** Antonyms as well as an implied comparison. Without government, you have anarchy, just as you have dissonance without harmony.
5. **(D)** **bull : taurine** The adjective describing a cat is *feline,* just as the adjective describing a bull is *taurine.* If you didn't know the word *taurine,* answer (A) could still be discarded immediately since a tomboy is not particularly feminine in behavior. The word describing a cow (or meaning cowlike) is bovine; *canine* refers to dogs. Answer (C) is in the wrong *order;* otherwise, it would have been acceptable. And (E) is silly, since a woman is not virile, a word that means manly.
6. **(A)** **viper : slay** Just as we customarily vilify (criticize strongly) a turncoat or traitor, so we typically slay a viper, which is a treacherous snake.

7. **(A)** **battle : slaughter** An analogy of cause and effect, this one says that a downpour may lead to a flood, just as a battle may lead to a slaughter. Any completion of this analogy depends on your realizing that a *bad outcome* to the downpour and battle is necessary, which is why (A) is such a nice answer. Answers (B), (C), and (D) are essentially synonyms, so they're out. Answer (E) is possible, but rain is not a "bad outcome," so it won't work.
8. **(C)** **pages : book** This analogy says that speech is composed of words, just as a book is composed of pages. Answer (A) says that an orange is composed of peeling, but this is inaccurate, as is answer (B), which says that a tree is composed of leaves. Both the tree and the orange have other major features. Answer (D) shows the items in incorrect order and wouldn't have worked anyway, mainly because it is too narrow. And (E) falls victim to the same problem: an apple is composed of more than seeds.
9. **(D)** **facade : building** Because your expression is what shows on your face, the analogy to the facade of a building is especially appropriate: the facade is what we see showing on the outside of a building. Answers (A) and (B) fail to make sense in this relationship. Hair shows on your head, but it doesn't reveal a "face" to the world in any sense, and so answer (C) is weak. Answer (E) says that look is to features as face is to expression, and that falls apart logically since features may individually not be expressive, may even be unattractive, yet the overall look can be appealing. (E) is too vague and unspecific for your purposes.
10. **(E)** **suggest : epitomize** This analogy is one of degree. To intimate is to subtly hint or suggest—much less powerful than to command. To suggest or give a hint—of a personality trait, for instance—is much less strong than epitomizing that trait (being its perfect example).

Practice Analogies 3, from p. 58

1. **(A)** **deer : timorous** Implied comparison. A tiger is customarily described as ferocious, just as the deer is described as timorous (shy, timid).
2. **(B)** **mulberry : tree** Part of a whole. A squash grows on a vine just as the mulberry grows on a tree. None of the other choices exhibits *exactly* this relationship. You may have a *quart of berries* (A); and a *handle* is on a *drawer,* and so is a part of it, but it does not GROW THERE, and that is the significant distinction in this analogy. Likewise, a *buckle* may be part of a *boot,* but it doesn't grow there. *Answer (E)* gives *peach* as one kind of *fruit.*
3. **(C)** **wine : cask** Implied comparison. Honey is stored in a hive, just as wine is stored in a cask.
4. **(E)** **midday : dawn** An analogy of degree, this relationship states that radiance is much brighter than a mere glimmer, just as midday is considerably brighter than dawn.
5. **(C)** **deer : venison** Animal related to its product. Even if you did not know for sure that we make cheese from cow's milk, it is a logical connection. None of the other answer choices gives us an animal first, followed by a common product of that animal. *Answer (E)* has correct items, but in the wrong order!
6. **(D)** **seamstress : garment** Worker related to the typical product. Remember that an engraver (E) does not work on the stamp itself but on the engraving plate.

7. **(C) tenuous : impalpable** Comparison of degree. Arcane is the extreme of difficult, just as impalpable (unable to be touched, felt, grasped) is an extreme for tenuous. If you have a tenuous hold on something, you can at least grasp it. If it is impalpable, it has gone beyond your reach.

8. **(A) bud : burgeon** Implied comparison. A child is expected to mature (grow and develop) into an adult, just as a bud is expected to burgeon (grow) into a flower, leaf, or shoot.

9. **(B) attempt : frustrate** Implied comparison. A plot that has been thwarted (foiled or frustrated) is just like any attempt that has been frustrated (foiled or thwarted). The first slots show the idea—the plot or attempt—and the second slots show an identical unsuccessful outcome.

10. **(D) ant : assiduous** Animal related to its most logical or expected characteristic. All sloths are described as torpid (sluggish, sleepy, slow-moving), just as ants are assiduous (diligent, hardworking). Answer (C) may have been tempting, but remember that not all mammals are carnivores (meat eaters).

Practice Analogies 4, from p. 58

1. **(C) wagon : rectangular** A cylinder is customarily round in shape, just as a wagon is customarily rectangular.

2. **(E) squander : spend** Analogy of degree. To drench something is the extreme of sprinkling it, just as squandering something (e.g., money or time) is the extreme of spending it. Answer (B), which may have been tempting, shows synonyms.

3. **(B) head cold : smell** Implied comparison. A mitten interferes with the sense of touch, just as a cold in the head is apt to interfere with the sense of smell. One impairs the other on both sides of this analogy.

4. **(A) curiosity : knowledge** Cause and result. Perseverance typically leads to success, just as curiosity leads to finding out, which is knowledge.

5. **(A) rejoice : good fortune** Implied comparison. We are expected to heed (pay attention to) advice; that is why advice is given. Likewise, we are expected to rejoice at good fortune. Do not be misled by other common, idiomatic expressions offered as answers, such as (D), if those answers don't complete the comparison suggested by the original pair.

6. **(D) thought : chaotic** Implied comparison. Sleep that is not going well is interrupted sleep, often described as fitful. Thought that is not going well, that is in a muddle, is chaotic. Both words in the first blank are intangibles—sleep and thought. Answer (E), which may have given you pause, offers *manuscript*, a tangible thing, which is *trite*—not similar to *fitful* and *chaotic*, which both suggest disorder.

7. **(C) spectator : throng** Part of a whole. A group of bees is often described as a swarm, just as a group of spectators is termed a throng. If you were tempted by (E), you should know that a group of actors is not called a bevy; a *bevy of girls* is a common expression as is a *bevy of quail*.

8. **(E) unguent : soothe** Product related to purpose. A narcotic usually dulls the senses, just as an unguent usually soothes (a burn or abrasion).

9. **(B) will : codicil** Implied comparison. On both sides, what is in the second slot altered the document in the first slot. An amendment modifies or changes or adds to a constitution, just as a codicil modifies, changes, or adds to a person's will.

10. **(D) mountebank : bilk** Person related to logical characteristic. A shyster diddles (fools, deceives) the public, just as a mountebank bilks (robs through trickery or deceit) the public. Both first slots show disreputable characters, and the second slots feature logical verbs for each.

How's it going? Are you finding unknown words? If so, make flashcards now to learn those strangers.

Practice Analogies 5, from p. 59

1. **(D) ground : mole** Animal related to home. The stream is a crayfish's home, just as the ground is home to a mole. Both live "in" their respective habitats.

2. **(C) spring : flower** Implied comparison. Not tough, though, right? This problem is here to remind you that *flower* is often a *verb*.

3. **(B) sneak : wily** Person related to typical characteristic. A toady is most often described as fawning (overly servile, obsequious), just as a sneak is said to be wily.

4. **(A) fodder : cattle** Implied comparison. We feed a computer data, just as fodder (silage, grain, hay, or any food) is fed to cattle.

5. **(D) historian : past** Implied comparison—the person and his or her special stock-in-trade. An augur predicts the future, just as a historian recounts the past.

6. **(E) sober : mien** Each of these word pairs are really clichés. They have been paired so many times that they no longer convey much meaning, but they *are* familiar to readers. On one side is a noun describing someone's carriage or bearing; the other side then shows an appropriate adjective, the cliché expression. This sort of analogy is a recent development on SATs. Only answer (E) completes the comparison given by the original pair.

7. **(D) forebear : descendant** This analogy shows people in time. The progenitor or forebear always precedes his or her heir or descendant in time by one or more generations.

8. **(E) agnostic : cleric** Person related to least logical or desirable characteristic. The stoic would never be rash (hasty, impetuous) in behavior, just as the cleric (minister, reverend, pastor, priest) would not be agnostic (unbelieving or doubtful of God's existence).

9. **(B) yoke : conjunction** Implied comparison. A jalopy always signifies dilapidation, or else it could not be termed a jalopy. A yoke signifies conjunction—joining or yoking together. On each side is a concrete item, followed by one of the most logical characteristics that could be used to describe it.

10. **(A) transient : permanence** Implied comparison. The wastrel (dissipated, purposeless) is one who lacks self-discipline and "wastes" himself or herself. Likewise, the transient lacks permanence and never stays anywhere very long.

Words to Remember: Antonyms A–D, from p. 59

Antonyms A
1. Zeal is the opposite of apathy.
2. Vigorous is the opposite of decrepit.
3. Burgeon is the opposite of atrophy.
4. Paucity is the opposite of plethora.
5. Resist is the opposite of capitulate.

Antonyms B
1. Sophisticated is the opposite of ingenuous.
2. Exuberant is the opposite of staid.
3. Biased is the opposite of indifferent.
4. Obtuse is the opposite of discerning.
5. Disdain is the opposite of revere.

Antonyms C
1. To talk pleasantly is the opposite of rant (and rave).
2. Esteem is the opposite of ignominy.
3. Confound is the opposite of elucidate.
4. Embroil is the opposite of extricate.
5. Sincerity is the opposite of hypocrisy.

Antonyms D
1. Irreplaceable and vital are opposites of expendable.
2. Extant is the opposite of defunct.
3. Sparse is the opposite of copious.
4. Broad-minded is the opposite of provincial.
5. Definite is the opposite of ambiguous.

Sentence Completion 1, from p. 65

1. **(B) tedious** Key words: mindless marathons
2. **(C) difficult** Key words: always/habit/scraping riders off
3. **(E) idiosyncrasies** Key words: age and *customary* good nature/occasional/with tact and *humor*
4. **(C) wariness. .consternation** Key words: feeling threatened/cat/ *young* puppy
5. **(A) sanguine. .detachment** Key words: If only/at the *very least*
6. **(A) subjective** Key words: *essay* tests/founded on teacher *opinion*
7. **(B) challenge. .security** Key words: *gamble* on sales/*safer* route/former/latter

8. **(C)** **satisfaction. .unique** Key words: your *own* house/excitedly
9. **(D)** **finesse. .perspicacious** Key words: *reflected* daily (this must be a parallel comparison)
Answer (E) makes sense, but *acuteness* is rarely used to refer to personnel relationships, so diction (word usage) is vital in making your decision.
10. **(E)** **indifference. .fervor** Key words: *assiduously* pursues/later/startling contrast to *earlier*
Answer (D), with *interest,* is too weak in feeling, given the sentence.

Sentence Completion 2, from p. 65

1. **(B)** **cliché** Key words: one . . . after *another*/hadn't altered/twenty years
2. **(A)** **arresting** Key words: originality/will discover
Answer (B), *delightful,* is close, but not as specific as *arresting.* Remember, you are asked to select the *best* answer of the choices.
3. **(C)** **novelty. .profound truths** Key words: in spite of/rarely revealed/or (indicates an idea parallel to the words *serious attention*)
4. **(C)** **labor-intensive. .dependence** Key words: machines . . . rescued farmers/still . . . weather plagues
Also note the little word *on* that makes the second word in (B), (D), and (E) impossible as answers.
5. **(E)** **abundance. .forestalled** Key words: natural/further afield/sustenance or sporting entertainment
6. **(D)** **beach. .investigate** Key words: normally intrepid/uncharacteristic/before we continued
7. **(E)** **inadequate. .heartwarming** Key words: although preparations/actual debate/turned/surprising *and* (indicates comparable or coordinate ideas)
8. **(B)** **convivial. .society** Key words: but/retreats
9. **(C)** **appealing. .virtuoso** Key words: always/popular/even more/Pete Fountain (unknown amateurs would never be cited; thus you have a major clue to a word meaning "pro" for your second blank)
10. **(A)** **conundrum. .defy** Key words: zealously study/its complexity/definitive relationships/years to come

Sentence Completion 3, from p. 66

1. **(E)** **unchanged** Key words: undergone redefinition/*yet*/role/essentially
2. **(C)** **persistence** Key words: often striving/unanswerable questions/is/always/ally
3. **(D)** **ponderously. .residual landmarks** Key words: **glaciers**/behind/hill-shaped debris
4. **(A)** **compassion. .obsessive** Key words: concern *and*/at times/misconstrued/*and* overly protective
In this sentence, *concern* equates with the negative *obsessive* in the second phrase, while *compassion* equates with the negative *overly protective* also in the second phrase. The *ands* tell you that the first two adjectives describing Marlene will be parallel and positive in connotation, while the last two adjectives will be parallel but negative because of the verb *misconstrued.*
5. **(B)** **freedom. .indiscriminate** Key words: inoculations/*from* disease/diseases long eradicated/questionable
(Although answer (E) may be tempting, logic tells you *habitual* use of inoculations for eradicated diseases would be a poor medical approach, not just a questionable practice. Also, good diction prevents the phraseology *absence from* in this sentence.)
6. **(A)** **sudden. .mushrooming** Key words: consequence/popularity/emphasis on physical fitness (the word *horde,* which usually refers to people or animals, could not be used with racquetball courts.)
7. **(D)** **deterioration. .deep regret** Key words: blamed/inbreeding/formerly lovable/respect/breed itself
8. **(E)** **consummately skilled. .retiring** Key words: boxer/*and* unusually shy/*surprised*/outside the ring
9. **(C)** **nonchalant. .gratified** Key words: unaware/she had expected/relieved *and*/dedication/serious purpose

10. **(B)** **persevered. .foretold** Key words: special insight/archaeologist/whereabouts/*just* as he had

Sentence Completion 4, from p. 67

1. **(B)** **modest** Key words: viewers did not flock/*only*
2. **(D)** **demanding** Key words: economics textbook/yet/read attentively
3. **(E)** **support** Key words: because/on my side
4. **(C)** **truth** Key words: Although (sets up contrast)/honestly
5. **(E)** **metamorphosis. .ruthless** Key words: considerate (requires sharply contrasting word for second blank)/underwent a total/bent on evil
6. **(A)** **harsh reality. .idealistic goals** Key words: moral good/imagination
7. **(C)** **epigram. .cynicism** Key words: (Entire quote is an epigram, determining first blank)/flawed human race
8. **(D)** **enigma** Key words: to puzzle
9. **(A)** **idyllic. .idol** Key words: now transformed/Industrial Progress
10. **(B)** **modicum. .chimera** Key words: more than/not/but/an actual man

Sentence Completion 5, from p. 68

1. **(D)** **obscure** Key words: clear and direct/yet/uncharacteristically
2. **(B)** **innovate** Key words: nevertheless/novelty for novelty's sake
3. **(D)** **heated. .tempered** Key words: lively discord/chillingly civilized discourse
4. **(A)** **eccentric. .accentuated** Key words: age/propensity/unpredictable behavior
5. **(E)** **relevant** Key words: confine testimony/learn the answers
6. **(C)** **virulent. .tenacious** Key words: like plague/grip (You must think about plague to answer this sentence correctly. Although *stubborn* [answer D], it is not *subtle.* However, it is exceedingly virulent.)
7. **(A)** **resignation. .repudiated** Key words: accepted/but/resolutely stayed in his cabin
8. **(E)** **acuity. .provocative** Key words: nonetheless/prompted careful study
9. **(C)** **reticence. .eloquence** Key words: rather than garrulity (The word in the first blank must be an opposite of garrulity; only (C) works logically.)
10. **(C)** **heresy. .scrutinize** Key words: Logic of the entire sentence depends on the second blank. Only (A), (C), and (D) have appropriate verbs, but only (C) has a logical word for the first blank.

Practice Passage 1, from p. 87

1. **(C)** Note lines 12–17, which indicate country, and lines 27–29, which say that cotton was a major crop, along with snakes known to live in the South.
2. **(A)** Note line 50, "toughest feet," and lines 62–65. Answer (D), a tempting one, cannot be considered because the passage states in lines 17–20 that *shoes* were the symbol of manhood.
3. **(B)** Note that the passage states this clearly in lines 23–25.
4. **(E)** The entire passage betrays a perceptive person looking back at his past in a nostalgic (somewhat sentimental) manner.

Practice Passage 2, from p. 88

1. **(D)** Compare lines 28–29 with lines 11–13, which state that similar magnitude in stars is helpful for distinguishing them.
2. **(E)** See lines 17–18.
3. **(C)** None of the other choices are essential for testing your own eyes. This was a difficult question; usually only one or two questions on the Verbal SAT are this difficult.
4. **(B)** The paragraph (lines 48–55) is about changes in the stars.
5. **(D)** See the preceding sentences (lines 64–69).
6. **(A)** Note the preceding sentence (lines 78–80), where the Arabs are claimed by some to have observed this star.

7. **(B)** Answers C, D, and E *are* discussed in Passage 1. Answer A is not specifically discussed in Passage 2, so it is not a difference between the two passages.

8. **(E)** See lines 42–43 and 70–72.

9. **(C)** Note lines 36–37, where this author suggests that the test was for bad vision.

10. **(A)** See lines 43–45, where the author mentions the medieval Arabs' lack of eyeglasses, which would have helped those with poor eyesight.

Practice Passage 3, from p. 90

1. **(C)** See lines 35–39, which express Stein's dissatisfaction with his country's leadership.

2. **(D)** This interpretation is supported by the man's actions as recounted in this passage.

3. **(A)** See lines 5–11. Answer (B) is too narrow, as it could not include the immense war indemnities incurred as the war progressed.

4. **(B)** See lines 25–28.

5. **(E)** Note lines 50–58.

Practice Passage 4, from p. 91

1. **(B)** Note lines 1–6 and 17–20, which express the author's feeling.

2. **(D)** Note line 16, where the author states that true responsibility is "sovereign and self-determining."

3. **(A)** This is stated in lines 26–28.

4. **(C)** Note lines 31–33, which state this almost word for word.

5. **(D)** Reread the entire sentence (lines 40–42), if you missed this one, and you would get: "Seldom does anything penetrate the other person, and if it does, it is usually a *garbled message*." This substitution fits the author's sense in the clearest way when compared with the other answer choices.

Practice Passage 5, from p. 92

1. **(D)** This is stated in line 6 and expanded on subsequently.

2. **(A)** See lines 14–15 and 23–27. It is the same preoccupation with his love life that causes Owen to forget the stamps later on.

3. **(C)** Note all of paragraph 2 and lines 36–39.

4. **(B)** The word "largess" nearly always connotes valuable gifts.

Practice Passage 6, from p. 92

1. **(A)** Webster will support this choice, especially in this context.

2. **(D)** Something is wrong with all the others. (A) is too narrow; (B), (C), and (E) give a wrong or skewed idea of the passage contents.

3. **(C)** Note lines 28–37 and 41–46.

4. **(B)** See lines 49–60. The passage shows him to be all of the other answer choices.

5. **(D)** Any answer choices containing either II or V are incorrect according to the passage.

Practice Passage 7, from p. 94

1. **(C)** Note lines 6–9. Not enough information is offered to support answer (A) or (B), if you were led astray.

2. **(D)** See lines 27–31, which explain the opposite actions of axons and dendrites.

3. **(D)** Stated in the last sentence of the passage.

4. **(B)** Note lines 34–40, which explain the contrast between vertebrate and invertebrate glial cell sheaths.

Practice Passage 8, from p. 95

1. **(C)** See lines 37–42. Answer (A) is true but too narrow.

2. **(A)** Note lines 37–52.

3. **(E)** Read lines 42–52 again.

4. **(C)** Remember the foregoing "how-to" information? Answers (A) and (E) are too negative to be correct answers.

UNIT 4: THE ROOTS OF ENGLISH WORDS

Prefixes quiz, from p. 98

I. Fill-ins

1. *ana* means back or again
2. *contra* means against, opposing
3. *epi* means outside, over, outer
4. *homo* means same
5. *inter* means among, between
6. *trans* means across
7. *sus, sub, suc,* and *sup* mean under or beneath
8. *re* means back, backward, or again
9. *orth* means straight or right
10. *meta* means change of, over, or beyond

II. Creating Words

1. beneficial
2. amorphous
3. antiseptic
4. circumnavigate
5. hyperthyroid
6. malevolent
7. disagree
8. foretell
9. heterodox
10. hypodermic
11. expel
12. neophyte
13. prediction
14. prolong
15. retrogression
16. transform
17. transitive
18. synchronize
19. superstar
20. subterranean

III. Matching

1. (b) small
2. (g) large, prominent
3. (h) after, following
4. (j) through, thoroughly
5. (f) amiss, wrong, bad
6. (c) both
7. (d) against, opposing
8. (e) first, chief
9. (i) good, well
10. (a) straight, right

IV. Antonyms

1. (g) biased
2. (o) agreement
3. (i) rule, order
4. (a) sincere
5. (m) cacophony
6. (j) acute
7. (k) good repute
8. (d) zeal
9. (n) alienate
10. (l) uniform
11. (b) vital, necessary
12. (c) nobility
13. (f) ill-tempered, cruel, miserly
14. (e) condemn or castigate
15. (h) preserve

Of Course You Speak Latin and Greek, from p. 109

I. Underlining Roots

1. agitate, re<u>act</u> (c) to do, drive, impel
2. <u>art</u>ifact, <u>art</u>ist—(f) skill, art
3. <u>acr</u>id, ex<u>acr</u>bate—(h) sharp
4. <u>audi</u>ence, in<u>audi</u>ble—(m) to hear
5. e<u>volv</u>e, con<u>volut</u>ed—(k) to roll or turn

6. <u>bon</u>us, <u>ben</u>evolent—(e) well, good
7. in<u>vinc</u>ible, <u>vanquish</u>—(l) to conquer
8. in<u>vert</u>, a<u>vers</u>ion—(o) to turn
9. <u>capit</u>al, <u>capt</u>or—(d) head
10. <u>corps</u>e, in<u>corp</u>orate—(p) body
11. ex<u>claim</u>, <u>clam</u>or—(q) to cry out
12. <u>theo</u>/<u>cracy</u>—(i) god—(j) rule, power
    <u>auto</u>/<u>crat</u>—(r) self—(j) rule
13. e<u>duc</u>ation, <u>duct</u>ile—(n) to lead, direct
14. <u>voc</u>ation, in<u>voke</u>—(a) to call
15. <u>culp</u>rit, ex<u>culp</u>ate—(b) guilt

II. *Fill-ins*

1. *err   wander, mistake*   erant, aberration
2. *flu, fluct   flow*   fluctuation, fluid (et al.)
3. *fer   carry, bear, yield*   transfer, ferry, infer (et al.)
4. *dem   people*   democracy, epidemic   *crac   rule*
5. *dic, dict   speak, say*   dictator, diction, edict (et al.)
6. *cosm   world, order*   cosmology, cosmic (et al.)
7. *chrom   color*   chromatic

III. *Decoding Roots*

1. in (among, within) the race (of people)
2. water fear
3. through go
4. through see
5. down (or away) send
6. down bad
7. hand writing
8. before warn
9. down spirit
10. star naming
11. again new
12. bone feelings
13. father kill
14. down sound
15. forth summon

IV. *Build-a-Word*

1. misanthrope
2. adhesive
3. precursor
4. interpose
5. inflexible

V. *Mystery Words*

1. *Re* = over or again + *iter* = way. If you said to go the same way twice, you were right on target. *To reiterate is to repeat.*
2. *Dis* = *not* plus *claim*, from the Latin root meaning *to call* or *cry out*. A *disclaimer* is a statement that says, basically, *"No, I don't, or didn't. It's nothing to do with me!"* It is a *notice of rejection, or denial.*
3. *Fict* = made or created, possibly *built*. If you guessed that *fictile* referred to something built or created, you were right. *Fictile means molded or made,* as pottery is molded. If this were applied to *people,* you'd know that fictile meant *easily swayed or led.*
4. *Pre* = before + *cognit* = know or recognize. To know ahead of time is an obvious guess here and would be exactly correct. *Precognition is clairvoyance, awareness of something not yet experienced.*
5. *Ideo* = idea + *log* = knowledge, study of. An *ideologue* is someone who is an expert in idea systems, or a person who is somewhat idealistic.
6. *Pan* = all, entire + *dem* = people. Something that affects all of the people is a logical conclusion to draw from this word's roots. *Pandemic* means *universal* and, when applied to a disease, means that the *disease is prevalent throughout* an entire region or the world.
7. *Bene* = well, good + *fic* = do, make, leads us to guess that a beneficence is something good that has been created. A formal definition is reassuringly similar: something good that has been produced; any good act or deed.

8. No doubt you saw the root, *rect*, and thought of the word *correct*. From that it's not too hard to guess that *rectitude* refers to being right or correct in some way. In fact, it refers to moral integrity, or righteousness, just as close to its root as we wish all words were.

VI. *Antonyms*

1. (g) to alleviate, soothe
2. (i) enmity
3. (l) petty, mean-spirited
4. (k) genuine
5. (a) philanthropic
6. (c) peaceful, pacific
7. (n) to stand firm, be adamant
8. (d) praise
9. (o) skinny, slender
10. (e) fondness
11. (f) straight, direct
12 (m) hidden
13. (b) to release
14. (h) apart, separate
15. (j) contained

Figure It Out, from p. 112

I. *Underlining Roots*

1. *deca* ten
2. *mega* million
3. *teen* ten and
4. *hexa* six
5. *tri* three
6. *bi* two
7. *tetra* four
8. *cent* hundred
9. *Sept* seven
10. *kilo* thousand

II. *Know Those Numbers*

1. A nonagenarian is 90 or in his or her nineties.
2. A quinquereme was an old galley with five banks of oars.
3. Paucity means lack; therefore, I cry.
4. The Pentagon has five sides.
5. We are worried about three witches. (Who wouldn't be?)
6. It means that the author's words seem a foot and a half long.
7. An ambiguous answer beats around the bush (maybe giving two points of view), but it is not a definite answer.
8. We think she meant her appeal was to other people in their sixties.
9. Mono means one.
10. The protagonist will be the main character, first in our thoughts.
11. A quadrille is a square—4-sided—dance.
12. Untrammeled means free, unfettered.
13. Seventy scholars produced the Septuagint.
14. A troika is pulled over the snow by three horses.
15. Zwieback is baked, sliced, and baked or toasted a second time. Zwei is German for two.

What's in a Name? from p. 124

I. *Giant Match-ups*

1. (e) a clean rewrite
2. (h) men mow lawns; women are nurses
3. (a) bully, torment
4. (g) sneaky, deceitful
5. (b) oracle, soothsayer
6. (d) wend your way slowly, with turns
7. (k) free, nontraditional
8. (n) disdainful, scornful
9. (j) hedonists
10. (o) refuse to budge
11. (m) stoic, brave beyond belief
12. (c) gross, robust humor
13. (f) all English people
14. (l) Erewhon, El Dorado, heaven
15. (i) succinct, pithy, terse

II. *Fill-ins*

1. Cinderella, Horatio Alger
2. Pollyanna
3. Casanova, Galahad, Iothario, Romeo
4. malapropism (He meant *varicose* veins.)

5. pooh-bah
6. quixotic
7. Simon Legree
8. Swiftian
9. Uriah Heep, Tartuffe (also Bumble and Babbitt)
10. lilliputian, Brobdingnagian

III. *Mythical Chaos (Answers may be in any order, by pairs.)*

1. Adonis—male hunk
2. Cassandra—doom prophet
3. Achilles' heel—weak spot
4. omnipotent—Jupiter or Zeus
5. chimera—Third Kind encounter
6. cupidity—avarice
7. furor—frenzy
8. halcyon—peaceful
9. Herculean—demanding
10. lethargy—torpor
11. jovial—good-humored
12. mentor—guide
13. mercurial—volatile
14. Mnemosyne—memory

15. muse—inspiration
16. odyssey—long journey
17. nemesis—jinx/bane
18. Promethean—life-giving
19. saturnalia—orgy, bacchanal
20. stentorian—loud
21. gorgon—scary hag

IV. *Names = Words to Remember*

All definitions are given in text. Antonyms only are given here.
1. Titan is the opposite of midget.
2. Quixotic is the opposite of practical.
3. Bacchanal and saturnalia are opposites of funeral.
4. Cupidity is the opposite of generosity.
5. Halcyon is the opposite of chaotic.
6. Iridescent is the opposite of dull, and sometimes of gloomy. An iridescent personality would be a sharp contrast to a gloomy one.
7. Jovial is the opposite of gloomy.
8. Lethargic is the opposite of active.
9. Mercurial is the opposite of unchangeable.
10. Saturnine is the opposite of jolly or jovial.

UNIT 5: BASIC VOCABULARY

Plagued Pairs—and Then Some, from p. 132

I. *Words in Context*

1. contemptuous
2. effects—affected
3. complement
4. elude
5. lose—loose
6. adopted
7. emigrated—immigrants
8. censure
9. demurred
10. allude

II. *Analogies*

1. ascetic (chief quality of a person)
2. complaisant (chief quality of a person)
3. capital (analogy of size: large to small)
4. effect (both sides show synonyms)
5. disinterested (both sides show antonyms)
6. equitable (main quality of person)
7. indigent (both sides antonyms)
8. indigenous (both sides antonyms)
9. perspicuous (most common quality of each noun)
10. discrete (switch only one letter on both sides to obtain entirely different word)

III. *Antonyms*

1. (e) to squander, waste
2. (h) inclined, apt to
3. (j) incorruptible
4. (l) disagreeable
5. (i) reckless
6. (b) ingenuous
7. (n) to cite
8. (o) to approve
9. (a) peaceable
10. (c) humble
11. (d) of minor importance
12. (g) straight
13. (f) aloof
14. (k) obtuse
15. (m) freedom

IV. *Quick Reminders*

1. abjure
2. Inclement
3. censure
4. credible
5. Factious
6. to prosecute
7. prophesying
8. prophecy
9. To adjure
10. elicit

List 1, from p. 136

I. *Words in Context*

1. accrue
2. agnostic, abstruse
3. aesthetic
4. allay
5. abate
6. abort
7. allegory
8. affinity
9. abet
10. altruism
11. abeyance
12. admonishes
13. advocate (noun)
14. alacrity
15. accolades
16. allude
17. advocate (verb)
18. acerbic

II. *Antonyms*

1. (c) soothing
2. (e) love
3. (a) object
4. (g) concrete, or (m) definite
5. (f) nadir
6. (j) sweetness, gentleness
7. (k) clumsy
8. (i) condemnation
9. (l) irritable
10. (h) poor
11. (m) definite, or (g) concrete
12. (n) accord, agreement
13. (o) involved, caring
14. (b) cite
15. (d) aggravate

III. *Favorite SAT Word Families*

A. ACER

1. exacerbate = to aggravate, make worse
2. acrid = burning, stinging, pungent
3. acrimony = acerbity, bitterness
4. acrimonious = rancorous, biting, caustic
5. acute = pointed or keenly perceptive

B. LEV

6. alleviate = to allay, relieve
7. levity = lightness, humor
8. leverage = power or effectiveness
9. levitation = buoyancy; the illusion of the human body in air without support
10. elevate = to lift up, raise

IV. Analogies

1. aborigine : bush :: advocate : court [Person related to appropriate environment. A human being acting as an advocate is found in a court of law. Answer (C) is weak because the conductor stands *on* the podium.]
2. behavior : aberrant :: response : ambiguous [Bad example of a general type. Answer (A) is the red herring, but it is wrong because the word in the first blank is negative, whereas *behavior* and *response* have neutral connotations.]
3. seats : assign :: portions : allocate (Implied comparison. Each side offers a logical verb that shows how each noun is apportioned.)
4. farm : agrarian :: skyscraper : urban (Relationship of nouns to their logical locations)
5. manager : acumen :: monk : abstemiousness (Person and most logical, desired attribute)

List 2, from p. 142

I. Matching

1. congenial	6. shocking	11. scornfully
2. dislike	7. demanding	12. reserved
3. abnormality	8. diligent	13. awry
4. opposite	9. curse	14. intrepid
5. indifference	10. intention	15. soothsayer

II. Synonyms

1. (c) pardon
2. (b) proverb
3. (b) poise
4. (a) intelligible
5. (d) degenerate

III. Words in Context

1. bailiwick	6. autocratic	11. apostate
2. anarchy	7. attest	12. arable
3. augurs	8. astute	13. anachronism
4. atavistic	9. auspices	14. annals
5. balm	10. augment	15. apprehension

IV. Antonyms

1. (f) to establish, found	6. (b) equitable, fair, just
2. (h) exacerbate	7. (c) humility
3. (i) well-known	8. (d) timid
4. (a) amity	9. (e) to mumble
5. (j) gentleness, kindness	10. (g) uninterested in, averse to

List 3, from p. 146

I. Antonyms

1. fresh, original, inventive
2. simple, unadorned, classic
3. malignant, evil, cruel
4. tolerance, open-mindedness
5. discreet, tasteful, quiet
6. sad, downhearted, sorrowful
7. appealing
8. urban, "citified"
9. destroy, tear down, raze
10. euphony (pleasing sound)
11. praise, encomium, accolade; any words showing reverence or strong approval or endorsement
12. insecure, timid, shy, withdrawn, self-effacing
13. praise, accolade; any words revealing strong approval or endorsement
14. genial, jovial, jolly; also serene or peaceable
15. mild, soothing, healing, etc.

II. Words in Context

1. brandished	6. cathartic
2. candid	7. beset
3. chagrin	8. bilked
4. bourgeois	9. bellwether
5. capitulated	10. capricious

III. Favorite SAT Word Families

A. BENE
1. benign = harmless or kindly
2. benevolent = philanthropic, well-meaning, generous
3. beneficient = kindly, generous
4. benediction = a blessing, literally good words
5. benefactor = one who sponsors or supports you in some way

B. CAP, CIP, CEIPT, CEPT
6. capitulate = to acquiesce, yield
7. perceptive = astute, intuitive, acute
8. susceptible = liable, impressionable, responsive
9. emancipate = to set free
10. conceit = arrogance, pride; a whimsical idea or metaphor

IV. Logical Connections

1. (B) undoing	9. (B) criticism
2. (C) pugilist	10. (A) jargon
3. (A) quibble	11. (C) wheedle
4. (C) pompous	12. (C) caricature
5. (B) patience	13. (A) curt
6. (A) pirate	14. (B) gun bore
7. (B) carp	15. (B) poll
8. (C) war	

List 4, from p. 151

I. Antonyms

1. (e) unknowing	6. (h) honesty
2. (g) indifferent	7. (i) rudeness
3. (b) commend	8. (j) severe
4. (c) acquired	9. (d) encourage
5. (f) certainty	10. (a) illogical

II. Words in Context

1. chaos	6. colloquy	11. conducive
2. chaste	7. commensurate	12. consummate
3. cite	8. condone	13. contingent
4. citadel	9. consorting	14. contemplate
5. cognate	10. consternation	15. connive

III. Favorite SAT Word Families

A. CIRCUM
1. circumvent = to foil by intelligence; to frustrate or get around
2. circumscribe = to limit, constrict
3. circumlocutory = evasive in speech or excessively wordy
4. circumspect = prudent, cautious
5. circuitous = roundabout, indirect

B. SPEC, SPIC, SPECT
6. speculate = to conjecture, guess
7. perspicacious = wise, shrewd, perceptive
8. conspicuous = highly noticeable
9. auspicious = promising, favorable in outlook
10. introspection = self-examination; looking inward
11. respite = welcome rest or lull in activity

IV. Definitions

1. (A) adjacent and (C) nearby
2. (B) defile and (E) pollute
3. (C) perfect and (D) achieve
4. (A) interpret and (D) decipher
5. (A) suggestion and (C) implication
6. (B) stoop and (E) unbend
7. (B) agree and (C) assent
8. (A) scruple and (E) qualm
9. (C) well-suited and (D) consonant
10. (A) pretty and (C) attractive
11. (B) related and (D) alike
12. (B) persuasive and (E) convincing
13. (A) harsh and (C) merciless
14. (B) lucidity and (C) clearness
15. (B) surreptitious and (E) secret

List 5, from p. 156

I. Synonyms

1. (d) repentant
2. (g) disdain
3. (j) plentiful
4. (a) substantial
5. (b) pledge
6. (i) dismay
7. (e) paucity
8. (f) congenial
9. (c) wicked
10. (h) profane

II. Fill in the Blanks

1. decrepit
2. crux
3. culpable
4. debility
5. Despondent
6. deference
7. derogatory
8. corollary
9. corroborates
10. cursory
11. dawdle
12. coterie
13. cowered
14. culinary
15. decorum

III. Analogies

1. crony
2. culmination
3. cynic
4. desiccated
5. desolate

IV. Antonyms

1. (d) lacking remorse, (h) unrepentant
2. (l) intrepid, (i) bold
3. (b) failure to credit or believe, (r) implausibility
4. (t) manageable, (o) lightweight
5. (q) to appreciate, (g) to revel in
6. (j) to lengthen, (m) to elongate
7. (c) expressing a high opinion, (e) revealing esteem
8. (n) to confuse, (k) to cloud
9. (f) to commence, (s) to begin
10. (a) favorable recognition, (p) applause

List 6, from p. 160

I. Words in Context

1. random reading with no set plan or order, reading without purpose
2. an achievement of doubtful or questionable value
3. absolute nonsense, words from the mouth of a fool
4. harsh, perhaps unusually gloomy native of Scotland (like the climate sometimes?)
5. carefully chosen belongings
6. noticeable error or mistake that cries out for all to see
7. worthless, nonproductive, decadent culture
8. for my enlightenment, betterment, or instruction
9. a moving, perhaps emotional, gesture that conveys more than words
10. hanged in the form of a dummy or likeness

II. Antonyms

1. (d) direct
2. (c) confident
3. (g) prompt
4. (a) connoisseur
5. (j) accord
6. (f) highly ordered, organized (also [d] direct)
7. (b) to conceal
8. (h) straightforwardness
9. (e) lifeless
10. (i) to draw in

III. Synonyms

1. (c) quandary
2. (a) radical
3. (d) adept
4. (a) opinionated
5. (b) instructive
6. (d) frustration
7. (b) belittle
8. (d) likeness
9. (a) tractable
10. (c) chutzpah

IV. Favorite SAT Word Families

A. FAC, FICT, FECT, -FY

1. efficacious = potent, effective
2. edify = to teach, enlighten
3. effect = to bring about, cause to happen
4. factious = disputatious, quarrelsome
5. exemplify = to act as an example of

B. LOC, LOG, LOQU, LOCUT

6. loquacious = extremely talkative
7. eloquent = verbally skilled
8. colloquial = of conversation or speech of a distinct time or place
9. epilogue = words at end of a book or play
10. monologue = talk or speech for one person
11. elocution = effective speech

V. Phrase Completion

1. discerning, discriminated
2. disparage, destitute
3. discomfiture, discrepancy
4. didactic, disseminate
5. deviate
6. dichotomy, dexterous
7. dissipated
8. duress, elixir
9. éclat
10. droll

List 7, from p. 165

I. Words in Context

1. (e) emanated
2. (i) emulates
3. (a) engender
4. (c) enigma
5. (j) ephemeral
6. (b) epicurean
7. (g) epithets
8. (d) erudite
9. (f) erratic
10. (h) enervating

II. Antonyms or Synonyms

1. (C) irrelevant—synonym
2. (A) common—antonym
3. (B) nonexistent—antonym
4. (D) efface—synonym
5. (A) indefinite—antonym
6. (B) impede—antonym
7. (C) expound—synonym
8. (D) absolve—synonym
9. (B) husky—antonym
10. (A) cacophony—antonym
11. (B) public—antonym
12. (A) improvise—synonym
13. (D) evasive—synonym
14. (A) entrance—synonym
15. (C) encourage—antonym

III. Favorite SAT Word Families

A. GEN

1. indigenous = native to an area
2. degenerate = to sink to a lower state
3. congenial = warm, amicable, sociable
4. ingenuous = innocent, trusting, naive

5. engender = to beget, produce, sponsor
6. ingenious = inventive, clever
7. congenital = connected with birth

B. SACR, SANC, SECR

8. desecrate = to profane or defile something sacred
9. consecrate = to dedicate; note as sacred
10. sanctify = to consecrate, set apart as holy
11. sacrosanct = literally holy of holies, the most sacred
12. execrable = wretched, revolting
13. execration = a curse
14. sacrilege = gross lack of reverence

IV. Truth or Fiction?

1. T	8. F
2. F	9. F
3. F	10. T
4. T (As long as John retains his U.S. citizenship.)	11. T
5. T	12. F (Phew!)
6. F	13. F
7. F	14. F (A perennial is supposed to bloom year after year.)

List 8, from p. 170

I. Words in Context

1. forensic	6. futile	11. facetious
2. formidable	7. fallacious	12. filch
3. fortuitous	8. germane	13. gentility
4. gamut	9. girth	14. foibles
5. generic	10. fetish	15. fulsome

II. Antonyms

1. (g) rear	7. (d) fragrant
2. (a) complex	8. (k) honesty
3. (e) casual	9. (l) muscular
4. (c) to compliment	10. (h) hide
5. (b) unfortunate	11. (i) discerning
6. (j) civilized	12. (f) warranted

III. Favorite SAT Word Families

A. FRA, FRAG, FRACT

1. fragmentary = incomplete, in parts
2. fractious = unruly, troublesome
3. frail = weak, slight; easily destroyed or broken
4. refractory = unmanageable, literally breaking back or away
5. infraction = a violation of rules
6. infringe = to encroach on, trespass

B. GREG

7. gregarious = convivial, sociable
8. segregate = to set aside or apart
9. congregate = to gather together
10. aggregate = the total, combined amount
11. egregious = outstandingly bad

IV. Analogies

1. complexion : florid :: error : flagrant
   (Implied comparison; a highly noticeable example of each general type)
2. garrulous : frugal :: fervent : apathetic
   (Implied comparison. One who is garrulous is never frugal [with words], just as one who is fervent is never apathetic.)
3. fluctuate : static :: gambol : fixed
   (Implied comparison. That which fluctuates is not static, just as that which gambols is not fixed.)

4. thief : furtive :: charlatan : facile (Most logical adjective for each noun)
5. remedy : drastic :: task : grueling (Implied comparison: a severe degree of each)

V. Remembering Definitions
Check in List 8.

List 9, from p. 176

I. Synonyms

1. (k) disdainful	9. (d) intangible
2. (g) hoax	10. (f) troublesome
3. (j) dialect	11. (e) abominable
4. (i) execration	12. (c) embroilment
5. (a) bigot	13. (o) fatuous
6. (l) eternal	14. (m) serene
7. (b) lapse	15. (n) hindrance
8. (h) compassionate	

II. Words in Context

1. inadvertent	6. impecunious
2. inane	7. imparting
3. implicit	8. immutable
4. impetus	9. implacable
5. impervious	10. idiosyncrasies

III. Antonyms

1. (B) (D) indigent, affluent
2. (B) (C) flawed, impeccable
3. (A) (C) honor, ignominy
4. (C) (D) iconoclast, traditionalist
5. (A) (C) fact, hypothesis
6. (A) (B) ascetic, hedonist
7. (C) (D) histrionic, understated
8. (B) (C) follower, harbinger
9. (B) (C) fortunate, hapless
10. (A) (D) fresh, hackneyed

IV. Truth or Fiction?

1. F	6. T	11. T
2. T	7. T	12. T
3. T	8. F	13. F
4. T	9. F	14. T
5. F	10. F	15. T

List 10, from p. 181

I. Word Meanings

1. (B) beginning	9. (B) imprison
2. (D) spell	10. (D) relentless
3. (C) inactive	11. (B) the unexpected
4. (B) not agreeing with	12. (C) habitual
5. (D) without pause	13. (D) ready perception
6. (C) unmanageable	14. (D) chant
7. (A) invincible	15. (A) treacherous
8. (A) depressing burden	

II. Analogies

1. irascible
2. insipid
3. incendiary
4. indifferent
5. incite

III. Antonyms

1. reduction, decrease
2. exculpate, absolve
3. dynamic, energetic
4. competent, skillful
5. believer, devotee
6. alienate, divorce
7. learned, acquired
8. harmful, stimulating
9. moderate, reasonable
10. innocuous, harmless

IV. Favorite SAT Word Families

A. COGN
1. being disguised or otherwise unrecognizable
2. aware, informed
3. referring to knowledge, acquiring knowledge, or what is known
4. one who really knows, an expert, a professional
5. identification of something one has already become acquainted with; awareness

B. FER
6. hint or indirect suggestion
7. to discuss, talk over
8. to yield or gracefully give way to another with more age, experience, power, etc.; deference is respectful yielding to the wishes or rights of another
9. unbiased, not prejudiced or not concerned, incurious, aloof, detached, disinterested
10. bearing cones (as some evergreens do)

V. Words in Context

1. innate
2. ineffable
3. incipient
4. inevitably
5. indolent
6. insolvent
7. incantation
8. interpolate
9. innocuous
10. inundated

List 11, from p. 185

I. Antonyms

1. (C) melancholic
2. (A) indiscreet
3. (B) separate
4. (C) failure to understand
5. (A) mend
6. (C) loquacious
7. (D) dynamism
8. (A) obvious
9. (B) sobriety
10. (D) inflexible
11. (A) trustworthy
12. (B) uplifting
13. (D) laud
14. (B) harboring a grudge
15. (C) blithe

II. Words in Context

1. litany
2. lexicon
3. livid
4. loquacious
5. lucid
6. lucrative
7. ludicrous
8. lurid
9. manifest
10. malevolent
11. jaundiced
12. jeopardize
13. laity
14. lampoon
15. linguistics

III. Analogies

1. adage : motto :: proverb : maxim (Related words)
2. karma : life :: design : building (Implied relationship; karma is defined as one's destiny in life, or how the life is laid out in advance—its plan, in other words, just as the design of a building is its plan.)
3. lawyer : litigation :: marauder : pillage (Person related to stock in trade)
4. language : jargon :: humor : lampoon (Implied relationship; one example of a general type)
5. gesture : magnanimous :: achievement : laudable (Implied relationship; a worthy or notable adjective for each general type)

IV. Favorite SAT Word Families

A. MAL
1. malign = to slander, defame
2. malevolent = exuding evil or hatred
3. malcontent = perennial complainer or discontented person
4. malefactor = literally *maker of bad;* one who creates trouble
5. malady = illness, ailment
6. malediction = curse, execration

B. JOC
7. (jocular) and 8. (jocund) and 9. (jocose) all mean fond of joking, witty, merry
10. (jocularity) and 11. (jocundity) mean merriment, joy

List 12, from p. 190

I. Puddle of Words

In any order: mendicant, beggar; specious, meretricious; servile, menial; demeanor, mien; alleviate, mitigate; moot, debatable; incisive, mordant; murky, gloomy; mundane, worldly; munificent, lavish

II. Words in Context

1. negligible
2. noisome
3. nadir
4. obloquy
5. obdurate
6. nuance
7. officious
8. negligence
9. nefarious
10. nebulous

III. Favorite SAT Word Families

A. NOM, NOMEN, NOMIN, ONYM
1. nominal = in name only
2. ignominy = utter shame, disgrace
3. renown = fame; wide acclaim or high honor
4. physiognomy = facial features; general character or makeup
5. anomaly = paradox, irregularity
6. nomenclature = a naming system for classification purposes
7. misnomer = incorrect or misleading name

B. SEQU, SECUT
8. obsequious = fawning, servile
9. sequel = that which follows or comes after
10. inconsequential = insignificant, negligible
11. execute = to carry out
12. subsequent = following, successive

IV. One More Time
Definitions or synonyms may be checked for accuracy in List 12. *Antonyms only are given here.*
1. (Example)
2. generous, altruistic, selfless
3. sloppy, uncaring, disheveled (personal appearance)
4. aggravate, annoy, irritate, pester, harass, tease
5. homogeneous, like, similar, identical
6. sophisticated, urbane, polished, knowing
7. pliable, yielding, weak, unsure, compliant, complaisant, flexible
8. professional, connoisseur, expert
9. diurnal (during the day)
10. stunt (as to stunt growth or development), deprive
11. slender, slim, skinny, trim
12. create, preserve, establish, found
13. keen or keenly perceptive, quick, intuitive, knowledgeable, acute
14. up-to-date, modern, state-of-the-art
15. appealing, desirable, beloved
16. auspicious, favorable in omen or outlook
17. obtuse, dull, lacking in perception or knowledge

V. A Need for Words?

Extremely Careful with Money: stingy, niggardly, parsimonious, penurious, "tight"

Rigidly Set in Feelings or Behavior: obdurate, adamant, unyielding, inflexible, stubborn

Lacking Worldly Knowledge: naive, ingenuous, natural, unaffected, innocent

List 13, from p. 196

I. Puddle of Synonyms

1. common, ordinary	7. evidently, obviously
2. annoy, discompose	8. rural, bucolic
3. noxious, deleterious	9. remedy, cure-all
4. flaw, fault	10. infamy, disgrace
5. scarcity, dearth	11. verve, flamboyance
6. pity, poignancy	12. example, archetype

II. Antonyms

1. (f) indigence	6. (c) excite
2. (a) flippant or lighthearted	7. (d) include
3. (i) covert	8. (e) obscure
4. (b) irritate	9. (g) praising
5. (j) disagreeable	10. (h) obtuse

III. Words in Context

1. perquisite	11. philanthropy
2. perfunctory	12. paradox
3. peremptory	13. orifice
4. plausible	14. pertinacity
5. pernicious	15. pariah
6. pervading	16. pedant
7. platitude	17. parable
8. perfidy	18. ossified
9. onus	19. paraphrase
10. phlegmatic	20. plethora

IV. Favorite SAT Word Families

A. TEND, TENS, TENT
1. ostentatious = showy
2. attenuate = to weaken; reduce strength or vitality
3. contend = to hold, maintain, believe
4. pretentious = showy
5. contention = opinion; rivalry
6. tenuous = flimsy, weak, thin
7. portent = omen, warning sign
8. ostensible = apparent, plausible; in appearance only

B. TEN, TIN, TAIN, TENT
9. pertinacity = ability to hold on, to persist no matter what; also answer (C)
10. tenacity = persistence, obstinacy; also answer (A)
11. abstain = to refrain from (usually strong drink or rich foods; also to avoid altogether)
12. abstinence = refraining from indulgence
13. retain = to keep or hold in place

V. A Need for Words?

Soothing Injured Feelings: placate, mollify, allay or alleviate, calm, pacify

Describing Smart Folk: keen, perceptive, discerning, perspicacious, acute (maybe aware)

For Plodding, Unemotional Types: phlegmatic, impassive, stolid, bovine, sluggish

List 14, from p. 201

I. Word Meanings

1. (D) prematurely bright	12. (D) preference known in advance
2. (D) appease	
3. (A) expected right	13. (A) scrupulously exact
4. (D) fecund	14. (B) put off
5. (C) sharp	15. (A) to forestall
6. (B) bulging	16. (B) after death
7. (A) childish	17. (B) useful
8. (C) preliminary	18. (B) of plundering
9. (C) skill	19. (A) be evasive
10. (C) kinship	20. (D) pen name
11. (B) cowardly	

II. Antonyms

1. emaciated	6. moral laxness
2. weak	7. dislike
3. secure	8. stingy
4. following act	9. meager
5. unassuming	10. maladroit

III. Favorite SAT Word Families

A. SCRIB, SCRIPT
1. Proscribe = to forbid, prohibit
2. Postscript = what follows other writing
3. Ascribe = to impute, attribute, assign
4. Transcribe = to write down, record
5. Circumscribe = to define, limit, or surround with limitations

B. PRO
6. Profess = to declare, affirm
7. Propitious = favorable, auspicious
8. Propriety = decorum, good manners
9. Propensity = strong natural tendency or inclination
10. Provident = prudent, providing for the future
11. Profligate = wildly extravagant, prodigal
12. Prodigy = extraordinary thing; highly gifted child

C. VOC, VOKE
13. Provoke = to pique, annoy
14. Evoke = to call forth subtly
15. Irrevocable = unchangeable, unable to be called back or undone
16. Advocate = to be in favor of, promote
17. Vociferous = noisily demanding
18. Equivocate = to prevaricate; evade by responding indirectly

IV. Sentence Completion

1. purporting, prurient	4. postulate
2. pragmatic	5. purged, prosaic
3. pugnacious, precluded	6. precipitate

List 15, from p. 206

I. Synonyms

1. (B), (D) quell, overwhelm
2. (A), (B) petulant, querulous
3. (B), (C) quiescent, inactive
4. (C), (D) rancid, offensive
5. (A), (D) reasonable, rational
6. (C), (D) revere, venerate
7. (A), (D) vibrating, resonant
8. (B), (D) retaliation, reprisal

428 The Answer Section/Unit 8

9. (A), (C) recompense, remuneration
10. (A), (D) object, remonstrate
11. (B), (C) set aside, relegate
12. (C), (D) drink, quaff
13. (A), (B) raconteur, storyteller
14. (A), (C) implications, ramifications
15. (B), (D) bitterness rancor

II. Sentence Completion

1. rhetoric
2. retribution
3. reticent
4. Resourceful
5. quietus
6. reprehensible
7. remorse
8. refutation
9. remiss
10. Recapitulation

III. Find the Oddball

1. (B) rectify
2. (A) debate
3. (C) elect
4. (D) decisive
5. (B) broken
6. (A) known
7. (B) message
8. (C) preliminary
9. (D) pronounce
10. (D) action

IV. Antonyms

1. (B) extraneous material
2. (C) lukewarm
3. (E) patently uninterested
4. (C) speak peaceably
5. (D) discord
6. (A) convivial
7. (D) satiated
8. (B) subtle
9. (C) forget
10. (E) refuse to barter

V. Favorite SAT Word Family

QUER, QUIR, QUIS
1. query = a question; any request requiring an answer
2. querulous = whining, petulant, questioning
3. required = necessary, needed; requisite = required, essential
4. inquisitive = questioning, inquiring; sometimes "nosy"
5. inquisition = interrogation; when capitalized, refers to the Spanish Inquisition
6. acquire = to get; acquisition = the thing gotten

List 16, from p. 212

I. Antonyms

1. proper
2. obscure
3. respectful
4. simple
5. pessimistic
6. svelte
7. slovenly
8. overt act
9. splenetic
10. haughty
11. mundane, worldly
12. genuine
13. dynamic
14. flexible
15. naive

II. Fill-ins

1. satiate
2. scathing
3. sagacity
4. salubrious
5. sedulous
6. scourge
7. serendipity
8. shibboleth
9. simulation
10. sinecure

III. Analogies

1. rung : ladder :: status : hierarchy (Part of whole; also, position in the ranking)
2. raucous : sound :: strident : voice (Disagreeable quality of each general type)
3. recant : adhere :: flow : stagnate (Antonyms)
4. minister : pulpit :: speaker : rostrum (Person related to most typical location for that person when giving a speech)
5. crime : punish :: error : rue (Implied relationship; typically, a crime is punished and an error rued)

IV. Truth or Fiction?

1. F
2. T
3. F
4. F
5. T
6. T
7. T
8. F
9. F
10. T

List 17, from p. 216

I. Find the Oddball

1. (D) warn
2. (A) lengthy
3. (C) big
4. (A) minister
5. (C) tractable
6. (C) pocketbook
7. (A) turgid
8. (C) servile
9. (B) fool
10. (A) identity

II. Synonyms and Definitions

1. hesitant
2. succinct
3. effrontery
4. tangible
5. amulet, fetish
6. redundancy
7. clandestine
8. curtail
9. tiresome
10. unspoken
11. disdainfully superior
12. unrestrained
13. sway rhythmically
14. juicy, appealing
15. indefensible

III. Words in Context

1. tenuous
2. tolerance
3. truculent, usurped
4. sully
5. surfeit
6. surpass
7. taciturn
8. trepidation
9. transcends

IV. Favorite SAT Word Families

A. TRA, TRANS
1. Transient = ephemeral, fleeting
2. Transcend = to go beyond certain limits
3. Travesty = mockery, caricature
4. Transgress = to go beyond a legal or moral boundary, to sin
5. Transpose = to alter position, shift, reverse
6. Transition = change

B. SUPER, SUR
7. Superficial = on the surface, shallow
8. Supercilious = haughty, proud
9. Surpass = to go beyond expectations
10. Supersede = to take precedence over
11. Superfluous = extra, unneeded, unimportant

V. In Need of a Word?

For Those Dull, Overused Expressions: cliché (noun), trite, hackneyed, banal, stale
To Describe Someone Spoiling for a Fight: belligerent, truculent, aggressive, bellicose, feisty, pugnacious
To Describe the Exceedingly Economical Use of Words: terse, curt, succinct, pithy

List 18, from p. 222

I. Synonyms

1. (A) vacillate and (C) fluctuate
2. (B) caprice and (D) vagary
3. (A) authenticate and (D) validate
4. (B) vehement and (C) zealous
5. (A) veracity and (C) truthfulness

6. (B) vilify and (C) malign
7. (B) wraith and (C) apparition
8. (B) debase and (C) vitiate
9. (C) vitriolic and (D) corrosive
10. (A) voluble and (C) glib

II. Legacy from England (phrase completion)

1. wizened
2. wan
3. wary
4. willful
5. winsome
6. wistful
7. wont
8. wreaked
9. wanton
10. wrest
11. wraith
12. waned

III. Antonyms

1. impregnable, invincible
2. skeptic, agnostic
3. stolid, impassive
4. understated, soft-spoken
5. benign, beneficent
6. tyro, novice
7. aged, decaying
8. deny, negate
9. succinct, terse
10. scorn, disparage

IV. Remembering Definitions

Please check your answers with List 18's definitions in the book. You will honestly learn more that way.

V. Favorite SAT Word Family

DIC, DICT
1. to exculpate; to justify
2. spiteful
3. to order, pronounce absolutely
4. complex problem
5. to renounce, give up
6. order, edict
7. to charge with an offense
8. adjudicated result
9. literally *good words*; blessing
10. curse
11. to surrender an alleged criminal to another authority with jurisdiction to try the offense
12. to speak against or in opposition

UNIT 6: MATH FOR SATS AND PSATS

Lesson 1

Addition, from p. 254

1. 2,205	6. 28,930
2. 2,721	7. 18,554
3. 2,471	8. 18,988
4. 3,494	9. 19,479
5. 14,448	10. 21,765

Subtraction, from p. 254

11. 28	16. 395	21. 222
12. 53	17. 109	22. 1,001
13. 187	18. 1,105	23. 499
14. 212	19. 752	24. 305
15. 414	20. 39	25. 3,709

Multiplication, from p. 255

26. 1,578,808	31. 2,592
27. 5,264,973	32. 128,352
28. 7,496,412	33. 105,985
29. 597,504	34. 412,156
30. 2,021,640	35. 637,332

Division, from p. 255

36. 807	41. 709
37. 70	42. 72
38. 81	43. 49
39. 373	44. 159
40. 32	45. 0

Quick Tests for Divisibility, from p. 257

1. Yes, 19 times.
2. Yes.
3. Yes, since 112 does not end in 0 or 5, it is not divisible by 5.
4. No, (7) + (1) + (8) = 16, which is not divisible by 3.
5. Yes, break 12 up into 4 × 3. Both the test for divisibility by 3 and the test for divisibility by 4 hold.
6. Yes, because the last three digits, 992, are divisible by 8.
7. Yes, because the sum of the digits, 19, is not divisible by 9.
8. Yes, because 793 is not divisible by 2.
9. Yes, because the sum of the digits, 18, is divisible by 3.
10. Yes, because the last two digits, 48, are divisible by 4.

Addition of Signed Numbers, from p. 258

1. −46	5. −179	8. −115
2. 17	6. 73	9. 0
3. −11	7. −51	10. −39
4. 11		

Subtraction of Signed Numbers, from p. 259

1. 114	5. 43	8. 254
2. 42	6. −185	9. −583
3. −46	7. 151	10. −257
4. 99		

Multiplication and Division of Signed Numbers, from p. 260

1. −4	5. 643	8. 240
2. −9	6. −72	9. 532
3. −15	7. −84	10. 221
4. 121		

Order of Operations, from p. 261

1. $4(28) + 6(−17) = 112 − 102 = 10$
2. $12 − 5 + 2 = 9$
3. $32 − [8 − (−22)] = 32 − [30] = 2$
4. $3(3)^2 = 3(9) = 27$
5. $6(7 − 3[5 − 2(2)]) = 6(7 − 3[1]) = 6(7 − 3) = 6(4) = 24$
6. $\dfrac{42 − 16}{2} = \dfrac{26}{2} = 13$
7. $[12 + 1 − 2 + (−2)] = [12 + 1 + 1] = 14$
8. $[4 − (−19)][42 − 6 + 1] = [23][37] = 851$
9. $24 − [96 − 6^2] = 24 − [96 − 36] = 24 − 60 = −36$
10. $24 − 2 + 3 = 25$

Lesson 2

Addition and Subtraction of Polynomials, from p. 263

1. $10x^2 + x + 2$
2. $18rp − 14rs − 10ps$
3. $8ab + 6b^2 + 24a^2$
4. $10xy − 4x^2$

5. $2x^2 + 4xy + 6y^2$
6. -22
7. $2x - 9y + 11$
8. $4x^3y - 6xy^2 + xy$
9. $p^4 - 9p^2 - p + 13$
10. $x^2 + 9x - 10$

Multiplication of Polynomials, from p. 264

1. $15a^2 + 12a$. Remember, when you multiply like bases you *add* the exponents.
2. $-6x^5 + 4x^4 + 8x^3 - 6x^2$. Hint—multiply the signs first, then the coefficients, then the bases.
3. $-16x^2y^2 + 24xy^3 + 32xy^2$
4. $6x^3y^2z^3 - 3x^2y^2z^4 + 15x^4yz^5$
5. $3x^{11}y^5z^8$
6. $x^2 + 3x + 3x + 9 = x^2 + 6x + 9$. Remember the FOIL method.
7. $6x^2 + 8x - 3x - 4 = 6x^2 + 5x - 4$. Remember to collect like terms.
8. $6x^2y^2 - 3xyz + 4xyz - 2z^2 = 6x^2y^2 + xyz - 2z^2$
9. $18x^3 - 30x^2 + 12x - 12x^2 + 20x - 8 = 18x^3 - 42x^2 + 32x - 8$
10. $15x^2 + 40xy - 6xy - 16y^2 = 15x^2 + 34xy - 16y^2$

Division of Polynomials, from p. 264

1. $-3x^3y^4$. Divide the numerical coefficients first, then the bases. If the bases are the same, subtract the exponents.
2. $-\dfrac{24a^2b^2c}{5}$. Divide – 144 and 30 by 6.
3. $6x$
4. $3x^2y$
5. $-3x^3y^5 + 2xy^3$. Divide each term of the dividend $(-12x^5y^8 + 8x^3y^6)$ by the divisor $(4x^2y^3)$.
6. $18a^2b^2 - 12a^3b + 4a$
7. $r^2s - \dfrac{2}{r}$
8. $18a^4b^6 - 9a^3b^2$
9. $3a^7 - 2b$. Remember that $\dfrac{a}{a} = 1$ or $b \div b = 1$.
10. $2 + \dfrac{3y}{x}$

Practice SAT Problems, from p. 265

1. C
2. C Simplify first within the parentheses.
3. D $-3(-4) = +12$
4. D Do the division $(-24 \div -6)$ before the subtraction.
5. D
6. C Simplify the fraction $\dfrac{10-4}{2}$ first.
7. E Remember that $y^0 = 1$.
8. C FOIL.
9. E Remember that a minus sign in front of a grouping symbol changes the sign of every term within the grouping symbol.
10. B
11. B Watch your signs. In division of like variables subtract the exponents.
12. E Combine the numerator. $\dfrac{5(.2)}{5} = .2$

Divide by 5.

13. B Rewrite as $(6x^2 - 4x + 7) - (2x^2 - 3x - 4)$.
14. C Divide $5pq$ into each term of the dividend.
15. D Distribute first, then collect like terms.

Lesson 3

Solving Linear Equations, from p. 268

1. C Multiply each term by 6 to eliminate the fraction.
$4x + 5 = x$. Then solve for x.
2. B Remember to change the signs of everything in the parentheses when you remove them since they are preceded by a – sign. *If you were having trouble*, try *plugging in and chugging through*. Only the right answer will work, and chances are you'll have found it by your *third* try.
3. C Remove the parentheses, collect like terms, and solve for y.
4. A If you got answer (C), you probably solved for $2y$ and not y. Other answers could mean you mixed up the + and – signs.
5. E Keep your operations straight. Do the right one!
6. C Answer (A) comes up if you solved for $2r$ and not r. Getting (B) is a result of multiplying when you were to divide, and (E) and (D) were put in for people who jump at tempting answers. Don't be one of them; *they* usually trip.
7. A Keep your signs straight.
8. E If $b = 4$ and $c = -4$, then $a = 4 - (-4) = 8$ and $d = -4 - 4 = -8$. So $d - a = -8 - 8 = -16$.
9. A Answer (B) comes from inverting each fraction separately, and you can't do this.
10. C Answer (A) is the answer for $y = \dots$. (Remember *what* you are solving for.) Answers (D) and (E) both have the wrong sign.

Word Problems, from p. 272

1. D The equation becomes $8(c) + (13 - 8)(2c) = ?$ Answers (A) and (B) occur if you forget that she is paid double after eight hours. Notice that $13 - 8$ is the number of hours that the woman is paid double.
2. A If you did this problem phrase by phrase, you should have had no problem.
3. E x dollars equals $100x$ cents.
y apples at 16 cents each equals $16y$ cents.
z pears at 12 cents each equals $12z$ cents.
The expression is then $100x - (16y + 12z)$ or $100x - 16y - 12z$.
4. B The equation is $x - 3 = 2x + 6$.
5. D d dollars equals $100d$ cents. The number of stamps that can be bought would be the total amount, divided by the cost of each stamp: $\dfrac{100d}{22}$.
6. 31 The equation becomes $19 - (-12) = ?$
7. 16 The equation becomes $(x - 4) = \dfrac{1}{2}(x + 8)$.
8. 50 The equation is $C - 10 = (100 - C) + 10 - 20$. C stands for Chris and $(100 - C)$ stands for Andrea.
9. 200 The equation becomes $\dfrac{1}{4}x + \dfrac{1}{5}x + 110 = x$.
10. 5 If x is the middle number, the equation is $5x = 3(x + 2)$. Remember to solve for the largest number, $x + 2$.
11. 10 The equation becomes $5x + 10x + 25x = 400$. Think that x represents the number of each type of coin and 400 is the total number of cents.
12. 9 The two equations are $a^2 - b^2 = 9$, and $a - b = 1$. Recall that $a^2 - b^2$ factors to $(a - b)(a + b)$. Substituting 1 for $a - b$ leaves $1(a + b) = a^2 - b^2$. Since the right side of the equation equals 9, you are left with $1(a + b) = 9$. The sum of $a + b$ is therefore 9.
13. 1 Volume = length times width times depth. Replacing the length and width by their given values leaves $24 = 8 \cdot 3 \cdot$ depth. Dividing both sides by 24 leaves $1 = d$. Make sure not to divide 24 by 24 and get 0. It may look silly now, but the mistake is somewhat common.
14. 2 The equation is $\dfrac{1}{3}(x + 13) = 2x + 1$. Multiply both sides by 3 to get $x + 13 = 6x + 3$; then solve for x.

15. 3   Let x = Tom's age. The equation is $\frac{1}{3}x$ (Tom's brother's age) + $3x$ (Tom's sister's age) + x (Tom's age) = $2(3x) - 5$.
Combine like terms

$$4\frac{1}{3}x = 6x - 5; \quad \frac{13}{3}x = 6x - 5;$$
$$13x = 18x - 15; \quad -5x = -15;$$
$$x = 3.$$

16. 2,400   Set up the equation $x - \frac{1}{4}x - \frac{1}{3}x = 1000$, and solve for x.

17. 4   If the meat loses $\frac{1}{4}$ of its weight, then she really bought $\frac{3}{4}$ of a pound for \$3.00. The equation is $\frac{3}{4} \cdot x = 3.00$. Multiply both sides by 4 and get $3x = 12.00$. Divide by 3 to get the cost, \$4.00 a pound.

18. 12   6 gallons filled $\left(\frac{5}{6} - \frac{1}{3}\right)$ or $\frac{1}{2}$ of the tank. So $2(6)$ or 12 gallons will fill the tank completely.

19. 45   Remember that odd integers differ by 2. If the first odd integer is x, then the sum of the first five would be $x + (x + 2) + (x + 4) + (x + 6) + (x + 8)$ and this would equal $3(x + 8) + 6$.
Combine like terms and solve for x.

20. 134   If x equals the average width of each house, then the equation will be $10x + 9(x + 60) + 2(60) = 3,206$. Solve for x to get $x = 260$. Note that between 10 houses will be 9 spaces plus 60 feet on each end.

Lesson 4

Solving Inequalities, from p. 278

1. A   Adding $3y$ to both sides and then subtracting x from both sides leaves $0 > 6y$. Divide both sides by 6 to get $0 > y$. Since answer (A) is the opposite of this, it is the one that must be false.

2. D   Subtract a^2 and b^2 from both sides to get $-2ab > 2ab$. Since $b < 0$, dividing both sides by b switches the direction of the sign giving $-2a < 2a$. Adding $2a$ to both sides and then dividing by 4 leaves $0 < a$, answer (D). Do not forget to *switch the direction of the inequality sign when dividing by a negative*.

3. D   Taking $p \geq 0$ and multiplying both sides by 4 gives $4p \geq 0$. Add $2p$ to both sides to get $6p \geq 2p$. To check the answer, try picking examples. In this case try $p = 0$ and $p = 1$. If you had chosen answer (A) for example, $p = 0$ would have proved it incorrect.

Remember, in all cases it never hurts to pick a couple of values and plug them in. If you find *one value that doesn't work* in the answer you chose, *the whole answer is wrong*.

4. E   The two inequalities say nothing about the signs of a, b, and c. So answers (A), (B), and (D) can't be true. Picking values such as $a = 3$, $b = 2$, and $c = 1$ disproves the validity of (D). So (E) is the only one left.

5. C   Subtracting b from both sides of $a > b$ leaves $a - b > 0$, answer (C). Getting answer (A) means you forgot that a and b could be negative. The same is true of the other answers. Answer (E) is an especially tricky example of this. Both $a = -3$ and $b = -4$ fulfill the given, but $9 > 16$ is *not* true.

6. B   When you multiply an inequality by a negative, you must reverse the sign: $-3a > 3$.

7. A   By the transitive property for inequalities $x < -4$.

8. D $-5x \geq 15$; $x \leq -3$. Remember to reverse the sign when you divide by a negative.

9. C

10. D x must be positive because a positive divided by a negative is a negative. Cross multiply to get $5 > x$.

11. A   If the numerator remains constant and the denominator increases, then the value of the fraction decreases.

12. E   Solve for x: $-8 \leq 4x$; $-2 \leq x$.

13. B $2 + $ (a positive number) > 2.

14. D   The whole is always greater than a part.

15. D   Solving for x, you get $x > -2$. (-2) is not $> (-2)$.

16. D   A number subtracted from a larger number will always result in a positive number.

17. E   Choose easy numbers to work with, like $a = 2$ and $b = 1$; then substitute these in for each part. Stop when you get a correct answer.

18. D   Substituting (-1) for x, you get $|2(-1) - 1| > 3$;
$|-3| > 3$; $3 > 3$, which is false.

19. D   If you multiply every term by 6 to eliminate the fractions, you get $2x + 12 > 3x$. Solve for x.

20. C   Let $q = 1$ and $p = 2$, and substitute these values in for each answer, or follow your rules.

Lesson 5

Factoring, from p. 280

1. $3(x^2 + 2x + 4)$
Always look for the greatest common factor first.
In this case we factored a 3 out of each term.

2. $4p^2q(q^2 + 6p - 4p^2q)$
Remember that when terms contain the same variables, you factor out the smallest exponent.

3. $-7xz^2(y^2z^2 - 3xy^3 + 12x^2z)$
We could have factored out a $(+7)$, but it is customary to factor out a negative if the first term is negative. Notice that we could not factor a y out of the last term.

4. $75p^2q^2(p^3 - 3q^3 + 5pq)$
Remember that factoring out a common factor means to divide each term of the expression by the common factor.

5. $(x - 3)(x + 5)$
There are two terms in the problem $x(x - 3)$ and $5(x - 3)$. The common factor is $(x - 3)$.

6. $(x + 5)[4(x + 5) - 3] = (x + 5)(4x + 17)$
The common factor is $(x + 5)$. Factor it out of each term; then simplify the last expression $[4(x + 5) - 3]$.

7. $(p^2 - 1)(p + 4)$ $(p^2 - 1)$ is the common factor.

8. $3ab^2(5a^2 - 6a^3b + 8b^3)$

9. $2r(r - h)$

10. $(3x + y)(3x - 4)$ The common factor is $(3x + y)$.

11. 1,200 $(12 \times 33) + (12 \times 67) = 12(33 + 67)$

12. 5,100 $(129 \times 51) + [51 \times (-29)] = 51(129 - 29)$

13. $5x^2y^3z^3(x^5z + 2x^2y^2 - y^5)$
Look for the greatest common factor first. Then factor it out of each term.

14. $4x(x + 9)$ Always look for the greatest common factor first!

15. $3(2x + y)^2[(2x + y) + 4]$ Do not expand $(2x + y)^3$ or $(2x + y)^2$.

Factoring the Difference of Two Perfect Squares, from p. 280

1. $(y + 9)(y - 9)$
Follow the rule: $A^2 - B^2 = (A + B)(A - B)$. Remember to take the square root of each term.

2. $(8 - p)(8 + p)$
The order of the $(+)$ and $(-)$ signs does not matter. $(8 + p)(8 - p)$ is also correct.

3. $(13x - 5y)(13x + 5y)$

4. $(11A^3 - 12B^2)(11A^3 + 12B^2)$
To take the square root of an exponent, divide the exponent by 2.

5. $(6x-15)(6x+15)$ or $9(2x-5)(2x+5)$

Notice here that the first step should have been to factor a 9 out of each term. Why? (It is the greatest common factor.)

6. $[(x-y)+z][(x-y)-z]$

7. $(x^n-2)(x^n+2)$ The square root of x^{2n} is $x^{\frac{2n}{2}}=x^n$.

8. $(a^{2^n}-3b^{3^n})(a^{2n}+3b^{3n})$

9. $2(16x^2-9)=2(4x-3)(4x+3)$

10. $3(25z^2-49b^2)=3(5z-7b)(5z+7b)$

Always look for the greatest common factor first!

11. $(16-9x)(16+9x)$ Memorize the perfect squares.

12. $[(2x+3)+4][(2x+3)-4]=(2x+7)(2x-1)$

Factor first then combine like terms.

13. $(7A^4-15B^2)(7A^4+15B^2)$

14. $(17A-25)(17A+25)$

15. $2(5x^3+7y)(5x^3-7y)$ Factor out the greatest common factor first.

Factoring Trinomials, from p. 282

1. $(p-10)(p+1)$

If the coefficient of the first term is 1 and the last sign is negative, look for factors of 10 that differ by 9. Always check by FOILing to make sure your numbers are in the right places. $(p+10)(p-1)$ would be incorrect because FOILing would give $p^2+9p-10$.

2. $(x+15)(x+1)$

If the coefficient of the first term is 1 and the last sign is positive, look for factors of 15 that add up to 16.

3. $(a-4)(a+1)$

4. $(x+9)(x+3)$

5. $(x-16)(x+9)$ Look for factors of 144 that differ by 7. $(9 \cdot 16.)$

6. $\left(x-\dfrac{1}{2}\right)\left(x-\dfrac{1}{2}\right)$ or $\left(x-\dfrac{1}{2}\right)^2$

The square root of $\dfrac{1}{4}$ is $\dfrac{1}{2}$ and $\left(\dfrac{1}{2}+\dfrac{1}{2}\right)=1$.

So the factors of $\dfrac{1}{4}$ that add up to 1 are $\dfrac{1}{2}$ and $\dfrac{1}{2}$.

7. $(x+2)(x+2)$ or $(x+2)^2$ Look for factors of 4 that add up to 4.

8. $(y+16)(y+16)$ or $(y+16)^2$

9. $\left(p+\dfrac{1}{4}\right)\left(p+\dfrac{1}{4}\right)$ or $\left(p+\dfrac{1}{4}\right)^2$

10. $(x^n-2)(x^n-2)$ or $(x^n-2)^2$

11. $x=5$ or -7 Set each factor equal to 0. Then solve for x.
$$x-5=0 \text{ or } x+7=0$$
$$x=5 \quad x=-7$$

12. $y=0$ or $\dfrac{5}{2}$

13. $p=4$ or 1 $p^2-3p-4=0$
$$(p-4)(p+1)=0$$
$$p-4=0 \text{ or } p+1=0$$
$$p=4 \text{ or } p=-1$$

14. $x=+4$ or -4

15. $y=0$ or $y=9$ $y^2-9y=0$; $y(y-9)=0$; 0 or $y=9$

16. 2,500 $(23)^2+2(23)(27)+(27)^2=(23+27)^2=(50)^2=2,500$

17. 400 $(38)^2-2(38)(18)+(18)^2=(38-18)^2=20^2=400$

18. .0004

19. 2,300 $(48)^2-(2)^2=(48+2)\cdot(48-2)=50(46)=2,300$

20. .0049 $(.25)^2-(.24)^2=(.25+.24)(.25-.24)=(.49)(.01)=.0049$

Lesson 6

Radicals, from p. 285

1. $5\sqrt{3}$ $\sqrt{75}=\sqrt{25}\cdot\sqrt{3}=5\sqrt{3}$

2. $9\sqrt{2}$ $\sqrt{162}=\sqrt{81}\cdot\sqrt{2}=9\sqrt{2}$

3. $15\sqrt{2}$ $\sqrt{450}=\sqrt{9}\cdot\sqrt{50}=\sqrt{9}\cdot\sqrt{25\cdot2}=3\sqrt{25}\cdot\sqrt{2}=15\sqrt{2}$

4. $7y\sqrt{6}$ $\sqrt{294y^2}=\sqrt{49y^2}\cdot\sqrt{6}=7y\sqrt{6}$

5. $11x^3\sqrt{2}$ $\sqrt{242x^6}=\sqrt{121x^6}\cdot\sqrt{2}=11x^3\sqrt{2}$

6. $8\sqrt{6}$ $\sqrt{12}\cdot\sqrt{32}=\sqrt{4}\cdot\sqrt{3}\cdot\sqrt{16}\cdot\sqrt{2}=2\sqrt{3}\cdot4\sqrt{2}=8\sqrt{6}$

7. 28 $\sqrt{98}\cdot\sqrt{8}=\sqrt{49}\cdot\sqrt{2}\cdot\sqrt{4}\cdot\sqrt{2}=7\sqrt{2}\cdot2\sqrt{2}$
$$=14\cdot2=28$$

8. 7 $\dfrac{\sqrt{196}}{\sqrt{4}}=\sqrt{\dfrac{196}{4}}=\sqrt{49}=7$

9. $5\sqrt{2}$ $\sqrt{\dfrac{150}{3}}=\sqrt{50}=\sqrt{25}\cdot\sqrt{2}=5\sqrt{2}$

10. $\dfrac{4}{5}$ $\dfrac{\sqrt{112}}{\sqrt{175}}=\dfrac{\sqrt{16.7}}{\sqrt{25.7}}=\dfrac{\sqrt{16}\cdot\sqrt{7}}{\sqrt{25}\cdot\sqrt{7}}=\dfrac{4}{5}$

11. $\sqrt{32}\cdot4\sqrt{6}=\sqrt{16.2}\cdot4\sqrt{6}=4\sqrt{2}\cdot4\sqrt{6}$
$$=16\sqrt{12}=16\sqrt{4.3}=32\sqrt{3}$$

12. $2\sqrt{18}\cdot7\sqrt{98}=2\sqrt{9\cdot2}\cdot7\sqrt{49\cdot2}-6\sqrt{2}\cdot49\sqrt{2}$
$$=294\sqrt{4}=588$$

13. $16\sqrt{\dfrac{50}{16}}=16\dfrac{\sqrt{50}}{\sqrt{16}}=\dfrac{16\sqrt{25\cdot2}}{4}=\dfrac{80\sqrt{2}}{4}=20\sqrt{2}$

14. $\dfrac{8\sqrt{50}}{5\sqrt{2}}=\dfrac{8\sqrt{25\cdot2}}{5\sqrt{2}}=\dfrac{40\sqrt{2}}{5\sqrt{2}}=8$

15. $2\sqrt{3}\cdot4\sqrt{8}\cdot\sqrt{54}=8\sqrt{24}\cdot\sqrt{54}=8\sqrt{4\cdot6}\cdot\sqrt{9\cdot6}$
$$=16\sqrt{6}\cdot3\sqrt{6}=48\cdot6=288$$

Radicals, from p. 287

1. 120 $(3\sqrt{25})(2\sqrt{16})=(3\cdot5)\cdot(2\cdot4)=15\cdot8=120$

2. 15 $\sqrt{(3\sqrt{25})(5\sqrt{9})}=\sqrt{(3\cdot5)(5\cdot3)}=$
$$\sqrt{15\cdot15}=\sqrt{15^2}=15$$

3. $\dfrac{1}{7}$ $7x=25-24; 7x=1; x=\dfrac{1}{7}$

4. $8\sqrt{2}$ $\sqrt{98}+\sqrt{2}=(\sqrt{49}\cdot\sqrt{2})+\sqrt{2}=7\sqrt{2}+\sqrt{2}=8\sqrt{2}$

5. 1.4 $\sqrt{1.96}=\sqrt{\dfrac{196}{100}}=\dfrac{\sqrt{196}}{\sqrt{100}}=\dfrac{14}{10}=1.4$

6. -1 $(\sqrt{3}-2)(\sqrt{3}+2)=3+2\sqrt{3}-2\sqrt{3}-4=-1$

7. $18-4\sqrt{6}-9\sqrt{2}+4\sqrt{3}$ $(2\sqrt{3}-\sqrt{6})(3\sqrt{3}-\sqrt{8})=$
$$6\sqrt{9}-2\sqrt{24}-3\sqrt{18}+\sqrt{48}$$
$$=18-2\sqrt{4}\cdot\sqrt{6}-3\sqrt{9}\cdot\sqrt{2}$$
$$+\sqrt{16}\cdot\sqrt{3}$$
$$=18-4\sqrt{6}-9\sqrt{2}+4\sqrt{3}$$

8. $6\sqrt{2}+5\sqrt{3}$ $\qquad$ $\sqrt{72}+\sqrt{75}=\sqrt{36}\cdot\sqrt{2}+\sqrt{25}\cdot\sqrt{3}$
$$=6\sqrt{2}+5\sqrt{3}$$

9. $\dfrac{2-\sqrt{14}}{2}\cdot\dfrac{4-\sqrt{56}}{4}=\dfrac{4-\sqrt{4}\cdot\sqrt{14}}{4}$
$$=\dfrac{4-2\sqrt{14}}{4}=\dfrac{2-\sqrt{14}}{2}$$

10. $2\sqrt{10}-5\sqrt{2}$ $\qquad$ $\sqrt{40}-\sqrt{50}=\sqrt{4}\cdot\sqrt{10}-\sqrt{25}\cdot 2$
$$=2\sqrt{10}-5\sqrt{2}$$

11. $\dfrac{\sqrt{105}}{50}$ $\qquad$ $\sqrt{.042}=\sqrt{\dfrac{42}{1,000}}=\dfrac{\sqrt{42}}{\sqrt{100}\cdot\sqrt{10}}=\dfrac{\sqrt{42}}{10\sqrt{10}}$
$$\dfrac{\sqrt{42}}{10\sqrt{10}}\cdot\dfrac{\sqrt{10}}{\sqrt{10}}=\dfrac{\sqrt{420}}{100}$$
$$=\dfrac{\sqrt{4}\cdot\sqrt{105}}{100}=\dfrac{\sqrt{105}}{50}$$

12. $\dfrac{\sqrt{14}}{2}$ $\qquad$ $\dfrac{7}{\sqrt{14}}=\dfrac{7}{\sqrt{14}}\cdot\dfrac{\sqrt{14}}{\sqrt{14}}=\dfrac{7\sqrt{14}}{14}=\dfrac{\sqrt{14}}{2}$

13. $\dfrac{\sqrt{2}}{6}$ $\qquad$ $\dfrac{\sqrt{6}}{\sqrt{108}}=\sqrt{\dfrac{6}{108}}=\sqrt{\dfrac{1}{18}}=\dfrac{\sqrt{1}}{\sqrt{18}}$
$$=\dfrac{1}{\sqrt{9}\cdot\sqrt{2}}=\dfrac{1}{3\sqrt{2}}=\dfrac{1}{3\sqrt{2}}\cdot\dfrac{\sqrt{2}}{\sqrt{2}}=\dfrac{\sqrt{2}}{6}$$

14. $\dfrac{2\sqrt{6}}{15}$ $\qquad$ $\sqrt{\dfrac{8}{75}}=\dfrac{\sqrt{8}}{75}=\dfrac{\sqrt{4}\cdot\sqrt{2}}{\sqrt{25}\cdot\sqrt{3}}=\dfrac{2\sqrt{2}}{5\sqrt{3}}\cdot\dfrac{\sqrt{3}}{\sqrt{3}}=\dfrac{2\sqrt{6}}{15}$

15. $\dfrac{\sqrt{3}}{3}$ $\qquad$ $\dfrac{3}{\sqrt{27}}=\dfrac{3}{\sqrt{9\cdot3}}=\dfrac{3}{3\sqrt{3}}=\dfrac{1}{\sqrt{3}}=\dfrac{\sqrt{3}}{3}$

16. $35\sqrt{3}$ $\qquad$ $\sqrt{3}\cdot\sqrt{35}\cdot\sqrt{35}=35\sqrt{3}$

17. $15\sqrt{2}$ $\qquad$ $\sqrt{6}\cdot\sqrt{75}=\sqrt{2}\cdot\sqrt{3}\cdot\sqrt{25}\cdot\sqrt{3}=\sqrt{2}\cdot\sqrt{9}\cdot\sqrt{25}$
$$=3\cdot5\sqrt{2}=15\sqrt{2}$$

18. $17-12\sqrt{2}$ $(2\sqrt{2}-3)^2=(2\sqrt{2}-3)(2\sqrt{2}-3)$ FOIL

19. $\sqrt{2}$ $\qquad$ $\dfrac{(\sqrt{6}^2-\sqrt{2})^2}{\sqrt{8}}=\dfrac{6-2}{\sqrt{8}}=\dfrac{4}{\sqrt{8}}=\dfrac{4}{\sqrt{4}\cdot\sqrt{2}}=\dfrac{4}{2\sqrt{2}}$
$$=\dfrac{2}{\sqrt{2}}=\dfrac{2\sqrt{2}}{2}=\sqrt{2}$$

20. 5 $\qquad$ $\dfrac{\sqrt{75}}{\sqrt{3}}=\dfrac{\sqrt{25}\cdot\sqrt{3}}{\sqrt{3}}=\sqrt{25}=5$

Practice SAT Problems, from p. 288

1. C $2^{x+2}=32$; $2^{x+2}=2^5$; therefore $x+2=5$ and $x=3$.

2. D First change .25 to a fraction, $\dfrac{1}{4}\cdot\dfrac{1}{y}=\sqrt{\dfrac{1}{4}};\dfrac{1}{y}=$
$$\dfrac{\sqrt{1}}{\sqrt{4}};\dfrac{1}{y}=\dfrac{1}{2};y=2.$$

3. E $4\sqrt{48}-3\sqrt{12}=4\sqrt{16\cdot3}-3\sqrt{4\cdot3}$
$$=4\sqrt{16}\cdot\sqrt{3}-3\sqrt{4}\cdot\sqrt{3}$$
$$=16\sqrt{3}-6\sqrt{3}=10\sqrt{3}$$

4. D $\left(\dfrac{1}{2}x^6\right)^2=\left(\dfrac{1}{2}\right)^2 x^{6\bullet2}=\dfrac{1}{4}x^{12}$

Do not forget to square the coefficient, $\dfrac{1}{2}$.

5. E $\sqrt{\dfrac{x^2}{4}+\dfrac{4x^2}{9}}=\sqrt{\dfrac{9x^2}{36}+\dfrac{16x^2}{36}}=\sqrt{\dfrac{25x^2}{36}}=\dfrac{\sqrt{25x^2}}{\sqrt{36}}=\dfrac{5x}{6}$

Do not take the square root of each term.

6. C $x^2-y^2=(x+y)(x-y)=48$.
  If $(x+y)=6$, then $(x-y)=8$.

7. D $3x-.3x=2.7x=54$; $x=\dfrac{54}{2.7}=\dfrac{540}{27}$; $x=20$.

8. B $x^2-y^2=(x+y)(x-y)=100$. If $(x-y)$
  $=100$, then $(x+y)=1$.

9. A $7x-7y=7(x-y)=20$; $(x-y)=\dfrac{20}{7}$.

10. B $\sqrt{.0121}=\sqrt{\dfrac{121}{10,000}}=\dfrac{\sqrt{121}}{\sqrt{10,000}}=\dfrac{11}{\sqrt{10^4}}$
$$=\dfrac{11}{10^2}=\dfrac{11}{100}=.11$$

11. A $2\sqrt{2}\cdot3\sqrt{32}=6\sqrt{64}=6\cdot8=48$
12. C Solve for x, then substitute.
13. C $2x+3y=17$
  $\underline{+\ x+2y=\ 7}$
  $3x+5y=24$ Therefore $\dfrac{3x+5y}{2}=\dfrac{24}{2}=12$

14. A Add both quantitites to get $12A+12B=48$.
  Divide by 12.
15. D $A^2-B^2=(A+B)(A-B)$; so $2(A+B)(A-B)=2(16)$.
16. D Substitute, then simplify; $3(1)^2-2(-2)=7$
17. C If $A=\dfrac{B}{5}$, then $5A=B$; If $10A=14$, then $5A=7$; so $B=7$.
18. C Simplify the fraction first, then square it.
19. E Watch your signs!
20. D Solve for p, or pick and plug.
21. A Pick and plug.
22. B $2+5+3+x=14$; so $x=4$.
23. B Add the exponents. DO NOT multiply the bases!
24. E $\dfrac{4}{5}\cdot\dfrac{5}{6}\cdot\dfrac{6}{7}\cdot\dfrac{7}{8}\cdot\dfrac{8}{9}\cdot\dfrac{9}{10}\cdot\dfrac{10}{11}\cdot\dfrac{11}{12}=\dfrac{4}{12}=\dfrac{1}{3}$
25. B Solve for x, then substitute.

Lesson 7

Fractions, from p. 293

1. $\dfrac{2}{3}$ $\dfrac{\cancel{8}^{1}}{\cancel{8}_{1}}\cdot\dfrac{\cancel{16}^{2}}{\cancel{27}_{3}}=\dfrac{2}{3}$ Use the equivalence rule on p. 290.

2. $\dfrac{9}{10}$ $\dfrac{\cancel{15}^{3}}{\cancel{24}_{1}}\cdot\dfrac{\cancel{72}^{3}}{\cancel{80}_{10}}=\dfrac{9}{10}$

3. $\dfrac{1}{2}$ $\dfrac{\cancel{5}^{1}}{\cancel{9}_{1}}\cdot\dfrac{\cancel{12}^{1}}{\cancel{25}_{5}}\cdot\dfrac{\cancel{45}^{\cancel{9}^{1}}}{\cancel{24}_{2}}=\dfrac{1}{2}$

4. $\dfrac{x-5}{x+5}$ $\dfrac{x^2-25}{x^2+10x+25}=\dfrac{(x+5)(x-5)}{(x+5)(x+5)}=\dfrac{x-5}{x+5}$

5. $\dfrac{A+4}{A+1}$ $\dfrac{A^2-16}{A^2-3A-4}=\dfrac{(A+4)(A-4)}{(A+1)(A-4)}=\dfrac{A+4}{A+1}$

6. $\dfrac{3}{2}$ $\dfrac{9}{8}+\dfrac{3}{4}=\dfrac{9}{8}\cdot\dfrac{4}{3}=\dfrac{36}{24}=\dfrac{12\cdot3}{12\cdot2}=\dfrac{3}{2}$

7. 3 $\dfrac{2}{3}+\dfrac{4}{9}+\dfrac{1}{2}=\dfrac{2}{3}\cdot\dfrac{9}{4}\cdot\dfrac{2}{1}=\dfrac{4\cdot9}{4\cdot3}=3$

8. $\dfrac{27}{5}$ $\dfrac{\frac{9}{16}}{\frac{5}{48}}=\dfrac{9}{\cancel{16}}\cdot\dfrac{\overset{3}{\cancel{48}}}{5}=\dfrac{27}{5}$

9. $\dfrac{13}{12}$ The least common denominator (LCD) is 12.

$\dfrac{1}{3}+\dfrac{3}{4}=\dfrac{4}{12}+\dfrac{9}{12}=\dfrac{13}{12}$

10. $\dfrac{13}{12}$ The LCD is 12.

$\dfrac{1}{2}+\dfrac{1}{3}+\dfrac{1}{4}=\dfrac{6}{12}+\dfrac{4}{12}+\dfrac{3}{12}=\dfrac{13}{12}$

11. $\dfrac{-1}{12}$ The LCD is 12.

$\dfrac{2}{3}-\dfrac{3}{4}=\dfrac{8}{12}-\dfrac{9}{12}=\dfrac{-1}{12}$

12. $\dfrac{5}{48}$ The LCD is 48.

$\dfrac{7}{24}-\dfrac{3}{16}=\dfrac{14}{48}-\dfrac{9}{48}=\dfrac{5}{48}$

13. $\dfrac{-23}{24}$ Follow the order of operation, MDAS.

$\dfrac{3}{8}-\dfrac{2}{3}+\dfrac{1}{2}=\dfrac{3}{8}-\dfrac{2}{3}\cdot2=\dfrac{3}{8}-\dfrac{4}{3}$. The LCD is 24.

$=\dfrac{9}{24}-\dfrac{32}{24}=\dfrac{-23}{24}$

14. $\dfrac{2}{5}$ $\dfrac{3}{5}\cdot\dfrac{4}{9}-\dfrac{8}{15}+\dfrac{2}{3}=\dfrac{12}{45}-\dfrac{8}{15}+\dfrac{2}{3}$

$=\dfrac{4}{15}-\dfrac{8}{15}+\dfrac{2}{3}$. The LCD is 15.

$=\dfrac{4}{15}-\dfrac{8}{15}+\dfrac{10}{15}=\dfrac{6}{15}=\dfrac{2}{5}$

15. $\dfrac{241}{72}$ $\dfrac{3}{4}+\dfrac{2}{3}+\dfrac{5}{6}+\dfrac{3}{8}=\dfrac{3}{4}\cdot\dfrac{3}{2}+\dfrac{5}{6}\cdot\dfrac{8}{3}$

$=\dfrac{9}{8}+\dfrac{40}{18}=\dfrac{9}{8}+\dfrac{20}{9}$. The LCD is 72.

$=\dfrac{81}{72}+\dfrac{160}{72}=\dfrac{241}{72}$

Fractions, from p. 295

1. $\dfrac{28}{39}$ $\dfrac{2\frac{1}{3}}{3\frac{1}{4}}=\dfrac{\frac{7}{3}}{\frac{13}{4}}=\dfrac{7}{3}\cdot\dfrac{4}{13}=\dfrac{28}{39}$

2. $\dfrac{9}{7}$ $\dfrac{\frac{1}{4}+\frac{1}{2}}{\frac{1}{3}+\frac{1}{4}}=\dfrac{\frac{1}{4}+\frac{2}{4}}{\frac{4}{12}+\frac{3}{12}}$

$=\dfrac{\frac{3}{4}}{\frac{7}{12}}=\dfrac{3}{\cancel{4}}\cdot\dfrac{\overset{3}{\cancel{12}}}{7}=\dfrac{9}{7}$

3. $\dfrac{16}{39}$ $\dfrac{3\frac{1}{6}-2\frac{1}{2}}{1\frac{5}{8}}=\dfrac{\frac{19}{6}-\frac{5}{2}}{\frac{13}{8}}=\dfrac{\frac{19}{6}-\frac{15}{6}}{\frac{13}{8}}$

$=\dfrac{\frac{4}{6}}{\frac{13}{8}}=\dfrac{4}{\underset{3}{\cancel{6}}}\cdot\dfrac{\overset{4}{\cancel{8}}}{13}=\dfrac{16}{39}$

4. $\dfrac{148}{27}$ $\dfrac{4\frac{1}{2}+1\frac{2}{3}}{2\frac{1}{4}-1\frac{1}{8}}=\dfrac{\frac{9}{2}+\frac{5}{3}}{\frac{9}{4}-\frac{9}{8}}$

$=\dfrac{\frac{27}{6}+\frac{10}{6}}{\frac{18}{8}-\frac{9}{8}}=\dfrac{\frac{37}{6}}{\frac{9}{8}}=\dfrac{37}{\underset{3}{\cancel{6}}}\cdot\dfrac{\overset{4}{\cancel{8}}}{9}=\dfrac{148}{27}$

5. $-\dfrac{13}{4}$ $\dfrac{\frac{3}{5}-2\frac{1}{3}}{1\frac{2}{15}-\frac{3}{5}}=\dfrac{\frac{3}{5}-\frac{7}{3}}{\frac{17}{15}-\frac{3}{5}}$

$=\dfrac{\frac{9}{15}-\frac{35}{15}}{\frac{17}{15}-\frac{9}{15}}=\dfrac{-\frac{26}{15}}{\frac{8}{15}}=\dfrac{-26}{15}\cdot\dfrac{15}{8}=\dfrac{-13}{4}$

Fractions, from p. 298

1. $\dfrac{9}{2}$ $\dfrac{3}{4}+\dfrac{7}{4}+\dfrac{8}{4}=\dfrac{18}{4}=\dfrac{9}{2}$

2. $\dfrac{45}{4}$ $2\dfrac{1}{3}+3\dfrac{1}{6}+4\dfrac{1}{2}+1\dfrac{1}{4}$

$=\dfrac{7}{3}+\dfrac{19}{6}+\dfrac{9}{2}+\dfrac{5}{4}$. The LCD is 12.

$=\dfrac{28}{12}+\dfrac{38}{12}+\dfrac{54}{12}+\dfrac{15}{2}=\dfrac{135}{12}=\dfrac{45}{4}$

3. $\dfrac{809}{20}$ $26.2+5\dfrac{3}{4}+\dfrac{17}{2}=26\dfrac{1}{5}+5\dfrac{3}{4}+\dfrac{17}{2}$

$=\dfrac{131}{5}+\dfrac{23}{4}+\dfrac{17}{2}$. The LCD is 20.

$=\dfrac{524}{20}+\dfrac{115}{20}+\dfrac{170}{20}=\dfrac{809}{20}$

4. $\dfrac{5}{12}$ $\dfrac{3}{4}-\dfrac{1}{3}=\dfrac{9}{12}-\dfrac{4}{12}=\dfrac{5}{12}$

5. $\dfrac{127}{20}$ $12\dfrac{3}{4}-6\dfrac{2}{5}=\dfrac{51}{4}-\dfrac{32}{5}$

$=\dfrac{255}{20}-\dfrac{128}{20}=\dfrac{127}{20}$

6. $\dfrac{5}{6}$ $5\dfrac{1}{2}-4\dfrac{2}{3}=\dfrac{11}{2}-\dfrac{14}{3}=\dfrac{33}{6}-\dfrac{28}{6}=\dfrac{5}{6}$

7. $\dfrac{297}{8}$ $5\dfrac{1}{2}\cdot6\dfrac{3}{4}=\dfrac{11}{2}\cdot\dfrac{27}{4}=\dfrac{297}{8}$

8. $\dfrac{25}{4}$ $2\dfrac{1}{2}\cdot3\dfrac{1}{3}\cdot\dfrac{3}{4}=\dfrac{5}{\underset{1}{\cancel{2}}}\cdot\dfrac{\overset{5}{\cancel{10}}}{\underset{1}{\cancel{3}}}\cdot\dfrac{\overset{1}{\cancel{3}}}{4}=\dfrac{25}{4}$

9. $\dfrac{92}{17}$ $\dfrac{13\frac{7}{3}}{2\frac{5}{6}}=\dfrac{46}{\underset{1}{\cancel{3}}}\cdot\dfrac{\overset{2}{\cancel{6}}}{17}=\dfrac{92}{17}$

10. $\dfrac{23}{26}$ $\dfrac{14\frac{3}{8}}{16\frac{1}{4}}=\dfrac{\frac{115}{8}}{\frac{65}{4}}=\dfrac{\overset{23}{\cancel{115}}}{\underset{2}{\cancel{8}}}\cdot\dfrac{\overset{1}{\cancel{4}}}{\underset{13}{\cancel{65}}}=\dfrac{23}{26}$

11. 2,050 $\dfrac{12.3}{.006} = \dfrac{12\frac{3}{10}}{\frac{6}{1,000}} = \dfrac{\frac{123}{10}}{\frac{6}{1,000}} = \dfrac{123}{10} \cdot \dfrac{1,000}{6} = 2,050$

12. 2 $\dfrac{3}{5} + \dfrac{4}{10} + 2\dfrac{1}{2} \cdot \dfrac{10}{3} = \dfrac{\cancel{10}}{\cancel{3}} \cdot \dfrac{\cancel{10}}{\cancel{4}} \cdot \dfrac{\cancel{2}}{\cancel{5}} \cdot \dfrac{\cancel{10}}{\cancel{3}} = 2$

13. $\dfrac{2}{5}$ $\dfrac{\frac{5}{3}}{4+\frac{1}{6}} = \dfrac{\frac{5}{3}}{\frac{25}{6}} = \dfrac{\cancel{5}}{\cancel{3}} \cdot \dfrac{\cancel{6}}{\cancel{25}} = \dfrac{2}{5}$

14. $\dfrac{1}{3}$ $\dfrac{\frac{7}{6}-\frac{1}{3}}{2+\frac{1}{2}} = \dfrac{\frac{7}{6}-\frac{2}{6}}{\frac{5}{2}} = \dfrac{\frac{5}{6}}{\frac{5}{2}} = \dfrac{\cancel{5}}{\cancel{6}} \cdot \dfrac{\cancel{2}}{\cancel{5}} = \dfrac{1}{3}$

15. $\dfrac{4}{21}$ $\dfrac{1\frac{2}{3}-\frac{5}{6}}{3\frac{1}{4}+1\frac{1}{8}} = \dfrac{\frac{5}{3}-\frac{5}{6}}{\frac{13}{4}+\frac{9}{8}} = \dfrac{\frac{10}{6}-\frac{5}{6}}{\frac{26}{8}+\frac{9}{8}} = \dfrac{\frac{10}{6}-\frac{5}{6}}{\frac{26}{8}+\frac{9}{8}} = \dfrac{\frac{5}{6}}{\frac{35}{8}} = \dfrac{\cancel{5}}{\cancel{6}} \cdot \dfrac{\cancel{8}}{\cancel{35}} = \dfrac{4}{21}$

Decimals, from p. 301

1. 1,018.425
2. 144.783
3. 2.63765
4. 57.93
5. 29.475
6. 36.085
7. 25.908
8. 180.792
9. .98556
10. 2.4
11. 9.6
12. 8,266.666...
13. 30.0555...216.4 + (5.3 + 1.9) = 216.4 + (7.2) = 30.0555...

14. 1.07 $\dfrac{6.42}{\frac{14.4}{2.4}} = \dfrac{6.42}{6} = 1.07$

15. 68.634   110.7 − (12.3 • 3.42) = 110.7 − 42.066 = 68.634

16. $\dfrac{125}{10,000} = \dfrac{1}{80}$

17. $\dfrac{234}{100} = \dfrac{117}{50}$

18. $\dfrac{34,215}{1,000} = \dfrac{6,843}{200}$

19. 16.8
20. 30.28333...

Averages, from p. 303

1. 1 $\dfrac{\frac{3}{2}+\frac{5}{6}+\frac{2}{3}}{3} = \dfrac{\frac{9}{6}+\frac{5}{6}+\frac{4}{6}}{3} = \dfrac{\frac{18}{6}}{3} = \dfrac{3}{3} = 1$

2. 22   Let $x =$ the number.

$$\dfrac{x+6+16+8}{4} = 13$$

$\dfrac{x+30}{4} = 13.$ Multiply both sides by 4.

$x + 30 = 52.$ Solve for x.

$x = 22$

3. 66   Let $x =$ Bill's fourth quiz.

His first three quizzes averaged a 78.

$$\dfrac{78+78+78+x}{4} = 75$$

$\dfrac{x+234}{4} = 75.$ Multiply by 4.

$x + 234 = 300.$ Solve for x.

$x = 66$

4. 55 inches   18 feet 4 inches equals 220 inches [(18 • 12) + 4].

$\dfrac{220}{4} = 55$ inches.

5. .75333...   Convert all terms to decimals.

$\dfrac{.75+.64+.87}{3} =$ average

$\dfrac{2.26}{3} = .75333...$

6. $x-1$ $\dfrac{x+(x-3)+(2x-5)+(2x+2)+(1-x)}{5} =$ average

$= \dfrac{5x-5}{5} =$ average

$= \dfrac{5(x-1)}{5} = (x-1)$

7. −2° $\dfrac{-7+5+1+(-10)+(-8)+2+0}{7} =$ average

$\dfrac{-17}{7} = 2\dfrac{3}{7} = (-2)°$ to the nearest degree.

8. $\dfrac{11}{2}$ or $5\dfrac{1}{2}$ $\dfrac{(2x-1)+4+6+12+13}{5} = 9$

$= \dfrac{2x+34}{5} = 9.$ Multiply by 5.

$= 2x+34 = 45.$ Solve for x.

$2x = 11$

$x = \dfrac{11}{2}$

9. $\dfrac{4}{3}$ $\dfrac{x+y}{2} = 4.$ Substitute $5y$ for x.

$\dfrac{5y+y}{2} = 4.$ Multiply both sides by 2.

$5y + y = 8.$ Solve for y.

$6y = 8$

$y = \dfrac{8}{6} = \dfrac{4}{3}$

10. $109\dfrac{1}{6}$ $\dfrac{108\frac{1}{2}+97\frac{1}{4}+121\frac{3}{4}}{3} =$ average weight

$\dfrac{\frac{217}{2}+\frac{389}{4}+\frac{487}{4}}{3} =$ average

$\dfrac{\frac{434}{4}+\frac{389}{4}+\frac{487}{4}}{3} = \dfrac{\frac{1,310}{4}}{3} = \dfrac{1,310}{4} \cdot \dfrac{1}{3}$

$= \dfrac{1,310}{12} = 109\dfrac{1}{6}$

Practice SAT Problems, from p. 303

1. C   If $\dfrac{4}{5} = \dfrac{x}{4}$, then $5x = 16$; $x = \dfrac{16}{5}$

2. D $\dfrac{95+87+84+84+61}{5} = \dfrac{410}{5} = 82$

3. E $\$15.00 - \$3.50 = \$11.50; \$20.00 - \$11.50 = \$8.50.$

4. A $\dfrac{1x}{3} - \dfrac{1x}{4} + 6.$ LCD = 12.

Multiply each term by 12.

$4x = 3x + 72.$ Solve for x.

5. C $\dfrac{\frac{3}{4}}{\frac{9}{8}} = \dfrac{3}{4} \cdot \dfrac{8}{9} = \dfrac{24}{36} = \dfrac{2}{3}$

6. A $(.53)^2 - (.52)^2 = (.53 - .52)(.53 + .52)$
          $= (.01)(1.05) = 0.0105$

7. C   The ratio must be in the same units.
          Convert both to minutes.
          120 seconds = 2 minutes, so
          $\dfrac{2 \text{ minutes}}{8 \text{ hours}} = \dfrac{2}{8(60)}$
          $= \dfrac{1}{8 \cdot 30} = \dfrac{1}{240}$

8. C $\dfrac{78 + 78 + 92 + x}{4} = 82$
          $78 + 78 + 92 + x = 328;\quad 248 + x = 328;\quad x = 80.$

9. C   LCD = 1,000 $\dfrac{23}{1,000} + \dfrac{60}{1,000} + \dfrac{700}{1,000} = \dfrac{783}{1,000}$

10. B   If $8x + 8y = 64$, then $x + y = 8$ and $\dfrac{x+y}{2} = \dfrac{8}{2} = 4.$

11. B $8 = 4 \cdot 2$ and $36 = 4 \cdot 9$; therefore N must be a number
          whose factors are 4, 2, and 9.

12. D   Let n = number of girls, $2n$ = number of boys,
          $\dfrac{1n}{6} + \dfrac{1(2n)}{4}$ = number of students who play
          soccer.
          $\dfrac{1n}{6} + \dfrac{1n}{2} = \dfrac{2n}{3};$
          $\dfrac{\frac{2n}{3}}{3n} \dfrac{\text{number of students who play soccer}}{\text{total number of students}}.$
          $= \dfrac{2}{9}$

13. B $\dfrac{2.0}{250} = .008 =$ thickness of each sheet
          $3(.008) = .024$

14. C $\dfrac{5 + 6 + 8 + x + 12}{5} = 12$
          $\dfrac{31 + x}{5} = 12;\quad 31 + x = 60;\quad x = 29.$

15. D $8 \cdot 42 \ne 12 \cdot 32$

Lesson 8

Percent, from p. 306

1. $\dfrac{144}{5}$ or 28.8 $x = \dfrac{40}{100} \cdot (72); x = \dfrac{2}{5} \cdot 72 = \dfrac{144}{5}.$

2. 30 $x = \dfrac{125}{100} \cdot 24; x = \dfrac{5}{4} \cdot 24; x = \dfrac{120}{4}; x = 30.$

3. .075 $x = \dfrac{.05}{100} \cdot 150; x = \dfrac{7.5}{100} = .075$

4. 40% $16 = \dfrac{x}{100} \cdot 40$
          $16 = \dfrac{40x}{100}.$ Multiply both sides by 100.
          $1,600 = 40x.$ Solve for x.
          $40 = x$

5. 400% $9 = \dfrac{x}{100} \cdot (2.25)$
          $9 = \dfrac{2.25x}{100}; 900 = 2.25x; x = 400.$

6. 16% $12 = \dfrac{x}{100} \cdot 75;\ 12 = \dfrac{75x}{100}; 1,200 = 75x;$
          $x = \dfrac{1,200}{75} = 16.$

7. 27.5 $4.4 = \dfrac{16(x)}{100};\ 440 = 16x;\ x = \dfrac{440}{16} = 27.5.$

8. 35 $42 = \dfrac{x}{100} \cdot 120;\ 4,200 = 120x;\ x = 35.$

9. 40 $\dfrac{5}{4} = \dfrac{x}{100} \cdot \dfrac{25}{8};\ \dfrac{5}{4} = \dfrac{25x}{800};\ (5) \cdot (800) = 4 \cdot (25x);$
          $4,000 = 100x; x = 40.$

10. 3.03 $x = \dfrac{101}{100} \cdot (3);\ x = \dfrac{303}{100} = 3.03.$
          (Move the decimal point 2 places to the left.)

11. $37\dfrac{1}{2}$% $\dfrac{3}{8} = \dfrac{x}{100};\ 8x = 300;\ x = \dfrac{300}{8} = 37\dfrac{1}{2}\%.$

12. $2.67 Let x = the original price.
          $\dfrac{75}{100}x = 2.00;\ 75x = 200;\ x = \dfrac{200}{75} = 2.67.$

13. 90% $\dfrac{15}{100} \cdot (300) = \dfrac{x}{100} \cdot 50;\ 45 = \dfrac{50x}{100};$
          $45 \cdot 100 = 50x;\ x = 90.$

14. 14 hours $12\dfrac{1}{2}\%$ is equal to the fraction $\dfrac{1}{8}$.
          Carlos drove for $\dfrac{1}{8}$ of the trip.
          He still needs to drive $\dfrac{7}{8}$ of the trip.
          $\dfrac{1}{8} = 2$ hours; $\dfrac{7}{8} = 7 \cdot 2,$ or 14 hours.

15. 574 girls   If 44% were boys, 56% were girls.
          $\dfrac{56}{100} \cdot (1,025) =$ number of girls
          $574 =$ number of girls

Ratio and Proportion, from p. 308

1. $\dfrac{47}{29}$ Convert the measurements to inches.
          Length = 15 feet 8 inches = $(15 \cdot 12) + 8 = 188$ inches
          Width = 9 feet 8 inches = $(9 \cdot 12) + 8 = 116$ inches
          The ratio of the length to the width is $\dfrac{188}{116} = \dfrac{47}{29}.$

2. $\dfrac{8}{1}$ Convert 3 pounds to ounces.
          3 pounds = $(3 \cdot 16)$ ounces; $\dfrac{3 \cdot 16}{6} = \dfrac{8}{1}$

3. 99   Let the ratio of the numbers be $\dfrac{3x}{5x}.$
          The larger number, $5x$, equals 165.
          Solve for x. $5x = 165; x = 33.$
          The smaller number is then $3 \cdot 33$, or 99.

4. $\frac{44}{75}$ The total number of students is 300.

The ratio of girls to the total number of students is

$\frac{176}{300}$, or $\frac{44}{75}$.

5. $\frac{dy}{x}$ Each baseball costs $\frac{d}{x}$ dollars.

y baseballs would cost $y \cdot \left(\frac{d}{x}\right)$ dollars.

6. 16   This is an inverse variation. The number of man-hours required to paint the house is (8 • 12), or 96. Six men

would take $\frac{96}{6}$, or 16, hours to paint the same house. For

a proportion, you would have $\frac{8}{6} = \frac{x}{12}$.

7. 10   Cross multiply and solve for x.

$\frac{18}{5x} = \frac{9}{25}$; $18 \cdot 25 = 9 \cdot 5x$; $x = \frac{\overset{2\,\cdot\,5}{\cancel{18} \cdot \cancel{25}}}{\underset{1\,\cdot\,1}{\cancel{9} \cdot \cancel{5}}} = 10$.

8. 166.4 miles   If 1 inch = 32 miles, 5.2 inches would equal (5.2) (32), or 166.4, miles.

9. 5

$\frac{\text{teaspoons}}{\text{tablespoons}} \cdot \frac{\text{tablespoons}}{\text{ounces}} \cdot \frac{\text{teaspoons}}{\text{ounces}}$

$\frac{3 \text{ teaspoons}}{1 \text{ tablespoon}} \cdot \frac{2 \text{ tablespoons}}{1 \text{ ounce}} = \frac{6 \text{ teaspoons}}{1 \text{ ounce}}$

So $\frac{6 \text{ teaspoons}}{1 \text{ ounce}} = \frac{30 \text{ teaspoons}}{x \text{ ounces}}$

$x = 5$

10. $\frac{5}{3}$ Set up a ratio: inches of snow to minutes.

Convert 2 hours to minutes.

$\frac{\frac{1}{3} \text{ inches}}{24 \text{ minutes}} = \frac{x \text{ inches}}{120 \text{ minutes}}$

$24x = 40$.   Solve for x.

$x = \frac{40}{24}$

$x = \frac{5}{3}$

Practice SAT Problems, from p. 309

1. B   The first step here is to do the subtraction in the denominator of

the fraction. This leaves a $\frac{1}{2}$ in the denominator. Since 1 over a

fraction simply flips the fraction, you get $1 - 2$ or -1 as an answer.

2. B   Cross multiplying is the quickest way to work this problem. To save even more time though, instead of going from $5 \cdot 9 = x \cdot 15$ to $45 = 15x$, divide a 5 from both sides *before* multiplying. This leaves $9 = 3x$, a fairly easy equation.

3. D   This problem must be done one card at a time. That is, take an X card from pile A and put it in pile B. Then find what fractional part of each pile the X cards make up. Do this until the fractional part of X cards is the same for each pile. Once the fractional parts are equal, go back and count how many X cards you moved. After taking one X card from A and putting it in pile B, the

fractional part of X cards in pile A is $\frac{3}{5}$ and the fractional part of

X cards in pile B is $\frac{1}{7}$. Notice that the "size" of the whole

changes when you move cards. After moving the third X card, the

fractional part of X cards in pile A is $\frac{1}{3}$ and in pile B is

$\frac{3}{9}$. Since $\frac{1}{3} = \frac{3}{9}$, 3 is the answer.

4. E   The distance runner B falls behind is given by the fraction

$\frac{x \text{ inches}}{y \text{ minutes}}$. Since you want the answer in terms of feet and

hours, you must multiply by unit fractions.

$\frac{1 \text{ foot}}{12 \text{ inches}}$ and $\frac{60 \text{ minutes}}{1 \text{ hour}}$ are the two unit fractions you use.

The multiplication looks like:

$\frac{x \text{ inches}}{y \text{ minutes}} \cdot \frac{1 \text{ foot}}{12 \text{ inches}} \cdot \frac{60 \text{ minutes}}{1 \text{ hour}}$ The inches and the minutes

drop out, leaving you with $\frac{60x \text{ feet}}{12y \text{ hours}}$. By dividing 12 from the

top and bottom, you can simplify the equation to $\frac{5x}{y}$ feet in 1

hour.

5. D   The steps for doing this problem are (1) change the mixed numbers to fractions; (2) find the difference between the distances in feet; and (3) convert the feet to inches with the unit fraction,

$\frac{12 \text{ inches}}{1 \text{ foot}}$.

6. D   Do not make the mistake of inverting $\frac{1}{a} - \frac{1}{b}$ and getting $a - b$!

You must first change the denominator into a *single fraction*

before you may invert it. To do this, find the difference between

$\frac{1}{a}$ and $\frac{1}{b}$. It should come out to be $\frac{b-a}{ab}$. Now you may invert

the fraction in the denominator and get $\frac{ab}{b-a}$ for an answer.

7. B   With this problem either you can convert the decimal to a fraction and then do the multiplication, or you can just do the multiplication with decimals. Doing the multiplication with

decimals looks like $\begin{array}{r} .125 \\ \times 8 \\ \hline 1.000 \end{array}$. There are three digits in front of the

decimal, so the answer must be 1.000 or just 1, answer (B).

8. E   Squaring the .2 gives you $.04 = \sqrt{x}$. Do not stop here and put answer (C). Square both sides of the equation to get $.04^2 = x$. Multiplying out $.04 \cdot .04$ leaves .0016, answer (E).

9. B   This is a problem in juggling equations, except the numbers used are decimals. The first thing you do is multiply both sides by 10. This changes the $-.6$ to a -6 and the 1.2 to a 12. From here you can divide both sides by 6, leaving you with $-(0.4 - p) = 2(.8p + .7p)$. Adding the $.8p$ and the $.7p$ and getting rid of the parentheses on both sides of the equations gives $p - .4 = 3p$. Subtract p from both sides and then divide by 2. You're left with $-.2 = p$, answer (B). If you had wanted, you could have changed all of the decimals to fractions and worked from there; the steps would be mostly the same. Finally, if nothing else seems to be working for you, plug answer choices in and chug them through. Only the correct answer works.

10. A   By subtracting the second given equation from the first one, all of the 3s after the decimal point become zeros, so you are left with $9n = 3$. Dividing both sides by 9 and then simplifying the fraction

leaves you with $\frac{1}{3}$, answer (A).

11. C $\frac{(2x+1)+(x+5)+(1-4x)+(3x+1)}{4}$

$= \frac{2x+8}{4} = \frac{1}{2}x + 2$

12. E   The least weight would be when two players weigh 150 and one weighs 175. Their average would be $\frac{150+150+175}{3}=158\frac{1}{3}$. The greatest weight would occur when two players weigh 175 and one weighs 150. Their average weight would be $\frac{175+175+150}{3}=\frac{500}{3}=166\frac{2}{3}$. Their average weight could not be 167.

13. D   Let x equal the other number. The average of A and x would be $\frac{A+x}{2}=P$. Solve for x.
$A+x=2P$; $x=2P-A$.

14. D   If the average grade of 10 students is x, then the total score is $10x$. Five students earned a grade of 84. The entire average would be $\frac{10x+5(84)}{15}$, or $\frac{10x+420}{15}$.

15. E   Setting up the percentage equation $(P=\frac{c}{100}\bullet W)$, you have
$12=\frac{x}{100}\bullet 120$. First dividing a 12 out of both sides and then canceling a 10 from the numerator and denominator of the second fraction leaves $1=\frac{x}{10}$, or $x=10$. Marking 10 is a mistake, however. You have just solved for the amount she has *eaten*. $100\%-10\%=90\%$ is the amount that *remains*.

16. A $P=\frac{75}{100}\bullet 12$ is the distance the boy has walked. By first dividing the numerator and the denominator by 25, and then by 4, the equation is reduced to $P=9$. But this is the distance the boy has *already* walked. Subtracting 9 from 12 leaves 3, the number of miles the boy has left to go.

17. C   Go back to the equation $P=\frac{c}{100}\bullet W$. The first statement, "60-gallon tank is 40% full of water," can be written as $P=\frac{40}{100}\bullet 60$. The part of the tank that is full, P, solves to be 24. *Don't stop here* and mark answer (A). Now ask what percent 24 is of 40. Algebraically, it reads $24=\frac{c}{100}\bullet 40$. Solving for c gives 60, answer (C).

18. B   Problems involving boys and girls usually leave out one important but obvious fact: the number of boys plus the number of girls equals the total number of people.
Call the number of people in the class x. This means the number of boys is 30% of x, or $\frac{30}{100}\bullet x$. Since the number of boys added to the number of girls equals the total number of people in the class, you can set up the equation $\frac{30}{100}x+21=x$. Solving for x, you get $x=30$; that is, there are 30 people *in the class*. Subtracting 21, the number of girls in the class, leaves 9, the number of boys in the class, which is answer (B).

19. B   The total number of "parts" of socks is $2+3+5=10$. The black socks are 5 of those parts. The fraction of the socks that are black socks is the part over the whole, $\frac{5\text{ parts}}{10\text{ parts}}$, or $\frac{1}{2}$. Half of 30 is 15, so there are 15 black socks.

20. D   The ratio of cost to side is constant since the lengths of all of the sides are the same. The algebraic equation becomes $\frac{6y\text{ dollars}}{3\text{ sides}}=\frac{N}{1\text{ side}}$. Divide the numerator and denominator of the first fraction by 3. What's left is $\frac{2y\text{ dollars}}{1\text{ side}}=\frac{N}{1\text{ side}}$. N must be $2y$ dollars to make the two fractions equal.

21. B   Convert the problem to fractions to get $\frac{3}{4}=\frac{a}{12}$. Cross multiplying and doing the simplification leaves $a=9$.

22. C   Forty-four percent of 25 students is 11, so there are 11 boys. The 14 other students must be girls. The ratio of boys to girls is therefore 11:14.

23. B   Call my age now M and my father's age now F. The two equations take the form $\frac{M+15}{F+15}=\frac{1}{2}$ and $\frac{M-5}{F-5}=\frac{1}{4}$. Cross multiply to get $2M+30=F+15$ and $4M-20=F-5$. Solve the two equations in two unknowns to get $M=15$ and $F=45$. M represents my age, so I am 15.

24. D   Set up the equality $\frac{6\text{ pages}}{9\text{ seconds}}=\frac{x\text{ pages}}{24\text{ minutes}}$. Since the units of time are not the same, you must make them so by multiplying the first fraction by the unit fraction $\frac{60\text{ seconds}}{1\text{ minute}}$. Then do the cross multiplication and cancellation to get $6\bullet 24\bullet 60=9x$. Divide both sides by 9 and do the multiplication so that you are left with $x=906$. Looking at the answers *before* doing the problem can also be very helpful here. Answers (A), (B), and (C) can be discarded because they are so small. If you decided to do this problem by plugging in, you would need to try only answers (D) and (E).

25. B   An equilateral triangle is defined as having three equal sides; so if the length of one side is called s, then the perimeter (the sum of the lengths of the sides) must be $3s$. The ratio of the length of one side to the perimeter is therefore s to $3s$ or $\frac{s}{3s}$, which equals $\frac{1}{3}$.

26. 1/20 or .05   Since the brown socks, the blue socks, the black socks, and the white socks all put together make up all of the socks in the drawer, the sum of all the different fractional parts must equal 1. Algebraically this can be said:
$\frac{1}{2}+\frac{1}{4}+\frac{1}{5}+w=1$, where w stands for the fractional part of the socks that are white. By substracting $\frac{1}{2},\frac{1}{4}$, and $\frac{1}{5}$ from both sides of the equation you are left with $w=\frac{1}{20}$.

27. 2.40   Dividing the 12 inches of ribbon into the number of $\frac{1}{4}$-inch pieces in it and then multiplying that number by 5, since each piece costs a nickel, gives the answer $2.40. Algebraically you have $(12+\frac{1}{4})\bullet .05$.

28. 1/12 or .083   Knowing the key words in this problem makes it one of the simpler questions. Remember that *of* implies multiplication and *more than* implies addition. Algebraically the problem takes the form $\left(\frac{1}{2}\bullet\frac{2}{3}\right)=\left(\frac{3}{4}\bullet\frac{1}{3}\right)+x$. By canceling the 2s in the first multiplication and the 3s in the second, you are left with $\frac{1}{3}=\frac{1}{4}+x$. By finding a common denominator of the two fractions, you can simplify the expression to $\frac{4}{12}-\frac{3}{12}=x$ or $\frac{1}{12}=x$.

29. 1/3 or .333   The trick here is remembering that Joan paints $\frac{1}{2}$ of what is left, *not* $\frac{1}{2}$ of the fence. You must first figure out how much of the fence is left before you can determine how much Joan painted. Subtracting $\frac{1}{3}$, the amount Jim painted, from 1 gives the amount left $\frac{2}{3}$. Half of $\frac{2}{3}$ is $\frac{1}{3}$. Subtracting the part Jim painted and the part Joan painted from 1 gives the part that was left unpainted. $1-\frac{1}{3}-\frac{1}{3}=\frac{1}{3}$, so $\frac{1}{3}$ was the fractional part left unpainted.

30. 163   This is a word problem dealing with containment. Containment implies division, so when you set up the algebraic equation, it should look like $16.3 + \dfrac{1}{10} = ?$ Changing 16.3 to $\dfrac{163}{10}$ and inverting $\dfrac{1}{10}$ gives you $\dfrac{163}{10} \cdot \dfrac{10}{1}$. The 10s cancel each other out, so you are left with 163.

31. 17/8 or 2.13 $\dfrac{2\frac{1}{2}+1\frac{3}{4}}{2}$ = average length of time

$\dfrac{\frac{5}{2}+\frac{7}{4}}{2}$ = average; $\dfrac{\frac{10}{4}+\frac{7}{4}}{2}$ = average;

$\dfrac{\frac{17}{4}}{2} = \dfrac{17}{8} = 2\frac{1}{8}$ hours.

Remember to always convert a mixed number to an improper fraction or a decimal for gridding-in.

32. 100   Set the equation up phrase by phrase: "30% of" "80" "is" "what percent" "of" "24." The algebraic expression for this is

$\dfrac{3}{100} \cdot 80 = \dfrac{x}{100} \cdot 24$. Canceling a 10 twice from the first fraction

leaves $3 \cdot 8 = \dfrac{x}{100} \cdot 24$. Divide both sides of the equation by 24

to get $1 = \dfrac{x}{100}$, or $x = 100$.

33. .9 or 9/10   Since both calls are made at the same rate, the ratio between the cost and the time of both calls is equal. That is:

$\dfrac{\$0.24}{4 \text{ minutes}} = \dfrac{\$x}{15 \text{ minutes}}$. Cross multiplying and canceling units leaves $(.24)15 = 4x$.
Solving for x gives $x = \$0.90$.

34. .5 or 1/2   The word *represents* implies that a ratio is being used. Call x the number of inches that represents 1 foot 6 inches in the drawing. The algebraic equation becomes

$\dfrac{x \text{ inches}}{1 \text{ foot } 6 \text{ inches}} = \dfrac{3 \text{ inches}}{9 \text{ feet}}$. Convert the feet to inches to get

$\dfrac{x \text{ inches}}{18 \text{ inches}} = \dfrac{3 \text{ inches}}{9 \cdot 12 \text{ inches}}$.
Cross multiplying and canceling units leaves
$x \cdot 9 \cdot 12 = 3 \cdot 18$.   Divide both sides by 9.
$x \cdot 12 = 3 \cdot 2$.   Divide both sides by 6.
$x \cdot 2 = 1$.   Divide both sides by 2.

$x = \dfrac{1}{2} = .5$.

So .5 inches represents 1 foot 6 inches in the scale drawing. Notice that you did not need to do the multiplication out. *Simplify before* you do the multiplication.

35. 16   The total number of parts is $6 + 2 + 1 = 9$. Ned receives 2 of them, so Ned's share is $\dfrac{2}{9}$ of \$72.00, or \$16.00.

Lesson 9

Two Equations in Two Unknowns, from p. 315

1. $x = 2$
   $y = 3$ Use the substitution method.
   Substitute $(2x - 1)$ for y in the second equation.
   $3x + 2(2x - 1) = 12$ Solve for x.
   $7x = 14$
   $x = 2$ Solve for y.
   $y = 2x - 1$
   $y = 2(2) - 1 = 3$

2. $a = 2$
   $b = 4$ Use the substitution method.
   Substitute $(6 - b)$ for a in the second equation.
   $-3(6 - b) + b = -2$ Solve for b.
   $-18 + 3b + b = -2$
   $4b = 16$
   $b = 4$ Solve for a.
   $a = 6 - b$
   $a = 6 - 4 = 2$

3. $y - x = -5$ Subtract the bottom equation from the top equation.
   $3y - 4x = 5$
   $\underline{-(2y - 3x = 10)}$ Change all of the signs before you
   $y - x = -5$
   add.

4. $p = -2$
   $q = -6$ Use the linear combination method. Multiply the bottom equation by (-2), and add it to the top equation to eliminate q.

   $\begin{aligned}3p - 2q &= 6\\-2(-2p - q = 10)\end{aligned} = \begin{aligned}3p - 2q &= 6\\4p + 2q &= -20\end{aligned}$ Add.

   Solve for p. $7p = -14$
   $p = -2$
   Solve for q. $3(-2) - 2q = 6$
   $-6 - 2q = 6$
   $-2q = 12;\ q = -6$.

5. 4   Add the two equations directly to get $a - b$.
   $-2a - 5b = -15$
   $\underline{3a + 4b = 19}$
   $a - b = 4$

6. $x = \dfrac{2}{5}$
   $y = 2$ Add the two equations to eliminate $\dfrac{1}{y}$; then solve for x by cross multiplying.

   $\dfrac{1}{x} + \dfrac{1}{y} = 3$ Add the two equations.
   $\dfrac{1}{x} - \dfrac{1}{y} = 2$
   $\dfrac{2}{x} = \dfrac{5}{1}$ Solve for x; cross multiply.

   $5x = 2$
   $x = \dfrac{2}{5}$ Substitute for x and solve for y.

   $\dfrac{1}{\frac{2}{5}} + \dfrac{1}{y} = 3$ $\dfrac{1}{\frac{2}{5}} = 1 \cdot \dfrac{5}{2} = \dfrac{5}{2}$

   $\dfrac{5}{2} + \dfrac{1}{y} = 3$
   $\dfrac{1}{y} = 3 - \dfrac{5}{2}$
   $\dfrac{1}{y} = \dfrac{1}{2}$
   $y = 2$

7. −14   Rearrange the terms and add the two equations.
   $\begin{aligned}12 &= 4a - 3b\\7a &= 5b - 2\end{aligned} = \begin{aligned}-4a + 3b &= -12\\7a - 5b &= -2\end{aligned}$
   $3a - 2b = -14$

8. $x = \frac{1}{2}$ Add the two equations to eliminate $\frac{1}{y}$; then solve for x by

$y = -\frac{1}{2}$ cross multiplying.

$$\frac{2}{x} + \frac{1}{y} = 2$$
$$\frac{3}{x} - \frac{1}{y} = 8 \qquad \text{Add.}$$
$$\overline{\frac{5}{x} \qquad = \frac{10}{1}}$$

$10x = 5$ Solve for x.

$x = \frac{1}{2}$

$\frac{2}{\frac{1}{2}} + \frac{1}{y} = 2$ Solve for y; substitute $\frac{1}{2}$ for x.

$4 + \frac{1}{y} = 2$

$\frac{1}{y} = -2$ Multiply both sides by y.

$-2y = 1$ Divide by (-2).

$y = -\frac{1}{2}$

9. $p = \frac{9}{4}$ Add the equations to eliminate q and then solve for p.

$q = \frac{1}{4}$

$$\frac{p}{3} + q = 1$$
$$\frac{p}{3} - q = 2 \qquad \text{Add.}$$
$$\overline{\frac{4p}{3} \qquad = 3}$$ Solve for p; multiply both sides by 3.

$4p = 9$

$p = \frac{9}{4}$ Solve for q; substitute $\frac{9}{4}$ for p in either equation.

$\frac{9}{4} - q = 2$

$-q = 2 - \frac{9}{4}; \ -q = -\frac{1}{4}; \ q = \frac{1}{4}$.

10. $x = 8$ Use the substitution method.
$y = 1$ $x = 2(2y + 2) = (4y + 4)$ Substitute for x.
$3(x - 3y) = 15$
$3[(4y + 4) - 3y] = 15$ Solve for y.
$3[y + 4] = 15$
$3y + 12 = 15$
$3y = 3$
$y = 1$
$x = 2[2(1) + 2] = 8$ Solve for x.

Lesson 10

Motion Problems, from p. 318

1. 750 miles $R \cdot T = D$

120 mph $\cdot 6\frac{1}{4}$ hours $= 750$ miles

2. 60 mph $R \cdot T = D$.   Let x = rate.

$x \cdot 15\frac{2}{3} = 940$

$x \cdot \frac{47}{3} = 940$.   Solve for x.

$x = 940\left(\frac{3}{47}\right) = 60$

3. q kilometers/ $R \cdot T = D$.   Let x = rate.
   hour $x \cdot p$ hours $= pq$ kilometers
   $xp = pq$ Solve for x.
   $x = q$ kilometers/hour

4. 70 mph   Mr. Smith has to drive 105 miles in $1\frac{1}{2}$ hours. Let x
   equal the rate.
   $R \cdot T = D$

$x \cdot \frac{3}{2} = 105$

$\frac{3}{2}x = 105; \ 3x = 210$.   Solve for x.

$x = 70$

5. $\frac{15}{2}$ mph $\dfrac{\frac{3}{4} \text{ mile}}{6 \text{ minutes}} = \dfrac{x \text{ miles}}{60 \text{ minutes}}$ Solve for x.

$6x = (60)\left(\frac{3}{4}\right)$

$6x = 45$

$x = \frac{45}{6} = \frac{15}{2}$

6. $9\frac{1}{5}$ mph   The boy walked 10 miles in 2 hours and bicycled 36
   miles in 3 hours.
   Average rate equals $\frac{D}{T} = \frac{46}{5} = 9\frac{1}{5}$ mph.

7. $\frac{x+y}{5}$ Average rate $= \dfrac{\text{Total distance}}{\text{Total time}} = \dfrac{x+y}{5}$

8. 2 hours   Let x = number of hours.

	R	· T =	D
Car 1	40	x	$40x$
Car 2	54	x	$54x$

$54x + 40x = 188$ Solve for x.
$94x = 188$
$x = 2$ hours

9. $60\left(\dfrac{x}{y}\right)$ $T = \dfrac{D}{R}$ T hours $= \dfrac{x \text{ miles}}{y \text{ mph}}$

The problem asks for minutes, so multiply your answer by 60.

10. $54 - 3x$ kilometers

	R	· T =	D
Boat 1	15	x	$15x$
Boat 2	18	$x-3$	$18x-54$

The difference is $15x - (18x - 54) = (54 - 3x)$ kilometers.

Mixture Problems, from p. 319

1. 18 grams Let x = the number of grams of silver.

	Unit Value	•	Amount	=	Value
Silver	4		x		$4x$
Gold	24		$(30 - x)$		$24(30 - x)$

$$4x + 24(30 - x) = 12(30)$$
$$4x + 720 - 24x = +360$$
$$-20x = -360$$
$$x = 18$$

2. 50 grams Let x = number of grams of pure acid.

	Unit Value	•	Amount	=	Value
25% solution	.25		200		50
Pure acid	1.00		x		$1x$
Mixture	.40		$200 + x$		$80 + .4x$

$$x + 50 = 80 + .4x$$
$$.6x = 30; \ 6x = 300; \ x = 50.$$

3. 10 gallons

	Unit Value	•	Amount	=	Value
80% solution	.80		30		24
Pure water	.00		x		.00
Mixture	.60		$x + 30$		$.6x + 18$

$$24 = .6x + 18; \ 6 = .6x$$
$$60 = 6x; \ 10 = x.$$

4. $1\frac{1}{2}$ quarts Let x = the number of quarts of grape juice.

	Unit Value	•	Amount	=	Value
Grape juice	1.20		x		$1.20x$
Apple juice	.90		3		2.70
Punch	1.00		$3 + x$		$3 + x$

$$1.20x + 2.70 = 3 + x$$
$$.2x = .3. \quad \text{Multiply both sides by 10.}$$
$$2x = 3. \quad \text{Solve for } x.$$
$$x = 1\frac{1}{2}$$

5. 210 Let x = the number of balcony seats sold.

	Unit Value	•	Amount	=	Value
Balcony	15		x		$15x$
Orchestra	20		$540 - x$		$20(540 - x)$
Total					\$9,750

$$15x + 20(540 - x) = \$9,750$$
$$15x + 10,800 - 20x = \$9,750$$
$$-5x = -1,050$$
$$x = 210$$

6. 18 pounds Let x = the number of pounds of cashews.

	Unit Value	•	Amount	=	Value
Cashews	2.00		x		$2.00x$
Peanuts	.80		30		24
Mixture	1.25		$x + 30$		$1.25(x + 30)$

$$2.00x + 24 = 1.25x + 37.50$$
$$.75x = 13.50. \quad \text{Multiply both sides by 100.}$$
$$75x = 1,350. \quad \text{Divide by 75.}$$
$$x = 18$$

7. $13\frac{1}{3}$ Let x = the number of ounces of water.

	Unit Value	•	Amount	=	Value
Water	.00		x		.00
10% solution	.10		20		2
Mixture	.06		$x + 20$		$.06(x + 20)$

$$2 = .06x + 1.2$$
$$.8 = .06x. \quad \text{Multiply both sides by 100.}$$
$$80 = 6x. \quad \text{Divide by 6.}$$
$$13\frac{1}{3} = x$$

8. 12 ounces Let x = the number of ounces of pure acid.

	Unit Value	•	Amount	=	Value
Pure acid	1.00		x		$1x$
Solution	.20		60		12
Mixture	.25		$x + 60$		$.25(x + 60)$

$$x + 12 = .25x + 21$$
$$.75x = 9. \quad \text{Multiply by 100.}$$
$$75x = 900$$
$$x = 12$$

9. 5 pounds Let x = the number of pounds of the 60-cent candy.

	Unit Value	•	Amount	=	Value
60-cent candy	.60		x		$.60x$
80-cent candy	.80		$20 - x$		$16 - .8x$
Mixture	.75		20		15

$$.60x + 16 - .8x = 15; \ -.2x = -1;$$
$$-2x = -10; \ x = 5.$$

10. 24 nickels Let x = the number of nickels.

	Unit Value	•	Amount	=	Value
Nickels	5 cents		x		$5x$
Dimes	10 cents		$34 - x$		$340 - 10x$
Mixture					220 cents

$$5x + 340 - 10x = 220$$
$$-5x = -120$$
$$x = 24$$

Work Problems, from p. 321

1. $\frac{8}{12}$ or $\frac{2}{3}$

2. 48 $\frac{16}{1} = \frac{x}{3}$; $x = 48$.

3. $\frac{40}{128} = \frac{5}{16}$

4. $\frac{6}{7}$ hour   Let x = the number of hours working together.

$$\frac{x}{2} + \frac{x}{\frac{3}{2}} = 1; \qquad \frac{x}{2} + \frac{2x}{3} = 1.$$

$$3x + 4x = 6$$
$$7x = 6$$
$$x = \frac{6}{7} \text{ hour}$$

5. $\frac{12}{7}$ hours   Let x = the number of hours working together.

$$\frac{x}{4} + \frac{x}{3} = 1; \; 3x + 4x = 12$$
$$7x = 12$$
$$x = \frac{12}{7} \text{ hours}$$

6. $\frac{252}{191}$ hours   Let x = the number of hours they work together.

$$\frac{x}{4\frac{1}{2}} + \frac{x}{4} + \frac{x}{3\frac{1}{2}} = 1$$

$$\frac{x}{\frac{9}{2}} + \frac{x}{4} + \frac{x}{\frac{7}{2}} = 1; \; \frac{2x}{9} + \frac{x}{4} + \frac{2x}{7} = 1.$$

Multiply each term by 252, the common denominator.

$$252\left(\frac{2x}{9}\right) = 252\left(\frac{x}{4}\right) + 252\left(\frac{2x}{7}\right) = 252(1)$$

$$56x + 63x + 72x = 252$$

$$191x = 252$$
$$x = \frac{252}{191} \text{ hours}$$

Number Problems, from p. 323

1. 83, 84, 85, 86, 87, 88

$$x + (x+1) + (x+2) + (x+3) + (x+4) + (x+5) = 513$$
$$6x + 15 = 513$$
$$6x = 498$$
$$x = 83$$

2. 41, 43, 45, 47, 49

$$x + (x+2) + (x+4) + (x+6) + (x+8) = 225$$
$$5x + 20 = 225$$
$$5x = 205$$
$$x = 41$$

3. $-11, -10$ Let x = the odd integer; $x + 1$ is the even integer.
$$4(x) = 3(x+1) - 14$$
$$4x = 3x + 3 - 14$$
$$x = -11$$

4. 4   The consecutive integers are $x, x+1, x+2, x+3,$ and $x+4$.
$$x + 4 = 2(x)$$
$$4 = x$$

5. 19   Let x = the first odd integer.
The four consecutive odd integers are then $x, x+2,$ $x+4,$ and $x+6$.

$$\frac{x + (x+2) + (x+4) + (x+6)}{4} = 16. \quad \text{The average} = 16.$$

$$4x + 12 = 64$$
$$4x = 52$$
$$x = 13. \qquad \text{Smallest.}$$
$$x + 6 = 19. \qquad \text{Largest.}$$

6. 20, 21, 22   The three consecutive integers are $x, x+1,$ and $x + 2$.

$$\frac{x + (x+1) + (x+2)}{9} = 7. \quad \text{Multiply both sides by 9.}$$

$$3x + 3 = 63$$
$$3x = 60$$
$$x = 20$$

7. 83   Let x = the smallest integer.
$$\frac{x}{3} + \frac{x+1}{3} + \frac{x+2}{3} = 84. \quad \text{Multiply each term by 3.}$$
$$x + (x+1) + (x+2) = 252$$
$$3x + 3 = 252$$
$$3x = 249$$
$$x = 83$$

8. 30   Let x = the second number;
$2x$ = the first number;
$2(x-5)$ = the third number.
$$x + 2x + (2x - 10) = 65$$
$$5x - 10 = 65; \; 5x = 75; \; x = 15; \; 2x = 30.$$

9. 59   Let x = number of games lost; $x + 32$ = number of games won.
$$x + (x + 32) = 150$$
$$2x = 118$$
$$x = 59$$

10. 23, 35   Let the numbers be x and $x + 12$.
$$x + 2(x + 12) = 93; \; x + 2x + 24 = 93;$$
$$3x + 24 = 93.$$
$$3x = 69$$
$$x = 23$$
$$x + 12 = 35$$

Age Problems, from p. 325

1. 16   Let x = Roger's age now.

$$x + 32 = 3x$$
$$32 = 2x$$
$$16 = x$$

2. 20   Let x = Sam now.
$x + 12$ = Brad now.

	Age Now	In 8 Years
Brad	$x + 12$	$x + 20$
Sam	x	

$$x + 20 = 2(x)$$
$$20 = x$$

3. 23   Let x = Krista's age now.
$x + 2$ = Barrie's age now.

	Age Now	In 15 Years
Krista	x	
Barrie	$x + 2$	$x + 17$

$$x + 17 = 2(x) + 2$$
$$15 = x = \text{Krista now.}$$
$$17 = \text{Barrie now.}$$
$$23 = \text{Barrie in 6 years.}$$

4. 45   Let x = Marcus's age now.
          $x + 10$ = John's age now.

	Age Now	In 5 Years	5 Years Ago
John	$x + 10$	$x + 15$	
Marcus	x		$x - 5$

$$3(x + 15) = 5(x - 5)$$
$$3x + 45 = 5x - 25$$
$$70 = 2x$$
$$35 = x = \text{Marcus now.}$$
$$45 = \text{John now.}$$

5. 19   Let x = Danielle's age now.

	Age Now	In 1 Year	In 10 More Years
Kristen	$4x + 3$	$4(x + 1)$	$(4x + 4) + 10$
Danielle	x	$x + 1$	$(x + 1) + 10$

$$4x + 14 = 2(x + 11)$$
$$4x + 14 = 2x + 22$$
$$2x = 8$$
$$x = 4 = \text{Danielle now.}$$
$$4 \bullet (4) + 3 = 19 = \text{Kristen now.}$$

6. 17   Let x = the daughter's age now.

	Age Now
Mother	$3x + 6$
Daughter	x

The difference between their ages is always 30.
$$(3x + 6) - x = 30$$
$$2x + 6 = 30$$
$$2x = 24$$
$$x = 12$$
$$17 = x + 5. \text{ In five years.}$$

7. 16   Let x = Joe's age now.

	Age Now	3 Years Ago	In 10 Years
Ralph	$2x + 3$	$2x$	
Joe	x	$x - 3$	$x + 10$

$$2x = 4(x - 3)$$
$$2x = 4x - 12$$
$$-2x = -12$$
$$x = 6 = \text{Joe now.}$$
$$x + 10 = 16 = \text{in 10 years.}$$

8. 10 years ago   Let x = the number of years ago.

	Age Now	x Years Ago
Lisa	15	$15 - x$
Father	40	$40 - x$

$$40 - x = 6(15 - x)$$
$$40 - x = 90 - 6x$$
$$5x = 50$$
$$x = 10$$

9. Bob is 33.   Let x = Bob's age now.
   Joel is 11.

	Age Now	In 7 Years
Joel	$\frac{1}{3}x$	$\frac{1}{3}x + 7$
Bob	x	$x + 7$

$$\left(\frac{1}{3}x + 7\right) + (x + 7) = 58$$
$$\frac{4}{3}x + 14 = 58$$
$$\frac{4}{3}x = 44; \ 4x = 132; \ x = 33 = \text{Bob.}$$
$$\frac{1}{3}x = 11 = \text{Joel.}$$

10. 13   Let x = Leigh Ann's age now. Tom is $3x$.

	Age Now	In 7 Years
Leigh Ann	x	$x + 7$
Tom	$3x$	$3x + 7$

$$\frac{1}{2}(3x) + \frac{1}{3}(x + 7) = 3x. \quad \text{Multiply every term by 6,}$$
$$\text{the LCD.}$$
$$9x + 2x + 14 = 18x$$
$$7x = 14$$
$$x = 2 = \text{Leigh Ann now.}$$
$$3x = 6 = \text{Tom now.}$$
$$3x + 7 = 13 = \text{Tom in 7 years.}$$

Practice SAT Problems, from p. 325

1. D   Set up ratios $\dfrac{5 \text{ pounds}}{\$10.00} = \dfrac{x \text{ pounds}}{\$6.00}$.

Solve for x: $10x = 30$; $x = 3$ pounds

$$\frac{3 \text{ pounds}}{\$10.00} = \frac{x}{\$6.00}; \ 10x = 18; \ x = 1.8.$$

Subtract 3 pounds − 1.8 pounds = 1.2 pounds

2. C

Age 4 years ago	Now	In 4 years
M	$M + 4$	$M + 8$

3. A

	Age Now	Age 3 Years Ago
Rocky	p	$p - 3$
Apollo	$p - 5$	$p - 8$

4. B

	1 Year Ago	Age Now
Lumpy's Weight	x	$x + 18$

Set up the equation $x = \dfrac{90}{100}(x + 18)$.

Solve for x. $100x = 90(x + 18)$
$$100x = 90x + 90 \bullet 18$$
$$10x = 90 \bullet 18$$
$$x = 9 \bullet 18 = 162$$

5. E   Let x = the smaller number;
        $x + 20$ = the larger number.

$$\frac{2}{3}x = \frac{1}{4}(x + 20). \quad \text{Multiply both sides by 12, the LCD.}$$
$$8x = 3x + 60$$
$$5x = 60; \ x = 12; \ x + 20 = 32.$$

444   The Answer Section/Unit 8

6. D   Let x = the number of hours working together.

$\dfrac{x}{8} + \dfrac{x}{12} = 1.$ Multiply each term by 24, the LCD.

$3x + 2x = 24$

$5x = 24;\ x = \dfrac{24}{5},$ or $4\dfrac{4}{5}$ hours.

7. C   Let x = the number of hours each travels.

	R	• T	= D
Twin A	35	x	$35x$
Twin B	45	x	$45x$

$35x + 45x = 640$

$80x = 640;\ x = 8$ hours.

8. C   Let x = the number of ounces of the 40% solution.

	Unit Value	• Amount	= Value
40% solution	.40	x	$.40x$
12% solution	.12	20	2.4
Mixture	.28	$(x+20)$	$.28(x+20)$

$.40x + 2.4 = .28x + 5.6$

$.12x = 3.2.$ Multiply both sides by 100.

Solve for x.

$12x = 320;\ x = 26\dfrac{2}{3}.$

9. A   Let x = the number of gallons of 94-octane gas.

	Unit Value	• Amount	= Value
94-octane	94	x	$94x$
89-octane	89	$(100-x)$	$8{,}900-89x$
Mixture	92	100	9,200

$94x + (8{,}900 - 89x) = 9{,}200.$ Solve for x.

$5x = 300$

$x = 60$

$100 - 60 = 40.$ Gallons of 89-octane gas.

10. C   Let x = younger brother's age now.

	Age Now	1 Year Ago
Younger brother	x	$x-1$
Older brother	$x+5$	

$\dfrac{1}{3}(x+5) = x-1.$ Multiply by 3 (both sides).

$x + 5 = 3x - 3$

$8 = 2x$

$4 = x$ = younger brother now

$x + 4 = 8$ = younger brother in 4 years

11. C   Combine both equations.

$\begin{aligned} 2x + 3y &= 7 \\ x - 4y &= 12 \\ \hline 3x - y &= 19 \end{aligned}$

12. D   Combine both equations.

$\begin{aligned} 6p - 5q &= 12 \\ 2p + 7q &= 10 \\ \hline 8p + 2q &= 22 \end{aligned}$

Divide by 4 to get $2p + \dfrac{1}{2}q = 5.5.$

13. E   Substitute $(2x - 6)$ for y in the equation $3x + y = 4$ and solve for x.

$3x + (2x - 6) = 4;\ 5x - 6 = 4;\ 5x = 10;\ x = 2.$

Solve for y.

$y = 2(2) - 6 = -2;\ 3y = -6.$

14. A   If $\dfrac{7}{x} = 1,$ then $x = 7.$

If $\dfrac{y}{4} = 6,$ then $y = 24.$

$\dfrac{3+x}{3+y} = \dfrac{3+7}{3+24} = \dfrac{10}{27}$

15. D $x^2 + 2xy + y^2 = (x+y)(x+y) = 12 \cdot 12 = 144$

Lesson 11

Geometry of Angles, from p. 330

1. $\angle Y = 62°$ — $\angle X = \angle Y$. Alternate interior angles are equal.

   $\angle Z = 118°$ — Same-side interior angles are supplementary.
   $\angle X + \angle Z = 180°$

   $\angle W = 62°$ — $\angle X = \angle W$. Corresponding angles are equal.

2. $\angle 2 = 50°$ — $\angle 1 = \angle 2$. Alternate interior angles are equal.

   $\angle 4 = 39°$ — $\angle 5 = \angle 4$. Alternate interior angles are equal.

   $\angle 3 = 91°$ — $\angle 1 + \angle 3 + \angle 4 = 180°$

3. $25°$ — $\angle 1 + \angle 2 = 90°;\ \angle 2 = 48°.$
   $\angle 1 + \angle 2 + \angle 3 + \angle 4 + \angle 5 = 180°$
   $42 + 48 + 17 + 48 + \angle 5 = 180°$
   $\angle 5 = 25°$

4. $59°$ — $(2x + 18) + (x - 15) = 180°$
   $3x + 3 = 180°$
   $3x = 177°;\ x = 59°.$

5. $20°$ — $2x + (x + 30°) = 90°.$ Solve for x.
   $3x + 30° = 90°;\ 3x = 60°;\ x = 20°.$

6. $110°$ — Let x = the supplement; $x + 40°$ = the angle.
   $x + (x + 40°) = 180°$
   $2x + 40° = 180°;\ 2x = 140°;\ x = 70°.$
   $x + 40° = 110°$ = the angle.

7. $42°, 48°$ — Let x = the angle; $(90° - x)$ = the complement.
   $3(x) = 2(90° - x) + 30°$
   $3x = 180° - 2x + 30°;\ 5x = 210°;\ x = 42°.$

8. $\angle ABE = 53°$ — $\angle ABE = \angle DBC = 53°$. Opposite angles are equal.

   $\angle EBC = 127°$ — $\angle EBC + \angle DBC = 180°$. There are 180° in every line.
   $\angle EBC + 53° = 180°;\ \angle EBC = 127°.$

9. $29°$ — $\angle PQR + \angle PQS = 90°$. ⌐ means 90°.
   $\angle PQR + 61° = 90°;\ \angle PQR = 29°.$

10. $PW \perp SW$ — Perpendicular lines form right angles (90°).
    $QW \perp TW$ — $\angle PWQ + \angle QWR + \angle RWS = 90°$
    $SW \perp WV$ — $\angle QWR + \angle RWS + \angle SWT = 90°$
    $\angle SWT + \angle TWU + \angle UWV = 90°$

11. $53°$ — $\angle COA = \angle BOD = 37°$. Opposite angles are equal.
    $\angle COE + \angle COF = 180°;\ 90° + \angle COF = 180°$
    $\angle COF = 90°$
    $\angle AOF = \angle COF - \angle COA;\ \angle AOF = 90° - 37° = 53°.$

12. 72°   Let x = the measure of $\angle 1$;

   $2x$ = the measure of $\angle 2$;

   $2x$ = the measure of $\angle 3$.

   $\angle 1 + \angle 2 + \angle 3 = 180°$

   $x + 2x + 2x = 180°$; $5x = 180°$; $x = 36°$.

   $\angle 2 = \angle 4$. Opposite angles.

   $\angle 2 = \angle 4 = 72°$

13. 73° $\angle AOF = \angle COF - \angle COA$

   $\angle AOF = 120° - 47° = 73°$

   $\angle AOF = \angle EOB$. Opposite angles.

14. $\angle ROT = 51°$ $\angle ROT + \angle TOS = 180°$

   $\angle POV = 91°$ $\angle ROT + 129° = 180°$

   $\angle ROT = 51°$

   $\angle TOQ = \angle ROS - \angle ROT$; $\angle TOQ =$

   $142° - 51° = 91°$.

   $\angle TOQ = \angle POV = 91°$.

15. 37°

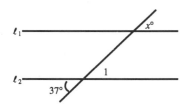

   $\angle 1 = 37°$. Opposite angles are equal.

   $\angle 1 = \angle x°$. Corresponding angles are equal.

16. 36° $118° = (2x + 10°) + x$. Alternate interior angles are equal.

   $118° = 3x + 10°$

   $108° = 3x$

   $36° = x$

17. 24° $(5x - 30°) + (3x + 18°) = 180°$. Same-side interior

   angles are supplementary.

   $8x - 12° = 180°$

   $8x = 192°$

   $x = 24°$

18. 20° $(3x + 10°) + (x - 6°) = 84°$. Corresponding angles are

   equal.

   $4x + 4° = 84°$

   $4x = 80°$; $x = 20°$.

19. 74° $\angle x = 74°$. Alternate interior angles are equal.

20. 56°   Extend one of the lines.

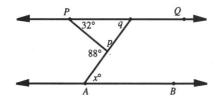

   $p = 92°$. Straight angles = 180°.

   $q = 180° - (92° + 32°) = 56°$. 180° in every triangle.

   $\angle x = \angle q = 56°$. Alternate interior angles are equal.

Lesson 12

Basic Definitions and Theorems for Triangles,
from p. 338

1. 30 square units $BC = 12$. $\triangle ABC$ is a 5-12-13 right triangle.

   Area $\triangle ABC = \frac{1}{2}(\text{leg}) \bullet (\text{leg})$

   Area $\triangle ABC = \frac{1}{2}(5) \bullet (12) = 30$ square units

2. 60 square units $XY = 8$. $\triangle XYZ$ is an 8-15-17 right triangle.

   Area $= \frac{1}{2}(\text{leg}) \bullet (\text{leg})$

   Area $\triangle XYZ = \frac{1}{2}(8) \bullet (15) = 60$

3. $(180 - 2x)°$

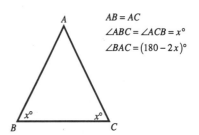

   $AB = AC$

   $\angle ABC = \angle ACB = x°$

   $\angle BAC = (180 - 2x)°$

4. $\angle QPR = 55°$ $\angle PRS$ is an exterior angle of $\triangle PQR$.

   $\angle PRS = \angle PQR + \angle QPR$

   $112° = 57° + \angle QPR$

   $55° = \angle QPR$

5. 78° $\angle QZP = \angle XZY$

   $\angle ZXY + \angle XYZ + \angle XZY = 180°$

   $43° + 59° + \angle XZY = 180°$

   $\angle XZY = 78° = \angle PZQ$

6. 168 square units

   $\triangle ADC$ is a right triangle; $BD = DC$.

   $(DC)^2 + (AD)^2 = (AC)^2$ Pythagorean theorem.

   $(DC)^2 + (24)^2 = 25^2$

   $(DC)^2 + 576 = 625$

   $DC^2 = 49$; $DC = \sqrt{49} = 7$.

   Area $= \frac{1}{2}(\text{base})(\text{height}) = \frac{1}{2}(14)(24) = 168$

7. $9\sqrt{3}$ square units   Area of an equilateral triangle equals

   $\frac{s^2\sqrt{3}}{4}$. Area $\triangle ABC = \frac{6^2\sqrt{3}}{4} = 9\sqrt{3}$

8. 2:1   The ratio of the areas of similar polygons equals the square of
   the ratio of the sides.

   $\frac{64}{16} = \left(\frac{XY}{AB}\right)^2$; $\frac{XY}{AB} = \frac{8}{4} = \frac{2}{1}$.

9. $\frac{9}{25}$ The ratio of the areas is equal to the square of the ratio of the

   sides.

   $\frac{\text{Area of } \triangle ABC}{\text{Area of } \triangle PQR} = \left(\frac{3}{5}\right)^2 = \frac{9}{25}$

10. 80 $16^2 + 30^2 = (\text{hypotenuse})^2$
$256 + 900 = (\text{hypotenuse})^2; (\text{hypotenuse})^2 = 1,156;$

$\text{hypotenuse} = \sqrt{1,156} = 34.$

or

Recognize that $16 = 8 \cdot 2$
$30 = 15 \cdot 2$
$\text{hypotenuse} = (x) \cdot 2$

The right triangle is a multiple of an 8-15-17 right triangle, so the hypotenuse is $17 \cdot 2$, or 34.
The perimeter is $16 + 30 + 34 = 80$.

11. 40°   The angles are in the ratio of $2x:3x:4x$.
The sum equals 180°.
$2x + 3x + 4x = 180°; 9x = 180°; x = 20°.$
The smallest angle is $2(20°) = 40°$.

12. $6\sqrt{3}$

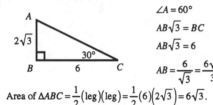

$\angle A = 60°$
$AB\sqrt{3} = BC$
$AB\sqrt{3} = 6$
$AB = \dfrac{6}{\sqrt{3}} = \dfrac{6\sqrt{3}}{3} = 2\sqrt{3}$

Area of $\triangle ABC = \dfrac{1}{2}(\text{leg})(\text{leg}) = \dfrac{1}{2}(6)(2\sqrt{3}) = 6\sqrt{3}$.

13. $25\sqrt{3}$

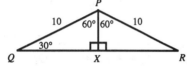

Draw an altitude from P to QR that bisects angle QPR.

$\triangle RPX$ and $\triangle QPX$ are 30 - 60 - 90 triangles.

$PX = \dfrac{1}{2}(10) = 5$

$QX = XR = 5\sqrt{3}$

Area $= \dfrac{1}{2}(\text{base})(\text{height}) = \dfrac{1}{2}(10\sqrt{3})(5) = 25\sqrt{3}$

14. 48 inches

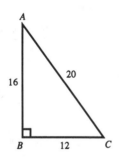

Look for multiples of the common right triangles.
$12 = 3 \cdot 4$
$20 = 5 \cdot 4 \text{ } or \text{ } (AB)^2 + (12)^2 = 20^2$

$(AB)^2 + 144 = 400$

$AB^2 = 256$

$AB = \sqrt{256} = 16$

The perimeter is $16 + 12 + 20 = 48$ inches

15. $\dfrac{7}{4}$ The ratio of the sides of similar polygons is equal to the square root of the ratio of the areas.

$\sqrt{\dfrac{49}{16}} = \dfrac{7}{4} =$ ratio of the sides.

Quadrilaterals, from p. 344

1. $(180 - x)°$ $\angle A = \angle D = 180°$.
   Same-side interior angles are supplementary.
2. 48 square inches   Area = (base) • (height) = 4 • 12 = 48

3. 36 inches

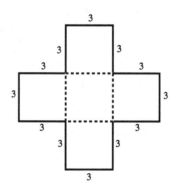

Perimeter = 12 • 3 = 36 inches

4. 45 square inches   The total area equals the sum of the areas of the five squares.
Area = 5 • 9 = 45 square inches
5. 60 square inches   Area of the shaded region is equal to the area of *PQRS* – area *ABCD*.
6 • 12 – 4 • 3 = 72 – 12 = 60 square units
6. 12 square units   *PQRS* is a trapezoid. *PQ* and *SR* are the bases.
PS is the height. The area of a trapezoid equals $\dfrac{1}{2}h(b_1 + b_2)$. Count the squares.
$PQ = 3; SR = 5; PS = 3.$

Area $= \dfrac{1}{2}(3) \cdot (3 + 5) = 12$ square units

7. 104   If the area of each square is 16, then each side is 4.
The perimeter is the distance around the outside of the figure. Count the outer segments and multiply by 4.
Perimeter = 26 • (4) = 104

8. 28 square units

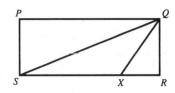

Add line segment SQ

The area of $\triangle QRS$ = area of

$\triangle SPQ = 16.\left(\dfrac{1}{2}\text{ area of the rectangle.}\right)$

Triangles QRX and QRS have the same height (QR).

$RX = \dfrac{1}{4}SR$, so the area of $\triangle QRX = \dfrac{1}{4}$ area of $\triangle QRS$.

Area of $\triangle QRS = \dfrac{1}{2}(QR)(RS)$

Area of $\triangle QRX = \dfrac{1}{2}(QR)(RX)$

The ratio of their areas is equal to the ratio of RX and RS, which

is $\dfrac{1}{4}$.

The area of triangle $QRX = \dfrac{1}{4}(16) = 4$.

The area of $\triangle SQX = 16 - 4 = 12$.
The area of $PQXS = 16 + 12 = 28$.

9. 16 square units   If the area of $ABCD = 100$, then $AB = 10$.
If the area of $PQBR = 36$, then $RB = 6$.
$AR = AB - BR = 10 - 16 = 4$
Area of $TSRA = 4^2 = 16$

10. $\left(48 + 18\sqrt{3}\right)$ square units

Draw an altitude from B to CD forming a 30-60-90 triangle.

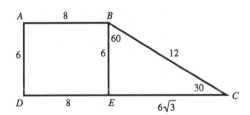

$BE = AD = \dfrac{1}{2}(12) = 6$

$EC = 6\sqrt{3}$, $DE = AB = 8$

Area of a trapezoid $= \dfrac{1}{2}(h) \bullet (b_1 + b_2)$

Area $= \dfrac{1}{2}(6) \bullet \left(8 + 8 + 6\sqrt{3}\right)$

Area $(ABCD) = 3\left(16 + 6\sqrt{3}\right) = 48 + 18\sqrt{3}$

Practice SAT Problems, from p. 345

1. C   There are several ways to proceed with this problem after you
have drawn in all of the given information. One way is to say BC
is half of one of the diagonals of $BFED$ and CF is half of the
other. The two diagonals are equal, so BC must equal CF. BC is a
side of square $ABCD$, so it has length 4. It follows then that
$CF = 4$.
Another, more roundabout way of finding the answer is to
determine that DB is the diagonal of a square with side 4.

Consequently $DB = 4\sqrt{2}$. DB, however, is the side of the square
that has DF as a diagonal. $DF = DB$ times the square root of $2 =$
$4\sqrt{2} \bullet \sqrt{2} = 8$. CF is half of DF, so it is half of 8, which is 4.

2. D   The side of the original sheet of metal is $x + 2 + 2 = x + 4$. Since
the original sheet is a square, its area is the length of one of its
sides squared $= (x + 4)^2$. However, the given information says that
the area also equals $x^2 + 24x$. To solve for x, set the two equal to
each other. $(x + 4)^2 = x^2 + 24x$ or $x^2 + 8x + 16 = x^2 + 24x$; $16x =$
16; $x = 1$. Area $= 25 - 16 = 9$.

3. A   Line 3 is intersecting two parallel lines, so by the parallel
intersector theorem $b = 135°$. Angle a is supplementary to $135°$;
that is, $a° + 135° = 180°$. Solving for a, you get $45°$. Taking the
equation $b - 2a = x$ and plugging in 45 for a and 135 for b gives
you $135 - 2(45) = 45$.

4. A   The given information has been drawn in for you, but you can go
no further; there are no theorems that allow you to conclude that
any lines in the figure are parallel.

A good way to convince yourself that something is not always
true is to redraw the picture without disturbing the given
information. Remember not to assume that pictures are drawn to
scale on standardized tests.

The figure for this problem could be redrawn as below without
disturbing the given information.

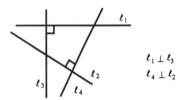

$\ell_1 \perp \ell_3$
$\ell_4 \perp \ell_2$

5. D   By adding two line segments (as below), this problem is greatly
simplified.

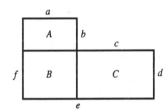

Now it is a lot easier to see that ab is the area of rectangle A and
de is the area of rectangles $B + C$. All three of the smaller
rectangles are accounted for, so answer (A) gives the correct area.
Breaking up each of the other answers this way shows that they
too give correct areas except for answer (D). In answer (D) you
have af, which is the sum of rectangles A and B, and ed, which is
the sum of the areas of rectanges B and C. Rectangle B is
accounted for twice, so $af + ed$ is *larger* than the area of the
figure.

6. B   The bottom of the box is the shaded region. It has a length of two
sides of the square tabs, or more simply $2s$. The width of the
bottom is $3s$. When the tabs are folded up, the height of the box
formed will be the height of one tab, s. The volume of the box is
length times width times height, $3s \bullet 2s \bullet 1s = 6s^3$. One hint to the
answer is the exponent. Length will always be given to a first
power, area to the second power, and volume to the third. Only
answers (B) and (D) fit this description.

7. A   The figure has already been drawn in this problem, so your next
step is to fill in any information that you can. Two sides of the
upper right triangle are equal (they are both 2), so the angles
opposite those two sides must also be equal. Call these angles x.
Now notice that $x°$, $x°$, and $40°$ make up a triangle, so their sum
must be $180°$. Algebraically you have $x + x + 40 = 180$. Solving
for x gives you $x = 70$. Now fill in the new information. One of

the 70° angles shares a vertical angle with an angle in the lower left-hand triangle; these two angles must be equal. (Some more information to fill in.)

In the lower left triangle you now have a 90° angle, a 70° angle, and a p° angle. Their sum must be 180°. Algebraically this is 90 + 70 + p = 180. Solving for p from this equation gives p = 20, answer (A).

8. C   The average equation says that the average equals the sum over the number. The sum of the angles in a triangle is always 180, and there are always three angles in a triangle. The average must be

$$\frac{180}{3} = 60.$$

9. D   This figure looks nice, but it has much more than you need. Find the triangle with angles 20°, 30°, and r°. As with any other triangle, their sum must be 180. 20 + 30 + r = 180. Solve the equation for r to get r = 130. Notice that the 100° and extra two line segments have absolutely no bearing on the problem.

10. A   This is a case where you must draw in an extra line. Drawing in BE, where BE is perpendicular to AC and E is on AC, forms a 45–90–45 triangle and a 30–60–90 triangle. (Numbers like 45, 30, and 60 are hints that something like this is afoot.)

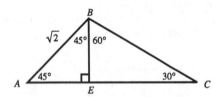

Using the rule for 45–90–45 triangles, you can solve for BE and AE to find that each equals 1. But now, since you know the length of one side of the 30–60–90 triangle (BE), you can solve for EC and get $\sqrt{3}$. The area of triangle ABC is half its base (AC) times its height (BE). BE = 1 and AC = 1 + $\sqrt{3}$. Area =

$$\frac{1}{2}(BE)(AC) = \frac{1}{2}(1)(1+\sqrt{3}) = \frac{1}{2} + \frac{\sqrt{3}}{2}.$$

11. 45   The only triangle that is both an isosceles and a right triangle is a 45–90–45 triangle, so an acute angle has measure 45. To prove to yourself that the 45–90–45 triangle is indeed the only triangle to fulfill both properties, draw a triangle. Label one of the angles a 90° angle to satisfy the condition that the triangle be a right triangle. Since the triangle is an isosceles triangle, the other two angles must be the same; call them x. This is a triangle, so the sum of the two x° angles and the 90° angle must be 180°. Putting this in an algebraic equation and solving for x gives you x = 45°.

12. 75   Call the length of a side of square ABCD s. Since E is the midpoint of CD, ED must have length $\frac{1}{2}s$. The area of triangle BED is half of its base times its height. Use ED as its base. The corresponding height is BC; it touches vertex B and is perpendicular to ED. The length of BC is s, and the length of ED is $\frac{1}{2}s$, so the area of triangle BED is $\frac{1}{2}\left(\frac{1}{2}s\right)(s) = \frac{1}{4}s^2$. The area of the square as a whole is s^2, which means that the triangle takes up 25% of the area. The shaded area, which is everything but the triangle, takes up 100 – 25% of the area, or 75%.

13. 104   If CD = DB, then $\angle DBC$ = $\angle DBC$ = 52°. $\angle ADC$ is an exterior angle of $\triangle DBC$, so x = 52° + 52° = 104°.

14. 155   If XY = YZ, then $\triangle XYZ$ is isosceles and $\angle XZY$ = $\angle ZXY$. $\angle XYP$ is an exterior angle of $\triangle XYZ$, so it is equal to the sum of $\angle XZY$ and $\angle ZXY$. Therefore $\angle XZY$ = 25 and $\angle QZX$ is its supplement.

15. 3/2 or 1.5   The ratio of the perimeters of similar triangles is equal to the ratio of their corresponding sides. $\frac{12}{8} = \frac{3}{2}$

Lesson 13

Geometry of Circles, from p. 354

1. A = 9π square inches   Area = $\pi r^2 = \pi(3)^2$ = 9π square inches
   C = 6π inches   Circumference = $2\pi r = 2\pi(3)$ = 6π inches

2. 8 inches   The ratio of the radii of two circles is equal to the square root of the ratio of their areas.

   $$\sqrt{\frac{1}{16}} = \frac{1}{4}$$

   Let x = the radius of the larger circle.

   $$\frac{2}{x} = \frac{1}{4}; x = 8.$$

3. Multiplied by 3 $C = 2\pi r$ If the radius is multiplied by 3, $C = 2\pi(3r) = 6\pi r$, which is 3 times the circumference.

4. Multiplied by 9 $A = \pi r^2$
   If the radius is multiplied by 3, the area = $\pi(3r)^2$ = $9\pi r^2$, which is 9 times the original area.

5. 18π inches $C = \pi d$; $C = \pi 18 = 18\pi$.

6. 24 $C = 2\pi r$; 48 = $2\pi r$; r = 24.

7. 40   The diagonal of the square passes through the center; so it is a diameter $C = \pi d$, 40π = πd; d = 40.

8. .45 inches   The thickness is equal to the difference of the radii. $T = 4.2 - 3.75 = .45$

9. 42,240 inches   1 revolution = $2\pi r$ inches = the circumference. 240 revolutions = 240($2\pi r$)

   $$\text{distance} = 240(2)\left(\frac{22}{7}\right)(28)$$

   d = 42,240 inches

10. 720   1 revolution = $2(\pi)(14) = 2\left(\frac{22}{7}\right)(14)$ = 88 inches

    1 mile = 5,280 feet = (5,280 • 12) inches

    The number of revolutions = $\frac{5,280 \cdot 12}{88}$ = 720

11. 8π inches   Arc length = $\frac{t}{360} \cdot 2\pi r$, where t = the number of degrees in the central angle. The measure of the central angle is equal to the measure of the arc.

    Arc length = $\frac{144}{360} \cdot (2)\pi(10) = 8$.

12. 120°   Arc length = $\frac{t}{360} 2\pi r$

    $8\pi = \frac{t}{360} 2\pi(12)$;

    $8\pi = \frac{24\pi t}{360}; 8\pi \cdot \frac{360}{24\pi} = t$

    $120° = t$

13. 6π   Arc length = $\frac{t}{360} (C)$ (C = circumference.)

    Arc length = $\frac{60}{360} (36\pi) = \frac{1}{6} (36\pi) = 6\pi$

14. 4π

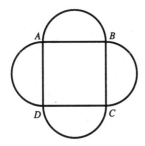

The radius of each circle is 1.

The circumference of each semicircle $= \frac{1}{2}[2\pi(1)] = \pi$.

The perimeter is 4π.

15. 26 inches $\qquad A = \pi r^2; \qquad 169\pi = \pi r^2$
$$169 = r^2$$
$$13 = r$$
$$26 = d$$

16. 324π square inches $\qquad C = 2\pi r; \quad 36\pi = 2\pi r; \quad r = 18$
$$A = \pi r^2 \quad A = \pi(18)^2 = 324\pi \text{ square inches}$$

17. 45π square inches $\qquad$ The area between two concentric circles is equal to the difference of the areas of the circles.
$$A_1 = \pi(9)^2 = 81\pi \text{ square inches}$$
$$A_2 = \pi(6)^2 = 36\pi \text{ square inches}$$
$$A_1 - A_2 = 81\pi - 36\pi = 45\pi \text{ square inches}$$

18. 17 $\qquad$ Let r = the radius of the circle.
$$\pi r^2 = \pi(8)^2 + \pi(15)^2$$
$$\pi r^2 = 64\pi + 225\pi; \quad \pi r2 = 289\pi; \quad r^2 = 289; \quad r = 17.$$
(Notice the 8-15-17 relationship.)

19. 5π square inches

Area of a sector $= \dfrac{t}{360} \cdot \pi r^2$, where t = the number of degrees in the central angle.

Area $= \dfrac{72}{360}\pi(5)^2 = \dfrac{1}{5}\pi(25) = 5\pi$.

20. $\dfrac{128\pi}{3}$ square inches

Area of sector equals $\dfrac{t}{360}(A)$ $\quad$ (A = area of the circle.)

Area of the sector $= \dfrac{240}{360}(64\pi) = \dfrac{2}{3}(64\pi) = \dfrac{128\pi}{3}$ square inches

21. 20° $\qquad$ Area (sector) $= \dfrac{t}{360}\pi r^2$

$$8\pi = \dfrac{t}{360}(12)^2$$

$$8\pi = \dfrac{144\pi t}{360}; \quad 8\pi\left(\dfrac{360}{144\pi}\right) = t.$$

$$t = 20$$

22. $8\sqrt{3}$ $\qquad \dfrac{45}{360}\pi r^2 = 24\pi; \quad \dfrac{1}{8}\pi r^2 = 24\pi$

$$r^2 = 24\pi \cdot \dfrac{8}{\pi}$$
$$r^2 = 192$$
$$r^2 = \sqrt{192} = \sqrt{64 \cdot 3} = 8\sqrt{3}$$

23. $\dfrac{64\pi}{3}$ square feet $\qquad r = 8$ feet; $t = 120°$

$$\text{Area (sector)} = \dfrac{120}{360}\pi(8)^2$$
$$= \dfrac{1}{3}64\pi = \dfrac{64\pi}{3}$$

24. $16 - 4\pi$

The area of the shaded region is equal to the area of the square minus the area of the circle.
$OX = 2 = r$; the sides of the square are $2r$ or 4.
(Area of the square) – (Area of the circle) $= 16 - 4\pi$ = Area of the shaded region.

25. $(288 - 72\pi)$ square inches

The area of the shaded region is equal to the area of the rectangle minus the areas of the circles. If the radius of each circle is 6, the area of each circle is 36π. The dimensions of the rectangle are 24×12. The area is 288. ($A = lw$.)
The area of the shaded region is $288 - 72\pi$.

26. 192π cubic inches

Volume of a cylinder $= \pi r^2 h$. The diameter = 8; so $r = 4$.
$V = \pi(4^2)(12) = 192\pi$ cubic inches.

27. 348π cubic inches

$V_1 = \pi(4)^2(12) = 192\pi$ cubic inches
$V_2 = \pi(6^2)(15) = 540\pi$ cubic inches
Subtract to find the answer. $540\pi - 192\pi = 348\pi$ cubic inches

28. $(96 + 12\pi)$ square inches

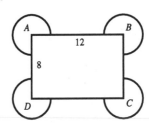

The total area is equal to the area of the rectangle $[(8 \cdot 12) = 96]$ plus the areas of the four circular regions. The area of each region is $\dfrac{3}{4}$ the area of a circle with a radius of 2.

$$\dfrac{3}{4}[\pi(2)^2] = \dfrac{3}{4} \cdot 4\pi = 3\pi = \text{Area of 1 region}$$

Total area $= 96 + 4 \cdot (3\pi) = 96 + 12\pi$ square inches

29. 432π cubic feet $\qquad V = \pi r^2 h$
$\qquad\qquad$ Volume $= \pi(12)^2 \cdot (3)$
$\qquad\qquad$ Volume $= 432\pi$ cubic feet

30. $12\pi - 9\sqrt{3}$

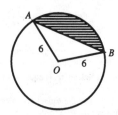

The area of the segment (shaded region) is equal to the area of the sector minus the area of the triangle.

$$\frac{t}{360}\pi r^2 - \frac{1}{2}b \cdot h = \text{Area of segment}$$

$$\frac{120}{360}\pi(6)^2 - (9\sqrt{3}) = \text{Area of segment}$$

$12\pi - (9\sqrt{3}) = \text{Area of segment}$

To find the area of the triangle, draw in an altitude from O to AB. This will form two 30-60-90 triangles.

$OX = \frac{1}{2}(6) = 3$

$AX = 3\sqrt{3}$

$BX = 3\sqrt{3}$

$AB = 6\sqrt{3}$

Area of $AOB = \frac{1}{2}(6\sqrt{3}) \cdot (3) = 9\sqrt{3}$

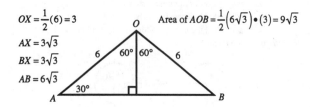

Lesson 14

Coordinate Geometry, from p. 359

1. $\sqrt{65}$ $d = \sqrt{(x_2 - x_1)^2 + (y_2 - y_1)^2}$; $(3,5)(-1,-2)$
   $\quad\quad\quad\quad\quad\quad\quad\quad\quad\quad\quad\quad\quad\quad\quad x_1,y_1 \quad x_2,y_2$

   $d = \sqrt{(-1-3)^2 + (-2-5)^2} = \sqrt{(-4)^2 + (-7)^2}$

   $\quad = \sqrt{16+49} = \sqrt{65}$

2. $(5,4)$ Midpoint $= \frac{x_1 + x_2}{2}, \frac{y_1 + y_2}{2}$

   Midpoint $= \frac{2+8}{2}, \frac{2+6}{2} = 5,4$

3. $\frac{5}{4}$ Slope $= \frac{y_2 - y_1}{x_2 - x_1}$ $(3,7)(-1,2)$
   $\quad\quad\quad\quad\quad\quad\quad\quad\quad x_1,y_1 \quad x_2,y_2$

   Slope $= \frac{2-7}{-1-3} = \frac{-5}{-4} = \frac{5}{4}$

4. $(-3,0)$ Midpoint $= \frac{x_1 + x_2}{2}, \frac{y_1 + y_2}{2}$

   $(2,3) = \frac{7+x}{2}, \frac{6+y}{2}$

   $2 = \frac{7+x}{2}; 4 = 7+x, x = -3$

   $3 = \frac{6+y}{2}; 6 = 6+y; y = 0$

5. -6 Substitute (-4) for x and (K) for y; then solve for K.
   $3(-4) - 2(K) = 0$
   $-12 - 2K = 0; -2K = 12; K = -6.$

6. $(-6,-6)$ If the coordinates are equal, then $x = y$. Substitute x for y, and solve for x.
   $x = 2x + 6; -x = 6; x = -6;$ so $y = -6.$

7. $\frac{2}{3}$ The y-coordinate on the x-axis is always 0.

The x-coordinate on the y-axis is always 0.
The points are (3,0) and (0,–2).

$$\text{Slope} = \frac{y_2 - y_1}{x_2 - x_1} = \frac{-2-0}{0-3} = \frac{-2}{-3} = \frac{2}{3}$$

8. $2\sqrt{2}$ Distance $= \sqrt{(x_2 - x_1)^2 + (y_2 - y_1)^2}$

$\left(\frac{8}{3}, \frac{1}{2}\right)\left(\frac{2}{3}, -\frac{3}{2}\right)$

$x_1, y_1 \quad x_2, y_2$

$d = \sqrt{\left(\frac{2}{3} - \frac{8}{3}\right)^2 + \left(\frac{-3}{2} - \frac{1}{2}\right)^2}$

$d = \sqrt{\left(\frac{-6}{3}\right)^2 + \left(\frac{-4}{2}\right)^2} = \sqrt{(-2)^2 + (-2)^2}$

$d = \sqrt{4+4} = \sqrt{8} = \sqrt{4 \cdot 2} = \sqrt{4} \cdot \sqrt{2} = 2\sqrt{2}$

9. $\left(\frac{19}{12}, \frac{5}{12}\right)$ Midpoint $= \frac{x_1 + x_2}{2}, \frac{y_1 + y_2}{2}$

$\left(\frac{5}{3}, \frac{1}{6}\right)\left(\frac{3}{2}, \frac{2}{3}\right) = \left(\frac{\frac{5}{3} + \frac{3}{2}}{2}, \frac{\frac{1}{6} + \frac{2}{3}}{2}\right)$

$x_1, y_1 \quad x_2, y_2$

$= \frac{\frac{19}{6}}{2}, \frac{\frac{5}{6}}{2}$

Midpoint $= \left(\frac{19}{12}, \frac{5}{12}\right)$

10. $-\frac{11}{35}$ Slope $= \frac{y_2 - y_1}{x_2 - x_1}$

$\left(1\frac{3}{4}, 2\frac{1}{3}\right)\left(-1\frac{1}{6}, 3\frac{1}{4}\right)$

$\left(\frac{7}{4}, \frac{7}{3}\right)\left(-\frac{7}{6}, \frac{13}{4}\right)$

$(x_1, y_1)(x_2, y_2)$

Slope $= \frac{\frac{13}{4} - \frac{7}{3}}{\frac{-7}{6} - \frac{7}{4}} = \frac{\frac{39}{12} - \frac{28}{12}}{\frac{-14}{12} - \frac{21}{12}} = \frac{+\frac{11}{12}}{\frac{-35}{12}}$

Slope $= \frac{11}{12} \cdot \frac{12}{-35} = -\frac{11}{35}$

11. $y = -2x + 1$ Use $y = mx + b$; $m = $ slope; $b = y$-intercept
$\quad\quad\quad\quad\quad\quad m = -2; b = 1; y = -2x + 1.$

12. $y = 5x - 32$ Use $y = mx + b$; $m = 5$; $y = 5x + b$.
The line goes through the point (6, – 2).
Substitute 6 for x and –2 for y; then solve for b.
$-2 = 5(6) + b; = -32$

13. $y = \frac{8}{5}x + \frac{1}{5}$ First find the slope of the line passing through the

points (–2, –3) and (3,5).

$m = \frac{5-(-3)}{3-(-2)} = \frac{8}{5}$

Then use the equation $y = mx + b$ to solve for b.
Plug in the coordinates of either point to solve for

b. Using the point (3,5), we get $5 = \frac{8}{5}(3) + b$.

$5 = \frac{24}{5} + b; b = \frac{25}{5} - \frac{24}{5} = \frac{1}{5}$

The equation of the line is $y = \frac{8}{5}x + \frac{1}{5}$.

14. $y = 3$ First find the slope of the line passing through the points (0,3) and (4,3).

$$m = \frac{3-3}{4-0} = \frac{0}{4} = 0$$

What line has a slope of 0 (horizontal)? The y-intercept is 3. The equation is $y = 0x + 3$ or $y = 3$.

15. $\frac{3}{4}$ Rearrange the equation to get it into the form $y = mx + b$,

where m is the slope.

$3x - 4y = 6$ Subtract $3x$ from both sides.
$-4y = -3x + 6$ Divide by -4.

$$y = \frac{3}{4}x - \frac{6}{4}$$

$$m = \frac{3}{4} = \text{Slope}$$

Practice SAT Problems, from p. 359

1. E The equation for the circumference of a circle is $C = 2\pi r$. Since 2 and π are constants, to double the circumference you must double the radius r. The area of a circle is given by the equation $A = \pi r^2$. Sticking in $2r$ for r in the area equation, since you're working with a doubled radius, you find that the new area equals $\pi(2r)^2 = 4\pi r^2$. The question asks how many times as large the new area, $4\pi r^2$, is compared with the old area, πr^2. $4\pi r^2 = 4(\pi r^2)$; so the answer is 4.

2. B The volume of a cylinder is given by the equation $V = \pi r^2 h$. You are given h and V; so it is a matter of shuffling the equation around to find r; $20 = \pi(r^2)5$. This becomes $r = \frac{2}{\sqrt{\pi}}$.

3. A Draw a circle around the five angles like the one below. The central angles of a circle add up to 360°, so $x + 2x + 3x + 4x + 5x = 360$. Adding all of the x's on the left side you get $15x = 360$. From this equation you can solve for x and find that $x = 24$.

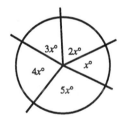

4. E The circumference of the right triangle and the diameter of the semicircle are the same line segment; so by applying the Pythagorean theorem you can solve for the diameter of the semicircle and get it to be $\sqrt{(3)^2 + (4)^2} = 5$. The radius of the semicircle is half the diameter, which is $\frac{5}{2}$. The area of a whole circle with this radius would be $\pi\left(\frac{5}{2}\right)^2$. Since you want only the area of the semicircle, you divide the whole circle's area by 2.

$$\frac{\pi\left(\frac{5}{2}\right)^2}{2} = \frac{\pi\frac{25}{4}}{2} = \frac{\pi 25}{8} = \frac{25}{8}\pi$$

5. C The trick in this problem is spotting the symmetry. Once you have done that, the actual work that you must do to solve the problem is very simple. An equilateral triangle is made up of 3 equal angles and 3 equal sides. The way that the triangle is drawn into the circle divides the circle up into 3 equal pieces. The total number of degrees in a circle is 360; the three equal pieces which are added together to form a circle must each be $\frac{1}{3}$ of 360°, which equals 120°.

6. E AB, the width of the rectangle, is a radius of a circle; so it must have length 2. AD, the length of the rectangle, is made up of two radii of the circles; so it must have length 4. The area equals the length times the width. $A = 1 \cdot w = 4 \cdot 2 = 8$.

7. D OA and OB are both radii of the same circle; so they must have equal lengths. Mark this on the diagram along with the fact that $\angle OAB$ has a measure of 20°, which was given. Using the rule that says, "Opposite angles of equal sides in a triangle are equal," you may fill in 20° for $\angle OBA$. Now you have a triangle, AOB, with an unknown angle and two 20° angles. The unknown angle, call it x, is the one you are asked to solve for. The angles of a triangle must add to 180; $x + 20 + 20 = 180$. Solving for x you find $x = 140$.

8. C The diameter of each of the smaller circles is equal to the radius of the larger circle. The radius of each of the smaller circles is half its diameter. The radius of the larger circle is 4; so the radii of the smaller circles are 2. Using the area equation $A = \pi r^2$, you can solve for the area of the large circle and the areas of the two smaller circles. The area of each of the smaller circles is 4π. The area of the larger circle is 16π. Subtracting 4π twice from 16π, you have the area of the larger circle minus the area of the two smaller circles, 8π. The shaded area is half of what is left and consequently has area 4π.

9. A The length of the line drawn by the roller after *one complete revolution* is 4; so 4 must be the circumference of the roller. The circumference equation says that $C = \pi D = 2\pi r$, where C is the circumference, D the diameter, and r the radius. Plugging 4 in for C, you have $4 = 2\pi r$, which reduces to $r = \frac{2}{\pi}$.

10. E The circumscribed (outside) circle has a diameter equal to the diagonal of the square. The inscribed (inner) circle has a diameter equal to the length of a side of the square. The length of a side of the square is 2; so the diagonal has a length $2\sqrt{2}$. Consequently the diameter of the outer circle is $2\sqrt{2}$ and the diameter of the inner circle is 2. Dividing the diameters by 2 to find the radii, you get 1 and $\sqrt{2}$. The areas of the circles are given by the equation $A = \pi r^2$. Plugging 1 and $\sqrt{2}$ into this equation, you find the areas to be π and 2π. The ratio of the larger area to the smaller area is 2 to 1.

11. B Drawing a set of axes and marking down where each point lies would help you decide which point to test first, but in the long run you must test each point using *the distance formula* until you find a distance that is not 5. There are, however, points which are easier and quicker to test than others. Any point with an x-coordinate of 3 lies on a vertical line with the point (3,4); so its distance from (3,4) is simply the difference of the two y-coordinates. The same rule applies to two points with the same y-coordinate except that the difference between the two x-coordinates is equal to the distance between the two points.

12. B The only quadrant in which x can *not* be greater than y is the quadrant in which x is negative and y is positive. This is the case in quadrant II.

13. A Using the formula for the midpoint would give you $(-x, -y)$ algebraically, but drawing a picture would make the answer a lot more obvious and would be faster. Put A (x,y) in the first quadrant. If (0,0) is the midpoint B must be in the third quadrant. In the third quadrant x and y must *both* be negative. Hence the answer is $(-x, -y)$.

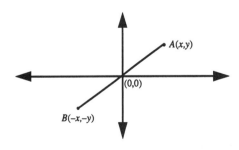

14. C   Plug the two points $(a,3)$ and $(b,9)$ and the distance 10 into the distance formula. What you get is $\sqrt{(b-a)^2 + (9-3)^2} = 10$. Squaring both sides of the equation and simplifying $(9-3)^2$, you are left with $(b-a)^2 + 36 = 100$. Subtract 36 from both sides and then take the square root of both sides to get $(b-a) = 8$.

15. B   The area of a triangle is given by the equation $A = \frac{1}{2}bh$. Call AB the base of the triangle. The altitude is then the distance from C to the x-axis, which is simply the y-coordinate of point C. Plug in 12 for A, y for the height, and 6 for the base (remember that length is always positive). What you have is $12 = \frac{1}{2}(6)(y)$. Solving for y, you get $y = 4$. Since C is in quadrant II, y is positive; so 4 is the correct answer.

16. C   The midpoint of a diameter is the center of the circle. If $CF = 6$, then $AC = 6$ and $AB = 3$. If $CD = EF$, then CD and $EF = \frac{6}{4} = \frac{3}{2}$.

Area of a semicircle $= \frac{1}{2}\pi r^2$

Area of the shaded region would be

$$\frac{1}{2}\pi(3)^2 + \frac{1}{2}\pi(6)^2 - \frac{1}{2}\pi\left(\frac{3}{2}\right)^2$$

$$= \frac{9\pi}{2} + 18\pi - \frac{9\pi}{8} = \frac{45\pi}{2} - \frac{9\pi}{8}$$

$$= \frac{180\pi}{8} - \frac{9\pi}{8} = \frac{171\pi}{8}$$

17. E   Let $OB = 3$; then $OA = \frac{1}{3}(OB) = \frac{1}{3}(3) = 1$.
Area of the larger circle $= \pi(3)^2 = 9\pi$ square units.
Area of the smaller circle $= \pi(1)^2 = \pi$ square units.
$$\frac{\text{Area of shaded region}}{\text{Area of the larger circle}} = \frac{8\pi}{9\pi} = \frac{8}{9}$$

18. B   Make $(4,5)$ the *midpoint* of the segment joining $(5,6)$ and (x,y).

A ————— B ————— C
(x,y) $(4,5)$ $(5,6)$

$AC = 2AB$

Use midpoint formula

$\frac{x+5}{2} = 4 \qquad \frac{y+6}{2} = 5$

$x+5 = 8 \qquad y+6 = 10$

$x = 3 \qquad y = 4$

19. D   Area of a sector of a circle =
$$\frac{t}{360}\pi r^2, \text{ so } \frac{t}{360}\pi(3)^2 = \pi; \ \frac{9\pi t}{360} = \pi;$$
$$\frac{\pi t}{40} = \pi; \ \pi t = 40\pi; \ t = 40.$$

20. D   Area of $\triangle XRY = \frac{1}{2}(3)(4) = 6$
Area of $\triangle YRZ = 28 - 6 = 22$
Area of $\triangle YRZ = \frac{1}{2}(4)(RZ); \ 2(RZ) = 22; \ RZ = 11.$

Lesson 15

Quantitative Comparisons: Arithmetic and Algebra, from p. 364

1. A $1.9980 > 1.9978$
2. A $44,544 > 44,500$
3. C   Multiply $(xy = 12)$ by (-2), and add the result to $x^2 + y^2 = 30$ to get $x^2 - 2xy + y^2 = 6$. Factor $x^2 - 2xy + y^2$ into $(x-y)(x-y)$ or $(x-y)^2$. Therefore $(x-y)^2 = 6$. Answer C.

4. C   Factors $A(B-4) + B(B-4)$ into $(A+B)(B-4)$ by taking out the common factor $(B-4)$. Both columns are then equal. Or FOIL both sides to find out that both columns are equal.

5. B   If $\frac{1}{A} > 1$, then $O < A < 1$. Example: If $A = \frac{1}{2}$, then
$$\frac{1}{\frac{1}{2}} = 1; \ \frac{2}{1} = 2. \text{ Therefore Column B > Column A.}$$

6. D   If $AB \neq 0$, then A and B could be positive or negative. Plug and chug different numbers in for A and B, remembering to use positive and negative numbers. If $A = 1$ and $B = -1$, then $AB^3 = 1(-1)^3 = -1$; $-A^3B = -(1)^3(-1) = 1$. In this case Column B > Column A. *But*, if $A = 1$ and $B = 2$, $AB^3 = 8$; $-A^3B = -2$, making Column A > Column B.

7. A   Solving the two equations gives $x = 3$ and $y = 2$. Here, subtracting the second equation from the first gives the quickest answer. Notice, though, that you get $-2y = -4$ when you do the subtraction.

8. A   Solving the equations gives $y = -3$ and $x = 0$. Looking at -3 and 0 and immediately deciding that -3 is greater can have disastrous results. Take the time to be careful.

9. D   This is tricky! Even though you have two equations, there is no way of solving for x and y. All of the methods leave you with $0 = 0$ or a statement that is always true. To check the fact that no relationship can be determined, find two different pairs for x and y that work in the first equation. If they both work in the second equation, (D) must be the correct answer. Two pairs that would work in this problem are $x = 3$ when $y = 0$ and $x = -5$ when $y = -4$.

10. A   Doing the addition and multiplication leaves a $\frac{5}{6}$ in Column A and a $\frac{1}{6}$ in Column B. By doing the cross-multiplying check for inequalities with fractions, you get a 30 above the $\frac{5}{6}$ and a 6 above the $\frac{1}{6}$. Consequently $\frac{5}{6}$ is bigger. Another commonsense way of looking at the problem is to say $\frac{1}{2}$ of something is surely less than $\frac{1}{2}$ plus the something when dealing with positive numbers. In this problem $\frac{1}{3}$ is the something.

11. A   Since the numerators are the same and the fraction in Column B has a greater denominator, the fraction in Column B must be less than the fraction in Column A. Cross multiplying confirms this since $6\sqrt{5}$ is greater than $3\sqrt{5}$ and it ends up above the fraction in Column A.

12. A   The mistake most commonly made here is that with a quick glance someone will say that the two fractions are equal. There is no rule for breaking up the denominator. Doing the arithmetic leaves $\frac{48}{18}$ in Column A and -6 in Column B. Without simplifying the fraction in Column A you know that it is positive; so it must be greater than the negative value in Column B.

13. A   There is a rule for breaking up the numerator of a fraction. The fraction in Column A becomes $\frac{1,001}{13} - \frac{26}{13}$ or, by simplification, $\frac{1,001}{13} - 2$. By inspection you can see that some number minus 2 is definitely larger than the same number minus 26. Using this logic, you do not have to waste time by simplifying $\frac{1,001}{13}$.

14. D   Since there are no rules that jump right out at you in this problem, try picking some possible values that satisfy the condition $x > y$. Usually picking first negative then positive values tests more possibilities. In this case if x and y are negative, Column B is greater, and if x and y are positive, Column A is greater; consequently a relationship between the quantity in Column A and the quantity in Column B cannot be determined.

15. A   The first step is to simplify the quantities in both columns by dividing out factors of 10. This leaves $(6.3 \cdot 2.9) + 10$ in the first column and $(6.3 \cdot 2.9) + 100$ in Column B. The quantity in Column A is larger since the quantity in the parentheses is only being divided 10 times and not 100.

16. A   Squaring the quantities in both columns does not disturb their relationship, but it does get rid of the radical sign and leaves a .036 in Column A and a .0036 in Column B. *Do not lose the extra 0 in Column B.* Dividing the quantity in Column A by 10 leaves the quantity in Column B, so the quantity in Column A must be larger.

17. C   By converting .25 to a fraction you can reduce the quantity in Column B to $\frac{1}{4}$. Since 1 over a fraction inverts the fraction, this quantity becomes 4, which is what is in Column A.

18. B   Although .026 is larger than .017, both quantities have been multiplied by negative 1, so their relationship has been switched. Now $-.026$ is less than $-.017$. The idea here is much the same as saying 3 is greater than 2 but -3 is less than -2.

19. B   By multiplying the numerator and the denominator of the fraction in Column A by 100 you get $\frac{4,992}{160}$. (Remember that you are allowed to do this by the equivalence rule.) Now both fractions have equal numerators, so the one with the larger denominator is smaller. Consequently the fraction in Column A is smaller.

20. B   Solving both equations gives $a = 15$ and $b = -5$. A common mistake is getting $b = 5$ and marking Column A as greater.

21. C $x = 7$ and $y = 0$. Don't be uncomfortable if one of the variables comes out to be zero—it makes the job of checking easier.

22. D   Column B is greater when $x > 1$, but when $x = 1$ the two columns are equal and when $x < 1$ Column A is greater. *The square root of a number between 0 and 1 is larger than the number;* consequently the relationship cannot be determined.

23. A $\sqrt{2} < \sqrt{3}$ since when x and y are greater than 1 and $x < y$, $\sqrt{x} < \sqrt{y}$ is a true statement. The larger quantity being *subtracted* from 2 results in a smaller sum, so $2 - \sqrt{2}$ is greater than $2 - \sqrt{3}$.

24. D   Remember that $\sqrt{x}$ is *never* negative, so if a represents a negative number, the quantity in Column A is larger, since it is positive. If a represents a positive number or zero, the quantities in the two columns are equal.

25. A   Changing $\frac{3}{2}$ to 1.5, it becomes obvious that the quantity in Column A is greater: $\sqrt{1.5} > \sqrt{1}$.

26. B   The trick here is that many people will square $2x$ and get $2x^2$. This is not the case, because $(2x)^2 = 4x^2$ [think of $(2x)^2$ as $2x \cdot 2x$, or $4x^2$]. Since x^2 is always positive when x is not equal to 0, you can divide the quantities in both columns by x^2 without disturbing their relationship. What's left is a 4 in Column B and a 2 in Column A. The relationship is easily determined from here.

27. A $6 + 5^2 = 6 + 25 = 31$, so Column A contains the greater quantity. The real mistakes that can occur here are glossing over the problem too quickly and missing the + sign, or multiplying 5 by 2 and not squaring it.

28. D   If n is an odd number, $(-1)^n$ is -1. If n is an even number, $(-1)^n$ is 1. 1^n is always 1, so the relationship between the two quantities cannot be determined. Picking and plugging here would be very helpful. First, try $n = 0$; then try $n = 1$. The answers come up differently, so the relationship cannot be determined.

29. C   The problem here is that the bases are not equal: one is 8 and one is 4. Change the 8 to 2^3 and the 4 to 2^2 so you have $(2^3)^{4a} = (2^2)^{6b}$. This simplifies to $2^{(3 \cdot 4a)} = 2^{(2 \cdot 6b)}$. The bases are the same, so now you can set up the equality $3 \cdot 4a = 2 \cdot 6b$ or $12a = 12b$. Divide both sides by 12 to get $a = b$.

30. A   Subtracting 2 from both sides leaves $x + 2 > 1$, so Column A must be greater.

31. A   Since $a > b + 1$ and $b + 1 > b$, you may say $a > b$.

32. D   Plugging in first a positive, then a negative, number gives you opposite results; so (D), undeterminable, is the correct answer.

33. B   This is as hard a problem as you're apt to see on a college entrance math test. Start with $b^2 - 4ac < 0$. Add $4ac$ to both sides to get $b^2 < 4ac$, and then divide both sides by 4. Divide both sides again by a, remembering to change the direction of the sign since $a < 0$. You now have $\frac{b^2}{4a} > c$. Since b^2 *is positive for any b as long as* $b \neq 0$, and a is negative, b^2 divided by a must be negative. The fact that c *is less than a negative implies that c is less than 0.* You can also attack this problem with reasoning—a tool everybody has. You want to subtract some value from b^2, a positive, to make it less than 0. If you were to subtract a negative value from b^2 it would become larger, so $4ac$ must be positive. If $4ac$ is positive, you can say that $4ac > 0$. Dividing both sides by a and switching the sign, since a is negative, leaves $4c < 0$. Dividing again leaves $c < 0$, which is the answer.

34. D   Don't be tricked here: q could be 0 and p could be 1 and still fulfill the requirements. The relationship between p and q is never given.

35. A   Factoring $x^2 - y^2$ gives $(x + y)(x - y)$. Set up an inequality: $(x + y)(x - y) ? (x - y)$. Since $x > y$, $(x - y)$ must then be positive and dividing by it on both sides of the inequality leaves $(x + y) ? 1$. Since $x > 1$ and $y > 1$, then $x + y > 1$. Thus the ? must stand for a > sign. Going back to the beginning, you can replace the ? by a > sign so that you get $(x + y)(x - y) > (x - y)$ or $x^2 - y^2 > x - y$.

36. A   Setting up the equation $P = \frac{c}{100} \cdot W$ and plugging in 30 for c and $63.90 for W gives you $19.17 for P. But $19.17 is the amount of the discount. The new price of the coat is $63.90 - $19.70, which is $44.20. The $44.20 is greater than $19.70, so answer (A) is the correct answer. A very common mistake is getting $19.17 as the discount, seeing $19.17 in Column B, and deciding the two quantities are equal. (Always keep in mind what you are looking for!)

37. C   X% of Y is $\frac{X}{100} \cdot Y$ and Y% of X is $\frac{Y}{100} \cdot X$. By the rules for multiplication of fractions, the product of both of these statements is $\frac{XY}{100}$. They are equal. The information in the center is extra and doesn't affect the outcome of the problem.

38. C $\frac{1}{2}$% is equal to $\frac{\frac{1}{2}}{100}$, which is equivalent to $\frac{1}{200}$. Changing this fraction to a decimal, you find $\frac{1}{2}$% is equal to .005, so the quantities in the two columns are equal.

39. B   The trickiness here is in the wording. By breaking the phrase up into two parts you have:

$$\frac{c}{100} \cdot 80 \qquad \text{"percent of 80"}$$

$$\frac{c}{100} \cdot 80 = 100 \qquad \text{"that 100 is"}$$

Solving this for c gives you 125%. 125% of 80 is greater than 80, so the answer is (B).

A quick way around the calculations of this problem is to notice that 100 is greater than 80. Thus, 100 is more than 100% of 80. Anything greater than 100% is greater than 80%, so the answer is (B).

40. B   The quickest way to do this problem is to notice that 16×2 and 4×8 both equal 32. Since dividing both quantities by a *positive* number respects their relationship, you may divide the 32 out of both sides to leave you with 13 in one column and 15 in the other column; the relationship between them is easily determined. If you did not notice the 32 contained in both sides, you could start off by dividing by smaller and more obvious factors such as 2.

41. A With this problem, approximating is the best method. 5 + .003 is a bit more than 5, and 3 + .005 is a bit more than 3. A bit more than 5 is greater than a bit more than 3.

42. A A rule that is worth remembering is that if you have two fractions with the same numerator the *lesser fraction* is the one with the *greater denominator*. If you didn't remember this rule, however, divide both sides by 1,058 and then multiply both sides by 46. A 2 is left in one column and a 1 in the other.

43. B x and y are both negative, since they are both less than –1. Column A is therefore negative, or less than 0. Column B, however, contains a negative times a negative, which gives a positive, a number greater than 0. Hence the quantity in Column B is greater than that in Column A.

44. A 1^p always equals 1 for any p. *Doing the addition* first in Column B gives 0^p, which is 0 for any positive p. 1 > 0, so the quantity in Column A is greater than the quantity in Column B.

45. D The product of two numbers is not always greater than their sum. Three examples that give different relationships are $a = b = 1$, $a = b = 2$, and $a = b = 3$. Remember, all you must do is find two different relationships and then answer D is the correct response.

46. B Dividing 1/3 and 1/7 from both sides leaves 1/11 in Column A and 1/5 in Column B. The same rule applies here as in problem 3.

47. B The given says y divided by a negative number is positive. You know that only a negative divided by a negative gives a positive, so y must be negative. This means the quantity in Column A is negative. The quantity in Column B, a negative divided by a negative, is positive. Since a positive number is always greater than a negative number, the quantity in Column B must be greater.

48. D The *less than or equals* allows $a = b = 5$ to be a true statement, but since a can equal 4 when b equals 7, there are two different relationships that can exist, so the answer must be "undeterminable."

49. B This is a test in logic. The perimeter is the sum of the lengths of the sides. Figure A has 8 sides of squares showing. Figure B has the same 8 sides showing, plus a little bit extra uncovered by the shift. Consequently, the perimeter of figure B is greater.

50. C Multiplying the first given equation by xyz on both sides gives $yz + xz = xy$. Replacing the xy by z gives $yz + xz = z$. Dividing both sides by z leaves $y + x = 1$.

51. C Replacing b and c by a, since they are all equal, leaves $2a$ in the first column and $2a$ in the second column.

52. B Substituting $x + 2$ for y in the second equation gives $x + 1 = t$. Thus, t is always one larger than x.

53. D Remember, multiplication does not always make a value bigger. If x were negative, y would be a larger negative, making it smaller. Test by plugging in –1, 0, 1.

54. B $40\% = \dfrac{40}{100} = \dfrac{4}{10} = \dfrac{2}{5}$; $\dfrac{2}{\frac{5}{2}} = 2 \cdot \dfrac{2}{5} = \dfrac{4}{5}$.

Column B > Column A.

55. B $\boxed{x} = 2^x$, so $\boxed{3} = 2^3 = 8$. 8 is less than 9, so answer B is the correct one. Don't make the mistake of flipping the 2 and the 3 to get $3^2 = 9$.

56. C Plug into the average equation to get:

$$80 = \frac{x}{3}$$

Shannon's total score is 240. The new percentage is 85, and the new number of quarters is 4. The equation becomes:

$$85 = \frac{240 + n}{4}$$

Solve for n to get 100%.

57. C Call the sum of the n numbers S. The average is then $\dfrac{S}{n}$. The sum divided by the average is $S \div \dfrac{S}{n} = \cancel{S} \cdot \dfrac{n}{\cancel{S}} = n$. The quantities are equal.

58. A $[3,3,3] = \dfrac{3 \cdot 3 \cdot 3}{3}$ by substituting 3 for a, b, and c. Doing the arithmetic simplifies this expression to $[3,3,3] = 9$. The average of 3, 3, and 3 can intuitively be set equal to 3, or you can use the average equation. In either case 9 is greater than 3, so Column A is greater.

59. D Don't get caught!

Even though $\sqrt{36} = 6$, saying that $y^2 = 36$ implies that y *can be either –6 or 6*. By the same reasoning x can be either –5 or 5. Since –5 < 6, and 5 > –6, the relationship between x and y cannot be determined.

60. D If $x = 50$ and $y = 1$, $x + y = 51$, which is greater than 15; but if $x = -10$ and $y = -5$, $x + y = -15$, which is less than 15. The correct answer is D.

Lesson 16

Quantitative Comparisons: Geometry, from p. 370

1. A Use the Pythagorean theorem. $(12)^2 + (16)^2 = x^2$;

$x^2 = 144 + 256$; $x^2 = 400$; $x = \sqrt{400}$; $x = 20$.

$y^2 = 8^2 + 15^2$; $y^2 = 64 + 225$; $y^2 = 289$; $y = \sqrt{289}$; $y = 17$.

2. A The volume of a rectangle solid equals lwh. The volume of $\text{box}_1 = 4 \cdot 3 \cdot 15 = 180$ cubic yards. The volume of $\text{box}_2 = 1 \cdot 12 \cdot 2 = 24$ cubic yards.

3. B The larger side is opposite the larger angle since $PS = QR$ and $PQ = PQ$.

4. B $C = 2\pi r$; $d = 2r$. The circumference of a circle with a radius of $r = 2\pi r$. The circumference of a circle with a diameter of $3r = $

$$2\pi \left(\frac{3r}{2} \right) = 3\pi r.$$

5. D $A = \pi r^2$; $d = 2r$. The area of a circle with a diameter of $x^2 = $

$$\pi \left(\frac{1}{2} x^2 \right)^2 = \frac{\pi}{4} x^4.$$

The area of a circle with a radius of $x = \pi x^2$. If $x = 1$, $B > A$; if $x = 2$, $B = A$.

6. C Extend one of the lines.

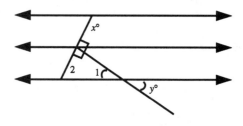

$1 + 2 + 90 = 180$; $1 = y$; $y + 2 + 90 = 180$.
$x + 2 = 180$ (Same-side interior angles are supplementary.)
$y + 2 + 90 = x + 2$; $y + 90 = x$; $90 = x - y$.

7. B The area of an equilateral triangle is $\dfrac{s^2}{4}\sqrt{3}$.

The area of $\Delta XYZ = \dfrac{4^2}{4}\sqrt{3} = 4\sqrt{3} < 8$.

8. C Use the Pythagorean theorem. $2^2 + (YZ)^2 = (2\sqrt{2})^2$
$4 + (YZ)^2 = 8$; $(YZ)^2 = 4$; $YZ = 2$.
Triangle XYZ is isosceles, so $\angle x = \angle z$.

9. C $[-1.5] = -2$; $[-2] = -2$; $A = B$.

10. B   The area of the unshaded region is equal to the area of the square
$[4^2]$ minus the areas of the two semicircles $2\left[\dfrac{1}{2}\pi r^2\right]$.

If $PQ = 4$, the radius of each semicircle is 2.

$\text{Area} = 16 - \left[\dfrac{1}{2}\pi(2)^2\right] = 16 - 4\pi.$

$16 - 4\pi < 4$

11. C   Area of $ABCD = 8h$. Area of $PQRS = 16\left(\dfrac{h}{2}\right) = 8h$.

12. C   An exterior angle of a triangle is equal to the sum of the two opposite interior angles. $x = 41 + 48 = 89$

13. C   If two chords of a circle are equal, then the central angles are equal.

14. B   Column A; the sum of the interior angles of any triangle is always 180°. Column B; the sum of the exterior angles of any polygon is always 360°.

15. B $\angle x = 49°$; $\angle y = 51°$.

16. A   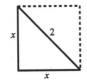 $= \dfrac{1}{3}(7) \cdot \dfrac{1}{4} = \dfrac{7}{12}$; $= \dfrac{1}{2}$; $\dfrac{7}{12} > \dfrac{1}{2}$ because
$7 \cdot 2 > 12 \cdot 1.$

17. A   Use the Pythagorean theorem to solve for x.
$6^2 + x^2 = 8^2$; $36 + x^2 = 64$; $x^2 = 28$; $x = \sqrt{28}$; $x < 6.$

18. C $AB = BC = CD = DA$, so $AB = BC = CD = DA$.
$ABCD$ must be a square whose diagonal is 2.

Use the Pythagorean theorem.
$x^2 + x^2$ $(2)^2$ $2x^2 = 4$; $x^2 = 2$; $x = \sqrt{2}$.

The perimeter of quadrilateral $ABCD$ is $4\sqrt{2}$.

19. B $\dfrac{3}{4}\,\square\,\dfrac{1}{2} = \dfrac{\frac{3}{4}-\frac{1}{2}}{\frac{3}{4}+\frac{1}{2}} = \dfrac{\frac{1}{4}}{\frac{5}{4}} = \dfrac{1}{5}$

$\dfrac{3}{8}\,\square\,\dfrac{1}{8} = \dfrac{\frac{3}{8}-\frac{1}{8}}{\frac{3}{8}+\frac{1}{8}} = \dfrac{\frac{2}{8}}{\frac{4}{8}} = \dfrac{2}{4} = \dfrac{1}{2}$

$\dfrac{1}{2} > \dfrac{1}{5}$

20. C $x + 90 + y = 180$; $x + y = 90$.

21. B $y + 105° = 180°$; $y = 75°$.
$\angle x = \angle y = 75°$ (They are alternate interior angles.)
$105° - x = 105° - 75° = 30°$

22. B $\angle B + 63° + 55° = 180$; $\angle B = 180° - 118° = 62°$.
$BC > AC$. The largest side of a triangle is opposite the largest angle.

23. D   Not enough information is given.

24. B $\angle PQR = 90°$ (definition of perpendicular lines). $90° + x = y$. An exterior angle of a triangle is equal to the sum of the two opposite interior angles. $y > 90 - x.$

25. D   We know that $\angle z > \angle x$, but we do not know anything about $\angle y$.
Example: $XY > YZ$ in both triangles.

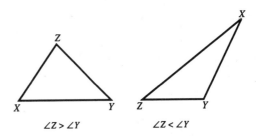

$\angle Z > \angle Y$ $\angle Z < \angle Y$

26. C $\angle x + \angle y = \angle z$. An exterior angle of a triangle is equal to the sum of the two opposite interior angles. Rearranging the equation, we solve for y and get $y = z - x$.

27. D $ABCD$ is a rectangle, but we do not know if it is a square. Not enough information given.

28. A $\angle y = 80°$. Opposite angles are equal.
$\angle B = 70°$. Sum of the angles of a triangle equals 180.
$\angle x = \angle B = 70°$. Alternate interior angles are equal.
$\angle y > \angle x.$

29. B $90° 44' + \angle R = 180°$
$\angle R = 46°$; $PQ > PR$.
The larger side of a triangle is opposite the larger angle.

30. C $XY = 12$
$\text{Area} = 48$

$\text{Area} = \dfrac{1}{2}(\text{base}) \cdot (\text{height})$

$48 = \dfrac{1}{2}(12)(YZ)$

$48 = 6YZ$; $YZ = 8.$

31. B $\triangle ABC$ is a 30-60-90 triangle.
$A = 60°$; $\sqrt{3}\ AB = BC$.
$\sqrt{3}\ AB = 4$

$AB = \dfrac{4}{\sqrt{3}} = \dfrac{4\sqrt{3}}{3} \approx \dfrac{6.8}{3} < 3[\sqrt{3} \approx 1.7]$

32. D   The average of x, y, and z is 60. We do not know about the size of y. Not enough information is given.

33. B   If the perimeter of square $ABCD = 12$, then each side is 3.
If the perimeter of an equilateral triangle is 18, then each side is 6.
Area of the square $= 3^2 = 9$. Area $= (s)^2$.

Area of the triangle $= \dfrac{6^2\sqrt{3}}{4} = 9\sqrt{3}$. Area $= \dfrac{s^2\sqrt{3}}{4}$.

$9\sqrt{3} > 9$

34. C $(3a + 4) + (2a + 6) + (4a - 1) = 27$
$9a + 9 = 27$
$9a = 18$; $a = 2.$

35. A   Triangle XYZ is a 30-60-90 triangle. We can represent the sides as

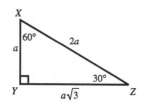

Area $= \frac{1}{2}(a) \cdot \left(a\sqrt{3}\right) = 16\sqrt{3}$

$\frac{1}{2}a^2\sqrt{3} = 16\sqrt{3}$

$a^2\sqrt{3} = 32\sqrt{3}$

$a^2 = 32;\ a = \sqrt{32};\ a = \sqrt{16} \cdot \sqrt{2};$

$a = 4\sqrt{2} = XY;\ XY > 4.$

36. B   Triangle ADE is similar to $\triangle ABC$ because $\angle ADE = \angle B$, $\angle AED = \angle C$, and $\angle A = \angle A$. The ratio of the areas of similar triangles is equal to the *square* of the ratio of their corresponding sides.

Since $AD = DB$ (definition of midpoint), $AD = \frac{1}{2} AB$.

$\dfrac{\text{Area } \triangle ADE}{\text{Area } \triangle ABC} = \left(\dfrac{1}{2}\right)^2 = \dfrac{1}{4}.$

The area of $\triangle ADE$ is $\frac{1}{4}$ of the area of $\triangle ABC$, which is less than

$\frac{1}{3}$ of the area of $\triangle ABC$.

37. C   If $PQ = PR$, then $\angle PQR = \angle PRQ$.

If $QR \parallel ST$, then $\angle PRQ = \angle T$. (Corresponding angles are equal.)
Therefore $y = z$ (substitution).

38. C   Since the distance between parallel lines is constant (otherwise trains would fall of the track), $\triangle PSR$ and $\triangle QSR$ have the same altitude. Triangle PSR and $\triangle QSR$ share a common base, SR.

$A = \frac{1}{2} b \cdot h$. Both triangles have the same height (altitude) and

the same base, SR; so they have the same area. The answer is C.

39. C   Call AD the base of $\triangle ACD$ and $\triangle ABD$. The bases are now obviously equal. The altitude of $\triangle ABD$ is the distance from B to the x-axis, which is simply the y-coordinate of B $(a,3)$, or 3. Point C $(b,3)$ has the same y-coordinate, so the altitude from point C in $\triangle ACD$ must also be 3. The two altitudes are equal; the two bases are equal; so the two areas must be equal.

40. D   The fact that point (a,b) is on the x-axis implies that b equals 0. It says nothing about a. Since a could be either positive or negative, the relationship between a and b cannot be determined.

41. B   The distance from C to D is b. Since $ABCD$ is a square, the lengths of the four sides are equal and the length of side AD is also b. The distance from the origin to point D is a. The origin is closer to D than A is, so the length from the origin to D, which is a, must be less than the length from A to D, which is b. Hence $b > a$.

42. B   The longest segment that can fit inside a circle is the diameter. The length of the diameter is 8, the distance between $(-4,0)$ and $(4,0)$. Since AB is not a diameter (it does not pass through the center of the circle), its length must be less than the length of the diameter. The length of AB is less than 8.

43. B   If a is less than 45° (which is given), then b must be greater than 45° so that the sum of the three angles will still total 180°. Since b is greater than a, the side opposite $\angle b$ must be greater than the side opposite $\angle a$. Hence $CB > AB$.

44. D   If you take 1 and $\sqrt{2}$ to be the legs of the triangle, then the hypotenuse squared equals $(1)^2 + \left(\sqrt{2}\right)^2 = 3$, and the hypotenuse equals $\sqrt{3}$. In this case the quantities in the two columns are equal, but now take the case where $\sqrt{2}$ is the hypotenuse of the right triangle, and 1 and the unknown length are the legs. In accordance with the Pythagorean theorem, the equation becomes

$\left(\sqrt{2}\right)^2 = (1)^2 + (x)^2$, or $2 = 1 + x^2$, or $x = 1$. In this case the quantity in Column A is less than the quantity in Column B. Because of the two different cases, the exact relationship between the two quantities cannot be determined.

45. D   It looks as though each interval is 3, but since this is not given anywhere as a fact, *don't assume* it to be true. In fact, the position of C cannot be determined beyond the fact that it is between B and D. *Since you can move C back and forth anywhere between B and D, the length of AC is undeterminable.*

46. C   The area of the two triangles is half their bases times their heights. Their bases are equal, since it is given that AC = DF.

$\ell_1 \parallel \ell_2$ implies that the distance between ℓ_1 and ℓ_2 is the same anywhere you choose to measure it. The heights of the two triangles are just the distance measured at two different points. Since the bases and the heights are equal, the areas must also be equal.

47. B   All triangles contain 180°, so $a + b + c = 180$. If you solve for c, you get $180 - (a + b)$. Pencil this into Column B and notice the resemblance between the two quantities. Column A contains 90 minus some quantity, and Column B contains 180 minus the same quantity. The quantity in Column B will always be 90 greater than that in Column A.

48. C   By using the vertical angle theorem and the straight angle definition, you can solve for a and b and get 90° for both. Hence, the quantities are equal.

49. B   Call the length of a side of each of the squares s. Six sides of squares are showing on the first figure, so its perimeter is $6s$. Eight sides of the squares are showing in the second figure, so its perimeter must be $8s$. Since s—a distance—must always be positive, $8s$ is greater.

50. C   Call the center angle x. Angle p and $\angle x$ add to be a right angle, so $p + x = 90$. Angle q and $\angle x$ also add to be a right angle, and the equation $q + x = 90$ can be set up. Both p and q equal $90 - x$, so they must be equal.

51. C   Vertical angles are equal so $p = r$.

52. C   Solve for x. $8x + 40 = 360$; $8x = 320$, $x = 40$. $2x - 20 = 80 - 20 = 60$. Each angle of an equilateral triangle equals 60°.

53. A $y = 40 + 95 = 135$ (exterior angle)
$x = 180 - 135 = 45$ (supplementary angles = 180)
$3x = 135, y - 10 = 125$

54. B   Area of a circle of radius $8 = \pi(8)^2 = 64\,\pi$

Volume of a sphere $= \frac{4}{3}\pi r^3 = \frac{4}{3}\pi(4)^3 = \dfrac{256\,\pi}{3}$

55. B $OA = OB$, = equal radii. $\angle OAB = \angle OBA = 59°$
$\angle AOB = 180 - 2\,(59) = 62°$. $AB > OA$ because in a triangle the largest side is opposite the largest angle.

56. A $C = 2\pi r$ $C = 2\pi(3) = 6\pi$
Perimeter of a square $= 4s = 4\,(3.5) = 14;\ 6\pi > 14.$

57. C $a + p + b + q + c + r + d + s = 4\,(180)$
(supplementary angles = 180)
$a + b + c + d = 360$. The sum of the interior angles of a quadrilateral is 360. Subtract, $720 - 360$ to get
$p + q + r + s = 360.$

58. B   Surface area of a cube is $6 \cdot$ (area of one face) $6 \cdot (4 \cdot 4) = 96$ square inches.

Area of a sphere of side $6\sqrt{3} = \left(6\sqrt{3}\right)\left(6\sqrt{3}\right) = 36\,(3) = 108$ square inches.

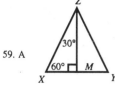

59. A

Remember the 30-60-90 triangle. Let ZM be the altitude to side XY. XMZ is a 30-60-90 triangle.

$$XM = \frac{1}{2}XY; \quad ZM = \frac{1}{2}(XY)\sqrt{3}. \text{ Therefore } ZM > \frac{1}{2}(XY).$$

60. C First find the x and y intercepts of the line $2x - 3y + 12 = 0$.
x intercept: let $y = 0$, solve for x
$2x - 3(0) + 12 = 0$
$2x = -12; x = -6$
y intercept: let $x = 0$; solve for y
$2(0) - 3y + 12 = 0; -3y = -12; y = 4$.

Area of the triangle equals $\frac{1}{2}$ (4) (6) = 12.

Lesson 17

Special Topics, from p. 387
1. 17   The pattern is +2, +3, +4, +5.
2. 17   The pattern is +6 −5, +4, −3.
3. 8   The pattern is 2, 4, 6, 8, ..., with alternating signs.
4. −139 Each term is (−2) times the preceding term, *minus 1*.
5. 2   Multiply the last term (−4) by $\left(-\frac{1}{2}\right)$.
6. $\frac{4}{27}$ Multiply the last term $\frac{2}{9}$ by $\frac{2}{3}$.
7. 10   Every other term is increased by 3.
8. 94   Multiply the last term by 2 and add 2.
9. 36   The pattern is $2^2, 3^2, 4^2, 5^2, 6^2$.
10. 32   The pattern is $2^1, 2^2, 2^3, 2^4, 2^5$.
11. 4.3 Subtract (3.7), the common difference, from 8.
12. $\sqrt{3}$ The pattern is 81, $\sqrt{81}, \sqrt{9}, \sqrt{3}$.
13. 196 The pattern is $18^2, 17^2, 16^2, 15^2, 14^2$.
14. 6   The pattern is +6, −5, +4,−3, +2, −1.
15. -2^9 or 512   The pattern is $-(2^3), 2^5, -(2^7), 2^9$.
16. 33   The pattern is +3, +0, +4,. +0, +5,+0, +6. Add 6 to 27 to get 33.
17. 3   The pattern is −11, −9, −7, −5. Subtract 5 from 8 to get 3.
18. blue $115 \div 4 = 28$ with a remainder of 3. Therefore, the 115th dress would be blue.
19. cheeseburger $76 \div 3 = 25$ with a remainder of 1. The 76th burger would be a cheeseburger.
20. Team A $53 \div 4 = 13$ with a remainder of 1. The 53rd student would then be on Team A.

Practice SAT Problems, from p. 388
1. 9/2 or 4.5 $\dfrac{3}{\frac{4}{6}} = 3 \cdot \dfrac{6}{4} = \dfrac{18}{4} = \dfrac{9}{2}$
2. 13 $(3+1)^2 - (3-1)^2 + 1 = 16 - 4 + 1 = 13$
3. 20 $(4,6 \uparrow 2,8) = 4 \cdot 8 - 2 \cdot 6 = 32 - 12 = 20$
4. 1/16 or .063 $\downarrow\frac{3}{4} = \left(\frac{3}{4} - 1\right)^2 = \left(-\frac{1}{4}\right)^2 = \frac{1}{16}$
5. 1 $2 \bigcirc (-3) = (-3)^2 - 2(2)^2 = 9 - 8 = 1$

6. .09 $\dfrac{3}{2} \square \dfrac{2}{3} = \left(\dfrac{\frac{3}{2}-1}{\frac{2}{3}+1}\right)^2 = \left(\dfrac{\frac{1}{2}}{\frac{5}{3}}\right)^2 = \left(\dfrac{1}{2} \cdot \dfrac{3}{5}\right)^2 = \left(\dfrac{3}{10}\right)^2 = \dfrac{9}{100} = .09$

Note: you can't enter "$\dfrac{9}{100}$" into the grid.

7. 3 $(3x)\left(\dfrac{x}{3}\right) = 1x^2; 1 + 2 = 3$
8. 12
9. 5 $[2.3] - [-2.3] = 2 - (-3) = 5$
10. 108 $(-2) \star 3 = (-2)^2 \cdot 3^3 = 4 \cdot 27 = 108$

Lesson 18

The Last Three SAT Problems, from p. 390
1. B When the set of integers is divided by a number, the *remainders form a repeating series*. Five divided into 1 has a remainder of 1, into 2 has remainder 2, into 3 remainder 3, into 4 remainder 4, into 5 remainder 0. Dividing 5 into 6, however, brings the remainder back to 1 again. The repetition means that the remainders from five consecutive numbers must include the numbers 0 through 4 independent of which number you begin dividing with. Ten equals 0 + 1 + 2 + 3 + 4; the sum of the numbers in the group is 10; the quantity of numbers in the group is 5; so the average equals 10 divided by 5, or 2.

2. A There are two methods with which you could approach this problem. Randomly, call a 1, b 2, and c 3. Plugging in shows that 1 is the only correct statement.
To do the problem algebraically, you plug the values of a, b, and c into the function, making sure to do what is in the parentheses first.

(1) $a * b = \dfrac{a+b}{ab}; b * a = \dfrac{b+a}{ba}$.

The two final expressions are equal, so statement I must be true.

(2) $(a * b) * c = \dfrac{a+b}{ab} * c = \dfrac{\frac{b+a}{ab} + c}{\left(\frac{a+b}{ab}\right) \bullet c} = \dfrac{a+b+abc}{ac+bc}$

$a * (b * c) = a * \dfrac{b+c}{bc} = \dfrac{a + \frac{b+c}{bc}}{a \bullet \left(\frac{b+c}{bc}\right)} = \dfrac{abc+b+c}{ab+ac}$

The two final expressions are *not* equal, so statement II must be false.

(3) $a * (b + c) = \dfrac{a+(b+c)}{a(b+c)} = \dfrac{a+b+c}{ab+ac}$

$a * b + a * c = \dfrac{a+b}{ab} + \dfrac{a+c}{ac} = \dfrac{ac+bc+ab+ac}{abc}$

The two final expressions are *not* equal, so statement III must be false.

3. C The diagonal of the square passes through the center of the circle and has endpoints on the circle, so it must be a diameter of the circle. The diagonal of the square is $\sqrt{2}$ times the length of a side. Since the length of the side is $a\sqrt{2}$, the length of the diagonal and consequently the length of the diameter of the circle is $a\sqrt{2} \bullet \sqrt{2} = 2a$. Half of the diameter, length $2a$, is the length of the radius, a. The area of the circle is π times the radius squared or simply πa^2.

4. D Call the number of adults who attended the movie A, and the number of students S. $A + S$ = the total number of people who attended the movie—500. The number of students times the cost per student, plus the number of adults times the cost per adult, is the total amount spent for the day. Algebraically, $1.5A + .75S = 450$. Now you have two equations in two unknowns. Using either of the methods to solve for A and S you will find that $A = 100$ and $S = 400$. The number of students is, therefore, 400.

5. A   Remember that you can never come up with a fraction of a dog while working this problem. (People are the same way.) $\frac{2}{5}$ of the number of unlicensed dogs must be an integer. $\frac{2}{5}$ of $\frac{3}{8}$ of the number of unlicensed dogs must also be an integer. $\frac{2}{5}$ times $\frac{3}{8}$ equals $\frac{3}{20}$. The only number less than 30 when multiplied by $\frac{3}{20}$ that gives an integer answer is 20. Hence there are 20 unlicensed dogs in the town.

6. B   Even with the extra twist, the average equation is still used here. After two quarters, Buffy's average is 87, so her total score must be 2(87) = 174. You are trying to find the lowest score Buffy can get in the third quarter and still have a chance of receiving 90% overall, so assume that she has a 100% average in the fourth quarter. Call X Buffy's average in the third quarter. Now the new equation takes the form:

$$\frac{87 + 87 + X + 100}{4} = 90$$

Solving the equation for X gives $X = 86\%$ as the lowest possible score Buffy can receive during the third quarter and still have a chance of receiving a 90% for the year.

7. A   Randomly plugging in 3 for the number of girls, 4 for the number of boys, 2 for the number of pizzas, and $1 for the cost per pizza is one way of doing the problem. Doing the problem algebraically, however, is the most straightforward way.
The total cost of the pizzas is the number of pizzas times the cost per pizza, which is $P \times D$ or simply PD. If only the girls pay for the pizza, the cost per girl is the cost divided by the number of girls, $\frac{PD}{G}$. When the boys come the cost is shared among the number of boys plus the number of girls, $\frac{PD}{B+G}$. Don't stop here! The question asks for the *difference*, which is $\frac{PD}{G}$ – $\frac{PD}{B+G}$. Using the rules for subtracting fractions, you first make the denominators the same and then subtract to get $\frac{PD(B+G) - PD(G)}{G(B+G)}$. Getting rid of the parentheses in the numerator leaves $\frac{PDB + PDG - PDG}{G(B+G)}$, which simplifies further to $\frac{PDB}{G(B+G)}$.

8. B   "The cycle is repeated . . ." The clue is right there—you are looking for a repeating series. After the first person is done, the booth has made a profit of 15¢ – 1¢, or 14¢. The second person loses a total of 10¢, the third 5¢; and the fourth *wins* 10¢. The pattern is then repeated. The net profit for every 4 people going to the booth is therefore 14¢ + 10¢ + 5¢ – 10¢ = 19¢. After 43 people have been to the booth, the net profit is 10 • 19¢ plus the amount the booth wins from the next three people: 14¢, 10¢, and 5¢. The total profit is (10 • 19¢) + 14¢ + 10¢ + 5¢ = $2.19.

9. E   Using polynomial multiplication, you can rewrite $(x - y)^2$ as $x^2 - 2xy + y^2$. Rearranging this expression, you have $x^2 + y^2 - 2xy$. Substitute 25 for $x^2 + y^2$, and –5 for xy, to get 25 – 2(–5) = 25 + 10 = 35.

10. E   When dealing with boy-girl problems, the unstated fact is that if one is not a boy, one must be a girl. In this problem the unstated fact is a bit less obvious: if the water comes to a fork and doesn't take one path, it must take the other. Since $\frac{5}{8}$ of the water flowing from path A takes path B, then the *other* $\frac{3}{8}$ *of the water must take path C.*
The $\frac{5}{8}$ of the water that takes path B comes to another fork. From here $\frac{3}{5}$ of the water from path B, which is $\frac{5}{8}$ of the water from path A, takes path D. By multiplying $\frac{3}{5}$ by $\frac{5}{8}$ you can deduce that $\frac{3}{8}$ of the water from path A follows path D. Path F is the sum of the water from path C, which is $\frac{3}{8}$ of the water from path A, plus the water from path D, which is also $\frac{3}{8}$ of the water from path A. Adding these two quantities together, we find that $\frac{3}{4}$ of the water coming in from path A leaves by path F.
Three fourths converted to a percent is 75%. Note that during the problem the water coming in from A is used to represent all of the water, which is true since it is the only path coming in.

UNIT 7: THE PRACTICE TEST

Practice SAT, p. 394

Verbal Sections

Section 1	Section 3	Section 5
1. E	1. D	1. B
2. D	2. C	2. C
3. B	3. B	3. A
4. B	4. B	4. B
5. A	5. E	5. C
6. C	6. B	6. D
7. D	7. C	7. B
8. D	8. D	8. A
9. E	9. A	9. E
10. C	10. E	10. E
11. C	11. C	11. C
12. D	12. E	12. D
13. B	13. A	13. D
14. E	14. C	
15. B	15. E	
16. C	16. D	
17. A	17. B	
18. D	18. A	
19. E	19. D	
20. B	20. D	
21. B	21. A	
22. A	22. C	
23. B	23. B	
24. A	24. D	
25. D	25. E	
26. C	26. A	
27. A	27. C	
28. B	28. D	
29. D	29. B	
30. E	30. D	
	31. A	
	32. E	
	33. C	
	34. A	
	35. C	

Math Sections

Section 2	Section 4	Section 6
1. C	*1. A	1. C
2. D	*2. C	2. D
3. D	*3. B	3. E
4. E	*4. C	4. E
5. A	*5. D	5. E
6. E	*6. B	6. C
7. A	*7. B	7. C
8. D	*8. A	8. A
9. E	*9. B	9. C
10. E	*10. C	10. E
11. D	*11. B	
12. A	*12. C	
13. B	*13. A	
14. E	*14. C	
15. D	*15. D	
16. E	†16. 980	
17. E	†17. 1/4 or .25	
18. C	†18. .045	
19. C	†19. 22.5 or 45/2	
20. E	†20. 71	
21. D	†21. 480	
22. B	†22. 3	
23. A	†23. 3/13	
24. C	†24. 20	
25. D	†25. 60	

16. 9 8 0

17. 1 / 4

18. . 0 4 5

19. 2 2 . 5

20. 7 1

21. 4 8 0

22. 3

23. 3 / 1 3

24. 2 0

25. 6 0

APPENDIX A: SAMPLE ANSWER GRIDS

If you will be taking the new PSAT or the SAT I beginning in March 1994, you will be asked to "grid in" answers to 10 questions. The grids that appear on this page and on those that follow are based on grids found in the first sample PSAT and SAT I released by Educational Testing Service in March 1993. Study the samples below to give you an idea of what you will be expected to do. Then use the blank grids on the next three pages to hone your "gridding-in" skills. (Notice that we wrote each answer in the top blank boxes. You should do the same to keep errors to a minimum.)

341   .7   1.8   1,495

$3\frac{1}{4} = 3.25$ OR→ $3\frac{1}{4} = \frac{13}{4}$ 0 (ZERO)   .842

$8\frac{1}{3} = \frac{25}{3}$ 1/5   33/2   1/16

APPENDIX B: PRACTICE ANSWER GRIDS

Use the blank grids on these three pages to practice "gridding-in" skills before test day. You may wish to photocopy these before using so you'll have all the space for practice that you need.

OFFICIAL ANSWER SHEET FOR DIAGNOSTIC TEST, pp. 5-22

Name: _____

Date: ___ / ___ / ___

School: _____

Class: _____

Start with number 1 for each new section. If a section has fewer questions than answer spaces, leave the extra answer spaces blank.

SECTION 1

1 ⊂A⊃ ⊂B⊃ ⊂C⊃ ⊂D⊃ ⊂E⊃	9 ⊂A⊃ ⊂B⊃ ⊂C⊃ ⊂D⊃ ⊂E⊃	17 ⊂A⊃ ⊂B⊃ ⊂C⊃ ⊂D⊃ ⊂E⊃	25 ⊂A⊃ ⊂B⊃ ⊂C⊃ ⊂D⊃ ⊂E⊃
2 ⊂A⊃ ⊂B⊃ ⊂C⊃ ⊂D⊃ ⊂E⊃	10 ⊂A⊃ ⊂B⊃ ⊂C⊃ ⊂D⊃ ⊂E⊃	18 ⊂A⊃ ⊂B⊃ ⊂C⊃ ⊂D⊃ ⊂E⊃	26 ⊂A⊃ ⊂B⊃ ⊂C⊃ ⊂D⊃ ⊂E⊃
3 ⊂A⊃ ⊂B⊃ ⊂C⊃ ⊂D⊃ ⊂E⊃	11 ⊂A⊃ ⊂B⊃ ⊂C⊃ ⊂D⊃ ⊂E⊃	19 ⊂A⊃ ⊂B⊃ ⊂C⊃ ⊂D⊃ ⊂E⊃	27 ⊂A⊃ ⊂B⊃ ⊂C⊃ ⊂D⊃ ⊂E⊃
4 ⊂A⊃ ⊂B⊃ ⊂C⊃ ⊂D⊃ ⊂E⊃	12 ⊂A⊃ ⊂B⊃ ⊂C⊃ ⊂D⊃ ⊂E⊃	20 ⊂A⊃ ⊂B⊃ ⊂C⊃ ⊂D⊃ ⊂E⊃	28 ⊂A⊃ ⊂B⊃ ⊂C⊃ ⊂D⊃ ⊂E⊃
5 ⊂A⊃ ⊂B⊃ ⊂C⊃ ⊂D⊃ ⊂E⊃	13 ⊂A⊃ ⊂B⊃ ⊂C⊃ ⊂D⊃ ⊂E⊃	21 ⊂A⊃ ⊂B⊃ ⊂C⊃ ⊂D⊃ ⊂E⊃	29 ⊂A⊃ ⊂B⊃ ⊂C⊃ ⊂D⊃ ⊂E⊃
6 ⊂A⊃ ⊂B⊃ ⊂C⊃ ⊂D⊃ ⊂E⊃	14 ⊂A⊃ ⊂B⊃ ⊂C⊃ ⊂D⊃ ⊂E⊃	22 ⊂A⊃ ⊂B⊃ ⊂C⊃ ⊂D⊃ ⊂E⊃	30 ⊂A⊃ ⊂B⊃ ⊂C⊃ ⊂D⊃ ⊂E⊃
7 ⊂A⊃ ⊂B⊃ ⊂C⊃ ⊂D⊃ ⊂E⊃	15 ⊂A⊃ ⊂B⊃ ⊂C⊃ ⊂D⊃ ⊂E⊃	23 ⊂A⊃ ⊂B⊃ ⊂C⊃ ⊂D⊃ ⊂E⊃	31 ⊂A⊃ ⊂B⊃ ⊂C⊃ ⊂D⊃ ⊂E⊃
8 ⊂A⊃ ⊂B⊃ ⊂C⊃ ⊂D⊃ ⊂E⊃	16 ⊂A⊃ ⊂B⊃ ⊂C⊃ ⊂D⊃ ⊂E⊃	24 ⊂A⊃ ⊂B⊃ ⊂C⊃ ⊂D⊃ ⊂E⊃	32 ⊂A⊃ ⊂B⊃ ⊂C⊃ ⊂D⊃ ⊂E⊃

SECTION 2

1 ⊂A⊃ ⊂B⊃ ⊂C⊃ ⊂D⊃ ⊂E⊃	8 ⊂A⊃ ⊂B⊃ ⊂C⊃ ⊂D⊃ ⊂E⊃	15 ⊂A⊃ ⊂B⊃ ⊂C⊃ ⊂D⊃ ⊂E⊃	22 ⊂A⊃ ⊂B⊃ ⊂C⊃ ⊂D⊃ ⊂E⊃
2 ⊂A⊃ ⊂B⊃ ⊂C⊃ ⊂D⊃ ⊂E⊃	9 ⊂A⊃ ⊂B⊃ ⊂C⊃ ⊂D⊃ ⊂E⊃	16 ⊂A⊃ ⊂B⊃ ⊂C⊃ ⊂D⊃ ⊂E⊃	23 ⊂A⊃ ⊂B⊃ ⊂C⊃ ⊂D⊃ ⊂E⊃
3 ⊂A⊃ ⊂B⊃ ⊂C⊃ ⊂D⊃ ⊂E⊃	10 ⊂A⊃ ⊂B⊃ ⊂C⊃ ⊂D⊃ ⊂E⊃	17 ⊂A⊃ ⊂B⊃ ⊂C⊃ ⊂D⊃ ⊂E⊃	24 ⊂A⊃ ⊂B⊃ ⊂C⊃ ⊂D⊃ ⊂E⊃
4 ⊂A⊃ ⊂B⊃ ⊂C⊃ ⊂D⊃ ⊂E⊃	11 ⊂A⊃ ⊂B⊃ ⊂C⊃ ⊂D⊃ ⊂E⊃	18 ⊂A⊃ ⊂B⊃ ⊂C⊃ ⊂D⊃ ⊂E⊃	25 ⊂A⊃ ⊂B⊃ ⊂C⊃ ⊂D⊃ ⊂E⊃
5 ⊂A⊃ ⊂B⊃ ⊂C⊃ ⊂D⊃ ⊂E⊃	12 ⊂A⊃ ⊂B⊃ ⊂C⊃ ⊂D⊃ ⊂E⊃	19 ⊂A⊃ ⊂B⊃ ⊂C⊃ ⊂D⊃ ⊂E⊃	26 ⊂A⊃ ⊂B⊃ ⊂C⊃ ⊂D⊃ ⊂E⊃
6 ⊂A⊃ ⊂B⊃ ⊂C⊃ ⊂D⊃ ⊂E⊃	13 ⊂A⊃ ⊂B⊃ ⊂C⊃ ⊂D⊃ ⊂E⊃	20 ⊂A⊃ ⊂B⊃ ⊂C⊃ ⊂D⊃ ⊂E⊃	27 ⊂A⊃ ⊂B⊃ ⊂C⊃ ⊂D⊃ ⊂E⊃
7 ⊂A⊃ ⊂B⊃ ⊂C⊃ ⊂D⊃ ⊂E⊃	14 ⊂A⊃ ⊂B⊃ ⊂C⊃ ⊂D⊃ ⊂E⊃	21 ⊂A⊃ ⊂B⊃ ⊂C⊃ ⊂D⊃ ⊂E⊃	28 ⊂A⊃ ⊂B⊃ ⊂C⊃ ⊂D⊃ ⊂E⊃

SECTION 3

1 ⊂A⊃ ⊂B⊃ ⊂C⊃ ⊂D⊃ ⊂E⊃	10 ⊂A⊃ ⊂B⊃ ⊂C⊃ ⊂D⊃ ⊂E⊃	19 ⊂A⊃ ⊂B⊃ ⊂C⊃ ⊂D⊃ ⊂E⊃	28 ⊂A⊃ ⊂B⊃ ⊂C⊃ ⊂D⊃ ⊂E⊃
2 ⊂A⊃ ⊂B⊃ ⊂C⊃ ⊂D⊃ ⊂E⊃	11 ⊂A⊃ ⊂B⊃ ⊂C⊃ ⊂D⊃ ⊂E⊃	20 ⊂A⊃ ⊂B⊃ ⊂C⊃ ⊂D⊃ ⊂E⊃	29 ⊂A⊃ ⊂B⊃ ⊂C⊃ ⊂D⊃ ⊂E⊃
3 ⊂A⊃ ⊂B⊃ ⊂C⊃ ⊂D⊃ ⊂E⊃	12 ⊂A⊃ ⊂B⊃ ⊂C⊃ ⊂D⊃ ⊂E⊃	21 ⊂A⊃ ⊂B⊃ ⊂C⊃ ⊂D⊃ ⊂E⊃	30 ⊂A⊃ ⊂B⊃ ⊂C⊃ ⊂D⊃ ⊂E⊃
4 ⊂A⊃ ⊂B⊃ ⊂C⊃ ⊂D⊃ ⊂E⊃	13 ⊂A⊃ ⊂B⊃ ⊂C⊃ ⊂D⊃ ⊂E⊃	22 ⊂A⊃ ⊂B⊃ ⊂C⊃ ⊂D⊃ ⊂E⊃	31 ⊂A⊃ ⊂B⊃ ⊂C⊃ ⊂D⊃ ⊂E⊃
5 ⊂A⊃ ⊂B⊃ ⊂C⊃ ⊂D⊃ ⊂E⊃	14 ⊂A⊃ ⊂B⊃ ⊂C⊃ ⊂D⊃ ⊂E⊃	23 ⊂A⊃ ⊂B⊃ ⊂C⊃ ⊂D⊃ ⊂E⊃	32 ⊂A⊃ ⊂B⊃ ⊂C⊃ ⊂D⊃ ⊂E⊃
6 ⊂A⊃ ⊂B⊃ ⊂C⊃ ⊂D⊃ ⊂E⊃	15 ⊂A⊃ ⊂B⊃ ⊂C⊃ ⊂D⊃ ⊂E⊃	24 ⊂A⊃ ⊂B⊃ ⊂C⊃ ⊂D⊃ ⊂E⊃	33 ⊂A⊃ ⊂B⊃ ⊂C⊃ ⊂D⊃ ⊂E⊃
7 ⊂A⊃ ⊂B⊃ ⊂C⊃ ⊂D⊃ ⊂E⊃	16 ⊂A⊃ ⊂B⊃ ⊂C⊃ ⊂D⊃ ⊂E⊃	25 ⊂A⊃ ⊂B⊃ ⊂C⊃ ⊂D⊃ ⊂E⊃	34 ⊂A⊃ ⊂B⊃ ⊂C⊃ ⊂D⊃ ⊂E⊃
8 ⊂A⊃ ⊂B⊃ ⊂C⊃ ⊂D⊃ ⊂E⊃	17 ⊂A⊃ ⊂B⊃ ⊂C⊃ ⊂D⊃ ⊂E⊃	26 ⊂A⊃ ⊂B⊃ ⊂C⊃ ⊂D⊃ ⊂E⊃	35 ⊂A⊃ ⊂B⊃ ⊂C⊃ ⊂D⊃ ⊂E⊃
9 ⊂A⊃ ⊂B⊃ ⊂C⊃ ⊂D⊃ ⊂E⊃	18 ⊂A⊃ ⊂B⊃ ⊂C⊃ ⊂D⊃ ⊂E⊃	27 ⊂A⊃ ⊂B⊃ ⊂C⊃ ⊂D⊃ ⊂E⊃	36 ⊂A⊃ ⊂B⊃ ⊂C⊃ ⊂D⊃ ⊂E⊃

BE SURE TO ERASE ANY ERRORS OR STRAY MARKS COMPLETELY.

Start with number 1 for each new section. If a section has fewer questions than answer spaces, leave the extra answer spaces blank.

SECTION 4

1 ⊂A⊃ ⊂B⊃ ⊂C⊃ ⊂D⊃	5 ⊂A⊃ ⊂B⊃ ⊂C⊃ ⊂D⊃	9 ⊂A⊃ ⊂B⊃ ⊂C⊃ ⊂D⊃	13 ⊂A⊃ ⊂B⊃ ⊂C⊃ ⊂D⊃
2 ⊂A⊃ ⊂B⊃ ⊂C⊃ ⊂D⊃	6 ⊂A⊃ ⊂B⊃ ⊂C⊃ ⊂D⊃	10 ⊂A⊃ ⊂B⊃ ⊂C⊃ ⊂D⊃	14 ⊂A⊃ ⊂B⊃ ⊂C⊃ ⊂D⊃
3 ⊂A⊃ ⊂B⊃ ⊂C⊃ ⊂D⊃	7 ⊂A⊃ ⊂B⊃ ⊂C⊃ ⊂D⊃	11 ⊂A⊃ ⊂B⊃ ⊂C⊃ ⊂D⊃	15 ⊂A⊃ ⊂B⊃ ⊂C⊃ ⊂D⊃
4 ⊂A⊃ ⊂B⊃ ⊂C⊃ ⊂D⊃	8 ⊂A⊃ ⊂B⊃ ⊂C⊃ ⊂D⊃	12 ⊂A⊃ ⊂B⊃ ⊂C⊃ ⊂D⊃	

ONLY ANSWERS ENTERED IN THE OVALS IN EACH GRID AREA WILL BE SCORED.
YOU WILL NOT RECEIVE CREDIT FOR ANYTHING WRITTEN IN THE BOXES ABOVE THE OVALS.

Grid-in answer boxes numbered 16, 17, 18, 19, 20 each containing:
⊂/⊃ ⊂/⊃ columns, ⊂•⊃ row, and digit ovals ⊂0⊃ through ⊂9⊃

Grid-in answer boxes numbered 21, 22, 23, 24, 25 each containing:
⊂/⊃ ⊂/⊃ columns, ⊂•⊃ row, and digit ovals ⊂0⊃ through ⊂9⊃

SECTION 5

1 ⊂A⊃ ⊂B⊃ ⊂C⊃ ⊂D⊃ ⊂E⊃	5 ⊂A⊃ ⊂B⊃ ⊂C⊃ ⊂D⊃ ⊂E⊃	9 ⊂A⊃ ⊂B⊃ ⊂C⊃ ⊂D⊃ ⊂E⊃	13 ⊂A⊃ ⊂B⊃ ⊂C⊃ ⊂D⊃ ⊂E
2 ⊂A⊃ ⊂B⊃ ⊂C⊃ ⊂D⊃ ⊂E⊃	6 ⊂A⊃ ⊂B⊃ ⊂C⊃ ⊂D⊃ ⊂E⊃	10 ⊂A⊃ ⊂B⊃ ⊂C⊃ ⊂D⊃ ⊂E⊃	14 ⊂A⊃ ⊂B⊃ ⊂C⊃ ⊂D⊃ ⊂E
3 ⊂A⊃ ⊂B⊃ ⊂C⊃ ⊂D⊃ ⊂E⊃	7 ⊂A⊃ ⊂B⊃ ⊂C⊃ ⊂D⊃ ⊂E⊃	11 ⊂A⊃ ⊂B⊃ ⊂C⊃ ⊂D⊃ ⊂E⊃	15 ⊂A⊃ ⊂B⊃ ⊂C⊃ ⊂D⊃ ⊂E
4 ⊂A⊃ ⊂B⊃ ⊂C⊃ ⊂D⊃ ⊂E⊃	8 ⊂A⊃ ⊂B⊃ ⊂C⊃ ⊂D⊃ ⊂E⊃	12 ⊂A⊃ ⊂B⊃ ⊂C⊃ ⊂D⊃ ⊂E⊃	16 ⊂A⊃ ⊂B⊃ ⊂C⊃ ⊂D⊃ ⊂E

SECTION 6

1 ⊂A⊃ ⊂B⊃ ⊂C⊃ ⊂D⊃ ⊂E⊃	4 ⊂A⊃ ⊂B⊃ ⊂C⊃ ⊂D⊃ ⊂E⊃	7 ⊂A⊃ ⊂B⊃ ⊂C⊃ ⊂D⊃ ⊂E⊃	10 ⊂A⊃ ⊂B⊃ ⊂C⊃ ⊂D⊃ ⊂E
2 ⊂A⊃ ⊂B⊃ ⊂C⊃ ⊂D⊃ ⊂E⊃	5 ⊂A⊃ ⊂B⊃ ⊂C⊃ ⊂D⊃ ⊂E⊃	8 ⊂A⊃ ⊂B⊃ ⊂C⊃ ⊂D⊃ ⊂E⊃	11 ⊂A⊃ ⊂B⊃ ⊂C⊃ ⊂D⊃ ⊂E
3 ⊂A⊃ ⊂B⊃ ⊂C⊃ ⊂D⊃ ⊂E⊃	6 ⊂A⊃ ⊂B⊃ ⊂C⊃ ⊂D⊃ ⊂E⊃	9 ⊂A⊃ ⊂B⊃ ⊂C⊃ ⊂D⊃ ⊂E⊃	12 ⊂A⊃ ⊂B⊃ ⊂C⊃ ⊂D⊃ ⊂E

BE SURE TO ERASE ANY ERRORS OR STRAY MARKS COMPLETELY.